ADVANCED METHODS IN FAMILY THERAPY RESEARCH

Research is vital in moving the field of family therapy forward, but the myriad of possibilities inherent in working with systems and individuals can overwhelm even the most seasoned researcher. *Advanced Methods in Family Therapy Research* is the best resource to address the day-to-day questions that researchers have as they investigate couples and families, and the best source for learning long-term theory and methodology. The contributors of this volume share their wisdom on a wide variety of topics, including validity concerns, measuring interpersonal process and relational change, dyadic data analysis (demonstrated through a sample research study), mixed methods studies, and recruitment and retention. The volume contains one of the most detailed descriptions of data collections and covers interviewing, using questionnaires, and observing brain activity. Also addressed are suggestions to meaningfully reduce cultural bias, to conduct ethical research, and, in the Health Services Research chapter, to examine interventions for clients in various income brackets. A separate, groundbreaking chapter also addresses psychophysiological research in a couple and family therapeutic context. As an added benefit, readers will learn how to become informed consumers of journal articles and studies, how to produce quality, publishable research, and how to write fundable grant proposals. Each chapter provides a clear and detailed guide for students, researchers, and professionals, and as a whole *Advanced Methods in Family Therapy Research* advances the field by teaching readers how to provide evidence that marriage and family therapy not only relieves symptoms, but also effects behavioral change in all family members.

Richard B Miller, Ph.D., is a faculty member in the Marriage and Family Therapy Program and a Professor and former Director of the School of Family Life at Brigham Young University.

Lee N. Johnson, Ph.D., is a faculty member in the Marriage and Family Therapy Program and an Associate Professor in the School of Family Life at Brigham Young University.

ADVANCED METHODS IN FAMILY THERAPY RESEARCH

A Focus on Validity and Change

Edited by
Richard B Miller
Lee N. Johnson

Routledge
Taylor & Francis Group

NEW YORK AND LONDON

First published 2014
by Routledge
711 Third Avenue, New York, NY 10017

and by Routledge
27 Church Road, Hove, East Sussex BN3 2FA

Routledge is an imprint of the Taylor & Francis Group, an informa business

© 2014 Taylor & Francis

Library of Congress Cataloging-in-Publication Data

Advanced methods in family therapy research : a focus on validity
    and change / edited by Richard B. Miller and Lee N. Johnson.
      pages cm
    Includes bibliographical references and index.
  1. Family psychotherapy—Methodology. 2. Family
psychotherapy—Research. 3. Couples therapy. I. Miller,
Richard B., editor of compilation. II. Johnson, Lee N., editor
of compilation.
    RC488.5A34 2014
    616.89'156—dc23
    2013029099

ISBN: 978-0-415-63750-3 (hbk)
ISBN: 978-0-415-71090-9 (pbk)
ISBN: 978-0-203-08452-6 (ebk)

Typeset in ITC Galliard
by Apex CoVantage, LLC

This book is dedicated to our wives (R. M.) Mary and (L. J.) Angela and our children (R. M.) Marc, Kaylyn, Rob, Janae, Elli, and David and (L. J.) Micaela, Camilla, and Alex. Without their love and support we could not have completed this project.

CONTENTS

About the Editors xi
About the Contributors xiii

1 Introduction: The Importance of Validity, Relationships,
   and Change in Marriage and Family Therapy Research 1
   LEE N. JOHNSON AND RICHARD B MILLER

SECTION I
Foundational Issues 13

2 Developing a Good Research Idea 15
   RICHARD B MILLER AND LEXIE PFEIFER

3 Integrating Theory and Research 28
   MAUREEN DAVEY, SENEM ZEYTINOGLU, AND LAURA LYNCH

4 Measurement Issues with Couple- and Family-Level Data 44
   DEAN M. BUSBY AND FRANKLIN O. POULSEN

5 Ethical Guidelines for Conducting Clinical Research
   in Relationship-Focused Therapy 59
   STEVEN M. HARRIS AND KATHARINE WICKEL

SECTION II
Data Collection 77

6 Recruitment and Retention of Couples and Families
   in Clinical Research 79
   MICHAEL M. OLSON AND RICHARD B MILLER

CONTENTS

7 Using Questionnaires in Clinical Couple and
   Family Research   94
   DEANNA LINVILLE, JEFF L. TODAHL, AND MAYA ELIN O'NEIL

8 Emergent Technologies in Marriage and Family
   Therapy Research   112
   CRAIG W. SMITH, KELLY A. MAXWELL, AND LEE N. JOHNSON

9 Physiological Research in Couple and Family Therapy   124
   KIM D. GREGSON AND SCOTT A. KETRING

10 Electroencephalography in Marriage and Family
   Therapy Research   142
   TRENT S. PARKER, KRISTYN M. BLACKBURN, AND
   RONALD J. WERNER-WILSON

SECTION III
Methodologies   159

11 Cultural Adaptation Research: A Critical Opportunity for
   Addressing Mental Health Disparities in the Couple and
   Family Therapy Field   161
   JOSÉ RUBÉN PARRA-CARDONA, MICHAEL R. WHITEHEAD,
   ANA ROCÍO ESCOBAR-CHEW, KENDAL HOLTROP, SARA N. LAPPAN,
   SHEENA R. HORSFORD, MELANIE M. DOMENECH RODRÍGUEZ,
   AND GUILLERMO BERNAL

12 Randomized Clinical Trials: Putting Marriage and
   Family Therapy Interventions to the Test   178
   WAYNE H. DENTON

13 Single-Case Research with Couples and Families   196
   KAYLA D. MENNENGA AND LEE N. JOHNSON

14 Examining Micro-Change in Clinical Populations Using
   a Daily Diary Approach   208
   JEREMY B. YORGASON, LEE N. JOHNSON, AND NATHAN R. HARDY

15 Observational Research   230
   KAREN S. WAMPLER AND JAMES M. HARPER

CONTENTS

16 Qualitative Research for Family Therapy   247
JERRY E. GALE AND MEGAN L. DOLBIN-MACNAB

17 Mixed Methods Clinical Research with Couples
and Families   266
MEGAN L. DOLBIN-MACNAB, JOSÉ RUBÉN PARRA-CARDONA,
AND JERRY E. GALE

18 Community-Based Participatory Research: Where
Family Therapists Can Make a Difference   282
DAVE ROBINSON, MICHAEL M. OLSON, RICHARD BISCHOFF,
PAUL SPRINGER, AND JENENNE GESKE

19 Health Services Research: Optimizing Delivery of Care   298
ADRIAN BLOW AND CHRIS MARCHIONDO

SECTION IV
Analysis   313

20 Applied Statistical Analysis and Interpretation   315
LEE N. JOHNSON AND RICHARD B MILLER

21 Missing Data   329
COLWICK M. WILSON, RUTH HOUSTON BARRETT,
AND SARAH C. STUCHELL

22 Mediation and Moderation: Conceptual Foundations
and Analytical Applications   347
JARED R. ANDERSON, JARED A. DURTSCHI, KRISTY L. SOLOSKI,
AND MATTHEW D. JOHNSON

23 Dyadic or Systemic Data Analysis   366
SUZANNE BARTLE-HARING, LENORE M. MCWEY, AND
JARED A. DURTSCHI

24 Observing Couple and Family Relationships:
Data Management and Analysis   383
RYAN B. SEEDALL

25 Statistical Analysis with Small Samples   401
RACHEL B. TAMBLING AND SHAYNE R. ANDERSON

CONTENTS

26 Integrating Costs into Marriage and Family
    Therapy Research   420
    JACOB D. CHRISTENSON AND D. RUSSELL CRANE

    Author Index   437
    Subject Index   456

ABOUT THE EDITORS

Richard B Miller is a Professor in the School of Family Life at Brigham Young University. During his tenure at BYU he has served as the Director of the School of Family Life and an Associate Dean in the College of Family, Home, and Social Science. Prior to becoming a faculty member at BYU, he taught at Kansas State University for eleven years, where he was associated with the marriage and family therapy program and served for four years as the Program Director. He received his bachelors degree in Asian Studies and masters degree in sociology from Brigham Young University and later earned his Ph.D. in sociology at the University of Southern California, with a graduate certificate in Marriage and Family Therapy.

He mainly teaches research methods and statistics courses in the MFT program at BYU, and he takes great satisfaction in helping research-adverse masters-level MFT students learn to tolerate and eventually appreciate the research side of MFT. He loves teaching research methods classes to doctoral students who share his passion for MFT research. His current program of research focuses on the process of change in couples therapy, and he also conducts cross-cultural research, with a focus on Asia. He has published numerous articles in peer-reviewed journals, including *Journal of Marital and Family Therapy, Family Process, Journal of Social and Personal Relationships, Journal of Marriage and Family, Family Relations,* and *Journal of Family Psychology.* He currently serves as a member of the Editorial Board of the *Journal of Marital and Family Therapy.*

Lee N. Johnson is an Associate Professor in the School of Family Life at Brigham Young University. Prior to becoming a faculty member at BYU, he taught at the University of Georgia for twelve years and at Friends University for three years. At each university he was associated with the marriage and family therapy program, and he served for five years as the Program Director at the University of Georgia. He received his bachelors degree in Family Science from Brigham Young University. He later earned his Master's degree from Utah State University and his Ph.D. from Kansas State University, both with an emphasis in Marriage and Family Therapy.

He teaches research methods and theory courses in the MFT program at BYU. He likes the challenge of teaching students who hate statistics or think that they cannot do research. He also enjoys mentoring graduate students who share his passion for research. His current program of research focuses on the process of change in couples therapy and the effects of using exercise as a catalyst to improve therapy outcomes. He has published numerous articles in peer-reviewed journals, including the *Journal of Marital and Family Therapy, Family Process, American Journal of Family Therapy,* and *Contemporary Family Therapy.* He currently serves as a member of the Editorial Board of the *Journal of Marital and Family Therapy* and *Contemporary Family Therapy.*

ABOUT THE CONTRIBUTORS

Jared R. Anderson, Ph.D., is an Associate Professor of Marriage and Family Therapy at Kansas State University. He earned his M.S. degree in Marriage and Family Therapy from Kansas State University and his Ph.D. in Family Science with a specialization in Marriage and Family Therapy from the University of Minnesota. His research interests include the study of marriage across the life course, specifically with military couples and couples experiencing chronic illness, and the development of romantic relationships among young adults in China. He is on the editorial boards of *the Journal of Marriage and Family* and the *Journal of Marital and Family Therapy*.

Shayne R. Anderson, Ph.D., is an Assistant Professor in the Department of Human Development and Family Studies at the University of Connecticut. His research interests center on understanding the change process in couples therapy. In particular, he is interested in how model-independent factors influence both immediate and long-term therapeutic outcomes in couples therapy. To facilitate studying the change process, his research also concentrates on issues of measurement in couple therapy.

Ruth Houston Barrett, Ph.D., is a consultant for the development of research and programs for the Marriage and Family Research Institute, a non-profit counseling center that emphasizes the integration of research and clinical practice. She also maintains a private practice. She earned her Ph.D. in MFT from Loma Linda University, where she pursued advanced training in research methodologies and statistics. She has also earned degrees in electrical engineering, including an M.S. from the University of Southern California and a B.S. from the University of California, Los Angeles.

Suzanne Bartle-Haring, Ph.D., is Director and Professor in the Couple and Family Therapy Ph.D. Program at The Ohio State University. Her research and clinical interests focus on Bowen Family Systems Theory and assessment of its key constructs. She has expertise in structural equation modeling, multilevel modeling, and dyadic data analysis. She has also published in other areas including adolescent substance abuse treatment, IPV, and thera-peutic alliance. She continues to revise and design survey instruments that assess differentiation from multiple perspectives and can be used with both community and clinical populations.

Guillermo Bernal, Ph.D., is Professor of Psychology at the University of Puerto Rico and Director of the Institute for Psychological Research. His work has focused on research, training, and the development of mental health services for ethno-cultural groups. He conducts efficacy trials on culturally adapted treatments for depression.

Richard Bischoff, Ph.D., is Chair and Professor in the Department of Child, Youth, and Family Studies at the University of Nebraska. Previously, he taught at the University of San Diego. He received his Ph.D. from Purdue University. His research interests include increasing access to mental health services for underserved populations, collaborative health care, and telecom-munications as a medium for delivering mental health care.

Kristyn Blackburn, M.S., is a doctoral student in the Department of Fam-ily Sciences at the University of Kentucky. Her research includes work on understanding client and therapist factors, including neurological and physi-ological factors that influence the therapy process. Her research also includes the study of factors influencing self-disclosure and secrecy in couples.

Adrian Blow, Ph.D., is an associate professor in the Department of Human Development and Family Studies at Michigan State University and is the Program Director of the couple and family therapy program. He obtained his doctorate from Purdue University, served on the faculty at Saint Louis University for six years, and joined Michigan State University in 2005. He is involved with several studies related to military deployment, including post-deployment adjustment of Michigan National Guard Couples (MING), evaluation of the Buddy-to-Buddy program (a peer-to-peer support program), resiliency processes in National Guard Families, and other family-based inter-ventions. Blow also studies spirituality, emotional well-being, and quality of life in women living with breast cancer.

Dean M. Busby, Ph.D., is a Professor and the Director of the School of Family Life at Brigham Young University. He received his Ph.D. in Family Ther-apy from Brigham Young University. Following his schooling, he taught at Syracuse University and Texas Tech University, where he was the depart-ment chair, before returning to Brigham Young University. His research focuses on the areas of marriage relationships, sexuality, relationship educa-tion and intervention, assessment of couples, and relationship trauma. He has taught at the university level for more than twenty years, primarily in the area of dating and marriage relationships, family violence, and research methods.

Jacob D. Christenson, Ph.D., is an Assistant Professor and Clinical Director for the Marriage and Family Therapy Program at Mount Mercy University in Cedar Rapids, Iowa. His professional areas of interest include interventions for treatment resistant children and adolescents, families and health, and family therapy training. He is an editorial board member for *Contemporary Family Therapy: An International Journal*.

D. Russell Crane, Ph.D., is a Professor of Marriage and Family Therapy in the School of Family Life at Brigham Young University. His primary research concerns the cost effectiveness of the profession and practice of marriage and family therapy, as well as the influence of family interaction on health outcomes. He is editor of *Contemporary Family Therapy: An International Journal*. He received the Cumulative Contributions to Marriage and Family Therapy Research Award from AAMFT in 2007. He is also a former Chair of AAMFT's Commission on Accreditation for Marriage and Family Therapy Education.

Maureen Davey, Ph.D., is an Associate Professor in the Department of Couple and Family Therapy at Drexel University. Her research focuses on the development of culturally relevant interventions for individuals, couples, and families coping with illness, as well as training medical and mental health providers to overcome health disparities.

Wayne H. Denton, M.D., Ph.D., is a Professor of Marriage and Family Therapy and Director of the Marriage and Family Therapy Program at Florida State University. He has conducted randomized clinical trials involving emotionally focused therapy for couples. He also conducts related research on couple communication and the role of relational issues in health and illness.

Megan L. Dolbin-MacNab, Ph.D., is an Associate Professor in the Marriage and Family Therapy Program in the Department of Human Development at Virginia Tech. She is also the Clinical Training Director at The Family Therapy Center of Virginia Tech. Her research focuses on relationship dynamics in grandparent-headed families and best practices for intervention with this population. Her research interests and experience also include dyadic research, mixed methods research, program evaluation, and community-based participatory research.

Melanie M. Domenech Rodríguez, Ph.D., is a Professor of Psychology at Utah State University. Her work has focused on research, teaching, practice, and training with diverse populations, with a particular emphasis on cultural adaptations of evidence-based interventions. She has also made substantive contributions to teaching, research, and training in professional ethics. She obtained her doctoral degree at Colorado State University.

Jared A. Durtschi, Ph.D., is an Assistant Professor of Marriage and Family Therapy at Kansas State University. He earned his M.S. degree in Marriage and Family Therapy from Purdue University Calumet and his Ph.D. in Marriage and Family Therapy from The Florida State University. He studies romantic relationships during the transition to parenthood, emerging adulthood, and early marriage. He analyzes dyadic, longitudinal data to identify predictors and processes associated with higher romantic relationship quality and stability.

Ana Rocío Escobar-Chew, M.A., is a Fulbright scholar born and raised in Guatemala. She is a doctoral candidate in the Couple and Family Therapy Program at Michigan State University. She has been actively engaged in research projects involving Latino populations and other minority groups, with a special focus on cultural adaptation of prevention programs, interaction with the welfare system, domestic violence, and clinical interventions for couples.

Jerry E. Gale, Ph.D., is an Associate Professor at the University of Georgia. He is the Director of the Family Therapy Doctoral Program. He is presently engaged with projects studying relational financial therapy and relational meditation. He has written extensively on discursive analysis.

Jenenne Geske, Ph.D., is an Assistant Professor in the Department of Family Medicine at the University of Nebraska Medical Center. She is trained in quantitative and qualitative research methods and statistics. Her research focuses on medical education research in primary care. In addition, she studies practice improvement processes and patient outcomes in primary care.

Kim D. Gregson, M.S., is a doctoral student in the Department of Human Development and Family Studies at Auburn University. She received her M.S. in Marriage and Family Therapy from Abilene Christian University. Her research interests focus on stress reactivity in the context of family relationships. In particular, she is interested in the effects of couple conflict on partners' own and their children's emotion regulation, measured physiologically.

Nathan R. Hardy, M.S., is a doctoral student in Marriage and Family Therapy at Kansas State University. He received his M.S. from Kansas State University in Marriage and Family Therapy. His current research interests include the study of couple relationships across various contexts, such as couples managing chronic illnesses and couples in the military. He is also interested in factors related to successful relationship formation and development.

James M. Harper, Ph.D., is the Zina Young Williams Card Professor in the Marriage and Family Program in the School of Family Life at Brigham Young University. His research interests include family assessment, family systems processes, and therapy process.

Steven M. Harris, Ph.D., is a Professor and the Director of the Couple and Family Therapy Program at the University of Minnesota. He received his graduate training in Family Therapy at Syracuse University and worked for thirteen years as a professor in the MFT program at Texas Tech University. His research interests include the ethical delivery of family therapy services and the impact of relationship education on marginalized populations. He recently co-authored a book entitled, *Seven Letters that Will Bring You Closer to Your College Student* that outlines a method for parents to reach out to their college-bound children to strengthen family bonds.

Kendal Holtrop, Ph.D., is an Assistant Professor in the Marriage and Family Therapy Program in the Department of Family and Child Sciences at The Florida State University. Her program of research focuses on the implementation, adaptation, and evaluation of evidence-based parenting interventions for underserved populations in community settings. She is currently working to adapt a parenting program to meet the needs of homeless families with children living in transitional housing.

Sheena R. Horsford, M.A., is a doctoral candidate in the department of Human Development and Family Studies at Michigan State University. Her current research focuses on resiliency and risk behaviors among African American females in higher education and family-based interventions among low-income families of color.

Matthew D. Johnson, Ph.D., is an Assistant Professor of Family Ecology at the University of Alberta. He earned his M.S. and Ph.D. in Human Ecology with an emphasis in Marriage and Family Therapy from Kansas State University. His research interests include the developmental antecedents of relationship functioning, young adult risky sexual behavior, and couples coping with chronic illness.

Scott A. Ketring, Ph.D., is an Associate Professor in the Department of Human Development and Family Studies at Auburn University. His research focuses on how the therapeutic relationship impacts couple and family therapy outcomes. He is especially interested in the therapeutic interactions that regulate therapist and client physiology and, subsequently, improve therapeutic outcomes.

Sara N. Lappan, M.A., is a doctoral student in the couple and family therapy at Michigan State University. Her research interests include the adaptation of efficacious parenting interventions to serve overweight and obese families and curb the worldwide obesity epidemic. She is also working on a research project that targets overweight and obese mothers by delivering educational media messages on healthy eating, exercise, and stress management.

Deanna Linville, Ph.D., is an Associate Professor and Program Director for the Couples and Family Therapy Program at the University of Oregon. She conducts intervention research in the areas of eating disorders, obesity, and couples. She is on the editorial board of the *Journal of Marital and Family Therapy* and *Contemporary Family Therapy*.

Laura Lynch, M.S., is a doctoral student in the Couple and Family Therapy Program at Drexel University. She received her Master's degree in Marriage and Family Therapy from the University of Rochester, where she completed clinical internships at a community mental health center, an OB-GYN practice, and a community hospital. Laura's research interests include the development of interventions to help families cope with chronic illness, specifically parental diabetes, couples coping with cancer, and women's health issues.

Chris Marchiondo, M.S., is a doctoral student in the Couple and Family Therapy Program at Michigan State University, where he studies resiliency in military families. He previously worked at the Ann Arbor Veterans Administration's Serious Mental Illness Treatment Resource and Evaluation Center, where he was part of a team conducting health services research on recently returned veterans.

Kelly A. Maxwell, M.A., is a doctoral student in the Department of Family and Community Medicine at Saint Louis University. Her research has centered on ambiguous loss theory, singleness, mate selection, emergent technologies in marriage and family therapy, and the impact of communication technologies on relationships.

Lenore M. McWey, Ph.D., is an Associate Professor in the Marriage and Family Therapy Doctoral Program at Florida State University. Her research and clinical interests involve working with families involved with the child welfare system.

Kayla D. Mennenga, M.S., is a doctoral student at Brigham Young University. She earned her masters degree from Abilene Christian University. Her research interests involve using exercise in couple therapy as a catalyst for creating change, and she is currently engaged in research exploring the benefits of using exercise in couples therapy.

Michael M. Olson, Ph.D., is the Director of Behavioral Medicine and an Associate Professor in the Department of Family Medicine, University of Texas Medical Branch. He earned his masters degree in MFT from Brigham Young University and doctorate in MFT from Kansas State University. He completed a post-doctoral clinical and research fellowship in Behavioral Medicine from the University of Texas Medical Branch. His research interests include biomarkers in marriage and chronic illness, spirituality in clinical medicine, community-based participatory research, and integrating motivational interviewing as a pedagogical approach in education.

Maya Elin O'Neil, Ph.D., is a licensed psychologist at the Portland VA Medical Center and Assistant Professor at Oregon Health and Science University in the departments of Psychiatry and of Medical Informatics and Clinical Epidemiology. She works on the Neuropsychology Service and is an investigator with the VA Evidence-Based Synthesis Program and AHRQ Scientific Resource Center.

Trent S. Parker, Ph.D., is Assistant Professor in the Department of Family Sciences at the University of Kentucky. He received his Ph.D. in marriage and family therapy from Texas Tech University. His research interests include couples therapy process research and technology's impact on couple interaction.

José Rubén Parra-Cardona, Ph.D., is an Associate Professor in the Couple and Family Therapy Program in the department of Human Development and Family Studies at Michigan State University. He is also Associate Director of the MSU Research Consortium on Gender-Based Violence. His current research is focused on cultural adaptation of evidence-based parenting interventions for Latino populations, evaluation of cultural relevance of services for Latina survivors, as well as Latino men who batter and abuse, and development of interventions aimed at reducing gender-based violence in Latino populations.

Lexie Pfeifer, M.S., is a doctoral candidate in the Marriage and Family Therapy program at Brigham Young University. Her research interests include family therapy process with young children and family processes associated with therapeutic presenting concerns of young children. She also is interested in cross-cultural research in China and Taiwan.

Franklin O. Poulsen, M.S., is a doctoral student at Arizona State University's T. Denny Sanford School of Family and Social Dynamics. His primary research focuses on adolescent and emerging adult romantic relationship development. More specifically, he is interested in the factors that predict differing pathways of romantic relationship development and in understanding the implications these differing pathways may have for individual well-being and future relationship success.

Dave Robinson, Ph.D., is the Director of the Marriage and Family Therapy Program at Utah State University. His research interests include collaborative health care, community-based participatory research, rural mental health, physician/patient relationships, and distance therapy.

Ryan B. Seedall, Ph.D., is an Assistant Professor in Marriage and Family Therapy at Utah State University. He received his doctoral degree from

Michigan State University. He has grown to genuinely enjoy research, with his primary interests centering on process research. Specifically, he is interested in understanding more about how social support and attachment-related processes influence couple relationships, as well as therapy process and outcomes.

Craig W. Smith, Ph.D., is Professor of Family and Community Medicine and Director of the Medical Family Therapy graduate programs in the Department of Family and Community Medicine in the School of Medicine at Saint Louis University. His research interests are in the psychosocial aspects of chronic illness and traumatic injury, the application of emergent technologies in mental health and medical care, and integrative care in primary care settings.

Kristy L. Soloski, M.S., is a doctoral student in the Marriage and Family Therapy program at Kansas State University. She earned her B.A. in Psychology from Kent State University and her M.S. in Marriage and Family Therapy from Purdue University Calumet. Her research interests include examining family relations and the development of substance use in the adolescent population. She is also interested in researching couple processes in an effort to strengthen marriages.

Paul Springer, Ph.D., is an Associate Professor in the Marriage and Family Therapy Program at the University of Nebraska-Lincoln. His research interests include working with rural underserved populations and how to address mental health disparities by emphasizing culturally sensitive collaborative care practices. He received his Ph.D. from Texas Tech University and his Master's degree from Auburn University, both in Marriage and Family Therapy.

Sarah C. Stuchell, Ph.D., is currently the Program Director and Lead Clinician at Malibu Vista, a women's residential psychiatric facility that is part of Elements Behavioral Health and Promises Treatment Centers. She is the founder of the Marriage and Family Research Institute, a non-profit counseling center for families that specializes in integrating research and clinical practice. Sarah earned her Ph.D. in Marital and Family Therapy from Loma Linda University.

Rachel B. Tambling, Ph.D., is an Assistant Professor in the Department of Human Development and Family Studies at the University of Connecticut. Her research interests are centered around understanding and modeling statistical factors that contribute to successful outcomes in therapy. Specifically, she is interested in factors known to influence therapy initiation, persistence, and outcome, such as expectations about therapy, motivation to change, and couple distress.

Jeff L. Todahl, Ph.D., is an Associate Professor for the Couples and Family Therapy program at the University of Oregon. He is the Director of the

Center for the Prevention of Abuse and Neglect. His research interests include child abuse and neglect prevention, intimate partner violence universal screening and assessment, and early intervention and prevention-oriented couples therapy.

Karen S. Wampler, Ph.D., is Professor and Chair of the Department of Human Development and Family Studies at Michigan State University. She is a past editor of the *Journal of Marital and Family Therapy*. Her primary interests are research methodology and the development of observational measures of marriage and family process. Her current research focuses on couple interaction from an attachment theory perspective. She also writes on issues related to mentoring and doctoral education in MFT.

Ronald J. Werner-Wilson, Ph.D., is Chair and Professor in the Department of Family Sciences at the University of Kentucky. He previously taught in the MFT programs at Colorado State University and Iowa State University. He earned his Ph.D. at the University of Georgia. He conducts research on adolescent development, including adolescent sexuality and positive youth development. His other main research interest focuses on MFT process research.

Michael R. Whitehead, M.S., is a doctoral student in the Couple and Family Therapy Program at Michigan State University. His current research is focused on cultural and parenting experiences of U.S.-born Latino's, the utilization of play therapy interventions with both parents and children, and the use of systemically oriented therapy interventions for the treatment of ADHD.

Katharine Wickel, M.S., is a doctoral candidate in the Couple and Family Therapy Program at the University of Minnesota. Her primary research interests focus on the integration of physical, mental, and relational health for couples and families. In keeping with this theme, her main clinical interest is in working with diverse families in medically oriented family therapy.

Colwick M. Wilson, Ph.D., is an Associate Professor in the School of Nursing and Research Associate Affiliate at the Institute of Social Research at the University of Michigan. He is former Chair, Director of Research, and Professor in the Department of Counseling and Family Sciences at Loma Linda University. He graduated from the University of Michigan with his Ph.D. in Sociology and has published in the areas of family, medical sociology- and health disparities.

Jeremy B. Yorgason, Ph.D., is an Associate Professor in the School of Family Life at Brigham Young University. He received his Ph.D. from Virginia Tech in human development, with an emphasis in marriage and family therapy. His current research efforts focus on later life couple relationships in the context of the effects of daily health stressors, managing multiple chronic illnesses, and on grandparent/grandchild relationships.

Senem Zeytinoglu, M.A, M.Ed., is a doctoral student in the Couple and Family Therapy Program at Drexel University. Her research interests include person-of-the-therapist issues and developing culturally sensitive interventions for families who are coping with illness and trauma, specifically the experiences of couples who are raising a child born with cleft lip and/or palate.

1

INTRODUCTION

The Importance of Validity, Relationships, and Change in Marriage and Family Therapy Research

Lee N. Johnson and Richard B Miller

I (L.J.) remember when I started graduate school as a new student in the field of marriage and family therapy (MFT). One of the required classes in my first semester was statistics. I was an engineering major and I enjoy math so I thought statistics would be fun. The teacher was great, and I learned a lot. The one downside to the experience was that the course was taught in the agriculture department. The class focused mostly on analysis of variance (ANOVA), and the instructor would draw a 2 × 2 or larger plot on the chalkboard and say something like, "You can randomly assign conditions to each square in your field, and then you plant your seeds in the randomly assigned quadrant, and you can 'see' what happens and calculate an ANOVA." After a few class periods of plot drawing and hearing examples from agriculture, I felt like I was starting to learn what an ANOVA was and how to calculate it. But I was missing the application to people. So, being the good graduate student that I was, I raised my hand and asked, "How do you do this with people?" The instructor replied, "You don't." I was dumbfounded. Why was I taking this class if I could not apply what I was learning to people? Why was I taking this class from someone who was a fine teacher but did not know how to apply this information to people? As I progressed through graduate school and took other statistics and research methods courses, I was able to fill in the gaps and learn how to apply statistics to people. I also learned how much more complicated research was when trying to apply what I had learned about researching individual people to researching more complex configurations that included couples and families.

I recall another experience during my (L.J.) dissertation proposal meeting. I was developing an understanding of the complex nature of researching couples and families and how their shared environment contributes to the nonindependent nature of their responses. However, I had overlooked another problem that MFT researchers need to grapple with. How do we measure and analyze change across time? My dissertation committee, (of which Rick was a member), was very helpful, and I remember having a lengthy discussion of the many ways to analyze change and how scores at the beginning of therapy may be related (the nonindependent word came up again) to scores at subsequent times during therapy.

Early in my career, I (L.J.) found it difficult to find answers to these questions about dealing appropriately with data from multiple family members in statistical analysis. Moreover, it wasn't well understood how to analyze change using clinical data because couples' and families' responses across waves were also nonindependent. Ignoring these issues when doing MFT research leads to inaccurate results and flawed conclusions, which makes appropriately dealing with them important.

It turns out that there are ways to deal with these methodological and statistical challenges of working with complex, nonindependent clinical data, but they haven't been very accessible to MFT researchers. The two of us (L.J. and R.M.) have had conversations about these issues over the past few years, and we finally decided that it might be a good idea for us to put together a research methods book that would address these issues in ways that could be easily applied to MFT clinical research.

On a more general level, we have also discussed the need for a book on MFT research methods that addresses more advanced topics. The excellent book edited by Sprenkle and Piercy (2005), *Research Methods in Family Therapy*, addresses concepts and principles of MFT research methods, but we believe that there has been a gap between what graduate-level research methods books teach and the methodological standards of the top journals in MFT, psychology, and psychotherapy. There are many challenges that MFT researchers face, such as handling missing data, statistically analyzing small datasets, and recruiting adequate clinical samples, that need to be addressed in order to conduct high quality research. There are also research methodologies, such as physiological research, mixed-methods research, and observation research, that are currently not commonly used by MFT researchers that offer considerable promise to advance our understanding of the process of change in MFT. In addition, cultural adaptation research and community-based participatory research provide methods to validly export models of MFT to other cultures and settings.

Thus, the purpose of this book is to address statistically valid ways of handling nonindependent data and to address more advanced research methods that will enable MFT researchers to conduct high-impact, state-of-the-art clinical research. This isn't a book about structural equation modeling, multilevel modeling, or other advanced statistical approaches. There are abundant resources for learning these statistics (including excellent chapters by Keiley and associates; Keiley, Dankoski, Dolbin-MacNab, & Liu, 2005; Keiley, Martin, Liu, &

Dolbin-MacNab, 2005). Rather, the focus of the book is on compiling methodological and statistical strategies from divergent disciplines, such as family studies, family sociology, family psychology, nursing, and clinical psychology, and *applying* them to clinical MFT research questions. We believe that this effort will lead to more valid and high-impact MFT research.

Nonindependence

Because the issue of nonindependence is so pervasive in MFT research, and is discussed in many of the book's chapters, we decided that it would be helpful to provide a brief introduction in this chapter. Kashy and Kenny (2000) stated: "Before we can have a genuinely social psychology [or MFT field], our theories, research methods, and data analysis will have to take into account the truly interpersonal nature of the phenomena under study" (p. 451). This statement can be applied to MFT; before we can truly show the benefits of MFT treatments, we need to account for the interpersonal nature or nonindependence of what we are studying in all facets of the research process. This requires MFT researchers to model, or account for (and not ignore), nonindependence (Kenny & Cook, 1999). The reason nonindepence is a problem is that ANOVA and regression models have the assumption that observations are independent (Kashy & Kenny, 2000; Kenny, Mannetti, Pierro, Livi, & Kashy, 2002). Consequently, when conducting clinical research with couples and families, researchers need to consider the nonindependence of the data.

It has been well documented that individuals in relationships (e.g., couples and families for this volume) are more similar to each other when compared with two random people in the population; thus, they are nonindependent (Atkins, 2005; Kashy & Kenny, 2000; Kenny & Cook, 1999; Kenny et al., 2002). There are two main ways that researchers fail to account for the fact that people in relationships are nonindependent. First, researchers remove the nonindependence by analyzing couple and family members separately. While this method enables the statistical assumptions of ANOVA and regression to be met and provides useful information about individuals in relationships, it does not give us information about couples, families, and their relationships. It essentially removes the part of the data that couple and family researchers are interested in studying.

Second, researchers have ignored nonindependence by including all couple or family members in the same analysis. Grouping all members together causes a bigger problem in that "nonindependence does distort the estimate of the error variance, so standard errors, p-values, confidence intervals, and most effect-size measures are invalid" (Kenny et al., 2002, p. 128). It is evident that removing or ignoring the nonindependence associated with relational data is not the best method for understanding relationships. On the other hand, using statistical strategies that have been developed for use with dependent data allows for valid conclusions to be made from the analysis that preserves the richness of relational data.

Change

As the two of us discussed how to provide coherence and unity to a book with scores of different chapter authors, we decided to have contributing authors, when appropriate, organize their ideas around two main research principles. The first organizing principle is change. Similar to individuals in couple and family relationships being more similar to each other, the same phenomenon also occurs when measuring individuals, couples, and families across time. Each observation of an individual, couple, or family tells us something about the subsequent observations of the same people and relationships. Thus, MFT researchers need to deal with nonindependence across time.

The problem of nonindependence of observations across time may have influenced the following statement made in 1963 and requoted in 2012: "Although it is commonplace for research to be stymied by some difficulty in experimental methodology, there are really not many instances in the behavioral sciences of promising questions going unresearched because of deficiencies in statistical methodology. Questions dealing with psychological [and MFT] change may well constitute the most important exception" (Bereiter, 1963, p. 58, cited in Hamaker, 2012; brackets added). Similar to ignoring nonindependence within relationships, ignoring nonindependence across observations has consequences (e.g., distorted estimates of the error variance making standard errors, p-values, confidence intervals, and most effect-size measures invalid; Kenny et al., 2002, p. 128). Thus, it is also important to model, and not ignore, nonindependence across time in order to accurately assess change.

Validity

The second organizing principle is validity (external, construct, internal, conclusion). In our experience of teaching research methods, it has become evident that students who understand validity and the relationship among the types of validity can adapt research methods to better answer research questions. With a working understanding of validity, they also do not try to design studies that are overly complex. Research with clinical couples and families is already complex without trying to do too much in one study. They are also better equipped to adapt and expand research methods in answering research questions, instead of taking a "cookbook" approach to research design.

Despite all the advances in research methods and statistics, the perfect research study does not exist (a fact that should relieve some pressure for those graduate students working to impress their dissertation or thesis committee). So, if the studies that we conduct as researchers, or read as consumers, are not perfect, how do we know the value of any given study or program of research? The key to understanding the value of research is validity. As Reis (2012) defined it, "[V]alidity, in the broadest sense of that term, depends on matching protocols, designs, and methods to questions, so that across a diverse program of studies, plausible alternative explanations are ruled out, important boundary conditions are determined, and the real-world relevance of a theory is established" (p. 9). As we apply the standards of validity to research, our goal is to learn how couples and families change by attending therapy, or to find "Truth" with a capital "T"—what is happening in reality. When we conduct research with our nonperfect studies, we learn "truth" with a lowercase "t." The key to knowing the value of any one research study, or program of research, is to understand the gap between Truth and truth. It would be nice if we could simple write it as an equation and do the math: $T - t$ = research value. Unfortunately, it is impossible to assign a value to most factors that go into each part of the equation. The best we can do is understand the types of validity and how they are related (Table 1.1). This allows us to make informed decisions as consumers on the value of studies we read, and as researchers we are able to understand the costs and benefits of our methodological decisions. Just a few of the many validity-related questions that need to be addressed in the planning stages of a research project are: (1) If I collect a random sample from the population (which improves external validity), does it have an impact on other types of validity? (2) What effect do my choices, in how I measure variables and what questionnaire I use to measure my variables, have on other types of validity? and (3) Do decisions I make to improve one type of validity have a potentially negative effect on other types of validity? Answers to these questions require a working knowledge of the four types of validity, and while many readers of this book have an understanding of validity, a brief review is always helpful.

External Validity

"External validity is the degree to which the conclusion in your study would hold for other persons in other places and at other times" (Trochim, 2005, p. 27). One of the goals of research is to be able to apply our results to other people, other places, and other times. Thus, by generalizing findings to a similar group of people, to similar settings, or similar times, we can know about a group of people without actually using them as research participants. Researcher decisions that fall under the area of external validity, while impacting external validity, also have implications for internal and conclusion validity. The main source of the relationship between these types of validity comes from the makeup of study participants. As researchers work to have a representative sample, they create more variability in the participants, which can have a negative effect on internal and conclusion validity.

Construct Validity

"Construct validity refers to the degree to which inferences can legitimately be made from the operationalizations in your study to the theoretical constructs on which those operationalizatons are based" (Trochim, 2005, p. 49). In research we often think about construct validity in connection to measurement. Measurement reliability/validity are a part of construct validity, which is important in the social sciences, where measuring many of our variables of interest is less than straightforward. However, construct validity needs to be examined anytime a researcher has operationalized a variable or intervention. For example, the idea of "reframing" the problem has been used as an intervention by many MFT models. How well a researcher is able to define and describe a reframe and provide information on when to and how to use a reframe are all part of construct validity. Additionally, how accurately and consistently the reframes are done during the study is a construct validity issue. The quality of operationalizations and the consistency with which they are implemented are key construct validity questions.

Construct validity issues have an effect on other types of validity. For example, poor measurement reliability, validity, or treatment implementation can introduce an alternative explanation (internal validity) to results, and poor measurement reliability and intervention implementation contribute to the likelihood of committing a type I or type II error (conclusion validity). Construct validity can even have implications for external validity. Trochim (2005) discussed the idea of the construct validity of the operationalization of study participants and how it is important to recruit participants that match the theoretical constructs you are researching (e.g., using college students to research adult attachment may be a good starting point, but it is not the best operationalization of study participants).

Internal Validity

"Internal validity is the approximate truth about inferences regarding cause-effect or *causal* relationships" (Trochim, 2005, p. 135; italics in original). Internal validity is mainly focused on the degree to which alternative explanations to your findings have been ruled out. This is done through research design and random assignment to groups or conditions (see Chapter 21 for a review of causal relationships). The criteria for showing a causal relationship via research are stringent and often difficult or unethical to carry out. Correlational research makes a valuable contribution to researching couples and families. However, when we do not control the assignment of participants to conditions, or control the independent variable, we are conducting research that has many alternative explanations and, thus, lower internal validity. In correlational research, we try to improve internal validity by measuring variables that, according to our guiding theory, may be alternative explanations and by showing statistically that these variables are not alternative explanations. Additionally, we try to improve internal validity in correlational studies by using covariates in our analysis to determine the effect of the covariates on the results. While these strategies help to somewhat improve internal validity, there are many other variables that we have not measured or controlled that may influence the results. Thus, correlational studies, while valuable and necessary, have limited internal validity.

Conclusion Validity

"Conclusion validity is the degree to which conclusions you reach about relationships in your data are reasonable" (Trochim, 2005, p. 206). The degree to which relationship conclusions are reasonable can best be summed up by asking: "Are your results correct? Did you make a type I or type II error?" If findings are correct, "Truth" in reality says that we should find a relationship in our results, and our research "truth" was that we found a relationship. The opposite, while not what we want as a researcher but still correct, is "Truth" in reality is that we should not find a relationship among our study variables, and our research "truth" is that we did not find a relationship. In both of these cases, we have done a good job of designing our study to maximize our conclusion validity. When we have threats to conclusion validity, we are more likely to commit a type I error (finding a relationship in our research when in reality there is not one) or type II error (missing a relationship in our research when in reality there is one).

Conclusion validity is not discussed much in the limitation sections of research articles. Many limitations focus on external validity (e.g., "Our external validity is low because of our low sample size, and participants came from a university clinic, so results are not generalizable"). Findings could be much better understood, and future research improved, if researchers provided information about the conclusion validity of their results. Conducting a power analysis is a part of the research planning process that is necessary to be able to discuss conclusion validity (see Chapter 26 for discussion of power analysis). Discussing conclusion validity also requires researchers to be forthcoming about the number of analyses they run and use an appropriate Bonferroni correction (Napierala, 2012).

Summary

It is our hope that this book adds to the professional discussions on validity and nonindependence in the area of clinical research with couples and families. Chapters provide valuable information on issues such as measurement, ethics, and using theory in researching clinical couples and families. Additional chapters provide information on methods ranging from physiology, dyadic data analysis, missing data, and analysis strategies for smaller samples.

We have learned much from working with the chapter authors. They are excellent researchers and have done a remarkable job of bringing a wide range of methodological issues to bear on MFT clinical research. We should note that the chapter authors come from a variety of backgrounds and educational settings. In this chapter and throughout this book we and our chapter authors have used couple, marriage, MFT, and CFT (couples and family therapy) as terms related to the research done within our field and therein have been discussed in the professional context. However, this book is focused on research methods and not on the professional debate. Thus, we have not edited or tried to unify these terms; rather, we have left them as written by the authors.

Table 1.1 Descriptions and Relationships Among Types of Validity*

	External	Construct	Internal	Conclusion
External	• Generalizability to other people, places, and times Threats • People • Places • Times	• Operationalization of sample needs to match theory (e.g., using undergraduates to test differentiation or adult attachment is not a good match).	• These two types of validity are generally inversely related. • As you implement more stringent controls to increase internal validity you decrease external validity. • As you increase the variability of your participants you introduce more possible alternative explanations.	• As you increase variables in your sample, you increase your chances of making a type II error.
Construct		• Are you consistently and accurately measuring your variables? • Is your program or intervention operationalized in a way that others can consistently and accurately carry it out? Threats • Low measurement reliability or validity • Only using one version of program • Only measure construct in one way • Participants learn from the tests • Did not give the proper dose of treatment • Hypothesis guessing • Evaluation apprehension • Researcher expectations	• Poor measurement reliability and validity introduce an alternative explanation to your findings. • Poor operationalization of your intervention or independent variable introduces an alternative explanation to your findings. • Poor monitoring of your intervention or independent variable can introduce alternative explanations.	• Low reliability of measures or lack of consistency in intervention or independent variable can increase the chances of making a type II error.

External	Construct	Internal	Conclusion
Internal		• Have you ruled out alternative explanations to the results? <u>Threats</u> • History—events outside causing the effect • Maturation—normal development causing the effect • Testing—pre-test made participants aware of study variables • Mortality—people dropout of the study • Regression to the mean—inaccurately makes participants appear more like the population • Imitation of treatment—control or comparison group gets a different but effective treatment • Rivalry—control or comparison group competes with treatment group • Demoralization—control or comparison group gives up • Equalization of treatment—someone provides treatment to control or comparison group to equalize treatment	• Internal and conclusion validity are not related. • Studies can be low or strong in both types. • Studies can be strong in either type and not the other type.

(*Continued*)

Table 1.1 (Continued)

	External	Construct	Internal	Conclusion
Conclusion				• Is there a relationship among the variables (e.g., are you making a type I or type II error)? Threats • "Fishing" for a statistically significant finding • Data entry errors • Low reliability of measures • Low reliability in intervention implementation • Violation of statistical assumptions • Inadequate power • Large variability in participants • Other factors that introduce variability in the setting

*Interpret as a correlation table with definitions and threats along the diagonal. Information in this table is from courses taught by the authors, Brewer (2000), Creswell (2014), and Trochim (2005).

References

Atkins, D. C. (2005). Using multilevel models to analyze couple and family treatment data: Basic and advanced issues. *Journal of Family Psychology, 19*(1), 98–110.

Brewer, M. B. (2000). Research design and issues of validity. In H. T. Reis & C. M. Judd (Eds.), *Handbook of research methods in social and personality psychology* (pp. 3–16). New York: Cambridge University Press.

Creswell, J. W. (2014). *Research design: Qualitative, quantitative, and mixed methods approaches.* Los Angeles: Sage.

Hamaker, E. L. (2012). Why researchers should think "within-person": A paradigmatic rationale. In M. R. Mehl & T. S. Conner (Eds.), *Handbook of research methods for studying daily life* (pp. 43–61). New York: Guilford.

Kashy, D. A., & Kenny, D. A. (2000). The analysis of data from dyads and groups. In H. T. Reis & C. M. Judd (Eds.), *Handbook of research methods in social and personality psychology* (pp. 451–477). New York: Cambridge University Press.

Keiley, M. K., Dankoski, M., Dolbin-MacNab, M., & Liu, T. (2005). Covariance structure analysis: From path analysis to structural equation modeling. In D. H. Sprenkle & F. P. Piercy (Eds.), *Research methods in family therapy* (2nd ed., pp. 432–460). New York: Guilford Press.

Keiley, M. K., Martin, N. C., Liu, T., & Dolbin-MacNab, M. (2005). Multilevel growth modeling in the context of family research. In D. H. Sprenkle & F. P. Piercy (Eds.), *Research methods in family therapy* (2nd ed., pp. 405–431). New York: Guilford Press.

Kenny, D. A., & Cook, W. (1999). Partner effects in relationship research: Conceptual issues, analytic difficulties, and illustrations. *Personal Relationships, 6*(4), 433–448.

Kenny, D. A., Mannetti, L., Pierro, A., Livi, S., & Kashy, D. A. (2002). The statistical analysis of data from small groups. *Journal of Personality and Social Psychology, 83*(1), 126–137.

Napierala, M. A. (2012). What is the Bonferroni correction? *AAOS Now, 6*(4), 40–40.

Reis, H. T. (2012). Why researchers should think "real-world": A conceptual rationale. In M. R. Mehl & T. S. Conner (Eds.), *Handbook of research methods for studying daily life* (pp. 3–21). New York: Guilford.

Sprenkle, D. H., & Piercy, F. P. (Eds). (2005). *Research methods in family therapy* (2nd ed.). New York: Guilford Press.

Trochim, W. M. K. (2005). *Research methods: The concise knowledge base.* Cincinnati: Atomic Dog Publishing.

Section I

FOUNDATIONAL ISSUES

2

DEVELOPING A GOOD RESEARCH IDEA

Richard B Miller and Lexie Pfeifer

I (R.M.) well remember when I first learned the importance of having a good research idea. Near the end of my master's thesis defense, consistent with tradition, my committee excused me while they deliberated their decision. A few minutes later they invited me back in the room, and they told me that I had passed. I was excited to hear the good news, but my excitement was quickly dampened by what a member of the committee said to me. He said, "We decided to pass your thesis because the design was solid. You have a well-developed questionnaire, a good sample, good data collection procedures, and good statistical analysis. Moreover, your thesis was fairly well written considering it is a master's thesis. However, your thesis is a complete waste of time because you asked a research question that no one cares about. You failed to answer the 'So what?' question. Although your thesis demonstrated very good methodology, it is basically worthless because you didn't have a good research idea."

Ouch! It was a tough lesson to learn, and the member of my thesis committee could have chosen a better, less harsh, way to communicate it to me. However, the point he emphatically made was correct. The first requirement for conducting a high-quality study is to have a good research idea, in other words, to ask a good research question. The truth is that the best research methodology cannot rescue a bad research idea. Indeed, "the selection and formulation of a good research question are important, if not the most important, parts of research" (Lipowski, 2008, p. 1667).

Having an important research idea is also an important consideration in obtaining external funding for a research project. For example, grant proposals that are submitted to the National Institutes of Health are evaluated on five criteria: the significance of the research idea, the qualifications of the investigators, the innovation of the study design, the methods used in the study, and the quality of the scientific environment, which is usually the principal investigator's university (National Institutes of Health [NIH], 2013). Thus, each proposal is evaluated on the significance of the research question and the aims of the proposed study. A poor score on the significance criterion will relegate the proposal to the rejection bin. When evaluating the significance of the research idea, reviewers are asked to consider whether the project addresses an important problem in society or a

15

critical barrier to progress in the field. Specifically, they ask themselves: "If the aims of the project are achieved, how will scientific knowledge, people's lives . . . and/ or clinical practice be improved? How will successful completion of the aims change the concepts, methods, technologies, treatments, services, or preventative interventions that drive this field?" (NIH, 2013).

What Is a Good Research Idea?

Interesting, Important, and Meaningful

What makes a research idea, or research question, good, and how can we tell the difference between a good idea and a bad one? Kwiatkowski and Silverman (1998) have stated: "Any good research question should be able to pass the 'so what' test; the answer to the question should be *important, interesting,* and *meaningful*" (p. 1114, emphasis added). In order to pass the "so what?" test, the research question needs to address an issue that marriage and family therapists (MFTs) care about and are interested in and that will have an impact on the field and clients' lives. For example, research by Law and Crane (2000) on medical offset asked the significant question: Do couples and families who receive marriage and family therapy (MFT) visit medical doctors less often, and thereby reduce medical costs? With the field of MFT struggling to receive insurance coverage for relationship problems (e.g., V-codes), their findings that MFT led to lower health care utilization were important, interesting, and meaningful.

When considering the value of a research idea, one important question that should be asked is: "How many MFTs will find this research question important, interesting, and meaningful?" For example, a study that asks the question "What are the perceptions of American therapists conducting MFT in Sweden?" would be of interest to only a handful of MFTs. On the other hand, a study that asks the question "What therapist behaviors in the first session predict positive therapy outcomes?" would be of interest to most MFTs because they would be interested in knowing what first-session therapist behaviors will lead to better therapy outcomes. In addition, the question is important because it holds the potential to improve clients' well-being as therapists apply the findings from the study in their clinical work. Thus, the impact of the research would be high because of widespread interest and its significant implications for clinical practice.

Original

An important criterion for a good research idea is to ask a research question that is original, that hasn't been asked before (Kwiatkowski & Silverman, 1998). The study needs to have the potential of producing new information. Sometimes, a case can be made for the replication of an existing study in order to increase the robustness of the findings, especially if the original study had a small, limited sample size or was being conducted in a different setting. However, in general, the research idea needs to hold the promise of asking a question that has not previously been addressed. For example, asking the question "Is behavioral marital therapy an effective model for treating couples' relationship distress?" wouldn't be a good idea because at least 30 randomized clinical trials have already demonstrated its effectiveness (Shadish & Baldwin, 2005). Thus, researchers must provide in their literature review evidence that the research idea is novel and will provide new information.

One mistake researchers often make is assuming that a gap in the literature automatically translates to a good research idea. For example, researchers could do a study of the effectiveness of structural family therapy in Luxembourg. While it is true that no clinical randomized trials have addressed that research question in Luxembourg, it would be difficult to make the case that it is an important and meaningful research idea. Alvesson and Sandberg (2011) have coined the term "gap-spotting," when it appears that researchers have merely identified a gap in the literature without developing an argument that the gap is an important and meaningful one to address. The managing editor of a major peer-reviewed business journal, after 26 years of working with the journal, stated, "If you can't make a convincing argument that you are filling an important gap in the literature, you will have a hard time establishing that you have a contribution to make to that literature. You might be surprised how many authors miss this fundamental point" (Johanson, 2007, p. 292). Finding a gap in the literature is not enough; researchers must also demonstrate that the idea generated by finding the gap is important, interesting, and meaningful.

Linked to Theory or Important Problem

Sjöberg (2003) adds to our understanding of a good idea by stating, "A good idea is new and original and it is related in an interesting way to theoretical developments in the field and/or to practical problems" (p. 12). Through this definition, Sjöberg suggests that good research ideas test MFT theories. Indeed, good research ideas test the validity or challenge an existing theoretical principle or a widely held assumption (Alvesson & Sandberg, 2011). A research question that is explicitly tied to theory has much more impact than a research question that merely addresses a specific topic. For example, researchers may want to find out whether emotionally focused therapy (EFT) is effective in China. This could be an interesting and meaningful research question because China has a population of 1.3 billion people, so there would naturally be widespread interest in the adaptability and applicability of EFT to the Chinese culture. However, the research idea would be much more interesting, important, and meaningful if the question were explicitly linked to cross-cultural theories of emotion (see Alonso-Arbiol, van de Vihver, Fernandez, Paez, & Campos, 2011) or to the cross-cultural theoretical concepts of *etic* and *emic*. The concept of *etic* refers to the assumption that cultures share universal characteristics, which suggests that EFT would be effective in other cultures, including China. The concept of *emic*, on the other hand, assumes that each culture has unique characteristics and, therefore, must be studied independently, with the recognition that specific therapy models might not be appropriate in other cultures, including China (Berry, 1989). Thus, a study of the effectiveness of EFT in China that was grounded in cross-cultural theory would not only address the specific issue of the effectiveness of EFT in China, but also inform cross-cultural MFT, which would provide important implications to the adaptability of EFT in other cultures as well. By adding the theory component, the research idea improves from being good to excellent.

In a similar way, research that challenges widely held assumptions within the field of MFT can also have high impact (Alvesson & Sandberg, 2011). For example, since the beginning of MFT training, the field has taken pride in the widespread use of live supervision; it seems to be considered the "gold standard" of supervision. However, a recent study on the effect of live supervision on perceived therapeutic progress found that while therapist-trainees who received live supervision reported more progress in therapy, the clients whose therapist-trainee received live supervision reported the same progress in therapy as those clients whose cases did not receive live supervision (Bartle-Haring, Silverthorn, Meyer, & Toviessi, 2009). The authors suggest that one explanation for the findings is that those clients whose cases involve live supervision might perceive that their therapists are less competent and, therefore, in more need of close supervision. The results of the study provide new information that challenges the assumption that the labor-intensive modality of live supervision is the gold standard in the field of MFT. Consequently, the research idea that spawned this study of live supervision was interesting, important, and meaningful.

Sjöberg (2003) also states that a research idea is good if it addresses an important practical problem. For example, at the time this chapter was being written, MFTs were not approved providers for Medicare mental health services and were ineligible to be reimbursed by Medicare. As a result, MFTs are generally not able to provide clinical services to the elderly in the United States. With the rapid growth of the number of elderly, especially as the "baby boomers" begin turning 65, the need for MFT services that target older adults will increase dramatically in the near future. This barrier to providing MFT services to older adults is a significant problem in the field of MFT in general and to many practicing MFTs specifically. Consequently, a study that demonstrated the clinical and cost effectiveness of MFT services to the older population would be a great idea.

Feasible

An additional important criterion of a good research question is that it must be feasible to conduct a study that will address the question (Kwiatkowski & Silverman, 1998). The issue of feasibility, of it being "doable," is crucial. The best idea, if it lacks feasibility, is heading toward a dead end. A major reason why the qualifications of the researchers and the quality of the research environment are included as evaluation criteria for NIH grant proposals (NIH, 2013) is that they are important markers of feasibility. The experience and skills of the researcher, as well as the level of institutional support from an agency or university where the research will be conducted (in addition to the proposed budget), give the reviewers a sense of whether or not the research idea and proposed design are feasible. Consequently, a good research idea must be doable, or else it is not a good idea. We recommend that researchers use validity threats as a guide in determining whether a research project is possible.

Interesting to Researcher

Finally, the research idea needs to be one in which the *researcher* is interested (Kwiatkowski & Silverman, 1998). Research is a demanding endeavor that requires a huge investment from the researcher. If researchers have a passion for the idea that they are investigating, the process can be engaging and exciting. However, if the researcher does not really care about the research topic, then the research process will be tedious, boring, and never-ending. Consequently, when deciding upon a research idea, researchers need to be introspective and honestly ask themselves whether this is an idea that really excites them. An otherwise wonderful research idea in which the researcher lacks passion and excitement is actually a bad idea.

How Does a Researcher Develop a Good Research Idea?

After understanding the characteristics of good research ideas, how does a researcher develop a good idea? Does it come with a flash of brilliance, or does it involve incremental steps? Developing a good research idea can seem like a daunting task. A resource for learning to develop good research ideas, surprisingly (for MFT researchers), comes from the business world. However, this shouldn't come as a surprise because the vitality and success of businesses lie in their ability to be innovative and introduce products that are novel and appealing to potential customers. Consequently, business scholars have focused substantial research into better understanding how good, innovative ideas are generated.

A team of researchers conducted a large study on innovation by distributing a series of surveys to business executives, as well as interviewing close to a hundred innovative inventors or business executives about the circumstances surrounding the generation of their most creative business ideas. Innovators interviewed included founders and inventors of Amazon.com, eBay, Dell, Skype, JetBlue, and BlackBerry products. They reported the findings of their research in the book *The Innovator's DNA: Mastering the Five Skills of Disruptive Innovators* (Dyer, Gregersen, & Christensen, 2011).

Their major finding was that great innovators *acted* in ways that were different than those of business leaders who were less innovative. They noted, "One's ability to generate innovative ideas is not merely a function of the mind, but also a function of behaviors," and "if we change our behaviors, we can improve our creative impact" (Dyer et al., 2011, p. 3). Specifically, they found that great innovators did five behaviors that facilitated the discovery process. The innovators were experts at making connections and associations. They asked questions, were keen observers of the world around them, and networked with a wide variety of persons. In addition, they experimented with new ideas.

Associating

Making associations is one way to generate research ideas. It involves taking seemingly unrelated questions, problems, and ideas and making connections between them. Dyer et al. (2011) suggest that we extract ourselves from the mire of "problems of detail" by zooming in and out on a problem and beginning to draw connections between elements of the larger picture and the problem of focus. They note that "the movement [between high-level things to really, really small details] often makes for new associations" (p. 54). Zooming out encourages us to look at the context connected with a problem of focus.

Associational thinkers are also what the IDEO design firm calls "T-shaped." They "hold deep expertise in one knowledge area but actively acquire knowledge broadly across different knowledge areas" (Dyer et al., 2011, p. 56). What have the fields of clinical psychology, child development, and neurophysiology contributed to our understanding of marriage and family phenomena? What could the fields of physiology and chemistry teach us about relational phenomena? *The Innovator's DNA* encourages "importing" ideas from other research and fields into our specific areas of research. They also discuss "exporting" ideas.

Dyer et al. (2011) also note that creative associational thinking occurs most naturally when one is in a relaxed state and engaged in normal everyday activities, rather than "deliberately attacking a problem" (p. 58). Activities suggested by *The Innovator's DNA* (2011) to jump-start associational thinking are to "force new associations" by making connections between ideas we wouldn't normally think to connect, taking on another's persona for a new perspective on the problem, generating metaphors for your research phenomenon, or starting a collection or file of interesting ideas from a variety of sources.

I (R.M.) had an experience with making associations that was very unexpected. As a department chair a couple of years ago, I was asked by my dean to attend a presentation by some business researchers. I had many things to do at that time, and I did *not* want to attend the presentation. Reluctantly (and with a really bad attitude), I went to the presentation and sat in the back of the room so that I could read a couple of articles that I needed to read. The professors started their presentation and talked about research on innovation in business. They mentioned that they had just published a book called *The Innovator's DNA*, which reported their main research finding that great business innovators had five behaviors that differentiated them from less innovative research leaders. I had been doing a lot of thinking during that period of time about the need for MFT researchers to develop better research ideas. I had done some reading and figured out the basic characteristics of good research ideas, but I was struggling with how to teach graduate students, as well as more experienced researchers, *how* to develop good research ideas.

As I reluctantly listened to these business researchers' presentation, I made a very unexpected association. I realized that these five behaviors of business innovators would also apply to MFT researchers striving to come up with good research ideas. After making that association, I listened to these business scholars' presentation with newfound interest, and their ideas have found their way into this chapter because it seemed obvious that they offer a guide to MFT researchers working on developing a good research idea.

Dr. Eliana Gil is an example of someone making associations in the practice of MFT. She received training in family therapy, but she struggled to develop a method for treating children and their families in developmentally appropriate ways. She was able to make an association with the field of play therapy, where she gleaned insight and techniques for engaging children in the therapy process through nonverbal play. She began to develop her own integrated model of family play therapy, which elicits more of the child's participation and voice in therapy through the use of play expression (Christensen & Thorngren, 2000).

Questioning

The authors of *The Innovator's DNA* (Dyer et al., 2011) found in their research that innovative executives asked a lot more questions than typical executives. Innovative thinkers are "suspended comfortably between faith in and doubt of their maps [of the research territory]" (Dyer et al., p. 71). Healthy doubt does not mean cynicism or rejection of existing theories and research, but a courageousness to question and challenge the tenets and assumptions of those theories and research. *The Innovator's DNA* describes types of questions to ask to get you started.

"**What is** _____? " and "**What causes** _____?" These questions bring you back to the basics of defining a phenomenon at its roots. Decades of research may have defined this very phenomenon countless times, but how would you define it in your own words? There will be parts of existing definitions and explanations that you both accept and reject. Pay attention to inconsistencies in definitions and the parts you are tempted to reject. These areas are fertile ground for generating good research.

"**Why?**" or "**Why not?**" Don't be afraid to challenge assumptions (Alvesson & Sandberg, 2011). The heart of the scientific method is in challenging rather than proving. However, we often set out to prove or defend a position with research, rather than seek deeper understanding through challenging authoritative sources and long-held traditional theories. We need to give ourselves permission to ask the incredible "whys" and even the rebellious "whys" that pertain to our passion for the depth of the field of MFT. *The Innovator's DNA* and Lipowski (2008) suggest the "five-whys" method, encouraging researchers to ask "why" at least five times to get to the heart of an issue.

"What if?" By imposing and eliminating constraints on a research question, it is possible to fully explore the "what ifs" that can lead to unique research discoveries. We should ask of our research questions and methodology: "What assumptions are being made? What constraints or conditions have been imposed? What constraints or conditions are being ignored?" These "what ifs" provide limitless opportunities for generation of relevant research.

Further, it is even encouraged to ask the absurd, such as: "What if something positive were actually negative?" or "What if something efficient was a problem?" These questions become less absurd when we are able to "transform what are commonly seen as truths or facts into assumptions" (Alvesson & Sandberg, 2011). Again, as researchers, we must cultivate the characteristic of courage to challenge authoritative sources to ask such questions.

An example of this is the historically accepted notion of repression, as introduced by Freud. Tavris and Aronson (2007) describe the "epidemic" of recovered memory therapy based on the theoretical notion that individuals unconsciously repress traumatic memories. Clients would uncover, in therapy, knowledge of sexual abuse that had never been in their conscious awareness. This practice of uncovering repressed traumatic memories was not isolated to a few eccentric therapists, but was widely disseminated in articles, books, and conferences. Therapists testified in trials against "abusers." The assumption that repression is a common reaction to sexual trauma has since been scientifically studied. Contrary to the theoretical notion of memory repression, research indicated that trauma victims seem to remember obsessively or to actively (not unconsciously) avoid details relating to trauma, but they do not forget (Tavris & Aronson).

There are many such theoretical notions (perhaps not as political or blatantly harmful) that exist in the field of MFT. Lipowski (2008) refers to these as "pet theories or practice traditions." These theoretical notions are often accepted and applied to therapeutic practice without strong scientific evidence supporting them. We must have the courage to treat commonly accepted premises as conditions and assumptions instead of truths.

Observation

A third behavior practiced by successful innovators is intense observation. They pay attention to and are curious about the world and people around them. Innovators pay attention to "a job and a better way to do it," workarounds, and surprises. A workaround is a way a system negotiates a resolution in a roundabout way, which is indicative of incomplete solutions and suggests rich areas of investigation. When a process is surprising, unexpected, or doesn't make sense, this is an opportunity to understand why the solution was worked out in this particular way or whether there is a more efficient answer. Innovators observe in many different environments, not just the context of interest (Dyer et al., 2011). Similarly, MFT researchers observe the family system and the therapeutic session and ask questions about what they see. First, in our observations, we will notice the functional, social, and emotional aspects of accomplishment of a goal. Then, we will look for workarounds and surprises (Dyer et al.; Lipowski, 2008), gaps (Alvesson & Sandberg, 2011), or half-truths (Sjöberg, 2003). The behaviors of innovators do not exist in isolation; rather, innovative business executives (and MFT researchers) will be observing, asking questions, and making associations about what they observe. For example, the history of the development of the systemic paradigm for treating individual pathology features innovative therapists who actively participated in the behaviors of observing, questioning, and making associations. Several of these pioneers independently observed that patients suffering from major mental illnesses would make significant improvement in psychiatric hospitals or other mental health institutions. During the course of treatment, they would go home to their families for a few days but come back with worse symptoms than when they left. This repeated observation led these pioneers to question the prevailing theories of the etiology and treatment of mental illnesses. In searching for answers, the association was made with general systems theory (Nichols, 2011). Thus, the idea of treating individual pathology from a systems perspective was born. It was a *great* idea, and it was the product of innovative therapists observing, asking questions, and making associations.

As researchers, we can follow in the footsteps of these innovative founders of our field. When we notice surprises, workarounds, gaps, and inconsistencies, rather than jump to intervene according to preconceived theory, we can ask: "Why did you do that? Why did that happen?" The answers our clients, supervisees, and colleagues give us to these questions may touch on something investigation worthy or something unique that will build upon or generate theory.

A final guideline for observation is to seek out new environments. As researchers, we can seek new environments and experiences that will lead to research innovation. Some examples of new environments are conferences outside the field of MFT, observing in-home family therapy versus traditional outpatient family therapy, observing the philosophies and maintenance of other clinics and agencies, and, in the growing field of multicultural family therapy, visiting other countries and cultures.

Indeed, MFTs are in a prime position to develop innovative research questions because our work as therapists calls on us to constantly observe the therapeutic process while we are working with couples and families. In turn, the observation of unexpected or persistently frustrating interactions in therapy leads us to ask questions about the therapeutic models we are using and their application to specific populations. These questions, as well as the process of making associations with other theories and assumptions, can lead to great research ideas.

Networking

The authors of *The Innovator's DNA* found that successful innovators are networkers, but generally not for the purpose of expanding professional connections. Rather, successful innovators network for ideas (Dyer et al., 2011). They are interested in other's ideas and perspectives and make associations back to development of their own research ideas. They seek out ideas within and outside their own field.

For example, Drury (1991), in an editorial for the *British Journal of General Practice*, commented on the limited communication between general practitioners and pharmacists. Despite their common roles to provide medical care to the community, there is little communication between the two professions.

This occurs across all professions. Specifically, as MFTs, we work with clinical psychologists, social workers, psychiatrists, neurologists, doctors, and school counselors. How often do we do more than simply try to represent our profession to the "other" fields? To develop innovative research ideas, in addition to making an intentional effort to share our research ideas and perspectives with professionals in other fields, we need to ask for their thoughts and ideas.

Thus, there is a reason why so many good research ideas are sketched out on a napkin at a restaurant. When a group of scholars get together for lunch or dinner, they come from different universities and agencies, and they each bring specific expertise and experience. During the course of the conversation, there is a natural synergism that comes with this networking of ideas. The process is invigorating, and the outcome is often some incredibly good research ideas.

Another good example of successful networking by MFT researchers is seen at the University of Georgia's MFT clinic. Marriage and family therapists work in concert with nutritionists, environmental/housing specialists, and financial counselors to provide care for families coming to the clinic (Johnson, Gale, Ford, & Goetz, 2012). They have recognized that these other fields offer something valuable to the well-being and functioning of those they see in MFT practice. Thus, they have developed an innovative multidisciplinary clinical model that holds great promise for good research ideas.

To improve our own networking behavior, Dyer et al. (2011) suggest that we seek to expand the diversity of our networking circles by seeking out people with different opinions and backgrounds from our own. They encourage us to ask their perspectives and what is cutting edge in their field. They also recommend planning to attend two conferences a year. At these conferences we are exposed to the ideas and work of others. But networking alone will not generate innovative research ideas. While networking, we need to observe, ask questions, make associations, and open up our minds to experimentation with new ideas.

Experimenting

The fifth behavior of successful innovators identified by Dyer et al. (2011) is a willingness to experiment. Successful innovators have experimented and failed a number of times before coming up with a groundbreaking idea. Dyer et al. suggest three ways in which innovators engage in experimentation. First, they are willing to try out new experiences. Second, they deconstruct processes and ideas. Third, they test ideas with informal pilot studies and prototypes. A spirit of experimentation was an important trait of many of the founders of the field of MFT. Jay Haley and Carl Whitaker's sessions were acts of experimentation. They manipulated family dynamics while being unsure of the outcome but being willing to learn from the process that unfolded (Keith & Whitaker, 1981). From this cyclical process of experience, experimentation, adjustment, and more experimentation, they generated innovative techniques and theories that have influenced the field of MFT. This spirit of experimentation requires researchers to be humble and willing to make mistakes. Sjöberg (2003) stated that researchers must not become stuck in the problem of "too little or too much self-confidence." At either extreme, we become hesitant to try new things and make mistakes.

The second way to engage in experimentation is to be like a little child who delights in taking things apart for the challenge of putting them back together again. Alvesson and Sandberg (2011) call this "unpacking of theory." Similar to a car mechanic who systematically takes apart an engine and examines the parts—how they fit and whirl together in the system—researchers can take apart theories and examine individual assumptions and theoretical cohesiveness.

A third way to engage in experimentation is through pilot studies and prototypes. Large, grant-funded research with large sample sizes and controlled conditions are difficult to plan and implement. Further, these studies are built upon smaller pilot studies. With smaller samples and less restrictive conditions, researchers can try out new ideas and innovative hypotheses. Case studies and single-case studies (see Chapter 13) are examples of smaller-scale experimentation, and it is expected that this is the process leading up to more formal experimentation. For example, the NIH grant proposal has a section for describing preliminary work that led up to the proposed research (Gordon, 1989). Lipowski (2008) recommends thinking of this kind of experimentation in terms of a working model, which is a framework that changes, adapts, and builds itself according to feedback from ongoing experimentation.

Reading

Although not mentioned explicitly by the authors of *The Innovator's DNA*, we suggest a sixth important behavior of innovative MFT researchers: reading extensively in the field of MFT and in other fields. In order to develop a novel and cutting-edge research idea, researchers must be familiar with the "frontiers" of MFT research in order to know what is cutting-edge. There is simply no substitute for immersion in the MFT clinical and research literature. Research is constantly being generated, and there is a never-ending flow of new information to update our own research. The best MFT researchers are well read in the MFT research literature, as well as in the literature of related fields. On the other hand, less innovative and less impactful researchers try to take shortcuts and don't pay the price to master the MFT clinical and research literature.

Conclusion

The most important step in conducting high-impact research is having a great research idea that generates a compelling research question. The best research design cannot compensate for a weak, low-impact, and uninteresting research idea. The best research ideas are original and address an important question that is interesting, important, and meaningful to a large number of MFTs. In addition, research ideas are best when they are couched in theory or examine a significant problem, and they need to be ideas that capture the passion of the researcher.

From business scholars who have studied innovation, we have gleaned five skills that can aid us as researchers in generating good research ideas. Innovative researchers will be constantly engaged in the process of making associations, questioning, observing, networking, and experimenting. In addition, they will be well-read, up-to-date scholars in the general field of MFT, as well as in their specialty areas. It should be easier for MFT researchers than other researchers to develop innovative and important ideas because MFTs practice these behaviors every day in their clinical work. The task, then, of MFT researchers is to transfer these behaviors and skills from their clinical work to their work in developing good research ideas. Excellent clinicians and researchers cultivate qualities of curiosity, humility, confidence, acceptance, courage, and interest in the world and people around them. Indeed, the qualities that make for creative family therapists make for innovative family therapy researchers.

References

Alonso-Arbiol, I., van de Vihver, F.J.R., Fernandez, I., Paez, D., & Campos, M. (2011). Implicit theories about interrelations of anger components in 25 countries. *Emotion, 11*, 1–11.

Alvesson, M., & Sandberg, J. (2011). Generating research questions through problematization. *Academy of Management Review, 36*, 247–271.

Bartle-Haring, S.B., Silverthorn, B.C., Meyer, K., & Toviessi, P. (2009). Does live supervision make a difference? A multilevel analysis. *Journal of Marital and Family Therapy, 35*, 406–414.

Berry, J.W. (1989). Imposed etics-emics-derived etics: The operationalization of a compelling idea. *International Journal of Psychology, 24*, 721–735.

Christensen, T.M., & Thorngren, J.M. (2000). Integrating play in family therapy: An interview with Eliana Gil, Ph.D. *Family Journal: Counseling and Therapy for Couples and Families, 8*, 91–100.

Drury, M. (1991). Doctors and pharmacists—working together. *British Journal of General Practice, 41*, 91.

Dyer, J., Gregersen, H., & Christensen, C. M. (2011). *The innovator's DNA: Mastering the five skills of disruptive innovators.* Cambridge, MA: Harvard Business School Press.

Gordon, S. L. (1989). Ingredients of a successful grant application to the National Institutes of Health. *Journal of Orthopaedic Research, 7,* 138–141.

Johanson, L. M. (2007). Sitting in your readers' chair: Attending to your academic sensemakers. *Journal of Management Inquiry, 16,* 290–294.

Johnson, L. N., Gale, J., Ford, M., & Goetz, J. (September, 2012). *Building cross-disciplinary bridges for client success.* Institute presented at the annual meeting of the American Association for Marriage and Family Therapy, Charlotte, North Carolina.

Keith, D. V., & Whitaker, C. A. (1981). Play therapy: A paradigm for work with families. *Journal of Marital and Family Therapy, 7,* 243–254.

Kwiatkowski, T., & Silverman, R. (1998). Research fundamentals: II. Choosing and defining a research question. *Academic Emergency Medicine, 5,* 1114–1117.

Law, D. D., & Crane, D. R. (2000). The influence of marital and family therapy on health care utilization in a health-maintenance organization. *Journal of Marital and Family Therapy, 26,* 281–291.

Lipowski, E. E. (2008). Developing great research questions. *American Journal of Health-System Pharmacy, 65,* 1667.

National Institutes of Health. (2013). Peer review process. Retrieved from http://grants.nih.gov/grants/peer_review_process.htm#scoring

Nichols, M. P. (2011). *The essentials of family therapy* (10th ed.). New York: Pearson.

Shadish, W. R., & Baldwin, S. A. (2005). Effects of behavioral marital therapy: A meta-analysis of randomized controlled trials. *Journal of Consulting and Clinical Psychology, 73,* 6–14.

Sjöberg, L. (2003). Good and not-so-good ideas in psychological research. A tutorial in idea assessment and generation. *VEST: Journal for Science and Technology Studies, 16,* 33–68.

Tavris, C., & Aronson, E. (2007). *Mistakes were made, but not by me.* New York: Harcourt.

3

INTEGRATING THEORY AND RESEARCH

Maureen Davey, Senem Zeytinoglu, and Laura Lynch

Introduction

The integration of theory, research, and validity is the hallmark of quality research. In this chapter, we examine how theory and research synergistically work together when designing, implementing, evaluating, and disseminating findings from couples and family therapy (CFT) research studies. This chapter lays the foundation for understanding the specific research topics discussed throughout the book. First, we want to identify our own epistemology, because ways of knowing inform our beliefs about integrating theory and research and this book chapter on integrating theory and research (Simon, 2006).

One of the hallmarks of science is that it is falsifiable, and scientific hypotheses cannot be developed without explicit expectations. In this chapter these expectations will, of necessity, represent an amalgam of previous research, theoretical principles, and our own biases, none of which should remain implicit. While positivists believe that the researcher and participants being studied are independent of each other, in contrast, as postpositivists, we believe that the theories, background, knowledge, and values of the researcher can all influence what is observed (Kuhn, 1962; Phillips & Burbules, 2000). As postpositivists we believe that there is an existing reality out there, as positivists do, but we differ because we can only *get close* to that reality. We can never fully capture objective truth because knowledge is not based on unchallengeable foundations, but on our own assumptions and locations, theory, and the process of scientific inquiry (Worrall, 2003).

Theories are very important in CFT research because they help to make connections between findings from different studies and can advance the field in theoretically meaningful ways (Barton & Haslett, 2007; Lavee & Dollahite, 1991). Theory should do three things: (1) explain findings, (2) have implications, and (3) generate further testable hypotheses for future studies (Babbie, 2011). If we do not use theory to inform each stage of our research, then we will have disparate findings with little to no relationship to each other. Consequently, it will be more difficult to move the field forward in a programmatic and theoretically meaningful way. Often, CFT research studies are disseminated with no mention of the theories informing the study design (e.g., Hawley & Geske, 2000; Torraco, 1997) and no consideration of what the findings mean regarding theoretical and clinical implications, as well as future research. We need to carry theory all the way through our studies and avoid making research decisions based on personal whims or the latest statistical tool. It should inform the review of relevant literature, development of the research question, design of the study (internal validity), choice of measures based on theoretically consistent constructs (construct validity), choice of a sampling frame (external validity), decision about the methodology, analysis plan (conclusion validity), report of findings, and dissemination. Theory provides the context and structure for each of these important decisions, which we describe in this chapter.

The integration of theory and research should start at the very beginning of the research design process. This means that while formulating a research question, researchers should choose theories that map onto existing gaps in the extant literature. It is also important for researchers to be aware of their own personal biases by locating themselves sociodemographically (e.g., gender, race, age, class, beliefs, values) at the start of the research process, because all researchers (qualitative, mixed-method, quantitative) influence each stage of a research study (Babbie, 2011). Consistently using theory throughout a study can provide a check on researcher bias, because decisions must fit within the chosen theory or theories and are not solely based on personal preferences. As CFT researchers, we believe that theoretical frameworks will have the greatest relevance if they accommodate the relational and systemic focus in our field (Barton & Haslett, 2007; Davey, Davey, Tubbs, Savla, & Anderson, 2012; Stanton & Welsh, 2012). It is also important to consider and evaluate salient contextual variables (race, ethnicity, class, sexual orientation, community) while conducting CFT research studies in order to better understand the larger systems that individuals, couples, and families live in (Huang & Coker, 2010; Madison, 1992; Rogoff, 2003; Turner, Wieling, & Allen, 2004).

Integrating Systemic Theory and Research

CFT researchers think about change differently from other, more individually focused disciplines. Why, then, do we tend to study and evaluate the same kinds of change as other disciplines? Given the historical underpinnings of our field, we are uniquely poised to offer new insights and strategies for studying and affecting meaningful changes in individuals, couples, and families. Second-order change, an alteration of the system itself, and the richness it connotes, provides a unique opportunity to consider how systems change (e.g., Bateson, 1972; von Bertalanffy, 1968). At the same time, many of the founding principles of CFT have not been operationalized clearly enough to inform clinical practice and research. While most CFT researchers who study individuals, couples, and families are informed by systems theory and principles, the field still does not have well-articulated theories of systemic change (Gottman, Murray, Swanson, Tyson, & Swanson, 2002; Heatherington, Friedlander, & Greenberg, 2005; Stanton & Welsh, 2012).

The unit of study and target of change for CFT researchers is often large and complex because, according to general systems theory (GST), it is multifaceted and comprises the contextual environment (e.g., the family, neighborhood, school community, culture), intrapersonal factors (personality, IQ, gender, race, socioeconomic status), and interpersonal variables (closeness in relationships, attachment, communication) that may affect the individual, couple, family, or unit of study. Another basic principle derived from GST is that the system (couple or family) is either in a state of homeostasis and/or in continuous change and the therapist or researcher (observer) is often part of the system and can also change with it. In other words, the system is like a moving target that one is trying to study and understand at the same time that a therapist is trying to effect meaningful systemic clinical change (Davey et al., 2012; Watzlawick, Weakland, & Fisch, 1974).

Although the principles of change, according to GST, have been described by several forward-thinking scholars (e.g., Bateson, Jackson), Watzlawick and his colleagues (1974) articulated these principles most clearly in their seminal work, *Change: Principles of Problem Formation and Problem Resolution.* Despite being almost 40 years old, it remains their most widely cited work and is especially useful for clarifying principles of change using GST. Change can occur on two levels, according to Watzlawick and colleagues: as first-order or as second-order change.

First-Order Change

First-order change tends to focus on symptom reduction in the individual to ameliorate the presenting problem. In other words, it consists of superficial changes within the already existing system, rather than changes to the structure or rules of the system itself. In terms of measuring change using first-order change principles, individual parameters would change up or down (e.g., depression or anxiety scores increasing or decreasing), but the structure of the system itself would not be altered. First-order research is most often targeted in psychological approaches to treatment—for example, changing the immediate behaviors or symptoms in an individual through insight or cognitive-behavioral clinical approaches. According to Watzlawick and colleagues (1974) this type of change will likely have little effect on changing the structure of the system itself and will not promote enduring change.

Second-Order Change

In contrast, second-order change represents what is unique about GST and systemic theory. A second-order change occurs when there is a qualitative shift in the system, such that the body of rules governing the structure of that system

30

itself changes. Rules, according to Jackson (1965), are defined as a formula for a relationship that can be inferred by what one sees between individuals in the many patterns of behaviors (e.g., both nonverbal and verbal communication). Second-order change is described as a transformation of the system itself, where the rules of the system change into a new configuration. This type of change refers to variations of process, structure, and rules of operation in a system. There are many ways to study change, and the introduction of a systems framework can move us from a symptoms orientation toward a systems orientation. Instead of focusing on individuals, we should focus on individuals in the context of their interactions and environment. All of this leads us from the traditional emphasis on first-order change (e.g., modifying individual parameters or characteristics) toward a more general notion of second-order change (e.g., modifying the system itself and changing the rules of interaction).

As CFT scholars and researchers, we are uniquely poised to offer new insights and strategies for studying meaningful relational changes by conducting research with individuals, couples, and families. We need to study systemic or relational change, a *transformation of the system itself*, in order to understand the various processes underlying it (Bateson, 1972; von Bertalanffy, 1968; Watzlawick, Weakland, & Fisch, 1974; Wiener, 1948). We all know systemic change when we see it (or perhaps simply assume it), but we should also be able to demonstrate it to others through research, in reliable and replicable ways (Davey et al. 2012). We can fill this gap by asking research questions and designing studies that better target relational constructs and measure systemic change rather than continuing to rely on an individual focus. Research questions, sampling, design, measurement, and analysis therefore should all be informed by systemic and relational theories.

How Epistemology and Theory Inform Research

Epistemology

Epistemology refers to approaches for understanding reality or the science of knowing that involve different understandings of reality (Barton & Haslett, 2007; Kuhn, 1962). These worldviews or paradigms refer to frameworks of beliefs, values, and methods within which research takes place (Worrall, 2003). In CFT, Bateson has been credited with the introduction of the term "epistemology," which he defined as a personal theory about the nature of reality. He was an early advocate for the adoption of a "cybernetic" epistemology, based on patterns and communication, over the more conventional "lineal" epistemology in the physical sciences (Bateson, 1972). In the late 1970s and early 1980s, several scholars emphasized the relevance of epistemological issues to the developing field of CFT (e.g., Keeney, 1979, 1982).

Positivists, for example, believe that the researcher and participant are independent of each other and, therefore, can be objectively observed to fully capture phenomena (Phillips & Burbules, 2000). As mentioned earlier, post-positivists like us believe that a reality does exist out there, but it can be known only imperfectly because our theories, background, knowledge, and personal values all influence what is observed. We believe that these competing philosophies should be valued equally when conducting CFT research studies (e.g., Sprenkle & Piercy, 2005). We need to promote a wide variety of epistemologies (positivism, postmodernism, postpositivism) and research methods (quantitative, qualitative, mixed-method) because individuals, couples, and families require a diverse range of approaches to observe and understand their complexity.

Theory

Theories help us to explain, predict, and understand phenomena and provide a larger framework for challenging and extending existing knowledge (Babbie, 2011; Hulley, Cummings, Browner, Grady, & Newman, 2006; Lavee & Dollahite, 1991). A theory makes generalizations about observations consisting of an interrelated and coherent set of ideas and models. Theories help us make sense of observed patterns and, in turn, shape and direct our research efforts. While conducting a research study, theory helps researchers choose what to focus on, as well as what not to. It provides the framework for determining what is most relevant for each step of a research study. Theories help researchers more clearly understand the important variables to examine in a study and provide a general framework for the research methods and data analysis. For example, theories tell us what key independent (predictor), dependent (outcome), moderator, and mediator variables are important to study to best explain a phenomenon. We can either use theories in a deductive model of research, where a study is used to confirm and test existing theories (e.g., quantitative, mixed-method), or use an inductive model of research, where we develop theories from the analysis of research data (e.g., qualitative) (Lambert, 2004).

A good theory predicts events in a general context and also helps us develop specific research hypotheses about how much two or more variables are associated with each other and in what direction (e.g., no association, positive association, negative association). Theories are different from working hypotheses, because hypotheses make specific predictions about a particular set of circumstances (Cook & Campbell, 1979; Cook, Campbell, & Peracchio, 1990). A hypothesis is a statement of something that ought to be observed in the "real world," if our theory is correct. In contrast, a theory has been extensively tested and is generally accepted among scholars, while a hypothesis is an educated guess or expectation that still has to be tested (Babbie, 2011). Finally, a model is often developed to describe the application of a theory for a particular CFT clinical situation, and further testing is needed in order for a model to be later established as an empirically validated treatment model (Lavee & Dollahite, 1991).

Choosing a Theory

There are several strategies for choosing a theoretical framework or frameworks, and below we provide an example from our recently completed study to illustrate this process. It is essential to first do a thorough review of the literature on your chosen topic in order to identify noteworthy gaps in the extant clinical and research literature. Theories operate on different levels and include different assumptions; considering the theoretical orientations that tend to dominate an area of research can help to point out what is missing and will help you choose theories that best address the research gap. Your chosen theories should inform the research questions, hypotheses, and choice of research methods and help you to identify which key variables or constructs seem to influence the phenomenon of interest (Torraco, 1997). As CFT researchers, we should always use at least one systemic or relational theory in order to stay true to the core principles of our field. It is also important to consider using more contextually sensitive theories, because these theories take into consideration the role and impact of culture in the lives of diverse individuals, couples, and families (Tucker & Herman, 2002).

Researchers should use contextually sensitive theories at the very beginning of a research project, because they are grounded in research that has been conducted with participants of a specific culture (Tucker & Herman, 2002). The development of more contextually sensitive theories has unfortunately been impeded by the following issues: (1) unacknowledged researcher biases, (2) a lack of reporting or focus on the ethnic and racial makeup of research participants, and (3) assumed generalizability of results to populations not represented in study samples (Tucker & Herman).

For example, in our work with African American families coping with parental cancer, we have rarely applied a single theory; instead, we have integrated, synthesized, and compared theories to see which ones best fit with the evidence and clinical research gap we want to address. Our recently completed 2-year pilot study was designed to develop and evaluate a culturally relevant family intervention for African American families coping with parental cancer (Davey, Kissil, Lynch, & Harmon, 2013). After first doing a thorough review of the extant clinical and research literature, we found that most prior studies were informed by individual stress theory and conducted with White middle-class parents coping with cancer (usually with the patient and his/her spouse, while not including their children and not having a family focus). We found that most clinics providing care to cancer patients had not adapted their psychosocial support services for culturally diverse patient populations. Based on our review of prior studies and the identified gap in the field, we decided to develop and design our recently completed 2-year pilot study using family systems (Becvar & Becvar, 2003) and sociocultural theories (Rogoff, 2003).

From a family systems perspective (Becvar & Becvar, 2003), family members are interconnected and should be viewed as a whole, so we developed a culturally adapted family-centered clinical intervention because the cancer experience of a parent involves the entire family and not just the individual diagnosed with cancer. Sociocultural theory (Rogoff, 2003) emphasizes that culture shapes how families see the world and how they function, cope, and adapt to stressors like parental cancer. Sociocultural theorists argue for the proximal and immediate influence of culture on individuals and on families. When developing psychosocial interventions for families coping with parental cancer, their culture needs to be considered to best promote family resilience (Davey et al., 2013).

How Theory Informs Methodology

Many methodological decisions need to be made that will influence the overall quality of your study and the ability to generalize results to other populations, and it all starts with your chosen theory or theories. Different types of research methods (e.g., quantitative, qualitative, mixed-methods) and time frames (e.g., prospective, retrospective, cross-sectional, longitudinal) can be used to answer different types of research questions based on the theory that informs the study and the research question (Babbie, 2011; Hulley et al., 2006; Johnson, Onwueg-buzie, & Turner, 2007; Pedhazur & Schmelkin, 1991; Silverman, 1993). Designs are chosen based on the epistemology of the researcher, theory, research question, and primary purpose of the study.

For example, in our study, 2 years before our 2-year pilot study, we first conducted six qualitative focus groups with African American parents recently diagnosed with cancer, along with their school-age children (phase I), with the goal of first understanding their needs in order to develop a culturally relevant family intervention. Building on this earlier qualitative study, and using family systems and sociocultural theories as our theoretical guides, we designed a quantitative quasi-experimental two-arm pre- and post-intervention prospective design to test the effectiveness of a culturally relevant family intervention (phase II) (Davey et al., 2013).

How Theory Informs the Sampling Approach

The sampling approach is determined by the theory and research question that is being examined. As CFT researchers who are informed by systems theory, ideally the sampling frame should include more than one member of a system (e.g., parent and child, both members of a couple) or an individual's experience of their relationships. Theory and the research question inform the sampling approach and will help you specify the inclusion/exclusion criteria because you want to choose participants who can best help you address your theory-based research question. For example, in our study, family systems theory informed our dyadic sampling approach (parents and their school-age children was the unit of analysis), and we additionally asked parents and school-age children to evaluate the effectiveness of the clinical provider who delivered the intervention, because the therapist is also a part of the system.

Sociocultural theory informed our decision to include only African American families in order to develop a culturally relevant intervention, and our review of the cancer literature informed the stage of cancer we included because we focused on parents with better chances for recovery, as our intervention was not developed to help families cope with the loss of a parent to cancer. Consequently, our theory and research questions led to a natural set of inclusion and exclusion criteria for our study: (1) African American families (parent–child dyads); (2) parent or caregiver diagnosed with stage I, II, or III cancer within the past 6 months; and (3) parent-child dyads with at least one school-age child between the ages of 10 and 18, still living at home, and told about the diagnosis. Exclusion criteria were (1) cancer patients with stage IV or stage 0 cancer, (2) cancer patients with serious mental health or mental retardation disorders, and (3) parent-child dyads with school-age children with severe mental health or mental retardation disorders (Davey et al., 2013).

It is also important to consider salient contextual factors while developing your sampling approach, such as age, gender, race, ethnicity, class, and institutional and structural barriers to participation. For example, in our study, sociocultural theory informed our understanding that African Americans often do not utilize psychosocial support services such as cancer self-help groups because of an understandable mistrust of providers, perceived lack of cultural sensitivity, and institutional and structural barriers to recruitment and participation. We learned that it is very important to understand the historical context of African Americans, to partner and build trust with community leaders, and to engage in our own self-examination as researchers (Huang & Coker, 2010). Consequently, we applied sociocultural theory to overcome recruitment barriers, including partnering with both oncology providers and senior pastors at a large African American church and their cancer ministry.

How Theory Informs Internal, External, Construct, and Conclusion Validity

Theory informs decision points about the following four different types of validity, which in turn influence the quality of research studies: (1) internal validity, (2) external validity, (3) construct validity, and (4) conclusion validity (Babbie, 2011; Cook, Campbell, & Peracchio, 1990; see Chapter 1). Variables are operationalized and defined based on attributes that we use to describe the theoretically meaningful qualities of people or objects (Babbie). For example, "single," "partnered," "divorced," and "married" are attributes used to operationalize the variable "relationship status." Operational definitions make it possible for us to target, observe, intervene, and measure variables derived from theoretically meaningful constructs. Naturally, GST's relational focus informs the variables and constructs we tend to evaluate in CFT research. In addition to intrapersonal and contextual factors, GST also targets salient environmental and interpersonal factors (e.g., quality of relationships).

CFT researchers should additionally evaluate these theoretically informed constructs and variables with more diverse samples in order to ensure that these constructs are culturally relevant. One should remember that defining, measuring, and studying theoretically derived constructs is an ongoing and cyclical process, which in turn revises theories (Smith, 2005). For example, in our research study with African American families coping with parental cancer, family systems and sociocultural theories informed the key constructs we chose to target, which were family communication and parent–child psychosocial distress. We then chose culturally sensitive measures of family communication in order to capture how African American parents and their school-age children, who participated in our culturally adapted family intervention, communicated with each other while navigating parental cancer (Davey et al., 2013).

Construct validity refers to the fit between what the theoretically derived construct should capture and what the instrument actually measures (Cook & Campbell, 1979; Cook et al., 1990) (see Table 3.1).

As Table 3.1 describes, construct validity of your chosen measures is evaluated by identifying other constructs that theoretically converge and diverge with the

Table 3.1 How Theory Informs Choices about Constructs and Validity

Type of Validity	How Theory Informs Choices about Constructs and Measurement
Construct/convergent validity	What are the key constructs we need to be measuring in order to test our theory? Which constructs should be associated and how should they be associated? (convergent validity)
Construct/discriminant validity	Which constructs should not be associated with each other (discriminant validity)?
Criterion validity	What should each construct predict (and/or under what circumstances should it predict)? (criterion-related validity, which includes concurrent and predictive validity as a function of design) All of this is essential to knowing what should and should not occur if our theory is correct/incorrect and how we would know it.
Content validity	What is and is not a part of each construct? Also, to what extent do our measures cover/include (sampling validity) all aspects of these constructs?

targeted constructs (Smith, 2005). In order to establish convergent validity, the associations between two theoretically related constructs are evaluated using different methods to find positive associations between the two constructs, independently of the method used. When establishing discriminant validity, we expect to find that two theoretically different constructs will not be associated with each other, when measured by different methods (Campbell & Fiske, 1959; Smith). Two other types of validity that are associated with construct validity are content validity and criterion-related validity. Content validity refers to the degree to which a measure includes different aspects of a construct (Babbie, 2011), and a theory will describe the different aspects of this construct. Criterion-related validity refers to the degree to which a measure predicts an external criterion—for example, what each construct should predict and under what circumstances it will be predicted (Babbie).

How Theory Informs Measurement Choices

Theory should inform the types of measures chosen for our research studies. Because a system is a hierarchically ordered network of relationships, each with greater complexity, CFT researchers should choose measures that capture these complex systemic phenomena (Bateson, 1972; Stanton & Welsh, 2012; von Bertalanffy, 1968). According to Stanton and Welsh, "Many Western models identify the individual as the focus of measurement . . . they tend to study the individual by removing the person from the context of his or her life . . . systemic thinking actively recognizes the connections between persons inherent in systems" (p. 18). Measures should be chosen that allow you to evaluate systemic phenomena—for example, at the individual, couple, and family levels—and CFT researchers who are using systemic or relational theories should choose measures that allow them to collect data from more than one of these levels. In most CFT outcome studies, to date, however, most researchers have chosen measures developed to capture an individual perspective, and few CFT studies have included data from multiple perspectives in the system (Sanderson et al., 2009). Choosing measures that capture multiple perspectives within the couple and family system and the larger system should become a central feature of CFT research, especially if we use theories that are relational.

It is also important for CFT researchers to consider the reliability and validity of the measures chosen for their studies. We should choose measures that not only have high reliability and validity, but have been normed on populations similar to those samples we are studying. It is additionally important to report the reliability and validity of these measures for our study samples. For example, we chose the following constructs and measures: (1) general and program descriptive, (2) family/parenting points of intervention, (3) school-age child outcomes, and (4) adult outcomes (Davey et al., 2013) (Table 3.2). We chose these particular parent and school-age child self-report measures to enhance our reliability and validity based on our two chosen theories (family systems and sociocultural theories), as well as prior research on health disparities and parental cancer. Finally, we

Table 3.2 Constructs, Measures, and Reporters

Construct	Measure	Reporter			
		Caregiver	School-age Child	Coder	Facilitator
General and Program Descriptive					
Demographic	Demographic Family Survey	X			
Attendance	Record				X
Treatment fidelity	Fidelity Checklist and videotape			X	
Consumer satisfaction	CS Measure	X	X		
Family/ Parenting Points of Intervention					
Parent–school-age child	Short Form Interaction	X	X		
Relationship	Infant Behavior Questionnaire (IBQ)				
General communication	General communication (parent and child)	X	X		
Family routines	Family Routines Inventory (FRI)	X	X		
School-age Child Outcomes					
Depression	Children's Depression Inventory (CDI)		X		
Anxiety	Revised Children's Manifest Anxiety Scale (RCMAS)		X		
Adult Outcomes					
Depression	Center for Epidemiologic Studies Depression Scale (CES-D)	X			

evaluated the reliability of the measures with our African American study sample and reported them (Davey et al., 2013).

How Theory Informs Plan for Analysis

One implication of having multiple ways of conceptualizing systemic change is that it can lead us to think about multiple ways of measuring change. Yet, Hetherington and her colleagues (2005) have noted the lack of well-articulated theories about systemic change in CFT and have suggested that "without an articulation of the processes that can and should propel therapeutic systemic change, researchers will flounder in deciding what variables to study, what instruments to apply, and what specific changes to anticipate" (p. 19); and, we would add, what analysis strategy to use.

Correlation/Factor Analysis/Regression Analysis

Correlation, factor analysis, and regression analysis are all statistical analysis tools that have been frequently used by CFT researchers (see Chapter 21). In our study, family systems and sociocultural theories informed the primary aim to test the effect of our culturally adapted family intervention on the quality of parent–school-age child communication in our sample (primary trial outcome; between-group comparison). Our main study hypothesis was that parents and school-age children who completed the culturally adapted family intervention would report improved communication with each other, in comparison with the psychoeducation group. We also tested the effect of the intervention on the parent's (Center for Epidemiologic Studies Depression Scale) and child's symptoms of depression (Children's Depression Inventory), child's symptoms of anxiety (Revised Children's Manifest Anxiety Scale), and their views of relationship (Infant Behavior Questionnaire) and levels of satisfaction. Finally we examined effect sizes for all study outcomes. All analyses were two-tailed. Following intention-to-treat principles, we included participants regardless of exposure level to treatment. For comparisons of intervention and control group participants at baseline, chi-square and Fisher's exact tests were used for categorical analysis and Student's t-tests were used for parametric data. For treatment effects, Mann–Whitney tests were conducted to evaluate the hypothesis that parents and children in the family intervention show improvements, on average, relative to the control group. Cohen d was calculated to measure and compare the effect sizes for the parents compared with their school-age children (Davey et al., 2013).

Dyadic Analysis

Dyadic analysis is a valuable statistical strategy to analyze data from two members of a family system. Dyadic analysis allows CFT researchers to evaluate interpersonal dynamics. Congruent with systems theory, data capturing individual and relational phenomena are collected from multiple members of a system (e.g., asking for both parent and school-age child reports about the quality of family communication in our study; see Chapter 24).

Hierarchical Linear Modeling

Hierarchical linear modeling (HLM) is a sophisticated data analysis tool that allows you to evaluate complex systemic phenomena within and between individuals, taking into consideration nested hierarchical structures by gathering data from multiple members of a system at multiple points in time (e.g., the couple, the family). We can then compare changes within and between groups over time and evaluate key variables that significantly change over time. Systemic theories can now be tested because of advanced statistical tools like HLM, which are designed to evaluate nested hierarchical contexts.

There are at least four levels of hierarchical contexts that we can consider when conducting systemic research using HLM: (1) macro-level context, (2) familial context, (3) individual context, and (4) time (Davey & Takagi, 2012). The macro-level context includes the community and/or neighborhood that the family is embedded in. Ethnic and cultural backgrounds of the family as well as the socio-political influences of the system on the community are considered macro-level factors impacting the family. The familial context consists of the family structure and the family norms, since they play a significant role in shaping family interactions. The individual context is also crucial to take into consideration, since the individual's social location, such as his/her demographics and generational location, affects his/her view of the family. HLM allows us to assess for change at different time points and at multiple levels between different family members and to examine whether these changes vary in a systemic way (Keiley, Martin, Liu, & Dolbin-MacNab, 2005).

Structural Equation Modeling

Structural equation modeling (SEM) is an advanced analysis tool designed to evaluate the associations between observed variables and underlying constructs derived from theoretical models. Underlying theoretical constructs are referred to as latent variables that cannot be directly measured, and observed variables are the indicators that represent these latent variables. One of the biggest advantages of SEM is that it can be used to study the relationships among latent constructs using multiple measures. SEM uses a confirmatory (hypothesis testing) approach to the multivariate analysis of a theory and evaluates causal associations among multiple variables (MacCallum & Austin, 2000). This systemic pattern of associations between variables is first developed using a theory and is then tested using SEM. The goal of SEM is to determine whether a hypothesized theoretical model is consistent with the data collected to reflect this theory, which is evaluated through model–data fit. SEM can help CFT researchers better test models derived from systems theory, because it is designed to evaluate complex individual, couple, and family phenomena over time (Chan, Lee, Lee, Kubota, & Allen, 2007; Cook, 1994; MacCallum & Austin).

Conclusion

In conclusion, when we finally disseminate our findings (e.g., publications, presentations), it is very important to make more explicit linkages among theory, research, and clinical practice. CFT research that is cumulative and based on theory can be integrated back into the original theories to further refine and expand them. Theories serve as a framework and context for new research to be conducted so that it better informs CFT practice and health policy. Although CFT clinicians often consider how theories can help them provide effective and culturally sensitive care to individuals, couples, and families, in contrast CFT researchers focus on a theory's ecological validity, which refers to how closely a theory captures reality when empirically evaluated (Babbie, 2011; Barton & Haslett, 2007). As professionals in our field, we need to do more of our own research explicitly linking systemic theory, research, and clinical interventions in order to programmatically build CFT clinical research that addresses complex systemic and relational phenomena.

References

Babbie, E. (2011). *The basics of social research* (5th ed.). Belmont, CA: Wadsworth.

Barton, J., & Haslett, T. (2007). Analysis, synthesis, systems thinking and the scientific method: Rediscovering the importance of open systems. *Systems Research and Behavioral Science, 24,* 143–155. doi:10.1002/sres.816

Bateson, G. (1972). *Steps to an ecology of mind.* New York: Ballantine.

Becvar, D.S., & Becvar, R.J. (2003). *Family therapy: A systemic integration* (5th ed.). Boston: Allyn & Bacon.

Campbell, D.T., & Fiske, D.W. (1959). Convergent and discriminant validation by the multitrait-multimethod matrix. *Psychological Bulletin, 56,* 81–105. doi:10.1037/h0046016

Chan, F., Lee, G.K., Lee, E., Kubota, C., & Allen, C.A. (2007). Structural equation modeling in rehabilitation counseling research. *Rehabilitation Counseling Bulletin, 51,* 44–57. doi: 10.1177/00343552070510010701

Cook, W. (1994). A structural equation model of dyadic relationships within the family system. *Journal of Consulting and Clinical Psychology, 62,* 500–509. doi:10.1037/0022-006X.62.3.500

Cook, T. D. & Campbell, D. T. (1979). *Quasi-experimentation: Design and analysis issues for field settings.* Boston: Houghton Mifflin.

Cook, T. D., Campbell, D. T., & Peracchio, L. (1990). Quasi experimentation. In M. D. Dunnette & L. M. Hough (Eds.), *Handbook of industrial and organizational psychology* (2nd ed., pp. 491–576). Palo Alto, CA: Consulting Psychologists Press.

Davey, A., & Takagi, E. (2012). Adulthood and aging in families. In G. W. Peterson & K. R. Bush (Eds.), *Handbook of marriage and the family* (pp. 377–399). New York: Springer.

Davey, M. P., Davey, A., Tubbs, C., Savla, J., & Anderson, S. (2012). Second order change and evidence-based practice. *Journal of family therapy, 34,* 72–90.

Davey, M. P., Kissil, K., Lynch, L., Harmon, L.-R., and Hodgson, N. (2012), A culturally adapted family intervention for African American families coping with parental cancer: Outcomes of a pilot study. *Psycho-Oncology. 22,* 1572–1580. doi: 10.1002/pon.3172

Gottman, J. M., Murray, J. D., Swanson, C. C., Tyson, R., & Swanson, K. R. (2002). *The mathematics of marriage: Dynamic nonlinear models.* London: MIT Press.

Hawley, D. R. & Geske, S. (2000). The Use of Theory in Family Therapy Research: A Content Analysis of Family Therapy Journals. *Journal of Marital and Family Therapy, 26,* 17–22.

Heatherington, L., Friedlander, M. L., & Greenberg, L. (2005). Change process research in couple and family therapy: Methodological challenges and opportunities. *Journal of Family Psychology, 19,* 18–27. doi:10.1037/0893-3200.19.1.18

Huang, H., & Coker, A.D. (2010). Examining issues affecting African American participation in research studies. *Journal of Black Studies, 40,* 619–636. doi:10.1177/0021934708317749

Hulley, S. B., Cummings, S. R., Browner, W. S., Grady, D., & Newman, T. B. (2006). *Designing clinical research: An epidemiologic approach* (3rd ed.). Philadelphia: Lippincott Williams & Wilkins.

Jackson, D. D. (1965). The study of the family. *Family Process, 4,* 1–20. doi: 10.1111/j.1545-5300.1965.00001.x

Johnson, R. B., Onwuegbuzie, A. J., & Turner, L. A. (2007). Toward a definition of mixed methods research. *Journal of Mixed Methods Research, 1,* 112–133. doi: 10.1177/1558689806298224

Keeney, B. P. (1979). Ecosystemic epistemology: An alternative paradigm for diagnosis. *Family Process, 18,* 117–129. doi: 10.1111/j.1545-5300.1979.00117.x

Keeney, B. P. (1982). What is an epistemology of family therapy? *Family Process, 21,* 153–168.

Keiley, M., Martin, N. C., Liu, T., & Dolbin-MacNab, M. (2005). Multilevel growth modeling in the context of family research. In D. Sprenkle & F. Piercy (Eds.), *Research methods in family therapy* (pp. 405–432). New York: Guilford Press.

Kuhn, T. (1962). *The structure of scientific revolutions.* Chicago: University of Chicago Press.

Lambert, M. J. (2004). *Bergin and Garfield's handbook of psychotherapy and behavior change* (5th ed.). New York: John Wiley & Sons.

Lavee, Y., & Dollahite, D. C. (1991). The linkage between theory and research in family science. *Journal of Marriage and the Family, 53,* 361–373.

MacCallum, R. C., & Austin, J. T. (2000). Applications of structural equation modeling in psychological research. *Annual Review of Psychology, 51,* 201–226.

Madison, A. M. (1992). Primary inclusion of culturally diverse minority program participants in the evaluation process. *New Directions for Program Evaluation, 1992,* 35–43.

Pedhazur, E. J., & Schmelkin, L. P. (1991). *Measurement, design, and analysis: An integrated approach.* Hillsdale, NJ: Lawrence Erlbaum Associates.

Phillips, D., & Burbules, N.C. (2000). *Postpositivism and educational research.* Lanham, MD: Rowman & Littlefield.

Rogoff, B. (2003). *The cultural nature of human development.* New York: Oxford University Press.

Sanderson, J., Kosutic, I., Garcia, M., Melendez, T., Donoghue, J., Perumbilly, S., Franzen, C., & Anderson, S. (2009). The measurement of outcome variables in couple and family therapy research. *American Journal of Family Therapy, 37,* 239–257.

Silverman, D. (1993). *Interpreting qualitative data: Methods for analyzing talk, text, and interaction.* Thousand Oaks, CA: Sage.

Simon, G. (2006). The heart of the matter: A proposal for placing the self of the therapist at the center of family therapy research and training. *Family Process, 45,* 331–344.

Smith, G.T. (2005). On construct validity: Issues of method and measurement. *Psychological Assessment, 17,* 396–408. doi:10.1037/1040–3590.17.4.396

Sprenkle, D., & Piercy, F. (2005). Pluralism, diversity and sophistication in family therapy research. In D. Sprenkle & F. Piercy (Eds.), *Research methods in family therapy.* New York: Guilford Press.

Stanton, M., & Welsh, R. (2012). Systemic thinking in couple and family psychology research and practice. *Couple and Family Psychology: Research and Practice, 1,* 14–30. doi:10.1037/a0027461

Torraco, R.J. (1997). Theory-building research methods. In R.A. Swanson & E.F. Holton III, (Eds.), *Human resource development handbook: Linking research and practice* (pp. 114–137). San Francisco, CA: Berrett-Koehler.

Tucker, C.M., & Herman, K.C. (2002). Using culturally sensitive theories and research to meet the academic needs of low-income African American children. *American Psychologist, 57,* 762–773. doi:10.1037/0003–066X.57.10.762

Turner, W.L., Wieling, E., & Allen, W.D. (2004). Developing culturally effective family-based research programs: Implications for family therapists. *Journal of Marital and Family Therapy, 30,* 257–270. doi:10.1111/j.1752–0606.2004.tb01239.x

von Bertalanffy, L. (1968). *General systems theory: Foundation, development, applications.* New York: George Braziller.

Watzlawick, P., Weakland, J.H., & Fisch, R. (1974). *Change: Principles of problem formation and problem resolution.* New York: W.W. Norton & Co.

Wiener, N. (1948). Cybernetics. *Scientific American, 179,* 14–18.

Worrall, J. (2003). Normal science and dogmatism, paradigms and progress: Kuhn 'versus' Popper and Lakatos. In T. Nichols (Ed.), *Thomas Kuhn* (pp. 65–100). Cambridge, UK: Cambridge University Press.

4

MEASUREMENT ISSUES WITH COUPLE- AND FAMILY-LEVEL DATA

Dean M. Busby and Franklin O. Poulsen

Introduction

Early in my (D.B.) training as a family therapist, I did some co-therapy with a clinical psychology student who wanted to learn how to work with couples. The couple we were working with was quite volatile, and it was not uncommon for the dialogue between the spouses to get heated. While it was challenging enough to keep the interactions between the partners moving in a productive direction, my co-therapist was quite uncomfortable with conflict and would emotionally "check out" of the session as soon as things became intense. Each time a session was challenging and conflict became intense, my co-therapist would suggest during our supervision or postsession discussions that we needed to meet with each person separately. Rather quickly the supervisor and I learned that his anxiety about intense emotions was driving this desire, rather than what was necessarily best for the couple. Unfortunately, rather than learning how to become better at couple therapy, the end result of our experience together was more clarity in the clinical psychology graduate student's mind that couple and family work was not what he wanted to spend the rest of his career doing.

Similarly, I have been teaching beginning and advanced research methods to clinical and nonclinical students for over two decades now, and it is quite common to experience graduate students wanting to make measurement and method decisions based on what is easiest to do, rather than what is best for the research question under consideration. Like my co-therapist, they often end up doing individual-level research because it is so much simpler to manage the complex statistical and methodological issues, when just dealing with a few variables from one person in the family system. In contrast, using multiple variables from multiple family members, and maybe even measures from observational coding and other "outsiders" seems overwhelming. We often fear that, like the previously mentioned co-therapist, what many researchers will learn when exposed to the measurement and statistical techniques required to do good couple and family clinical research is that they would prefer to do individual research.

Measurement decisions with couple and family data clearly relate to the concept of validity with a small "v" and validity with a capital "V." Validity with a small "v" has to do with how accurate the measure is at capturing the construct under consideration, such as, "Do the items measuring an individual's depression accurately measure depression?" This type of validity is often called construct validity. Validity with a capital "V" has to do with how much validity the overall study (external, construct, internal, conclusion) has for addressing the couple and family research question under consideration. For example, a researcher who conducts relational research might want to know how depression in the parental system influences important child outcomes. Although it is crucial to make sure the self-report measure of depression of a parent is valid with a small "v," if all the researcher does is correlate self-report measures of depression of one parent to self-report measures of the same parent about child outcomes, very little is learned and overall *Validity* is likely low in the study. It would be surprising if an individual's measure of her own depression were not associated with her ratings of her child's outcomes, but this may not be a *Valid* answer to the research question. Instead it may just be yet another study that shows that a depressed individual's attitudes about almost everything become bleaker, or another example of a study that shows that shared method variance continues to be a problem in research (Gottman, 1998). The child may or may not be actually functioning worse.

To answer the original complex research question about how depression in the parental system influences child outcomes, it is likely that the researcher will want to find out how the partners each assess their own and their partner's depression across time. It may also be important to evaluate how depressed parents interact uniquely between themselves and with their child, as compared with nondepressed parents. In terms of the child outcomes, it would probably be best to measure these from within the family system by asking each parent how the child is doing in important areas and by having teachers and, possibly, the child evaluate the same thing.

This more sophisticated approach to measurement will allow the researcher to understand the influence of depression from many angles. The researcher can evaluate the interaction of one parent's depression on the other and how this interaction influences the child, and it will allow the researcher to evaluate how changes in depression between the parents are related to child outcomes. It may be that a particular parent's level of depression influences only his or her own ratings of the child, but not the teacher's, the other parent's, or the child's ratings of the outcomes. Over time it may be that one parent's depression begins to erode the child's outcomes more than does the influence from the other parent. The researcher can also see whether the influence of depression on interaction patterns makes the most difference for the child or the direct relationship between depression and child outcomes is more influential. Finally, there may be many measurement-oriented studies that could result from this sophisticated measurement approach, such as whether there is measurement invariance for either depression or the child outcomes and whether the level of measurement invariance influences the outcomes. Obviously this more complex approach to the role of depression in the family system will take substantially more effort and more advanced methods and statistical skills, but the potential wealth of knowledge that can be learned is exponentially greater than simply measuring the mother's self-reported depression on her ratings of child outcomes. Additionally, the added information can be used to rule out alternative explanations to improve internal validity while reducing the chances of a type I and type II error to improve conclusion validity. Conducting *V*alid couple and family clinical research is more intense and complex than conducting research on the individual, but we would contend it is more rewarding, informative, and useful in the practical world, where children and parents interact dynamically with each other and depression influences emotions, cognitions, and behaviors within the individual and between individuals.

While an entire book could easily be written on the topic, in this chapter we will address what we see as the most common and most crucial measurement issues faced by scholars conducting clinical couple and family research. To do so, we will consider the following issues: general measurement issues in clinical couple and family research; unit of interest, measurement, and analysis; nonindependence of data; measurement invariance; and unidimensional measurement and validity.

General Measurement Issues in Clinical Couple and Family Research

Good measurement is the foundation of all good research, and good measurement is usually based on sound theory. While developing a measure that is relatively reliable is a straightforward process, developing a measure that has multiple types of validity is much more challenging. Beyond basic reliability and validity issues, when it comes to measurement in couple and family research, concepts such as congruence, accuracy, bias, and enhancement become relevant and add exciting new opportunities for scholars. For example, consider the graph in Figure 4.1. If we gather measures from each partner about self and other, and we have an observer such as a therapist or coder rate each partner, there will be at least six different measures to manage. While agreeableness has consistently been shown to be one of the crucial Big Five personality constructs that influence relationship dynamics (Donnellan, Larsen-Rife, & Conger, 2005; McCrae & Costa, 2008), most measures of this construct are just from the individual self-report. For the example in Figure 4.1, this would be either the first or the third bars from the left, depending on whether the person measured was a male or female. In this instance, the researcher would know that agreeableness was relatively high, so the assumption might be made that the relationship would be functioning better than those where agreeableness was low. If the researcher happened to take the time to evaluate both members of the dyad through self-report, the

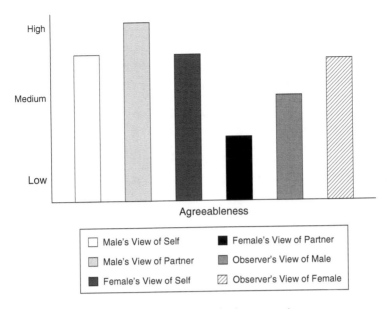

Figure 4.1 Measures of agreeableness from multiple perspectives.

researcher might make the additional conclusion that because both individuals rated themselves high and there was high congruence between the two ratings, this relationship is doing well. Almost all of the conclusions drawn about couple relationships regarding personality are derived from one or both of these ratings of the self (Cooper & Sheldon, 2002).

Unfortunately, these are the least predictive and informative ratings available to the relationship researcher (Busby, Holman, & Niehuis, 2009). With just a little more effort, the researcher can begin to understand much more of the important aspects of the relationship than two self-report measures can provide. Consider how much more informative it is to ask the partners to each rate each other, as well as themselves. This is where a more complete picture of the couple emerges, as this comparison between self and other appears to uncover crucial attitudinal and perceptual issues that drive relationship quality and stability (Busby & Gardner, 2008). It is evident that without this information, our findings from a research study would have been biased, leading to decreased conclusion validity. With the data in Figure 4.1, the important dynamics of this couple are evident. The male views self and partner in positive ways and even views his partner as more agreeable than himself. This partner enhancement is an important characteristic of strong relationships (Busby et al.). However, of more serious concern is the pattern for the female. She sees her partner as substantially less agreeable than herself, and this partner-diminishing perspective, especially from females toward their male partners, is the most serious pattern that can emerge in cross-ratings such as this. In fact, the observer's ratings mirror this perspective, and even the male's ratings demonstrate the same pattern of there being considerably less agreeableness coming from the male than the female, though he seems to give himself higher ratings than anyone else. Is this couple in trouble? It is very likely that they are, and the most typical type of relationship assessment with just self-ratings would not have uncovered this.

Of equal interest and importance is evaluating the observer ratings. If this observer is the therapist, interesting questions arise. Does the fact that the therapist mirrors the female's pattern represent a reality that the male is, in fact, much less agreeable than the female, and/or does it represent an unequal alliance in that the therapist is more connected and empathic of the female perspective? Is this couple at risk of dropping out of therapy because the male doesn't feel that his perspective is shared by the therapist? Obviously much more information is needed, but the patterns suggest intriguing possibilities that could lead to interventions that might help alleviate patterns that are beginning to develop in the therapist/client alliances.

These multiple measures also provide many new opportunities for the researcher and clinician in that now evaluations of congruence (how close self-report measures for each partner are), accuracy or bias (how similar ratings of the partner or self are with observers' ratings of the same person), enhancement (within person comparison of self and partner ratings) or idealization (across person comparisons of ratings of the partner with the partner's ratings of the self) can be calculated and used to predict couple outcomes (Busby et al., 2009; Morry, Reich, & Kito, 2010; Priem, Solomon, & Steuber, 2009). Very little is known about these different types of couple measures that may, in fact, uncover other important relationship dynamics that are crucial for interventions and basic couple research. These couple measures allow the researcher and clinician to try and capture something that is between people, rather than just within the individual, as is usually the case with simple self-report measures. Still, one can develop a severe headache just by trying to label and keep straight all of the different permutations and scores that can be calculated with six measures of the same phenomenon, especially if the research design contains multiple independent and dependent measures.

Unit of Interest, Measurement, and Analysis

Unit of Interest

To help with organizing multiple measures and multiple perspectives, it is useful to consider questions about the unit of interest, measurement, and analysis. Whenever a marriage and family therapy (MFT) researcher begins a research study, the most important questions that need to be addressed are "What is the unit of interest?" and "Is the unit of measurement and analysis consistent with the unit of interest?" (Draper & Marcos, 1990; Ganong, 2003; Olson, 1977). Snyder, Cavell, Heffer, and Mangrum (1995) present a model that includes five levels, or what we call units of interest, that could be measured in research: (1) individuals, (2) dyads, (3) the nuclear family, (4) the extended family system, and (5) the community or larger systems, to which we add two therapeutic levels: (6) the therapist/client system, and (7) the clinical setting system. On the surface, it may seem a simple matter to just determine which of these seven units a researcher is interested in and then proceed. However, it is often the case that a researcher is interested in more than one unit, and often the independent and dependent variables of interest are from different levels. If decisions are not made in a theoretically sound manner and with clear research questions, the units of interest can be confused in a study, and validity will suffer (Ganong; Wampler & Halverson, 1993). For example, if a scholar is primarily interested in a couple outcome, such as relationship quality, it would seem obvious that the unit of interest is the couple. This may be true for the dependent variable, but what if the theory the researcher is working from is attachment theory? This would suggest that the independent variables that might influence the quality of the couple relationship might originate from each partner's family of origin as well as from the couple's attachment behaviors and processes. This theoretical preference crosses different units from the family of origin, the individual, and the couple. The researcher must carefully consider what the primary levels of interest and the basic research questions are, as these will help set clear boundaries around which units are measured and analyzed.

While we might assume that usually family therapists will at least be primarily interested in the dyad or higher units because they are using some type of systems theory, there are also many circumstances where they might be primarily interested in the individual unit. Perhaps the scholar is evaluating what factors are associated with dropout rates for a particular intervention being tested. Even though the intervention may be a couple or family therapy approach, if the available research is very sparse, an exploratory qualitative study is needed to first figure out the general reasons that explain why people are dropping out of the study. In this scenario the individual's attitude or opinion may be all that is necessary to measure. A simple survey that is administered over the phone by clinic staff may be enough to begin to discover the crucial factors that are contributing to dropouts, such as cost, inconvenience of the clinic location, relationship with the therapist, or problems in the couple relationship. In this example, if a common reason for dropout has to do with the couple's dynamics or the therapeutic alliance, it may be necessary in a second study to carefully evaluate each member of the dyad, and the therapist must figure out more details about these issues. In these examples, for the first qualitative study, the unit of interest, measurement, and analysis is the individual. In the second study, where the couple's dynamics and/or the therapeutic alliance is inherently involved, the unit of interest might be the couple or the therapeutic system, requiring that the scholar ask questions of two or three individuals instead of just one.

If the unit of interest includes a couple or family subsystem, the scholar must begin to answer unit of measurement questions that are more complex. Does the scholar want to measure something that occurs between the members of the dyad, such as communication that is coded by observers outside the couple? Or does the scholar want to understand something that exists within the individual members of the dyad, such as attitudes or thoughts? In many instances, scholars will want to do both. Even if the interest is only about individual attitudes or thoughts, the scholar may want to link the attitudes or cognitions of one member of the dyad to the other, such as when a researcher wants to understand how one partner's attitudes influence the other partner's behaviors or attitudes. The answers to these questions guide measurement and analysis decisions. In most instances, the research is stronger when there is congruence between the units of interest, measurement, and analysis (Draper & Marcos, 1990).

Often the clinical scholar can answer the unit of interest question by considering the end goal of the intervention. If the end goal is to develop an effective program for addressing school truancy, measurement of the family members and school personnel will be necessary. If the end goal is to find out what individual factors of clinicians-in-training lead to better clinical training outcomes, perhaps only the clinician needs to be measured and analyzed. Usually when working with clinical researchers, we ask them whether their research is applied or basic research. If it is applied research, the next question is which of the seven levels (individuals, dyads, nuclear families, extended family systems, community or larger systems, therapist/client system, clinical setting systems) they hope the intervention influences. Once this is clear, who and how people are measured becomes easier to answer.

Unit of Measurement

Unit of measurement issues are complicated by what unit of interest is selected and the differences in these units of interest for the dependent and independent variables. They are further complicated by the different theories and assumptions behind each measure that is selected. In addition, there are many different domains that can be measured. Kashy and Snyder (1995, p. 338) indicate that each of the units of interest could be evaluated on five different domains: "(a) cognitive, (b) affective, (c) communication and interpersonal, (d) structural and developmental, and (e) control, sanctions, and related behavioral domains." We would suggest that one additional domain overlooked by Kashy and Snyder is the physiological/biological domain. This would mean that clinical family researchers have the possibility of 7 levels of interest and 6 domains, for 42 different combinations that they could measure. Then when we consider collecting these measures from more than one level, and by using different assessment strategies, such as from insiders or outsiders of the family (Olson, 1977), from surveys to physiological instruments, etc., there are literally hundreds of combinations researchers could choose from when trying to match their unit of interest, the domains that are measured, and the assessment strategy.

A recent example from the clinical research literature illustrates how the units of interest and these domains can be used to categorize and evaluate studies. Rohrbaugh, Shoham, Skoyen, Jensen, and Mehl (2012) studied how communal language, such as the use of the pronouns "we," "our," and "us," might be indicative of couples who held a communal problem-solving perspective that might be predictive of success in a smoking cessation program for people who already had compromised health. In this interesting study, although the unit of interest was how well the smoker was able to abstain from cigarettes over the course of time, which means that the unit of interest was the individual, it was measured on the domain of control, sanctions, and related behavioral domains. The primary unit of interest for the independent variable was at the couple level of communal language, although the authors measured it from only the individual level. If the authors had been more overt or thoughtful about the incongruence between their unit of interest for the independent variable, the couple, and their measurement approach, they might have included more interesting findings. This couple-level variable of communal language was measured in the communication and interpersonal domain by a textual analysis program that was used to simply count the number of "we"-like pronouns used by each partner during pretreatment and posttreatment discussions. In addition, the researchers created ratios of we/I pronouns for each partner and created change scores in these pronouns from pretreatment to posttreatment. These individual measures were quite predictive of smoking cessation. This creative approach to measurement at the individual level could be enhanced in future studies, where researchers want to evaluate the communal language of a couple or family. This could be done by creating difference scores between partners or family members. Perhaps if one person used a great deal of communal language but another family member didn't, this might be indicative of lower levels of commitment.

Unit of Analysis

If scholars have been careful in planning their studies so that the unit of interest and measurement are congruent and consistent with their theory, the next step is to figure out how to analyze the data. While other chapters in this book will focus more extensively on analytic techniques, it is important to discuss some analysis issues here, as they are related to measurement. Typically, most of the analytic choices will be tied to the theoretical and measurement issues that are made as the study is designed. The important point to focus on here is that the unit that is analyzed needs to be consistent with the units of interest and measurement, or all of the hard work that is exerted to collect appropriate couple or family data will be for naught. In our experience, most of the problems in the analytic area are due to researchers either relying on analytic methods they are most familiar with, but which may not be well suited to their data, or not thinking in terms of units at all so they are vulnerable to mismatches between the unit of measurement and analysis. These problems are particularly acute when researchers use secondary data for their research.

Much of the research in the therapy journals is research on individual attitudes and behaviors with individual analytic techniques. The only couple or family aspect of the research is often the fact that people were in a relationship or may have children. To make conclusions about the couple or family units, the data not only must be collected from these units, but they must be analyzed through either a structural or a hierarchical model, where the associations between the different individual, couple, or higher units are part of the analysis.

Nonindependence of Data

When the unit of interest, measurement, and analysis is any of our seven levels outside the individual, one issue that must be dealt with is nonindependence of observation. Nonindependence is also a problem in longitudinal studies, as one measure of a variable, such as relationship satisfaction at a second or third time point, would be dependent on the first measure of relationship satisfaction when the study began. In social science disciplines, the dominant research design assumes that a data point gathered from one individual has no necessary relationship with a data point collected from another individual. Thus, we conclude that our data are composed of independent observations. This is important because most statistical estimators (e.g., ordinary least squares) have a strict assumption of independence of the data (Kenny, Kashy, & Cook, 2006). However, this assumption does not hold when data are gathered from individuals in a marriage or family relationship and/or from the same people across time. This is primarily because individuals within these relationships have mutual influence (Grawitch & Munz, 2004); that is, when we attempt to measure couple or family interactions (e.g., marital or family conflict), or when we measure individuals' perceptions of and attitudes toward the relationship (e.g., marital satisfaction), the responses to these measures are inherently dependent on the influence of other individuals within the system. In short, individuals cannot provide information about marital satisfaction as if their partners have no influence. In this way, responses are nonindependent. As an analytical definition, Kashy and Snyder (1995) propose that "nonindependence of observations occurs when (a) there is a natural link between two scores and (b) the two scores are related in such a way that knowing the value of one provides information about the value of the other" (p. 339).

Because couple- and family-level data are nonindependent, it is essential that researchers studying these relationships be cognizant of this in their research, especially when considering how data are analyzed. Although this issue will be discussed more in the chapter on dyadic analysis, for now it is important to consider how the nonindependence of couple and family data dictates analytic choices. Specifically, ignoring nonindependence between romantic partners, families, and other close or intimate systems can threaten the validity of the statistical results. For example, when using both husband and wife scores on the same construct to predict individual or couple outcomes, failure to account for the nonindependence of observations, both within the couple and across time, may result in biased coefficients and significance levels, which can raise questions of internal and conclusion validity for the results. Although multiple techniques have been utilized to deal with nonindependence, strategies presented by Kenny and colleagues (2006) that analyze the data by modeling the nonindependence should become the norm rather than the exception in family therapy research.

Measurement Invariance

In addition to issues of nonindependence within samples, researchers who conduct research wherein the unit of interest, measurement, and analysis is the family or the couple also frequently neglect to consider whether measures are invariant across family members and across time. Researchers have noted that parental reports of family interactions often do not coincide with the reports of outside observers (Maccoby & Martin, 1983) and thus may not be valid measures of the interaction. Furthermore, researchers have found that family members often do not agree with each other on ratings of the same constructs (Noller & Callan, 1988), leading researchers to wonder about the reliability of family responses. Many have attempted to address this problem by merely aggregating the scores of multiple family members to create a summary score (Schwarz, Barton-Henry, & Pruzinsky, 1985). Until recently this has been a common way to construct a family or couple variable. Two specific problems occur with this approach.

First, this approach assumes that all of the variance from multiple informants represents a common perspective and, in so doing, ignores the possibility that some variance may actually reside in the unique perspective of the individual rater. A summary score does not allow for the measurement of both common and unique variance. Secondly, summary scores assume that any correlation between constructs for the two raters reflects a shared perspective about the construct. However, Kenny and Berman (1980) have noted that collecting data from multiple raters who are asked to rate another interdependent person who is also providing information often introduces correlational bias. That is, the correlation between constructs may be due to one person's consistent overestimation or underestimation of the other on several items or constructs. This bias cannot be accounted for or removed when scores are summed.

To deal with the two problems presented above, Cook and Goldstein (1993) have suggested that a latent variable approach be used to separate the unique variance of independent raters from what may be common among the raters, and to account for any bias that may exist when interdependent persons rate each other on different constructs. The creation of a latent variable makes explicit the estimation of residual error for each item, thus separating what is unique from what is common (the factor score). It also allows researchers to correlate the residual error for the same rater across different constructs, which accounts for and thus removes the correlational bias (see Figure 4.2.) Although this alone does not ensure that

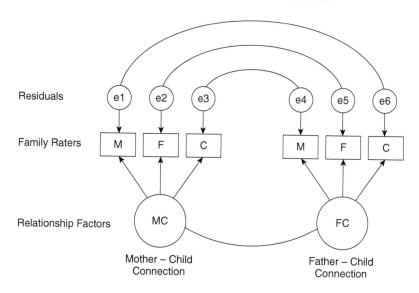

Notes: M = Mother, F = Father, C = Child

Figure 4.2 Latent measures representing reports of three family members on the same constructs.

measures are invariant across family members, it explicitly accounts for correlational bias that may exist.

Of equal or greater importance to the family researcher is the question of whether measurement invariance exists between family members and across time within the same family member. Recent research has called into question the assumption that the same questions given to different family members are conceptually equivalent (Dyer, Day, & Harper, in press) at one time point, in addition to across time. What appears to be the more accurate stance is that concepts, such as parental involvement, have distinct meaning to mothers, fathers, and children and that these meanings change across time (Dyer et al.). This makes common techniques, such as creating aggregate scores across family members or using growth curve analyses, where the same measures are considered equivalent across time, questionable practices. At the very least these issues demand that researchers carefully consider measurement invariance in all longitudinal designs, and if it is weak to consider alternatives to common growth curve analysis.

An additional important issue with measurement invariance is whether the same questions are invariant across cultures. Far too little research has been done to verify measures across different cultures within one country and among different countries. It is likely that common constructs, such as relationship quality and self-esteem, have very different meanings and need to be measured differently among cultures. The issue of measurement invariance and the implications for clinical, relational, and longitudinal research are complex, and each researcher should carefully consider this issue before planning a study and proceeding with analyzing data by referring to good publications where these issues are discussed (Dyer et al., in press; Vandenberg & Lance, 2000; Widaman, Ferrer, & Conger, 2010).

Unidimensional Measurement and Validity

One of the ongoing concerns that family scientists struggle with is the validity of common measures of marital quality (Glenn, 1990). Fincham and Linfield (1997) suggested that at least in part, the validity of such measures is threatened by the tendency to regard global marital quality as a single construct that typically asks questions anchored by response options ranging from *very dissatisfied* to *very satisfied*. Such concerns could easily be applied to other global measures of relationship, or family-level constructs, that have initially been conceived as unidimensional. Fincham and Linfield proposed that rather than representing polar ends of a scale, positive and negative may actually represent two distinct dimensions of marital quality. Their work has shown that positive and negative marital quality may, indeed, be two distinct constructs, and subsequent research has indicated that this conceptualization may be true of relationship satisfaction among engaged couples (Mattson, Paldino, & Johnson, 2007), as well as couple communication (e.g., adversarial vs. collaborative; Sanford, 2010).

As an example of how these constructs are operationalized, a respondent may be asked to "evaluate good feelings you have about your relationship [while] ignoring the bad ones" in their assessment of positive marital quality, and then "evaluate bad feelings you have about your relationship while ignoring the good ones" when evaluating negative marital quality (Fincham & Linfield, 1997). Participants are instructed to evaluate each item on a scale from 0 (not at all) to 10 (extremely). Scholars have shown that these two constructs may provide more information about marital and relationship quality than do other widely used unidimensional measures of marital quality (Mattson et al., 2007; Sanford, 2010).

We suggest that family therapy researchers consider the possibility that many of the constructs they desire to measure may not be unidimensional and measurable on a single continuum. Such thoughtful conceptualization of measures will likely enhance measurement validity and lead to a more accurate understanding of couple and family interactions.

Conclusions

In sum, we have introduced far more questions than solutions in the area of measurement. As the foundation of all research, measurement is not something to quickly "accomplish" by picking the most valid and reliable measures available and proceeding on to "more important" issues. Measurement should be an organizing issue that helps researchers decide what, how, and who will be studied, and how data will be analyzed to most appropriately answer the research questions of a study. In many instances, when clinically oriented researchers begin a study, they will discover that another study needs to be done first, a measurement study, before the original research questions can be fully answered. Developing high-quality measures of important couple and family constructs and therapeutic outcomes with couples and families is one of the most important contributions scholars can make. Pinsof and colleagues (2009, p. 144) recently said,

> Progress research has produced methodologically sound instruments as well as findings that suggest that providing therapists with feedback about client change improves efficacy and efficiency. However, this research has been limited to individual clients in individual outpatient or inpatient therapy. . . . None of the measures has been developed to study change in family or couple therapy or from a multisystemic perspective in individual therapy. Whether the promising findings from individual therapy will generalize to family and couple therapies remains to be seen.

We concur with this assessment. The measures available for couples and families, especially regarding the therapeutic process and change, are very sparse and the development of these measures should be the highest priority of both applied and basic family scholars.

References

Busby, D. M., & Gardner, B. C. (2008). How do I analyze thee? Let me count the ways: Considering empathy in couple relationships using self and partner ratings. *Family Process, 47*, 229–242.

Busby, D. M., Holman, T. B., & Niehuis, S. (2009). The association between partner- and self-enhancement and relationship quality outcomes. *Journal of Marriage and Family, 71*, 449–464.

Cook, W. L., & Goldstein, M. J. (1993). Multiple perspectives on family relationships: A latent variables model. *Child Development, 64*, 1177–1388.

Cooper, M. L., & Sheldon, M. S. (2002). Seventy years of research on personality and close relationships: Substantive and methodological trends over time. *Journal of Personality, 70*, 783–812.

Donnellan, M. B., Larsen-Rife, D., & Conger, R. D. (2005). Personality, family history, and competence in early adult romantic relationships. *Journal of Personality and Social Psychology, 88*, 562–576.

Draper, T. W., & Marcos, A. C. (Eds.). (1990). *Family variables: Conceptualization, measurement, and use.* Newbury Park, CA: Sage.

Dyer, J., Day, R. D., & Harper, J. (in press). Measuring father involvement: The central role of context and reporter. *Journal of Marriage and Family.*

Fincham, F. D., & Linfield, K. J. (1997). A new look at marital quality: Can spouses feel positive and negative about their marriage? *Journal of Family Psychology, 11*, 489–502.

Ganong, L. H. (2003). Selecting family measurements. *Journal of Family Nursing, 9,* 184–206.

Glenn, N. D. (1990). Quantitative research on marital quality in the 1980's: A critical review. *Journal of Marriage and Family, 52,* 818–831.

Gottman, J. M. (1998). Psychology and the study of marital processes. *Annual Review of Psychology, 49,* 169–197.

Grawitch, M. J., & Munz, D. C. (2004). Are your data nonindependent? A practical guide to evaluating nonindependence and within-group agreement. *Understanding Statistics, 3,* 231–257.

Kashy, D. A., & Snyder, D. K. (1995). Measurement and data analytic issues in couples research. *Psychological Assessment, 7,* 338–348.

Kenny, D. A., & Berman, J. S. (1980). Statistical approaches to the correction of correlational bias. *Psychological Bulletin, 88,* 288–295. doi:10.1037/0033-2909.88.2.288

Kenny, D. A., Kashy, D. A., & Cook, W. L. (2006). *Dyadic data analysis.* New York: Guilford Press.

Maccoby, E. E., & Martin, J. A. (1983). Socialization in the context of the family: Parent-child interaction. *Handbook of Child Psychology, 4,* 1–101.

Mattson, R. E., Paldino, D., & Johnson, M. D. (2007). The increased construct validity and clinical utility of assessing relationship quality using separate positive and negative dimensions. *Psychological Assessment, 19,* 146–151.

McCrae, R. R., & Costa, P. T. (2008). The five factor theory of personality. In O. P. John, R. W. Robins, & L. W. Pervin (Eds.), *Handbook of personality, theory, and research* (pp. 159–181). New York: Guilford Press.

Morry, M. M., Reich, T., & Kito, M. (2010). How do I see you relative to myself? Relationship quality as a predictor of self- and partner-enhancement within cross-sex friendships, dating relationships, and marriages. *Journal of Social Psychology, 150,* 369–392.

Noller, P., & Callan, V. J. (1988). Understanding parent-adolescent interactions: Perceptions of family members and outsiders. *Developmental Psychology, 24,* 707–714.

Olson, D. H. (1977). Insiders' and outsiders' views of relationships: Research strategies. In G. K. Levinger & H. L. Rausch (Eds.), *Close relationships: Perspectives on the meaning of intimacy* (pp. 115–135). Amherst: University of Massachusetts Press.

Pinsof, W. M., Zinbarg, R. E., Lebow, J. L., Knobloch-Fedders, L. M., Durbin, E., Chambers, A., Latta, T., Karam, E., Goldsmith, J., & Friedman, G. (2009): Laying the foundation for progress research in family, couple, and individual therapy: The development and psychometric features of the initial systemic therapy inventory of change. *Psychotherapy Research, 19,* 143–156.

Priem, J. S., Solomon, D. H., & Steuber, K. R. (2009). Accuracy and bias in perceptions of emotionally supportive communication in marriage. *Personal Relationships, 16,* 531–552.

Rohrbaugh, M. J., Shoham, V., Skoyen, J. A., Jensen, M., & Mehl, M. R. (2012). We-talk, communal coping, and cessation success in a couple-focused intervention for health-compromised smokers. *Family Process, 51,* 107–121.

Sanford, K. (2010). Assessing conflict communication in couples: Comparing the validity of self-report, partner-report, and observer ratings. *Journal of Family Psychology, 24*(2), 165.

Schwarz, J. C., Barton-Henry, M. L., & Pruzinsky, T. (1985). Assessing child-rearing behaviors: A comparison of ratings made by mother, father, child, and sibling on the CRPBI. *Child Development, 56,* 462–479.

Snyder, D. K., Cavell, T. A., Heffer, R. W., & Mangrum, L. F. (1995). Marital and family assessment: A multifaceted, multilevel approach. In R. H. Mikesell, D. D. Lusterman, & S. H. McDaniel (Eds.), *Integrating family therapy: Handbook of family psychology and systems theory* (pp. 163–182). Washington, DC: American Psychological Association.

Vandenberg, R. J., & Lance, C. E. (2000). A review and synthesis of the measurement invariance literature: Suggestions, practices, and recommendations for organizational research. *Organizational Research Methods, 3,* 4–17.

Wampler, K. S., & Halverson, C. F. (1993). Quantitative measurement in family research: In P.G. Boss, W. J. Doherty, R. LaRossa, W. R. Schumm, & S.K. Steinmetz (Eds.), *Sourcebook of family theories and methods: A contextual approach* (pp. 181–194). New York: Plenum Press.

Widaman, K. F., Ferrer, E., & Conger, R. D. (2010). Factorial invariance within longitudinal structural equation models: Measuring the same construct across time. *Child Development Perspectives, 4,* 10–18.

5

ETHICAL GUIDELINES FOR CONDUCTING CLINICAL RESEARCH IN RELATIONSHIP-FOCUSED THERAPY

Steven M. Harris and Katharine Wickel

Mental health codes of ethics are in place to protect the public, the profession, and the clinician. Most of these outline certain behaviors that clinicians should practice (confidentiality, informed consent, respect for client autonomy, etc.) and warn against others (sexual contact with clients, multiple role relationships, etc.). Most also make some recommendations as to how clinicians who are engaged in research should conduct themselves (offering informed consent, protecting identity, responsible dissemination of findings, etc.). Any clinical intervention or treatment modality that is subjected to a research protocol must also be ethical, and those delivering the treatment are held to the ethical standards that guide the profession. In clinical practice, ethical dilemmas can arise despite our best efforts to practice ethically. Similarly, in clinical research, where the art of practice meets the science of inquiry, ethical dilemmas can arise, but they can also be anticipated and dealt with in a successful manner. While attending to each and every possible ethical dilemma that can arise in relationship-focused clinical research is beyond the scope of this chapter, we present a guide that can help scientist-practitioners ethically navigate these waters.

Like others, we contend that from the beginning, conducting clinical research is a difficult endeavor (McWey, James, & Smock, 2005; Sprenkle & Piercy, 2005; Thyer, 1991). So many moving parts need to be lined up and accounted for at multiple stages of the project, regardless of whether one is conducting a single-case design or a randomized clinical trial. Clearly, clinical research involves much more than having people fill out a survey or mere observation of a phenomenon. The intersection of practice and research is especially challenging when the client or unit of observation is a couple, family, or other relationship. This makes for a unique proving ground for our code of ethics and our skills as scientist-practitioners.

59

We have chosen to organize our chapter according to the three main sections of *The Belmont Report* (1979): respect for persons, beneficence, and justice. *The Belmont Report* was initially authored in 1979 by the National Commission for the Protection of Human Subjects of Biomedical and Behavioral Research from the then federal Department of Health, Education, and Welfare (now Health and Human Services). The report was a direct outgrowth of the discovery of the inequitable treatment of persons involved in the now infamous Tuskegee Syphilis Experiments (more on this later in the chapter). The document continues to be a trusted guide for researchers working with human subjects. The document has its limitations. For example, it was written from an individual-oriented and linear-causal model of research (and practice, for that matter). Using this report as a guide, as well as the Code of Ethics of the American Association for Marriage and Family Therapy (2012 [AAMFT]), we will discuss the principles of ethical research practice as they specifically pertain to research that focuses on engaging relationships in clinical practice. Also, we will focus attention on the topic of vulnerable populations, as many marriage and family therapists (MFTs) have the opportunity to work with individuals who might fall under this classification or work in organizations that house and serve such individuals. To encourage group or in-class discussion of these principles and concepts, we have included hypothetical clinical-research scenarios throughout the chapter.

Respect for Persons—Autonomy and Self-Determination

From a practice perspective, respecting the client is the very first ethical principle an MFT-in-training ever learns. MFTs are encouraged to advance the "welfare of families and individuals" (AAMFT, 2012), and we learn quickly that respecting our clients is one way we do this. This respect comes as the MFT professional embraces client autonomy and clients' ability to choose for themselves the course their lives should take (self-determination). Accompanying this respect is the ethical obligation to help clients understand the consequences of their decisions. This seems simple enough: Give clients the space they need to sort out their life dilemmas and help them see the ramifications of their decisions. However, we're also a profession that sees relationships first, and respecting the autonomy and self-determination of one person in the family or system may unintentionally bump up against our ability to respect the autonomy and self-determination of another member of that family system. If this dynamic is present in our clinical practice, it will also be present in our clinical research.

Early in my (S.H.) training, I remember one of my systems theory professors saying something to the effect of, "there are no individuals." This comment launched a 3-hour-long conversation about the existence of "self," the incompatibility of the medical model to adequately address systemic issues, and a host of theoretical postulates regarding the role of relationships in all that we do at multiple levels. We ended up agreeing that the self is probably possible to define only as it exists within the context of relationships. Given the possibility that relationships define the self, it is to be expected that within the realm of clinical research, where much of what we are studying involves choices people make and how those choices impact relationships (e.g., what happens between people), the very idea of respecting an individual would be difficult to accomplish and would entail a constant balancing of the competing autonomous wills of all members of the family relational system. Clinical researchers who develop projects to investigate the impact of interventions on relationships must be aware of this tension. They must assess, during the conceptualization stage of the project, how all members of a family system will be impacted by the study and how they will balance a respect for the autonomy of all family members involved.

Clinical Research Scenario: Respecting Autonomy and the "Battle for Structure"

You are on a research team that is testing a family-based treatment protocol for clinically depressed adults that requires all family members living with the depressed person to attend all seven sessions of a manualized family therapy treatment approach. As a member of the research team assigned to macro-code (look for general patterns) video recordings of the sessions, you begin to see a pattern of behaviors demonstrated by preteen family members around the third session. In the mildest form, you observe them tuning out of the sessions (turning their backs to both their parents and the therapist) and not being involved. More overt behaviors from this cohort include complaining about having to be in the treatment, nagging the parents about why they have to be there, and statements such as, "Why do I have to be here if all we do is talk about Dad?" Despite having reviewed the majority of the data, you have yet to observe the therapist address any of the concerns raised by the children.

- What are the major ethical dilemmas in this scenario?
- How could this dilemma have been avoided? (Give two or more solutions.)
- Given that manualized approaches to clinical treatment have some inherent rigidity to them, what do you think could be said to the treatment team about respect for the autonomy of the preteen cohort you've observed?
- How would you propose respectfully balancing the will of the parents (their decision to enroll the family in the clinical trial) with the will of the children (or at least their stated dissatisfaction with their involvement in the research project)? How does the concept of "relative power" (the idea that members of a system influence and are influenced differently by one another based on the level of power they have in the system) figure into your understanding of this balancing act?
- Discuss other situations that come to your mind when you think about balancing respect for competing agendas that inevitably will be present when working with relational systems.

One way of being respectful of the autonomy and self-direction of clinical research participants is to have an adequate informed consent process. In all likelihood this will be a requirement of the institution's human subjects review board. However, having an informed consent process assumes that all participants are able to consent on their own behalf. This is typically not the case with minors. Also, informed consent can be as minimal as reviewing and signing a sheet of paper or as involved as reading a consent document but also receiving a consent interview that can help ensure that each participant is fully aware of the risks involved in participation (Brandon, Shivakumar, Lee, Inrig, & Sadler, 2009). The range of informed consent practices is wide in clinical research, and researchers are cautioned to err on the side of informing more as opposed to less (Wittenborn, Dolbin-MacNab, & Keiley, 2012). Specific consent protocols should be developed for those who have limited capacity to offer consent (i.e., children in a family context). Of course, parents will have the right to consent on behalf of their children, but out of respect for the developing autonomy of children and recognizing that when children are included in therapy they want to be heard (Stith, Rosen, McCollum, Coleman, & Herman, 1996), researchers are encouraged to engage children at an appropriate developmental level to explain what their participation in the study will look like and how it will benefit them and others. This may also have the effect of increasing participation rates of those children involved in treatment (Adelman, Kaser-Boyd, & Taylor, 1984).

Another part to respecting participant autonomy is understanding the role of self-determination, or the right of the participant to shape the events in his or her life. This can be a difficult thing to accomplish when a particular research protocol calls for participants to make choices without having access to all options due to random assignment or other experimental design limitations. In some cases, divulging key elements of a study will compromise the data, and keeping the main objective of the inquiry hidden from the participants is necessary. Further, in marriage and family therapy (MFT), where some of our foundational clinical theories seem to advocate a degree of deception (structural and strategic family therapies—prescribing the symptom, paradoxical injunctions, etc.) as part of the standard practice, some participants would be shielded from full knowledge of the purpose of a clinical study designed to judge the effectiveness of these techniques, thereby limiting their ability to be self-determining in how they approach their decision to participate fully informed in a particular study.

Clinical Research Scenario: Incentive Conflict

As part of her research on families who participate in therapy, a researcher offers incentives to participants in the form of gift cards to a retail superstore. As part of the project protocol, families are supposed to receive a gift card each time they meet with the researcher. Due to the nature of the research question and population of interest, each of the families is simultaneously attending therapy while also participating in the research. One family is uncomfortable with receiving the gift card because they disapprove of the business practices of the superstore and have made a decision not to shop there. After two research interviews, the family mentions this dilemma to their therapist and presents the gift cards back to her. The therapist decides that because the family won't use the gift cards, she will take them. The researcher, who also happens to be the therapist's supervisor, witnesses the conversation replayed from a video recording of the session.

- What is the major dilemma in the scenario?
- How could this dilemma have been avoided? (Give two or more solutions.)
- How does the "reward" aspect of this research project conflict with the participants' autonomy and self-determination?
- Discuss multiple role relationships as an educator, researcher, and clinical supervisor.
- From a research perspective, do you have an opinion about the data collected from this particular couple?
- Should the researcher try to provide similar compensation to this couple, perhaps from a different store? What are the barriers to doing so?
- How do incentives aid or become a barrier to a project's success?
- What are the logistics involved in providing gift cards or other monetary incentives when a researcher is part of a larger system?

Beneficence

The Hippocratic Oath, taken by medical professionals, asserts, among other things, that those responsible for patient care will "first do no harm" as they attempt to alleviate human suffering. This standard of care, often referred to as "nonmalfeasance," is the same standard to which mental health professionals are held (Kitchener, 2000). In essence, it means that the things we do for our clients are intended to, first and foremost, not make them any worse. This can sound a bit dismal. After all, is that the best our clients can expect from us, that we won't make things worse? A different standard of care is discussed in ethics circles and is also reflected in *The Belmont Report*: beneficence. This standard basically suggests that the practitioner will do all in his or her power to ensure that interventions and treatments will, at the very least, do good for the client. There is a marked difference in the two standards of care, with one (beneficence) requiring much more thoughtfulness and intentionality on the part of the practitioner than the other (nonmalfeasance). Indeed, doing good for our clients requires that we practice at a higher level than merely not causing harm would demand.

The balance between doing no harm and benefiting clients is at the forefront of scholarly inquiry, especially as it pertains to clinical research. In order for practitioners to do no harm, they must be equipped with theories, techniques, and practices that are proved to do no harm and to be effective (Emanuel, Wendler, & Grady, 2000). This information can only be known through the research process

(Sprenkle & Piercy, 2005). Hypothesis testing and the implementation of experimental designs contribute to knowing what is harmful or beneficial for our clients. So, all clinical research must carefully balance exposing participants to some degree of risk while ensuring their safety. The clinical researcher must be prepared to justify how the benefits outweigh the risks involved, as well as abandon a certain design because the risks outweigh the potential benefits.

As a standard for research, beneficence has to do with ensuring that research participants will benefit from their participation in a project. This can be defined either directly, that participating in the research will help the individual or family on a personal level (participating in an experimental couple treatment will improve the couple's marriage), or indirectly (participating in research benefits the community at large and, as such, is a benefit to the individual). Furthermore, the benefits need to obviously outweigh the risks involved. The challenge for many scholars is to adequately describe the risk–reward ratio to members of an institution's human subjects review panel. Most institutional review board (IRB) applications specifically request a detailed description of the risks involved in the research. Indeed, if a researcher is unable to identify any risks inherent in the project, the proposal is likely to be returned as unapproved until some risks are identified. Most IRB documents, in discussing risk, indicate that no research involving human subjects is risk free. Therefore, researchers must do their best to identify the risks and discuss ways to minimize the impact of those risks to the participants.

In clinical research with couples and families, it is often the case that those in the most need of the services we provide (a clinical population of couples and families in distress) are often the most desperate for the services. They need services to strengthen or improve their relationships or to alleviate emotional distress. However, with family therapy being a mix of art and science, combined with the fact that we are working with people who have their individual will, it is impossible to say with any confidence that one particular intervention will guarantee a specific outcome. There is always the risk that an intervention we intend will not produce the desired outcome. Balancing risk and reward, and factoring in the will of multiple individuals in any relationally focused treatment unit, can help clinical researchers meet the standard of beneficence in their research designs and implementation.

Clinical Research Scenario: Treatment Progress and Randomized Controlled Trials

A research team organizes a clinical trial for a treatment protocol for couples who experience interpersonal violence. The sample comprises solely couples who are court mandated due to the extensive nature of the violence they have experienced. The study calls for monitoring both the treatment and control group for a 3-year period. Preliminary data analysis (3 months after treatment) indicates that those in the treatment condition experience dramatic changes in their relationships and the elimination of any violent behavior on the part of either person in the couple. Further data analysis indicates that the changes these couples experience persist over time (6-month follow-up after termination). The findings are very positive. One member of the research team suggests that they have an ethical obligation to provide the same treatment to couples in the control group despite the experiment having not run its full course.

- What are the major ethical dilemmas in this scenario?
- How could this dilemma have been avoided? (Give two or more solutions.)
- In clinical trial research (given that the study is theoretically grounded, well conceived, empirically based, etc.), one would expect that the treatment condition would naturally bring about favorable targeted outcomes to those in the treatment group. Those in the control group would, most likely, experience little to no change. In cases where those favorable outcomes are dramatically significant (not just statistically significant), does the researcher have an obligation to alert the participants in the control group of the findings and make the treatment available to them?
- What would constitute a "dramatically significant" outcome that would prompt such a course of action?
- Discuss two standards of care: nonmalfeasance and beneficence, and which of these standards should guide clinical research.

Justice

Justice is a principle that necessitates each participant in a research project be treated in a fair and equitable way. Additionally, it requires that the distribution of benefits and burdens be equal among participants (Zimmerman, 1997). For example, it is not just that one participant be unknowingly exposed to different risks than others. *The Belmont Report* describes equity in distribution as the following: individual investment, individual need, individual effort, societal contribution, and merit of the research (Belmont Report, 1979). This means that each individual should be required to contribute relatively the same amount of time, resources, and effort to participate in the research and, consequently, receive similar benefits and compensation as other participants. Additionally, data gathered from each participant should contribute equally to the findings from the study. To further understand the meaning of these concepts, it is helpful to know some background information that explains the intent and reasoning that support the principle of justice in a research context.

In 1972, the U.S. Public Health Service concluded a 40-year study on 399 African American men who had syphilis, known as the Tuskegee Syphilis Experiment. During the course of the study, participants were not told they had syphilis and were not given treatments that had been found to be effective, so as not to disrupt the study. After the Associated Press exposed the study (Heller,

1972), the U.S. Assistant Secretary for Health and Scientific Affairs convened an advisory panel to investigate and subsequently called for termination of the study and legal action on behalf of the participants.

Although the Tuskegee Syphilis Experiment is one of the most well-known studies for its unethical practices, it was certainly not the only one of its kind; around this same time, there were many other studies with grievous ethical concerns (Cain, Harkness, Smith, & Markowski, 2003). This type of unethical research prompted the creation of *The Belmont Report* and the setting of standards to ensure the safety and protection of human subjects. These standards have protected countless individuals since their inception and implementation. However, *The Belmont Report*'s principle of justice is yet another area where guidelines developed for individually oriented therapy and research may come up short for those conducting research of a more systemic nature. When designing relationally focused, clinically based research, researchers must hold themselves not only to this standard, but to the additional one of ensuring justice within each system of analysis.

Often with couple and family research, there are at least two family members participating, and the requirements of justice are the same. However, with additional participants comes a much bigger task of assessing the risks and benefits to each participant within the couple or family. To be clear, the principle of justice is not the balance of risks and benefits themselves, but the balance of both across all participants. Justice is an essential aspect of any research study, and it becomes increasingly complex when conducting research with couples, families, and communities. The complexity arises with multiple family members participating because the principles of justice may be difficult to determine when each family member may be affected differently by the focus of the research project. For example, if the research is about drug addiction, ensuring that the risks and benefits are similar for the addict and additional family members may become very difficult. This is due to the fact that each family member may be at risk in different ways and may stand to benefit differently from the intervention. Researchers are given the challenge to determine what is equitable for each individual participant in the study, but also within each family subsystem participating as well. The AAMFT (2012) Code of Ethics reiterates the concern of risk/benefit: "Investigators respect the dignity and protect the welfare of research participants, and are aware of applicable laws, regulations, and professional standards governing the conduct of research." It is essential for researchers to have discussions early in their treatment/research design to determine what is just for each participant and to be aware that each member of the family may experience the risks and benefits differently.

Clinical Research Scenario: Client Experiences in Therapy

A researcher interested in knowing more about clients' experiences of therapy meets with clients after their therapy session. During the conversation, the clients report that they are not pleased with the direction therapy is going. In fact, when pressed, they indicate that they do not believe the thera-pist is very good at all. The researcher, also a faculty member at the training program where the research is being conducted, happens to be the therapist's clinical supervisor. The researcher has information that could change the course of therapy and be beneficial to the clients' treatment, as well as to their therapist's development. And it would be well within the researcher's scope of practice as a supervisor to recommend changes to the therapist's clini-cal approach, but she has this information only by virtue of conducting the research. Knowing that the clients agreed to participate in the research on the basis of confidentiality, the researcher/supervisor now faces a dilemma. If she does not share any information with the therapist, she is risking the clients having a bad experience in therapy and possibly dropping out of treatment (and dropping out of the study as well). If she divulges the information, she's violating the confidentiality of the research participants.

- What is the major dilemma in the scenario?
- How could this dilemma have been avoided? (Give two or more solutions.)
- Knowing how hard it is to recruit couples for clinical research, should the researcher's emphasis be on keeping the participants in the study (as much as possible)?
- Discuss the pros and cons of subtly "leading" the supervisee into a dialogue about how to be more effective with this particular couple without mention-ing anything about the research project.
- Imagine that the student approaches the supervisor and says, "I love working with that couple, they are doing great!" How would you advise the supervi-sor/researcher to respond?
- How do you make a decision about which code of ethics "trumps" or takes precedence over another code when enforcing or supporting one code seems to come at the expense of another?
- Contextual information: How do your answers change if the following vari-ables are introduced?
  o Researcher is under pressure to increase sample size for grant funding
  o The problem reported by the participants is one that the therapist has received supervision for on multiple occasions.

Clinical Trials

An increasing amount of MFT research focuses on assessing the validity of treat-ment interventions (Lyness, Walsh, & Sprenkle, 2005). Such studies include, but are not limited to, clinical trials. While clinical trials are not a new phenom-enon, most of the published literature addressing concerns of justice and clinical trials comes from fields other than MFT (Tremaine et al., 2005). In treatment-based research, randomized clinical trials have been accepted as the pinnacle of methodological design, and are often referred to as the "gold standard."

However, when a research protocol calls for participants to be grouped together and receive different types of treatment (or no treatment), concerns of justice surface. It is not our intent to call into question the ethical nature of randomized clinical trials but to point out concerns that must be addressed while conducting such research.

Clinical trials, by definition, treat research participants differently, citing theoretical and/or empirical evidence for doing so. While it is necessary for there to be evidence for giving the treatment, there must also be some basis for not giving the treatment. In other words, there must be sufficient evidence that the treatment *may* work, but also a lack of evidence that would suggest that there is a *potential* that giving no treatment may be just as effective or could even be preferable to treatment outcomes. The goal, of course, is to see which treatment is most successful. However, researchers must also be prepared to address principles of justice that may arise. Many protocols call for a control group being assigned to a wait list, while others may call for no treatment. There is not a single solution that can be applied to every study; instead, the researcher must take the population of interest into account and be sensitive to issues of justice. For example, a particular clinical trial study may indicate the importance of employing a wait list condition. However, if the population that participates in the study has been historically marginalized, those in the wait list condition may perceive their situation as unjust and even unethical, and indeed it may be. In these situations, sensitivity and creativity may need to be employed.

Researchers who work with populations that have histories of marginalization need to be aware of the past actions of other researchers and take purposeful steps to design research protocols in a sensitive manner. Imagine an urban community that is located close to a university. This community has experienced higher than average levels of violence, abuse, addiction, poverty, unemployment, and poor health outcomes. Because of its proximity to the university and its complex challenges, its population is a natural focus for many university-based research studies. Imagine also that traditionally the researchers have gone into the community, collected data, and left without giving back to the community in return. Research findings were rarely shared with the community, and sustainable plans to aid the challenges being researched were never introduced. This scenario represents a serious violation of the spirit of the principle of justice. Over time, this community will develop a mistrust of the university as a whole, and research opportunities will be closed off. In this case, the researchers lose, and the community loses an opportunity to benefit from all that the research findings could have provided.

In a community such as this, creating a protocol that involves a wait list may be insensitive and unjust. In the case of a wait list, the community members may not trust that the researchers will actually include wait-listed participants at a later date. Additionally, communities that want all members to benefit from the study may have difficulty understanding control group protocols that call for some members to receive treatment and others to go without. They may see this as another example of research being done *on* them rather than *with* them. New researchers, interested in an underserved population such as this, who have developed an intervention-based study, would have to spend considerable time developing a relationship of trust with the major stakeholders in the community before the study could begin with a solid footing in the principle of justice. It is the researcher's obligation to balance treating the community justly while ensuring methodological rigor.

Additionally (and as discussed earlier), researchers may need to be prepared for an instance where the treatment is so successful that it seems unethical to withhold treatment, and thus discontinue the research. The intent of performing a randomized clinical trial is to develop a successful treatment for the problem of interest. Concerns may arise if the treatment is proved to be so successful that it becomes unethical to not include participants who have been assigned to no-treatment or wait-list groups. If this concern were to arise midstudy, it may be cause for reevaluation of the research protocol. It may be difficult to determine when this line is crossed, particularly for professionals who have invested time and effort into the research. This may call for outside consultation if the question surfaces during the implementation of the treatment protocol.

Clinical Research Scenario: Randomized Clinical Trial

In the developmental stages of a research proposal, a research team meets to plan how to develop the procedure for a randomized clinical trial. The purpose of the project is to find if there is empirical evidence for a particular parenting intervention. Although the intervention has been tested with Euro-American populations, this research team wants to focus its work on local immigrants. Furthering their understanding about parenting interventions with this particular population could be useful to inform advocacy and policy within the community. The project follows the community-based participatory research model, with members of the community contributing as members of the research team. In planning the intervention, however, the team comes to a disagreement. Some members of the team want to assign participants to the intervention and control groups, following traditional randomized controlled trial methodology. However, other members are concerned with this direction. They express their belief that putting people into a control group would harm relationships with the community and reinforce sentiments of mistrust. At the same time as wanting to be respectful of the people and community, these members of the team also recognize that some sort of compromise is needed to enable methodological and statistical rigor in the process. That is to say, there needs to be a comparison between those who receive the intervention and those who do not.

- What are the major ethical dilemmas in this scenario?
- How could this dilemma have been avoided? (Give two or more solutions.)
- What might be some ethical ramifications if the researchers didn't listen to the community members within the research team?
- How do you balance the ethical needs of rigorous research and community input?
- How might this dilemma be different if it weren't targeting a population that had a history of oppression and marginalization?

It is clear that this third principle is a complex part of the ethical considerations in any project design. Adding the considerations for relationship-focused clinical research can cause it to grow in complexity very quickly. Concerns of justice must be addressed within each system, as well as across all family systems participating. Further, recently MFT as a field has been increasingly focusing on the concept of social justice as it pertains to our clinical and educational practices (Baumann, Rodriguez, & Parra-Cardona, 2011; McDowell, Fang, Brownlee, Young, & Khanna, 2002; McDowell, Goessling, & Melendez, 2012). We address this particular dimension of justice in the following section.

Vulnerable Populations

One of the important aspects of justice is the consideration of vulnerable populations. There are three different types of vulnerable populations that relationship-focused clinical researchers need to consider. Traditionally, the label of vulnerability has been applied to populations that either have their ability to consent compromised (prisoners, cognitively impaired persons, students, terminally ill patients, etc.) and/or are in a sensitive stage of life (children, pregnant women, elderly, etc.) (Goldman, 2001). However, this view may be inadequate; due to circumstances and context, other populations, such as historically underrepresented or marginalized people, may also be viewed as vulnerable. This may be because of historical discrimination or oppression. Within many social science fields, this consideration is referred to as social justice. When vulnerable populations participate in research, it is important that the researchers recognize ways to do research *with* participants rather than *on* them. This has been exemplified with community-based participatory research, which has introduced new ways of engaging community members to co-create research that is meaningful to, rather than exploitative of, their community (Wallerstein & Duran, 2010).

For clinical researchers, there is a third consideration in determining the definition of a vulnerable population: the clients. In many ways those who seek therapeutic services are already, at a minimum, vulnerable—emotionally and mentally. It may even be an additional concern of justice if one of the family members is more emotionally or mentally vulnerable than others. This may occur when one person has been diagnosed with a mental health disorder or has experienced personal trauma (abuse, violence, etc.). Additionally, this vulnerability may differ slightly in each study, depending on the problem of interest; however, it is essential that clinical researchers recognize all three types of vulnerable populations and how to treat each participant and each relationship justly.

Clinical Research Scenario: Working With Vulnerable Populations

A research team is progressing well as it starts to implement the testing of an intervention with an immigrant population. Several months into the study, a lot of preliminary data have been collected about each of the families; however, every family that has participated still has more steps within the study to finish the project and ensure complete data collection. In the area where the study is taking place, there is increased enforcement by government around illegal immigration. Several participants in the study are forced to frequently change residence and many have family members who are arrested and then deported. Seeing this, the researchers are concerned about the well-being of the participants and the research project. They realize that a lot of resources and grant money have been invested into this study and are concerned that this might shut down the project. There is a concern about wanting to help the people but in a way that will minimally influence research findings and allow the project to continue.

- What are the major ethical dilemmas in this scenario?
- How could this dilemma have been avoided? (Give two or more solutions.)
- What responsibilities does the research team have to the population it is working with?
- How should the team go about balancing fidelity to the research design and sensitivity to issues of social justice?

The Belmont Report (1979) does address some concerns of social justice by stating:

> selection of research subjects needs to be scrutinized in order to determine whether some classes (e.g., welfare patients, particular racial and ethnic minorities, or persons confined to institutions) are being systematically selected simply because of their easy availability, their compromised position, or their manipulability, rather than for reasons directly related to the problem being studied. (p. 3)

However, in the principles addressed in the AAMFT Code of Ethics (2012), an additional guideline for relationship-focused clinicians engaged in research helps to clarify how these principles may apply to professionals within the field of MFT. It is clear that while the purpose of this document is to address ethical concerns as a whole, it also incorporates ideas of social justice within many of the principles, reflecting an important value of the profession.

One of the first principles addressed in the Code of Ethics that govern our practice is the concept of social justice: "Marriage and family therapists provide professional assistance to persons without discrimination on the basis of race, age, ethnicity, socioeconomic status, disability, gender, health status, religion, national origin, sexual orientation, gender identity or relationship status." While this statement is essential to the profession, therapists are left to themselves to determine what this may mean within a clinical research setting.

In current research, however, it may be more difficult to determine what it means to consider the concept of protecting the welfare of each research participant. The meaning of welfare is nuanced and researchers have the responsibility to ensure that each part of the research process is just. Cain and colleagues (2003) spoke to this when they discussed the importance of "[selecting] participants equitably" (p. 49). However this becomes an additional challenge when doing research with couples and families. Researchers who want to look at clinical outcomes cannot just look at the outcomes of a person within the family who exhibits the behaviors of interest. For example, if the treatment is addressing families who have one member dealing with depression, it is not adequate to just look at depression levels of that individual. If the inclusion of families is essential for the study, there may also be a need to examine family-level outcomes. This would provide information on whether or not the treatment is equitably beneficial for all participants, not just the one who has the diagnosis. This protocol would, understandably, look different, depending on the topic of interest; however, the needs of all participants must be considered.

Clinical Research Scenario: Attending to Vulnerability and Power Within a Relationship

A group of researchers develop a sex therapy treatment for couples designed to improve overall relational outcomes. In keeping with the protocol to test the effectiveness of the treatment, therapists at a specific clinic are trained in the treatment, and as part of the study the clinic is advertised as a place where people can participant in the study and receive the treatment for free. As part of the study, the sessions will be recorded and the information will be both transcribed and coded by a team of researchers, including students. The clinic services clients who both do and do not participate in the study. A couple contacts the clinic stating that they want treatment and would like to participate in the study. However, in the initial session, it becomes clear to the therapist that although both members of the couple agree to participate, one individual is resistant to the idea of participating in the study. During the initial session, the wife expresses concerns about privacy and just wanting to get appropriate treatment; she is also concerned that the treatment that focuses on the couple's sexual relationship is not the appropriate level of care for her specific relationship concerns. The husband, however, voices excitement about the free services and states that he is willing to consent to the sex therapy intervention because, in his opinion, "it should be good enough" to help their relationship.

- What are the major ethical dilemmas in this scenario?
- How could this dilemma have been avoided? (Give two or more solutions.)
- Is there a way to avoid couples having differences of opinion about their level of participation or investment in a research protocol?
- How might the power of one individual overshadow the interests of another in a research scenario?
- How can we, as researchers, provide incentives to participate that do not play to the vulnerabilities of the people we wish to have participate in our research?

Additional principles that allude to justice within the AAMFT Code of Ethics are those that address the protection of research participants, informed consent, and participants' right to withdraw from any study at any time or decline participation altogether. This may become a concern, as some family members may have stronger motivations to participate in a particular study and influence others to participate in a study for a variety of reasons, as depicted in the scenario above. The principle of justice mandates that all participants be treated the same in terms of protection of their confidentiality, consent, and decisions to participate or withdraw from the study. While these are helpful guidelines, they lack an explicit discussion of justice and concerns specific to relationship-focused clinical research.

Clinical Research Scenario: Children as a Vulnerable Population

After many submissions to the IRB, a researcher receives clearance to conduct a (therapeutic) process effectiveness study with families where child abuse had occurred but was no longer an imminent threat. The purpose of the study is to discover what works well in a natural (non-experimental) therapeutic setting with these particular families. According to the protocol, each session was observed live, and two research assistants coded process variables. For liability purposes, the IRB denied a request to video-record the therapy sessions. Upon completion of the therapy session, participants were asked to remain in the room and were told that a researcher would be with them shortly. After the therapist leaves the room, the researcher joins the family to begin the "research" portion of the project. During the interview with the researcher, one of the children discloses that he doesn't like being hit by his father and he hopes therapy will "make it stop." After the session, the research team is debating whether or not they have an obligation to report the child's disclosure. One researcher suggests that reporting this disclosure to Child Protective Services is not necessary, since the disclosure came out during the "research" phase of the project and not during therapy. Another suggests that a report is not necessary because the family already has a history with Child Protective Services, and the information was known prior to the beginning of the project. Finally, a third disagrees entirely and suggests that they have a duty to report this information.

- What are the major ethical dilemmas in this scenario?
- How could this dilemma have been avoided? (Give two or more solutions.)
- If the researchers are mandated reporters in one setting (i.e., therapy), are they still mandated reporters as researchers?
- If we are trying to "first do no harm" as clinicians, how does that mandate conflict with the potential of family dissolution once a report of child abuse is made?
- In what ways might the participants be considered a vulnerable population? (Discuss as many as possible.)

Conclusion

Successfully conducting clinical research is demanding and difficult. But it is one way to demonstrate that mental health intervention and prevention strategies are effective. Furthermore, it has been successfully undertaken by a host of researchers in individually oriented mental health disciplines. Adding a relational dimension to the already challenging endeavor of conducting clinical research complicates things further. It introduces more moving parts, more individual wills, more voices to honor and respect. However, well-conceived and ethically implemented research on relationship-focused therapy will move the field further and help to establish the legitimacy of relationship-focused interventions for a host of mental and emotional problems. In fact, it will be the only thing that will move the field forward. The challenge to relationship-focused clinical researchers is to also attend to a host of ethical dilemmas that may be present as we empirically validate the claim that attending to relationships is of paramount importance to healthy human functioning at multiple levels.

References

Adelman, H.S., Kaser-Boyd, N., & Taylor, L. (1984). Children's participation in consent for psychotherapy and their subsequent response to treatment. *Journal of Clinical Child Psychology, 13,* 170–178. doi: 10.1080/15374418409533186

American Association for Marriage and Family Therapy. (2012). Code of Ethics. Washington, DC: American Association for Marriage and Family Therapy.

Baumann, A., Rodriguez, M. D., & Parra-Cardona, J. R. (2011). Community-based applied research with Latino immigrant families: Informing practice and research according to ethical and social justice principles. *Family Process, 50,* 132–148.

Belmont Report (1979). The Belmont Report: Ethical principles and guidelines for the protection of human subjects of research. Retrieved from hhs.gov/ohrp/humansubjects/guidance/belmont.html

Brandon, A. R., Shivakumar, G., Lee, S. C., Inrig, S. J., & Sadler, J. Z. (2009). Ethical issues in perinatal mental health research. *Current Opinion in Psychiatry, 22,* 601–606. doi:10.1097/YCO.0b013e3283318e6f

Cain, H. I., Harkness, J. L., Smith, A. L., & Markowski, E. M. (2003). Protecting persons in family therapy research: An overview of ethical and regulatory standards. *Journal of Marital and Family Therapy, 29,* 47–57. doi: 10.1111/j.1752–0606.2003.tb00382.x

Emanuel, E. J., Wendler, D., & Grady, C. (2000). What makes clinical research ethical? *Journal of the American Medical Association, 31,* 2701–2711. doi: 10.1001/jama.283.20.2701.

Goldman, E. (2001). Vulnerable subjects. Retrieved from http://poynter.indiana.edu/sas/ress/vs.pdf

Heller, J. (1972, July 26). Syphilis victims in U.S. study went untreated for 40 years. *New York Times,* Al.

Kitchener, K. S. (2000). *Foundations of ethical practice, research, and teaching in psychology.* Mahwah, NJ: Lawrence Erlbaum.

Lyness, K. P., Walsh, S. R., & Sprenkle, D. H. (2005). Clinical trials in marriage and family therapy research. In D. H. Sprenkle & F. P. Piercy (Eds.), *Research methods in family therapy* (pp. 297–317). New York: Guilford Press.

McDowell, T., Fang, S.-R., Brownlee, K., Young, C. G., & Khanna, A. (2002). Transforming an MFT program: A model for enhancing diversity. *Journal of Marital and Family Therapy, 28,* 179–191.

McDowell, T., Goessling, K., & Melendez, T. (2012). Transformative learning through international immersion: Building multicultural competence in family therapy and counseling. *Journal of Marital and Family Therapy, 38,* 365–379. doi: 10.1111/j.1752–0606.2010.00209.x

McWey, L. M., James, E. J., & Smock, S. A. (2005). A graduate student guide to conducting research in marriage and family therapy. In D. H. Sprenkle & F. P. Piercy (Eds.), *Research methods in family therapy* (pp. 19–40). New York: Guilford Press.

Sprenkle, D. H., & Piercy, F. P. (2005). Pluralism, diversity, and sophistication in family therapy research. In D. H. Sprenkle & F. P. Piercy (Eds.), *Research methods in family therapy* (pp. 3–18). New York: Guilford Press.

Stith, S. M., Rosen, K. H., McCollum, E. E., Coleman, J. U., and Herman, S. A. (1996). The voices of children: Preadolescent children's experiences in family therapy. *Journal of Marital and Family Therapy, 22,* 69–86. doi: 10.1111/j.1752–0606.1996.tb00188.x

Thyer, B. A. (1991). Guidelines for evaluating outcome studies on social work practice. *Research on Social Work, 1,* 76–91. doi: 10.1177/104973159100100105

Tremaine, W. J., Carlson, M. R., Isaacs, K. L., Motil, K. J., Robuck, P. R., & Wurzelmann, J. I. (2005). Ethical issues, safety, and data integrity in clinical trials. *Inflammatory Bowel Diseases, 11*(S1) S17-S21. doi: 10.1097/01.MIB.0000184850.46440.ea

Wallerstein, N., & Duran, B. (2010). Community-based participatory research contributions to intervention research: The intersection of science and practice to improve health equity. *American Journal of Public Health, 100* (S1) S40-S46. doi: 10.2105/AJPH.2009.184036

Wittenborn, A. K., Dolbin-MacNab, M. L., & Keiley, M. K. (2012). Dyadic research in marriage and family therapy: Methodological considerations. *Journal of Marital and Family Therapy.* doi:10.1111/j.1752–0606.2012.00306.x

Zimmerman, J. F. (1997, Summer). The Belmont Report: An ethical framework for protecting research subjects. *The Monitor.*

Section II

DATA COLLECTION

6

RECRUITMENT AND RETENTION OF COUPLES AND FAMILIES IN CLINICAL RESEARCH

Michael M. Olson and Richard B Miller

The Importance of Successful Recruitment and Retention

The recruitment and retention of an adequate sample poses one of the biggest challenges to high-quality marriage and family therapy (MFT) research. Gul and Ali (2010) have called recruitment and retention a "constant challenge to the success of clinical research" (p. 228). Indeed, even a study that has a compelling research question, with a research design that is state-of-the-art, will fail if researchers are unable to recruit a suitable sample and retain participants for the duration of the study. Unfortunately, the difficulty in recruiting the targeted sample is a problem that plagues many clinical studies. Scholars have estimated that about 60% of U.S. federally funded clinical trials fail to meet their targeted sample size or are required to extend the time period needed to recruit an adequate sample (Puffer & Torgerson, 2003). In the United Kingdom, only 31% of health care clinical trials were able to successfully meet their recruitment needs (Bower et al., 2009). Low response rates of face-to-face, mail, and Internet MFT-related surveys also present a significant challenge to mental health researchers (Galea & Tracy, 2007).

Challenges in Recruiting

The willingness of people to participate in health- and mental health-related research has been declining for a number of years (Probstfield & Frye, 2011). One reason for the decreased willingness is that adults and families have become increasingly busy, with little discretionary time, with parents working full-time (Bianchi & Milkie, 2010) and children involved in an increasing number of extracurricular activities (Anderson & Doherty, 2005). The result is that families perceive that they have little time to participate in research studies.

The widespread use of telemarketing in today's culture has further decreased the willingness of couples and families to participate in research studies. Families have grown weary of telemarketers, who sometimes disguise their sales approach as some kind of research (Dillman, Smyth, & Christian, 2009). In addition, the proliferation of junk mail in our mail boxes, as well as spam in our email inboxes, has led individuals to almost instinctively throw away junk mail and delete email spam without reading its contents. Email users have also become cautious of scams from unscrupulous hackers who want to either steal personal information or infect our computer with viruses. The result is that email users are leery of opening and reading email from unknown senders.

MFT researchers face an exponentially difficult challenge as the unit of recruitment and retention moves from the single patient/client to a dyad or family. Obtaining the willingness of both partners, in the case of couples research, and all relevant family members, in the case of family research, to voluntarily consent to participate in a study is difficult (Bonvicini, 1998). This compounding problem increases methodological complexity, as loss of one subject can result in the loss of the unit of analysis for study purposes. Consequently, strategies to recruit and retain research subjects must account for this complexity. MFT researchers face the additional challenge of recruiting and retaining subjects who are often in distress or crisis, thus increasing the likelihood of attrition due to emotional and relational instability. Consequently, it is not coincidental that much of the published clinical literature on couples and families involves patients who are mildly distressed and middle class. MFT researchers must focus efforts to engage and retain couples and families that are more severely distressed, often with comorbid conditions and subjects of diverse ethnic and racial backgrounds, to increase internal and external validity of their research.

Challenges to Validity

The inability to successfully recruit an adequate sample creates serious issues regarding the validity of the study. Conclusion validity is compromised when the statistical power of the study is insufficient due to an inadequate sample size. Statistical power refers to the probability of rejecting the null hypothesis, given the effect size, alpha, and sample size (Cohen, 1992). Hence, statistical power is partly a function of sample size, and type II error, indicating that the statistical analysis erroneously found nonsignificant results, is much more likely when the statistical power is too low to accurately determine statistical significance (Del Boca & Darkes, 2007; Watson & Torgerson, 2006). Inadequate recruitment can also weaken the external validity of a study. In some cases, nonparticipation in research is not random; rather, specific groups may be less likely to participate in a study. For example, depressed individuals or severely distressed couples may be less inclined to participate in a clinical study, which will bias the study toward representing less depressed individuals and more mild to moderately distressed couples. This results in a selection bias, and the findings of the study may have limited generalizability (Andersen, 2007; Watson & Torgerson; Woodall, Howard, & Morgan, 2011).

The concern of validity extends to sample retention. Similar to problems caused by a recruitment process that results in a small sample size, participants prematurely dropping out of the study can similarly reduce sample size, also leading to low statistical power and type II error. In addition, participant attrition can lead to attrition bias, where participants who drop out of a clinical study are different from those who remain in the study (Miller & Wright, 1995). For example, if the composition of the treatment and control groups in a clinical trial change because of nonrandom attrition, the statistical comparisons of the two groups at posttest can be contaminated (Gul & Ali, 2010). In correlational studies, differential dropout can lead to inaccurate tests of association between variables (Miller & Wright). Systematic, nonrandom attrition can also affect the overall results of outcome studies. For example, clinical studies of substance abuse have found that the first 70% of participants contacted at follow-up have significantly different levels of substance use than those who are more difficult to contact, thereby altering the results of the study (Del Boca & Darkes, 2007). Thus, the retention of participants is important in making accurate conclusions about any study. Each of these issues results in lower conclusion validity. In addition, excessive attrition can affect the external validity of the study by changing the sample characteristics that were present at the beginning of the study, thus reducing generalizability.

Despite the significant challenges to recruit and retain an adequate sample, the situation isn't hopeless. Methodologists have carefully studied the principles and practices necessary for successful recruitment and retention and have provided evidence-based strategies and recommendations to recruit and retain subjects in clinical research. Paramount among the researchers' suggestions is that adequate planning and consideration for the recruitment and retention of the clinical sample cannot be a methodological afterthought, but must be central to research design (Gul & Ali, 2010). MFT researchers who use scientifically validated recruitment and retention strategies and devote sufficient time, energy, and resources to the process will experience success for their efforts.

Establishing an Adequate Census

A key component when constructing a research protocol involving couples or families is the need to establish the presence of an adequate clinical population, or census, being studied at data collections site(s). For example, clinical researchers will fail if their research design calls for two randomized groups of 50 distressed couples when, in fact, their university clinic sees only about 100 couples annually. In that scenario, some couples will fail to meet the inclusion criteria and others will refuse the invitation to participate in the study. Gul and Ali (2010) call this the "funnel effect"; consequently, it is important that the population census be significantly larger than the research design demands.

Researchers often overestimate the population census and rates of consent and underestimate the time and resources required to enroll an adequate sample (Hunninghake, Darby, & Probstfield, 1987; Swanson & Ward, 1995). The consequence of overestimating the population census is that researchers will be unable to recruit an adequate sample. In settings where client records are maintained electronically, a simple electronic query by diagnosis, marital status, or presenting problem can give realistic population census figures, thus ascertaining the number of existing clients currently being treated at the clinic that meet research criteria and parameters. If no electronic database is available, researchers should conduct a manual census. By conducting a power analysis (Cohen, 1992), researchers will know the appropriate sample size for their study, which will help them better estimate the needed size of their population census. In today's external funding environment, demonstrating an adequate census and having access to the population is usually required by federal and state funding agencies.

Collaboration

An important strategy for increasing the population census is to establish collaborative relationships with clinical sites that can provide adequate access to a population of interest. Collaboration is a "willing cooperation" for the good of both entities. In unfunded research, particularly at university-based MFT clinics and small agencies, researchers may need to rely on collaborators' altruism as a means of conducting research. Just as providing incentives have proven to increase the recruitment and retention of research subjects (Guyll, Spoth, & Redmond, 2003), so should there be incentives, or a "quid pro quo," for collaborators. Most individuals and systems respond (change behavior) to rewards, real or perceived. While well meaning and sincere, many potential collaborators in research studies often fail to provide the necessary support, not because of disregard or ambivalence, but, rather, due to lack of real incentive to do so. The use of a decisional balance matrix (see Table 6.1) may be helpful in exploring the pros and cons of participation with potential collaborators.

Note that the incentives and obstacles to collaboration are likely to be very specific to the individual collaborator. While, as researchers, we might anticipate certain types of rewards and costs associated with working together, these may be

Table 6.1 Decisional Balance Matrix

	Incentives/ Benefits	*Concerns/ Obstacles*
Change (participation in research)		
No change (nonparticipation in research)		

very different for the potential collaborator. At a minimum, a decision matrix will help clarify the key reasons that a potential collaborator may or may not be interested in participation. The researcher proposing the idea may offer suggestions regarding potential incentives and acknowledge potential barriers and obstacles to working together.

The work of clinical researchers W. Miller and S. Rollnick on motivational interviewing (MI) can be instructive in providing a framework for engaging and collaborating with others for clinical research purposes. At a basic level, three central constructs are imperative; first, establishing *rapport/relationship*; second, ascertaining how *important* the collaborative relationship is to the other party; and third, being *confident* that the researchers can provide the necessary support. Even if importance is high for collaborators, if confidence is low, their productive participation will likely be limited. The first challenge is to determine those who will view the collaboration as important (a colleague will benefit from participating in any publications that may come from the work, a clinic may benefit from access to clinical data about its therapists or clients, etc.). MFT researchers should keep in mind what kinds of things will likely increase importance for collaborators. Additionally, researchers might engage potential collaborators to determine ways of increasing importance. The second step is to determine the level of involvement (behavior change, essentially) that collaborators feel most confident with.

A stepped approach is similar to the MI approach in a counseling environment, where the clinician offers choices to the patient in a collaborative style, emphasizing autonomy and choice. The aim of using an MI-based approach is to acknowledge collaborators' own reasons for participation (or nonparticipation), determine levels of importance and confidence, and establish the steps (specific and realistic) the researcher and collaborator might take together to increase the likelihood of a successful partnership. It is possible that the level of involvement agreed upon may not be sufficient to carry out the research protocol. If this is the case, the researcher should engage in identifying real and perceived barriers or obstacles to a necessary level of engagement. This may include, for example, offering to provide additional support, education, or oversight or enlisting others to provide such ancillary support.

Collaboration is seldom a relationship between two peoples. More often, it involves multiple levels of participation across varied groups of individuals who interact with the clients, including administrators, clinical supervisors, and therapists. "Buy-in" at all levels to collaborate on the research project is needed in order for the research study to be successful. Thus, it is necessary to consider the decisional matrix for each group of collaborators. For example, it is common to rely on the therapists to identify eligible clients for participation in a research protocol. Therapists, as with anyone else we collaborate with, including our research participants, have their own importance/confidence axis for making decisions whether to act (participate). Moreover, experience has demonstrated the importance of having at least one collaborator at each research site who is a "champion" for the research project. This person, who is enthusiastic about the project, helps the others at the site "buy into" the project and willingly become collaborators who cooperate with the research protocols.

A recent study investigating recruitment into a randomized controlled trial following contact with a counseling service found that out of 34,722 calls to the counseling agency during the recruitment period, only 9% of callers were invited to participate (despite being required to do so), with only 2.6% agreement by potential participants (Burgess, Christensen, Griffiths, & Farrer, 2010). When therapists were asked about not referring potential patients into the study, reasons given included that it was inappropriate to ask their clients to participate in the research project, they felt uncomfortable about asking the question, they were concerned that the invitation might affect the therapeutic relationship, and they simply forgot to ask. MFT researchers must take appropriate steps to ensure that all collaborators involved (therapists, administrative personnel, academic institutional representatives, and participants) are on the same page and that concerns and obstacles are identified and resolved. The presence of an on-site research manager, regular encouragement and feedback, and tailored and specific recruiter training may improve collaboration/participation. In addition, there is evidence that financial incentives to referring therapists increase the rate of therapists referring their clients for a research study (Unger, Wylie, Fallah, Heinrich, & O'Brien, 2010).

Maximizing Positive Response from Subjects

Recruitment in Clinical Research

Research and practical experience has suggested procedures to enhance the likelihood of success in recruiting subjects into clinical trials, clinical process research, mental health services research, and qualitative research that explores in-depth clinical issues. There is consensus among clinical researchers of the importance of using multiple methods to market clinical studies to attract potential subjects (Striley, Callahan, & Cottler, 2008). For example, an intervention study of HIV-infected persons used multiple ways to market the study, including making presentations to community groups; posting flyers on public bulletin boards at local grocery stores, bookstores, and hair salons; placing short announcements in church bulletins and community newspapers; hosting information and recruitment tables at community events; and meeting with providers at medical and community service agencies (Baigis, Francis, & Hoffman, 2003).

It is important that researchers do not underestimate the efforts and resources required to recruit a suitable sample. Instead, researchers must allocate sufficient time, staffing, and resources to be successful in the recruiting process. In addition, Gul and Ali (2010) report that active methods of recruitment are more successful than passive methods in clinical research. For example, they have found that a letter of invitation to participate in a clinical research project that is followed up by a telephone call from a member of the research team is much more successful than using only a letter of invitation. A passive method, such as a flyer or announcement in a newspaper, may pique interest in a study, but an active follow-up recruitment strategy, such as a telephone call or a face-to-face visit, will lead to a much higher recruitment rate. In fact, research suggests that recruitment strategies that include telephone contact with potential participants leads to three times more success, compared with strategies that don't include telephone contact (Watson & Torgerson, 2006).

There is substantial evidence that financial incentives increase the success of recruiting for clinical research (Berger, Begun, & Otto-Salaj, 2009; Watson & Torgerson, 2006), and the provision of remuneration has become common practice in clinical research. One study examined the effect of offering potential research subjects $100 to participate in an intervention study and found that the financial incentive had a significant influence on people's decision to participate. Additionally, the study by Striley, Callahan, and Cottler (2008) found that the financial incentive reduced selection bias by increasing participation rates among individuals who would be less likely to participate in the research, including people with low education and those who initially reported that they were not inclined to participate in the research project (Guyll et al., 2003). In another study, researchers used qualitative methods to interview people who had consented to participate in a clinical research project. The researchers reported that most of the participants mentioned financial incentives as a significant reason for their decision to participate (Woodall et al., 2011).

Unfortunately, there are no clear guidelines as to the appropriate level of remuneration. Researchers need to offer a large enough incentive to motivate people to participate in the study but not too large that it unduly influences people to participate in the study, thereby reducing the voluntariness of their consent to participate (Largent, Grady, Miller, & Wertheimer, 2012). To use an extreme hypothetical example, if a person were offered $10,000 to participate in a clinical experiment that required them to attend only four sessions of therapy, they would almost feel compelled to agree to participate because it would be "a deal that they couldn't refuse." Consequently, their ability to make a voluntary choice would be compromised. Scholars who have examined the ethical considerations of offering incentives to potential research subjects have suggested that the amount of the incentive should be based on the level of effort, inconvenience, and time required to participate in the research project. Thus, decisions concerning the level of incentives should be made on a study-by-study basis (Berger et al., 2009).

In addition to financial incentives, there is evidence that people are motivated by altruistic factors to participate in clinical research studies. For some people, the decision to participate in a research project is based on their perception of the relevance or importance of the project, as well as the potential benefits of the results of the study to themselves and the community (Gul & Ali, 2010), similar to the decision matrix presented earlier. For example, families with a disabled child are usually highly motivated to participate in research because of their strong desire to better understand their child's disease or disorder, as well as discover viable treatments. They also have a strong sense of empathy for other families in similar situations and want to help them live less stressful lives. In order to elicit this altruistic and intrinsic motivation to participate in research, it is crucial for researchers to clearly communicate the purpose and potential benefits of the study (Bonvicini, 1998) while recognizing that what the potential participants perceive as a benefit will be grounded in culture, language, and community values. In order to "market" the study, it is helpful to demonstrate that there is a need or a problem (e.g., "research suggests that nearly one out of two marriages end in divorce"). Presenting the problem that the study is going to address makes the need for a solution more compelling. In addition, the potential benefits need to be specific and relevant to potential participants. For example, saying that "the results of the study will reveal ways that couples can repair distressed relationships and prevent divorce" is much more motivating than "the results of the study have the potential to benefit society."

Retention of Participants

After people have been recruited into a clinical study, the research team must make specific and sustained efforts to retain the participants. Experience has shown that it is crucial for the research team to develop an extensive tracking system. At the conclusion of one major clinical study, the researchers concluded that the "listing of contact information was the vital key to retention and hence the success" of the clinical study (Striley et al., 2008, p. 21). Part of the contact information included the names and telephone numbers of at least five people who would always know how to reach the participant. At least one member of the research team had specific responsibilities for tracking research participants, and the team reviewed and updated contact information during each visit to the clinic or contact with the researchers.

It is also important to "brand" the research project so that participants can identify themselves as members of the study. The study should have an easily identifiable name, and it is helpful for participants to receive branded material incentives, such as T-shirts, pens, mugs, and magnets, to help them identify themselves with the study (Del Boca & Darkes, 2007). As they begin to identify themselves as important participants of the "Marriage and Depression Study," for example, they will be much more likely to continue to participate in the study. In addition, sending birthday and holiday cards helps researchers maintain contact with participants, as well as communicate that the researchers are interested in them (Del Boca & Darkes).

Financial incentives that are given *throughout the course of the clinical study* are effective in preventing premature dropout (Berger et al., 2009; Pollastri, Pokrywa, Walsh, Kranzler, & Gelernter, 2005; Striley et al., 2008), but research suggests that positive interactions between the research team and the participants may be even more important for retention. For example, a clinical study

86

had participants who had completed the study fill out a questionnaire regarding the study and their continued participation. The participants reported that although they appreciated the material and cash incentives, their greatest motivation to continue to participate in the study was the positive "staff attributes such as friendliness, responsiveness, and encouragement" (Andersen, 2007, p. 50). Based on several studies that have found similar results, Andersen argues that *relational engagement*, where members of the research team show empathy, caring, and understanding to study participants, is an important component in retaining them.

Postal Mail Surveys

Clinical research often involves the use of surveys. Most follow-up assessments to clinical studies are conducted through the mail (or the Internet, which will be discussed below). In addition, many mental health services and epidemiologic studies are conducted using mail surveys, as well as surveys that are directed to clinicians concerning their attitudes about mental health issues and current practice patterns.

Unfortunately, survey research often has low response rates. Similar to other methods used in clinical research, low response to surveys can introduce validity concerns by reducing the statistical power and creating selection bias (Nakash, Hutton, Jorstad-Stein, Gates, & Lamb, 2006). The good news, though, is that survey methodologists have extensively studied nonresponse in survey research and have developed empirically based methods for maximizing response rates. For example, Don Dillman, a professor of sociology at Washington State University, has spent his career studying ways to increase response rates in survey research. Interestingly, much of this research uses experimental designs, where researchers randomly assign members of the sample to different groups, such as a group receiving financial incentives and a control group, to see if the treatment approach leads to higher response rates.

One obvious finding is that studies that use longer questionnaires consistently have lower response rates (Nakash et al., 2006). However, the length of the questionnaire should be judged by the number of questions that are included in the questionnaire, rather than the number of pages (Dillman et al., 2009). Formatting questionnaires with lots of "white space" and easy-to-answer designs, even if it means more pages in the questionnaire, is associated with higher response rates. Pages that are crowded with questions in a packed and dense format are overwhelming and discouraging to potential respondents.

A great deal of research has explored the effect of offering incentives on response rates in survey research, and the research has consistently found a positive effect. Similar to other forms of clinical research, an advantage of using incentives in survey research is that it tends to pull in respondents who otherwise might not participate in the study (Dillman et al., 2009). A substantial amount of research indicates that the most successful method for providing incentives is to prepay potential respondents, usually in the packet that contains the questionnaire. Thus, along with an invitation to participate in the study, the potential respondent also receives some cash in the envelope. Of course, some people will simply pocket the money and not return a completed questionnaire, but for many people, receiving unsolicited money creates a motivation for them to reciprocate and "give back" to the researchers by sending back the completed questionnaire. There is also evidence that providing cash cards is not as effective as giving cash, with one study finding that giving a cash card worth twice as much as the cash incentive still resulted in lower response rates (Dillman et al., 2009). Some universities may express some "heartburn" about giving a faculty researcher 250 five-dollar bills, but our experience is that a clearly articulated justification memo that is accompanied by research evidence is usually able to convince the university bureaucracy to grant the request.

Research indicates that the amount of the cash incentive can be small. Dillman and colleagues (2009) found that between $2 and $5 is adequate to substantially increase response rates and that higher levels of incentives do not do so. However, there are two exceptions to this general rule. First, survey questionnaires that are especially long or ask particularly delicate questions may require a higher level of financial incentive. This is because these burdensome questionnaires go beyond the principle of reciprocity, where a person receives a favor (e.g., a token amount of cash) and then returns the favor (e.g., a completed questionnaire). In the case of arduous questionnaires, the principle changes to that of reimbursement for time and effort, which requires a higher level of financial compensation. Second, research indicates that surveys that involve professionals, such as physicians, require a higher level of financial incentives. For example, Dillman and colleagues (2009) reported that surveys that include physicians typically need to provide financial incentives of $25–$100 to get a reasonable response rate. This exception probably extends to practicing marriage and family therapists and MFT professors, who have a lot of demands on their professional time.

In recent years, lotteries have become a popular form of incentive. These usually take the form of offering people who participate in the survey a chance to win something valuable, such as an iPad. The idea is that potential participants will be motivated to respond to the questionnaire because of the chance to win a valuable prize. The thinking is that the possibility of winning an iPad is much more motivating than simply receiving $5 in the mail. However, research has found that lotteries are only marginally successful in increasing response rates. One study compared response rates among a group that received no financial incentive, a group that received a $2 cash payment that came with the invitation to participate in the study, and a group that was promised a chance to win a $300 lottery. The results of the study indicated that 53% of the no incentive group responded to the study, 72% of the $2 cash payment group responded, but only 58% of the $300 lottery group responded. Another experimental study compared a lottery with a token prepaid cash incentive and found that only the prepaid cash incentive increased response rates (Warriner, Goyder,

Gjertson, Hohner, & McSpurren, 1996). Thus, research clearly indicates that token cash prepayments are the most effective incentive-based way to increase response rates.

In addition to financial incentives, there is clear evidence that follow-up reminders increase response rates. Researchers found in one study that reminding potential participants to return the questionnaire (which they called "chasing") increased the response rate from 47.5% to 72.0% (Gates et al., 2009). Dillman and researchers (2009) recommend making at least three follow-up contacts with potential participants. In addition, they make the point that the three types of contact need to be different. If the same type of reminder is used, such as three email reminders, the effect of the reminders is substantially diminished. It is much more effective to use a combination of mail, email, and telephone reminders. In the case of mail reminders, postcards are an inexpensive and convenient form of contact.

Internet Surveys

Internet surveys have become increasingly popular, especially among younger researchers who are comfortable navigating the Internet and programming Internet survey software, such as Survey Monkey and Qualtrics (Galea & Tracy, 2007). An obvious advantage of using Internet surveys is that they are substantially less expensive than having to pay for the paper supplies and postage required for mail surveys. Another advantage is that researchers can make all of the responses to the questionnaire be electronically transferred to statistical software, such as SPSS. This eliminates the time, costs, and data entry errors of manually entering the responses into the statistical software.

Despite the advantages of using Internet surveys, this method faces some unique challenges. For example, most invitations to participate in an Internet survey are sent via email, and because it is coming from an unknown source, it is commonly marked as spam or junk mail and doesn't reach the potential respondent. Consistent with other recommendations for recruitment, having a "champion" or a local contact "on the ground" who can distribute electronic and Internet-based surveys from within a group can make that important personal connection for the invitation to be successful. Another challenge of Internet surveys is that it is more difficult to offer cash incentives. The most common solution is for Internet researchers to offer an online gift card, such as a $5 gift card to an online merchant. However, researchers have found that online financial incentives are less effective than cash incentives that potential respondents receive in the postal mail. One study of Internet survey response rates compared the responses of a group who received an invitation through postal mail that included $5 cash, a group who received a $5 electronic gift card as part of their emailed invitation, and a group who received a $5 electronic gift card when they completed the Internet survey. Results showed that completion rates were 57% for the group who received cash via postal mail, 40% for the group who received the electronic gift card prepayment, and 32% for the group who received the electronic gift card payment after completing the survey. Moreover, substantial research has found that offering a lottery or prize drawing for those who completed the questionnaire does not significantly increase response rates to Internet surveys (Dillman et al., 2009).

Based on this research, Dillman recommends that researchers who use Internet surveys send a letter to those in the sample with an invitation to participate in such a survey with clear instructions about how to access and complete it. In order to maximize response rates, the survey should include a cash incentive.

Minority and Gender Considerations

Unfortunately, MFT clinical research has been dominated by the ethnic majority, with findings erroneously generalized to minority groups. Yet, many researchers continue to pursue research agendas without adequate strategies to accommodate ethnicity, culture, and other underrepresented voices in the study design, thus perpetuating an unrepresentative pattern in the literature. In response, the National Institutes of Health (NIH) in the United States, among other federal and state agencies, have required investigators to make accommodations for underrepresented or disadvantaged research participants for nearly two decades (National Institutes of Health, 2001). Further, the Surgeon General in a research report (U.S. Department of Health and Human Services, 2001) raised the concerns that minorities were generally underrepresented in clinical trials and that even studies that included ethnic minorities typically failed to examine the treatment effects of ethnic minorities separately (Burlew et al., 2011).

Much of what has been published about recruitment and retention of ethnic minorities has focused on barriers to inclusion (Mason, 2005; Yancey, Ortega, & Kumanyika, 2006), rather than on strategies to successfully recruit ethnic minorities. In a recent publication, Burlew and colleagues (2011) make several recommendations for increasing ethnic minority participation in clinical research. The two broad areas of recommendation are community involvement and cultural adaptation. The concepts of community involvement via community outreach, taking the research team into the community, and including community representatives in roles on the research team are consistent with a community-based participatory research approach, as described in detail in Chapter 18. (Methodological issues regarding the cultural adaptation of research are described in Chapter 11.) For example, Rodriguez, Rodriguez, and Davis (2006) found that the most effective strategy for recruitment of Spanish-speaking Latino families was "word of mouth" (meaning that participants reported enrolling as a direct result of the encouragement of a former study participant). These authors recommend targeting recruitment efforts at those who will, in turn, be able to facilitate and encourage others to participate. Most successful were recruitment activities from research assistants who were longtime members of the Latino community. This "insiders" principle is an important one and is again consistent with the principles of community-based participatory research. These approaches take more time than other strategies and require trust building, but they have been shown to be the most effective ways to substantively increase minority participation in clinical research (Burlew et al., 2011).

Conclusion

An important challenge facing MFT researchers is the recruitment and retention of adequate samples for clinical research. Failure to recruit and retain leads to significant threats to the validity of the research. However, a large research literature has emerged that provides empirically based strategies for enhancing the recruitment and retention of clinical samples. As MFT researchers learn and follow these strategies, they will be able to successfully obtain and retain the samples they need to conduct high-quality and impactful clinical research.

References

Andersen, E. (2007). Participant retention in randomized, controlled trials: The value of relational engagement. *International Journal for Human Caring, 11,* 46–51.

Anderson, J.R., & Doherty, W.J. (2005). Democratic community initiatives: The case of overscheduled children. *Family Relations, 54,* 654–665.

Baigis, J., Francis, M.E., & Hoffman, M. (2003). Cost-effectiveness analysis of recruitment strategies in a community-based intervention study of HIV-infected persons. *AIDS Care, 15,* 717–728.

Berger, L.K., Begun, A.L., & Otto-Salaj, L.L. (2009). Participant recruitment in intervention research: Scientific integrity and cost-effective strategies. *International Journal of Social Research Methodology, 12,* 79–92.

Bianchi, S. M., & Milkie, M.A. (2010). Work and family research in the first decade of the 21st century. *Journal of Marriage and Family, 72,* 705–725.

Bonvicini, K.A. (1998). The art of recruitment: The foundation of family and linkage studies of psychiatric illness. *Family Process, 37,* 153–165.

Bower, P., Wallace, P., Ward, E., Graffy, J., Miller, J., Delaney, B., & Kinmonth, A.L. (2009). Improving recruitment to health research in primary care. *Family Practice, 26,* 391–397.

Burgess, N., Christensen, H., Griffiths, K.M., & Farrer, L. (2010). Recruitment challenges associated with a randomized controlled trial within a general telephone counseling service. *Journal of Telemedicine and Telecare, 16,* 409–413.

Burlew, K., Larios, S., Suarez-Morales, L., Holmes, B., Venner, K., & Chavez, R. (2011). Increasing ethnic minority participation in substance abuse clinical trials: Lessons learned in the National Institute on Drug Abuse's Clinical Trials Network. *Cultural Diversity and Ethnic Minority Psychology, 17,* 345–356.

Cohen, J. (1992). A power primer. *Psychological Bulletin, 112,* 155–159.

Del Boca, F.K., & Darkes, J. (2007). Enhancing the validity and utility of randomized clinical trials in addictions treatment research: II. Participant samples and assessment. *Addiction, 102,* 1194–1203.

Dillman, D.A., Smyth, J.D., & Christian, L.M. (2009). *Internet, mail, mixed-mode surveys: The tailored design method* (3rd ed.). Hoboken, NJ: John Wiley & Sons.

Galea, S., & Tracy, M. (2007). Participation rates in epidemiologic studies. *Annals of Epidemiology, 17,* 643–653.

Gates, S., Williams, M.A., Withers, E., Williamson, E., Mt-Isa, S., & Lamb, S.E. (2009). Does a monetary incentive improve the response to a postal questionnaire in a randomised controlled trial? The MINT incentive study. *Trials, 10,* 44–50.

Gul, R.B., & Ali, P.A. (2010). Clinical trials: The challenge of recruitment and retention of participants. *Journal of Clinical Nursing, 19,* 227–233.

Guyll, M., Spoth, R., & Redmond, C. (2003). The effects of incentives and research requirements on participation rates for a community-based preventive intervention research study. *Journal of Primary Prevention, 24,* 25–41.

Hunninghake, D.B., Darby, C.A., & Probstfield, J.L. (1987). Recruitment experience in clinical trials: Literature summary and annotated bibliography. *Controlled Clinical Trials, 8,* 6S-30S.

Largent, E.A., Grady, C., Miller, F.G., & Wertheimer, A. (2012). Money, coercion, and undue inducement: Attitudes about payments to research participants. *IRB: Ethics & Human Research, 34,* 1–8.

Mason, S. (2005). Offering African Americans opportunities to participate in clinical trials research: How social workers can help. *Health & Social Work, 30,* 296–304.

Miller, R.B., & Wright, D. (1995). Correction for attrition bias in longitudinal analyses. *Journal of Marriage and Family, 57,* 921–929.

Nakash, R.A., Hutton, J.L., Jorstad-Stein, E.C., Gates, S., & Lamb, S.E. (2006). Maximising response to postal questionnaires: A systematic review of randomised trials in health research. *BMC Medical Research Methodology, 6,* 1–9.

National Institutes of Health. (2001). NIH policy and guidelines on the inclusion of women and minorities as subjects in clinical research. Retrieved from http://grants.nih.gov/grants/funding/women_min/guidelines_amended_10_2001.htm

Pollastri, A.R., Pokrywa, M.L., Walsh, S.J., Kranzler, H.R., & Gelernter, J. (2005). Incentive program decreases no-shows in nontreatment substance abuse research. *Experimental and Clinical Psychopharmacology, 13,* 376–380.

Probstfield, J.L., & Frye, R.L. (2011). Strategies for recruitment and retention of participants in clinical trials. *Journal of the American Medical Association, 306,* 1798–1799.

Puffer, S., & Torgerson, D. (2003). Recruitment difficulties in randomised controlled trials. *Controlled Clinical Trials, 24,* S214–S215.

Rodriguez, M.D., Rodriguez, J., & Davis, M. (2006). Recruitment of first-generation Latinos in a rural community: The essential nature of personal contact. *Family Process, 45,* 87–100.

Striley, C.L.W., Callahan, C., & Cottler, L.B. (2008). Enrolling, retaining, and benefiting out-of-treatment drug users in intervention research. *Journal of Empirical Research on Human Research Ethics, 3,* 19–25.

Swanson, G.M., & Ward, A.J. (1995). Recruiting minorities into clinical trials: Toward a participant friendly system. *Journal of the National Cancer Institute, 87,* 1747–1759.

Unger, S., Wylie, L., Fallah, S., Heinrich, L., & O'Brien, K. (2010). Motivated by money? The impact of financial incentive for the research team on study recruitment. *IRB: Ethics & Human Research, 32,* 16–19.

U.S. Department of Health and Human Services. (2001). *Mental health: Culture, race and ethnicity. A supplement to mental health: A report of the Surgeon General.* Rockville, MD: Author. Retrieved from http://www.surgeongeneral.gov/library/mentalhealth/cre/execsummary-1.html

Warriner, K., Goyder, J., Gjertsen, H., Hohner, P., & McSpurren, K. (1996). Charities, no; lotteries, no; cash, yes: Main effects and interactions in a Canadian incentives experiment. *Public Opinion Quarterly, 60,* 542–562.

Watson, J. M., & Torgerson, D. J. (2006). Increasing recruitment to randomised trials: A review of randomised controlled trials. *BMC Medical Research Methodology, 6,* 34–43.

Woodall, A., Howard, L., & Morgan, C. (2011). Barriers to participation in mental health research: Findings from the Genetics and Psychosis (GAP) study. *International Review of Psychiatry, 23,* 31–40.

Yancey, A., Ortega, A., & Kumanyika, S. (2006). Effective recruitment and retention of minority research participants. *Annual Review in Public Health, 27,* 1–28.

7

USING QUESTIONNAIRES
IN CLINICAL COUPLE AND
FAMILY RESEARCH

Deanna Linville, Jeff L. Todahl, and Maya Elin O'Neil

The use of questionnaires in couples and family therapy (CFT) research is prevalent, popular, and efficient, but there are many considerations for researchers deciding whether or not to use questionnaires as part of their data collection processes. The majority of measurement development research has been focused on measuring individual outcomes (e.g., health outcomes) and treatment efficacy, with lesser consideration to process variables, tracking change, and relational interaction measurements (Heatherington, Friedlander, & Greenberg, 2005). We believe that it is important to include questionnaires that measure interpersonal process and relational change while not sacrificing important individual-level information, especially because there is strong support for the reciprocal relationship between relational distress and individual mental health issues (Cano & O'Leary, 2000; Whisman & Uebelacker, 2006). For example, if a researcher is examining the effects of infidelity on partner depression, it will be essential to measure the effects of the infidelity on relationship dynamics and vice versa while also measuring depression at an individual level. In addition, we believe that it is essential for relational theories to lay the foundation for questionnaires that are used in CFT research (see Chapter 3). Too often, individual-focused psychological theory underlies the items in questionnaires being used to measure relational outcomes and processes, which can lead to inaccurate or incomplete assessment of complex couple and family dynamics. Also, using measures that are not designed to assess interactions or relational outcomes can yield invalid results. For example, the interactive nature of relational stress is likely inaccurately assessed by measures designed to assess individual stress levels. Similarly, generalizing the assessment data from one partner to the other partner can also result in an invalid assessment. Therefore, this chapter will focus on the use of questionnaires in tracking change and, specifically in couples and family contexts, in considerations for the four major types of validity: external, construct, internal, and conclusion.

Validity Considerations

There are many advantages and disadvantages to data collection through questionnaires, often having to do with issues of validity, and we think that it is important to critically evaluate both before hastily concluding that the best way to answer a research question is through collecting and analyzing questionnaire data. Commonly cited advantages of questionnaire data collection include efficiency, accessibility, ease of disclosure, comparability, and neutrality (Gillham, 2000). Additionally, researchers can quickly get a lot of data from many people, anonymously, for low cost. Participants may feel less pressure to answer immediately and there is less chance for interviewer bias. Some questionnaires may be used repeatedly as a way to measure change over time.

Disadvantages include concerns associated with mono-method bias (only one reporter of the data, using one method), respondents skewing answers to increase social desirability, and participants being reactive to the questionnaire itself (Fricker & Rand, 2002; Gillham, 2000). These issues can be intensified when trying to collect questionnaire data from couples and families. For example, consider a couple who are filling out questionnaires at home together about their satisfaction with their sexual relationship. As one partner is filling out the questionnaire, the other partner is leaning over her/his shoulder and looking at the partner's response. The one partner may want to make sure that the other rates their sexual relationship as positively as she/he does, out of concern about hurting the partner's feelings. Obviously, this interaction will bias the data. In addition, as with other types of research methods, there can often be a low response rate, which limits the generalizability, or external validity, of the findings. Misunderstanding of the items and response options can be a major issue, resulting in poor reliability; therefore, careful attention to item wording and piloting of questionnaire items is an important step to achieve adequate reliability (Nunnally, 1978). Finally, although it is tempting to simply repeat an administration of a questionnaire to assess change over time, some questionnaire responses can be influenced by repeat testing. For example, simply by having been asked the question previously, the respondent may have increased knowledge of the content of the item and answer it differently, indicating a change that did not actually occur. In short, creating or selecting a questionnaire that will allow the researcher to collect worthwhile data is, at best, challenging. Yet, questionnaires can be a useful single method of data collection for some research questions, but they are often most effectively used in tandem with other data collection methods that are more objective or rely less on self-report (e.g., physiologic measures, observer ratings).

Pertaining to the selection of questionnaires, researchers need to give significant attention to measurement validity and reliability. Types of measurement validity predominantly include construct, criterion, and content validity. When designing, choosing, and using questionnaires for data collection, research results are never better than the quality of the data collected (Bickman & Rog, 1998). Some of the threats to construct validity that are particularly relevant for data collected through questionnaires are mono-method bias, respondent bias, inadequate preoperational explanation of constructs, and the potential interactions between the testing and treatment. A frequently cited concern, mono-method bias, is when the researcher uses a measure that captures only a part of the construct of interest or unnecessary facets of the construct (Kane, 2006). The ways in which items on a questionnaire are worded may also increase the chance for response or respondent bias. The researchers may have lacked clarity when they developed the research questions, the items may not be worded in a manner that is clear for the intended audience, or cultural differences may contribute to a misunderstanding of the items as worded—all of which create operational bias and threaten construct and external validity. Finally, several authors have described the interactions that may occur between the questionnaires and the "treatment" in an intervention study, which could threaten construct and internal validity (Kane). An example of this occurs when a treatment is being investigated and participants are assessed in conjunction with the treatment. Would treatment have had the same effect without the concurrent assessment? In many study designs, it becomes difficult to separate the effect of the treatment from the effect of the assessment.

In addition, external validity, specifically cultural validity (Quintana, Troyano, & Taylor, 2001), should be a major consideration when selecting and implementing questionnaires to ensure that measures are culturally sensitive and translatable to marginalized populations. Some measures may function differently in different populations based on demographic or cultural considerations (e.g., age, length of relationship, other aspects of cultural background). Though not always possible, it is ideal for questionnaires to be validated in populations similar to the population of interest in a study or clinical setting in order to assure externally and culturally valid assessment.

Characteristics of High-Quality Measures

Identifying and selecting measures with high construct validity is one of the most important research design tasks. Measurement selection typically centers on conventional measurement characteristics, including reliability and validity properties of the instrument and the alignment among theory, the research question(s), and the construct(s) measured by the instrument (see Chapter 3). Selecting a high-quality *relational* measure, though, includes several additional considerations. In addition to the above-mentioned conventional questionnaire properties, features to consider when selecting a relational measure include (a) whether the instrument is designed to measure an interpersonal (nonindependent) process, (b) *who* is included in the measurement protocol (e.g., if a couple, is the questionnaire designed to collect information from both parties?), (c) the degree to which the measure selected will contribute to the larger body of relational research knowledge, and (d) whether the instrument has shown construct validity for the relational, cultural, and important demographic characteristics in the population targeted for the study (Cook & Snyder, 2005; Massey & Tourangeau, 2012; Sue, 2003; Tran, 2009).

There is no consensus in the research community about the best relational measures. Many self-report measures of relational features, such as couple satisfaction and distress, now exist (Lebow, Chambers, Christensen, & Johnson, 2012; Sanderson et al., 2009; Snyder, Heyman, & Haynes, 2005; Stanton & Welsh, 2012). In one review (Sanderson et al.), 87.2% of the questionnaires in 274 CFT outcome studies used self-report instruments. Most of these questionnaires were validated (though often not with the population of interest) and used several subscales for multidimensional assessment of constructs. However, the majority of questionnaires used in family therapy research continue to focus solely on the individual as the unit of analysis. Among the 274 CFT outcome studies reviewed by Sanderson and colleagues, only 27% focused explicitly on the couple or family as the unit of analysis. Given this, researchers who more fully investigate relational variables are contributing both to the literature at the level of their individual study and to a larger effort that explicitly embeds systemic thinking in research methodology (Stanton & Welsh).

Many validated measures of couple functioning are brief (Lebow et al., 2012) and designed to measure distinct features of family functioning, such as parent and child relationship quality and parenting practices. Some of the self-report family functioning questionnaires measure situation-specific issues, such as parent report of their child's serious illness (Pritchett, Kemp, Wilson, Minnis, & Bryce, 2011). Indeed, an explosion of measures has occurred. Sanderson and colleagues (2009) counted a total of 480 different outcome measures in their review of CFT outcome studies. Among these 480 measures, only 8 instruments were used in 10 or more studies. In addition, Christensen, Baucom, Vu, and Stanton (2005) concluded that relationship satisfaction is the most common category of measurement in couple therapy research, followed in popularity by observational measures of couple interaction.

Despite the lack of consensus about which relational measures are best, many researchers agree that multiple points of view should be elicited much more often in CFT research (Cook & Snyder, 2005; Eisikovits & Koren, 2010; Keiley, Keller, & El-Sheikh, 2009; Pritchett et al., 2011). Multi-informant data are particularly important toward advancing the knowledge base of couples and family process, family therapy theory, and CFT research outcomes. To date, the vast majority of family therapy research draws information from only one family member or uses data collection strategies that do not allow for optimal analysis of an interpersonal process. Consequently, we recommend that researchers select measures that meet at least minimum reliability and validity standards, that are adapted for the population of interest, and, importantly, that are designed to elicit self-other data matched to the same variable.

Dyadic research design is an example of a strategy that uses self-report questionnaires and multiple informants to measure interpersonal process. Dyadic research designs aim to address a relationally focused question and include gathering data about relationship and individual characteristics from multiple members (Wittenborn, Dolbin-MacNab, & Keiley, 2013). Dyadic research allows researchers to investigate connectedness, relational processes, and interdependence and is therefore very well suited for researchers interested in systemic change. Moreover, dyadic strategies can reduce the loss of information that occurs when researchers simply combine information from multiple informants, or separate members of dyads, prior to analysis. Proponents of dyadic research urge the use of identical or near-identical questionnaires, suggest that at least key constructs within a study be measured from the vantage point of multiple informants (e.g., both members of the dyad in a couple, each member of a family), and that when questionnaires that measure key constructs from multiple informants are not available or suitable, one can search for individually oriented measures that have at least been "used across linked participants (spouses, parent/child, etc.)" (p. 7).

Each of these strategies—eliciting multiple points of view, collecting multi-informant data, matching self-other data to the same variable, and designing dyadic research—shows promise for increasing the accuracy, i.e., the validity of relational constructs. For additional information, we refer the reader to Wittenborn et al. (in press) as an excellent overview of dyadic methodology for CFT research.

Considerations in Questionnaire Selection

Despite the lack of consensus existing about the best relational measures, there is wide agreement about the characteristics of high-quality measures. Naturally, this includes minimum standards of reliability and validity shown with the population under investigation. Though CFT researchers should be cautioned that there are no absolute standards of excellence and that adequate reliability depends on the specific area of research, examining reliability is still an important consideration when using questionnaires, specifically pertaining to conclusion validity. Researchers should consider standard, commonly cited reliability cutoffs for questionnaires in addition to being familiar with reliability standards in their specific area of research. Alderfer and colleagues (2008) evaluated the merits of 29 family measures and argued that "well-established" instruments should meet or exceed the following psychometric criteria:

> We define "good" psychometric properties as follows: internal consistency > .70 (Nunnally, 1978), test-retest reliability consistent with the purported stability of the construct, inter-rater reliability > .70 and/or inter-rater agreement > .61 (Landis & Koch, 1977), and at least two forms of evidence of concurrent/predictive or convergent validity. (p. 1048)

Yet, despite these recommendations, in their review of 274 CFT outcome studies, Sanderson et al. (2009) concluded, "in 624 out of 805 instances (77.5%), none of four types of reliability data were reported for the sample under investigation" (p. 250). Researchers also caution against the overreliance on inappropriate methods of establishing reliability depending on sample and measure characteristics, and propose a more detailed examination of appropriate cutoffs and choices of reliability coefficients (see Yang & Green, 2011 for a more detailed discussion of these decisions and recommendations). Additional general considerations for questionnaire selection include whether content, criterion, and construct validity are known and the theoretical fit of those constructs with the research question. Responsiveness of the instrument, inadequate differentiation among most low scorers (floor effects) or among most high scorers (ceiling effects), and interpretability of scores are also important considerations for questionnaire selection (Terwee et al., 2007).

Finally, in order to track trajectories of change in CFT research, multiple observations are necessary and measures need to be sensitive to change processes and need to measure variables/processes that will change as a result of attending therapy. For example, as described by Cook and Snyder (2005), "observations over the first three sessions of therapy may reveal a pattern of continuing growth in (each partner's) negativity, whereas observations from later points in therapy may reveal a decline in negativity" (p. 139). CFT research methods that are designed to evaluate growth curves and that seek to test the effects of individual stability and interpersonal influence on rates of change over time require multiple observations (i.e., participants must complete the same instrument on many occasions). In this situation, the use of brief and precise questionnaires, such as Funk and Rogge's (2007) Couples Satisfaction Index, is particularly important because questionnaires of this nature likely lower rates of attrition and reduce missing data percentages (Williams, Edwards, Patterson, & Chamow, 2011). Also, assessing change requires a definition of what constitutes change for a given outcome. For example, repeated use of a relationship satisfaction questionnaire may result in a statistically significant improvement from the start of therapy compared with after-therapy completion.

Selection of Culturally Appropriate Measures

Many methodologists, psychometrists, health care providers, and consumers have urged researchers to develop measures that account for diversity, which improves both external and construct validity. As Tran (2009) articulated well, "One cannot draw meaningful comparisons of behavioral problems, social values, or psychological status, between or across different cultural groups in the absence of cross-culturally equivalent research instruments" (p. 3).

In response, researchers have, for example, translated well-established instruments into a variety of languages, invited diverse populations to scrutinize existing questionnaires, developed questionnaires in partnership with members of targeted research audiences, and developed sampling and data collection strategies that reduce barriers to research participation (Mitchell, Patterson, & Boyd-Franklin, 2011; Quintana et al., 2006; Sindik, 2012). These efforts, largely, are rooted in cultural validity (Sue, 2003).

Leong and Brown (1995), early proponents of the notion of "cultural validity," described it in this way: "Cultural validity is concerned with the construct, concurrent, and predictive validity of theories and models across cultures, that is, for culturally different individuals" (p. 144). Validity, or the degree to which a questionnaire captures the construct of interest (Williams et al., 2011), is threatened by cultural bias. Sindik (2012) points to three types of test bias—construct, method, and item bias—and their important implications for threats to cultural validity. Construct bias is the degree to which research instruments fail to accurately account for cultural variation in the meaning attributed to the concepts purportedly measured by the questionnaire. The appropriateness of parent and child co-sleeping, for example, is perceived in widely varying ways between and within cultural groups (e.g., perceptions of differentiation, perceptions of adult-child boundaries). Questionnaires that are not validated on specific groups and cultures can easily misrepresent the construct of interest and introduce construct validity errors into research data, as well as conclusion validity problems with research findings and research implications. Due to long-standing failure to properly establish construct validity of measures, cultural bias is potentially embedded in many measures and can greatly bias existing findings. Sanderson and colleagues (2009), in their review of CFT outcome research questionnaires, determined that 94% of the instruments ($N = 480$) had not established construct validity for ethnic groups other than European Americans. In their review, Sanderson et al. did not investigate construct validity as it relates to additional dimensions of diversity (e.g, gender, sexual orientation).

Couples and family therapy researchers can meaningfully reduce cultural bias in the literature by selecting culturally valid questionnaires and developing instruments that are normed for diverse populations. Of equal importance, researchers can systemically amend cultural bias in existing measures. This process, which may include decontextualizing and recontextualizing the theoretical assumptions underpinning the questionnaire, is a strategy for assessing cultural assumptions embedded in the questionnaire and reformulating the instrument in light of culturally-adapted versions of targeted research constructs. Geisinger (1994) recommended a multi-step process for translating a questionnaire and adapting it to a new cultural group. Participatory research methodology applied to measurement development is another strategy for creating instruments that are likely to include valid constructs and items that are sensitive to those constructs (Cortez et al., 2011). We refer the reader to Sindik's (2012) excellent set of recommendations for reducing the influence of bias in cross-cultural research and to Okazaki and Sue's (1995) summary of methodological issues

Testing for equivalence in measurement across cultures can be accomplished by testing for invariance (or "nonequivalence") using a multisample confirmatory factor analysis (CFA). The general idea of invariance testing is to examine the measurement properties of the measure in the two samples (in this case, representing different aspects of culture or identity) to see if they measure functions in a similar manner between groups. The process of invariance testing is complex, and readers are encouraged to consult technical texts for detailed descriptions of the procedures specific to their chosen structural equation modeling (SEM) software package (e.g., Byrne, 2009). Generally, invariance testing involves a series of comparisons of models representing the initial model and a constrained model with values forced to be equivalent between comparison groups. Akin to omnibus testing prior to subgroup comparisons, invariance testing involves conducting a global test of similarity between the models by comparing the variance-covariance structures. If the global test indicates statistically significant model differences, a series of progressively restrictive hypotheses are tested to determine the specific differences between the models. Such comparisons involve an examination of χ^2 values. In SEM, the χ^2 statistic is used to quantify how much a model of interest differs from a comparison model. Traditional SEM measure development methods compare a proposed model to a saturated model (in which all possible relationships among constructs are represented), and the χ^2 value represents how different the proposed model is from the mathematically saturated model, with larger values indicating worse model fit. In invariance testing, differences in model components (e.g., relationships among items or latent constructs represented by factor loadings, variances, and covariances) between the two groups are compared; a statistically significant *difference* in χ^2 values across the models represents significant differences between the groups on the measure of interest. If the χ^2 value is significantly larger for the globally constrained model, the next in a series of hierarchically nested models is then constrained and compared. This process is repeated to test progressively restrictive hypotheses until the specific components of the model for which there are significant differences between groups are isolated. If there are no statistically significant differences across the models being compared, the interpretation is that the measure functions in an equivalent manner between the two groups or cultures being compared.

One particularly complex issue in culturally competent questionnaire implementation relates to translating measures into other languages. This issue is complex and requires detail beyond the scope of this chapter; therefore, we refer readers to the studies by Okazaki and Sue (1995) and Herrera, DelCampo, and Ames (1993) for an expanded discussion of strategies for translation of questionnaires from one language to another. However, for the purposes of this chapter, we summarize Herrera et al.'s steps as follows. First, the translation should be completed by two or more translators who have experience not only with translation but also with the population of interest, and these translations should be completed separately and then merged. In addition, someone skilled with grammar in the particular language should edit for accuracy. Next, the translation needs to be assessed for clarity and equivalence and then back-translated by bilingual persons of varying backgrounds. This back-translation should be audiorecorded and then listened to by a trained translator, who will make any additional and necessary changes. The last steps are to take the translation through field testing and then to assess reliability. Finally, the reliability indexes are interpreted with an eye on extraneous variables so that the researcher can distinguish between such variables and translation issues (Herrera, DelCampo, & Ames). Ultimately, ensuring that best practices are used for translations increases cultural validity and is crucial to consider when selecting a questionnaire and assessing external validity.

Considerations for Questionnaire Implementation

The primary considerations for implementing questionnaires are feasibility, access, frequency, delivery, ethics, and maximized validity. Since one of the advantages of data collection through questionnaires is efficiency, it is important that the researcher consider feasibility when implementing the questionnaires. Issues such as the time and place that the respondents will be asked to complete the questionnaire should be factored into the decision-making process, as well as how accessible the questionnaire is to the respondents. That is, the language in the questionnaire needs to be both readable and understandable for the respondents. Considering the context of the couple and family is essential. The researchers might ask, "What are the barriers to this couple or family filling out the questionnaire?" To put this simply, the researchers are asking more people within a system to complete the questionnaire, and if they are expected to do this at the same time, there is greater possibility for an increase in barriers. An example of this is when the first and second authors were conducting a randomized control trial, testing the effectiveness of a new parent, three-session intervention. The primary mode of data collection was through questionnaires. Issues of child-care options for the family, whether or not the mother was breastfeeding, how long parents could be away from their new baby, whether or not the couple should fill out the questionnaires together, etc., were important to consider; otherwise, there were significant barriers to both members of the couple participating. Without taking such participant factors into account, it is possible for couples and family researchers to inadvertently leave out large segments of their population of interest, which could skew results and yield invalid assessment of constructs.

Another important consideration is the frequency with which the researchers will administer the questionnaires. In order for the researchers to answer this question, they need to have developed good research questions, understand the best methods for answering those research questions, and know whether longitudinal or cross-sectional data are necessary. Researchers often have an easier time collecting data at one time point (cross-sectional) than they do at multiple time points.

Strategies for administration of questionnaires are also a big consideration for questionnaire data collection with couples and families and will ultimately influence the validity of a research study. Essential to consider prior to implementation are questions like, "Do the researchers want the couple or family to fill out the questionnaires at the same time?" "Is it okay for the members of the system to talk about the questions and their answers?" "Are the family members or partners allowed to show their responses to each other?" and "How will the researcher(s) intervene, if at all, if conflict arises from the family or couple as they are or after they are filling out the questionnaires?" In addition, will the questionnaires be delivered online, face-to-face, through the mail, or by group administration? There are pros and cons to each of these methods of delivery. For example, it might be easier for researchers to ensure that participants do not compare answers if they are sitting in the room with the couple or family as they fill out the questionnaires. Yet, this method will require more resources (time and expense) than delivering through mail, and it also means that the participants have to organize their lives in such a way to be at the appointment at the same time. If a questionnaire is delivered through the Internet, it may be harder to ensure that the participants are independently filling it out and that the same person is not completing the same questionnaire more than one time. Additionally, it may be more difficult for researchers to be in control of their sampling methods, and little may be known about the online community being sampled (Andrews, Nonnecke, & Preece, 2003; Dillman, 2000). At the same time, delivery through the Internet is obviously efficient and inexpensive.

In thinking about the ethics of any research data collection method, a researcher must consider its purpose or goal. As with all research in the field of mental health, primary objectives are to protect the well-being of participants and produce scientifically valid data (Margolin, Chien, Duman, Fauchier, & Gordis, 2005). It might be that participants will personally benefit from just completing the questionnaire. In fact, clinicians often use questionnaires throughout the course of therapy to receive and give feedback about progress toward goals, process indicators for change, and what is working and not working in the therapy arrangement. The scientist-practitioner needs to consider how participants will experience filling out the questionnaire as part of their ethical decision making. How likely is it that the questions could cause psychological distress? What resources will be provided for participants if the questions do cause distress in some way? Will the participants experience burnout or fatigue because there are too many items? Are there apparent microaggressions (brief and commonplace daily verbal, behavioral, or environmental indignities, whether intentional or unintentional, that communicate hostile, derogatory, or negative racial slights and insults toward people of color; Sue et al., 2007) in the questionnaire items that may cause marginalized participants to experience discrimination? How confident is the researcher that the participants will receive some benefit from being asked to reflect on and answer the questions? In addition to considering the experience of the questionnaire itself, the researcher(s) must be informed by ethics when deciding how they will recruit couples and families, incentivize study participation, and plan for the unique challenges and conflicts that may arise from having multiple members of a family participate in the study. The couples and family researcher must be prepared to evaluate benefits versus harms for the family as a unit, for all family members who are participating, and perhaps even for family members who are not participating, as well as the effects of all of this on internal and external validity of the study (Margolin et al., 2005, p. 157).

Considerations and Strategies for Relational Instrument Development

Though there are many existing instruments that have been developed for assessing aspects of couples and family relationships, there are many research and clinical questions that existing tools may not adequately address. Additionally, even when existing questionnaires are well validated in research contexts, clinical contexts may involve modifications to measures to make them appropriate for alternative settings and populations. It is important, therefore, to understand how to create new questionnaires to fill these research and clinical gaps. There are useful strategies for instrument development and validation, including exploratory, confirmatory, and predictive analyses (e.g., Brown, 2006).

Before any questionnaire is researched, the clinical researcher must determine if there is truly a gap in the literature that needs to be filled by the creation of a new or altered assessment tool. The process of measure development and validation is lengthy and complex and should not be undertaken unless there is a strong need for such research (de Leeuw, Hox, & Dillman, 2008). Too many measures assessing the same construct can lead to problems when attempting to compare results across studies. For example, if five intervention trials each use a different measure to assess the outcome 'relationship satisfaction,' it is very difficult to compare the effectiveness of the interventions because differences could be related to how relationship satisfaction is measured rather than whether or not there was similar change across the trials (Brown, 2006). More detailed discussions of the scale development process that are applicable to CFT research are included in a recently updated book by DeVellis (2012) and an article by Worthington and Whittaker (2006).

Before any statistical methods are employed, the clinical researcher must engage in the process of measure creation, which ideally involves many iterations of item construction based on the literature, consultation and revision based on expert opinion, and additional revision based on pilot testing. It is very important to consider the populations who will be assessed by the measure (demographic characteristics, familiarity with the topic, etc.), as well as other practical limitations, such as length and ease of understanding. Item wording must be clear and parsimonious: When creating items, it is important to ensure that each item clearly asks about only one concept (e.g., rating enjoyment of an activity) rather than multiple concepts (e.g., rating enjoyment of an activity and the person with whom you do the activity), since the respondent could be responding to either individual component or both (de Leeuw et al., 2008). Another practical consideration for measure development involves the availability of participants and resulting sample size. Though statisticians do not agree on firm rules for ratios of sample size to number of items in a measure, testing the validity and factor structure of longer measures requires larger samples than measures with fewer items. Recommended sample size is generally at least 100 when conducting exploratory factor analysis, and 200 for SEM regardless of survey length (e.g., see Kline, 2010 for a discussion of sample size requirements relative to measure length for CFA). Multiple items are often necessary to assess multicomponent or latent constructs; yet, participant fatigue and the increased sample size needed to adequately analyze obtained data should also be considered, and redundant or otherwise unnecessary items should be eliminated.

Exploratory analyses focus on development of new measures, for which there is no preexisting research or validation. In this instance, clinical researchers must be aware of research gaps as well as clinical and research needs. Though exploratory analyses are the necessary first step in the process of measure creation, placing too much faith in exploratory results can be problematic. This is because results based on only one sample are largely specific to that particular sample, and it is unknown whether the findings generalize to other samples (de Leeuw et al., 2008).

Exploratory research to develop an assessment tool can involve many different types of statistical methods (e.g., Crocker & Algina, 2006; DeVellis, 2012). Often, questionnaire development and validation involves an examination of the factor structure of the measure through analyses such as exploratory factor analysis (EFA). Once factors or subscales are established, exploratory research should also examine subscale and full scale reliability. Though EFA can be an important part of measure development, it is a complex statistical technique very specific to the type of questionnaire and area of research being examined. A detailed description of EFA methods is beyond the scope of this chapter, though readers are referred to statistics texts with software examples such as that by Stevens (2012).

Finally, an important part of measure validation is to establish the relationship between scores on the measure under development and established constructs. To achieve this, one can use many types of analyses (e.g., correlations, regression analyses, mean score comparisons like analysis of variance) to establish a relationship between scores on a measure and other constructs (convergent validity) or *lack* of such a relationship (discriminant validity). Both types of validity are important to establish. For example, not only would one want to know that a measure of relationship satisfaction is associated with factors such as length of relationships, but one would also want to show that it is less related to more peripheral constructs such as mental health diagnoses, and perhaps also show that it is not significantly related to other factors such as demographic variables. Both types of validity are necessary to demonstrate that the questionnaire is assessing the construct you are interested in measuring.

Confirmatory analyses are generally the second step in the measure validation process. The purpose of confirmatory research is to replicate initial results from exploratory research to see if the findings can be repeated across samples. This replication provides assurance that the initial, exploratory results are not simply due to chance associations among variables or items within a specific sample. Frequently, confirmatory research will be conducted in the same manner as the original, exploratory research. There are also some statistical techniques that particularly lend themselves to confirmatory research questions, such as CFA (Brown, 2006). This statistical method requires clinical researchers to test a theoretical model that is determined a priori. Generally, the theoretical model is based on previous, exploratory results.

If conducted with a similar population, confirmatory research would be expected to produce comparable results to the prior exploratory analyses. Confirmatory analyses, however, can also be conducted with different populations in order to determine different ways that measures function when used in different populations. This type of confirmatory research is part of the norming process, where scores are established for specific groups of individuals so that clinicians and researchers in the future can compare results with the norm. For example, if you are a couples therapist who wants to use an assessment tool with a couple, you would want to know what their obtained scores mean. To this end, you would compare their scores on a measure with established norms. Other ways of comparing sets of results obtained by different populations can be completed by using CFA and other SEM techniques referred to as invariance testing. These methods compare score patterns for subgroups of participants so that researchers can examine and potentially explain group differences. Though these relatively complex statistical methods are beyond the scope of this chapter, interested readers are referred to SEM texts by Brown (2006) and Kline (2010) and articles by Byrne, Shavelson, and Muthen (1989), and Byrne (1994).

Predictive analyses are generally conducted once initial validity has been established for a measure. Predictive analyses can involve many types of statistical techniques, though the purpose is always to demonstrate a predictive relationship between scores on a measure and another construct (predictive validity). Such analyses involve the measurement and association of constructs at different time points, so that a predictive relationship can be established. For example, once preliminary validation of a measure in a certain population has been established, a researcher might choose to examine how scores on that measure (or on subscales of the measure) are related to other constructs of interest. One might examine how scores change over time, or change in relation to participation in an intervention or treatment. More general research design and statistical texts will describe in more detail the wide variety of predictive analyses that can be conducted when using continuous outcomes based on measures (e.g., Tabachnick & Fidell, 2013).

A final, related type of measurement analysis involves assessment of change. Once questionnaires have been established to be valid assessments of constructs for the population(s) of interest, then they can be used to examine change over time, a central question to many CFT researchers given the need to examine treatment efficacy and effectiveness. There are many types of statistical methods that can be employed to examine change in questionnaire data over time, ranging from simple pre- and post-intervention mean score comparisons to more complex multilevel modeling techniques that can simultaneously account for factors such as therapist effects, relational data, and change patterns. For a detailed discussion of specific statistical techniques, including dyadic data analysis and reliable change index, see the studies by Jacobson and Truax (1991) and Kenny, Kashy, and Cook (2006).

Conclusion

Weighing the advantages and disadvantages of questionnaire use in research is essential when designing a study, especially keeping different types of validity at the forefront of the researcher's mind and decision-making process. As CFT researchers select, implement, and develop valid measures, they can consider how they will measure clinical change and relational constructs in a meaningful way in order to contribute meaningfully to the broader field. Finally, CFT researchers can significantly reduce cultural bias in the literature by selecting culturally valid measures and developing instruments that are then validated and made relevant for diverse populations.

References

Alderfer, M., Fiese, B., Gold, J., Cutuli, J., Holmbeck, G., Goldbeck, L., . . . Patterson, J. (2008). Evidence-based assessment in pediatric psychology: Family measures. *Journal of Pediatric Psychology, 33*(9), 1046–1061. doi:10.1093/jpepsy/jsm083

Andrews, D., Nonnecke, B., & Preece, J. (2003). Electronic survey methodology: A case study in reaching hard-to-involve Internet users. *International Journal of Human-Computer Interaction, 16*(2), 185–210. doi:10.1207/S15327590IJHC1602_04

Bickman, L., & Rog, D. (1998). *Handbook of applied social research methods.* Thousand Oaks, CA: Sage.

Brown, T. A. (2006). *Confirmatory factor analysis for applied research.* New York: Guilford Press.

Busby, D., & Gardner, B. (2008). How do I analyze thee? Let me count the ways: Considering empathy in couple relationships using self and partner ratings. *Family Process, 47*(2), 229–242. doi:10.1111/j.1545-5300.2008.00250.x

Byrne, B. (1994). Testing for factorial validity, replication, and invariance of a measurement instrument: A paradigmatic application based on the Maslach Burnout Inventory. *Multivariate Behavioral Research, 29*(3), 289–311. doi: 10.1207/s15327906mbr2903_5

Byrne, B. M. (2009). Structural equation modeling with AMOS: Basic concepts, applications, and programming (2nd ed.). New York: Routledge/Taylor & Francis.

Byrne, B., Shavelson, R., & Muthen, B. (1989). Testing for the equivalence of factor covariance and mean structures: The issue of partial measurement invariance. *Psychological Bulletin, 105*(3), 456–468.

Cano, A., & O'Leary, K. (2000). Infidelity and separations precipitate major depressive episodes and symptoms of non-specific depression and anxiety. *Journal of Consulting and Clinical Psychology, 68*(5), 774–781. Retrieved from http://psycnet.apa.org/journals/ccp/68/5/774/

Christensen, A., Baucom, D. H., Vu, C. T., & Stanton, S. (2005). Methodologically sound, cost-effective research on the outcome of couple therapy. *Journal of Family Psychology, 19*, 6–17. doi:10.1037/0893-3200.19.1.6

Cook, W. L., & Snyder, D. K. (2005). Analyzing nonindependent outcomes in couple therapy using the actor-partner interdependence model. *Journal of Family Psychology, 19*(1), 133–141. doi:10.1037/0893-3200.19.1.133

Cortez, P., Dumas, T., Joyce, J., Olson, D., Peters, S., Todahl, J., . . . Rose, W. (2011). Survivor voices: Co-learning, re-connection, and healing through community action research and engagement. *Progress in Community Health Partnerships: Research, Education and Action, 5*(2), 133–142. doi:10.1353/cpr.2011.0020

Crocker, L. M., & Algina, J. (2006). *Introduction to classical and modern test theory.* Manson, OH: Wadsworth.

de Leeuw, E., Hox, J., & Dillman, D. (Eds.). (2008). *The international handbook of survey methodology.* New York/London: Erlbaum/Taylor & Francis.

DeVellis, R. (2012). *Scale development: Theory and applications* (3rd ed.). Thousand Oaks, CA: Sage.

Dillman, D. A. (2000). *Mail and Internet surveys: The tailored design method.* New York: John Wiley & Sons.

Eisikovits, Z., & Koren, C. (2010). Approaches to and outcomes of dyadic interview analysis. *Qualitative Health Research, 20*, 1642–1655. doi:10.1177/1049732310376520

Fricker, R., & Rand, M. (2002). Advantages and disadvantages of Internet research surveys: Evidence from the literature. *Field Methods, 14*(4), 347–367. doi:10.1177/152582202237725

Funk, J., & Rogge, R. (2007). Testing the ruler with item response theory: Increasing precision of measurement for relationship satisfaction with the Couples Satisfaction Index. *Journal of Family Psychology, 21*(4), 572–583. doi:10.1037/0893-3200.21.4.572

Geisinger, K. (1994). Psychometric issues in testing students with disabilities. *Applied Measurement in Education, 7*(2), 121–140. doi:10.1207/s15324818ame0702_2

Gillham, B. (2000). *Developing a questionnaire*. New York: Continuum.

Heatherington, L., Friedlander, M., & Greenberg, L. (2005). Change process research in couple and family therapy: Methodological challenges and opportunities. *Journal of Family Psychology, 19*(1), 18–27. *doi:10.1037/0893-3200.19.1.18*

Herrera, R. S., DelCampo, R. L., & Ames, M. H. (1993). A serial approach for translating family science instrumentation. *Family Relations, 42*(3), 357–360. doi:10.2307/585567

Howe, G., Dagne, G., & Brown, C. (2005). Multilevel methods for modeling observed sequences of family interaction. *Journal of Family Psychology, 19*(1), 72–85. doi:10.1037/0893-3200.19.1.72

Jacobson, N., & Truax, P. (1991). Clinical significance: A statistical approach to defining meaningful change in psychotherapy research. *Journal of Consulting and Counseling Psychology, 59*(1), 12–19. doi: 10.1037/0022-006x.59.1.12.

Kane, R. (2006). *Understanding healthcare outcomes research* (2nd ed.). Sudbury, MA: Jones and Bartlett Publishers.

Keiley, M., Keller, P., & El-Sheikh, M. (2009). Effects of physical and verbal aggression, depression, and anxiety on drinking behavior of married partners: A prospective and retrospective longitudinal examination. *Aggressive Behavior, 35*(4), 296–312. doi:10.1002/ab.20310

Kenny, D., Kashy, D., & Cook, W. (2006). *Dyadic data analysis*. New York: Guilford Press.

Kline, R. B. (2010). *Principles and practice of structural equation modeling* (3rd ed.). New York: Guilford Press.

Landis, J. R.; & Koch, G. G. (1977). "The measurement of observer agreement for categorical data". *Biometrics 33* (1): 159–174. doi:10.2307/2529310

Lebow, J., Chambers, A., Christensen, A., & Johnson, S. (2012). Research on the treatment of couple distress. *Journal of Marital and Family Therapy, 38*(1), 145–168. doi:10.1111/j.1752-0606.2011.00249.x

Leong, F. T. L., & Brown, M. (1995). Theoretical issues in cross-cultural career development: Cultural validity and cultural specificity. In W. B. Walsh & S. H. Osipow (Eds.), *Handbook of vocational psychology* (2nd ed., pp. 143–180). Hillsdale, NJ: Erlbaum.

Margolin, G., Chien, D., Duman, S., Fauchier, A., & Gordis, E. (2005). Ethical issues in couple and family research. *Journal of Family Psychology, 19*(1), 157–167. doi:10.1037/0893-3200.19.1.157

Massey, D. S., & Tourangeau, R. (2012). Introduction: New challenges to social measurement. *Annals of the American Academy of Political and Social Science, 645*, 6–22. doi:10.1177/0002716212463314

Mitchell, M., Patterson, C., & Boyd-Franklin, N. (2011). Commentary: Increasing cultural diversity in pediatric psychology family assessment research. *Journal of Pediatric Psychology, 36*(5), 634–641. doi:10.1093/jpepsy/jsr019

Nunnally, J. C. (1978). *Psychometric theory* (2nd ed.). New York: McGraw Hill.

Okazaki, S., & Sue, S. (1995). Methodological issues in assessment research with ethnic minorities. *Psychological Assessment, 7*(3), 367–375. doi:10.1037/1040-3590.7.3.367

Pritchett, R., Kemp, J., Wilson, P., Minnis, H., & Bryce, G. (2011). Quick, simple measures of family relationships for use in clinical practice and research: A systematic review. *Family Practice, 28*(2), 172–187. doi:10.1093/fampra/cmq080

Quintana, S. M., Aboud, F. E., Chao, R. K., Contreras-Grau, J., Cross, W. E., Hudley, C., . . . Vietze, D. L. (2006). Race, ethnicity, and culture in child development: Contemporary research and future directions. *Child Development, 77*(5), 1129–1141. doi:10.1111/j.1467-8624.2006.00951.x

Quintana, S. M., Troyano, N., & Taylor, G. (2001). Cultural validity and inherent challenges in quantitative methods for multicultural research. In J. G. Ponterotto, J. M. Casas, L. A. Suzuki, & C. M. Alexander (Eds.), *Handbook of multicultural counseling* (pp. 604–630). Thousand Oaks, CA: Sage.

Sanderson, J., Kosutic, I., Garcia, M., Melendez, T., Donoghue, J., Perumbily, S., . . . Anderson, S. (2009). The measurement of outcome variables in couple and family therapy research. *American Journal of Family Therapy, 37*(3), 239–257. doi:10.1080/01926180802405935

Sindik, J. (2012). Data analysis strategies for reducing the influence of the bias in cross-cultural research. *Collegium Antropologicum, 36*(1), 31–37.

Snyder, D., Heyman, R., & Haynes, S. (2005). Evidence-based approaches to assessing couple distress. *Psychological Assessment, 17*(3), 288–307. doi:10.1037/1040-3590.17.3.288

Stanton, M., & Welsh, R. (2012). Systemic thinking in couple and family psychology research and practice. *Couple and Family Psychology: Research and Practice, 1*(1), 14–30. doi:10.1037/a0027461

Stevens, J. P. (2012). *Applied multivariate statistics for the social sciences* (5th ed.). New York: Taylor & Francis.

Sue, D. W., Capodilupo, C. M., Torino, G. C., Bucceri, J. M., Holder, A., Nadal, K., Esquilin, M. (2007). Racial microaggressions in everyday life: Implications for clinical practice. *American Psychologist, 62*(4), 271–286. doi:10.1037/0003-066X.62.4.271

Sue, S. (2003). Science, ethnicity, and bias: Where have we gone wrong? In A. E. Kazdin (Ed.), *Methodological issues and strategies in clinical research* (pp. 173–188). Washington, DC: American Psychological Association.

Tabachnick, B. G., & Fidell, L. S. (2013). *Using multivariate statistics* (6th ed.). Boston: Allyn and Bacon.

Terwee, C. B., Bot, S. D., de Boer, M. R., van der Windt, D., Knol, D. L., Dekker, J., . . . de Vet, C. W. (2007). Author reply: Criteria for good measurement properties. *Journal of Clinical Epidemiology, 60*(12), 1315–1316. doi:10.1016/j.jclinepi.2007.06.002

Tran, T. V. (2009). *Developing cross-cultural measurement.* New York: Oxford University Press.

Whisman, M., & Uebelacker, L. (2006). Impairment and distress associated with the relationship discord in a national sample of married or cohabiting adults. *Journal of Family Psychology, 20,* 369–377. doi:10.1037/0893-3200.20.3.369

Willett, J. B. (1989). Some results on reliability for the longitudinal measurement of change: Implications for the design of studies of individual growth. *Educational and Psychological Measurement, 49,* 587–602. doi:10.1177/001316448904900309

Williams, L., Edwards, T., Patterson, J., & Chamow, L. (2011). *Essential assessment skills for couple and family therapists.* New York: Guilford Press.

Wittenborn, A. K., Dolbin-MacNab, M. L., & Keiley, M. K. (in press). Dyadic research in marriage and family therapy: Methodological considerations. *Journal of Marital and Family Therapy.* doi:10.1111/j.1752-0606.2012.00306.x

Worthington, R., & Whitaker, T. (2006). Scale development research: A content analysis and recommendations for best practices. *Counseling Psychologist, 34,* 806–838. doi: 10.1177/0011000006288127.

Yang, Y., & Green, S. (2011). Coefficient alpha: A reliability coefficient for the 21st century. *Journal of Psychological Assessment, 29,* 377–392. doi: 10.1177/0734282911406668

8

EMERGENT TECHNOLOGIES IN MARRIAGE AND FAMILY THERAPY RESEARCH

Craig W. Smith, Kelly A. Maxwell, and Lee N. Johnson

Introduction

Marriage and family therapy (MFT) emerged from disparate lines of intervention and inquiry, with researchers exploring paradigm-shifting concepts in novel ways (Broderick & Schrader, 1991). That pioneering spirit fueled innovative explorations into the dynamics of interpersonal relationships and projected us into new ways of understanding human interaction. However, it would seem that, to some extent, the field has lost that pioneering spirit, at least insofar as how research is approached. When we were asked to prepare a chapter for this book looking at how technology was being used in MFT research, we anticipated that there would be much to report. The task was to describe the use of technologies beyond the ubiquitous therapy room or laboratory use of video and audio recording. While the methods for collecting physiological and self-report data are expertly described in Chapters 7, 9, and 10, the focus of this chapter is on the use of "emergent technologies" in clinical and interactional research, little of which has been used in marriage and family therapy research.

Emergent technologies are those technologies that "introduce a significant break in the way individuals, groups, and society as a whole conduct their everyday activities, as well as add new dimensions to our understanding of the social world" (Hesse-Biber, 2011, p. 4). Such technologies encompass the broad spectrum of hardware and software developments that are, on a daily basis, impacting and altering our lives and the ways that we interact socially, cognitively, and emotionally with others. Such emergent technologies encompass social networking, weblogs, wikis, photo sharing sites, content management systems, and applications for analysis of such data. However, for the purpose of this chapter we will limit our discussion to emergent technologies that have potential for application in direct clinical intervention research, technologies that provide experiential real-time data relevant to interactional processes.

Emerging Research Technological Devices

Electronically Activated Recording

Historically, in an effort to obtain valid data, researchers have incurred the dilemma of selecting between self-report measures and intrusive collection of data during the therapy session, attempting to balance the tradeoffs because each method may compromise data integrity. Data collected by self-report is subject to inaccurate and incomplete recall by the study participants, while the process of in situ data gathering by the researcher may disturb the data being collected (Wilhelm & Grossman, 2010). Particularly, Reddy and colleagues (2013) cited the use of self-report measures as a limitation in their quest to understand changed psychosocial functioning of at-risk adolescents in response to compassion training. Reddy et al. later reflected that the technology of electronically activated recording (EAR) may be the ideal solution to remedy this data-collection problem, as the EAR device would allow for the frequency of compassionate and empathetic responses to conflict and stress to be measured directly, increasing the validity of the data. New methods and tools for data collection that capture the participant's lived experiences in the moment provide an effective alternative to self-report and in situ researcher data-collection methods, and thus eliminate the problems of inaccurate, incomplete, or invalid data.

The EAR and the SenseCam (described in the next section) are two recently developed tools that may be used for such context-aware data collection (Berry et al., 2007; Mehl & Pennebaker, 2003). The EAR was developed by Mehl and Pennebaker at the University of Texas at Austin near the end of the 1990s in response to their interest in more fully understanding the day-to-day lives of people. In its third generation, EAR is a software application that can be installed on iPhones and iPods, permitting investigator-defined recording segments and sampling periods (http://dingo.sbs.arizona.edu/~mehl/EAR.htm). The second generation consisted of a lightweight and portable audio recording device that could be easily worn by study participants and set to record 30 seconds of audio periodically every 12 minutes for a specific period of days (Mehl, Pennebaker, Crow, Dabbs, & Price, 2001; Wilhelm & Grossman, 2010). The original device relied upon microcassette tape to capture the audio.

The EAR device is particularly useful in providing insight into individuals' natural social, linguistic, and psychological lives. Specifically, Mehl and Holleran (2007) assert that EAR recordings may be coded by relational experts for either psychological or behavioral measures. Researchers may be trained to ascertain the presence of a specific construct under investigation. For example, EAR was used to capture the presence of self-reference in participants' daily conversations in a study investigating the relationship between self-reference in everyday speech and symptoms of depression (Mehl, 2006). Furthermore, aiming to discern whether swearing mediates received emotional support, EAR was used to track the frequency of spontaneous swearing among women coping with a significant illness

(Robbins, Mehl, Holleran, & Kasle, 2011). The EAR device's ability to record in situ data was particularly valuable for this study, as it allowed the participant's relational context to be known in order to discern whether swearing in the presence of others or while alone had a unique effect on emotional support and depressive symptoms. Given the nature of swearing, self-report measures would likely be inaccurate, as individuals may inadvertently underreport swearing in an effort to maintain a positive image (social desirability) with the research team. Thus, the EAR device proved particularly valuable given the dynamics of this study. Similarly, the capabilities of the EAR allowed researchers to probe how parents' negative emotionality impacted their preschool children on a very practical, specific level (Slatcher & Robles, 2012). Slatcher and Robles used the EAR device to capture in situ data of the frequency of negative word use by the preschoolers. By gathering data at this level of specificity, instead of relying on often inaccurate self-report, the impact of parent negative emotionality on preschool children was able to be understood more fully. The EAR device's functionality to capture in situ data offers researchers the power to measure specific variables with increased accuracy.

Furthermore, audio samples from the EAR can be used to ascertain information about participants' particular activities and environment in addition to the content of their conversations (Mehl & Pennebaker, 2003). The sound files often reveal behaviors or tasks that the participant is involved with, such as working, shopping, reading, typing, eating, watching TV, and other activities for amusement, and recorded sounds can be used to determine the participant's location, such as a restaurant or other public building, at home, or outdoors. For example, Mehl, Robbins, and Deters (2012) report on the use of the EAR to capture naturalistic observation of social processes, including determination of time spent in social settings, in order to interpret the psychosocial impact on psychosomatic health symptoms. Slatcher and Robles (2012) used the EAR to track preschoolers' conflicts at home in order to discern whether a relationship existed between conflict at home and diurnal cortisol levels, aiming to understand the biological pathway that may mediate childhood conflict and physical health problems later in life. The EAR provided a valuable window into everyday conflict interchanges as they unfold, allowing the research team to determine which interchanges constituted a conflict. Self-reported conflict would have left the preschool participants' parents in the position of determining the definition of a conflict, subjecting the study to inconsistent reporting among the participants.

Although the EAR offers a method to collect naturalistic data without the intrusiveness of a researcher, its viability does depend on its perceived unobtrusiveness and participant compliance (Mehl & Holleran, 2007). Synthesizing data from two separate studies, Mehl and Holleran (2007) report that participant conversations referenced the EAR most frequently during the first 2 hours wearing the device, and then this heightened self-awareness dropped markedly thereafter. In contrast, compliance rates were very high initially at the onset of participants wearing the EAR device and then dropped gradually as the time of the study continued. Yet, Reddy et al. (2013) suggested that an adolescent population would be particularly receptive to using the device given their familiarity, enjoyment, and use of novel technology. However, much of these concerns are moot when using the third generation EAR. With the application loaded onto the participants' smartphones, the data-collection method is integrated into most participants' daily behavior and the devices they interact with on a daily basis.

SenseCam

SenseCam is a wearable digital camera that can be programmed to take pictures at specific times, based on input from other context-aware sense receptors programmed in conjunction with the device. The SenseCam (currently marketed under the name Vicon Revue) is a context-aware recording device developed by Microsoft Research Cambridge in 2003 with the aim to create a type of human "black box recorder" (Hodges, Berry, & Wood, 2011). Essentially, the SenseCam is a small, lightweight digital camera that can be worn around the neck and is programmed to take pictures automatically every 30 seconds and in response to changes in the environment. Sensors that detect environmental cues, such as changes in ambient light and the presence of a person, trigger the camera to take a photograph, in addition to the photographs taken every 30 seconds. The camera is equipped with a fish-eye lens, allowing photographs to reflect nearly the complete range of vision of the wearer (Byrne et al., 2007). Additionally, the camera is engineered with a privacy shut-off switch that the wearer can use to prevent the camera from taking pictures for up to 4 minutes, and the device has a traditional shutter button providing the wearer the ability to take a picture on demand (Hodges et al., 2011). In comparison to time-intensive video documentation viewing, a day's collection of SenseCam images can be viewed in a matter of a few minutes. This relatively quick speed at which large quantities of data from the SenseCam can be reviewed is a benefit for many researchers (Berry et al., 2009; Byrne et al., 2007).

To date, the SenseCam has proved its worth in a number of fields, including tourism, patient care, education, business accessibility, and counseling (Byrne et al., 2007). Most salient to marriage and family therapy, the SenseCam has been implemented in therapeutic services to assist memory-impaired individuals. Later in 2003, the year of the SenseCam's inception, Narinder Kapur, neuropsychologist, recognized the possibility that the SenseCam could be implemented to alleviate severe memory impairments. Kapur, in collaboration with Addenbrooke Hospital and Microsoft Research, postulated that if memory-impaired patients reviewed an aggregate collection of images captured throughout their day, their memory recall would be augmented significantly. This hypothesis was confirmed, and additionally the study demonstrated that the SenseCam contributed to the patient's ability to recall thoughts, feelings, and behaviors subsequent to those found in the images (Hodges et al., 2011). Furthermore, SenseCam images have been deemed so powerful that memories associated with the pictures have become consolidated into these patients' long-term memories, available for later recall (Berry et al., 2009; Brindley, Bateman, & Gracey, 2011).

The plethora of possibilities stemming from one's memory being aided by a digital surrogate, in the form of images from the SenseCam, remains untapped in the field of MFT research. Not only may the SenseCam benefit memory recall for the research participant/wearer, but also images from the SenseCam may provide a useful means for the researcher to conduct ethnographic studies (Byrne et al., 2007; Hodges et al., 2011). Ethnography often requires a subject to be shadowed for a period of time while the researcher takes extensive notes in an effort to capture the lived experience. The need for the ethnographer to be present continually with the subject is often experienced as a significant burden during the research process. Use of the SenseCam can diminish this hardship and allow for data to continue to be gathered in the absence of the researcher. Furthermore, such an unobtrusive device can be useful in collecting data in locales not feasible for traditional ethnographic methods (Byrne et al.).

Despite the apparent value of the SenseCam's use as a digital surrogate memory device and ethnographic data-collection tool, specifically improving duration and location of obtaining data, the context-aware technology does have its limitations. Limitations linked both to design and use of the SenseCam are important to consider for implementation of the tool in research. Byrne et al. (2007) reported that the image quality is often blurry, preventing the wearer's surroundings from being fully known. However, since that time, the resolution of the device has been increased to 3 megapixels, which has improved the images. Additionally, the digital image is subject to being obscured by the wearer's clothing. Wearer forgetfulness to turn on the camera also has resulted in data-collection problems. Thus, it has been argued that the SenseCam is best utilized as an ancillary device to accompany other traditional data-collection processes (Byrne et al.).

MyExperience

MyExperience is a system that captures both in situ objective and subjective data on a computing device. Device usage, user context, and other environmental factors are logged alongside active, context-prompted user subjective feedback and report. Technological advances in cellular communication in the form of smartphones allow for a singular device to facilitate voice and text communication and provide media capture and storage (digital photographs and video), in addition to accommodating full Internet access. MyExperience is an open source software designed to run on smartphones and equipped with the power to translate usage data into action triggers for the collection of both objective and subjective in situ data (Fisher, 2009; Froehlich, Chen, Consolvo, Harrison, & Landay, 2007). MyExperience can be programmed to trigger questionnaires aimed at gathering both quantitative and qualitative user data in response to a variety of sensors, including device geographic positioning, communication activity, and time (Stumpp, Anastasopoulou, & Hey, 2010).

Given the rapidly increasing prevalence of smartphones, recruiting research subjects who already use the communication device would not likely pose a significant challenge. Furthermore, MyExperience has demonstrated a minimal impact on cell phone function and battery power usage (Froehlich et al., 2007).

SocioXensor

Similar to MyExperience, SocioXensor is another context-aware measurement tool that uses devices like smartphones and personal digital assistants (PDAs) to capture in situ data about human behavior and social context, including subjective data about user experience (such as needs, frustrations, and emotions). Essentially, extant device functions can be exploited by sensors for information gathering about user context from logged calendar appointments, location via a Global Positioning System (GPS), and application usage (Mulder & Kort, 2008; Mulder, ter Hofte, & Kort, 2005). The SocioXensor can synthesize these data points to trigger a specific quantitative or qualitative survey to appear to ascertain more about the user's experience in a given moment/context/situation (ter Hofte, Otte, Peddemors, & Mulder, 2006). Capturing user data in situ protects data integrity by minimizing or eliminating the need for retrospective recall present in traditional survey methods. Additionally, SocioXensor allows data to be gathered at places, times, and durations not afforded by ethnography (ter Hofte et al.).

Although SocioXensor was originally designed to augment the development of context-sensitive technological applications (Mulder & Kort, 2008), the device function can be adapted for use as a valuable social science research tool.

Accelerometers

Accelerometers are used mainly in exercise science and kinesiology fields to track how much people exercise or move. There are many models on the market with various software packages, and we recommend that prior to purchase, you consult with someone who has used them. Generally, accelerometers are watch-sized devices that can be worn on the wrist or ankle or clipped to a belt. Recently, smartphone accelerometers have been developed (Mitchell, Monaghan, & O'Connor, 2013). In addition to being able to assess physical activity, accelerometers are able to assess sleep patterns (Natale et al., 2012; Tomoyuki, Hiroko, Shimizu, & Katsumata, 2012). With an add-on, researchers can also track heart rate.

WiShare

The WiShare tool, a context-aware application designed specifically to assess social connectedness and social presence experiences, relies upon similar technologies as does the MyExperience and SocioXensor sampling methods. Social connectedness is defined as "an emotional experience, evoked by, but independent of, the other's presence [or] psychological involvement" (Rettie, 2003) and as a "feeling of staying in touch" (IJsselsteijn, van Baren, & van Lanen, 2003), whereas social presence is defined as "the sense of being with another in a mediated environment" (Biocca, Harms, & Burgoon, 2003, p. 456). Ultimately, the aim of WiShare is to capture the difference between what people wish to share and what they actually share in an interpersonal encounter (Visser & Mulder, 2011).

When WiShare is active on the user's communication device (e.g., a smartphone, a personal computer [PC]), two avatars appear in a square box on the screen, depicting the user and the person with whom the user is sharing. The user can move and position the two avatars to reflect their sharing experience, with closer proximity indicating a stronger sharing experience. If the user does not experience sharing with her counterpart, this can be indicated by selecting a radio button for "I don't share." Following a submission indicating a shared experience or a desire to share, the WiShare application triggers the user to receive a short questionnaire inquiring about her thoughts and feelings and her expectations about her partner's thoughts and feelings (Visser & Mulder, 2011).

Digital Pens

Digital pens integrate the convenience and ease of use of traditional pen and paper methods of fieldnote taking with the benefits of digital technology. Specifically, many researchers value the dependability and light weight of pen and paper in comparison with laptops and other handheld PCs that add weight to the researcher's extensible toolkit and can malfunction or become depleted of battery power. Yet, data recorded via pen and paper are not easily archived, preserved, organized, or shareable for collaboration or dissemination purposes. Digital pens, manufactured by Hewlett-Packard, Logitech, Maxell, and Nokia, bridge this chasm of traditional and digital ethnographic methods, as the tool functions like a standard ballpoint pen while also capturing writing into a digital file with a time and date stamp attached. Special digital-pen paper printed with a pattern of dots must be used with the device. A small camera embedded within the pen reads pen strokes on the dotted paper and records the pen strokes' location and pressure into an XML file that can be transmitted wirelessly via Bluetooth to the researcher's computer located off-site (Becvar & Hollan, 2005).

The value and acceptance of digital pens as a worthy emergent technology is evident in their adoption as a foundational component in several digital ethnographic systems. For example, both ButterflyNet and Ethno-Goggles integrate the use of digital pens into their data capturing methods (Tennent, Crabtree, & Greenhalgh, 2008; Yeh et al., 2006). Champions of digital ethnography cite the benefit of digital pens to create a backup copy of data as one of their most important features (Yeh et al.). If the pen and paper notes are lost, the digital file is available, or if the digital file becomes corrupted, the pen and paper version can be referenced. Furthermore, notes taken with a digital pen can be easily annotated and linked with synchronous audio and/or video files (Yeh et al.).

Ethno-Goggles

Ethno-Goggles is a multimodal qualitative field data-collection system. The benefit of this system is that large amounts of data can be collected and tagged in real time, which is especially useful in covert ethnography (Murthy, 2011, p. 167).

Integrating several digital capture devices, Ethno-Goggles is useful to mitigate some of the challenges of other data-collection methods inherent to ethnography. Specifically, the Ethno-Goggles qualitative field data-collection system comprises a camera embedded in unobtrusive glasses, a microphone integrated into headphone buds, a digital pen, a laptop computer, GPS, and a PDA component. Because the camera is positioned in glasses worn by the researcher, the researcher is not distracted by the action of focusing a video camera on the scene to be recorded; instead, the event is automatically recorded without the researcher needing to devote part of his focus to the video capture. Furthermore, the position of the camera on the researcher's glasses affords the video to more closely mimic the researcher's vision than a traditional handheld camera. Similarly, microphones placed within earbuds allow for audio recordings to more closely reflect exactly what the researcher hears, in contrast to the audio captured on a camera microphone that is not located near the researcher's ears (Murthy, 2011; Tennent et al., 2008).

In addition to augmenting the quality of lifelike (eye of the observer) video and audio data, the camera and microphone disguised in the researcher's glasses and earbuds, respectively, are less noticeable to the respondent/observed individual. The discrete data-gathering devices may contribute to interactions between the researcher and researched participant being more natural and less impacted by the presence of data recording devices, thus reducing the Hawthorne effect. Also, because the data-collection means of Ethno-Goggles are quite concealed, it is possible to conduct covert ethnography with the digital data-capturing device. However, covert ethnography is not without its ethical controversies surrounding human privacy. Thus, researchers aiming to conduct covert ethnography, or other undisclosed research, ultimately must be able to convince their local institutional review boards of the value and sound ethics of their studies. Even in overt research, informed consent ought to remind participants that the veiled data-collection means may contribute to their forgetting that they are being recorded (Murthy, 2011, pp. 167–168; Tennent et al., 2008).

Another advantageous feature of Ethno-Goggles is its data synchronization and real-time tagging capabilities. During the data analysis process, researchers often struggle to realign contemporary audio, visual, and written data.

Ethno-Goggles digital integration of audio, visual, and written fieldnote data eliminates this difficulty, as these data threads are automatically assigned time stamps tagged to real time. Additionally, the GPS component allows for data localization to occur instantaneously (ET book, pp. 167–168; Tennent et al., 2008). Ethno-Goggles represents a definitive feat in the development of digital ethnography that bolsters both the quality and the quantity of data collection.

ButterflyNet

One of the challenges of the research process for social scientists is the need to organize and access vast quantities of heterogeneous digital data. Butterfly-Net was originally developed at Stanford University in an effort to attenuate this difficulty for biologists (http://hci.stanford.edu/research/butterflynet/butterflynet/). This open source software is designed to integrate audio, video, digital pen, GPS, and other digital data into one software application, allowing an array of data to be accessed in one domain, essentially creating a comprehensive digital field notebook (Murthy, 2011; Yeh et al., 2006). ButterflyNet allows for researchers to choose among a variety of possible data browsing layouts. Additionally, this software is equipped with search features that assist researchers in easily locating stored data (Yeh et al.). ButterflyNet may be most useful for MFT research that requires analysis of synchronized data, including audio, video, and digitally captured written notes.

Conclusion

Emergent technologies offer MFT researchers an array of data-collection methods that are uniquely appropriate for investigating the complex and multidimensional aspects of research on interpersonal processes. When combined with the traditional instruments used in studying therapeutic processes, these technologies can effectively extend data collection into the lived experience of the participants. For example, does an intervention in the consulting room change behavior and interactions in other contexts? With these technologies, that question can be answered. Responding to immediate prompts through technologies such as MyExperience or SocioXensor allows participants to offer data that are immediate and context sensitive, which a post-hoc questionnaire or daily journal cannot approach. EAR and SenseCam can unobtrusively gather data that would be inaccessible otherwise.

Research in the field of MFT has always struggled with the extant data-collection tools that could not address the richness of interpersonal dynamics. Today, the technologies that are becoming an everyday part of our lives offer a rich opportunity to understand interpersonal behavior in ways that we have never encountered before. Marriage and family therapy emerged from those who thought outside the box and considered the world through lenses that were not the standard viewpoint. MFT research can do the same by broadening its armamentarium beyond the standard data-collection methods.

References

Becvar, L. A., & Hollan, J. D. (2005). *Envisioning a paper augmented digital notebook: Exploiting digital pen technology for fieldwork.* Distributed Cognition and Human-Computer Interaction Laboratory, Department of Cognitive Science. La Jolla, CA: UCSD.

Berry, E., Hampshire, A., Rowe, J., Hodges, S., Kapur, N., Watson, P., . . . Owen, A. M. (2009). The neural basis of effective memory therapy in a patient with limbic encephalitis. *Journal of Neurology, Neurosurgery & Psychiatry, 80*(11), 1202–1205. doi: 10.1136/jnnp.2008.164251

Berry, E., Kapur, N., Williams, L., Hodges, S., Watson, P., Smyth, G., . . . Wood, K. (2007). The use of a wearable camera, SenseCam, as a pictorial diary to improve autobiographical memory in a patient with limbic encephalitis: A preliminary report. *Neuropsychological Rehabilitation, 17*(4-5), 582–601. doi: 10.1080/09602010601029780

Biocca, F., Harms, C., & Burgoon, J. K. (2003). Toward a more robust theory and measure of social presence: Review and suggested criteria. *Presence: Teleoperators & Virtual Environments, 12*(5), 456–480.

Brindley, R., Bateman, A., & Gracey, F. (2011). Exploration of use of SenseCam to support autobiographical memory retrieval within a cognitive-behavioural therapeutic intervention following acquired brain injury. *Memory, 19*(7), 745–757. doi: 10.1080/09658211.2010.493893

Broderick, C. B., & Schrader, S. S. (1991). The history of professional marriage and family therapy. In A. S. Gurman & D. P. Kniskern (Eds.), *Handbook of family therapy, vol. 2.* Philadelphia: Brunner/Mazel.

Byrne, D., Doherty, A., Jones, G., Smeaton, A., Kumpulainen, S., & Järvelin, K. (2007). *The SenseCam as a tool for task observation.* British Computer Society. http://doras.dcu.ie/639/

Fischer, J. E. (2009). Experience-sampling tools: a critical review. *Mobile Living Labs, 9.*

Froehlich, J., Chen, M. Y., Consolvo, S., Harrison, B., & Landay, J. A. (2007, June). MyExperience: A system for in situ tracing and capturing of user feedback on mobile phones. In *Proceedings of the 5th international conference on Mobile systems, applications and services* (pp. 57–70). ACM.

Hesse-Biber, S. (2011). Emergent technologies in social research: Pushing against the boundaries of research practice. In S. Hesse-Biber (Ed.), *Handbook of emergent technologies in social research* (pp. 3–24). New York: Oxford University Press.

Hodges, S., Berry, E., & Wood, K. (2011). SenseCam: A wearable camera that stimulates and rehabilitates autobiographical memory. *Memory, 19*(7), 685–696.

IJsselsteijn, W., van Baren, J., & van Lanen, F. (2003). Staying in touch: Social presence and connectedness through synchronous and asynchronous communication media. *Human-Computer Interaction: Theory and Practice (Part II), 2,* 924–928.

Mehl, M. R. (2006). The lay assessment of subclinical depression in daily life. *Psychological Assessment, 18*(3), 340.

Mehl, M. R., & Holleran, S. E. (2007). An empirical analysis of the obtrusiveness of and participants' compliance with the electronically activated recorder (EAR). *European Journal of Psychological Assessment, 23*(4), 248–257.

Mehl, M. R., & Pennebaker, J. W. (2003). The social dynamics of a cultural upheaval: Social interactions surrounding September 11, 2001. *Psychological Science, 14*(6), 579–585. doi: 10.1046/j.0956-7976.2003.psci_1468.x

Mehl, M. R., Pennebaker, J. W., Crow, D. M., Dabbs, J., & Price, J. H. (2001). The electronically activated recorder (EAR): A device for sampling naturalistic daily activities and conversations. *Behavior Research Methods, 33*(4), 517–523.

Mehl, M. R., Robbins, M. L., & Deters, F. G. (2012). Naturalistic observation of health-relevant social processes: The electronically activated recorder methodology in psychosomatics. *Psychosomatic Medicine, 74*(4), 410–417. doi: 10.1097/PSY.0b013e3182545470

Mitchell, E., Monaghan, D., & O'Connor, N. E. (2013). Classification of sporting activities using smartphone accelerometers. *Source, 13*, 5317–5337. doi: 10.3390/s130405317

Mulder, I., & Kort, J. (2008). Mixed emotions, mixed methods: The role of emergent technologies to study user experience in context. In S. Hesse-Biber & P. Leavy (Eds.), *Handbook of emergent methods in social research.* (pp. 601–612). New York: Guilford Publications.

Mulder, I., Ter Hofte, G. H., & Kort, J. (2005, August). SocioXensor: Measuring user behaviour and user eXperience in conteXt with mobile devices. In *Proceedings of Measuring Behavior* (pp. 355–358). Wageningen, the Netherlands.

Murthy, D. (2011). Emergent digital ethnographic methods for social research. In S. Hesse-Biber (Ed.), *Handbook of emergent technologies in social research* (pp. 158–179). New York: Oxford University Press.

Natale, V., Derjak, M., Erbacci, A., Tonetti, L., Fabri, M., & Martoni, M. (2012). Monitoring sleep with smartphone accelerometer. *Sleep and Biological Rhythms, 10*, 287–292. doi: 10.1111/j.1479-8425.2012.00575.x

Reddy, S. D., Negi, L. T., Dodson-Lavelle, B., Ozawa-de Silva, B., Pace, T. W. W., Cole, S. P., Craighead, L. W. (2013). Cognitive-based compassion training: A promising prevention strategy for at-risk adolescents. *Journal of Child and Family Studies, 22*(2), 219–230. doi: 10.1007/s10826-012-9571-7

Rettie, R. (2003, October). *Connectedness, awareness, and social presence.* Paper presented at the 6th Annual Workshop on Presence. Aalborg, Denmark.

Robbins, M. L., Mehl, M. R., Holleran, S. E., & Kasle, S. (2011). Naturalistically observed sighing and depression in rheumatoid arthritis patients: A preliminary study. *Health Psychology, 30*(1), 129–133. doi: 10.1037/a0021558

Slatcher, R. B., & Robles, T. F. (2012). Preschoolers' everyday conflict at home and diurnal cortisol patterns. *Health Psychology, 31*(6), 834–838. doi: 10.1037/a0026774

Stumpp, J., Anastasopoulou, P., & Hey, S. (2010, August). Platform for ambulatory assessment of psycho-physiological signals and online data capture. In *Proceedings of the 7th International Conference on Methods and Techniques in Behavioral Research* (p. 30). ACM. Tennent, P., Crabtree, A., & Greenhalgh, C. (2008). *Ethno-goggles: Supporting field capture of qualitative material.* Paper presented at the 4th International e-Social Science Conference.

Ter Hofte, G. H., Otte, R. A. A., Peddemors, A., & Mulder, I. (2006). What's your lab doing in my pocket? Supporting mobile field studies with socioxensor. In *Conference Supplement of CSCW 2006* (pp. 109–110). Banff, AB, Canada.

Tomoyuki, K., Hiroko, S., Shimizu, T., & Katsumata, M. (2012). Agreement in regard to total sleep time during a nap obtained via a sleep polygraph and accelerometer: A comparison of different sensitivity thresholds of the accelerometer. *International Journal of Behavioral Medicine, 19,* 398–401. doi: 10.1007/ s12529-011-9180-7

Visser, A., & Mulder, I. (2011). Emergent technologies for assessing social feelings and experiences. In S. N. Hesse-Biber, (Ed.) *Handbook of emergent technologies in social research* (p. 369). New York: Oxford University Press

Wilhelm, F. H., & Grossman, P. (2010). Emotions beyond the laboratory: Theoretical fundaments, study design, and analytic strategies for advanced ambulatory assessment. *Biological Psychology, 84*(3), 552–569. doi: 10.1016/j.biopsycho.2010.01.017

Yeh, R., Liao, C., Klemmer, S., Guimbretière, F., Lee, B., Kakaradov, B. et al. (2006). ButterflyNet: A mobile capture and access system for field biology research. In Proceedings of the SIGCHI Conference on Human Factors in Computing Systems, Chicago, IL (pp. 571–580). New York: ACM Press.

9

PHYSIOLOGICAL RESEARCH IN COUPLE AND FAMILY THERAPY

Kim D. Gregson and Scott A. Ketring

Abbreviations Glossary

ANS—Autonomic nervous system
BP—Blood pressure
ECG—Electrocardiogram
HR—Heart rate
PNS—Parasympathetic nervous system
RSA—Respiratory sinus arrhythmia
SCL—Skin conductance level
SNS—Sympathetic nervous system

Introduction

Historically the measurement of therapeutic change has perplexed researchers. Self-report and observational measures provide subjective perspectives, but objective assessments have been nearly impossible to acquire. Nevertheless, human development researchers have increasingly used physiological measures as more objective assessments of intra-individual changes in emotion regulation, along with interindividual differences. Indeed, contemporary developmental perspectives contend that individual differences in physiological response to environmental stressors shape the psychological and behavioral outcomes among individuals (Porges, 2001). This approach can be adapted to couple and family therapy research in an attempt to identify change in social engagement and emotion regulation within the family unit as it relates to behavioral and cognitive changes.

The utility of psychophysiological research to the field of marriage and family therapy has remained somewhat mysterious, particularly since no researchers, of whom we are aware, have conducted this type of research with couple or family groupings in the therapeutic context. Nevertheless, in the past few decades, a few prominent studies have launched this body of literature by assessing physiological processes of couples during naturalistic interactions (Holland & Roisman, 2010;

Jacobson et al., 2000; Newton & Sanford, 2003; Roisman, 2007). Significantly absent from this newly developing area of research are samples with other familial dyads (e.g., mother-child, siblings, father-child). In fact, numerous studies (primarily in the field of child development) have been performed with familial pairs during which *one* is assessed physiologically (for landmark studies, see Connell, Hughes-Scalise, Klostermann, & Azem, 2011; Hane & Barrios, 2011; Lorber & O'Leary, 2005). However, we are aware of no research examining physiological processes of *both* family members. While this approach to analyzing human behavior is undoubtedly both novel and complex, it also opens invaluable options for the study of mediators of therapy outcomes, moderators influencing therapy outcomes, and objective physiological outcomes in determining therapeutic benefit.

Measures of clients' physiological responses during sessions could potentially illuminate arousal processes that are potentiated through therapeutic intervention. Therapy models with an affective or experiential focus (structural, strategic, experiential, emotion-focused therapy, etc.) suggest that emotional arousal *in session* facilitates the effects of therapy on clients. Other models concentrate on cognitive or behavioral change (narrative, solution-focused, cognitive-behavioral, psychoeducation, etc.), rather than explicitly focusing on affective arousal. Considering the wide variety of theoretical perspectives, psychophysiological research may help illuminate the extent to which therapy models effectively modulate adaptive arousal (i.e., arousal that facilitates therapeutic effects), such as social-attentional engagement (perhaps reflected in vagal withdrawal) versus the less adaptive fight-or-flight response triggered by the sympathetic nervous system (SNS; reflected in electrodermal reactivity).

Evaluating various arousal responses to therapy interventions (e.g., vagal withdrawal, vagal augmentation, sympathetic activation) will also accentuate individual differences in relation to environmental context. Individuals who respond to behavioral interventions with heightened, sustained parasympathetic arousal may be affected quite differently than individuals who respond with moderate, sustained parasympathetic arousal. Likewise, social, family, and sex differences may contribute to the different responses of individuals participating in therapy. Hence, autonomic nervous system (ANS) parameters could be examined as mediators or moderators of therapy techniques or therapy processes to test these possibilities.

Finally, physiological measures provide opportunities to examine therapy outcomes in more reliable and objective ways than is possible in self-report and observational measures. For example, understanding the potential longitudinal shifts in vagal withdrawal or sympathetic responses related to specific therapy interactions can significantly impact our view of effective interventions and approaches. Likewise, physiological research in family therapy can address therapy interactions associated with changes in arousal recovery rates following conflict. The research options facilitated by psychophysiology are both stimulating and countless. This research is based on a theory of psychophysiology outlining the stages of ANS reactivity related to different behavioral coping strategies.

Autonomic Nervous System and Human Behavior

The ANS is a survival/engagement network that coordinates communication between the central nervous system and the visceral organs (e.g., heart, lungs, digestive system, liver, bladder). According to polyvagal theory (Porges, 2007), the ANS includes three subsystems, or stages of reactivity, that serve different regulatory and behavioral functions in normal and stressful situations (see Figure 9.1). In hierarchical order, the ventral vagal complex (VVC) facilitates social engagement, the SNS mobilizes resources for fight or flight, and the dorsal vagal complex (DVC) primarily functions to immobilize metabolic resources of the body and conserve energy.

The VVC, a component of the parasympathetic nervous system (PNS) branch of the ANS, includes the vagus nerve, which operates as a heart rate "brake" (see Figure 9.2). Decelerating the heart allows the individual to maintain calmness during social engagement and other periods of mild arousal. The VVC also

---

Level 1: *Social Communication*

Branch of ANS: Parasympathetic Nervous System (ventral vagal complex; VVC)

Associated Behaviors: Facial expression, vocalization, listening

Function: To promote self-soothing and maintain attention during social engagement

Physiological Measures: Respiratory Sinus Arrhythmia (RSA)

Level 2: *Mobilization*

Branch of ANS: Sympathetic Nervous System

Associated Behaviors: Active approach or avoidance (i.e., fight/flight)

Function: To mobilize and obtain needed resources to deal with current stressor

Physiological Measures: Skin Conductance Level (SCL)

Level 3: *Immobilization*

Branch of ANS: Parasympathetic Nervous System (dorsal vagal complex; DVC)

Associated Behaviors: Passive avoidance through production of fear/anxiety; physiological shut down or feigning death

Function: To immobilize and conserve metabolic resources

Figure 9.1 Overview of the three hierarchical physiological stress response subsystems of the ANS.

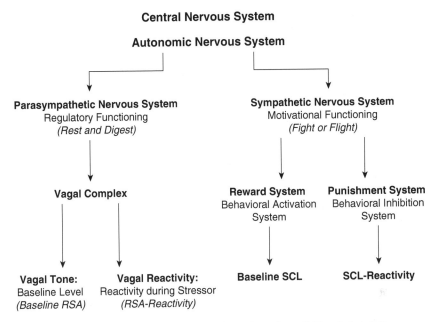

Figure 9.2 Conceptual diagram of the two branches of the ANS and their influence on physiological affect regulation.

controls facial expressions, speaking, and listening behaviors conducive to social engagement (Porges, 2001). During calm couple interactions, the VVC serves to increase social engagement and decrease hypervigilance (Porges, 2006). In more stressful interactions, the vagal brake is withdrawn incrementally to increase heart rate and facilitate attention and active coping.

The most common parameter of PNS functioning and vagal activity is respiratory sinus arrhythmia (RSA; measurement of variability in heart rate that accompanies the respiratory cycle). Vagal tone (baseline RSA) and vagal reactivity to challenges (RSA-Reactivity; RSA-R) are two measures of PNS activity (Bornstein & Suess, 2000; see Table 9.1). Vagal tone refers to baseline functioning (i.e., the ability to maintain homeostasis while the PNS is at rest) and characterizes the ability of the system to maintain focus and socially engage within nonthreatening environments (Porges, 2007). Vagal reactivity refers to changes in RSA as a result of environmental stress or challenge. It can be characterized by vagal withdrawal (decreased RSA) or vagal augmentation (increased RSA).

In the face of greater threat or stress, the second level of stress response (SNS) is activated (refer to Figure 9.1). The SNS is an active monitoring system that mobilizes the body's fight/flight response by raising the heart rate, activating sweat glands, and opening breathing passages (Brodal, 2004). The most

Table 9.1 Overview of Vagal Tone and Vagal Reactivity and How They Affect an Individual's Response to Stress

	Vagal Tone (Baseline RSA)	
	Low VT	High VT
Heart rate variability	Low	High
Ability to respond to stress	Restricted ability to withdraw heart rate "brake" (i.e., harder to regulate reactivity appropriately)	Enhanced ability to withdraw heart rate "brake" (i.e., easier to regulate reactivity appropriately)
Communication	Self-expression difficult, restricted range of emotions, engagement skills low	Self-expression easier, wide range of emotions, engagement skills high
Associated outcomes	Externalizing/internalizing problems and emotional dysregulation in children (Beauchaine, 2001)	Normative development (e.g., enhanced social functioning, communication, emotion regulation; Thayer & Lane, 2009)

	Vagal Reactivity (RSA-Reactivity; RSA-R)	
	Vagal Withdrawal (low RSA-R)	Vagal Augmentation (high RSA-R)
Effects on heart	Release of heart rate "brake" (i.e., increase in heart rate and metabolic output)	Utilization of heart rate "brake" (i.e., decrease in heart rate and metabolic output)
Stress response	Facilitates active coping with stressor	Facilitates calm, lack of attunement to stressor
Associated outcomes	Protective factor for children exposed to marital conflict (Katz & Gottman, 1997)	When faced with a challenge, this can be less functional and is related to negative outcomes (Porges, 2007)

common parameter of SNS activity is skin conductance level (SCL), a measure of sweat gland (i.e., electrodermal) activity (see Figure 9.2). Well validated as a parameter of the behavioral inhibition system of the SNS, it is often understood as a physiological indicator of anxiety under threatening/stressful circumstances (Beauchaine, 2001; Fowles, Kochanska, & Murray, 2000). Measures can be taken of baseline SCL or SCL-Reactivity to challenges. Lower baseline SCL (representing insensitivity to threat) is related to externalizing behaviors in children (van Goozen, Matthys, Cohen-Kettenis, Buitelaar, & van Engeland, 2000) and conduct disorder diagnoses in adolescents (Raine, Venables, & Williams, 1990). Additionally, SCL-Reactivity to stressful circumstances is conceptualized in adult research as representing exertion of inhibitory self-control (voluntary or involuntary), whether it be cognitive reappraisal (Sheppes, Catran, & Meiran, 2009), thought suppression (Wegner & Gold, 1995), or emotion suppression (Sheppes et al.). As a moderator of children's outcomes, high SCL-Reactivity has also been found to mitigate the externalizing responses among children exposed to harsh parenting (Erath, El-Sheikh, & Cummings, 2009).

If the SNS stress response is insufficient, the third and final level (DVC) is activated, immobilizing the individual (refer to Figure 9.1). The heart rate is slowed and digestive system temporarily halted. This physiological freezing/immobilizing system conserves resources in extremely threatening situations when more active responses are not likely effective. Since the DVC is the most primitive response subsystem requiring extreme life-threatening fear response, researchers rarely assess its activity; thus, no parameters of the DVC are identified for the purpose of this chapter.

The VVC, SNS, and DVC systems typically work together to offer sequential and/or simultaneous responses during arousing stress encounters (Matveev, Prokopova, & Nachev, 2006). Evaluating both vagal (e.g., RSA) and SNS (e.g., SCL) functioning can exhibit a combined response (Cacioppo, Uchino, & Berntson, 1994). For example, both physiological systems are predictors and moderators of child behavior in the context of marital discord (El-Sheikh, Harger, Whitson, 2001; El-Sheikh, Keller, & Erath, 2007). Since the PNS and SNS operate concurrently and are intertwined to enable social engagement, measurement of the co-influence of both ANS branches is necessary.

Review of Physiological Research in the Couple and Family Context

Dysfunctional relational cycles for which couples and families seek therapy are often rooted within the inability to regulate affect (Porges, 2001, 2007). As previously reviewed, at the physiological level, the ANS may regulate emotions and behaviors related to positive engagement, disengagement, and defensiveness, fundamentally influencing family members' interactions. When individuals are highly emotionally aroused, cognitive functioning is disrupted, resulting in anxiety-ridden or impulsive reversion to habitual and often maladaptive behaviors (Porges, 2001, 2007). Couple and family therapy presents an ideal context to examine the physiological responses of multiple members of a family. The very nature of couple and family therapy is to identify maladaptive responses at the physiological, cognitive, and behavioral levels and alter these response patterns by constructing new relational interactions during times of high arousal or sustained low arousal (depending on the therapy model).

129

While no published physiological research to date has been conducted within the therapeutic context, groundbreaking couple research examining physiological functioning during dyadic interactions has laid a strong foundation for the importance of studying physiology in the family context (see the following sections for review of literature). Indeed, the last few decades of psychophysiological research have solidified linkages between physical and psychological well-being within familial/romantic relationships as significant contexts of physical and psychological health. With these landmark studies as a guide, the psychophysiological field is indeed ripe for novel research questions to be addressed within the couple and family therapy context.

An historical overview of previous psychophysiological research examining couple interactions is necessary to set the framework for couple/family therapy research using psychophysiology as an additional measure of change. Past research has primarily focused on physiological markers of general ANS functioning (e.g., cardiovascular responses, general arousal) and, more recently, specific indices of the SNS and PNS branches of the ANS. While other physiological measures have also been assessed (hormonal responses, somatic activity, etc.), those fields of literature lie beyond the scope of this chapter and thus will not be cited. Following the review of past research, we present our current physiological research to highlight issues specific to collecting data in a couple therapy setting.

General ANS Functioning

Multiple measures of general ANS functioning (focusing on cardiovascular response and reactivity) have been utilized in physiological studies with couples. While these indicators are instrumental to understanding the role of general arousal in dyadic interactions, they limit specific interpretation of emotional/behavioral processes that may be more directly linked to the two ANS branches. Nevertheless, compared with parameters of PNS and SNS functioning, general ANS measures often guarantee less invasive data collection procedures, cost less, and offer greater ease of interpretation.

Blood pressure (BP) is typically assessed manually with a stethoscope, BP cuff, and sphygmomanometer. Involving a more complex procedure, the electrocardiogram (ECG) is usually conducted by placing electrodes on the chest, ribs, collarbones, finger, and/or earlobe. Heart rate (HR; beats per minute), the most oft used measure of general ANS functioning, may be obtained from ECG data, BP cuff, or simple pulse count. Multiple other cardiac indices can be calculated from an ECG and used in physiological analyses (e.g., interbeat interval, pulse transmission time, finger pulse amplitude), but for the sake of clarity in the following literature review, we will interpret all of these measures as indicators of general cardiac output.

The majority of studies utilizing cardiac measures of physiological regulation have focused on couples' conflict interactions, overall demonstrating higher cardiac response in conflict-ridden couples (Newton & Sanford, 2003)

130

or among partners with insecure attachment styles (Roisman, 2007) and lower response in supportive couples (Heffner, Kiecolt-Glaser, Loving, Glaser, & Malarkey, 2004). Two particular studies focused on violent couples and found elevated cardiac responses in wives (Jacobson et al., 2000) and differences between types of male batterers according to their physiological responses (Gottman et al., 1995). These studies confirm that couples' conflict does, indeed, generate physiological arousal, which can be particularly heightened among couples with relationship difficulties. Continuing research is necessary to illuminate arousal processes that might facilitate conflict resolution and to examine longitudinal shifts in affect regulation abilities due to conflict processes, among other noteworthy research topics.

Findings are mixed about whether men or women display greater cardiac arousal during conflict with their partner. However, there is preliminary evidence that wives' heightened arousal is associated with negative *cognitions* about the marriage (Menchaca & Dehle, 2005), while husbands' heightened arousal is linked with negative *affect* (Levenson, Carstensen, & Gottman, 1994). Additionally, husbands who converse under some sort of imposed pressure (i.e., trying to persuade their wives, perceiving evaluation by researchers) appear to raise their cardiac responses as well (Brown & Smith, 1992; Smith, Gallo, Goble, Ngu, & Stark, 1998). Future research topics could include gender differences in partners' behaviors/cognitions associated with cardiac arousal and their effect on therapy outcomes and links between cardiac arousal and experienced affect, among various options.

Longitudinal data are particularly uncommon for physiological studies. Nevertheless, Levenson and Gottman (1985) found that higher HR during conflict discussions predicted declines in marital satisfaction 3 years later. Additionally, Gottman et al. (1995) surprisingly discovered that domestic violence partnerships with a type 1 batterer (identified by lower physiological responses during conflict) had a 0% separation-divorce rate 2 years later, compared with a 27.5% rate for marriages involving type 2 batterers (identified by higher physiological responses during conflict).

In addition to examining cardiac responses alone, several researchers have measured cardiac and electrodermal parameters in concert, illuminating general "physiological arousal" as a dynamic interplay of various aspects of ANS functioning. Overall, reduced autonomic arousal during relational interactions is related to a sense of togetherness (Seider, Hirschberger, Nelson, & Levenson, 2009) and positive emotionality (Yuan, McCarthy, Holley, & Levenson, 2010). One unique study examined husband-wife physiological linkage (i.e., similarity between partners' concurrent cardiac/electrodermal responses) during conflict discussions and found greater physiological linkage (either high or low arousal) strongly associated with lower marital satisfaction (Levenson & Gottman, 1983).

Consistently both heightened cardiac arousal and greater cardiac reactivity during partners' interactions have been linked with maladaptive interactional behaviors and relationship distress. In fact, the long-term impact of heightened cardiac arousal during relational interactions is quite destructive to marital satisfaction (Levenson & Gottman, 1985). These findings are critical for informing therapists of the function of couple conflict and utility of therapeutic interventions.

PNS Functioning: Respiratory Sinus Arrhythmia

Other human development fields (particularly child development) have recently begun measuring respiratory sinus arrhythmia (RSA), but only one study has assessed RSA during couple interactions (Roisman, 2007). Relationship type (married versus engaged) significantly predicted baseline RSA (measured during couple conflict discussion), with engaged partners displaying greater RSA responses to the problem discussion than married individuals. With such minimal research examining RSA among both partners of familial dyads, there is particular need for couple/family therapists to initiate such studies. As reviewed, RSA (as a measure of parasympathetic activation) can provide critical details about the arousal processes involved in social engagement and attentional focus, a necessary component of healthy relationships and effective therapy.

SNS Functioning: Skin Conductance Level

SCL (an estimate of electrodermal activity) is typically assessed by placing two electrodes on the palm or two fingers of the nondominant hand. Again, most SCL research has concentrated on couples' interactions. Heightened SCL reactivity during interactions (i.e., anxious sensitivity to threat) has been linked with diminished attachment security (Holland & Roisman, 2010; Roisman, 2007) and subsequent longitudinal declines in relationship satisfaction (Levenson & Gottman, 1985). In addition, preliminary findings may signify that men are particularly sensitive to SCL responses, whether they are nonresponsive during conflict (Levenson & Gottman, 1983) or demonstrate high affect during conflict (Levenson et al., 1994).

Couple research has successfully identified some physiological markers related to positive and negative interactions within relationships. However, the next step is to evaluate individual, couple, and family physiological responses within the therapeutic context, considering both immediate and longitudinal associations. Understanding the contextual differences in relationship dynamics and functioning associated with differing physiological responses is essential. This research will open up new avenues in understanding how therapeutic interventions impact client physiology.

Our Current Research: Physiological Responses of Couples in Therapy

Drs. Scott Ketring, Margaret Keiley, and Thomas Smith, faculty at the Marriage and Family Therapy training program at Auburn University, along with Kim

Gregson, have collaborated to design a research study examining physiological processes among married couples over the course of multiple therapy sessions. The overarching hypothesis is that physiological changes in individuals' affect regulation capabilities (occurring as a result of new relational interactions constructed during couples' therapy) are associated with behavioral, emotional, and cognitive changes. To capture whether couples' therapy does, indeed, function in this manner, we collect three physiological measures (RSA, SCL, and HR) from heterosexual, married partners during three or four 1-hour therapy sessions. RSA and HR are measured via two electrodes (placed on the individual's right collarbone and lower left rib); SCL is assessed via two electrodes placed on the individual's palm. In addition, we also collect the same measures from the therapist during each session, potentially to address research questions related to therapist's arousal, intervention effectiveness, and physiological linkage of therapist and client(s) arousal. Therapy sessions are videoed and coded by trained observers for critical therapeutic events (which will be explained further below). In addition, both partners report on individual and couple functioning at the first and fourth sessions.

Using both presession baseline levels of physiological functioning and stress levels during critical therapeutic events for both partners, we plan to use longitudinal modeling to analyze change in physiological affect regulation over the course of multiple therapy sessions and how these changes are associated with individual and couple functioning. As noted previously, understanding affect regulation enhancement in the context of couples' therapy has significant import for designing clinical interventions and highlighting the mechanisms through which these interventions affect individual/couple functioning.

Throughout the remaining sections of the chapter, we will highlight specific validity issues related to collecting and analyzing physiological data, noting both approaches used by past researchers and unique issues we have faced in our physiological clinical couples' study at Auburn University.

Validity Issues in Physiological Research: Data Collection and Analysis

Sample Composition

Similar to other couple/family research, psychophysiological studies have primarily utilized small samples, focused on the couple dyad, focused on married couples over cohabiting couples, undersampled racial/ethnic minorities, not included lesbian-gay-bisexual-transgender (LGBT) couples, and not sampled from clinical populations. A minority of the cited studies had samples with over 100 dyads (Heffner et al., 2004; Holland & Roisman, 2010; Levenson et al., 1994; Seider et al., 2009; Yuan et al., 2010). In addition, two studies examined maritally distressed, violent/nonviolent couples, rather than sampling solely from nonclinical populations (Gottman et al., 1995; Jacobson et al., 2000).

Finally, a few researchers enhanced their study of married couples by comparing groups of newlywed or young married couples with older married couples (Heffner et al.; Roisman, 2007; Seider et al.; Yuan et al.).

Recruitment for physiological studies of couple/family therapy is particularly difficult due to the limited pool of eligible participants (i.e., clinically distressed family groupings willing to participate in therapy) and the invasiveness of the procedure, which can compromise external validity. In order to meet these challenges and enhance external validity, we have publicized our study in the community (via radio programs, flyers, church ministers, etc.) and have offered to waive counseling fees for the first four sessions as incentive for participation. Luckily, new clients' receptivity has been high, with few people reticent to participate. Although clinical samples may be more problematic to procure, it is nevertheless essential that researchers enhance the generalizability of physiological research by addressing issues of sample size, familial grouping, racial/ethnic diversity, inclusion of cohabiting and/or LGBT couples, and diversity in types of clinical distress.

Dyadic Interactions

Another critical consideration is the type of dyadic interaction to sample within session. Previous couple studies have included a conflict discussion, which is typically focused on the dyad's previously identified disagreement area. Lengths of the discussion last from 5 to 30 minutes, with most researchers assessing an average of 10–15 minutes. Several researchers asked their couples to engage in a problem discussion about an area of continuing disagreement (Gottman et al., 1995; Heffner et al., 2004; Holland & Roisman, 2010; Jacobson et al., 2000; Roisman, 2007), and Newton and Sanford (2003) had partners take turns discussing an issue on which they requested change from their spouses.

While conflict discussions may provide a fairly realistic (and externally valid) portrayal of the couple relationship, it may be helpful to include other types of interactions as well to get a more complete picture. For example, some researchers began the interaction sequence with an events-of-the-day discussion and/or concluded with a pleasant topic discussion (Holland & Roisman, 2010; Levenson et al., 1994; Levenson & Gottman, 1983; Menchaca & Dehle, 2005; Roisman, 2007; Seider et al., 2009; Yuan et al., 2010).

The therapy setting actually provides an ideal context to assess couple functioning (and thus enhance external validity without using a contrived "conflict discussion" in a laboratory setting). Our current study is the first physiological study, of which we are aware, to examine couples' interactions during therapy sessions. As such, we have encountered multiple challenges associated with collecting physiological data in this interactional context: (a) physiological equipment hinders gestures and movement during the session, (b) the amount of data collected is enormous (e.g., three physiological measures assessed continuously for 50 minutes from three individuals) and, thus, difficult to clean and analyze, and

(c) session length is prolonged by at least 30 minutes, due to equipment hookup/ removal and baseline readings. Encouragingly, clients and therapists consistently report that session flow is not greatly altered by their attachment to physiological equipment during session, nor has participation in the study been associated with higher therapy dropout rates.

It is probable that external validity of physiological research is particularly enhanced by conducting it during therapy sessions. Nevertheless, the naturalistic process of therapy (or other unstructured dyadic interactions) poses unique problems not presented by standardized challenge tasks (e.g., conflict discussion, family interaction task, events-of-the-day discussion), thus threatening construct validity. Even with an imposed coding system, "critical events" during therapy interactions (e.g., cognitive interventions, behavioral interventions, therapist anxiety) can vary by length, prompt, content, and sequence, among many other factors. Obviously, without standardized segments of interactions, it is impossible to conduct analyses examining between-individual differences. Precautions should be made to ensure some standardized elements (e.g., mode of therapy, interventions, goals of session). Developing a coding system shapes the entire research process and increases the validity and reliability of the measurement of events.

Interactional Coding Systems

For observational coding purposes, it is essential that video software be linked with the physiological recording software. Since the coding of therapy sessions (to be linked with physiological responses) is quite novel, we have recently created a coding system for marking critical therapeutic events in session. As this study is in the early stages, we have opted against concurrently coding clients' affect/behavior, because the time involved would be extensive. Our coding system focuses on three groups of therapeutic behaviors, with associated subgroups: (1) cognitive interventions (e.g., reframing, point processing, interrupting/stopping, goal-setting, exception-finding), (2) behavioral interventions (e.g., enactment, showing affection, sculpting, turning toward, active listening), and (3) therapist anxiousness (e.g., inactivity, "manic" behavior). In addition, we use modifiers to code both the intensity of the intervention (i.e., high versus low) and the focus of the intervention (i.e., directed at husband, wife, or the couple). There is much research to be done in the creation, validation, and replication of coding systems to be used for studies of physiological responses during couple/family therapy sessions.

Laboratory and Participant Setup

Some general considerations should be made when setting up the laboratory environment for physiological data collection (per our research experience and advice from other physiological researchers), in order to enhance measurement validity. It is important to record room temperature and humidity before and after each session of data collection (and keep it relatively consistent across participants), as these variables particularly affect accuracy of SCL readings. Additionally, instructions about electrode storage (airtight bags, cool temperature, etc.) should be followed explicitly, since incorrect storage may obscure accurate readings.

For physiological measures that are collected via electrode readings, several other precautions should be taken during participant hookup. Prior to attaching electrodes to participants' bodies, it is important that each area for electrode placement be cleaned (e.g., alcohol swabs on areas other than palms, hands washed with soap and scrubbed with brillo pads). Jewelry should be removed because it may also interfere with electromagnetic signals. Additionally, participants should be instructed to minimize their movements, since these create artifacts in the physiological data. It is, however, important to note that movement restriction may detract from external validity. Luckily, participants in our current study have not complained about restricted mobility, and the data cleaning process has not been overly problematic due to movement artifacts.

Assessment of Baseline Periods

In order to calculate change in participants' physiological responding (based on coded interactional events), researchers must measure baseline periods prior to the interactions. In general, baseline periods are conducted prior to the engagement tasks and range from 2 to 10 minutes, with a length of 3 minutes being most common. These are best conceptualized as pre-task periods (rather than pure baseline periods) because participants may experience anxiety induced by the lab environment and/or informed consent procedures (including knowledge of the upcoming task, whether it be conflict discussion or therapy session). The previously cited researchers consistently assess physiology during a nonspeaking, pre-task period. In addition, psychophysiologists in related fields of human development research assess physiology during a speaking pre-task period, since motor effects of speech production have been associated with cardiovascular reactivity and respiratory rate (Denver, Reed, & Porges, 2007). None of the cited researchers within our review of the literature conducted a speaking baseline period, although many listed this as a limitation.

Several validity issues related to baseline assessment are worth reviewing. Since the interaction tasks involve two (or more) participants, one dilemma is whether the baseline period should be assessed while the participants are alone or together. Although a joint baseline period may be a more valid assessment of pre-task functioning (because the task involves both participants), it also may be affected by individuals' engagement in surreptitious conversation and/or their raised discomfort due to sitting silently with another person. Thus, either option presents validity concerns. In the cited literature, baseline readings were usually taken with both partners in the room (Heffner et al., 2004; Holland & Roisman, 2010; Menchaca & Dehle, 2005; Roisman, 2007). Additionally, a few of the researchers addressed this construct validity issue specifically by trying to minimize silence-discomfort and/or conversation. Gottman et al. (1995) requested participants to relax with eyes closed, Smith et al. (1998) seated them across from each other with a removable partition between, and Newton and Sanford (2003) swiveled partners' chairs to face away from each other.

A related validity concern is whether participants should sit silently or complete a focused, yet nonchallenging activity (in order to maintain consistent involvement in a minimally demanding task, rather than allowing mindless drifting). Most of these studies had participants sit silently without participating in an activity, even requesting that they attempt to empty their minds of thoughts/feelings (e.g., Holland & Roisman, 2010; Roisman, 2007). Nevertheless, Smith et al. (1998) had participants view consecutive pairs of photographs and indicate which of the two they preferred.

For our current research study, we collect a 3-minute nonspeaking baseline measurement reading with all three participants (i.e., male/female clients and therapist) in the therapy room. In order to minimize discomfort and potential conversation, we show a video segment of calming nature scenes. In addition, we also collect a 3-minute speaking baseline measurement, during which each of the three participants alternate reading from an elementary reading–level script (unrelated to therapy topics).

Potential Confounding Variables

Physiological functioning can be affected by numerous other demographic and health-related factors. The ANS is influenced by age. In particular, older individuals display decreases in sympathetic and parasympathetic innervation and may be less aroused by conflict (Levenson et al., 1994). Additionally, health condition and behaviors (e.g., body mass index, physical exercise, nicotine/caffeine/alcohol use, medication usage, menstrual cycle phase) may affect HR (De Geus, Boomsma, & Snieder, 2003).

Sex and race/ethnicity also affect physiological responding. There is limited evidence that men and women have different tolerance levels for heightened physiological arousal (Gottman & Levenson, 1988), lending support to Pennebaker and Roberts' (1992) gender differences model that men are more attentive to internal cues of their affective states, while women more often consider external, situational cues. Additionally, several researchers have found links between race/ethnicity and physiological activity, with African Americans displaying decreased electrodermal responses (El-Sheikh & Erath, 2011).

Calculating Physiological Responses During Interactions

There are two primary methods used to calculate change in physiological responding from baseline period to coded interactions. The more oft-used and simple method involves calculating a "change score" by subtracting the mean baseline score from the mean interaction score; this method was defended conceptually and statistically by Rogosa (1995). A more complex method is particularly useful, since it accounts for between-subject differences in baseline readings. For this, a "reactivity score" (i.e., residualized change score) is calculated as the unstandardized residuals of the change score (i.e., mean interaction value minus mean baseline value) regressed onto the mean baseline score. These residualized change scores are particularly useful because they account for the influence of baseline levels on the range of potential reactivity (e.g., ceiling or floor effects). In addition to the primary methods of calculating change scores and residualized change scores, others simply use the physiological level during the target experience (e.g., conflict discussion) and others model change "longitudinally" during the course of an interaction. These change scores and residualized change scores are used in an analytic model as predictor or outcome variables.

Final Remarks

As our knowledge increases concerning physiology within the context of couple and family relationships, there will be increasing examples of interventions designed to affect physiological responding. There is encouraging preliminary evidence that ANS responses may be influenced by psychosocial interventions (e.g., Raine et al., 2001). Over the last 40 years, theoretical models of intervention have been based upon a symptom perspective. Groundbreaking physiological research ushers us into an age of adaptation based upon psychophysiology, which has potential to unlock innumerable mysteries about mechanisms of change and adaptive outcomes.

Acknowledgment: We gratefully acknowledge contributions made by Stephen Erath, Ph.D. of Auburn University as an adviser and editor of this chapter.

References

Beauchaine, T. (2001). Vagal tone, development, and Gray's motivational theory: Toward an integrated model of autonomic nervous system functioning in psychopathology. *Development and Psychopathology, 13,* 183–214.

Bornstein, M., & Suess, P. (2000). Child and mother cardiac vagal tone: Continuity, stability, and concordance across the first 5 years. *Developmental Psychology, 36,* 54–65.

Brodal, A. (2004). The vestibular nuclei in the macaque monkey. *Journal of Comparative Neurology, 227,* 252–266.

Brown, P. C., & Smith, T. W. (1992). Social influence, marriage, and the heart: Cardiovascular consequences of interpersonal control in husbands and wives. *Health Psychology, 11,* 88–96.

Caciopppo, J., Uchino, B., & Berntson, G. (1994). Individual differences in the autonomic origins of heart rate reactivity: The psychometrics of respiratory sinus arrhythmia and pre-ejection period. *Psychophysiology, 31,* 412–419.

Connell, A. M., Hughes-Scalise, A., Klostermann, S., & Azem, T. (2011). Maternal depression and the heart of parenting: Respiratory sinus arrhythmia and affective dynamics during parent–adolescent interactions. *Journal of Family Psychology, 25,* 653–662.

De Geus, E. J. C., Boomsma, D. I., & Snieder, H. (2003). Genetic correlation of exercise with heart rate and respiratory sinus arrhythmia. *Official Journal of the American College of Sports Medicine, 35,* 1287–1295.

Denver, J. W., Reed, S. F., & Porges, S. W. (2007). Methodological issues in the quantification of respiratory sinus arrhythmia. *Biological Psychology, 74,* 286–294.

El-Sheikh, M., & Erath, S. A. (2011). Family conflict, autonomic nervous system functioning, and child adaptation: State of the science and future directions. *Development and Psychopathology, 23,* 703–721.

El-Sheikh, M., Harger, J., & Whitson, S. (2001). Exposure to parental conflict and children's adjustment and physical health: The moderating role of vagal tone. *Child Development, 72,* 1617–1636.

El-Sheikh, M., Keller, P., & Erath, S. (2007). Marital conflict and risk for child maladjustment over time: Skin conductance level reactivity as a vulnerability factor. *Journal of Abnormal Child Psychology, 35,* 715–727.

Erath, S. A., El-Sheikh, M., & Cummings, E. M. (2009). Harsh parenting and child externalizing behavior: Skin conductance level reactivity as a moderator. *Child Development, 80,* 578–592.

Fowles, D. C., Kochanska, G., & Murray, K. (2000). Electrodermal activity and temperament in preschool children. *Psychophysiology, 37,* 777–787.

Gottman, J. M., Jacobson, N. S., Rushe, R. H., Shortt, J., Babcock, J., La Taillade, J. J., & Waltz, J. (1995). The relationship between heart rate reactivity, emotionally aggressive behavior, and general violence in batterers. *Journal of Family Psychology, 9,* 227–248.

Gottman, J. M., & Levenson, R. W. (1988). The social psychophysiology of marriage. In P. Noller & M. A. Fitzpatrick (Eds.), *Perspectives on marital interaction* (pp. 182–200). Clevedon, England: Multilingual Matters.

Hane, A., & Barrios, E. S. (2011). Mother and child interpretations of threat in ambiguous situations: Relations with child anxiety and autonomic responding. *Journal of Family Psychology, 25,* 644–652.

Heffner, K. L., Kiecolt-Glaser, J. K., Loving, T. J., Glaser, R., & Malarkey, W. B. (2004). Spousal support satisfaction as a modifier of physiological responses to marital conflict in younger and older couples. *Journal of Behavioral Medicine, 27,* 233–254.

Holland, A. S., & Roisman, G. I. (2010). Adult attachment security and young adults' dating relationships over time: Self-reported, observational, and physiological evidence. *Developmental Psychology, 46,* 552–557.

Jacobson, N. S., Gottman, J. M., Waltz, J., Rushe, R., Babcock, J., & Holtzworth-Munroe, A. (2000). Affect, verbal content, and psychophysiology in the arguments of couples with a violent husband. *Prevention & Treatment, 3,* 19a.

Katz, L., & Gottman, J. (1997). Buffering children from marital conflict and dissolution. *Journal of Clinical Child Psychology, 26,* 157–171.

Levenson, R. W., Carstensen, L. L., & Gottman, J. M. (1994). Influence of age and gender on affect, physiology, and their interrelations: A study of long-term marriages. *Journal of Personality and Social Psychology, 67,* 56–68.

Levenson, R. W., & Gottman, J. M. (1983). Marital interaction: Physiological linkage and affective exchange. *Journal of Personality and Social Psychology, 45,* 587–597.

Levenson, R.W., & Gottman, J.M. (1985). Physiological and affective predictors of change in relationship satisfaction. *Journal of Personality and Social Psychology, 49,* 85–94.

Lorber, M.F., & O'Leary, S.G. (2005). Mediated paths to overreactive discipline: Mothers' experienced emotion, appraisals, and physiological responses. *Journal of Consulting and Clinical Psychology, 73,* 972–981.

Matveev, M., Prokopova, R., & Nachev, C. (2006). *Normal and abnormal circadian characteristics in autonomic cardiac control.* New York: Nova Science Publishers.

Menchaca, D., & Dehle, C. (2005). Marital quality and physiological arousal: How do I love thee? Let my heartbeat count the ways. *American Journal of Family Therapy, 33,* 117–130.

Newton, T.L., & Sanford, J.M. (2003). Conflict structure moderates associations between cardiovascular reactivity and negative marital interaction. *Health Psychology, 22,* 270–278.

Pennebaker, J.W, & Roberts, T.A. (1992). Toward a his and hers theory of emotion: Gender differences in visceral perception. *Journal of Social and Clinical Psychology, 11,* 199–212.

Porges, S.W. (2001). The polyvagal theory: Phylogenetic substrates of a social nervous system. *International Journal of Psychophysiology, 42,* 123–146.

Porges, S.W. (2006). Asserting the role of biobehavioral sciences in translational research: The behavioral neurobiology revolution. *Developmental Psychopathology, 18,* 923–933.

Porges, S.W. (2007). The polyvagal perspective. *Biological Psychology, 74,* 116–143.

Raine, A., Venables, P.H., Dalais, C., Mellingen, K., Reynolds, C., & Mednick, S.A. (2001). Early educational and health enrichment at age 3–5 years is associated with increased autonomic and central nervous system arousal and orienting at age 11 years: Evidence from the Mauritius Child Health Project. *Psychophysiology, 38,* 254–266.

Raine, A., Venables, P., & Williams, M. (1990). Autonomic orienting responses in 15-year-old male subjects and criminal behavior at age 24. *American Journal of Psychiatry, 147,* 933–937.

Rogosa, D. (1995). Myths and methods: "Myths about longitudinal research" plus supplemental questions. In J.M. Gottman (Ed.), *The analysis of change* (pp. 3–65). Mahwah, NJ: Erlbaum.

Roisman, G.I. (2007). The psychophysiology of adult attachment relationships: Autonomic reactivity in marital and premarital interactions. *Developmental Psychology, 43,* 39–53.

Seider, B.H., Hirschberger, G., Nelson, K.L., & Levenson, R.W. (2009). We can work it out: Age differences in relational pronouns, physiology, and behavior in marital conflict. *Psychology and Aging, 24,* 604–613.

Sheppes, G., Catran, E., & Meiran, N. (2009). Reappraisal (but not distraction) is going to make you sweat: Physiological evidence for self-control effort. *International Journal of Psychophysiology, 71,* 91–96.

Smith, T.W., Gallo, L.C., Goble, L., Ngu, L.Q., & Stark, K.A. (1998). Agency, communion, and cardiovascular reactivity during marital interaction. *Health Psychology, 17,* 537–545.

Thayer, J., & Lane, R. (2009). Claude Bernard and the heart-brain connection: Further elaboration of a model of neurovisceral integration. *Neuroscience and Biobehavioral Reviews, 33,* 81–88.

van Goozen, S., Matthys, W., Cohen-Kettenis, P., Buitelaar, J., & van Engeland, H. (2000). Hypothalamic-pituitary-adrenal axis and automatic nervous system activity in disruptive children and matched controls. *Journal of the American Academy of Child and Adolescent Psychiatry, 29,* 1438–1445.

Wegner, D.M., & Gold, D.B. (1995). Fanning old flames: Emotional and cognitive effects of suppressing thoughts of a past relationship. *Journal of Personality & Social Psychology, 68,* 782–792.

Yuan, J.W., McCarthy, M., Holley, S.R., & Levenson, R.W. (2010). Physiological down-regulation and positive emotion in marital interaction. *Emotion, 10*(4), 467–474. doi: 10.1037/a0018699

10

ELECTROENCEPHALOGRAPHY IN MARRIAGE AND FAMILY THERAPY RESEARCH

Trent S. Parker, Kristyn M. Blackburn,
and Ronald J. Werner-Wilson

Introduction

A variety of noninvasive methods exist that measure brain structure and activity associated with human behavior (Harmon-Jones & Winkielman, 2007). Data gathered from these methods provide unique insight into a wide range of behavioral and psychological topics that are relevant to marriage and family therapy (MFT). We will provide a brief review of the primary methods of collecting data associated with brain structure and activity that may be of interest to MFT researchers.

There has been increasing interest in implications of brain structure, brain organization, and brain development on relationships between couples and families. These implications also carry over to psychotherapy. These approaches are from the field of social neuroscience, which refers to an integrative field that examines how nervous (central and peripheral), endocrine, and immune systems are involved in sociocultural processes (Harmon-Jones & Winkielman, 2007, p. 4). Cozolino (2006) suggests that the brain is a social organ and that there is a bidirectional relationship between brain development and social development. Mona Fishbane (2007) highlighted this relationship by suggesting: "Many of our best systemic practices and theories are strengthened by the field of interpersonal neurobiology. . . . Our basic beliefs about systems, contexts, and socially constructed meanings are validated by brain science" (p. 410). Electroencephalography (EEG) has the potential to increase our understanding of the impact of brain activity via basic research on couple and family interactions and direct measurement of brain activity during therapy sessions and outcome studies.

Within the past few years, MFT researchers have begun to incorporate EEG methodology into their research. For instance, a study conducted by Blackburn, Parker, Werner-Wilson, and Wood (2012) used EEG methodology to examine the effects of client self-disclosure on the therapist's level of engagement during therapy sessions. Engagement of the therapist was assessed by measuring therapist's brain activity via EEG. They found that the more clients self-disclosed, the more engaged therapists became in session. Additionally, therapists' engagement in session was positively correlated with clients' ratings of session smoothness and the therapeutic relationship. Studies like this have the potential to provide MFT researchers with unique insight into the therapy process and interpersonal processes that occur between couple and family members.

This chapter provides a context for EEG, a cost-effective and minimally invasive method to measure electrical brain activity. Functional magnetic resonance imaging (fMRI) and positron emission tomography (PET) are two other frequently used imaging methods, which are beyond the scope of this chapter. However, to provide a context for research in this area, a brief review of fMRI and PET methods will be provided.

Putting EEG in Context

Functional magnetic resonance imaging assesses brain activity as indicated by increases or decreases in regional blood flow (Wager, Hernandez, Jonides, & Lindquist, 2007). This imaging technique has been used to provide information on brain activation that occurs in response to cognitive and behavioral tasks, as well as in the study of emotion (Ryan & Alexander, 2008; Wager et al.). Functional MRI, compared with other methods like EEG, has higher spatial and temporal resolution. The images are obtained quickly from any clinically available scanner. The method requires that the subject be lying down and is not suitable for individuals who have metal implants. Recent studies that have used fMRI have studied topics including meditation, personality, emotion, and addiction (Canli et al., 2001; Engelmann et al., 2012; Lutz, Dunne, & Davidson, 2007; Ochsner, Bunge, Gross, & Gabrieli, 2002).

Positron emission tomography measures glucose metabolism, oxygen consumption, and cerebral blood flow (Wager et al., 2007). Images of physiological and metabolic responses within the brain are constructed through the use of positron-emitting radiotracers (Ryan & Alexander, 2008; Wager et al.). The radiotracers are compounds that bind to molecules like oxygen and glucose found in the brain. The radiotracer is injected into the bloodstream and produces a steady concentration of the tracer within the brain. Scans produce a three-dimensional image that displays areas of the brain where metabolic activity has occurred.

With the development of other methods, like EEG, the use of PET has lessened for cognitive activation studies. PET requires a great deal of space, and the cost of operation is high. Additionally, the method relies on the introduction of radiotracers into the subject's bloodstream. Compared with other methods, PET does offer more flexibility for monitoring the activity of many molecules within the brain. Topics that have been examined with the use of PET methods include schizophrenia, substance abuse, mood disorders, and autism (Andreasen, Calage, & O'Leary, 2008; Conway et al., 2012; Pagani et al., 2012; Weerts et al., 2011).

Together, fMRI and PET methods have made valuable contributions to the field of social neuroscience. However, as discussed, the methods are invasive and costly. The remainder of the review will focus on the use of EEG, which is an imaging method that is more accessible to the MFT researcher.

Measuring Electrical Brain Activity: EEG

EEG is a relatively inexpensive and noninvasive method to measure brain function and make inferences about electrical brain activity. Data gathered from EEG studies have contributed to research concerning cognitive processes, emotional function, and development (Davidson, Jackson, & Larson, 2000). Studies that use EEG are advantageous in that they provide researchers the ability to collect data with millisecond temporal resolution (i.e., how quickly brain activity can be collected after it occurs; Harmon-Jones & Beer, 2009; Pizzagalli, 2007), providing near-instantaneous feedback related to regional brain activity associated with various behavioral tasks, which is particularly useful for social science research. For example, the temporal resolution would allow the measurement of brain activity within a millisecond after the introduction of an intervention.

EEG records electrical brain activity directly from the scalp of the participant through the systematic placement of electrodes. The electrodes are designed to detect brain activity resulting from changes in electrical voltages inside of the brain that result from action potentials and postsynaptic potentials (Davidson et al., 2000; Harmon-Jones & Beer, 2009; Pizzagalli, 2007). The timing and arrangement of the neurons involved in action potentials prevent the changes in voltage that they create from being detected by EEG. However, the ability of postsynaptic potentials to summate makes it possible for EEG to record electrical brain activity (Pizzagalli).

The electrical activity generated by individual neurons is small (Davidson et al., 2000; Harmon-Jones & Beer, 2009; Pizzagalli, 2007). Therefore, any brain activity recorded at the scalp is a reflection of thousands of neurons acting synchronously. The consistent orientation of these neurons allows for the summation of recordable electrical activity at the scalp (Pizzagalli, 2007). Synchrony found to exist between neighboring neurons is referred to as local-scale synchronization, while synchrony between large neuronal assemblies of distant brain regions is referred to as large-scale synchronization.

The raw EEG signal appears as a complex waveform analyzed in a temporal or frequency domain (Harmon-Jones & Beer, 2009). In other words, the waveform appears as a graph, with the x-axis representing time and the y-axis representing the oscillations in EEG activity. These oscillations are produced via the interaction between the thalamic and cortical networks of the brain (Pizzagalli, 2007). These oscillations, also referred to as brain waves, are used to determine levels of

Table 10.1 Frequently Studied Brain Waves

Wave	Frequency	Comments
Delta	< 4 Hz	Associated primarily with sleep. High amplitude in awake adult suggests cerebral dysfunction
Theta	4–8 Hz	Increased in theta suggests drowsiness. Excessive presence that is asymmetrical may suggest depression or other emotional disorder
Alpha	8–13 Hz	Tend to be stronger when eyes closed. Associated with relaxation and meditation. High frontal alpha may be present in ADHD and depression
Beta	13–21 Hz	Present during tasks requiring cognitive activity. Excessive beta may also be present with sleep disorders and learning disorders
High beta	20–32 Hz	Peak performance, cognitive processing, worry, anxiety, overthinking, ruminating, and obsessive-compulsive disorder
Gamma	38–42 Hz	Emotion and negative emotion processing
Mu	8–13 Hz	Located over the sensorimotor cortex

brain activity. The brain waves most frequently used in research are presented in Table 10.1. For a more in-depth reading, see the studies by Rowan and Tolunsky (2003) and Demos (2005).

EEG signals are representative of the potential difference between two electrodes, an active electrode and a reference electrode (Pizzagalli, 2007). The quality of data obtained from an EEG recording is, in part, dependent upon the positioning of the electrode and the contact made between the electrode and the participant's scalp. The 10–20 system of electrode placement introduced by Jasper (1958) is a widely used system that ensures uniform and homogeneous coverage of the scalp for reliable measurement, as well as the ability to make comparisons between studies (Davidson et al., 2000; Pizzagalli, 2007).

EEG is measured from electrodes, commonly made of tin (Sn) or silver/silver chloride (Ag/AgCl) placed on the scalp. It is imperative that all electrodes be of the same metallic composition to ensure accurate recording of electrical activity (Davidson et al., 2000). The International 10–20 system (see Figure 10.1) involves a series of numbers and letters that represent different locations on the brain (Jasper, 1958). The first letter of the name of the electrode refers to the name of the brain region over which the electrode sits: Fp (frontal pole), F (frontal region), C (central region), P (parietal region), T (temporal region), and O (occipital region). Immediately following the letter is a number. Odd numbers represent the left hemisphere, while even numbers represent the right hemisphere. As the distance from the middle of the head increases, the numbers also increase. The letter "z" designates the midline that runs from the

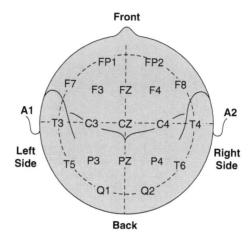

Figure 10.1 International 10–20 system of electrode placement.

front to the back of the head. Recording eye movement is common during the recording of EEG, as it facilitates artifact removal, which will be discussed later.

Equipment/Software

There are many excellent resources that describe equipment associated with collecting psychophysiologial data, software for data processing and reduction, and training to collect EEG data (cf. Curtin, Lozano, & Allen, 2007; Harmon-Jones & Peterson, 2009; Mendes, 2009). These resources primarily describe data collection from one person at a time rather than from couples or families. We will present: (a) basic considerations for collecting data, including collecting data from couples and families, (b) laboratory design, (c) data collection equipment, and (d) data processing and reduction software.

Basic Considerations for Collecting Data

There are at least four basic considerations associated with collecting psycho-physiological data (Curtin et al., 2007). First, you need to invest in your own lab or collaborate with someone who has already developed a lab. While it may be cost-efficient to collaborate, you may have difficulty adapting your research protocol to an existing lab, especially if you intend to collect physiological data during interactions, because most labs are designed to collect data from one person at a time. Second, what is your degree of technical proficiency and experience associated with collecting these data? Designing a lab, obtaining equipment, training personnel, and interpreting results requires a high degree

146

of knowledge about human anatomy, physiology, brain structure, and brain function. It also requires some comfort with using technology. Third, will your lab be multipurpose to provide flexibility or dedicated to a particular research area? Purchasing dedicated equipment may be more cost-effective, but it may limit future research. Once the initial purchase has been made, it might be difficult to locate funds to obtain more sophisticated equipment or update current equipment. Fourth, will you collect data from multiple physiological channels (e.g., EEG, heart rate, skin conductance)? EEG equipment will require an investment of at least $25,000. In addition, a computer will need to be dedicated to each EEG unit. Thus, collecting data from multiple family members simultaneously during interactions will require a budget of at least $50,000 to $75,000 for EEG equipment. We recommend collaborating with an existing lab in order to gain experience prior to investing in the development of your own lab.

Laboratory Design

The present material is based on recommendations made by Curtin, Lozano, and Allen (2007). A basic psychophysiological laboratory must be free of electrical interference that impacts data acquisition and ambient noise that distracts the research participant. At minimum, a lab needs to include an amplifier for collecting physiological signals, a computer to digitize and record the signals, and an observation room to monitor data collection processes. In most physiological labs designed to collect data from individuals, some method will be included to introduce a stimulus and assess the participant's response to a particular event of interest, such as the introduction of an anxiety-provoking visual stimulus. Curtin and colleagues provide a detailed description of issues to consider for this type of research. For couple and family research, the stimulus is likely to be interactions between family members. As such, a family interaction lab should include some mechanism for recording these interactions, usually a video recording system capable of recording each participant. The observation room should be in close proximity (ideally adjacent) to the data collection lab so that problems (e.g., an electrode coming loose) associated with data collection can be remedied quickly. The observation room should include video screens to permit viewing participants and the data acquisition computer to monitor problems with recording EEG activity.

Data Collection Equipment

Earlier, we suggested that it is important to identify the scope of your research in order to determine your equipment needs. Some of the autonomic nervous system (ANS) equipment that is used to measure heart rate, skin conductance, or respiration is also capable of measuring EEG from a limited number of sites. It is not uncommon for researchers to focus on a single site, such as Cz, to assess

general functioning. We recommend that researchers obtain equipment that can measure at least two sites from the 10–20 system in order to collect data associated with site or wave coherence. More sophisticated EEG data acquisition includes amplifiers that measure at least 19 sites based on the International 10–20 system described earlier (see Figure 10.1); other amplifiers, known as a dense array system, can measure 32, 64, 128, and even 256 sites. The increased number of sites provides better spatial resolution, but at a high cost (at least $75,000 per unit for a 32 channel system). Because of the cost, we do not recommend obtaining the dense array systems. Collecting data from the 10–20 system to map influences of family interaction on electrical brain activity is more than adequate at this point in time. In order to take better advantage of the temporal resolution offered by EEG, a vertical interval time code (VITC) system is recommended. This type of system allows research to identify correspondence between a video recording of therapy, couple, or family interactions and physiological measurements such as EEG.

Participant Preparation

Many EEG systems have calibration routines that can be used. It is highly recommended that researchers run these routines prior to participant arrival to ensure that the hardware and software is working properly. Failure to do so may result in unusable data.

When preparing participants for the collection of EEG data, it is important to make them feel comfortable throughout the entire process. The equipment used is often unfamiliar and may appear intimidating to the participants. Therefore, showing each participant the materials that will be used during the study and explaining each step of the process is recommended. Researchers should be encouraged to act in a professional manner so as to avoid altering the mood of the participants prior to data collection.

The majority of EEG systems require that the electrical impedance of the scalp be less than 5,000 ohms (Harmon-Jones & Beer, 2009). Impedance refers to the measure of opposition that a circuit presents to the passage of a current when a voltage is applied. The reduction of impedance can be accomplished in several ways. The participant may first be asked to brush his or her hair for approximately 5 minutes. This reduces any charge that the participant's hair may carry. The next thing to be done is to exfoliate the areas of the scalp on which the electrodes will be positioned. An alcohol prep pad may be used to do this.

In order to place the electrode cap on the participant, there are several steps that must be followed. The first thing to do is to use a metric tape to measure the distance from the nasion (point just below the eyebrows where there is an indentation at the top of the nose) to the inion (the bump on the occipital lobe at the back of the head). Ten percent of this total distance (in centimeters) is calculated and measured up from the nasion. This spot is marked with a wax pencil on the participant's head. Cap size is then determined by measuring the circumference of the participant's head. The caps often come in small, medium, and large sizes. It is important to select the cap size that will allow for the snuggest but most comfortable fit. The cap is then lined up with the wax mark and stretched over the participant's head. The cap is then remeasured to ensure that it is in the correct location on the scalp. The midline electrodes should sit on the midline of the scalp. To ensure this fit, the distance from the preauricular indentation in front of each ear is measured and the midpoint is calculated. The Cz electrode should sit on the calculated midpoint.

EEG Research of Interest to MFT

The field of social neuroscience as it relates to EEG provides a standardized and well-established set of brain waves and areas of activation that are of potential interest to the field of MFT. While many of these procedures have not yet been introduced into MFT research, this section of the chapter will focus on these sets of procedures and how they may be used in MFT research.

Theta-beta Ratio

Theta and beta waves (see Table 10.1) are used in the assessment of attention deficit/hyperactivity disorder (ADHD). Since theta is a slow wave, its presence in comparison with beta, a fast wave, is an indication that the area of the brain being measured is functioning relatively slowly. This slowing of brain functioning is associated with ADHD. Research has empirically established the ability of EEG to differentiate between those with ADHD and those without (see Monastra, Lubar, & Linden, 2001).

Lubar (1995) demonstrated that a single site, Cz, could be used to determine the presence of ADHD. Monastra et al. (2001) have developed a procedure to assess for ADHD, as well as established cutoff scores for the theta-beta ratios that suggest the presence of ADHD for several age groups. Linden (2011) recommends that additional instruments be used to assess for ADHD, such as a computer program designed to measure impulsivity and attention. Doing so increases the confidence of the construct validity of the measurement. In terms of conducting research on ADHD, it is also preferred to have an additional assessment tool to increase the validity of the study.

Outcome studies in MFT exist for children with ADHD. While medication is considered the treatment of choice, the literature suggests that MFT can have an impact on ADHD symptoms (Northey, Wells, Silverman, & Bailey, 2003). One potential use of EEG in MFT research is in examining how MFT changes the theta-beta ratio. This would demonstrate not only behavioral changes, but changes with brain functioning as well. If considering using EEG to measure ADHD, it must be noted that making changes in brain waves that impact behavior can require 6 months (Linden, Habib, & Radojevic, 1996). Thus, ample time must be allowed.

Frontal Cortical Alpha Asymmetry

The frontal lobe of the brain is generally recognized as being involved with attention, as well as emotional states. Developing within the social neuroscience literature are empirical findings that different levels of activity between the left and right frontal lobes are related to emotion (Coan & Allen, 2004). The differences in activity are measured by the amount of alpha wave (see Table 10.1) present on each side of the frontal lobe. This difference is referred to as frontal alpha asymmetry. By examining frontal alpha asymmetry, two models have developed. The first focuses on emotional valence, which suggests that greater left frontal activity, compared with the right, indicates the experience and expression of positive emotions (e.g., happiness), while the inverse indicates negative emotions (e.g., sadness). For example, increased right frontal activity has been demonstrated to be related to depression (Gotlib, Ranganath, & Rosenfeld, 1998). Due to some inconsistency of findings, the second model developed that focuses on the motivational direction. This model suggests that greater left frontal activity, compared with right frontal activity, indicates approach tendencies, while the inverse indicates withdrawal tendencies (Harmon-Jones, 2007).

To measure frontal alpha asymmetry, any of the frontal sites may be used (FP1/2, FP3/4, or FP7/8), but it is recommended that more than one pair be measured. To maintain consistency in research, the frontal alpha asymmetry is calculated by subtracting the log of the left alpha absolute power from the log of the right alpha absolute power (Harmon-Jones & Allen, 1997). Since alpha is considered a slow wave, a result from this formula that is positive indicates greater left activity, whereas a negative number indicates greater right activity.

Frontal alpha asymmetry has been used in examining couple interactions (Kimberly, Werner-Wilson, Parker, Lianekhammy, 2012; Werner-Wilson et al., 2011), as well as the therapy process (Blackburn et al., 2012). Parker, Blackburn, Hawks, Werner-Wilson, and Wood (2013) collected EEG data from clients and therapists in six therapy sessions. After each couple and therapist had electrodes placed on their heads according to the 10–20 system of electrode placement (see above), baseline measurements were taken. This involved having the couple and therapist sit quietly with their eyes open and then with their eyes closed. A 40-minute therapy session was then conducted. Frontal alpha asymmetry calculations were made during baseline and the therapy session. These calculations were then correlated to how empathic the clients perceived the therapist and how the therapist perceived the therapeutic relationship. The results indicated that the greater the change in therapists' frontal alpha asymmetry toward left activation, the more empathic the clients perceived the therapist. Additionally, there was a positive correlation between therapists' perception of the therapeutic relationship and their change in frontal alpha asymmetry toward greater left activation.

Cross-frequency Coupling

Schutter and Knyazev (2012) suggest that examining the coherence between different waves is another important part of understanding the human brain. In other words, it is important to examine various brain waves (see Table 10.1) being in sync with each other and any correlated phenomena. Evidence is emerging that suggests that the presence of anxiety is indicated by coherence between delta and theta (Knyazev, 2007). It has been demonstrated experimentally that administering cortisol increases this correlation (van Peer, Roelofs, & Spinhoven, 2008), which strengthens the findings that increased correlations between delta and theta suggest the presence of anxiety. More recently, Putman (2011) found a negative correlation between delta-beta coherence and attentional avoidance of threatening pictorial stimuli. Miskovic, Moscovitch, McCabe, Antony, and Schmidt (2011) have used this developing area of research to demonstrate that changes in the EEG take place during treatment for social anxiety disorder. Similar procedures can be taken to determine the impact that MFT has on brain processes and anxiety. It can also play a role in measuring the presence of anxiety in therapy sessions and in couple and family interactions.

Mirror Neuron System

The mirror neuron system (MNS; Rizzolatti & Craighero, 2004) is described as a system in the brain that activates when observing behavior or emotion in another individual (see Pfeifer & Dapretto, 2009). Suppression of the mu wave (see Table 10.1) has been validated as a way to measure the activity of the MNS (Oberman, Pineda, & Ramachandran, 2007). The MNS has been suggested to play a role in empathy (Pfeifer, Iacoboni, Mazziotta, & Dapretto, 2008), which has implications for researching the therapeutic relationship, as well as couple or family interactions. In couple interactions where there is a high degree of empathy, we would also expect to see an increase in the activation of the MNS. However, it also has interesting implications for the idea of interpersonal boundaries or differentiation (Bowen, 1978), for example. Exploring the relationship between MNS activation and levels of differentiation within therapeutic, couple, and family relationships would be an important contribution to the existing literature that fits within an MFT perspective.

Measuring the mu wave presents some challenges during social interactions. The mu wave lasts for only a brief period (0.5 to 2 seconds) and is recorded over C3, C4, and Cz in the absence of movement. Because of the temporal resolution offered by EEG, it is possible to measure mu waves, but its presence will not last as long as those of other waves. It should also be noted that the mu wave (8–13 Hz) overlaps with alpha. There are differences between the two, such as alpha being located more in the visual processing area of the occipital region, while mu is located in the frontoparietal networks (Pineda, 2005). Care should be taken in distinguishing between the two waves.

Advantages and Challenges

Artifact

EEG is the only measure of brain activity capable of tolerating some head movement and that does not require the subject to be lying down (Davidson et al., 2000). However, EEG is susceptible to both biological and nonbiological sources of artifact. An artifact is any electrical signal of noncerebral origin. It is best to first attempt to eliminate all possible sources of artifact prior to data collection, but it is still likely that artifact will need to be removed before analysis is conducted.

Sources of biological artifact include muscle activity, eye blinks and movements, heartbeat, and sweating (Pizzagalli, 2007). Signals obtained from muscle artifact are usually at a higher frequency than those obtained from brain activity. However, some artifact does occur within the range of brain activity; consequently, it is best to ask participants to limit movement. Research that evokes emotion is often susceptible to artifact because of the associated facial expressions. Eye movement artifact also exists. It is recommended that participants be instructed to limit head movement as much as possible during EEG recording. However, this must be balanced with the understanding that some movement will take place as a process of social interaction. Measuring eye movement through the use of electrodes is often practiced when using EEG. To record eye movement, electrodes are attached to the face and are referenced to each other. For measuring horizontal eye movement, one electrode is placed on the right temple and another placed on the left temple.

Nonbiological artifact also exists. This includes external electrical signals detected from elevators, electrical lights, computers, and other electronic devices (Pizzagalli, 2007). Most of these artifact sources can be handled through filtering the signal during data collection. It is important to mention that electrodes themselves may also be a source of nonbiological artifact. Electrodes must be washed after each use to prevent corrosion.

As mentioned, it is very likely that EEG data will contain artifact. This has implications for internal validity because it is important to be confident that the relationships between variables found are based on brain activity and not eye and head movement or environmental factors. This also has implications for external validity. If brain activity is not being measured, any conclusions made are questionable. Because of the threat to internal and external validity, visual and automatic artifact removal is therefore important before any analyses are conducted. Removing artifact from data may occur in the proprietary software or in aftermarket software that may include automatic or semiautomatic rejection of bad data, as well as a database that provides the opportunity to compare research subjects with normed data by age. These databases may be particularly useful for therapists who use EEG.

Another threat to construct validity and internal validity is the removal of artifact in EEG data. After artifacts are removed, only a percentage of the actual EEG data remains. There is no rule in the literature at the time of this writing as to what percentage should remain, although some software packages require a minimum amount in order to perform analyses. In any case, the higher the percentage of remaining EEG data, the better the validity of the study.

Additional Comments

An advantage of research conducted with EEG methodology is its relatively inexpensive cost of operation and the excellent temporal resolution it offers (Pizzagalli, 2007). The millisecond temporal resolution offered by EEG is ideal for linking behavior that dynamically changes over time with brain activation or deactivation. Any change in neuronal activation can be instantaneously detected by changes in EEG signal (Davidson et al., 2000).

However, EEG provides poor spatial resolution compared with other techniques that rely on metabolic or hemodynamic imaging methods (Davidson et al., 2000). Because of the nature of EEG, we cannot assume that a particular activation reflects a specific underlying neuroanatomical localization. The inability to use EEG to infer specific sources of change in electrical potential has methodological implications that make it difficult for researchers to arrive at definitive conclusions. This can threaten a study's construct validity when attempting to study specific brain structures. If studying specific brain structures, it is more appropriate to use one of the other brain imaging techniques.

Most EEG researchers have their own equipment rather than relying on someone else's (Harmon-Jones & Beer, 2009). This often makes the technique more accessible for research purposes and reduces the cost of operation. For systemic studies, this equipment can also be situated in the same room and multiple family members can be connected to individual machines, as was earlier discussed. Because some movement is tolerated by the devices and the participants do not need to be lying down, EEG makes the collection of data regarding systemic interaction feasible.

Although using EEG is cheaper than other brain imaging techniques, it still requires a monetary investment. For example, because of the cost, research using EEG in social neuroscience tends to have a smaller sample size, ranging between 8 and 160 (Werner-Wilson et al., 2011). Studies that fall into the smaller sample sizes are limited in their external validity. An additional threat to external validity stems from the participants having several electrodes, which can be cumbersome, attached to their scalps during interactions. Clearly, this is different from interactions they would have outside of the lab.

As a result of the smaller sample sizes, the number of statistical operations available is also limited due to power considerations. Most research using EEG in social neuroscience relies on correlation analyses. While this is not inherently a disadvantage, it does limit the conclusion validity. In addition, with smaller sample sizes, it can be difficult to achieve the traditional level of statistical significance ($p < .05$). In these cases, researchers can discuss findings in terms of trends and strength of correlations.

When conducting research using EEG, awareness of any brain injury a participant may have experienced is also an important consideration. Some software packages have normative databases that can report the likelihood that a participant experienced a brain injury. Assessing participants' medical history in a questionnaire is also a possible way of determining the appropriateness of someone to participate in a research protocol. Unless the study of brain injuries is part of the research question, brain injuries will cause unexpected waves (i.e., delta) to be more present than what is expected. Similarly, participants with epilepsy will also demonstrate unexpected wave patterns that could affect the outcome of the study. These become especially important to consider if the sample size is relatively small.

Conclusion

The use of EEG methodology in MFT research has promising implications. EEG provides researchers and clinicians alike with unique insight into many of the issues and topics of interest in systemic research. However, just like many other brain imaging methodologies, EEG possesses several advantages and disadvantages that must be taken into consideration prior to data collection. Information gathered using EEG has the potential to allow for the collaboration of systemic and neuroscientific researchers.

References

Andreasen, N. C., Calage, C. A., & O'Leary, D. S. (2008). Theory of mind and schizophrenia: A positron emission tomography study of medication-free patients. *Schizophrenia Bulletin, 34,* 708–719.

Blackburn, K. M., Parker, T. S., Werner-Wilson, R. J., & Wood, N. D. (2012). Effects of client self-disclosure on frontal alpha asymmetry in therapists. Manuscript submitted for publication.

Bowen, M. (1978). *Family therapy in clinical practice.* New York: Jason Aronson.

Canli, T., Zhao, Z., Desmond, J. E., Kang, E., Gross, J., & Gabrieli, J. D. E. (2001). An fMRI study of personality influences on brain reactivity to emotional stimuli. *BehavioralNeuroscience, 115,* 33–42.

Coan, J. A., & Allen, J. J. B. (2004). Frontal EEG asymmetry as a moderator and mediator of emotion. *Biological Psychology, 67,* 7–49. doi: 10.1016/j.biopsycho.2004.03.002

Conway, C. R., Sheline, Y. I., Chibnall, J. T., Bucholz, R. D., Price, J. L., Gangwani, S., & Mintun, M. A. (2012). Brain blood-flow change with acute vagus nerve stimulation in treatment-refractory major depressive disorder. *Brain Stimulation, 5,* 163–171.

Cozolino, L. (2006). *The neuroscience of human relationships: Attachment and the developing brain.* New York: Norton.

Curtin, J. J., Lozano, D. L., & Allen, J. J. B (2007). The psychophysiology laboratory. In J. A. Coan & J. J. B. Allen (Eds.), *The handbook of emotion elicitation and assessment* (pp. 398–425). New York: Oxford University Press.

Davidson, R. J., Jackson, D. C., & Larson, C. L. (2000). Human electroencephalography. In J. T. Cacioppo, L. G. Tassinary, & G. G. Berntson (Eds.), *Handbook of psychophysiology* (2nd ed., pp. 27–52). New York: Cambridge University Press.

Demos, J. H. (2005). *Getting started with neurofeedback*. New York: W.W. Norton & Co.

Engelmann, J.M., Versace, F., Robinson, J.D., Minnix, J.A., Lam, C.Y., Cui, Y., Brown, V.L., & Cinciripini, P.M. (2012). Neural substrates of smoking cue reactivity: A meta-analysis of fMRI studies. *Neuroimage, 60,* 252–262.

Fishbane, M. (2007). Wired to connect: Neuroscience, relationships, and therapy. *Family Process, 46,* 395–412. doi: 10.1111/j.15455300.2007.00219.x

Gotlib, I. H., Ranganath, C., & Rosenfeld, J.P. (1998). Frontal EEG alpha asymmetry, depression, and cognitive functioning. *Cognition and Emotion, 12,* 449–478. doi:10.1080/02699939879673

Harmon-Jones, E. (2007). Asymmetrical frontal cortical activity, affective valence, and motivational direction. In E. Harmon-Jones & P. Winkielman (Eds.), *Social neuroscience: Integrating biological and psychological explanations of social behavior* (pp. 137–156). New York: Guildford Press.

Harmon-Jones, E., & Allen, J.J.B. (1997). Behavioral activation sensitivity and resting frontal EEG asymmetry: Covariation of putative indicators related to risk for mood disorders. *Journal of Abnormal Psychology, 106,* 159–163. doi: 10.1037/0021-843X.106.1.159

Harmon-Jones, E., & Beer, J.S. (2009). *Methods in social neuroscience*. New York: Guilford Press.

Harmon-Jones, E., & Peterson, C.K. (2009). Electroencephalographic methods in social and personality psychology. In E. Harmon-Jones & J.S. Beer (Eds.), *Methods in social neuroscience* (pp. 170–197). New York: Guilford Press.

Harmon-Jones, E., & Winkielman, P. (2007). *Social neuroscience: Integrating biological and psychological explanations of social behavior*. New York: Guilford Press.

Jasper, H. H. (1958). The 10–20 system of the international federation. *Electroencephalography and Clinical Neurophysiology, 10,* 371–375.

Kimberly, C., Werner-Wilson, R., Parker, T.S., & Lianekhammy, J. (2012). Alpha to omega: A neurological analysis of marital conflict. Manuscript submitted for publication.

Knyazev, G.G. (2007). Motivation, emotion, and their inhibitory control mirrored in brain oscillations. *Neuroscience & Biobehavioral Reviews, 31,* 377–395. doi:0.1016/j.neubiorev.2006.10.004

Linden, M.K. (2011, March). *The ADD/Aspergers/autism connection: QEEG subtype based assessment and treatment*. Presented at the annual conference of Applied Psychophysiology and Biofeedback, New Orleans, LA.

Linden, M.K., Habib, T., & Radojevic, V. (1996). A controlled study of the effects of EEG biofeedback on cognition and behavior of children with attention deficit disorder and learning disabilities. *Biofeedback and Self-Regulation, 21,* 35–49. doi:10.1007/BF02214148

Lubar, J.F. (1995). Neurofeedback for the management of attention deficit hyperactivity disorders. In M.S. Schwartz (Ed.), *Biofeedback: A practitioner's guide* (pp. 493–522). New York: Guilford Press.

Lutz, A., Dunne, J.D., & Davidson, R.J. (2007). Meditation and the neuroscience of consciousness: An introduction. In P. Zelazo, M. Moscovitch, & E. Thompson (Eds.), *The Cambridge handbook of consciousness* (pp. 499–551). New York: Cambridge University Press.

Mendes, W. B. (2009). Assessing autonomic nervous system activity. In E. Harmon-Jones & J. S. Beer (Eds.), *Methods in social neuroscience* (pp. 118–147). New York: Guilford.

Miskovic, V., Moscovitch, D. A., McCabe, R. E., Antony, M. M., & Schmidt, L. A. (2011). Changes in EEG cross-frequency coupling during cognitive behavioral therapy for social anxiety disorder. *Psychological Science, 22,* 507–516. doi: 10.1177/0956797611400914

Monastra, V. J., Lubar, J. F., & Linden, M. (2001). The development of a quantitative electroencephalographic scanning process for attention deficit-hyperactivity disorder: Reliability and validity studies. *Neuropsychology, 15,* 136–144. doi:10.1037/0894-4105.15.1.136

Northey, W. F., Wells, K. C., Silverman, W. K., & Bailey, C. E. (2003). Childhood behavioral and emotional disorders. *Journal of Marital and Family Therapy, 29,* 523–545. doi:10.1111/j.1752-0606.2003.tb01693.x

Oberman, L. M., Pineda, J. A., & Ramachandran, V. S. (2007). The human mirror neuron system: A link between action observation and social skills. *Social Cognitive and Affective Neuroscience, 2,* 62–66. doi: 10.1093/scan/nsl022

Ochsner, K. N., Bunge, S. A., Gross, J. J., & Gabrieli, J. D. E. (2002). Rethinking feelings: An fMRI study of the cognitive regulation of emotion. *Journal of Cognitive Neuroscience, 14,* 1215–1229.

Pagani, M., Manouilenko, I., Stone-Elander, S., Odh, R., Salmaso, D., Hatherly, R., Brolin, F., Jacobsson, H., Larsson, St., & Bejerot, S. (2012). Brief report: Alterations in cerebral blood flow as assessed by PET/CT in adults with autism spectrum disorder with normal IQ. *Journal of Autism and Developmental Disorders, 42,* 313–318.

Parker, T. S., Blackburn, K. M., Hawks, J., Werner-Wilson, R. J., & Wood, N. D. (2013). Frontal alpha asymmetry, empathy and the therapeutic relationship in MFT. Manuscript submitted for publication.

Pfeifer, J. H., & Dapretto, M. (2009). "Mirror, mirror, in my mind": Empathy, interpersonal competence, and the mirror neuron system. In J. Decety and W. Ickes (Eds.), *The social neuroscience of empathy* (pp. 183–197). Cambridge, MA: MIT Press.

Pfeifer, J. H., Iacoboni, M., Mazziotta, J. C., & Dapretto, M. (2008). Mirroring others' emotions relates to empathy and interpersonal competence in children. *Neuroimage, 39,* 2076–2085.

Pineda, J. A. (2005). The functional significance of mu rhythms: Translating "seeing" and "hearing" into "doing." *Brain Research Reviews, 50,* 57–68. doi:10.1016/j.brainresrev.2005.04.005

Pizzagalli, D. A. (2007). Electroencephalography and high-density electrophysiological source localization. In J. T. Cacioppo, L. G. Tassinary, & G. G. Berntson (Eds.), *Handbook of psychophysiology* (3rd ed., pp. 56–84). New York: Cambridge University Press.

Putman, P. (2011). Resting state EEG delta-beta coherence in relation to anxiety, behavioral inhibition, and selective attentional processing of threatening stimuli. *International Journal of Psychophysiology, 80,* 63–68.

Rizzolatti, G., & Craighero, L. (2004). The mirror-neuron system. *Annual Review of Neuroscience, 27,* 169–192. doi: 10.1146/annurev.neuro.27.070203.144230

Rowan, J. A., & Tolunsky, E. (2003). *Primer of EEG.* Philadelphia: Elsevier.

Ryan, L., & Alexander, G. E. (2008). Neuroimaging: Overview of methods and applications. In L. J. Luecken & L. C. Gallo (Eds.), *Handbook of physiological research methods in health psychology* (pp. 371–394). Thousand Oaks, CA: Sage.

Schutter, D. J. L. G., & Knyazev, G. G. (2012). Cross-frequency coupling of brain oscillations in studying motivation and emotion. *Motivation and Emotion, 36*, 46–54. doi:10.1007/s11031-011-9327-6

van Peer, J. M., Roelofs, K., & Spinhoven, P. (2008). Cortisol administration enhances the coupling of midfrontal delta and beta oscillations. *International Journal of Psychophysiology, 67*, 144–150. doi: 10.1016/j.ijpsycho.2007.11.001

Wager, T. D., Hernandez, L., Jonides, J., & Lindquist, M. (2007). Elements of functional neuroimaging. In J. T. Cacioppo, L. G. Tassinary, & G. G. Berntson (Eds.), *Handbook of psychophysiology* (3rd ed., pp. 19–55). New York: Cambridge University Press.

Weerts, E. M., Wand, G. S., Kuwabara, H., Munro, C. A., Dannals, R. F., Hilton, J., Frost, J.J., & McCaul, M.E. (2011). Positron emission tomography imaging of mu- and delta-opioid receptor binding in alcohol-dependent and healthy control subjects. *Alcoholism: Clinical and Experimental Research, 35*, 2162–2173.

Werner-Wilson, R. J., Lianekhammy, J., Frey, L. M., Parker, T. S., Wood, N. D., Kimberly, C., . . . Dalton, M. (2011). Alpha asymmetry in female military spouses following deployment. *Journal of Feminist Family Therapy, 23*, 202–217. doi: 10.1080/08952833.2011.604534

Section III

METHODOLOGIES

11

CULTURAL ADAPTATION RESEARCH

A Critical Opportunity for Addressing Mental Health Disparities in the Couple and Family Therapy Field

*José Rubén Parra-Cardona, Michael R. Whitehead,
Ana Rocío Escobar-Chew, Kendal Holtrop,
Sara N. Lappan, Sheena R. Horsford, Melanie M.
Domenech Rodríguez, and Guillermo Bernal*

Mental Health Disparities in the United States and Abroad

Evidence-based treatments (EBTs) have benefited large segments of the U.S. population by promoting mental health, as well as couple and family relationship satisfaction (Kazdin, 2008a). Unfortunately, EBTs continue to be out of reach for the most vulnerable individuals and families. For example, at least two thirds of the worldwide population are in need of mental health treatment and do not have access to such services. In the United States alone, 67% of people affected by serious mental illness have not received adequate mental health treatment (Chisholm et al., 2007). Investment in applied research, treatment, and prevention continues to be disproportionately low across nations compared with existing rates of mental health disease (Collins et al., 2011). For example, behavioral problems such as noncompliance, defiance, aggression, and substance abuse constitute the most frequent request for mental health services for children and adolescents. However, only between 20% and 23% of children in greatest need receive adequate mental health services (Kazdin, 2008a). In the United States, ethnic minorities tend to receive lower-quality health and mental health care than non-Hispanic Whites; Latino children are the most likely group to be uninsured; and African American children tend to report the poorest health status among children from all ethnic groups (Flores, Olson, & Tomany-Korman, 2005). In a

161

time when ethnic minority children represent a numeric majority, these findings are striking.

Scholars have highlighted the need to address mental health disparities by taking into consideration sociohistorical frameworks. Based on this premise, emotional problems are exacerbated by stressors resulting from chronic poverty, racism, sexism, and homophobia. For example, there is a sizable body of evidence demonstrating that perceived discrimination is associated with a variety of negative health and mental health outcomes (Flores et al., 2005). Therefore, there is a need for researchers and mental health professionals to identify oppression "not only as a contextual factor but also as a direct, specific cause of emotional and physical trauma" (Smith, Chambers, & Bratini, 2009, p. 160).

A solution to this dilemma consists of reaching out and serving populations in greatest need by disseminating efficacious interventions capable of improving various mental health outcomes (Kazdin, 2008b). This chapter elaborates on how cultural adaptation research constitutes a key opportunity for reducing mental health disparities among diverse and underserved populations. To address this goal, we will first examine research and service disparities in the field of couple and family therapy (CFT). Next, we will define cultural adaptation research and summarize the most relevant literature associated with this area of scholarship. To illustrate the impact of cultural adaptation research, we will describe a program of prevention research with Latino immigrant populations, as informed by two well-defined models of cultural adaptation. Finally, we will discuss research implications for the field.

Research and Service Disparities in the CFT Field

While cultural competence is strongly emphasized in CFT training programs, there continues to be a gap that needs to be bridged between general practitioner cultural competence and comprehensive programs of intervention research aimed at benefiting diverse and underserved populations such as ethnic minorities, individuals with disabilities, and the lesbian-gay-bisexual-transgender (LGBT) community (Sprenkle, 2012). This disconnect has led to calls to address service and research disparities in our field, and inroads are being made, thanks to CFT scholars representing diverse and marginalized groups. For example, Turner, Wieling, and Allen (2004) proposed specific guidelines to promote culturally relevant research in the field.

Despite these gains, a recent review of articles published in relevant CFT journals (i.e., *Journal of Marital and Family Therapy, Family Process, American Journal of Family Therapy*) indicated that the implementation of comprehensive programs of applied research with underserved populations continues to be seriously limited (Seedall, Holtrop, & Parra-Cardona, in press). Specifically, researchers utilized a content analysis approach to examine published articles focused on specific diversity issues (e.g., low socioeconomic status, race and ethnicity, sexual orientation) associated with individuals, couples, and families and found that only 27.3% of all articles published in the selected journals over an 8-year period (2004–2011) addressed at least one diversity issue.

With regard to the potential impact that cultural adaptation can have among underserved populations in the United States and abroad, scholars have stated that this line of applied research can be used in the "service of empowerment, decolonization, and liberation" (Bernal & Domenech Rodríguez, 2012, p. 10). For example, in México, where there is a scarcity of resources to engage in generative and applied science, we have used the lessons learned in our U.S.-based studies to collaborate with scholars and service providers in the dissemination of EBTs. Our United States–México collaboration has been a great learning experience, as we have confirmed that interventions originally developed in the United States can have a significant and positive effect on low-income Mexican families earning an average monthly family income of US$300–$400. Furthermore, and because the most effective models of cultural adaptation are collaborative in nature, international cultural adaptation research should be characterized by a mutual learning process, contrasting with the sole imposition of U.S.-generated interventions that would lead to cultural and scientific imperialism (Bernal & Domenech Rodríguez, 2012).

Cultural Adaptation

Cultural adaptation research refers to "the systematic modification of an [EBT] or intervention protocol to consider language, culture, and context in such a way that is compatible with the client's cultural patterns, meaning, and values" (Bernal, Jimenez-Chafey, & Domenech Rodríguez, 2009, p. 362). While cultural adaptation research often targets ethnic or racial minority populations, it is important to consider multiple dimensions of culture and how cultural elements intersect (Castro, Barrera, & Holleran Steiker, 2010). Thus, cultural characteristics such as race, ethnicity, socioeconomic status, gender, religious background, sexual identity, ability/disability status, and immigration history are highly relevant in cultural adaptation research.

Cultural adaptation scholars highlight the need to clarify the type of cultural adaptation that will be undertaken in any given study. Specifically, *surface level adaptations* refer to adaptations that, although relevant, remain limited in scope. Examples of these are solely relying on client-therapist racial and/or ethnic matching and providing translated intervention materials to participants (Borrego, 2010). In contrast, *deep structure adaptations* involve a more detailed analysis of the role of culture in the lives of people (Borrego; Zayas, 2010). Examples of these adaptations include carefully reviewing how cultural values, traditions, and heritage inform engagement and retention strategies, measurement protocols, manual development, and intervention delivery activities. In practice, cultural adaptations take place along a continuum and vary in the degree to which they alter the original intervention (Castro et al., 2010).

163

Need for Cultural Adaptation Research

There is a great need to promote comprehensive lines of cultural adaptation research. According to Bernal and colleagues (2009), "basic questions regarding how much adaptation is needed, and when . . . the adaptations [should] occur can be answered with research projects that engage in cultural adaptation efforts in very distinct ethno-cultural groups with varied clinical presentations" (p. 366). Based on their initial meta-analytic research on 76 cultural adaptation studies, Griner and Smith (2006) concluded that more rigorous cultural adaptation studies were necessary, particularly because several of the studies included in their review had important methodological limitations, such as using single intervention groups, quasi-experimental designs, or pre-post designs without follow-up measurements. In a more recent meta-analysis focused on cultural adaptation, Smith, Domenech Rodríguez, and Bernal (2011) found that "culturally adapted mental health therapies are moderately superior to those that do not explicitly incorporate cultural considerations" (p. 172). The authors also state that "studies describing more cultural adaptations tended to be more effective than studies describing fewer cultural adaptations" (p. 171). The type of adaptations that were most associated with effect size magnitude were those that matched clients' goals and utilization of metaphors/symbols in therapy with clients' cultural worldviews (Smith et al., 2011).

An Integrative Model of Cultural Adaptation Prevention Research with Latino Immigrant Populations

In our program of research, we have guided our efforts according to two inter-related models: the Cultural Adaptation Process (CAP) model (Domenech Rodríguez & Wieling, 2005) and the Ecological Validity Framework (Bernal, Bonilla, & Bellido, 1995). We selected these models because they assist researchers in achieving two relevant goals: (a) to develop a community-based program of cultural adaptation research in close collaboration with targeted communities, and (b) to culturally adapt relevant mental health interventions that target the most salient life experiences of the population of interest.

Cultural Adaptation Process Model

Domenech Rodríguez and Wieling (2005) have proposed a model of cultural adaptation research characterized by an emphasis on establishing close collaborations with targeted communities. In the first phase of the model, three players are identified: (a) the change agent, (b) the opinion leader, and (c) members of the focal community. The change agent promotes innovation, the opinion leader is typically a leader of the community with the capacity to promote local and permanent change, and the members of the focal community are the ultimate beneficiaries of the proposed adapted interventions. The inclusion and interaction among these agents prevent a cultural adaptation process from becoming a colonizing experience (Domenech Rodríguez, Baumann, Schwartz, 2011; Domenech Rodríguez & Wieling).

During phase 2 of the model, three critical goals must be accomplished: (a) selection and evaluation of measures, (b) adaptation of the intervention, and (c) pilot work on both the adapted intervention and measures to evaluate them. Selecting appropriate measures is a time-consuming process, as these need to be reliable and valid for the target population. The adaptation of the intervention must be efficacious by retaining the core components that have established its efficacy while also being characterized by high cultural relevance. Finally, phase 3 consists of an iterative process to keep refining intervention materials and measurement protocols, as well as plans for larger dissemination and sustainability. For a full description of the CAP model, the reader is referred to the original source (Domenech Rodríguez & Wieling, 2005).

Phase 1

In 2005, we (*cultural adaptation change agent*) initiated a program of research aimed at culturally adapting and disseminating an evidence-based parenting intervention among low-income Latinos residing in the Midwestern United States. The evidence-based intervention that is the focus of our investigation is known as Parent Management Training—the Oregon Model (PMTO™) (*original EBT change agent*). Longitudinal research has confirmed the long-term positive effects of the intervention spanning 9 years posttreatment (Forgatch, Patterson, DeGarmo, & Beldavs, 2009). In addition, PMTO is highly syntonic with Latino parenting practices and traditions (Domenech Rodríguez et al., 2011). With regard to our target population (*members of the focal community*), we decided to focus on low-income Latino immigrants in Detroit because this immigrant population is exposed to intense contextual challenges, such as strenuous working conditions, discrimination, an anti-immigration climate, poverty, and community violence. Finally, we initiated collaborations with key community leaders, such as religious leaders and CEOs of the most important health and mental health agencies in the area (*opinion leaders*).

Having identified all key agents, we implemented qualitative studies to learn about the needs and experiences of the community. We also maintained close communication with opinion leaders to ensure an adequate understanding of these experiences, which was a critical step to prevent our program of cultural adaptation from becoming a colonizing experience. The results of this phase of investigation are described in an article entitled "Shared Ancestry, Evolving Stories: Similar and Contrasting Life Experiences Described by Foreign Born and U.S. Born Latino Parents" (Parra-Cardona, Córdova, Holtrop, Villarruel, & Wieling, 2008), which provides detailed descriptions of the life experiences of Latino immigrant parents residing in Michigan. Based on findings from this study, we adapted intervention materials and study procedures according to the participants' most relevant life and cultural experiences. In addition, we examined the expectations that Latino immigrant parents held regarding their participation in

165

parenting programs to be offered in the community. Study findings confirmed that Latino immigrant parents were highly interested in participating in a culturally adapted parenting intervention and highlighted ways in which the intervention could be relevant, respectful, and responsive to their life experiences (Parra-Cardona et al., 2009).

Selecting the Optimal Research Design: Reaching Consensus

The final goal of phase 1 consisted of reaching agreement about the general research design and study protocol characteristics. In this process, it was critical to engage in honest conversations about the priorities associated with all agents. Thus, the cultural and life experiences of members of the community, as well as the expertise of opinion leaders and change agents, were equally relevant throughout this phase of the cultural adaptation process.

For example, critical input by members of the community and opinion leaders led to the selection of a local church as the main site of implementation for our study, as it was the most trusted location for community members. A wait-list control condition versus services as usual or no treatment was chosen based on the high expectations that this study generated in the community. In addition, it was confirmed that all data collection and intervention delivery procedures had to be carried out by members of the local community because they could generate a level of trust that university-based graduate students could not offer, as they were not perceived as members of the community.

Our voice as change agents was also critical in this process, particularly as it referred to the need to advance the science of cultural adaptation research. Specifically, scholars have challenged cultural adaptation researchers to go beyond asking *if* adaptations are warranted to investigating the more complex question regarding *how much* adaptation is needed to produce positive outcomes among diverse cultural groups (Bernal et al., 2009). In response, we proposed to opinion leaders a randomized controlled trial (RCT) that would allow us to compare and contrast two differentially culturally adapted versions of the PMTO intervention. Following this design, we agreed to randomize participants into one of three conditions: (a) *CAPAS-Original,* (b) *CAPAS-Enhanced,* or (c) a wait-list control group. Measurements of parent/child interactions, parenting skills, and child internalizing and externalizing behaviors would be taken at baseline, intervention completion, and 6-month follow-up. Clearly communicating the scientific value of this design and the need for rigorous evaluation was essential to earn the trust and full support from opinion leaders and community-based research staff.

Phase 2

Three critical goals must be accomplished in this phase: (a) selection and evaluation of measures, (b) adaptation of the intervention, and (c) pilot work. The selection and evaluation of measures were accomplished by Domenech Rodríguez and colleagues in their program of research with Latino immigrants in the Southwest (see Domenech Rodríguez et al., 2011).

Adapted Interventions Being Tested

In our study, we proposed to our community collaborators the implementation of two differentially culturally adapted versions of the PMTO intervention. The first intervention, CAPAS-Original, was completed by Domenech Rodríguez and colleagues with funding support from the National Institute of Mental Health. The title of the translated version is "Criando con Amor, Promoviendo Armonía y Superación" (CAPAS), which translates "raising children with love, promoting harmony, and self-improvement." The cultural adaptation process followed specific sequential steps: (a) literal translation of the manual by Dr. Domenech Rodríguez, (b) refinement of the Spanish version of the intervention according to the eight dimensions of the Ecological Validity Framework (Bernal et al., 1995), (c) implementation of focus group interviews with 41 Latino immigrant parents residing in the United States in order to confirm the appropriateness and relevance of the Spanish version of the intervention, (d) implementation of the curriculum in an exploratory study with first-generation Latino immigrant parents, and (e) modification of the intervention based on feedback provided by participants and interventionists. Because back-translation of manuals is costly, Spanish-speaking scholars in the United States and México were asked to review and evaluate the linguistic and cultural appropriateness of the translated manual. Performing these steps was necessary to ensure that CAPAS went beyond a surface level adaptation. All the sessions included in the CAPAS-Original intervention correspond exclusively to the core components of PMTO. Additional details of the process of adaptation of the CAPAS-Original intervention can be found in the original source (Domenech Rodríguez et al., 2011).

The second intervention being used in our investigation, CAPAS-Enhanced, consists of all the components of the CAPAS-Original intervention plus specific sessions focused on culturally relevant issues. The selected topics were chosen according to the findings of our exploratory qualitative studies and include topics such as life as an immigrant parent, Latino cultural values and traditions, biculturalism, managing cultural conflicts in the family, and cultural identity formation. Interventionists also inform the discussion of parenting situations by addressing these cultural themes throughout the intervention. For example, when discussing with parents strategies for helping children to master new behaviors (e.g., brushing their teeth by themselves), interventionists emphasize how promoting independence in children is a skill that will help them in various U.S. contexts (e.g., schools). Similarly, interventionists talk with parents about how effective discipline also promotes cultural values that are important in the Latino community, such as the sense of family (i.e., *familismo*) and respect between parents and children (i.e., respect). The last session of the intervention is fully focused on issues of biculturalism, such as managing bicultural conflicts in the family and cultural identity formation.

Cultural Adaptation Framework Utilized to Adapt the Proposed Interventions

The CAPAS-Original and CAPAS-Enhanced interventions were developed by following the theoretical tenets of the Ecological Validity Framework developed by Bernal and colleagues (1995). This model focuses on eight specific dimensions that are necessary to address to culturally adapt an intervention: (a) language, (b) persons, (c) metaphors, (d) content, (e) concepts, (f) goals, (g) methods, and (h) context. The model has been used to inform culturally adapted psychosocial interventions for Latinos, including treatment of depression for Latino adolescents and their families (Domenech Rodríguez et al., 2011).

According to the Ecological Validity Framework, *language* refers to the importance of delivering interventions in the native language of the target population. Language also takes into consideration cultural norms of verbal and nonverbal expressions. The dimension of *persons* refers to the type and quality of the relationship between the recipients of interventions and the professionals who deliver the intervention. *Metaphors* refers to the symbols and concepts that are shared by a particular cultural group. For example, there are several metaphors in the Latino culture regarding the importance of parents in the lives of children. The dimension of *content* refers to the cultural knowledge that is communicated as embedded within the original intervention, particularly as it refers to the cultural values, customs, and traditions of a target population. The construct *concepts* makes reference to the theoretical models utilized in a culturally adapted intervention, which should be culturally relevant for the target population. For example, the PMTO intervention was developed according to principles of social learning theory. This theoretical framework is relevant for Latino populations because parents are placed in a position of high influence and authority with regard to their children. The dimension of *goals* refers to the objectives that are pursued when culturally adapting interventions. In our work we are testing the impact of focusing on highly relevant cultural issues for participants, such as immigration, cultural identity formation, and biculturalism. The category *methods* is associated with the characteristics of culturally relevant research procedures. For instance, cultural sensitivity should thoroughly inform engagement and retention strategies, as Latino parents have often experienced discrimination, work exploitation, and segregation. Finally, *context* refers to the consideration of a population's greater economic, social, and political environment. Table 11.1 illustrates the comparison between the CAPAS-Original and the CAPAS-Enhanced interventions according to the eight dimensions of the Ecological Validity Framework.

Table 11.1 Comparison of CAPAS-Original and CAPAS-Enhanced Interventions*

CAPAS-Original	CAPAS-Enhanced
1. *Language.* Intervention materials are linguistically appropriate.	In addition to items 1–8 of the CAPAS-Original intervention, the CAPAS-Enhanced intervention focuses on the following:
2. *Persons.* Interventionists are Latino/a bilingual professionals, members of the Detroit community	*Content.* The introductory session presents an overview of the PMTO intervention and its guiding principles. This session also focuses heavily on issues associated with immigration and Latino/a cultural values and traditions. The last session addresses issues of biculturalism, within-family cultural conflicts, and cultural identity formation.
3. *Metaphors.* Latino-specific phrases (i.e., *dichos*) and culturally relevant metaphors are utilized throughout the intervention.	
4. *Content.* An introductory session provides an overview of the PMTO intervention. Materials are fully focused on original PMTO parenting content. Cultural issues are emphasized whenever these discussions are initiated by participants.	*Concepts.* Each core component of the PMTO intervention is introduced to participants within culturally relevant frameworks associated with immigration and biculturalism. The concepts of cultural identity and within-family cultural conflict are addressed throughout the intervention. The benefits associated with biculturalism are continuously emphasized across all sessions.
5. *Concepts.* PMTO core concepts are highlighted throughout the intervention, as stated in the original PMTO manual.	
6. *Goals.* Focus on the core components of the PMTO intervention (i.e., giving good directions, teaching children through encouragement, setting limits, family problem solving, and monitoring).	*Goals.* The intervention seeks to integrate PMTO goals within immigration and bicultural frameworks.
7. *Methods.* In addition to didactic materials, intervention delivery heavily relies on role plays of parenting situations. Midweek calls are made to troubleshoot parenting skills at home.	*Methods.* Discussions on how PMTO parenting skills reinforce Latino/a cultural values and biculturalism are actively promoted by interventionists.
8. *Context.* Addressed by providing case management (e.g., health or mental health services, assistance programs, job training). Full dinner is served to participants, and child care is provided at every session. Intervention is delivered in a safe setting for participants.	

*Expanded from the original description of the CAPAS intervention (Domenech Rodríguez, Baumann, & Schwartz, 2011).

Pilot Testing of the Adapted Interventions

A critical step in phase 2 of the CAP model consists of pilot testing the intervention. Thus, we implemented a nonrandomized pilot study with a small number of Latino immigrant parents ($n = 24$) in order to evaluate the cultural acceptability of the adapted interventions, as well as cultural appropriateness of all study procedures, such as recruitment, measurement protocols, and intervention delivery. Preliminary findings from the pilot study related to intervention feasibility and cultural acceptability were promising and are described in detail in a refereed publication (see Parra-Cardona et al., 2012). These findings indicated to us that the adapted interventions were relevant to participants and that the study procedures were culturally appropriate. Following this small pilot study, we engaged in the implementation of an RCT in which CAPAS-Original and CAPAS-Enhanced were compared and contrasted. Parents in the wait-list control group received the intervention after all 6-month follow-up measurements for the intervention conditions were completed.

Recruitment and Participants

Several recruitment strategies have been used in this study, including referrals from community partners and religious organizations, as well as the posting of flyers in settings such as churches and mental health offices. Word-of-mouth from former group participants has been the most effective recruitment strategy.

The final goal of the project will be to recruit 88 families in the RCT. To date, a total of 26 families have participated in the first two waves of the randomized phase of the project. This included 24 two-parent families and two single-parent families, for a total of 49 parents (26 mothers, 23 fathers). Thirteen families (25 parents) participated in the CAPAS-Original intervention and 13 families (25 parents) participated in the CAPAS-Enhanced intervention. Families reported an average annual family income of $22,933. Families in both interventions also reported an average of 2.77 children living in the household. Parents' average age in CAPAS-Original was slightly lower ($M = 34.16$, $SD = 4.54$) than parents in CAPAS-Enhanced ($M = 36.73$, $SD = 9.71$). Parents in CAPAS-Original lived in the United States slightly longer ($M = 14.33$, $SD = 5.18$) than parents in CAPAS-Enhanced ($M = 13.75$ years, $SD = 6.71$). Neither difference was statistically significant. All parents reported México as their country of origin.

Preliminary Findings

Preliminary findings indicate high participant satisfaction with both culturally adapted versions of the intervention. Quantitative data on session satisfaction indicate high levels of satisfaction with both interventions and no statistical differences between CAPAS-Original and CAPAS-Enhanced on any of the weekly session satisfaction ratings.

Qualitative data provide detailed information regarding the reasons for parents to highly value the shared, core content of the PMTO sessions. In summary, participants expressed high satisfaction with the core components of the PMTO, particularly with those skills that have the most direct impact on their parenting practices, such as learning how to motivate their children to engage in independent behaviors (e.g., completing homework and chores), implementing effective discipline without corporal punishment, and monitoring and supervision. In addition, participants in the CAPAS-Enhanced intervention expressed high satisfaction with the culturally focused sessions on immigration, how immigration differs among families, and biculturalism. Furthermore, participants in both groups expressed the need for expanding culturally focused themes in order to devote sufficient time to address issues of culture and parenting, learning how to expose their children to PMTO practices while also preparing them for future exposure to prejudice and discrimination, challenges to maintaining cultural practices and traditions, and barriers to accessing culturally relevant mental health services. The reader is referred to the original source for a detailed presentation of these findings (Parra-Cardona et al., 2012).

Phase 3

The last phase of the CAP model refers to an iterative process to keep refinements of the intervention and measurement protocols, as well as plans for larger dissemination and sustainability. Definitive conclusions cannot be reached at this time in our program of research, as we are still implementing the RCT component of the study; however, we will refine the intervention and study procedures in the future based on final findings from the RTC.

In addition, we are already initiating efforts to move toward increasing the scope of our study. Specifically, we have been approached by schools and other community stakeholders, as they would like to see an expansion of our program of applied research to benefit the larger community. Thus, we are currently integrating a group with community leaders who are collaborators in our project, as well as new members (e.g., representatives from schools, business leaders). The goal of integrating this group of diverse stakeholders is to apply for private foundation and federal grants with the main goal of achieving the final refinement and long-term sustainability of the intervention. Reaching a place in which the intervention can be "owned and sustained" by the local community is critical in our process of cultural adaptation research, as we are temporary agents of change, and only the members and leaders of the community can become permanent agents of change.

Research Implications

The CFT field continues to have deficiencies with regard to the implementation of comprehensive programs of applied research aimed at reducing mental health disparities among diverse populations. There is an urgent need to address this issue, particularly because "numerous researchers agree that the single most important reason both for the underutilization of mental health services by ethnic minority clients and for the high dropout rates is the inability of psychotherapists and counselors to provide culturally sensitive/responsive therapy" (Gelso & Fretz, 2001, p. 153). In the face of these challenges, cultural adaptation research constitutes a key opportunity for disseminating efficacious practices in culturally relevant ways among diverse, underserved populations.

Guiding Frameworks for Cultural Adaptation Research

It is critical to inform cultural adaptation studies according to well-established cultural adaptation frameworks. In our program of research, we have guided our efforts according to two interrelated models: the CAP (Domenech Rodríguez & Wieling, 2005) and Ecological Validity (Bernal et al., 1995). Adhering to comprehensive cultural adaptation frameworks is essential to prevent the implementation of designs that overlook critical research considerations that directly influence the process of cultural adaptation (i.e., surface versus deep-structure adaptation). Because the field of cultural adaptation is flourishing with various models and examples of application, we refer the reader to an excellent source on cultural adaptation literature. This edited book provides an overview of the historical development of the field of cultural adaptation research and provides examples of cultural adaptation with a variety of diverse populations. Critical considerations for expanding cultural adaptation research with underserved populations at national and international levels are also included (see Bernal & Domenech Rodríguez, 2012).

Attention to social justice issues in cultural adaptation research is also critical, particularly because this line of work is likely to involve populations that have been historically marginalized in service delivery and research. Central to the CAP model is the engagement in honest and transparent conversations with opinion leaders who are advocates of targeted communities. For example, based on these interactions, we chose to utilize a wait-list control group rather than a no-treatment control condition. Although this approach carries methodological challenges due to treatment expectation, parents of the targeted community expressed a strong desire to receive the intervention. Operating from a social justice framework, we strongly believed that every family signing up for the intervention had the right to receive it, a conviction that informed our study design. Otherwise, we would have disregarded the needs of our target population and the history of oppression they have endured for many years.

Empirically Informed Cultural Adaptation Knowledge

In the current study, families experienced the PMTO parenting skills as highly relevant to their parenting efforts. This finding is critical, because it challenges the preconceived notion that diverse populations have highly unique or "different" parenting experiences. For example, we have received feedback in professional forums asserting that limit-setting skills, such as time out and privilege removal, are irrelevant to minority populations because they were developed with primarily Euro-American families. However, participants in this study have consistently challenged this notion by confirming that PMTO limit-setting skills are highly relevant to their parenting efforts.

At the same time, parents reported the high need to incorporate meaningful consideration of issues associated with immigration, ways in which the immigration experience greatly differs among families, challenges to maintaining cultural practices and traditions, and barriers to accessing culturally relevant mental health services. Thus, the value of cultural adaptation research lies in its potential to help identify which elements of an original intervention, as well as which culturally adapted components, are considered by target populations to be most relevant.

Selecting the Optimal Research Design

Research designs in cultural adaptation research should be determined according to clearly defined objectives and thorough knowledge of the cultural adaptation literature. While it is appropriate for programs of intervention research to proceed in stages, rigorous experimental designs with random assignment to conditions are critical for advancing the field of cultural adaptation research. Less rigorous designs, such as single group experiments, quasi-experimental designs, and nonrandomized trials, limit internal validity and prevent researchers from reaching solid conclusions about the process of cultural adaptation and the impact of adaptations on original efficacious interventions (Smith et al., 2011). Even randomized trials with one intervention condition and one comparison control group prevent investigators from analyzing the impact of differential levels of cultural adaptation (Martinez & Eddy, 2005). Based on these considerations, the research design described in our current study allows us to compare and contrast the impact of two differentially culturally adapted interventions (CAPAS-Original vs. CAPAS-Enhanced). Thus, when selecting research designs in cultural adaptation studies, investigators should carefully review the existing cultural adaptation literature in their area of interest and determine the usefulness and limitations of their proposed design.

Fidelity Issues

To promote rigorous cultural adaptation science, it is critical for researchers to implement safeguards to ensure that personal biases are carefully monitored and controlled throughout the process of investigation (Bernal & Domenech Rodríguez, 2012). To reach this goal, we highly recommend incorporating mechanisms to monitor intervention fidelity in cultural adaptation research projects. Assessing fidelity helps ensure that the core components of original efficacious interventions are adequately being implemented while reducing internal and conclusion validity threats (Forgatch, Patterson, & DeGarmo, 2005).

For example, the focal intervention in our research, PMTO, has an observation-based rating system that allows for the analysis of fidelity to the original PMTO core components (see Knutson, Forgatch, & Rains, 2003). The principal investigator for our project was trained in this fidelity rating system in order to monitor PMTO implementation. At the same time, the principal investigator has maintained close consultation with interventionists and co-investigators regarding emerging satisfaction findings to ensure that the intervention and intervention delivery procedures are characterized by cultural sensitivity and relevance.

The Critical Importance of Ecological Validity

Developing rigorous prevention and clinical trials is a challenging process that requires comprehensive knowledge of key research design issues, such as internal, external, construct, and statistical conclusion validity. Addressing these constructs in detail is beyond the scope of this chapter, but we refer the reader to an excellent source (Shadish, Cook, & Campbell, 2002). Thus, whereas consideration of these issues must thoroughly inform cultural adaptation studies, experts agree on the critical need to give special emphasis to issues of *ecological validity* in cultural adaptation research (Wallis, Amaro, & Cortés, 2012). In essence, ecological validity refers to the degree to which "the environment as experienced by the participant is the same as the environment the investigator assumes it to be. . . . The question 'Does the intervention work in the real world' (ecological validity) is thus expanded to 'Does the intervention work in the real world for people with different cultural contexts?" (Domenech Rodríguez & Wieling, 2005, p. 324). To this end, we have utilized two frameworks that allow us to respond to critical ecological questions at multiple levels. First, the CAP model particularly facilitates the examination of macro-level ecological validity issues. That is, is the intervention responsive to the needs and life experiences of the community and potential beneficiaries? Are study procedures responsive to the history and most pressing challenges of the community? Are members and key leaders of the community convinced of the benefits of the proposed program of cultural adaptation research, as well as being invested in identifying alternatives to achieve long-term sustainability?

Embedded within the CAP model, we have adopted the Ecological Validity Framework, which guides the researchers in achieving critical goals as detailed in eight well-defined dimensions of cultural adaptation. These guidelines assist researchers in achieving linguistic appropriateness of the intervention, culturally appropriate fit of interventionists, cultural relevance of intervention materials and procedures, and cultural congruency between the goals of the adapted interventions and the intervention delivery contexts. By following the aforementioned models, we are implementing a program of cultural adaptation research that is increasingly characterized by ecological validity. Adopting this framework allows us to maximize our external validity in the context of an RCT.

Furthermore, in addition to examining the ecological validity of adapting interventions in the United States, we are gathering preliminary data indicating the possibility of reaching ecological validity in international contexts. For instance, based on the lessons learned from our U.S.-based experience, we are following similar implementation guidelines in collaborative research in México. To date, we have found that community partners deeply value the collaborative nature of the CAP model and Ecological Validity Framework in that they ensure the shared expertise of all agents of change. As we engage in efforts to disseminate U.S.-based generated science in international contexts through cultural adaptation research, the active participation in this process of international community members and opinion leaders will help us to ensure an ecological process of cultural adaptation, rather than an experience of international scientific colonialism.

Conclusion

As we enter the 21st century, great accomplishments have been achieved in the CFT field. Yet, we continue to face clear limitations regarding our research and evidence-based service delivery with diverse populations. Cultural adaptation research constitutes a critical opportunity for enhancing the lives of underserved groups by advancing strong science within culturally relevant frameworks. We encourage CFT practitioners to engage in this area of applied scholarship in order to expand current knowledge on cultural adaptation processes. Most importantly, by developing applied programs of cultural adaptation research, we have the potential to reduce health disparities and promote social justice among populations that we have historically overlooked.

Endnote: This investigation was supported by award no. R34MH087678 from the National Institute of Mental Health. The content is solely the responsibility of the authors and does not necessarily represent the official views of the National Institute of Mental Health or the National Institutes of Health. Supplementary funding was provided by the Michigan State University (MSU) Office of the Vice-President for Research and Graduate Studies (OVPRGS), the MSU College of Social Science, and the MSU Department of Human Development and Family Studies (HDFS).

We express our most sincere gratitude to Drs. Marion Forgatch and Gerald Patterson. Their unconditional support and generosity have been essential for the successful implementation of our program of applied research.

References

Bernal, G., Bonilla, J., & Bellido, C. (1995). Ecological validity and cultural sensitivity for outcome research: Issues for the cultural adaptation and development of pyschosocial treatments with Hispanics. *Journal of Abnormal Child Psychology, 23,* 67–82.

Bernal, G., & Domenech Rodríguez, M. M. (2012). Cultural adaptation in context: Psychotherapy as a historical account of adaptations. In G. Bernal & M. M. Domenech

Rodríguez (Eds.), *Cultural adaptations: Tools for evidence-based practice with diverse populations* (pp. 3–22). Washington, DC: American Psychological Association.

Bernal, G., Jiménez-Chafey, M. I., & Domenech Rodríguez, M. M. (2009). Cultural adaptation of treatments: A resource for considering culture in evidence-based practice. *Professional Psychology: Research and Practice, 40,* 361–368.

Borrego, J., Jr. (2010). Special series: Culturally responsive cognitive and behavioral practice with Latino families. *Cognitive and Behavioral Practice, 17,* 154–156.

Castro, F. G., Barrera, M., & Holleran Steiker, L. K. (2010). Issues and challenges in the design of culturally adapted evidence-based interventions. *Annual Review of Clinical Psychology, 6,* 213–239.

Chisholm, D., Flisher, A. J., Lund, C., Patel, V., Saxena, S., Thornicroft, G., & Tomlinson, M. (2007). Scale up services for mental disorders: A call for action. *Lancet, 370,* 1241–1252.

Collins, P. Y., Patel, V., Joestl, S. S., March, D., Insel, T. R., & Daar, A. S. (2011). Commentary: Grand challenges in mental health. *Nature, 475,* 27–30.

Domenech Rodríguez, M. M., Baumann, A. A., & Schwartz, A. L. (2011). Cultural adaptation of an evidence-based intervention: From theory to practice in a Latino/a community context. *American Journal of Community Psychology, 47,* 170–186.

Domenech Rodríguez, M. M., & Wieling, E. (2005). Developing culturally appropriate, evidence-based treatments for interventions with ethnic minority populations. In M. Rastogi & E. Wieling (Eds.), *Voices of color: First-person accounts of ethnic minority therapists* (pp. 313–334). Thousand Oaks, CA: Sage.

Flores, G., Olson, L., & Tomany-Korman, S. C. (2005). Racial and ethnic disparities in early childhood health and health care. *Pediatrics, 115,* 183–193.

Forgatch, M. S., Patterson, G. R., & DeGarmo, D. S. (2005). Evaluating fidelity: Predictive fidelity for a measure of competent adherence to the Oregon model of Parent Management Training. *Behavior Therapy, 36,* 3–13.

Forgatch, M. S., Patterson, G. R., DeGarmo, D. S., & Beldavs, Z. G. (2009). Testing the Oregon delinquency model with 9-year follow-up of the Oregon Divorce Study. *Development and Psychopathology, 21,* 637–660.

Gelso, C. J., & Fretz, B. R. (2001). *Counseling psychology* (2nd ed.). Fort Worth, TX: Harcourt.

Griner, D., & Smith, T. B. (2006). Culturally adapted mental health interventions: A meta-analytic review. *Psychotherapy: Theory, Research, Practice, Training, 43,* 531–548.

Kazdin, A. E. (2008a). Evidence-based treatments and delivery of psychological services: Shifting our emphases to increase impact. *Psychological Services, 5,* 201–215.

Kazdin, A. E. (2008b). Evidence-based treatment and practice. New opportunities to bridge clinical research and practice, enhance the knowledge base, and improve patient care. *American Psychologist, 63,* 146–159.

Knutson, N., Forgatch, M. S., & Rains, L. A. (2003). *Fidelity of implementation rating system (FIMP): The training manual for PMTO.* Eugene: Oregon Social Learning Center.

Martinez, C. R., & Eddy, J. M. (2005). Effects of culturally adapted parent management training on Latino youth behavioral health outcomes. *Journal of Consulting and Clinical Psychology, 73,* 841–851.

Parra-Cardona, J.R., Córdova, D., Holtrop, K., Villarruel, F.A., & Wieling, E. (2008). Shared ancestry, evolving stories: Similar and contrasting life experiences described by foreign born and U.S. born Latino parents. *Family Process, 47*, 157–172.

Parra-Cardona, J.R., Domenech Rodríguez, M., Forgatch, M.S., Sullivan, C., Bybee, D., Tams, L., . . . Dates, B. (2012). Culturally adapting an evidence-based parenting intervention for Latino immigrants: The need to integrate fidelity and cultural relevance. *Family Process, 51*, 56–72.

Parra-Cardona, J.R., Holtrop, K., Córdova, D., Escobar-Chew, A.R., Tams, L., Horsford, S., . . . Fitzgerald, H.E. (2009). "Queremos aprender": Latino immigrants call to integrate cultural adaptation with best practice knowledge in a parenting intervention. *Family Process, 48*, 211–231.

Seedall, R.B., Holtrop, K., & Parra-Cardona, J.R. (in press). Diversity, social justice, and intersectionality trends in C/MFT: A content analysis of three family therapy journals, 2004–2011. *Journal of Marital and Family Therapy.*

Shadish, W.R., Cook, T.D., & Campbell, D.T. (2002). *Experimental and quasi-experimental designs for generalized causal inference.* New York: Houghton Mifflin.

Smith, L., Chambers, D.A., & Bratini, L. (2009). When oppression is the pathogen: The participatory development of socially just mental health practice. *American Journal of Orthopsychiatry, 79*, 159–168.

Smith, T.B., Domenech Rodríguez, M., & Bernal, G. (2011). Culture. *Journal of Clinical Psychology, 67*, 166–175.

Sprenkle, D.H. (2012). Intervention research in couple and family therapy: A methodological and substantive review and an introduction to the special issue. *Journal of Marital and Family Therapy, 38*, 3–29.

Turner, W.L., Wieling, E., & Allen, W.D. (2004). Developing culturally effective family-based research programs: Implications for family therapists. *Journal of Marital and Family Therapy, 30*, 257–270.

Wallis, F., Amaro, H., & Cortés, D.E. (2012). Saber es poder: The cultural adaptation of a trauma intervention for Latina women. In G. Bernal & M.M. Domenech Rodríguez (Eds.), *Cultural adaptations: Tools for evidence-based practice with diverse populations* (pp. 157–178). Washington, DC: American Psychological Association.

Zayas, L.H. (2010). Seeking models and methods for cultural adaptation of interventions: Commentary on the special section. *Cognitive and Behavioral Practice, 17*, 198–202.

12

RANDOMIZED CLINICAL TRIALS

Putting Marriage and Family Therapy
Interventions to the Test

Wayne H. Denton

"My spouse is unhappy in our marriage but is willing to go to therapy. What type of therapy should we go to?"

"We just found out our teenager has been skipping school and smoking marijuana. We need family therapy, but what kind?"

"My partner is very depressed and the doctor suggested we go to therapy as a couple. Is that a good idea?"

As a marriage and family therapist, it is not inconceivable that you may be asked such questions by a relative or friend. Or perhaps you have asked yourself how you can best help couples and families in these and other situations. If a loved one is diagnosed with a serious medical condition, we want to know "what is the best treatment?" Should we expect less if a problem is "relational" rather than "medical"? Perhaps you would actually like to contribute to discovering the effectiveness of couple and family interventions—but how can we honestly evaluate the good (or harm) that an intervention is producing? The current "gold standard" for evaluating the efficacy and effectiveness of any intervention (including marriage and family therapy [MFT] interventions) is the randomized clinical trial. Yet, there are many aspects of randomized clinical trials to consider. Anyone who has planned and carried out a randomized clinical trial knows that there are dozens of decisions to be made in the design of such a study. Each decision is a choice, and as there are usually no perfect choices, there will be necessary compromises in the internal and external validity of the study.

This chapter will present current thought on "state-of-the-art" elements of randomized clinical trials, areas of controversy regarding these elements, and proposals to improve the internal, external, and conclusion validity of randomized clinical trials. The student of intervention research will have to remain current and updated on the latest developments in clinical trials, but this chapter will give you a starting point.

An Overview of Randomized Clinical Trials

A randomized clinical trial is a prospective test of at least one clinical intervention and includes two or more groups of study participants. "Randomized" means that participants have an equal chance of being assigned to each study group. "Clinical" means that the intervention is being applied to humans (as opposed to other animals, plants, etc.). "Trial" means that the intervention(s) in question is being evaluated or tested.

Stage Model of Psychotherapy Model Development

Onken, Blaine, and Battjes (1997) proposed that progress in psychotherapy research would be "accelerated by a goal-oriented, systematic approach to the development and testing of behavioral therapies" (p. 479). Borrowing from the model for pharmaceutical research, they proposed that behavioral therapy research be conceptualized as progressing in stages.

Stage I Research

Stage I research is therapy development. This stage involves identifying and developing promising treatments. Other tasks of stage I are developing a treatment manual and a way to evaluate whether therapists are implementing the intervention faithfully (Onken et al., 1997; Rounsaville, Carroll, & Onken, 2001). Hopefully, data providing some preliminary evidence of the efficacy of the new therapy will be collected in stage I—often through a small randomized clinical trial. It should be noted that federal research funding agencies consider a "small" randomized clinical trial to have about 15–30 participants/couples/families per group (Rounsaville et al.). Rounsaville and colleagues have written, in essence, a manual for conducting stage I psychotherapy development research that is essential reading for anyone attempting such research.

Stage II Research

The main task of stage II is to establish the efficacy of the new therapy through a larger randomized clinical trial (Onken et al., 1997). A distinction is made in clinical trial research between "efficacy" and "effectiveness." "Efficacy" trials "refer to what the intervention accomplishes in an ideal setting" (Friedman, Furberg, & DeMets, 2010, p. 3) and seeks to maximize internal validity. For example, an efficacy trial may be done in a university clinic with carefully screened research participants and highly trained therapists supervised by the developers of the intervention. An "effectiveness" trial "refers to what the intervention accomplishes in settings closer to actual practice" (Friedman et al., p. 3) and is more related to external validity. For example, an effectiveness trial may be conducted in community agencies utilizing agency therapists who have had less training in the model and includes the regular clients of the agencies. Stage II research includes an efficacy trial to demonstrate that under ideal conditions, the intervention accomplishes what is intended.

Stage III Research

Once the efficacy of an intervention has been demonstrated, the next step is to demonstrate that the intervention can "work in the real world"—an effectiveness study. Interventions with high efficacy in carefully controlled conditions do not necessarily achieve the same level of effectiveness in community treatment settings. Multisystemic therapy (MST; Henggeler, Schoenwald, Borduin, Rowland, & Cunningham, 2009), for example (one of the most studied MFT models) has been found to have lower rates of change in effectiveness-type studies than in efficacy-type studies (Curtis, Ronan, & Borduin, 2004). Stage III research may involve modifications in the model or methods of training and supervision to enhance transportability to the community (e.g., Henggeler, Schoenwald, Liao, Letourneau, & Edwards, 2002).

Design Elements Common to All Randomized Clinical Trials

Some elements in the design of an MFT randomized clinical trial will be common to any randomized clinical trial, whether it be testing a behavioral intervention, a pharmaceutical agent, or a medical device. These design elements will be covered briefly here before turning to design elements more unique to psychotherapy research. The reader can reference a general text on randomized clinical trials for more details (e.g., Friedman et al., 2010).

Randomization

An alternative to randomization in a clinical trial would be matching participants to try and create two equivalent groups. The problem with this approach is that it is impossible to exactly match people on all known variables. Also, there are likely important variables we are not able to assess or may not even be aware of. These problems are theoretically solved through the process of randomization (with a caveat to follow below). Randomization means that "each participant has the same chance of being assigned to either intervention or control" (Friedman et al., 2010, p. 97). All variables, both known and unknown, will be equally likely to appear in each group. Randomization increases the internal validity of the study and is considered the "gold standard" for comparative treatment research. At the same time, many people will not volunteer for a randomized clinical trial, which raises issues of both external and internal validity (Corrigan & Salzer, 2003).

A statistical problem MFT researchers often face regarding randomization is that when sample sizes are less than 100, there is a significant potential for simple randomization to produce groups with an imbalance of covariates at baseline that could impact treatment outcome (Matthews, Cook, Terada, & Aloia, 2010). That is, there can be a "failure" of randomization. For this reason, baseline characteristics of groups should be statistically compared and controlled for when necessary. A sample size greater than 200 is preferable (yet more challenging to recruit) to avoid these problems (Lachin, 1988).

Recruitment

Recruitment is addressed more fully in Chapter 6. A barrier to recruitment unique to randomized clinical trials is that prospective participants may worry that they will be randomized to wait-list or a nondesired treatment (Thomson, Morley, Teesson, Sannibale, & Haber, 2008). Participants may drop out if not randomized to the desired group (Bale et al., 1980), weakening the internal validity of the study. It can be helpful to have a discussion with participants before randomization as to what it will be like for them if they are randomized to one group or the other. If participants would not be willing to participate in one of the study arms, it is preferable that they withdraw prior to randomization.

Design Elements Unique to Randomized Clinical Trials of Psychotherapy

Treatment Manuals

Why have a treatment manual? An essential purpose of the report of a scientific study is to allow other investigators to replicate the study. In an MFT randomized clinical trial, the independent variable is the MFT intervention (Carroll & Nuro, 1997). Thus, operationalizing the intervention is arguably the most crucial aspect of the report. The results of the study are meaningless if the intervention cannot be delivered consistently or repeated. Having a treatment manual increases the transparency of the research and facilitates replication (Schoenwald et al., 2011). If a researcher claims to be testing an intervention but, in fact, is implementing it with significant differences from the intentions of the original developers, this weakens the conclusion validity of the study.

There is not space in a journal article to include all the details pertaining to the intervention, but these details can be included in a separate treatment manual. Having a defined intervention not only allows interpretation of results from a single study, it allows comparison of results between studies. Being able to build upon previous studies (by either using the same intervention or being able to specify modifications in the intervention) is how the science of MFT will advance.

Finally, as clinical researchers, we strive to make our research relevant to MFT clinicians. If an intervention proves to have some degree of efficacy and effectiveness, the research is of no use to clinicians unless they are able to understand and replicate the intervention studied. As discussed below, treatment manuals from successful MFT models have been made available in forms accessible to clinicians.

What is included in a treatment manual? A simple answer to what goes in a treatment manual is that "[t]he fundamental purpose of a psychotherapy manual is to specify a treatment and provide guidelines to therapists for its implementation" (Carroll & Nuro, 2002, p. 397). There is variability in research treatment manuals in terms of the amount of detail, contents, length of the document, etc. In general, the manual should include "the theoretical underpinnings of a treatment, the goals of a treatment, the strategies the therapist uses to reach those goals, and how that treatment is different from other treatments" (Carroll & Nuro, 1997, p. 50).

It has been proposed that, just as there is a stage model of psychotherapy model development, there is an analogous stage model of treatment manual development (Carroll & Nuro, 2002). In brief, a stage I manual will "define the treatment in broad strokes for preliminary evaluation of feasibility and efficacy" (Carroll & Nuro, p. 397). A stage II manual will elaborate on material presented in the stage I manual, while including new material based on having more experience with the intervention and initial manual. Finally, a stage III manual provides guidelines for delivering the intervention in "real world" circumstances rather than just "ideal" circumstances (Carroll & Nuro). Carroll and Nuro (2002) note that there likely will not be three distinct versions of the treatment manual, but rather they suggest a course of manual evolution as experience with a model develops. The reader is referred to their paper for detailed guidelines of what could be included in treatment manuals at each stage of development (Carroll & Nuro).

What does a treatment manual look like? Probably the best way to get a sense of the composition of a treatment manual is to actually look at some examples. Fortunately, some examples of treatment manuals from mature MFT models are publicly available. These examples would correspond to at least stage II manuals and some may qualify as stage III manuals according to the guidelines of Carroll and Nuro (2002). Some treatment manuals can be downloaded at no charge via the Internet. *Brief Strategic Therapy for Drug Abuse* (Szapocznik, Hervis, & Schwartz, 2003) (http://archives.drugabuse.gov/pdf/Manual5.pdf) and *Multidimensional Family Therapy for Adolescent Cannabis Users* (http://www.chestnut.org/LI/cyt/products/MDFT_CYT_v5.pdf) (Liddle, 2002) are two examples. Manuals from other well-developed models of MFT have been published as books. *Bipolar Disorder: A Family-Focused Treatment Approach* (Miklowitz, 2010) and *The Practice of Emotionally Focused Couple Therapy: Creating Connection* (Johnson, 2004) are two examples of published research treatment manuals. Thus, some

MFT books, such as Johnson's, serve the dual purpose of teaching clinicians how to conduct therapy according to the model and act as a treatment manual for research purposes.

How to write a treatment manual. If you plan to study (or implement) a mature MFT model, treatment manuals may already be available. However, many popular MFT models continue to have had little or no empirical evaluation (Lebow, Chambers, Christensen, & Johnson, 2012). A first step in being able to conduct randomized clinical trials on these models would be the development of a treatment manual. Undoubtedly, many (and perhaps all) untested, yet popular, MFT models would be found efficacious and effective if studied—what they are lacking are scientific "champions" to conduct such studies. It may be argued that some of these treatments cannot be manualized. However, I would maintain that if (a) it is possible to train therapists to conduct these therapies, (b) expert supervisors can tell when the therapy is being implemented skillfully versus poorly, and (c) expert supervisors can distinguish the therapy from other models, then it is possible to write a treatment manual for that model. Some steps for writing a treatment manual for a developed therapy follow.

Most graduates of MFT programs are familiar with writing a "theory of change" paper. A treatment manual can begin with a theory section—written from the point of view of the model in question. A partial list of questions that could be included are: What are values/beliefs/assumptions about therapy? What does the model say about the development of problems? What are stages of change in this model? What are the goals of therapy? What are critical elements of the model? What is the role of the therapist?

A good strategy is to watch video recordings of the therapeutic model in action and start writing down everything the therapist does to begin developing a list of interventions and techniques used in the model. You might group the therapist's actions using the four classes of therapist behaviors proposed by Waltz, Addis, Koerner, and Jacobson (1993): (1) behaviors unique to the model and essential to it, (2) behaviors that are essential to the model but not unique to it, (3) behaviors that are compatible with the model and therefore not prohibited, but neither necessary nor unique, and (4) behaviors that are prohibited. This will be helpful in distinguishing unique aspects of the model and will help future users of the manual see the place of common factors in the model (Blow & Sprenkle, 2001).

Other aspects of the video recordings to note are examples of what the interventions look like when done poorly, adequately, or in an exemplary manner. This will be helpful later in developing a therapist fidelity scale. You may begin to note special situations (i.e., client behaviors) and how these are handled within the model.

Hopefully you have developed colleagues who are experts in this model. Particularly if you are not the original developer of the model, you will want to have your preliminary treatment manual evaluated by the model developers or other recognized experts in the model. The goal is to improve the manual and receive an "endorsement" for your research from leaders associated with the model. At the conclusion of this process, you will have a stage I (or perhaps higher) treatment manual (Carroll & Nuro, 2002).

Monitoring Therapist Treatment Fidelity

After having a treatment manual, the next issue in evaluating the results of your randomized clinical trial is whether your therapists actually implemented the therapy as intended. This is referred to as the "fidelity" of their implementation of the treatment manual. Fidelity is determined by adherence to the model and competence in implementing it (Schoenwald et al., 2011; Waltz et al., 1993). "Adherence" is defined as "the extent to which a therapist used interventions and approaches prescribed by the treatment manual and avoided the use of intervention procedures proscribed by the manual" (Waltz et al., p. 620). Adherence can be assessed by having a trained observer or rater mark a checklist of behaviors prescribed or proscribed for the model (Waltz et al.). Adherence measures can be useful in assessing whether two therapies can be distinguished (Hogue et al., 1998). "Competence" is defined as "the level of skill shown by the therapist in delivering the treatment" (Waltz et al., p. 620).

Competence requires a judgment of whether an intervention was carried out skillfully or poorly and, therefore, requires that the raters be experts in the therapeutic model (Waltz et al., 1993). The full interpretation of the results of a randomized clinical trial requires knowing how skillfully the intervention model was implemented. Thus, while competence is more challenging to assess than adherence, it is also more important. The term "fidelity" has been used to encompass the concepts of both adherence and competence (Forgatch, Patterson, & DeGarmo, 2005).

Measuring fidelity of manual implementation is challenging and resource intensive (Schoenwald et al., 2011). In an evaluation of 147 randomized clinical trials testing models of psychotherapy, only 3.5% were rated as having adequately addressed treatment integrity (Perepletchikova, Treat, & Kazdin, 2007). The determination of fidelity is a growing trend and an increasing standard for randomized clinical trials involving MFT and other psychotherapeutic interventions.

General Principles of Developing Therapist
Fidelity Rating Scales

The first step in developing a therapist fidelity rating scale that measures competence is to identify the core skills/interventions comprised in the model. A Likert rating scale is then usually used, where the lowest score represents "poor," the midpoint score represents "satisfactory," and the highest rating represents "excellent." Anchor point descriptions will then be written for about half of the Likert rating—an anchor description for every other point. An "anchor point" is a brief narrative description, generally a sentence or two, that describes what the intervention would look like at that level of competence. This description is intended to help improve reliability by providing an "anchor" for the ratings. However, even with anchor points, the rater must be an expert in the therapy model to be able to distinguish different levels of competence for each skill/intervention.

Some rating scales will have an accompanying manual. The manual may provide an overview of the rating process, discuss how the scale is to be used, outline training of raters, etc. It will then provide some expanded discussion of each of the skill/intervention items. Generally, therapist rating scales are "macro" ratings rather than "micro" coding. That is, the rater will usually watch an entire video-recorded session and then make global ratings based on everything observed in the session. The possible contents of a treatment manual have been previously described (Carroll & Nuro, 1997).

Examples of Therapist Fidelity Rating Scales

As with treatment manuals, perhaps the best way to learn about therapist fidelity rating scales is to examine published examples. The Emotionally Focused Therapist—Therapist Fidelity Scale (EFT-TFS) (Denton, Johnson, & Burleson, 2009) was patterned after the Cognitive Therapy Scale (Vallis, Shaw, & Dobson, 1986). The EFT-TFS consists of 13 items representing core skills in emotionally focused therapy for couples (Johnson, 2004) such as "alliance making, alliance maintenance, creating safety in session" and "continually reframing the problem in terms of the cycle." Items on the EFT-TFS are rated on a 5-point Likert-type scale where "1" represents "poor," "3" represents "satisfactory," and "5" represents "exemplary." The EFT-TFS consists of a rating scale and an accompanying manual. The 13 items, anchor points, and accompanying text from the manual are contained in the work by Denton and colleagues (2009).

As an example, Skill 7 from the EFT-TFS is "placing emerging emotions into the cycle." The anchor point for 1 ("poor") is: "This skill is poorly demonstrated when the therapist does not place emerging emotions into the cycle at all or inadequately does so." The anchor point for 3 ("satisfactory") is: "This skill is adequately demonstrated when the therapist appropriately places emotion into the emerging cycle." Finally, the anchor point for 5 ("exemplary") is: "This skill is demonstrated in an exemplary manner when the therapist regularly and skillfully places emotion into the emerging cycle in an impactful manner." Likert ratings of 2 and 4 are for when an observed skill falls in between the anchor points.

Other examples of published fidelity measures include the Fidelity of Implementation Rating System (FIMP) (Forgatch et al., 2005) based on the Oregon model of Parent Management Training (Forgatch, Bullock, & Patterson, 2004). The BFM Therapist Competence/Adherence Scale (Weisman et al., 1998) is based on the behavioral family management model for treating patients with bipolar disorder and their families (Miklowitz, 2010). An example of an adherence measure is the MST Adherence Scale (Schoenwald, Henggeler, Brondino, & Rowland, 2000).

Does Fidelity Matter?

A valid question is whether higher levels of fidelity to a model of psychotherapy are associated with better outcomes. In the broader field of psychotherapy research, there have been mixed findings in answer to this question (Perepletchikova & Kazdin, 2005). Looking specifically at MFT randomized clinical trial research, fidelity has generally been associated with superior outcomes. High fidelity to the Oregon model of Parent Management Training (PMTO) was associated with predicted changes in observed parenting practices (Forgatch et al., 2005), and these results were replicated in a study conducted in Norway (Forgatch & DeGarmo, 2011). The relationship of fidelity to outcomes was evaluated in a study of juvenile offenders and their primary caregivers treated with MST (Henggeler et al., 2009). At 1.7-year follow-up, rearrest and incarceration were significantly higher in cases where treatment adherence had been low (Henggeler, Melton, Brondino, Scherer, & Hanley, 1997). In another study, of 118 juvenile offenders, overall outcomes using community therapists were not as good as had been the case in earlier MST efficacy studies (Henggeler, Pickrel, & Brondino, 1999). It was also found that adherence to MST was lower among these therapists—supporting the idea that high treatment adherence and good outcomes are linked. Further, it was found in this study that cases where MST adherence was higher had better outcomes (Henggeler et al., 1999). In other secondary analyses, it has been found that greater adherence to MST is associated with greater improvement in family relations and decreased delinquent peer affiliation (Huey, Henggeler, Brondino, & Pickrel, 2000). Therapist fidelity to the Family Focused Treatment for bipolar disorder model, though, was not associated with better overall outcomes, although it was associated with greater time until hospitalization (Weisman et al., 2002). However, these results were from a highly supervised efficacy study and the authors noted that there may not have been enough range in therapist fidelity to observe differences in outcome.

Ethical Issues in Randomized Clinical Trials

Randomization

If you believe in the effectiveness of your intervention, is it ethical to randomize a research participant to a control group? Although, as scientists, we strive to have no vested interest in the outcome of a randomized clinical trial, in most instances, as clinicians, we do have a preferred outcome. A concept that guides the scientific community in addressing this conflict is "clinical equipoise" (Freedman, 1987). "Equipoise" refers to a state of equilibrium, and "clinical" equipoise means that there is an "equilibrium" in the scientific community, a balance of opinion, as to the merits of the treatment in question (Friedman et al., 2010). It has been said that clinical equipoise exists when "there is a split in the clinical community, with some clinicians favoring A and others favoring B" (Freedman, p. 144). Thus, the existence of clinical equipoise is based on the presence, or lack thereof, of consensus in the scientific community regarding a particular intervention. If the consensus of the scientific community is that an intervention is not empirically supported, then, in general, it is considered ethical to randomize a research participant to the intervention of interest or to an alternative appropriate control condition.

Control Groups

Planning the control group is one of the most important issues in designing a randomized clinical trial (Friedman et al., 2010). The results from the experimental group will be compared with the control group, so the interpretation of results is heavily influenced by the composition of the control condition. There is a hierarchy of control groups, in terms of statistical power, ranging from "no treatment" groups to "active alternative treatment" groups (Freedland, Mohr, Davidson, Schwartz, 2011). The greatest power is obtained by comparing the experimental group with a no treatment group, because there is usually a large effect size when comparing the outcomes of the two groups. A variation on the no treatment control group is the wait-list control. Participants are randomized to active treatment versus a waiting list. After the waiting period, the participants are offered the active treatment outside of the randomized clinical trial.

A question is whether it is ethical to deny treatment to participants. One guide to answering this question is to judge whether the experimental treatment "deprives participants of a proven better treatment that they would otherwise receive" (Friedman et al., 2010, p. 22). With regard to the treatment of relationship distress, for example, it has been argued that given the existence of empirically supported treatments, it is no longer ethical to place clients on a waiting list (Baucom, Hahlweg, & Kuschel, 2003).

More stringent control groups would include "attention control" (Freedland et al., 2011). This is the closest to a placebo that can be obtained in MFT research. The goal is to give participants "attention" that is "nontherapeutic." Of course, any attention may have a therapeutic effect, so the design of the attention control group requires careful consideration. Often, these groups may include education and nonspecific support (e.g., Kendall, Hudson, Gosch, Flannery-Schroeder, & Suveg, 2008). Using components of the active treatment is another option that has been employed with a control group. For example, Jacobson and colleagues randomized participants to a complete package of cognitive therapy (Beck, Rush, Shaw, & Emery, 1979), the behavioral activation component of cognitive therapy alone, or behavioral activation plus teaching of skills to counteract automatic thoughts without focusing on core schemas

(Jacobson et al., 1996). They found that the components were as efficacious as the complete package of treatment.

More stringent control groups will be those that include active treatment. These groups will require larger sample sizes to detect a difference, but they are easier to justify ethically. The comparison treatment might be a known, manualized therapy. For example, in an evaluation of Integrative Behavioral Couple Therapy (Jacobson, Christensen, Prince, Cordova, & Eldridge, 2000), traditional behavioral marital therapy (Jacobson & Margolin, 1979) served as the control (Christensen et al., 2004). The results showed that the two interventions were equally efficacious.

Another option is to use as a control group existing clinical care as delivered by an agency (often called "treatment-as-usual," or TAU) (e.g., Henggeler et al., 1986). An advantage of TAU is that it is easy to implement, as it does not require the investigator to have expertise in or monitor delivery of an alternative treatment. A disadvantage is that it is not known what treatments were delivered in TAU. For example, youth and families referred from a youth diversion program were randomized to either MST or one of several social service agencies or community mental health centers (Henggeler et al.). The youth randomized to MST had better outcomes than those assigned to community treatment. The authors noted that they did not have access to treatment records from the community agencies and centers, so did not know what treatment was received by the youth randomized to community treatment (Henggeler et al.).

Another stringent design is the "add on" design. Here, all participants receive an established intervention and are randomized to receive either the established intervention alone or the established intervention augmented by an add-on intervention (e.g., Denton, Wittenborn, & Golden, 2012). This design is desirable where the clinical condition being treated is a serious one (e.g., major depressive disorder), and it might be considered unethical to treat participants with an experimental intervention alone. The downside is that it will be more challenging to detect a statistically significant difference between groups because all participants are receiving the same established intervention.

Ethical Responsibilities Related to the Scientific Community and the Larger Public Good

Clinical Trials Registration

There is increasing emphasis on transparency in randomized clinical trials. Areas of special concern have been the nonpublishing of negative results and the selective reporting of outcomes (Tse, Williams, & Zarin, 2009). Since 2007, the United States Food and Drug Administration has required the registration of randomized clinical trials of certain medications, biological products, and medical devices prior to the beginning of the trial (Tse et al., 2009). Registration is done at the ClinicalTrials.gov website, which is maintained by the U.S. National

Institutes of Health. For each study entered, the investigator specifies the condition under study, the intervention, eligibility criteria, primary outcome(s), and other information. In doing this, the investigators have publicly "laid their cards on the table" prior to beginning the study so that future readers of reports based on the study data can have more confidence that the investigators did not go "data mining" to find the outcome that was most favorable.

MFT clinical trials are not required by law to be registered at ClinicalTrials. gov, although MFT researchers may register their trials voluntarily. Some scientific journals, however, have adopted a policy of not publishing results of clinical trials (including those with behavioral interventions) that were not registered at an approved registry such as ClinicalTrials.gov (International Committee of Medical Journal Editors, 2004).

Transparency in Reporting

To properly assess the report of a randomized clinical trial, the reader must have sufficient information about the methods and results of the trial. This requires transparency on the part of authors (Schulz, Altman, & Moher for the CONSORT Group, 2010). One of the leading groups in developing standards for transparency in the reporting of randomized clinical trials has been the CONSORT group (Consolidated Standards of Reporting Trials)—an international group of journal editors and scientists. The main product of the CONSORT group is the "CONSORT statement," which is periodically revised and simultaneously published in several journals, where it is available for free download (e.g., Schulz et al., 2010). The statement includes a checklist of information (the "CONSORT checklist") to include when reporting a randomized clinical trial and a flow diagram to indicate how participants flowed through the study from initial assessment to final data analysis (Schulz et al.). Randomized clinical trials of some interventions have specialized reporting needs—such as trials of psychotherapies. Recognizing this, the CONSORT group has produced a series of "extensions" to the CONSORT statement for specialized needs. MFT interventions come under the "nonpharmacological treatment interventions" extension (Boutron, Moher, Altman, Schulz, & Ravaud, for the CONSORT Group, 2008).

Many journals, such as the *Journal of Family Psychology*, now require submissions of randomized clinical trials to include (i) a CONSORT-style participant flow diagram in the manuscript and (ii) a CONSORT checklist with an indication where each item on the checklist can be found in the manuscript. A template of the checklist formatted in Microsoft Word is available on the CONSORT group website (www.consort-statement.org). If some items on the checklist are not included in the study, this is to be mentioned in the manuscript as a limitation of the study. A systematic review found that journals requiring use of the CONSORT checklist had better reporting of randomized clinical trials than did journals not requiring the checklist (Plint et al., 2006).

New Developments in Clinical Trials

A criticism of the traditional randomized clinical trial design is that it is not reflective of clinical practice—a critique related to its external validity. Many chronic clinical conditions require more than one course of treatment, and the traditional randomized clinical trial, testing only one intervention per group and usually at a fixed "dose," gives little or no guidance on the sequencing of treatment (Collins, Murphy, & Bierman, 2004). In response to this criticism, the "adaptive" design has been developed. Adaptive treatment research designs have more than one course of treatment, with subsequent treatments being selected based on factors such as response to a prior treatment (e.g., Brooner et al., 2007) and baseline participant characteristics (Marlowe, Festinger, Dugosh, Lee, & Benasutti, 2007).

Adaptive treatments more closely parallel clinical practice and thus may have greater external validity. Differing from clinical practice, however, there are specified decision rules to make regarding treatment assignments. MFT randomized clinical trials have not utilized adaptive designs to this point, although they could in the future. Couple or family therapy could be one component of a stepped treatment design with other treatments, or an adaptive design could utilize only MFT interventions. For example, participants not responding to an MFT intervention after a certain number of sessions could be randomized to alternative, more intensive treatments, while those with a good response to the intervention might be randomized to receive booster sessions or no additional treatment.

A variation of the adaptive design was utilized in the STAR*D treatment of major depressive disorder study (Gaynes et al., 2009). As noted above, many prospective research participants are reluctant to participate in a randomized clinical trial, as they give up their choice of health care to the process of randomization. The STAR*D study took patient preference partially into account with a design called "equipoise stratified randomization" (Lavori et al., 2001). Patients with major depressive disorder were allowed to choose treatments from a list that they would be willing to be randomized to. After initial treatment with citalopram, participants who did not experience remission of depressive symptoms were randomized to one of the treatments they had endorsed and could have up to three additional courses of treatment (Rush, Trivedi, & Fava, 2003). The largest randomized clinical trial for the treatment of depression ever conducted (beginning with over 4,000 participants), over 100 scientific papers have been published from the STAR*D data, and the results have been previously summarized (e.g., Gaynes et al.; Rush, 2011).

A challenge with the adaptive designs is the large sample size needed to allow for comparing multiple steps and account for attrition as the study proceeds. It may be most feasible that MFT interventions would be included as one treatment option along with non-MFT interventions in a large study. For example, in the STAR*D study, cognitive therapy was one of the treatment options participants could select to include in their randomization list (Thase et al., 2007).

The STEP-BD study (Systematic Treatment Enhancement Program for Bipolar Disorder) was a large effectiveness study that utilized a hybrid of standardized care and randomized care (Sachs et al., 2003) in which one treatment was Family Focused Therapy for bipolar disorder (Miklowitz, 2010).

Self-of-the-Researcher

Although challenging to carry out, randomized clinical trials have their rewards. For investigators who are clinicians at heart, randomized clinical trials provide a way to combine research and practice. It is satisfying to look for answers to very fundamental questions about the effectiveness of our clinical work, and it is enjoyable to work closely with colleagues on a research team. Once completed, randomized clinical trials are "high impact" studies that are of interest to researchers, policymakers, and practicing clinicians and can lead the way to a successful academic career.

While there will undoubtedly be design improvements in the future, randomized clinical trials are presently the "gold standard" for evaluating clinical interventions. Hopefully, this chapter has been of help to readers in becoming informed "consumers" of journal articles reporting on randomized clinical trials. Even better, perhaps some will be inspired to embark on the journey of becoming a clinical trialist!

References

Bale, R. N., Van Stone, W. W., Kuldau, J. M., Engelsing, T. M., Elashoff, R. M., & Zarcone, V. P., Jr. (1980). Therapeutic communities vs methadone maintenance. A prospective controlled study of narcotic addiction treatment: Design and one-year follow-up. *Archives of General Psychiatry, 37,* 179–193.

Baucom, D. H., Hahlweg, K., & Kuschel, A. (2003). Are waiting-list control groups needed in future marital therapy outcome research? *Behavior Therapy, 34,* 179–188.

Beck, A. T., Rush, A. J., Shaw, B. F., & Emery, G. (1979). *Cognitive therapy of depression.* New York: Guilford.

Blow, A. J., & Sprenkle, D. H. (2001). Common factors across theories of marriage and family therapy: A modified Delphi study. *Journal of Marital and Family Therapy, 27,* 385–401.

Boutron, I., Moher, D., Altman, D. G., Schulz, K. F., & Ravaud, P., for the CONSORT Group. (2008). Extending the CONSORT statement to randomized trials of nonpharmacologic treatment: Explanation and elaboration. *Annals of Internal Medicine, 148,* 295–309.

Brooner, R. K., Kidorf, M. S., King, V. L., Stoller, K. B., Neufeld, K. J., & Kolodner, K. (2007). Comparing adaptive stepped care and monetary-based voucher interventions for opioid dependence. *Drug and Alcohol Dependence, 88,* S14–S23.

Carroll, K. M., & Nuro, K. F. (1997). The use and development of treatment manuals. In K. Carroll (Ed.), *Improving compliance with alcoholism treatment* (pp. 50–68). Bethesda, MD: National Institute on Alcohol Abuse and Alcoholism.

Carroll, K.M., & Nuro, K.F. (2002). One size cannot fit all: A stage model for psychotherapy manual development. *Clinical Psychology: Science and Practice, 9,* 396–406.

Christensen, A., Atkins, D.C., Berns, S., Wheeler, J., Baucom, D.H., & Simpson, L.E. (2004). Traditional versus integrative behavioral couple therapy for significantly and chronically distressed married couples. *Journal of Consulting and Clinical Psychology, 72,* 176–191.

Collins, L.M., Murphy, S.A., & Bierman, K.L. (2004). A conceptual framework for adaptive preventive interventions. *Prevention Science, 5,* 185–196.

Corrigan, P.W., & Salzer, M.S. (2003). The conflict between random assignment and treatment preference: Implications for internal validity. *Evaluation and Program Planning, 26,* 109–121.

Curtis, N.M., Ronan, K.R., & Borduin, C.M. (2004). Multisystemic treatment: A meta-analysis of outcome studies. *Journal of Family Psychology, 18,* 411–419.

Denton, W.H., Johnson, S.M., & Burleson, B.R. (2009). Emotion-focused therapy-therapist fidelity scale (EFT-TFS): Conceptual development and content validity. *Journal of Couple and Relationship Therapy, 8,* 226–246.

Denton, W. H., Wittenborn, A. K., & Golden, R. N. (2012). Augmenting antidepressant medication treatment of depressed women with emotionally focused therapy for couples: A randomized pilot study. *Journal of Marital and Family Therapy, 38* (Supplement 1), 23–38.

Forgatch, M.S., Bullock, B.M., & Patterson, G.R. (2004). From theory to practice: Increasing effective parenting through role-play: The Oregon model of Parent Management Training (PMTO). In H. Steiner (Ed.), *Handbook of mental health interventions in children and adolescents: An integrated developmental approach* (pp. 782–813). San Francisco: Jossey-Bass.

Forgatch, M.S., & DeGarmo, D.S. (2011). Sustaining fidelity following the nationwide PMTO (TM) implementation in Norway. *Prevention Science, 12,* 235–246.

Forgatch, M.S., Patterson, G.R., & DeGarmo, D.S. (2005). Evaluating fidelity: Predictive validity for a measure of competent adherence to the Oregon model of Parent Management Training. *Behavior Therapy, 36,* 3–13.

Freedland, K. E., Mohr, D. C., Davidson, K. W., & Schwartz, J. E. (2011). Usual and unusual care: Existing practice control groups in randomized controlled trials of behavioral interventions. *Psychosomatic Medicine, 73,* 323–335.

Freedman, B. (1987). Equipoise and the ethics of clinical research. *New England Journal of Medicine, 317,* 141–145.

Friedman, L.M., Furberg, C.D., & DeMets, D.L. (2010). *Fundamentals of clinical trials* (4th ed.). New York: Springer.

Gaynes, B.N., Warden, D., Trivedi, M.H., Wisniewski, S.R., Fava, M., & Rush, A.J. (2009). What did STAR*D teach us? Results from a large-scale, practical, clinical trial for patients with depression. *Psychiatric Services, 60,* 1439–1445.

Henggeler, S.W., Melton, G.B., Brondino, M.J., Scherer, D.G., & Hanley, J.H. (1997). Multisystemic therapy with violent and chronic juvenile offenders and their families: The role of treatment fidelity in successful dissemination. *Journal of Consulting and Clinical Psychology, 65,* 821–833.

Henggeler, S.W., Pickrel, S.G., & Brondino, M.J. (1999). Multisystemic treatment of substance-abusing and -dependent delinquents: Outcomes, treatment fidelity, and transportability. *Mental Health Services Research, 1,* 171–184.

Henggeler, S. W., Rodick, J. D., Borduin, C. M., Hanson, C. L., Watson, S. M., & Urey, J. R. (1986). Multisystemic treatment of juvenile offenders: Effects on adolescent behavior and family interaction. *Developmental Psychology, 22,* 132–141.

Henggeler, S. W., Schoenwald, S. K., Borduin, C. M., Rowland, M. D., & Cunningham, P. B. (2009). *Multisystemic therapy for antisocial behavior in children and adolescents.* New York: Guilford Press.

Henggeler, S. W., Schoenwald, S. K., Liao, J. G., Letourneau, E. J., & Edwards, D. L. (2002). Transporting efficacious treatments to field settings: The link between supervisory practices and therapist fidelity in MST programs. *Journal of Clinical Child and Adolescent Psychology, 31,* 155–167.

Hogue, A., Liddle, H. A., Rowe, C., Turner, R. M., Dakof, G. A., & LaPann, K. (1998). Treatment adherence and differentiation in individual versus family therapy for adolescent substance abuse. *Journal of Counseling Psychology, 45,* 104–114.

Huey, S. J., Henggeler, S. W., Brondino, M. J., & Pickrel, S. G. (2000). Mechanisms of change in multisystemic therapy: Reducing delinquent behavior through therapist adherence and improved family and peer functioning. *Journal of Consulting and Clinical Psychology, 68,* 451–467.

International Committee of Medical Journal Editors. (2004). Clinical trial registration: A statement from the International Committee of Medical Journal Editors. *Lancet, 364,* 911–912.

Jacobson, N. S., Christensen, A., Prince, S. E., Cordova, J., & Eldridge, K. (2000). Integrative behavioral couple therapy: An acceptance-based, promising new treatment for couple discord. *Journal of Consulting and Clinical Psychology, 68,* 351–355.

Jacobson, N. S., Dobson, K. S., Truax, P. A., Addis, M. E., Koerner, K., Gollan, J. K., Gortner, E., & Prince, S. E. (1996). A component analysis of cognitive-behavioral treatment for depression. *Journal of Consulting and Clinical Psychology, 64,* 295–304.

Jacobson, N. S., & Margolin, G. (1979). *Marital therapy: Strategies based on social learning and behavior exchange processes.* New York: Brunner/Mazel.

Johnson, S. M. (2004). *The practice of emotionally focused couple therapy: Creating connection* (2nd ed.). New York: Brunner-Routledge.

Kendall, P. C., Hudson, J. L., Gosch, E., Flannery-Schroeder, E., & Suveg, C. (2008). Cognitive-behavioral therapy for anxiety disordered youth: A randomized clinical trial evaluating child and family modalities. *Journal of Consulting and Clinical Psychology, 76,* 282–297.

Lachin, J. M. (1988). Properties of simple randomization in clinical trials. *Controlled Clinical Trials, 9,* 312–326.

Lavori, P. W., Rush, A. J., Wisniewski, S. R., Alpert, J., Fava, M., Kupfer, D. J., . . . Trivedi, M. (2001). Strengthening clinical effectiveness trials: Equipoise-stratified randomization. *Biological Psychiatry, 50,* 792–801.

Lebow, J. L., Chambers, A. L., Christensen, A., & Johnson, S. M. (2012). Research on the treatment of couple distress. *Journal of Marital and Family Therapy, 38,* 145–168.

Liddle, H. A. (2002). *Multidimensional family therapy for adolescent cannabis users. Cannabis Youth Treatment Series, Volume 5. DHHS Pub. No. 02–3660.* Rockville, MD: Center for Substance Abuse Treatment, Substance Abuse and Mental Health Services Administration.

Marlowe, D. B., Festinger, D. S., Dugosh, K. L., Lee, P. A., & Benasutti, K. M. (2007). Adapting judicial supervision to the risk level of drug offenders: Discharge and 6-month outcomes from a prospective matching study. *Drug and Alcohol Dependence, 88, Supplement 2,* S4–S13.

Matthews, E. E., Cook, P. F., Terada, M., & Aloia, M. S. (2010). Randomizing research participants: Promoting balance and concealment in small samples. *Research in Nursing & Health, 33,* 243–253.

Miklowitz, D. J. (2010). *Bipolar disorder: A family-focused treatment approach* (2nd ed.). New York: Guilford Press.

Onken, L. S., Blaine, J. D., & Battjes, R. J. (1997). Behavioral therapy research: A conceptualization of a process. In S. W. Henggeler & A. B. Santos (Eds.), *Innovative approaches for difficult-to-treat populations.* Washington, DC: American Psychiatric Press.

Perepletchikova, F., & Kazdin, A. E. (2005). Treatment integrity and therapeutic change: Issues and research recommendations. *Clinical Psychology–Science and Practice, 12,* 365–383.

Perepletchikova, F., Treat, T. A., & Kazdin, A. E. (2007). Treatment integrity in psychotherapy research: Analysis of the studies and examination of the associated factors. *Journal of Consulting and Clinical Psychology, 75,* 829–841.

Plint, A. C., Moher, D., Morrison, A., Schulz, K., Altman, D. G., Hill, C., & Gaboury, I. (2006). Does the CONSORT checklist improve the quality of reports of randomised controlled trials? A systematic review. *Medical Journal of Australia, 185,* 263–267.

Rounsaville, B. J., Carroll, K. M., & Onken, L. S. (2001). A stage model of behavioral therapies research: Getting started and moving on from stage I. *Clinical Psychology–Science and Practice, 8,* 133–142.

Rush, A. J. (2011). Star-D: Lessons learned and future implications. *Depression and Anxiety, 28,* 521–524.

Rush, A. J., Trivedi, M., & Fava, M. (2003). Depression, IV: STAR*D treatment trial for depression. *American Journal of Psychiatry, 160,* 237.

Sachs, G. S., Thase, M. E., Otto, M. W., Bauer, M., Miklowitz, D., Wisniewski, S. R., . . . Rosenbaum, J. F. (2003). Rationale, design, and methods of the systematic treatment enhancement program for bipolar disorder. *Biological Psychiatry, 53,* 1028–1042.

Schoenwald, S. K., Garland, A. F., Chapman, J. E., Frazier, S. L., Sheidow, A. J., & Southam-Gerow, M. A. (2011). Toward the effective and efficient measurement of implementation fidelity. *Administration and Policy in Mental Health and Mental Health Services Research, 38,* 32–43.

Schoenwald, S. K., Henggeler, S. W., Brondino, M. J., & Rowland, M. D. (2000). Multisystemic therapy: Monitoring treatment fidelity. *Family Process, 39,* 83–103.

Schulz, K. F., Altman, D. G., & Moher, D., for the CONSORT Group. (2010). Consort 2010 statement: Updated guidelines for reporting parallel group randomized trials. *Annals of Internal Medicine, 152,* 726–733.

Szapocznik, J., Hervis, O. E., & Schwartz, S. J. (2003). *Brief strategic family therapy for adolescent drug abuse.* Rockville, MD: National Institute on Drug Abuse.

Thase, M. E., Friedman, E. S., Biggs, M. M., Wisniewski, S. R., Trivedi, M. H., Luther, J. F., . . . Rush, A. J. (2007). Cognitive therapy versus medication in augmentation and switch strategies as second-step treatments: A STAR*D report. *American Journal of Psychiatry, 164,* 739–752.

Thomson, C. L., Morley, K. C., Teesson, M., Sannibale, C., & Haber, P. S. (2008). Issues with recruitment to randomised controlled trials in the drug and alcohol field: A literature review and Australian case study. *Drug and Alcohol Review, 27,* 115–122.

Tse, T., Williams, R. J., & Zarin, D. A. (2009). Reporting "basic results" in Clinical-Trials.gov. *Chest, 136,* 295–303.

Vallis, T. M., Shaw, B. F., & Dobson, K. S. (1986). The cognitive therapy scale: Psychometric properties. *Journal of Consulting and Clinical Psychology, 54,* 381–385.

Waltz, J., Addis, M. E., Koerner, K., & Jacobson, N. S. (1993). Testing the integrity of a psychotherapy protocol: Assessment of adherence and competence. *Journal of Consulting and Clinical Psychology, 61,* 620–630.

Weisman, A., Tompson, M. C., Okazaki, S., Gregory, J., Goldstein, M. J., Rea, M., & Miklowitz, D. J. (2002). Clinicians' fidelity to a manual-based family treatment as a predictor of the one-year course of bipolar disorder. *Family Process, 41,* 123–131.

Weisman, A. G., Okazaki, S., Gregory, J., Tompson, M. C., Goldstein, M. J., Rea, M., & Miklowitz, D. J. (1998). Evaluating therapist competency and adherence to behavioral family management with bipolar patients. *Family Process, 37,* 107–121.

13

SINGLE-CASE RESEARCH WITH COUPLES AND FAMILIES

Kayla D. Mennenga and Lee N. Johnson

This chapter provides information on single-case research design, the different variations of the design, and the benefits. Single-case designs are simple to implement and best used when studying the effectiveness of a specific intervention or multiple interventions, but not a course of therapy (e.g., eight sessions of cognitive-behavioral therapy). The unique aspect of single-case design is that you can conduct a rigorous study, with a high degree of internal validity, with one or a small number of subjects (Kazdin, 2011) while avoiding the constraints and ethical issues associated with randomly assigning research participants. Single-case research methods originated in psychology and are ideally suited for fields interested in showing change via intervention. These methods are less likely to be used in the social and biological sciences (Kazdin).

Historically, single-case designs were used "to conduct experimental investigations with the single case (i.e., one subject)" (Kazdin, 1982, p. 3); studies including such experimentation would be called single-subject research design. Contemporary uses of single-case designs may be to investigate a single subject or to evaluate the effects of interventions, especially the ability to rigorously evaluate such effects repeatedly across multiple participants. Single-case research designs study one couple or family using a repeated measures process or using replication of multiple single cases. For example, in the context of therapeutic intervention, a particular couple or family may undergo a particular therapy model. By intervening at different times, the effectiveness of the particular model may be observed. In addition, this model can be used with other couples or families to further investigate the effectiveness of the model with a similar presenting problem, such as depression, anxiety, or couple satisfaction. Additionally, by using the couple or family as their own control, implementing the intervention at different phases allows the therapist to observe changes that may be occurring across time for the cases individually and show that the intervention causes the changes in the dependent variable.

Single-case research designs are often confused with case studies; however, single-case designs are distinctly different from case studies. The main difference is that case studies generally lack experimental manipulation, so causal effects are not tested or observed (Rizvi & Nock, 2008; Tate et al., 2008). Additionally, case studies often are descriptive, detailed, and qualitative, and are used to offer explanations and connect different variables together through an anecdotal or narrative method. Single-case research, on the other hand, is quantitatively measured, uses some form of experimental manipulation, and uses replication as a means to understand the effects of intervention (Kazdin, 2011; Nock, Michel, & Photos, 2008).

To be carried out successfully, single-case designs have two key requirements: (1) continuous assessment of the dependent variables over time and (2) the ability to manipulate the independent variable, often by removing and reintroducing the intervention (Crane, 1985) or by changing the intervention. By manipulating the intervention by its removal or changing it, participants serve as their own controls. This provides multiple data points from different conditions, allowing researchers the ability to evaluate the impact of the intervention and know across multiple incidents whether the change is accounted for by the intervention.

The main downside to single-case research is that this methodology has not been used much and is less likely to be taught to students. We believe there are several reasons for these past trends. First, with the increase in funding for randomized clinical trials, fewer researchers are exploring options that do not involve funding (Rizvi & Nock, 2008). However, many funding agencies require pilot data to provide proof of concept prior to receiving funding. Single-case research designs can be a great resource for gathering valid pilot data. Second, increasingly sophisticated statistics and research methods are being developed that are used for collecting and analyzing large amounts of data, and because of the small numbers associated with single-case research, single-case designs continue to fly under the radar and are not being taught (Nock et al., 2008). Third, when single-case research designs were first introduced, continuous measurement of variables was more problematic. With advancing technology, there have been great strides in our ability to continuously measure dependent variables. A review of technology advances is beyond the scope of this chapter (see Chapter 8 for a review). Finally, many researchers struggle with how to remove interventions once they have been delivered. However, there are ways this can be addressed in the design of single-case research.

This chapter will describe single-case designs and how to use them in a couple and family therapy setting. These designs are simple to implement, provide evidence of causal relationships, and are lower in cost than a randomized controlled trial. These designs also have great potential to advance our knowledge of interventions used in marriage and family therapy (MFT).

Unit of Analysis

Previous uses of single-case research methodologies have investigated an individual. In such single-case experimental designs, the unit of analysis was a single individual or a group of individuals, and information was obtained concurrently on the individuals; therefore, the n tends to be rather small (Barlow & Hersen, 1984; Lundervold & Belwood, 2000; Robinson & Foster, 1979). Bloom, Fischer, and Orme (1995) state that this is a process of using the system as a single unit and gathering all information possible on that unit. Single-case research designs provide a treatment score at each observation time (Gorman & Allison, 1996), and this is considered the unit of analysis. The unit of analysis in single-case research designs may refer to many different observational units. The unit of analysis can be the individual, the couple, or the family. In such cases, for example, you could observe the individual, couple, or family throughout the process of the different phases and assess whether the intervention was effective. Additionally, researchers could observe particular sessions to see the outcome of implementing the intervention. For example, if a researcher were implementing a certain intervention in one session but withholding it in the second session, using the session as the unit of analysis would be appropriate in investigating that particular intervention. The same could occur with using parts of the sessions as the units of analysis. In this case, the researcher is considering the number of observations, rather than only the unit(s) for which information is gathered. In the previous example, n could be the sessions or it could be the couples across the sessions. Furthermore, the unit of analysis could be the individuals within the couples or the families. Even while seeing a couple in session, the researcher could use the individuals within the couple as the unit of analysis, thus allowing research to track changes in couples and individuals within couples at the same time. Consequently, depending on the goals of the study, the unit of analysis varies for single-case research designs.

Using Single-Case Research Design

The goal and purpose of single-case designs is to "make and test predictions about performance" (Kazdin, 2011, p. 142), but knowing when to use a small n or single-case design is important. In clinical research, a randomized control trial has been held up as the "gold standard" for showing causal relationships. However, when random assignment to different conditions is not ethical or possible, using single-case research is an equally rigorous option. Similar to expanding a basic randomized control trial to meet design needs to answer the research questions under investigation, single-case research also has many different design options. Each design continuously assesses the dependent variable over time and shows what happens when an intervention is not used (Kazdin). When and how the intervention takes place varies with different research questions. We will look at the most basic elements of single-case designs and then discuss how these designs can be adapted to fit specific, applied, and clinical settings related to MFT.

The most basic design in single-case research is the AB method. The method is designed to show the effects of an intervention on an individual, couple, or family unit (Dugard, File, & Todman, 2012). The letter "A" represents the baseline phase or measurements of behavior before the independent variable is introduced (Crane, 1985), and the letter "B" represents the intervention phase, or the time at which the intervention is implemented. In this basic design, a series of measurements are taken. After establishing a baseline, the intervention is implemented, and the effects are observed as it is compared with the baseline, or "A" phase. If you are doing research on couples or families, we also recommend that you establish a baseline for each person in the system, as well as for each couple- or family-level variable. Adding additional baseline phases or additional intervention phases creates an expanded design to show replication of the effect across time. For example, if a researcher used the ABAB design, the goal would be to examine the intervention by alternating the baseline or no intervention condition (A phase) with the intervention (B phase). The intervention is deemed effective if performance returns close to baseline after the intervention is withdrawn and then increases again when the intervention is implemented. While the AB design is the most basic, it is recommended that "at the minimum, the design include three phases" (Kazdin, 2011, p. 136); these three phases can include either two baselines and an intervention or two interventions and one baseline. For example, a therapist may begin therapy by giving homework to a couple in the first session, not giving homework in the next session, and giving homework again in the third session. However, having four phases allows researchers to replicate the effects of the intervention within the individual, couple, or family. For example, in couples therapy, a researcher may want to investigate the influence that exercising before the session during one week has on the therapy session versus not exercising before the session during the next week. In this case, the researcher is removing the intervention of exercise from the design to see how therapy proceeds without exercising before the session. The researcher would then be able to see whether a trend appears after repeating this process.

Having a baseline is important because it describes what is happening and shows future behavior if an intervention is not implemented (Kazdin, 1978, 2011). The baseline phase is established before the intervention is implemented to create a standard by which change is judged; furthermore, the baseline provides the researcher information on targets or variables that change (Lundervold & Belwood, 2000). During the intervention phase, the researcher is able to see whether or not deviation from the baseline occurs. For example, a couple presents to therapy for issues in their marriage. Each person fills out a measure that assesses his or her level of couple satisfaction and level of anxiety. Having this baseline understanding on these two variables for what their behaviors would be like in the future, the therapist begins sessions with the couple. After some time with the couple, the therapist begins using emotionally focused therapy (EFT) with the couple. During the session, the therapist introduces an EFT intervention. The couple seems to respond well to it, comes back for the next session, and fills out the same measure assessing their level of satisfaction within their relationship. While the wife's satisfaction increased and her anxiety has decreased, the husband's satisfaction has increased but his anxiety has stayed the same. This may indicate that the intervention was successful and effective for the couple's satisfaction, but the husband's anxiety was not affected.

Understanding the intention of the intervention, the baselines from which the individuals started, and knowing how their behaviors would proceed in the future helps the therapist tailor interventions that are necessary for issues that are presented to therapy. The figure below provides a visual example of understanding how prediction can influence intervention effectiveness and why having a baseline is important.

In addition, the accuracy of predictions can be observed through using single-case designs, and the effectiveness of different interventions can be compared. From the previous example, the therapist might try a different or an additional intervention specifically for the husband that would target his anxiety. Understanding the trajectory of present behaviors provides insight into which interventions a therapist might use, as well as the ability to observe the effectiveness of the intervention through measures. Kazdin (2011) states that the effectiveness of interventions is achieved by projecting a continuation of the current baseline behavior. For example, if a couple is having trouble with communication, and a major complaint of the husband is that the wife interrupts him while talking, then the therapist could get a baseline of the number of times the wife complains over a week's time. Once the therapist is able to see how the current behavior is displayed, he or she will be able to make a prediction, or a projection, of what her future behavior might be.

In the case of clinical research or research where the intervention can't be completely removed, a more useful design might be the ABCBC method. This method includes the baseline phase (A), which might be measured before therapy

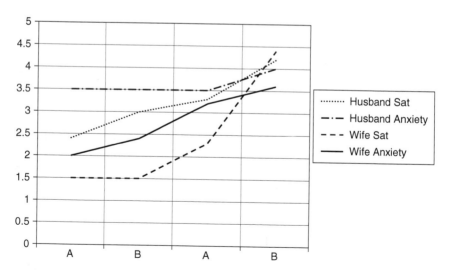

Figure 13.1 Hypothetical example of ABAB data.

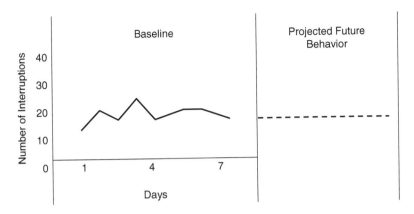

Figure 13.2 Hypothetical example of baseline observations of frequency of interruptions. The data in the baseline are used to predict or project the potential rate of future behavior.

occurs, and the intervention phases (B and C). This type of design would be helpful if a researcher wants to investigate the effectiveness of multiple or separate interventions. The ability to see the effects of an intervention and then to change or add a new intervention to improve the outcome is a benefit to using the ABCBC single-case design (Kazdin, 1982, 2003, 2011).

For example, Anderson, Templeton, Johnson, Childs, and Peterson (2006) used an ABCBC design to examine the differences in how therapy is structured. After establishing a baseline (A phase), where clients sat alone and waited for their therapist, they proceeded with two different therapy structures. During the B phase, the therapist structured therapy sessions to have the clients talk to the therapist and not to each other. Therapists were instructed to block clients when they tried to talk to each other. After 6 minutes, the researcher behind the mirror called into the session and instructed the therapist to start the C phase by changing the structure to having clients in couple therapy talk to each other and not to the therapist. The therapist was instructed to actively direct clients to talk to each other when they tried to talk to the therapist. The B and C phases were then repeated for an additional 6 minutes. Immediately following the session, couples viewed the video recording of their session and rated their emotional closeness using the Perception Analyzer to rate their level of emotional closeness continuously over the session. Couples generally reported that their emotional closeness was higher when they were talking with each other, as opposed to talking to the therapist.

Analysis in Single-Case Research Designs

Researchers using single-case research designs are interested in the ability to assess the efficacy of the different interventions implemented with clients. According to Kazdin (1978, 1982), there are two criteria that have been used to evaluate intervention effects: the experimental criterion and the therapeutic criterion. The experimental criterion refers to comparing the behavior during the intervention with the behavior before the intervention was implemented. Replicating treatment effects over time and showing change in behavior meet the experimental criterion. The experimental criterion involves the use of visual inspection; this is the process of "reaching a judgment about the reliability or consistency of intervention effects by visually examining the graphed data" (Kazdin, 1982, p. 232). Knowing whether the intervention effects are consistent and reliable depends on many characteristics: changes in means, changes in level, changes in trend, the length of time for change to take place (latency of the change), and using quality measures.

One strategy for visual inspection of the data is the degree to which data from each phase do not overlap (i.e., the values of the data points during the baseline phase do not approach the values observed during the intervention phase). Effects of the intervention are considered valid when the intervention phase does not overlap with behavior during the baseline phase across the different observation points (Kazdin, 1978). Scruggs and Mastropieri (1998) discuss the importance of the percentage of nonoverlapping data (PND) and provide some ranges that are useful. In general, PND scores of 90% or higher are considered very effective, scores of 70% to 90% are considered effective, scores of 50% to 70% are moderately effective, and scores below 50% are considered ineffective treatments. Generally, the lower the percentage of overlap, the greater the impact of the intervention. An important benefit of using PND is that it provides meaningful information about the effectiveness of the intervention. Kazdin (1978) suggests that the "replication of nonoverlapping distributions during different treatment phases strongly argues for the effects of the treatment" (p. 637). Finding the PND involves drawing a line through the highest baseline data point and through the subsequent treatment phase (Scruggs & Mastropieri, 1998). Visual inspection requires the researcher to make judgments about the patterns evident in the data. The use of visual inspection may be sufficient when the intervention effects are very large. The therapeutic value or importance of the results is determined by the effect the behavior change actually has for enhancing the client's functioning (Kazdin, 1978, 1982, 2011).

The complexity of projects and situations in which studies are conducted may make observing the intervention effects more difficult (Kazdin, 1982, 2011). In some complicated settings, the criterion for visual inspection may not be met, so additional statistical analysis is necessary. The use of statistical analysis can be for many reasons, such as trends in the data, increased intrasubject variability, investigation of new research areas, small changes that may be important, and replicability in data evaluation. Kazdin (1982) further suggests that statistical analysis is valuable when the baseline is not stable, when a new treatment is under evaluation, when the treatment effect is unclear, or when controlling for extraneous factors. Covering all possible statistical analyses used in single-case research is beyond the scope of this chapter; however, understanding some basic ideas is helpful.

Researchers suggest using a time series analysis to compare data for observations across different phases and over time (Kazdin, 1982). Time series analysis computes t-tests to evaluate the changes in level and in trend, taking into account the nonindependence of the data. Using time series analysis provides insight into the statistical meaningfulness of change in the level and trend from one phase to another and can be used in any design in which change occurs across phases. Time series analysis can be used with only one case or many cases and depends on the unit of analysis that fits the research questions. For example, using the ABAB design in single-case research, we can make separate comparisons for each set of adjacent phases (e.g., A_1B_1, A_2B_2, B_1A_2). Time series can assess each baseline to investigate whether there is a change in the level or trend (Kazdin, 1982).

Another statistical analysis in single-case research design that may be useful is the repeated-measures analysis of variance, ANOVA, which is used to compare the dependent measures of a single sample under more than two different conditions (treatment phases). This particular analysis is useful in understanding trends and, as well, it eliminates the variability due to individual (unit) differences because participants (or units) can each serve as their own control. Making a decision about whether to use visual inspection, statistical analyses, or both will be dependent on many factors and should be based on the experimental design and the goals and hypotheses of the study.

Validity Issues

Internal validity describes the level that the independent variable produced the effect it appears to have on the dependent variable. In addition, having high internal validity rules out the alternative explanations of the results (Kazdin, 2011; Monette, Sullivan, & DeJong, 2005). Well-implemented single-case designs have high internal validity because the persons, couples, or families each serve as their own control; this allows the relationship between independent and dependent variables to be demonstrated (Kazdin, 2011). Dugard, File, and Todman (2012) suggest that the key to achieving internal validity lies in randomization. The process of randomization uses chance to reduce the variation between different groups and can be reached through different processes. In regard to single-case designs, randomization occurs when and only when intervention and withdrawal of the intervention are chosen at random from the possible times (Dugard et al.). You could also randomly assign participants to different groups, with one group sequence being ABCBD and the other group sequence being ACBCB. Therefore, the process of randomization can occur in single-case research design even when using the same person as the control by randomly allocating treatments. Increasing the possibility for randomization increases the internal validity of the study.

In addition, by design, single-case designs involve repetition. By involving repetition in the design, internal validity increases by showing repeatedly that the independent variable causes the effect in the dependent variable, rather than extraneous influences (Kazdin, 2003). It is important to consider the value in monitoring the intervention throughout the study. Making sure the independent variable is consistent throughout the different phases is important because it increases the likelihood that the visual inspection will point to the effect being attributed to the intervention. This is particularly important if you have different individuals giving the intervention to participants. For example, if you have one therapist using a specific model and another therapist using a different model, this would influence the intervention given to the participants. Monitoring this provides consistency in the intervention, thus increasing internal validity and conclusion validity. Generally, single-case designs are high in internal validity, with the tradeoff being lower external validity.

One goal of research is to generalize findings to a greater population. Higher external validity means that "the results can be applied to a wider population than only those participating in the study" (Dugard et al., 2012, p. 40). Due to the small number of participants and highly controlled structure, single-case designs are lower in external validity. This is true even in situations where the researcher relies on random sampling from the population. However, single-case designs are simplistic enough that repeating the experiment is possible as well as replicable in other contexts. Replication with different participants and contexts can improve external validity.

Construct validity refers to the operationalization of the intervention that was responsible for the change or for the relationship between variables (Kazdin, 2011) and for the quality of measures in establishing a baseline and measuring changes. One goal in research is to figure out which part of the intervention explains the change. It is important to figure out whether or not the relationship between the intervention and the behavior change is due to the interpretation given by the researcher. In addition, it is important to consider confounds present in the study that might also contribute to the relationship between variables. Using single-case research design lessens the gap of confusion in interpretation of the results and describing the relationship between variables because of the use of a baseline and the individuals as their own controls (Kazdin). Single-case designs, as mentioned before, use a replication method in which the intervention is introduced more than once. Presenting the intervention repetitively increases the construct validity by fully understanding where the cause or relationship is taking place. Through replication, researchers are able to increase their understanding of how effective the intervention is and how the change is taking place; by nature, this increases the construct validity of the design.

Another important consideration when using single-case research designs is how the results are qualitatively constructed and how inferences are gathered from the results. Although this is usually referred to as conclusion validity, in the context of single-case research, authors have described it as data evaluation validity. Kazdin (2003) states that conclusion validity reflects "this level of concern with quantitative evaluation and is often the Achilles' heel of research" (p. 67). Because conclusion validity is not often considered at the beginning of a study, researchers run the risk of dealing with type I and type II errors. A type I error is committed when the researcher concludes that the intervention produced an effect when actually the results are attributed to chance. A type II error is committed when the researcher concludes that the intervention did not produce an effect when it in fact did (Kazdin, 1978, 1982).

There are many ways in which the conclusion validity of a study can be compromised. A few will be discussed. First, large variability in the data can obscure the ability to identify an intervention effect. Single-case research designs depend on the ability to detect trends or patterns in the data at different phases; large variability lessens that ability and makes it harder to draw proper conclusions about the results, potentially causing the researcher to commit a type I error. In this case, it is hard to tell whether the intervention created the impact that visual inspection might indicate (Kazdin, 2011). Additionally, unreliability of the measure can obscure the ability to draw proper conclusions about the intervention effect and potentially lead the researcher to commit a type II error. Measurement plays an important part in experimentation and in single-case research designs. Reliability refers to the "extent to which the measures assess the characteristics of interest in a consistent fashion" (Kazdin, p. 42). Reliability refers to the extent of variability in scoring of the participants, as well as coders. Unreliability amongst the scoring and interpretation can be a major threat to the conclusion validity of a study. Furthermore, a study that possesses low power and/or smaller sample sizes could potentially threaten the conclusion validity of the study. Large samples are often needed in order to observe small or medium effects. Single-case research designs, in most cases, use a smaller n; having a smaller n increases the threat to conclusion validity.

Strengths and Limitations of Single-Case Research Designs

An important benefit of single-case design includes the short time frame needed to collect data and the low cost associated with implementing the design. Single-case designs are a much faster and cheaper alternative to randomized clinical trials (Rizvi & Nock, 2008). Because single-case research designs allow the ability to conduct a rigorous experimental study, the time and cost of recruiting participants for a large randomized controlled experiment is not necessary. This saves researchers the time it takes to recruit and the cost of providing measures or protocol to the participants, as well as the incentives it would cost to compensate participants. In addition, the ability to see effects of an intervention and to change or add a new intervention to improve outcomes is also a strength of using single-case research designs (Kazdin, 2011). The ability to have ongoing feedback while applying the intervention is a tremendous benefit for clinicians as they work with clients to improve everyday life. Using different interventions, as in the ABCBC design, researchers can evaluate the effectiveness of multiple or different interventions at a time.

Conclusion

Single-case research designs differ from anecdotal studies or case studies in that they tend to be quantitative and involve manipulation of the independent variable; they provide an intense study of individuals, couples, or families in which observation and intervention take place over time (Tate et al., 2008). Single-case research designs provide a powerful tool for revealing intervention effects. In single-case research designs, a baseline phase is observed, which provides information about the level of functioning before the independent variable, or intervention, is implemented. Once the baseline is observed, intervention phases are implemented. When data exhibit changes in outcome based on the implementation of phases, evidence is provided that the intervention has been successful (Kazdin, 1982, 2003). One powerful benefit of single-case research designs involves the "reliance on repeated observations of performance over time" (Kazdin, 2003, p. 274). Single-case research designs also provide researchers with a unique opportunity to tailor the intervention to the couple or family in order to provide an application to clinical practice on the outcomes, as well as the effectiveness of the intervention.

References

Anderson, S. R., Templeton, G. B., Johnson, L. N., Childs, N. M., & Peterson, F. R. (2006, October). *Enactments and connection in couple therapy: A process research study.* Poster presented at the meeting of the American Association for Marriage and Family Therapy, Austin, Texas.

Barlow, D. H., & Hersen, M. (1984). *Single-case experimental designs: Strategies for studying behavior change.* Elmsford, NY: Pergamon.

Bloom, M., Fischer, I., & Orme, J. G. (1995). *Evaluating practice: Guidelines for the accountable professional* (2nd ed.). Upper Saddle River, NJ: Prentice-Hall.

Crane, E. R. (1985). Single-case experimental designs in family therapy research: Limitations and considerations. *Family Process, 24,* 69–77.

Dugard, P., File, P. & Todman, J. (2012). *Single-case and small-n experimental designs: A practical guide to randomization tests* (2nd ed.). New York: Routledge.

Gorman, B. S., & Allison, D. B. (1996). Statistical alternatives for single-case designs. In R. D. Franklin, D. B. Allison, & B. S. Gorman (Eds.), Design and analysis of single-case research (pp. 159–214). Mahwah, NJ: Lawrence Erlbaum.

Kazdin, A. E. (1978). Methodological and interpretive problems of single-case experimental designs. *Journal of Consulting and Clinical Psychology, 46,* 629–642.

Kazdin, A. E. (1982). *Single-case research designs: Methods for clinical and applied settings.* New York: Oxford University Press.

Kazdin, A. E. (2003). *Research design in clinical psychology* (4th ed.). Boston: Allyn and Bacon.

Kazdin, A. E. (2011). *Single-case research designs: Methods for clinical and applied settings* (2nd ed.). New York: Oxford University Press.

Lundervold, D. A., & Belwood, M. F. (2000). The best kept secret in counseling: Single-case (N = 1) experimental designs. *Journal of Counseling and Development, 78,* 92–102. doi: 10.1002/j.1556-6676.2000.tb02565.x

Monette, D.R., Sullivan, T.J., & DeJong, C.R. (2005). *Applied social research: A tool for the human services* (6th ed.). Belmont, CA: Brooks/Cole/Thomson Learning.

Nock, M.K., Michel, B.D., & Photos, V. (2008). Single-case research designs. In D. McKay (Ed.), *Handbook of research methods in abnormal and clinical psychology* (pp. 337–350). Thousand Oaks, CA: Sage Publications.

Rizvi, S. L., & Nock, M.K. (2008). Single-case experimental designs for the evaluation of treatment for self-injurious and suicidal behaviors. *Suicide and Life-Threatening Behavior, 38*, 498–510.

Robinson, P.W., & Foster, D.F. (1979). *Experimental psychology: A small-n approach.* New York: Harper & Row.

Scruggs, T.E., & Mastropieri, M.A. (1998). Summarizing single-subject research: Issues and applications. *Behavior Modification, 22*, 221–242.

Tate, R.L., McDonald, S., Perdices, M., Togher, L., Schultz, R., & Savage, S. (2008). Rating the methodological quality of single-subject designs and *n*-of-1 trials: Introducing the single-case experimental design (SCED) scale. *Neuropsychological Rehabilitation, 18*, 385–401. doi: 10.1080/09602010802009201

14

EXAMINING MICRO-CHANGE IN CLINICAL POPULATIONS USING A DAILY DIARY APPROACH

Jeremy B. Yorgason, Lee N. Johnson, and Nathan R. Hardy

Introduction

Daily diary studies "capture life as it is lived" (Bolger, Davis, & Rafaeli, 2003) through daily assessments of behaviors, perceptions, and experiences, typically across several days. Daily diary studies assess a "micro" perspective of life, compared with panel surveys, for example, where assessments can span several years and be a year or more between each assessment period. Mental health clinical research often involves assessments of clients' experiences on a weekly or monthly basis; again, less often than a daily approach. Daily diary approaches do not differ drastically from other research methods that examine phenomena across time. The main difference is that these methodologies assess variables at more frequent intervals, usually on a daily or more frequent basis. Because assessments occur at more frequent intervals, additional attention needs to be paid to measures used to gather data, to recruitment and retention procedures, and to data analysis techniques.

The daily diary methodology holds substantial promise for clinical research with couples and families, where an understanding of how couples change between therapy sessions can provide valuable information about the process of change and what influence therapy has in clients' daily experiences. To deepen an understanding of how clients change, researchers need data on what happens in clients' daily lives and how the therapy process is brought into daily living. The daily diary approach is an emerging research methodology in developmental psychology and family studies where a systematic evaluation of people's experiences occurs on a daily basis.

Other names for daily diary research include ecological momentary assessment, experience sampling methods, and real-time data capturing. Some have used "intensive longitudinal methods" as a broader description of daily diary and similar methods (Bolger & Laurenceau, 2013). These approaches may involve multiple assessments across several days within a relatively brief period, one assessment per day across several days, or multiple assessments within the same day (Laurenceau & Bolger, 2005). In this chapter, this group of methods will be referred to as daily diary studies, although great variability in these approaches is acknowledged.

Benefits and Challenges of the Daily Diary Approach

Various benefits and disadvantages of daily diary methods have been identified in research literature (see Bolger et al., 2003; Gunthert & Wenze, 2012; Laurenceau & Bolger, 2005). To summarize these, daily diary methods allow researchers to capture micro family processes in their natural contexts shortly after they have taken place. Findings gain ecological validity when they occur in their natural settings. Further, recall bias or effects of retrospection are reduced when assessments are made soon after they occur. Daily diary methods allow researchers to track changes across short periods of time (such as from one day to the next). Generally speaking, daily diary studies have procedures in place for participants to receive reminders of assessments, which often greatly reduce missing data (e.g., Yorgason, Almeida, Neupert, Spiro, & Hoffman, 2006). Reminders can come in the form of phone calls, electronic reminders (e.g., from personal digital assistants, cell phones, computers), or in-person assessments.

As a profession, marriage and family therapy is interested in (a) how families differ from each other, (b) what happens between individuals within families, and (c) ways that individuals change across time. Most clinical research focuses on between-person differences. For example, a between-person approach could address the general characteristics that distinguish between less versus more happily married couples as they terminate therapy services. These characteristics might include desire and willingness to change, family support during therapy, or therapist characteristics, like level of directive intervention or therapist/client relationship. Other research is focused on interaction patterns between family members. For example, patterns of communication, problem solving, and coping with stress might be identified or targeted with interventions. Last, some studies explore ways that individuals fluctuate across days, as well as correlates of fluctuations. For example, daily diary assessments allow clients to provide information about their individual and relationship experiences on a daily basis between sessions. Although some daily diary research focuses solely on within-person variation across days, others also consider between-person and between–family member questions. In other words, daily diary research is not exclusively focused on within-person change, but, rather, it can additionally explore between-person and between–family member associations.

When between-person differences or within-person changes are examined exclusively of each other, important information can be lost. For example, consider the association between emotional well-being at the outset of therapy and

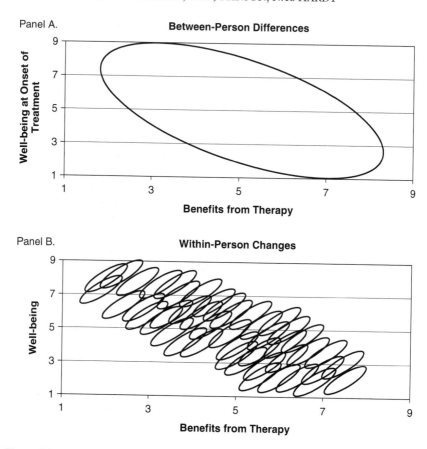

Figure 14.1 Comparison of overall between-person differences versus individual within-person change.

relative benefits of treatment. When the between-person trend is the only one that is considered, one might conclude that the benefits of treatment are less for clients who begin treatment with higher emotional well-being (see panel A, Figure 14.1). In contrast, when individual within-person change is tracked across days (see panel B, Figure 14.1), many may exhibit an upward linear trend, suggesting increased benefit from therapy as well-being increases, even at high levels. When both of these trends are considered together, they provide even greater insight.

Challenges associated with daily diary methods are that repeated assessments can be cumbersome to complete, sometimes respondents (or potential respondents) may feel that daily information is too personal to share, and methods of analyzing daily diary data can be somewhat complex. Because daily diaries often require substantial time and effort to complete, it is important that clients or respondents see the benefits of participating. In a clinical setting, researchers may share with clients the benefits of tracking daily processes and the benefits this information can provide. For example, research in client-centered progress monitoring indicates that clients whose' progress is routinely monitored have greater improvements in therapeutic outcomes (Anker, Duncan, & Sparks, 2009). This may in part be due to therapists having useful information to enhance their approach, or the act of self-monitoring may improve individuals' motivation to change. Research with strong theoretical grounding that will provide meaningful information about family life may also be motivating for potential respondents. Financial or other types of research incentives are also often helpful (see Chapter 6). As with much family-related research, daily diary surveys are often intrusive by requesting personal and relationship information; it is important for clients or participants to feel that their answers will be valued, safeguarded, and kept confidential. Generally, names can be omitted from surveys, and respondents of research studies can be reassured that others will view their assessments only in aggregate.

Brief Review of Relevant Daily Diary Research

In general, daily diary studies have the potential to provide clinicians with information about patterns in symptom variability, predictors of symptom variability, and sometimes the correlation of symptoms between family members. In addition, results from daily diary studies provide the information both across individuals and within couples. Consequently, information can be gained about how couples change and how individuals within a relationship change. Daily diary methodologies have been used in research with three groups relevant to this chapter. First, daily variations in symptoms and well-being have been examined among nonclinical samples of individuals and couples. Second, daily variability in symptoms and well-being have been examined among clinical samples. Third, treatment effectiveness has been examined in a daily diary context among clinical samples.

A growing body of literature addresses patterns and correlates of daily stress and daily mood among nonclinical samples. Findings generally indicate significant associations among daily stress, health, mood, and relationship interactions. Almeida and Kessler (1998) examined everyday stressors in males and females across 42 days. Their findings suggest that females tend to have more distressed days and fewer nondistressed days compared with males. In a study involving 169 Israeli dual-earner couples, Lavee and Ben-Ari (2007) examined the daily links between work-related stress and dyadic closeness, as mediated through partner mood. These authors described the average daily work stress, dyadic closeness, and partner mood, and then used work stress levels as predictors of dyadic closeness and mood. Shahar and Herr (2011) examined links between depression and "experiential avoidance" among 178 college students. They found that students with higher average depression symptoms had "inflexibly high levels of experiential avoidance in response to daily negative affect" (p. 676). To provide additional examples, perceived sleep quality has been linked to daily mood (McCrae et al., 2008), daily health symptoms have been linked to spousal mood (Yorgason et al., 2006), daily events have been associated with individual depressive symptoms (Zautra, Schultz, & Reich, 2000), and positive mood has been found to buffer the link between daily pain and negative mood (Zautra, Johnson, & Davis, 2005). The patterns examined in nonclinical samples provide helpful information for therapists and their clients, indicating that daily stressors often correlate with daily mood and relationship interactions.

Among clinical samples, daily diary studies have been useful in tracking important clinical symptoms, such as eating disorder episodes (Munsch et al., 2009; Smyth et al., 2009) and substance abuse behaviors (Shiffman, Kirchner, Ferguson, & Scharf, 2009). One line of research, headed by Cohen and colleagues (2008), has examined clinical symptoms in the context of cognitive therapy (Gunthert, Cohen, Butler, & Beck, 2005; Parrish et al., 2009). For example, 54 clients being treated for depression were surveyed daily (7 diary days beginning after session 1, and 7 diary days beginning after session 6) about positive and negative events, positive and negative mood, and negative thoughts. Findings from that study indicated that treatment was linked with decreased (a) depression symptoms, (b) daily negative mood, (c) daily negative thoughts, and (d) daily negative reactivity to negative events, and to increased daily positive mood. In one other daily diary study involving a clinical sample, Starr and Davila (2011) examined whether daily anxiety symptoms temporally preceded daily depression symptoms among 55 clients with generalized anxiety disorder. These researchers explored same-day associations between anxiety and depression symptoms, as well as 1-, 2-, 3-, and 4-day lags (i.e., anxiety on one day predicting depression symptoms the next day, 2 days later, 3 days later, and 4 days later). Their findings indicated concurrent associations between anxiety and depression symptoms, and associations across each of the lags, with the strongest association being with a 2-day lag.

Clinical research to date using daily diary methods has provided valuable information about daily stressors, daily symptoms, daily outcomes, as well as longer-term therapy outcomes as predicted by daily processes. Studies examining treatment approaches through a daily diary methodology have focused mainly on drug treatments. For example, daily studies of medication effectiveness have included samples of persons with depression (Barge-Schaapveld & Nicolson, 2002) and attention deficit/hyperactivity disorder (ADHD; Whalen et al., 2010). Compared with follow-up doctor visits that occur weeks or months after treatment has started, daily assessments of symptoms can provide a current picture of treatment effectiveness. Further, this approach provides micro, or small-scale, snapshots of symptom management and intervention effectiveness.

Unfortunately, each of the clinical daily diary studies we were able to locate involved only individuals. More research is needed among clinical samples with couples and families to better understand daily relationship processes. Daily interactions such as positive communication, working through challenges, and even failed attempts at closeness could be addressed using daily diary methods.

Tips for Carrying Out a Daily Diary Study

Published daily diary studies, as well as published resources specific to daily diary methods, provide interested individuals with excellent guides. For example, in the recently published *Handbook of Research Methods for Studying Daily Life,* Mehl and Conner (2012) provide details about (a) the theoretical groundings of daily diary research, (b) study design considerations, (c) data analysis methods, and (d) some applied examples. In the following paragraphs, we share ideas that can be helpful for researchers interested in collecting and analyzing their own daily diary data, including tips about recruitment and retention, modes of data collection and study design, and considerations when multiple family members are involved in daily diary research.

Recruiting for daily diary studies can be challenging. Participant involvement is intensive and often necessitates disclosure of personal and private information. Engagement in the research process is aided by carefully communicating the importance of the research and crucial nature of the participants' involvement. In therapy settings, clients may see greater reason to dedicate their time to an intensive research study if they see personal benefits, such as insight into their own daily experiences. Monetary incentives are often not sufficient for participants to feel they have been paid for their time but offer a kind gesture of gratitude for participants' efforts, and often boost response and retention rates. One study found that populations typically more difficult to recruit into research studies were more likely to participate when offered a monetary incentive (Guyll, Spoth, & Redmond, 2003). Also, in a study of mothers and children diagnosed with ADHD, both the mother and the child were offered an incentive of $100, and the child was given a bonus incentive of up to $10 depending on how many diaries were completed (Whalen, Odgers, Reed, & Henker, 2011).

Retention in daily diary studies can be aided through daily reminders to participate in the research each day of the study. Personal contact with participants during the first couple of days of a study allows participants to ask any questions as they get into a routine with research protocol. Daily reminders during the study can range from phone calls (messages left) to emails to text messages. Although they can be cumbersome, the daily reminders improve the chances of collecting data on all study days and decrease chances for missing data. For example, mobile phone reminders have been shown to improve response rates when they were sent well before the appointed collection time of each day (Rönkä, Malinen, Kinnunen, Tolvanen, & Lämsä, 2010).

Daily diary data collection can take various forms. Some researchers use a paper/pencil approach or daily phone interviews. Paper/pencil surveys can be beneficial with groups that don't always have Internet access, yet data has to be entered, and mailing costs for stacks of surveys can add up. Some researchers tap into technology and collect data using online, tablet, laptop, or smartphone surveys, or they may have the participants send text message responses. For instance, smartphones were used in a study of patients with type 2 diabetes in which diary data were collected, and, in response, interventive feedback was provided to support self-care management (Nes et al., 2012). In many of these electronic approaches data are automatically entered into formats that can be used in data analysis software packages. Traditional research methods can be integrated well with the daily diary approach. For example, qualitative, experimental, and mixed designs can involve daily repeated measures. Researchers may want to consider whether open-ended or closed-ended responses to daily questions will best address their research questions. Qualitative researchers could consider using a journaling approach, with a qualitative analysis of the text to answer research questions.

Researchers should be mindful of their goals when determining how many and which days they plan to collect data. Some considerations include: (a) On how many diary days should they ask respondents to provide data? (b) Will data be collected across holidays? (c) Will data be collected on weekdays and weekends? (d) Will clients have less involvement as they begin or terminate therapy services? Researchers studying rare events may collect data across more days, while those more interested in everyday experiences may need fewer days of data.

Precautions are in order when multiple family members are completing daily diaries at the same time, such as when both spouses in a marriage complete assessments of their marital relationship. Instructions can be provided that encourage partners to complete assessments on the same days (e.g., so that husband and wife experiences on the same days can be compared) and discourage cross-partner data contamination. For example, in a study of intimacy in marriage, researchers provided adhesive labels and asked each spouse to seal each paper-based diary shut after completing it (Laurenceau, Barrett, & Rovine, 2005). Specifically, couples can be asked to not discuss their responses with each other until after the study is over. Researchers may also want to be careful to not discourage natural conversations about topics in the diary questionnaires, so as to support the natural environment from which data are collected.

Data Analysis

We will present the basic steps in data analysis of daily diary data, beginning with data setup for multilevel models (i.e., data restructuring), ways to describe the data (e.g., plotting the data, modeling trends across time), and a few technical aspects of analysis (e.g., calculating intraclass correlation coefficients, modeling within- and between-person variation in predictors, calculating a pseudo-R^2).

In many statistical analysis programs you will need to restructure your data before any further analyses are conducted. This step is often necessary to plot data and to run the multilevel models that account for nonindependence in the data. This restructuring of data is often called "stacking" the data and consists of

Panel A: Wide or Unstacked data

ID	Support Day1	Support Day2	...	Support Day14	LifeSat Day1	LifeSat Day2	...	LifeSat Day14
104	1	2	...	3	2	2	...	4
106	1	4	...	1	4	4	...	4

Panel B: Long or Stacked data

ID	Day	Support	LifeSat
104	1	1	2
104	2	2	2
104	3	1	3
104	4	4	3
104	5	5	3
104	6	4	2
104	7	2	2
104	...	...	...
104	14	3	4
106	1	1	4
106	2	4	4
106	3	3	4
106	4	5	3
106	5	2	3
106	6	1	2
106	7	3	3
106	...	...	...
106	14	1	4

Figure 14.2 Data in wide (unstacked) and long (stacked) formats across 14 days.

moving repeated measures for a given individual from the same row (see panel A of Figure 14.2) to separate rows for each time point (see panel B of Figure 14.2). This restructuring enables each observation to have its own row in the data set. For example, in a daily diary across 14 days, each person in a sample would have 14 rows of data. Each row of data maintains some important variables, including a subject ID and a "time" or "day" variable. This data structure is sufficient when considering individual data (as we do below) and in cases where predictors in one family member (e.g., husband) are linked with outcomes from another family member (e.g., wife), in which case data from the same day from all family members will be on the same row in a data set. When outcomes are considered for multiple family members simultaneously (e.g., in actor/partner types of models), then the data have to be double stacked (see resources listed at the end of this section for more information about multivariate multilevel models).

Once the data are stacked, a good next step is to plot individual and aggregate trajectories. By looking at trends in your data, you can get a sense of whether there are linear trends across time, whether your outcomes have a lot of variability, and whether your data suggest more variability within subjects versus between subjects. Spaghetti plots can be created in all major statistical packages, such as SPSS, SAS, and Stata. Sometimes it is helpful to create one plot per individual in the sample, for small groups of individuals, and sometimes for the whole sample (see Figure 14.3 for examples of these). Although plots do not provide a statistical analysis of your data, they do provide a visual representation of your data across days and can provide direction with how you set up your specific analyses.

One of the first things you may notice with plots of data across days is whether your data show trends across time, such as decreasing levels of depression across days or weeks, or show more of a variable pattern. As seen in panel B of Figure 14.1, systematic trends across time either increasing or decreasing likely indicate linear changes, while patterns of variability that do not include systematic change across time indicate daily fluctuations (see all panels of Figure 14.3). These two patterns are modeled differently, with systematic trends indicating linear or higher-order changes being modeled as growth curves and what appear to be random fluctuations across time being modeled as "variability" in an outcome that can be predicted. These two models would be set up differently in a statistical software program, with the systematic trend model including time as a predictor. In the output for such a model, the slope associated with the time variable would then indicate the slope of the outcome across days. In a random fluctuations or variability model, no time slope is included (although some suggest you control for time to demonstrate no linear trends).

Regardless of whether data follow a growth or variability pattern, it is often of interest to researchers to determine how much variability in the outcome variable is due to between-person differences versus within-person change. This can be determined by estimating a multilevel model with only the outcome in the model (no predictors, often called an "empty" or "unconditional" model) and then calculating an intraclass correlation coefficient (ICC). Output from unconditional models provide covariance parameters, including a residual variance component and an intercept variance component. These numbers are used to create a ratio of between- versus within-person variance as follows:

Equation 1.

Between subjects variance/Between subjects variance + Residual variance

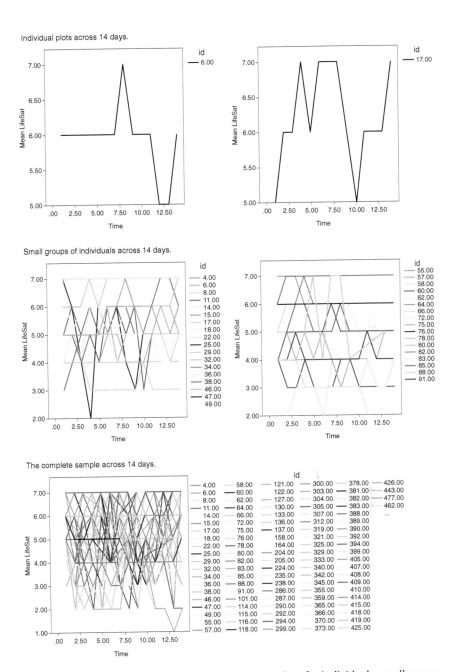

Figure 14.3 Spaghetti plots of life satisfaction across days for individuals, small groups of individuals, and the whole sample.

For example (using the output in Appendix B), if the residual variance is .31 and the intercept variance is .89, then the equation would be .89/.89 + .31 = .74, or 74% of the variance in the variable is due to between-person differences. Conversely, using this same information, one can determine that 26% of the variance in the variable is due to within-person changes across days. In this case, between-person predictors may be of greater relevance, as nearly three times the amount of variance (i.e., 74% compared with 26%) in the outcome is due to between-person differences.

The same variance components used to create the ICC can be compared with their counterparts in your final model with predictors and controls added (referred to as a "conditional" model) to calculate the amount of variance at each level that has been accounted for by predictors (see Singer & Willet, 2003). This statistic is called a pseudo-R^2 and is calculated by subtracting the variance in the conditional model from the variance in the unconditional or empty model, and then dividing by the variance in the unconditional or empty model as follows:

Equation 2.

Proportion reduction in variance or pseudo-R^2 = variance$_{unconditional}$ − variance$_{conditional}$ / variance$_{unconditional}$.

For example, if the residual variance from the unconditional model is .31 and the residual variance from the conditional with predictors model is .27, then the pseudo-R^2 would be: .31 − .27 / .31 = .13, or the residual variance for this variable will have decreased by 13%. Alternatively, as seen in Appendix B, a pseudo-R^2 for the intercept variance could also be calculated using the same approach.

Predictors in daily diary studies contain both between- and within-person variance. It is recommended that researchers separate this variance so as to better capture variation due to within-person changes versus variation due to between-person differences (see Bolger & Laurenceau, 2013). This is typically done by computing a within-person variable as follows (see Appendix A for related syntax): A person's mean across days is computed (person mean variable), and then the original variable is subtracted from that mean to create a variable that indicates how a person's score on a given day differs from the person's average across days. This new within-person variable is often referred to in daily diary literature as person-a mean centered predictor. Bolger and Laurenceau (2013) suggest that the predictor be grand-mean centered before creating the within-person variable, although coefficients don't change when this approach is taken and the intercept has different meaning. Specifically, the intercept is the average of the sample in the outcome variable when all predictors have a value of zero. If a variable is grand-mean centered before it is person-mean centered, the meaning of zero is relative to the overall sample (with a mean of zero, centered on the sample grand mean) and not just to a person's average daily report (which would also place the mean at zero, but only in context to a person's average across days). Next, a between-person variable is also computed, by grand-mean centering the person-mean variable that was calculated earlier. That is, the sample average for the predictor is subtracted from the person-mean variable that was created. This variable helps the researcher to consider how reports made by research participants with different averages across days relate to their reports of the outcome variable in consideration. Multilevel models should include both between and within predictors so as to show the influence of each while accounting for the other.

There are a number of other complexities that can be explored regarding analysis of daily diary data but are not described in this chapter. Among others, these include (a) considering different error structures that most appropriately fit the data being examined, (b) studies that include multiple "bursts" of daily diaries, (c) and multivariate multilevel modeling where outcomes from multiple family members are considered simultaneously.

Daily diary research requires a unique analysis approach that takes into account "nonindependence" or a correlation in responses to repeated measures of the same construct. For example, if a client completes an assessment about his mood on multiple consecutive days, those responses are more likely to be correlated with each other than with the responses of other clients completing the same assessment. Typically, multilevel modeling is used to account for the correlation between repeated measures. Analytic methods for daily diary data are becoming more accessible, with statistical software that is available to most social science researchers (e.g., SPSS, SAS, Stata, *Mplus*). Resources that can guide researchers in the specific details of data analysis include "Applied Longitudinal Data Analysis" by Singer and Willett (2003), "Intensive Longitudinal Methods" by Bolger and Laurenceau (2013), and the "Handbook of Research Methods for Studying Daily Life" by Mehl and Conner (2012). Other resources are available on the Internet through, for example, the UCLA statistics website (https://idre.ucla.edu/stats). It is beyond the scope of this chapter to provide more details about conducting multilevel analysis to analyze daily diary data.

Data Case Example

A few years ago I (L.J.) was talking with some colleagues and discussing some of the problems associated with current clinical research and how we believed that family therapy researchers needed to do something different to move our field forward. As part of this conversation, we started discussing daily diary methods. I had previously taught daily diary methods to my research methods class, and others were familiar with how these methods could provide different data to answer some important questions. The outcome of our discussions was the Daily Diary in Couple Therapy study. The four main research questions of this study are: (1) What are key relational events (positive and negative) that happen in client's lives? (2) Do clients use information they have learned in therapy on a daily basis? (3) Does therapy work to reduce stress and improve relationships on a daily basis? and (4) Do daily relational events influence a person's willingness to participate in therapy and the therapy alliance? To answer these questions, we developed the Daily Diary of Events in Couple Therapy (Johnson, Tambling, Anderson, Oka, & Mennenga, 2010). The development of the Daily Diary of Events in Couple Therapy was patterned after the Daily Inventory of Stressful Events (Almeida, McGonagle, Rodney, Kessler, & Wethington, 2002). The importance of developing a good assessment cannot be understated in daily diary research. We went through several iterations of the assessment working on question wording and the flow of the questions. We finally decided on the following main questions:

(1) Did you implement anything you learned in therapy since you last reported?
(2) Did you have an argument or disagreement with your partner since you reported yesterday?
(3) Since you reported yesterday, did anything happen that you could have argued about but you decided to let pass?
(4) Since you last reported yesterday, did anything positive happen in your relationship?
(5) Since you last reported yesterday, did anything happen at school or work that had an impact (positive or negative) on your relationship?
(6) Since you last reported, did you spend time exercising?

Each of these questions is a stem question that clients answer either yes or no. Based on their answers, they go on to a series of follow-up and clarifying questions related to the stem question. Participants are also asked how much the events of today influenced their willingness to attend therapy and try ideas from therapy, their hopefulness in changing, and their opinion of their therapist.

After assessment development, the diary was pilot tested to get feedback and see how long it took to complete. We recruited students, friends, and family to take the survey for 7 days and provide feedback on flow, question wording, and overall thoughts. We also discovered a possibility that people may learn that there were only follow-up questions when they answered yes. So if they were in a hurry one day, they could simply answer no to each question and be done with the survey in less than a minute. To remedy this situation, parallel follow-up questions were added to the survey when clients also answered no to each stem question.

Procedurally, we decided to deliver the survey to clients via a Web-based program called Qualtrics (http://www.qualtrics.com). Our reasons for this were that many clients have access to email and computers or smartphones (we do have a paper copy available for those who prefer it). This allowed us to set up Qualtrics to email each client in the relationship a link each day to complete the survey. This also allowed us to track whether the survey was completed on the day clients received the email or later. It also helped with the "skip logic" of the survey. Qualtrics also put the data in a form that is easily transferable to most statistical packages, streamlining the data entry process. Our survey takes up to 20 minutes depending on what clients report happened that day. Each member of the couple completes the survey each day for the first 28 days they are in therapy. As compensation, clients received free therapy for all sessions during the 28-day period. We also built in procedures to help reduce missing diaries. In addition to receiving the daily email with the survey link, clients receive a personal email or phone call after 2 days of not completing a diary.

These procedures have been successful in collecting quality data. Ideally people would complete the diary each day, which may not be a realistic expectation for clinical couples who are experiencing higher levels of stress. In our data collection experience, the average delay in completing a survey is 0.85 days, meaning that for most days clients are completing the survey on the day of the events.

Extensions

Although daily diary studies have been most commonly used with nonclinical samples, there are various advantages in extending this method to clinical populations going through treatment. First, daily diary studies can examine the unique impact of therapy on daily processes. Second, they provide the ability to explore micro-level changes among multiple family members going through couple or family therapy together. Third, daily diary studies provide a unique way of considering contextual factors, or moderators, of daily processes. Last, daily diary studies can include cutting edge extensions, such as the measuring of physiologic data.

Therapy and Daily Processes

Most studies that examine therapy outcomes consist of self-reports given at the beginning and end of the treatment to identify whether treatment is significantly associated with mean differences in the dependent variable from pretest to posttest. One major advantage in utilizing daily diary methods with samples of clients going through therapy is the ability to identify the effects of therapy on daily behaviors, emotions, and interpersonal interactions. As an example, Forbes et al. (2012) investigated the treatment effects in an 8-week clinical trial using cognitive-behavioral therapy, pharmacotherapy, or a mix of both treatments among adolescents with depressive and anxiety disorders. Findings from the study indicated that daily assessments of higher positive affect, lower negative affect, a higher positive to negative affect ratio, and more time spent with fathers predicted lower depressive and anxiety symptoms posttreatment. Furthermore, Forbes and colleagues found greater validity of daily assessments in predicting treatment outcomes over "retrospective" self-reports of depressive and anxiety symptoms. Daily diary clinical studies could provide clinicians with recommendations for treatment to encourage certain daily behaviors.

Clinical studies using daily diaries not only provide information about whether the therapy is working in alleviating symptoms, but also help to uncover *how* this daily change might be occurring. Treatment factors, therapist factors, and client characteristics can be identified that link with change across days. For example, considering therapist characteristics as predictive of daily change processes can provide information about how therapists directly influence change in their clients over a short period of time.

Multiple Family Members

There are no known published clinical studies using diary methods with couples or multiple family members in therapy. However, findings from this type of study could help validate and/or fine-tune the theories behind the systemic based therapies utilized by marriage and family therapists (MFTs). Systems theory posits that a change within one individual can lead to changes in other individuals within the same system. One way to capture the systemic process that MFTs are interested in when analyzing diaries would be to position the daily changes in one spouse/family member as a predictor (independent variable) of the daily changes of another spouse/family member. For example, couple therapy research using diaries could look at how one spouse's change in daily communication predicts the other spouse's change in daily life satisfaction. Or one could look at how a parent's change in stress is linked with a child's symptoms of depression. Furthermore, changes in clinical outcomes for both spouses can be modeled simultaneously, within a multivariate framework. (See Chapter 23 for further information as to how this modeling procedure works.)

Moderators

Moderators examine how one variable changes the relationship between two other variables. In other terms, a moderator is a "variable that affects the direction and/or strength of the relation between an independent or predictor variable and a dependent or criterion variable" (Baron & Kenny, 1986, p. 1174). Moderators can be a powerful tool for examining the conditions under which an independent/predictor variable influences clinical outcomes. A moderator can be applied to links between daily predictors and outcomes, to a pretreatment predictor and a daily outcome, or to a daily predictor and an outcome measured posttreatment. For example, treatment itself could be considered a moderator in examining the association between one spouse's stress and the other spouse's mood. It might be that those in treatment (compared with a wait-list control group) are more connected, and so stress in one has a stronger link with mood in the other. Alternatively, couples in therapy (compared with a wait-list control group) may learn to manage stress and therefore experience less spillover into their marriage.

Physiological Data

Most MFTs give attention to the biopsychosocial nature of individuals and families in therapy; however, most research investigates only subjective experience and behavior, while physiological data is often ignored (Wilhelm & Roth, 1998). These data, especially as it pertains to clinical research, can provide a more comprehensive picture of the change process for clients. Often these types of data collection fall under the umbrella term of *ambulatory assessment/monitoring* used in the field of psychology and clinical psychology (see Fahrenberg, Myrtek,

Pawlik, & Perrez, 2007). This term technically has reference to diary methods in general, but often it is associated with the assessment of physiological changes captured in diary research studies. Multiple studies have examined physiological changes with clinical populations in individual therapy. As an example, Meuret et al. (2012) examined physiological precursors to panic attacks among clients with panic disorder. It was found that there was greater instability in heart rate and breathing 1 hour before the onset of a panic attack than during or after the panic attack. This finding contradicted traditional belief about the nature and onset of panic attacks.

Physiological data can be useful in both individual treatment and family treatment. For example, a couple can measure their heart rates after a stressful interaction. Although this method of data gathering has become popular in clinical psychology, physiological data with multiple family members could provide valuable information on how each individual in the family is affected by certain events. For further information on how ambulatory assessments have been used in clinical psychology, see the study by Trull and Ebner-Priemer (2012).

Conclusion

Daily diary methods compose a unique and sophisticated research tool that has great potential to expand clinical process research in the mental health arena. Using this approach, marriage and family therapy researchers can explore important clinical microprocesses that capture change in the context of clients' natural environments. Data collection is less retrospective than weekly or less common assessments. This chapter provides a primer for marriage and family therapy researchers to understand and prepare to collect daily diary data in marriage and family therapy contexts.

References

Almeida, D. M., & Kessler, R. C. (1998). Everyday stressors and gender differences in daily distress. *Journal of Personality and Social Psychology, 75*, 670–680.

Almeida, D. M., McGonagle, K. A., Rodney, C. C., Kessler, R. C., & Wethington, E. (2002). Psychosocial moderators of emotional reactivity to marital arguments. *Marriage and Family Review, 34*, 89–113.

Anker, M. G., Duncan, B. L., & Sparks, J. A. (2009). Using client feedback to improve couple therapy outcomes: A randomized clinical trial in a naturalistic setting. *Journal of Consulting and Clinical Psychology, 77*, 693–704.

Barge-Schaapveld, D. Q., & Nicolson, N. A. (2002). Effects of antidepressant treatment on the quality of daily life: An experience sampling. *Journal of Clinical Psychiatry, 63*, 477–485.

Baron, R. M., & Kenny, D. A. (1986). The moderator-mediator variable distinction in social psychological research: Conceptual, strategic, and statistical considerations. *Journal of Personality and Social Psychology, 51*, 1173–1182.

Bolger, N., Davis, A., & Rafaeli, E. (2003). Diary methods: Capturing life as it is lived. *Annual Review of Psychology, 54,* 579–616.

Bolger, N., & Laurenceau, J-P. (2013). *Intensive longitudinal methods: An introduction to diary and experience sampling research.* New York: Guilford.

Cohen, L. H., Gunthert, K. C., Butler, A. C., Parrish, B. P., Wenze, S. J., & Beck, J. S. (2008). Negative affective spillover from daily events predicts early response to cognitive therapy for depression. *Journal of Consulting and Clinical Psychology, 76,* 955–965.

Fahrenberg, J., Myrtek, M., Pawlik, K., & Perrez, M. (2007). Ambulatory assessment—monitoring behavior in daily life settings: A behavioral-scientific challenge for psychology. *European Journal of Psychological Assessment, 23,* 206–213.

Forbes, L. J. L., Forster, A. S., Dodd, R. H., Tucker, L., Laming, R., Sellars, S., . . . Ramirez, A. J. (2012). Promoting early presentation of breast cancer in older women: Implementing an evidence-based intervention in routine clinical practice. *Journal of Cancer Epidemiology.* Retrieved from http://www.hindawi.com/journals/jce/2012/835167

Gunthert, K. C., Cohen, L. H., Butler, A. C., & Beck, J. S. (2005). Predictive role of daily coping and affective reactivity in cognitive therapy outcome: Application of a daily process design to psychotherapy research. *Behavior Therapy, 36,* 77–88.

Gunthert, K. C., & Wenze, S. J. (2012). Daily diary methods. In M. R. Mehl & T. S. Conner (Eds.), *Handbook of research methods for studying daily life* (pp. 144–159). New York: Guilford Press.

Guyll, M., Spoth, R., & Redmond, C. (2003). The effects of incentives and research requirements on participation rates for a community-based preventive intervention research study. *Journal of Primary Prevention, 24,* 25–41.

Johnson, L. N., Tambling, R. B., Anderson, S. R., Oka, M., & Mennenga, K. D. (2010). *Daily diary of events in couple therapy.* Available from Lee Johnson, School of Family Life, Brigham Young University, Provo, UT.

Laurenceau, J., Barrett, L. F., & Rovine, M. J. (2005). The interpersonal process model of intimacy in marriage: A daily-diary and multilevel modeling approach. *Journal of Family Psychology, 19,* 314.

Laurenceau, J., & Bolger, N. (2005). Using diary methods to study marital and family processes. *Journal of Family Psychology, 19,* 86–97.

Lavee, Y., & Ben-Ari, A. (2007). Relationship of dyadic closeness with work-related stress: A daily diary study. *Journal of Marriage and Family, 69,* 1021–1035.

McCrae, C. S., McNamara, J. P. H., Rowe, M. A., Dzierzeqski, J. M., Dirk, J., Marsiske, M., & Craggs, J. G. (2008). Sleep and affect in older adults: Using multilevel modeling to examine daily associations. *Journal of Sleep Research, 17,* 42–53.

Mehl, M. R., & Conner, T. S. (2012). *Handbook of research methods for studying daily life.* New York: Guilford.

Meuret, A. E., Rosenfield, D., Wilhelm, F. H., Zhou, E., Conrad, A., Ritz, T., & Roth, W. T. (2012). Do unexpected panic attacks occur spontaneously? *Biological Psychiatry, 70,* 985–991.

Munsch, S., Meyer, A. H., Milenkovic, N., Schlup, B., Margraf, J., & Wilhelm, F. H. (2009). Ecological momentary assessment to evaluate cognitive-behavioral treatment for binge eating disorder. *International Journal of Eating Disorders, 42,* 648–657. doi: 10.1002/eat.20657

Nes, A. A., van Dulmen, S., Eide, E., Finset, A., Kristjánsdóttir, Ó. B., Steen, I. S., & Eide, H. (2012). The development and feasibility of a Web-based intervention with diaries and situational feedback via smartphone to support self-management in patients with diabetes type 2. *Diabetes Research and Clinical Practice, 97*, 385–393.

Parrish, B. P., Cohen, L. H., Gunthert, K. C., Butler, A. C., Learuenceau, J.-P., & Beck, J. S. (2009). Effects of cognitive therapy for depression on daily stress-related variables. *Behaviour Research and Therapy, 47*, 444–448.

Rönkä, A., Malinen, K., Kinnunen, U., Tolvanen, A., & Lämsä, T. (2010). Capturing daily family dynamics via text messages: Development of the mobile diary. *Community, Work & Family, 13*, 5–21.

Shahar, B., & Herr, N. R. (2011). Depressive symptoms predict inflexibly high levels of experiential avoidance in response to daily negative affect: A daily diary study. *Behaviour Research and Therapy, 49*, 676–681.

Shiffman, S., Kirchner, T. R., Ferguson, S. G., & Scharf, D. N. (2009). Patterns of intermittent smoking: An analysis using ecological momentary assessment. *Addictive Behaviors, 34*, 514–519.

Singer, J.D., & Willett, J.B. (2003). *Applied longitudinal data analysis: Modeling change and event occurrence.* New York: Oxford University Press.

Smyth, J.M., Wonderlich, S. A., Sliwinski, M.J., Crosby, R.D., Engel, S.G., Mitchell, J.E., & Calogero, R.M. (2009). Ecological momentary assessment of affect, stress, and binge-purge behaviors: Day of week and time of day effects in the natural environment. *International Journal of Eating Disorders, 42*, 429–436.

Starr, L. R., & Davila, J. (2011). Temporal patterns of anxious and depressed mood in generalized anxiety disorder: A daily diary study. *Behaviour Research and Therapy, 50*, 131–141.

Trull, T. J., & Ebner-Priemer, U. W. (2012). Using experience sampling methods/ecological momentary assessment (ESM/EMA) in clinical assessment and clinical research: Introduction to the special section. *Psychological Assessment, 21*, 457–462. doi: 10.1037/a0017653

Whalen, C. K., Henker, B., Ishikawa, S. S., Emmerson, N. A., Swindle, R., & Johnston, J. A. (2010). Atomoxetine versus stimulants in the community treatment of children with ADHD: An electronic diary study. *Journal of Attention Disorders, 13*, 391–400.

Whalen, C.K., Odgers, C.L., Reed, P.L., & Henker, B. (2011). Dissecting daily distress in mothers of children with ADHD: An electronic diary study. *Journal of Family Psychology, 25*, 402–411.

Wilhelm, F.H., & Roth, W.T. (1998). Trusting computerized data reduction too much: A critique of Anderson's ambulatory respiratory monitor. *Biological Psychology, 49*, 215–219.

Yorgason, J. B., Almeida, D., Neupert, S., Spiro, A., & Hoffman, L. (2006). A dyadic examination of daily health symptoms and emotional well-being in later life couples. *Family Relations, 55*, 613–624.

Zautra, A. J., Johnson, L. M., & Davis, M.C. (2005). Positive affect as a source of resilience for women in chronic pain. *Journal of Consulting and Clinical Psychology, 73*, 212–220.

Zautra, A.J., Schultz, A.S., & Reich, J.W. (2000). The role of everyday events in depressive symptoms for older adults. In G.M. Williamson, P.A. Parmelee, & D. R. Shaffer (Eds.), *Physical illness and depression: A handbook of theory, research, and practice* (pp. 65–92). New York: Plenum.

APPENDIX A

SPSS Syntax for Data Analysis of Daily Diary Data

1. Syntax for restructuring or stacking the data
VARSTOCASES
/ID = id
/Make Support FROM supportDay1 SupportDay2 SupportDay3
    SupportDay4 SupportDay5 SupportDay6 SupportDay7 SupportDay8
    SupportDay9 SupportDay10 SupportDay11 SupportDay12 SupportDay13
    SupportDay14
/Make Lifesat FROM LifeSatDay1 LifeSatDay2 LifeSatDay3 LifeSatDay4
    LifeSatDay5 LifeSatDay6 LifeSatDay7 LifeSatDay8 LifeSatDay9
    LifeSatDay10 LifeSatDay11 LifeSatDay12 LifeSatDay13 LifeSatDay14
/INDEX = Time(14)
 /KEEP =   all
 /NULL = KEEP.
Save Outfile = 'C:\MLM\SupLifesatstacked.sav'.
*(You'll have to specify your own file location and name here.)
Execute.

2. Syntax for plotting the data
* The "temporary select" command allows the selection of few or a group of
  cases to plot.
* In the Ggraph command replace the word "lifesat" in each case with the
  variable you want to
* plot across days. The word "time" can be replaced with whatever the time,
  wave, or day variable is
* called in your data set.
Temporary.
Select if ID = 8.
GGRAPH
/GRAPHDATASET NAME="graphdataset" VARIABLES=time
    MEAN(LifeSat)[name="MEAN_LifeSat"] id
MISSING=LISTWISE REPORTMISSING=NO
 /GRAPHSPEC SOURCE=INLINE.

```
BEGIN GPL
  SOURCE: s=userSource(id("graphdataset"))
  DATA: time=col(source(s), name("time"))
  DATA: MEAN_LifeSat=col(source(s), name("MEAN_LifeSat"))
  DATA: id=col(source(s), name("id"), unit.category())
  GUIDE: axis(dim(1), label("Time"))
  GUIDE: axis(dim(2), label("Mean LifeSat"))
  GUIDE: legend(aesthetic(aesthetic.color.interior), label("id"))
  ELEMENT: line(position(time*MEAN_LifeSat), color.interior(id),
  missing.wings())
END GPL.
```

3. Syntax for an unconditional multilevel model using daily diary data
*   Replace "LifeSat" with whatever your dependent variable is.
*   "id" should be replaced with whatever the id variable is called in your data set.
*   "Time" can be replaced with whatever the time variable is called in your data set.

```
Mixed LifeSat with time
/fixed = | SSTYPE(3)
/random = intercept |subject (id) covtype(un)
/Print = solution testcov.
Execute.
```

4. Syntax for a growth curve (with time in the model) multilevel model using
    daily diary data

```
  Mixed LifeSat with time
  /fixed = | SSTYPE(3)
  /random = intercept time |subject (id) covtype(un)
  /Print = solution testcov.
```

5. Syntax for a conditional multilevel model using daily diary data

```
Mixed LifeSat with time support
/fixed = time support| SSTYPE(3)
/random = intercept time|subject (id) covtype(un)
/Print = solution testcov.
```

APPENDIX B

Select Output from Unconditional, Growth Curve (time added to the model), and Conditional Models

1. Unconditional Model

Estimates of Fixed Effects[a]

Parameter	Estimate	Std. Error	Df	t	Sig.	95% Confidence Interval	
						Lower Bound	Upper Bound
Intercept	5.400327	.069684	187.020	77.498	.000	5.262859	5.537794

[a] Dependent Variable: Lifesat.

Estimates of Covariance Parameters[a]

Parameter	Estimate	Std. Error	Wald Z	Sig.	95% Confidence Interval	
					Lower Bound	Upper Bound
Residual	.309668	.009096	34.044	.000	.292344	.328019
Intercept [subject = id] Variance	.889133	.094404	9.418	.000	.722087	1.094822

[a] Dependent Variable: Lifesat.

2. Growth Curve Model, or Model with Time as a Predictor

Estimates of Fixed Effects[a]

Parameter	Estimate	Std. Error	df	t	Sig.	95% Confidence Interval	
						Lower Bound	Upper Bound
Intercept	5.391353	.072901	188.658	73.955	.000	5.247548	5.535159
time	.001343	.003954	181.421	.340	.734	−.006458	.009145

[a] Dependent Variable: Lifesat.

Estimates of Covariance Parameters[a]

Parameter		Estimate	Std. Error	Wald Z	Sig.	95% Confidence Interval	
						Lower Bound	Upper Bound
Residual		.281957	.008593	32.811	.000	.265607	.299312
Intercept + time	UN (1,1)	.912872	.103971	8.780	.000	.730234	1.141188
[subject = id]	UN (2,1)	−.008005	.004180	−1.915	.055	−.016197	.000187
	UN (2,2)	.001604	.000309	5.181	.000	.001098	.002341

[a] Dependent Variable: Lifesat.

3. Conditional Model

Estimates of Fixed Effects[a]

Parameter	Estimate	Std. Error	df	t	Sig.	95% Confidence Interval	
						Lower Bound	Upper Bound
Intercept	5.733641	.104683	199.441	54.771	.000	5.527213	5.940069
time	.000958	.003935	177.385	.243	.808	−.006808	.008725
w_support	.090906	.016467	2302.195	5.520	.000	.058614	.123198
b_support	.338290	.076453	185.859	4.425	.000	.187462	.489118

[a] Dependent Variable: Lifesat.

Estimates of Covariance Parameters[a]

Parameter		Estimate	Std. Error	Wald Z	Sig.	95% Confidence Interval	
						Lower Bound	Upper Bound
Residual		.275355	.008474	32.494	.000	.259237	.292475
Intercept + time	UN (1,1)	.864614	.099605	8.680	.000	.689863	1.083633
[subject = id]	UN (2,1)	−.009675	.004118	−2.350	.019	−.017746	−.001604
	UN (2,2)	.001569	.000307	5.113	.000	.001070	.002302

[a] Dependent Variable: Lifesat.

15

OBSERVATIONAL RESEARCH

Karen S. Wampler and James M. Harper

This chapter focuses on the challenges and opportunities of collecting observational data for family therapy research. Collecting quantitative data using trained observers is important to clinical practice, testing theories underlying family therapy, and establishing treatment effectiveness. While use of self-report measures is well understood, methodological issues in the use of observational measures and related validity issues are not as familiar to family therapy researchers. Good resources on general methodological issues in observational research are available (cf. Aspland & Gardner, 2003; Bakeman & Gottman, 1997; Furr & Funder, 2007; Furr, Wagerman, & Funder, 2010; Hill & Lambert, 2004; Snyder, Heyman, & Haynes, 2005). Sources providing a broad view of observational methods in family therapy research have been less available. For example, *Research Methods in Family Therapy* (Sprenkle & Piercy, 2005) included only one chapter on observational research, which was focused specifically on task analysis (Bradley & Johnson, 2005).

Observational methodologies are used to study therapy process, evaluate treatment fidelity, test assumptions underlying family therapy theories, examine the effectiveness of family therapy approaches, and study family therapy training. Documentation of change in behavior as a result of family therapy is essential to clients, third-party payers, professionals who refer to family therapists, and to the profession. It is not sufficient to depend only on client or therapist report to provide evidence of change. Even "hard" outcomes such as drug use, family reunification, recidivism, and school attendance are not sufficient. To be credible, data in terms of behaviors (e.g., problem solving, positive interaction, lessened conflict, positive parenting) directly related to longer-term outcomes must be routinely collected and available.

This chapter is written from the perspective of a strong belief in the importance of multimethod approaches to research and clinical assessment in family therapy, especially the need to rely on measures in addition to self-report. The importance of multimethod assessment has been emphasized by many (Eid & Diener, 2005; Snyder et al., 2005), and frustration has been consistently expressed about the lack of basic description of interpersonal behavior central to the study of human beings in context (Agnew, Carlston, Graziano, & Kelly, 2010). Observational measures are an essential component in a multimethod approach and have surprisingly been underutilized in both research and clinical practice in family therapy. "Surprising" because family therapy focuses on the observed interaction of families, couples, parents, and children and, even when focusing on individuals, conceptualizes the individual in an interactional, systemic context.

Clinicians may use observational methodologies for assessment. Formal coding is likely to sharpen therapist ability to discriminate behaviors (Carpenter, Escudero, & Rivett, 2008; Ray & Ray, 2008), including those identified as crucial in family therapy theory (e.g., taking an "I position" in Bowen theory, blamer softening) or research (e.g., "disgust," Gottman, 1979). Observational measures can help determine when to move to the next phase or when to terminate therapy.

Regardless of the purpose, there are common methodological issues involved in developing, using, and evaluating observational measures. Unfortunately, this methodology is usually presented in a specific context (e.g., therapy process, couple interaction, parent-child interaction, treatment fidelity), rather than in a general framework for family therapy researchers who consider all aspects of the therapist-client and family system. This chapter provides a guide to decisions about when to use observational measures, choosing the type of measure, finding appropriate measures, developing a new measure, and training of coders.

Considering Observational Methods?

The design of observational research involves a series of steps. Figure 15.1 shows that every decision about observational research flows from the nature of the first step, which is the research question. These decisions are not as linear as the figure represents because, in reality, they are interconnected, making it impossible to consider one without also considering the others. A basic issue is whether the construct is most validly measured through observation. A second issue is whether to use an existing coding system or develop a new one.

Can the Relevant Constructs Be Observed?

Whether the relevant construct is best captured through observation is essential to establishing the validity of the measure. This decision will be easier when researchers have participated in extensive informal observation of the relevant behaviors in a variety of settings.

Observation or another approach? Many constructs do not readily lend themselves to self-report questionnaires or interviews. For example, family members are often unaware of some behaviors that observers can see, such as demand-withdraw patterns, sequences of communication, and prevalence of certain language use. On the other hand, because they require looking forward or back in time, constructs central to family therapy research such as satisfaction, happiness, and intention are not captured by the "slice in time" of observation.

231

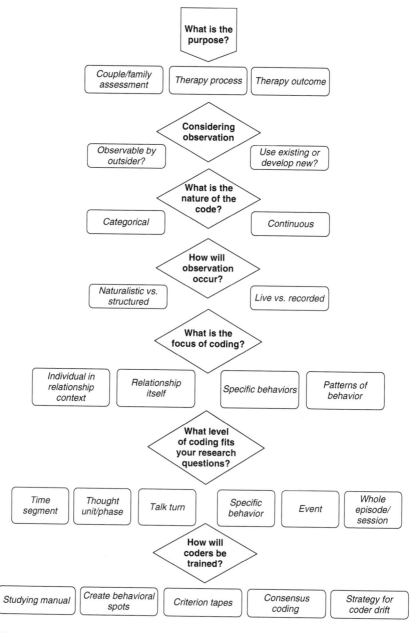

Figure 15.1 Steps in observational research.

Some behaviors, such as physical touch, may occur too infrequently to observe during a therapy session. One of the authors planned a study of couple interaction using a clinic archive of couple sessions, but sufficient lengths of couple interaction were too infrequent because of the therapist talking. Another validity problem is distinguishing constructs that the researcher sees as distinct but cannot be reliably coded. For example, a researcher may be interested in warmth and approachability but may not be able to reliably differentiate the two constructs.

Ethics and acceptability of observation. Researchers must decide whether the behavior can be observed in an ethical manner acceptable to participants. In taped interaction, participants usually remain identifiable, making it impossible for family members to be assured of anonymity. Participants are in control when completing questionnaires, but in interaction tasks, participants cannot control what will happen, especially what other family members will do or say. As part of debriefing, researchers should again offer an opportunity to withdraw consent for all/part of the procedures.

Participants must know who will view the recorded interaction and how confidentiality will be protected. Coders must be extensively trained in confidentiality. Technical advances allow coders to code outside of the laboratory—for example, on their home computer. Researchers must ensure confidentiality of coding and eventual disposal of all records. Increasingly, tapes are sent to centralized coding centers, taking them outside of immediate control of the investigator, which requires additional protections.

Participants being identified is not the only type of ethical issue faced by observational researchers. In conflict discussion tasks, participants receive a list of topics and indicate areas of disagreement. While "drug use" and "sexuality" are usually included on such lists, such topics may create dilemmas of how honest family members can be, which is a possible threat to validity. Snyder et al. (2005) explicitly address possible power and control in couple interactions, especially around conflict, and recommend careful screening to make sure that participants are not in danger from discussing difficult topics.

Using Existing Observational Measures vs. Developing a New Coding System

While most family therapy researchers and clinicians would probably agree that observational measures are valuable, there are also many barriers to their use. Coding systems take a long time to develop. Reliable and valid coding systems are available, but they may not capture the phenomenon that the researcher wants to observe or what the clinician wants to include as part of assessment. Extensive training is needed to attain and maintain adequate levels of interrater agreement, a basic requirement for observational coding. Many coding systems are complex and require extensive data management and data reduction before meaningful measures can be extracted. Fortunately, there are a range of measures in terms of complexity and ease of use, and more are becoming available.

If researchers identify an existing coding system that fits their research question, they should first informally pilot-test the coding system and assess its strengths and weaknesses in addressing the research question. Researchers take extensive notes in this phase, developing a narrative of what is being seen (Bakeman & Gottman, 1997). Involving others allows intensive observation and then periods of discussion, which is helpful. Over time it becomes apparent whether an existing coding system is sufficient (as is or with some modification) to address the research question. If a new coding system is needed, informal notes and discussions gradually yield lists of codes and their definitions. While this phase could be considered qualitative in nature (immersing oneself in the data, intensive observation), it is not formal qualitative research. Formal qualitative research often involves observation of interaction, and it is not uncommon for researchers to move back and forth between quantitative and qualitative methods to address a research question (Gnisci, Bakeman, & Quera, 2008).

Reliability and validity. As with any measure, establishing the reliability and validity of an observational coding system is a major consideration and of particular relevance in deciding whether to use an existing coding system or to develop a new one. Psychometric evidence of a measure is accumulated over time through multiple research studies. When developing a new measure, researchers must establish some evidence of reliability and validity of the new coding system. At minimum, reliability is established by acceptable levels of agreement across coders, which is also related to content validity when codes are clearly defined. Rarely are other types of reliability reported, most likely because assumptions are made that behaviors of participants vary across time, making the use of test-retest or split-half reliabilities questionable. Construct validity is crucial for a new coding system. The study by Gottman (1979) is an example of using discriminant validity to guide the development of a coding system based entirely on which codes distinguished between high and low couple relationship satisfaction. Predictive validity can be demonstrated when the observational codes predict an outcome, such as divorce (Gottman & Levenson, 2002). To establish convergent validity for the Adult Attachment Behavior Q-sort (AABQ), Wampler, Riggs, and Kimball (2004) analyzed how well AABQ scores on attachment security of individuals interacting with their partner correlated with attachment security as measured by the Adult Attachment Interview (George, Kaplan, & Main, 2002). That the AABQ scores on attachment security were not highly related to couple satisfaction was considered evidence of divergent validity.

Examples of determining psychometric properties of coding systems are available. We recommend classics such as Gottman's (1979) couple coding system; Ainsworth, Blehar, Waters, and Wall's (1978) strange situation codes of child behavior; as well as recent examples such as McLeod and Weisz's (2010) development of a process measure for adolescent psychotherapy. Furr and colleagues'

(2010) development of the Revised Riverside Behavior Q-sort (RBQ) is also a good example of the process of establishing reliability and validity.

Sources of measures. The availability of appropriate observational measures is another consideration. In comparison with self-report measures, observational measures tend to be developed and used by one researcher for a specific research question or related research questions. Increasingly, however, reliable and well-validated observational measures are available, all with coding manuals. Some systems even have training workshops available. Snyder et al. (2005) have developed a valuable set of criteria for evaluating the usefulness of observational measures.

Good sources of couple coding systems measures are from Kerig and Baucom (2004) and Snyder et al. (2005). Aspland and Gardner (2003) describe parent-child observational measures. McCrae and Weiss (2007) include systems focused on the individual. Reviews of family measures are available (Alderfer et al., 2008; Kerig & Lindahl, 2001). Manusov's (2005) edited volume of nonverbal measures contains copies of several useful coding systems.

Nature of the Code

Aspects of Behavior to Be Observed

Constructs of interest to family therapy researchers are best captured by "socially based" rather than "physically based" coding schemes (Bakeman & Gottman, 1997). "Socially based" systems require coders to track verbal and nonverbal cues and to use human ability to decode the meaning of behaviors (Gottman, 1979; Waldinger, Hauser, Schulz, Allen, & Crowell, 2004). Much meaning in human interaction is lost if only verbal content is tracked (e.g., coding from a transcript or visually blocking out an individual in order to focus on another individual). Ideally, coders have access to both content and nonverbal cues, such as facial expression, physical movement, and voice tone. Ray and Ray (2008) distinguish between coding "functional behavior" (coded only when it is completed) and "physical/structural behavior" (coded at initiation). Obtaining reliability is easier for low-inference physical codes (e.g., "who talks to whom," distance between chairs, number of head nods), but connecting such behaviors to meaningful constructs can be difficult.

Categorical vs. Continuous

As depicted in Figure 15.1, a coding system can contain categorical codes, continuous codes, or both. Categorical codes require observers to determine whether a behavior occurs or not, such as in Gottman's Specific Affect Coding System (Coan & Gottman, 2007), with coders identifying whether disgust, withdrawal, etc. occurred. Another example is the Cognitive-Affective Rating

Scale (Harper & Hoopes, 1987), with coders categorizing predicates as cognitive or affective. Measures of frequency or duration can be derived from categorical codes. Codes can also be continuous, such as ratings of intensity or negativity. For example, Ainsworth et al. (1978) coded child behavior in the Strange Situation with a paragraph describing behavior that would be rated 1 through 9. Q-sorts code interaction on a continuum from "least like" to "most like" the interaction. Most constructs can be measured by a continuous or a categorical code. For example, "positive interaction" could be a categorical code (yes–no) or an intensity rating. The decision depends on the research question and the associated analyses a researcher anticipates.

How Will Observation Occur?

Structured vs. "Naturalistic"

The context for observing behavior is a major consideration. Contexts can be thought of as varying along a dimension of naturalistic to highly structured. Unless one is observing public behavior that does not require permission, contexts cannot be completely natural. Observing therapy sessions with no special instructions or tasks could be considered "naturalistic." An example of a more structured context would be requiring the inclusion of a family sculpture in a therapy session. A central issue of external validity is whether observed behaviors are typical and generalizable to behaviors of the family system outside of the observation context. A common concern about observation, in general, including behavior in family therapy sessions, is that participants' awareness of taping or observation causes them to modify their typical behavior. A related issue is that behavior is observed as a "slice in time" (a particular time on a particular day in a specific setting) and may not be generalizable to other days or longer periods of time. Gottman (1979) was the first to systematically address the issue of generalizability with extensive research on observing behavior in different situations. He and others (Gardner, 2000; Jacob, Tennenbaum, Seilhamer, Bargiel, & Shron, 1994; Lorenz, Melby, Conger, & Surjadi, 2012) have consistently found that behavior coded in different contexts is generalizable and predictive of outcomes.

Researchers may use a structured task to elicit the behavior they wish to observe and record the interaction for later coding. Tasks are designed to elicit interaction relevant to the research question. Types of tasks can generally be grouped into "positive" (plan a vacation together, play a game, talk about what attracted you to each other, talk about a recent time you had fun together) or "negative" (discuss a recent problem or concern, talk about a time when you felt hurt by the other person, pick up the toys). Conflict tasks are most commonly used (Snyder et al., 2005), along with instructions to try to solve the problem. Tasks can also be structured into "process experiments." For example, Seedall and Wampler (2012) asked couples to first interact with each other

236

with a facilitator who watched but did not participate, followed by a second discussion of the same issues with the same facilitator, who then actively worked to create a softening event. The Strange Situation, which is coding a series of separations/reunions between parent and toddler (Ainsworth et al., 1978), is a process "experiment."

Structuring the interaction task is usually important for most research questions. Structuring to raise intensity is more likely to elicit behavior related to the constructs of interest to family therapy researchers. For example, one of the authors was evaluating whether to code a set of taped tasks in which couples expecting their first child discussed changes they expected after the baby was born. Partners sat side-by-side, and the task elicited positive behavior (much patting of pregnant bellies) with little variability. This comfortable social situation did not yield sufficient range and variability to capture differences in the quality of couple interaction.

Structuring the task is also needed to ensure that all participants are involved. One of the authors watched tapes of family interaction meant to involve both parents and a child, but, almost invariably, fathers sat off to the side in a chair and watched mother and child playing a game. In another study, a family task that involved building increasingly complex structures out of "Lincoln Logs" evoked such prescribed gender roles (mother dug pieces out of the box and handed them to father and child, who built the structure) that the intended family interaction was not elicited. Creativity can be used to design tasks. In one study, family members were given a poster board and a large box of materials and asked to "build their dream house." To raise intensity, one child was the only one allowed to use the scissors, and the other child was the only one allowed to use the glue. In addition to coding the family interaction, one could code the "product," as some families built elaborate, complex "houses" and others had sparse drawings.

Interaction should not be interrupted by broken equipment, dogs, cell phones, crying infants, drinking or eating, or bathroom breaks. It takes extensive pilot testing to eliminate most (alas, never all) possible problems. In addition to developing backup systems to mitigate equipment problems, the behavior of interest needs to be within view of the camera.

Live vs. recorded. The behaviors of interest and the nature of the coding system often determine whether the task is coded live or taped for later coding. A system with numerous and complex codes necessitates recorded tasks so coders can rewind and watch the behaviors again. Coding live interaction is possible only when the codes are simple (counting how many times one specific behavior occurs during time intervals or positive, neutral, or negative affect). Even when the system is simple, the number of family members in the task creates challenges for coding "live." Recording tasks has its challenges, including equipment failures, sound not loud enough, images not clear enough, and issues of organizing and managing videotapes, DVDs, or computer storage space for digital recordings.

What Is the Focus of Coding?

Observational methods have been developed for studies of (a) individuals; (b) dyads, such as couples, parent-child, therapist-client, or siblings; (c) triads, such as two parents and a child, sibling groups, or therapist and a couple; and (d) groups and families. Researchers must decide whether the initial code is focused on the individual in context or on a relationship pattern. Each has its advantages; however, the majority of systems code individual behaviors that can then be linked and "built up" to measure the relationship. When the relationship is the initial code, it is impossible to "break down" codes into representing individuals.

Individual

Sometimes coders focus on a specific individual regardless of how many individuals are present. The other individuals are background, with the focal individual in the foreground; however, the interactional context is almost always taken into account. For example, to code sensitive responding for a parent (the "target" person being coded), the behavior of the child is a crucial part of the context. The Client Experiencing Scale, EXP (Klein, Mathieu-Coughlan, & Keisler, 1986), is an example of an observational measure focused on a single client's depth of emotional experiencing in therapy process and outcome studies in emotionally focused therapy research (cf. Zuccarini, Johnson, Dalgleish, & Makinen, 2012).

Sometimes researchers are interested in only individual behavior. Most family therapy researchers want to combine codes of individuals into relationship-level constructs. Coding is done in a way that allows codes for each individual to be linked. To do this, observers must assign codes to individuals for the same piece of interaction being observed. In addition, the data file will require a family-level approach when data from two or more individuals are linked into a relationship variable. (See Chapter 24 for more on data management.)

Decisions about who to code and when and how to build relationship constructs from codes of individuals are related to participant sampling. Three types of participant sampling include focal, multiple pass, and conspicuous sampling (Yoder & Symons, 2010). Focal sampling involves coding one participant for a period of time, then coding a different participant for the same period until all participants are coded. Multiple pass sampling is when one participant is selected and her/his behavior coded for the entire session. Software is available to aid this sampling process (cf. "Observer XT" sold by Noldus; "VideoScribe" sold by Intranel; and "Interact" sold by Mangold). Conspicuous sampling involves watching a whole family and coding which individual engages in any predefined behaviors.

Directly Coding the Relationship

Directly coding the relationship may better fit some research questions. An advantage of coding the relationship as a whole is that coding does not depend on the number of individuals present. For example, a code of the quality of the therapeutic relationship could encompass the therapist (or even two therapists) and the client system, whether an individual, couple, or family. The process of coding family enjoyment is the same, regardless of four family members being present one week when only three were present the previous week.

An example of relationship-level coding is the Family Relational Communication Control Coding System (Friedlander et al., 2006), which requires coders to assign a one-up, one-down, or one-across categorization to every speech exchange between two people, with codes assigned to each exchange. Examples of coding systems that focus on the whole family, regardless of numbers of family members, include the Georgia Family Q-sort (Wampler, Halverson, Moore, & Walters, 1990) and the group codes from the Iowa Family Interaction Rating Scales (IFIRS; Melby et al., 1998).

What Level of Coding Fits the Research Question?

As indicated in Figure 15.1, behavior occurs in time, and in order to code, the researcher has to determine what period of time to code. Equally important, the researcher must determine what exactly "triggers" the observer entering a code. The approach chosen depends on the conceptual framework, the type of data that has been or will be collected, and resources.

Length of Time

Decisions need to be made about the total length of time to be observed and whether separate coding is done for segments within the total time. Again, the research question and whether the length of time is sufficient to reliably code the phenomenon in question are essential considerations for validity. Coding whole therapy sessions is seldom practiced because the resources in coder time are too costly; consequently, only segments of therapy sessions are usually coded. For example, one of us chose to code a 10-minute segment 30 minutes after the couple therapy session began in sessions at the beginning, middle, and end of treatment.

A useful approach to determining what segment to code within the total time of interaction available is to use an event, such as softening, a period of high conflict, therapist initiating a family sculpture, or an enactment (Woolley, Wampler, & Davis, 2012). Task analysis (Bradley & Johnson, 2005) is a classic example of event coding that begins with experienced clinicians identifying a specific part of a session in which change occurred. When an event triggers the segment of interaction to be coded, observers must agree on whether or not the event occurred as well as agreeing on the codes associated with the event. The segment of interaction surrounding the event to be coded is also defined—for example, coding for 3 minutes prior and 10 minutes after the event. For a more detailed discussion of sampling segments of interaction, see the work by Yoder and Symons (2010).

Collecting more structured observational data often involves different segments or tasks. For example, Wampler et al. (1990) included a series of family interaction tasks of about 5–7 minutes each. Observers only watched the two middle tasks, however, and coded both together as if they were continuous. The first and last tasks were used as "warm up" and "cool down." In contrast, when the difference in interaction between types of segments is important (e.g., Seedall & Wampler, 2012; semi-natural vs. therapy-like), each segment must be coded separately.

Preserving Sequence

Researchers must define what "triggers" a code within the segment. Usually a sequence of interaction contains codes of small "slices" of behavior. A common approach is to identify these slices of behavior by time (coding the target behavior at a set interval, such as every 30 seconds). A signal, in the form of a sound, cues coders to tally the behavior. One of the authors used a laptop to assign codes to 13 nonverbal behaviors at the beginning of the segment to be observed and then coders assigned changes in nonverbal categories as they occurred. The software program corrected for each coder's reaction lag time. Other small "slices" might be "thought units" (Gottman, 1979) or "talk turns." These small "slices" preserve sequence in a meaningful way.

These "fine-grained" codes are best fitted to questions about patterns and sequences of interaction and counts of specific behaviors. The more fine-grained the focus of coding, the simpler the codes must be, although either categorical or continuous codes can be applied even to small slices of behavior. For example, degree of negativity could be rated in 30-second slices. Disadvantages of such coding systems are the cost in time to code tasks, additional training time, and the large number of data points to be managed.

Coding Segments as a Whole

Some coding systems require observers to code after watching a whole segment. While whole segments lend themselves to ratings or Q-sorts, finer-grained codes can also be applied to whole segments. For example, coders could count how many times "disgust" occurs, regardless of when during the segment it occurs. Coding whole segments requires more judgment on the part of coders because longer lengths of interaction are viewed before codes are assigned. Examples of "whole segment" coding include the Adult Attachment Behavior Q-sort (AABQ; Wampler et al., 2004) and the IFIRS (Melby et al., 1998). The AABQ is designed to assess the attachment security of individuals when interacting with a romantic partner. IFIRS is a comprehensive system that includes ratings of individual, dyadic, and group characteristics. Coders consider frequency, intensity, affect, and context associated with each of the 55 coded behaviors. Generally, these types of codes are more feasible for use in clinical assessment (Snyder et al., 2005) because constructs related to more global family functioning (e.g., alliances, roles, structure, boundaries, narrative themes) can be examined.

Training of Coders

How coders are trained depends on the type of coding system. Complex coding systems require more training time. The Cognitive-Affective Rating Scale (CARS; Harper & Hoopes, 1987) requires coders to read transcripts and tally the number of times each person uses affective verbs and adjectives and cognitive verbs and adjectives. Because the categories are few, coders were trained and reached criterion interrater agreement in less than 4 hours. On the other hand, a complex coding system like IFIRS (Melby et al., 1998) takes an average of 90 hours of training. Researchers must decide what percentage of tasks is reliability coded, when during the study tasks are checked for agreement, and whether reliability coding can be "blind."

Adequate interrater agreement is accomplished through intensive training of coders and then establishing agreement between two or more coders. (See Chapter 24 on how to calculate interrater agreement.) However, an alternative way of obtaining reliable coding is to use large numbers of coders to code each interaction. If many individuals see the phenomenon in the same way, researchers can be confident the phenomenon "exists." Waldinger et al. (2004) describe encouraging results of a study using "naïve" coders to obtain consensual ratings of emotion descriptors. Baker, Messinger, Ekas, Lindahl, and Brewster (2010) provide another example of such an approach using 10 non-expert coders.

Typical Process of Training

Training in complex coding systems requires the development of an extensive coding manual that provides clear definitions of each code, rules for decision making, and examples and non-examples of the behavior. The methods used in training coders in the IFIRS system illustrate processes of training as recommended by Sharpe and Koperwas (2003). Coders in training are first given the 329-page coding manual and after a few days are required to pass a quiz on it.

They are then asked to code a couple task that requires "digging down" into the manual, and they watch "behavioral spots," taped examples of behavior representing different codes. The task they coded has also been coded by a "certified research coder," providing immediate feedback about their accuracy. They continue coding one to three tasks per week and receiving feedback. They are also introduced to a workbook that covers frequently made mistakes and frequently misunderstood codes. Once the trainees consistently reach 80% agreement with the certified coders, they code a criterion tape coded by those in the IFIRS coding lab at another university. Only after this does their coding become part of the research database. Twenty-five percent of the tasks are chosen at random to be double coded, with both coders blind to the fact that the task is being double coded. When there are discrepancies between coders on these double-coded tasks, they hold a consensus meeting in which both coders are blind to their initial ratings, watch the task together, and come to consensus only for those codes where they disagreed. Interrater reliabilities for each coder are examined weekly, and specific corrective attention is given to coders who consistently get lower reliabilities.

Maintaining High Coder Agreement

An issue in training is coder drift (Hill & Lambert, 2004). Coder accuracy is affected by many things, including not spending enough time coding, mood, daily experience of the coder, affinity toward persons being coded, specific bias related to culture, fatigue if a coder works too long, and coding in isolation for long periods. Each of these problems requires retraining. One maintenance strategy is to require all coders to participate in "call out" meetings, where they watch a taped task together and call out behaviors and levels as they see them. An additional approach is to do a group consensus meeting in which all coders rate a tape, and then all of their ratings are compared and examined for discrepancies. Individual and group instruction can focus on parts of the coding manual or on "behavior spots." If interrater reliabilities are examined regularly, then individual coders who are struggling are easily identified, as is any drift in the whole group.

Coder mood and daily experience can be handled by asking coders to respond to Likert-scaled questions about their mood at the beginning and end of the coding session and about their affinity toward and empathy with the persons they code. IFIRS (Melby et al., 1998) includes codes for the physical attractiveness of the person being coded and rater responsiveness to the person being coded. These codes can then be used in statistical analyses to control for observer bias. Of course, randomly assigning tasks to coders and ensuring that one coder does not code all the sessions of therapy or all of the tasks a family participates in helps to ensure that bias does not systematically affect the results.

Cultural Bias

One important consideration of possible observer bias is the culture/ethnicity of the coders and the individuals or families they are coding. Melby, Hoyt, and Bryant (2003) examined race of coder and race of family as sources of bias in coding. European American coders rated families more favorably regardless of race of family, and coders tended to rate same-race families less favorably. Most of the bias disappeared over time as training addressed this issue. Another approach might be to train coders of different races/ethnicities so that they can do this type of comparison and so that the bias is at least randomly distributed in the coding.

Conclusion

The increased availability of valid and reliable observational measures and knowledge of how to develop and use them are hopeful signs. The current focus of research funding on effectiveness studies and transportability to real-world clinical practice has encouraged development of more feasible approaches to observational measures (cf. McLeod & Islam, 2011) that are accessible to clinicians. For example, McLeod and Weisz (2010) describe a system of observational coding of "usual care" in child and adolescent therapy as practiced in the community. Another new development of promise is the use of multiple, untrained coders (Baker et al., 2010; Waldinger et al., 2004).

In writing this chapter, we were particularly struck by two issues. One relates to the need for more process research specifically tailored to couple and family therapy. Existing family therapy process measures are tailored to specific evidence-based approaches, and there is a need for more general family therapy measures. For example, a study of factors that clients identify as important (Chenail et al., 2012) included items such as "let them answer questions without interruptions," "give partners equal time," "connect with child," "provided feedback on goals." These could be an excellent source of codes for a general measure of family therapy process.

A second issue is related to family therapy training. While studied extensively, evaluation of family therapy training has depended almost entirely on questionnaires or interviews. This is particularly surprising because family therapy sessions are routinely recorded, providing multiple opportunities to code and examine changes in behavior over the entire period of training. Observational data would help document whether student learning outcomes are met and guide improvements in training.

The rewards of using observational measures, as well as the costs of the failure to use them to document observable outcomes, suggest that observational research will become more common in family therapy research and practice. Equally important, the dramatically increased availability of reliable, portable, and relatively inexpensive equipment in conjunction with the ability to transport, store, and manage large datasets, should also expand the use of observational measures in both family therapy research and clinical practice.

References

Agnew, C. R., Carlston, D. E., Graziano, W. G., & Kelly, J. R. (Eds.). (2010). *Then a miracle occurs: Focusing on behavior in social psychological theory and research.* New York: Oxford.

Ainsworth, M. D. S., Blehar, M. C., Waters, E., & Wall, S. (1978). *Patterns of attachment: A psychological study of the Strange Situation.* Hillsdale, NJ: Erlbaum.

Alderfer, M. A., Fiese, B. H., Gold, J. I., Cutuli, J. J., Holmbeck, G. N., Goldbeck, L., . . . Patterson, J. (2008). Evidence-based assessment in pediatric psychology: Family measures. *Journal of Pediatric Psychology, 33,* 1046–1061. doi:10:1037/a0021275

Aspland, H., & Gardner, F. (2003). Observational measures of parent-child interaction: An introductory review. *Child and Adolescent Mental Health, 8,* 136–143.

Bakeman, R., & Gottman, J. M. (1997). *Observing interaction: An introduction to sequential analysis* (2nd ed.). Cambridge, UK: Cambridge University Press.

Baker, J. K., Messinger, D. S., Ekas, N. V., Lindahl, K. M., & Brewster, R. (2010). Non-expert ratings of family and parent-child interaction. *Journal of Family Psychology, 24,* 775–778. doi: 10.1037/a0021275

Bradley, B., & Johnson, S. M. (2005). Task analysis of couple and family change events. In D. H. Sprenkle & F. P. Piercy (Eds.), *Research methods in family therapy* (2nd ed., pp. 254–271). New York: Guilford.

Carpenter, J., Escudero, V., & Rivett, M. (2008). Training family therapy students in conceptual and observation skills relating to the therapeutic alliance: An evaluation. *Journal of Family Therapy, 30,* 411–424.

Chenail, R. J., St. George, S., Wulff, D., Duffy, M., Scott, K. W., & Tomm, K. (2012). Clients' relational conceptions of conjoint couple and family therapy quality: A grounded formal theory. *Journal of Marital and Family Therapy, 38,* 241–264. doi: 10.111/j.1752-0606.2011.00246x

Coan, J. A., & Gottman, J. M. (2007). The Specific Affect Coding System (SPAFF). In J. A. Coan & J. B. Allen (Eds.), *Handbook of emotion elicitation and assessment* (pp. 267–285). New York: Oxford University Press.

Eid, M., & Diener, E. (Eds.). (2005). *Handbook of multimethod measurement in psychology.* Washington, DC: American Psychological Association.

Friedlander, M. L., Escudero, V., Horvath, S., Heatherington, L., Cabero, A., & Martens, M. P. (2006). System for Observing Family Therapy Alliances: A tool for research and practice. *Journal of Counseling Psychology, 53,* 214–225.

Furr, R. M., & Funder, D. C. (2007). Behavioral observation. In R. W. Robins, R. C. Fraley, & R. F. Krueger (Eds.), *Handbook of research methods in personality psychology* (pp. 273–291). New York: Guilford.

Furr, R. M., Wagerman, S. A., & Funder, D. C. (2010). Personality as manifest in behavior: Direct behavioral observation using the Revised Riverside Behavioral Q-sort (RBQ-3.0). In C. R. Agnew, D. E. Carlston, W. G. Graziano, & J. R. Kelly (Eds.), *Then a miracle occurs: Focusing on behavior in social psychological theory and research* (pp. 186–204). New York: Oxford.

Gardner, F. (2000). Methodological issues in the direct observation of parent-child interaction: Do observational findings reflect the natural behavior of participants? *Clinical Child and Family Psychology Review, 3,* 185–198. doi: 1096-4037/00/0900-0185

George, C., Kaplan, N., & Main, M. (2002). *The Adult Attachment Interview* (3rd ed.). Unpublished manuscript, University of California, Berkeley.

Gnisci, A., Bakeman, R., & Quera, V. (2008). Blending qualitative and quantitative analyses in observing interaction: Misunderstandings, applications and proposals. *International Journal of Multiple Research Approaches, 2,* 15–30.

Gottman, J. M. (1979). *Marital interaction: Experimental investigations.* New York: Academic Press.

Gottman, J. M., & Levenson, R. W. (2002). A two-factor model for predicting when a couple will divorce: Exploratory analysis using 14-year longitudinal data. *Family Process, 41,* 83–96.

Harper, J. M., & Hoopes, M. H. (1987). *The Cognitive-Affective Rating Scale.* Provo, UT: Family Studies Center, Brigham Young University.

Hill, C. E., & Lambert, M. J. (2004). Methodological issues in studying psychotherapy processes and outcomes. In M. J. Lambert (Ed.), *Bergin and Garfield's handbook of psychotherapy and behavior change* (pp. 84–135). New York: Wiley.

Jacob, T., Tennenbaum, D., Seilhamer, R. A., Bargiel, K., & Shron, T. (1994). Reactivity effects during naturalistic observation of distressed and nondistressed families. *Journal of Family Psychology, 8,* 354–363. doi: 10.1037/0893–3200.8.3.354

Kerig, P. K., & Baucom, D. H. (2004). *Couple observational coding systems.* Mahwah, NJ: Erlbaum.

Kerig, P. K., & Lindahl, K. M. (Eds.). (2001). *Family observational coding systems: Resources for systemic research.* New York: Psychology Press.

Klein, M. H., Mathieu-Coughlan, P., & Kiesler, D. J. (1986). The Experiencing Scales. In W. M. Pinsof & L. S. Greenberg (Eds.), *Guilford clinical psychology and psychotherapy series* (pp. 21–71). New York: Guilford.

Lorenz, F. O., Melby, J. N., Conger, R. D., & Surjadi, F. F. (2012). Linking questionnaire reports and observer ratings of young couples' hostility and support. *Journal of Family Psychology, 26,* 316–327. doi: 10.1037/a0028319

Manusov, V. (Ed.). (2005). *The sourcebook of nonverbal measures.* Mahwah, NJ: Erlbaum.

McCrae, R. R., & Weiss, A. (2007). Observer ratings of personality. In R. W. Robins, R. C. Fraley, & R. F. Krueger (Eds.), *Handbook of research methods in personality psychology* (pp. 259–272). New York: Guilford.

McLeod, B. D., & Islam, N. Y. (2011). Using treatment integrity methods to study the implementation process. *Clinical Psychology: Science and Practice, 18,* 36–40.

McLeod, B. D., & Weisz, J. R. (2010). The Therapy Process Observational Coding System for Child Psychotherapy Strategies scale. *Journal of Clinical Child & Adolescent Psychology, 39,* 436–443. doi: 10.1080/15374411003691750

Melby, J. N., Conger, R., Book, R., Reuter, M., Lucy, L., Repinski, D., . . . Scaramella, L. (1998). *The Iowa Family Interaction Rating Scales.* Ames: Institute for Social and Behavioral Research, Iowa State University.

Melby, J. N., Hoyt, W. T., & Bryant, C. M. (2003). A generalizability approach to assessing the effects of ethnicity and training on observer ratings of family interactions. *Journal of Social and Personal Relationships, 20,* 171–191. doi: 10.1177/02654075030202003

Ray, J. M., & Ray, R. D. (2008). Train-to-Code: An adaptive expert system for training systematic observation and coding skills. *Behavior Research Methods, 40,* 673–693. doi:10.3758/BRM.40.3.673

Seedall, R. B., & Wampler, K. S. (2012). Emotional congruence within couple interaction: The role of attachment avoidance. *Journal of Family Psychology, 26,* 948–958. doi: 10.1037/a0030479

Sharpe, T., & Koperwas, K. (2003). *Behavior and sequential analyses: Principles and practice.* Thousand Oaks, CA: Sage.

Snyder, D. K., Heyman, R. E., & Haynes, S. N. (2005). Evidence-based approaches to assessing couple distress. *Psychological Assessment, 17,* 288–307.

Sprenkle, D. H., & Piercy, F. P. (2005). *Research methods in family therapy* (2nd ed.). New York: Guilford.

Waldinger, R.J., Hauser, S.T., Schulz, M.S., Allen, J.P., & Crowell, J.A. (2004). Reading others' emotions: The role of intuitive judgments in predicting marital satisfaction, quality, and stability. *Journal of Family Psychology, 18,* 58–71. doi: 10.1037/0893-3200.18.1.58

Wampler, K.S., Halverson, C.F., Moore, J.J., & Walters, L.H. (1990). The Georgia Family Q-sort: An observational measure of family functioning. *Family Process, 28,* 223–238.

Wampler, K.S., Riggs, B., & Kimball, T.G. (2004). Observing attachment behavior in couples: The Adult Attachment Behavior Q-set (AABQ). *Family Process, 43,* 315–335.

Woolley, S.R., Wampler, K.S., & Davis, S.D. (2012). Enactments in couple therapy: Identifying therapist interventions associated with positive change. *Journal of Family Therapy, 34,* 284–305. doi: 10.1111/j.1467-6427

Yoder, P., & Symons, F. (2010). *Observational measurement of behavior.* New York: Springer.

Zuccarini, D., Johnson, S.M., Dalgleish, T.L., & Makinen, J.A. (2012). Forgiveness and reconciliation in emotionally focused therapy for couples: The client change process and therapist interventions. *Journal of Marital and Family Therapy.* doi: 10.1111/j.1752-0606.2012.00287

16

QUALITATIVE RESEARCH FOR FAMILY THERAPY[1]

Jerry E. Gale and Megan L. Dolbin-MacNab

'Get to your places!' shouted the Queen in a voice of thunder, and people began running about in all directions, tumbling up against each other; however, they got settled down in a minute or two, and the game began. Alice thought she had never seen such a curious croquet-ground in her life; it was all ridges and furrows; the balls were live hedgehogs, the mallets live flamingoes, and the soldiers had to double themselves up and to stand on their hands and feet, to make the arches.

The chief difficulty Alice found at first was in managing her flamingo: she succeeded in getting its body tucked away, comfortably enough, under her arm, with its legs hanging down, but generally, just as she had got its neck nicely straightened out, and was going to give the hedgehog a blow with its head, it would twist itself round and look up in her face, with such a puzzled expression that she could not help bursting out laughing: and when she had got its head down, and was going to begin again, it was very provoking to find that the hedgehog had unrolled itself, and was in the act of crawling away: besides all this, there was generally a ridge or furrow in the way wherever she wanted to send the

---

1 In qualitative research, it is common for the researcher, as the instrument of the research, to provide a statement that informs the reader of the contextual aspects of the researcher's identity that might influence the study. In this spirit, we have created subjectivity statements for this chapter. *Jerry Gale*: I had a speech impediment at about ages 4–8, such that few understood me when I spoke. I attended speech therapy classes at school and after school. I tended to be a loner. Looking back, I can see how this shaped my interest in language, interpersonal meaning making, and observation. This was also influential in my career moves toward both family therapy and qualitative research. My years of training in Ericksonian hypnosis were influential in attending to the nuances of language, and my years of meditation practice shaped my interest in phenomenology. *Megan Dolbin-MacNab*: I was raised in a family that loves stories, which has influenced my interest in hearing others' stories either as a therapist or as a qualitative researcher. Additionally, my years on my grandparents' dairy farm were instrumental in developing my sense of pragmatism when it comes to my selection of research methods and willingness to consider multiple methodological approaches to tackling a research question.

hedgehog to, and, as the doubled-up soldiers were always getting up and walking off to other parts of the ground, Alice soon came to the conclusion that it was a very difficult game indeed.

Lewis Carroll's *Alice's Adventures in Wonderland*

Qualitative inquiry invites the researcher into the world of meaning making. Rather than looking for patterns to be generalized across contexts, qualitative inquiry seeks contextually entwined patterns, in that meanings and patterns are better understood in relation to aspects of the social/political/historical/cultural context. As in Carroll's game of croquet, each action can be viewed from the meaning-motivation perspective of each particular character, the systemic interplay between characters, as well as the sociopolitical context.[2] Alice's experience and taken-for-granted assumptions of cause and effect, control, and prediction are challenged as she maneuvers the fluid flamingo to hit the ever-moving hedgehog through the shifting targets. As in family therapy, how each member of the client system, as well as the therapist system, attributes meaning and moral characterization and responds to each other's comments and behaviors can vary significantly. The purpose of this chapter is not to teach the reader how to do qualitative research (that would be beyond the scope of the chapter, and there are many excellent resources for that purpose, including studies by Creswell [2013], Glesne [2011], and Silverman and Marvasti [2008]), but to invite the reader into a discussion of a different set of rules and a new game toward understanding, studying, and potentially changing human behavior—the structure and rigor that goes along with qualitative inquiry.

Qualitative inquiry has a number of strengths that can benefit family therapy research. Some of these include gaining an understanding of people's lived experiences and exploring rational and nonrational decision making, emotional reactivity, attributions, and personal meaning of self and other. Qualitative approaches can also be valuable in gaining insight into how behavioral change occurs, both in and outside of family therapy. They can also provide clinicians with useful information about factors that influence the outcome of therapy.

As educators of qualitative researchers, we have experienced the difficulties and misconceptions associated with conducting rigorous qualitative inquiry. Common concerns include: "Why don't all the texts and authors use words the same way and to mean the same thing?" "Are 'grounded theory' and 'phenomenology' methods, methodologies, or theories?" "Why does it matter about whose ideas I am using when I do grounded theory (e.g., Glaser and Strauss, Strauss, Charmaz), phenomenology (Husserl, Heidegger, Gadamer, Moustakas, Ricoeur, Levinas, Schütz, etc.), narrative analysis (Riesman, Labov, Mishler, etc.), discourse analysis (Edwards and Potter, Fairclough, etc.), and any other qualitative methodologies?" "Why does epistemology matter in doing qualitative research?" "Just tell me how to do it,

---

2 We use the phrase "can be viewed" because, depending on the epistemology and methodology of the research, more or less of the context is considered.

and don't say 'it depends' so often." And we have heard from beginning research-ers that "qualitative research is easier than quantitative research, and I am going to use such and such methodology [even before they have their research question] for my dissertation." It is for these (and many other) reasons that we believe it is important for family therapy researchers and educators to understand the different qualitative frameworks and the "rules"[3] of these different methodologies, and what entails coherent rigor for a particular qualitative methodology.

There is rigor, imagination, and narrative coherence[4] in qualitative research, and to access these qualities requires iterative, reflective engagement in multiple con-texts of one's inquiry, including scrutinizing the research procedures. For example, the iterative quality of the qualitative research process, also referred to as analytical induction, can lead to new directions of inquiry *throughout* the research process (Atkinson & Delamont, 2005). The research process itself can be analyzed by exam-ining how interview questions shape responses (Roulston, 2010). Family therapy qualitative researchers, however, often embrace these and other complexities and are able to use the strengths of qualitative research and its associated complexity by generating useful insights about family processes and the process of family therapy.

Orienting to Qualitative Inquiry

The concept of 'qualitative research' is broad and varied and not easy to define. Denzin and Lincoln (2005) provide a broad definition: "Qualitative research is a situated activity that locates the observer in the world. It consists of a set of inter-pretive, material practices that make the world visible. These practices transform the world" (p. 3). To help the reader better understand the variety of approaches to qualitative inquiry, and the rules that guide the rigorous application of differ-ent qualitative methodologies, it is useful to first consider the role of epistemol-ogy in qualitative inquiry.

Epistemology

Crotty (1998) wrote a seminal book about how the researcher's epistemic per-spective, or implicit paradigm for understanding and explaining how we know what we know, shapes all aspects of the research endeavor and even determines how one defines and privileges 'science' and 'research.' Crotty discusses exten-sively how various epistemologies are associated with different frames of logic and rules for the conduct of research, including what is considered research, how one relates to participants (e.g., co-researchers, collaborators, participants), what is considered data, how research is conducted, and how the results of research

---

3 Rules here refer both to methodological and procedural differences as well as paradigmatic differences based on different epistemic framings.

4 Narrative coherence means that the various parts of the study logically hold together to present a persuasive story.

are analyzed and disseminated. Crotty maintains that there are four main conceptual elements that underlie all research inquiry, including qualitative inquiry. These include epistemology, theoretical perspective, methodology, and methods. Regardless of the research framework, each of these elements must be logically consistent with one another. This logical consistency is necessary if the research process is to be considered rigorous and the findings valid.

In his book, Crotty (1998) presents three major epistemic distinctions that are relevant to rigorous qualitative research in the field of family therapy—objectivism, constructionism, and subjectivism.[5] Summarizing Crotty, objectivism is based on assumptions of positivism (or postpositivism[6]) such that we can know the world independently of human meaning making through "hypothetico-deductive" scientific methods (proposed by Popper in 1959) and that scientific theories lead to hypotheses that can be tested objectively (often using experimental and quasi-experimental approaches) and with large enough samples to achieve statistical claims and generalize findings across populations. For research based on objectivism, issues of methodological and statistical validity and reliability are fundamental and necessary.

In contrast to objectivism, Crotty (1998) presents constructionism as an epistemology that argues that knowledge of the world cannot be achieved objectively but is always created from a social/historical/political meaning-making process. This epistemic orientation is often associated with such theories as symbolic interactionism, interpretivism, phenomenology, and hermeneutics, among others. Methodologies associated with constructionism are often qualitative approaches and include grounded theory, narrative analysis, phenomenology, ethnography, discourse analysis, and heuristic inquiry. Analyses are typically achieved through nonstatistical inductive methods such as constant comparison, creating taxonomies of themes, and the use of exemplars. In this context, issues of validity and reliability are better articulated as aspects of trustworthiness, authenticity, and narrative coherence (Glesne, 2011).

Finally, with regard to subjectivism, which views people's experiences as being independent of a fixed reality, Crotty (1998) offers the example of Paulo Freire, for whom consciousness is "already an active intervention on reality" and praxis is "reflection and action upon the world in order to transform it" (p. 151). Thus, a subjectivist epistemic view tends toward participatory action research (PAR) approaches where the purpose of the research, analysis, and results is to involve the communities being studied and achieve emancipatory change. In this type of

---

5 To further confound beginning students, it is relevant to note that different scholars articulate different categories of epistemologies. For example, Glesne (2011) presents four categories: positivism, interpretivism, critical theory, and poststructuralism, which she refers to as paradigms (not epistemologies).

6 Postpositivism is an extension of positivism in that there is the view that an independent world exists, but that it is not possible to achieve total precision in objectively knowing the world, and every statement must remain tentative forever (Crotty, 1998).

inquiry, the strength of a study is based less on criteria such as validity and reliability, and more on the extent to which a social agenda is advanced.

The implication of these different epistemic frameworks for clinical qualitative research in family therapy is that each epistemology leads to different definitions of research, varied research agendas, diverse ways of using theory, and different rules for research procedures, methods, analysis, and presentation. This includes variations in the definition of data, how data are collected and analyzed, and why the results are what they are. For example, grounded theory can be used from a postpositivist framework and is consistent with Glaser and Strauss's (1967) work. It can also be used from a constructionist perspective, which is consistent with Charmaz' (2006) approach. Depending on the epistemic view that the researcher takes, a grounded theory approach could look very different.[7]

Patti Lather and Bettie St. Pierre (cited in Lather, 2007) note that, depending on one's epistemological paradigm, research is used to predict, understand, emancipate, or deconstruct. As such, the different epistemic perspectives can, therefore, lead to different types of research questions and associated approaches to gathering data. For example, predictive research can be useful research to examine the effectiveness or efficacy of a family therapy approach and tends to be objectivist and primarily quantitative. Research seeking to understand might examine the clinical process and participants' experiences in treatment and can be both qualitative and quantitative. Research seeking to emancipate can be mixed method and is part of the action research movement (Reason & Bradbury, 2008). As such, this research is sensitive to issues of power, social hierarchies, and norms while addressing social justice. Finally, research that is deconstructing examines how both clinical and research practices are not independent of one's societal environment and how practices of power, identity, and meaning are culturally imposed. Deconstructing research tends to be qualitative and critically examines the implicit cultural/social biases and practices of its own procedures and methods (Guilfoyle, 2003).

For family therapy researchers, it can be problematic when trying to achieve research goals that sometimes conflict with the logic of different epistemic frameworks. For instance, this can occur in clinical research, such as when applying an objectivism epistemology in order to achieve scientific rigor and control while simultaneously seeking to attend to individual characteristics, context, power relations, social transformation, as well as critically and reflexively considering one's research practices. This is one of the confounding issues of clinical research that has contributed to the practitioner/research gap, such as when postmodern clinicians reject objectivist research for uncritically maintaining cultural norms and relational power disparity (Strong & Gale, in press). While resolving these complexities is not simplistic, qualitative family therapy researchers must work to ensure that their qualitative

---

7 A recent paper about Bronfenbrenner's theory is relevant here (Tudge, Mokrova, Hatfield, & Karnik, 2009), as this paper challenges researchers to be clear about which "ecological" theory is being used; over time, the theory has been articulated differently.

research questions, designs, and procedures are connected and consistent with specific methodological traditions and aligned with their epistemological positions.

Methodological Approaches

While there are numerous methodological approaches to qualitative inquiry, some commonly used among family therapy researchers include phenomenology, ethnography, grounded theory, and narrative and discourse analysis (Creswell, 2013; Silverman & Marvasti, 2008). As a methodology,[8] phenomenology, generally speaking, is an approach to learning about people's lived experiences. In phenomenological studies, a small number of participants are interviewed intensively (often across multiple interviews) to get very rich and detailed descriptions of a particular phenomenon of interest. Different scholars, such as Moustaka and van Manen, present different strategies for conducting a phenomenological study (for additional information, see Creswell, 2013).

Ethnographic studies examine the cultural beliefs, values, language, and practices of a community, which may entail the study of an entire culture (e.g., Samoa) or a small group (e.g., a classroom, a clinic). The researcher is often a participant observer and spends extensive time in the community doing field work. Ethnographic data often include interviews, observations, and document analysis with the goal of developing a "complex, complete description of the *culture* of a group" (Creswell, 2013, p. 91). Working from theory is very important in ethnographies, with attention to emic perspectives (participant views) contrasted with the etic (researcher's theoretical) perspective. There are different approaches to ethnographies, ranging from realist ethnography (van Maanen, 1995) to critical ethnographies, such as Denzin's (2003) performance ethnography.

Grounded theory was originally developed by Barney Glaser and Anselm Strauss in the late 1960s for the purpose of theory discovery and creation. Glaser and Strauss felt that, too often, scientific theory was disconnected from the experiences of the people being studied. As such, they argued that it was necessary to build theory from data gathered from participants. While the original approach to grounded theory was based on a positivist paradigm, more recently Charmaz (2006) has approached grounded theory from a constructivist perspective, while Clarke (2005) has used a postmodern perspective. Researchers conducting grounded theory often use terms like theoretical saturation, open coding, axial coding, selective coding, and the constant comparative method (Creswell, 2013). However, depending on whose philosophical approach to grounded theory one is using, there are variations in the methods. Therefore, qualitative researchers using grounded theory must situate their approach.

---

8 Phenomenology is also a term that is used to describe theory, such as those theories based on the different philosophies of Husserl, Schutz, Heidegger, and Merleau-Ponty, among others (see Lock & Strong, 2010).

Narrative approaches cover a wide range of methodologies. While building on the work of narrative theorists (including Brunner [1986] and Sarbin [1986], among others), one can study narratives as the phenomenon itself (*what* the story presents: plot, characterization of people, etc.) or as a method of how narratives are constructed (*how* the narrative is co-constructed in the telling of it; Creswell, 2013). Narrative approaches cover a range of epistemological frameworks, from viewing a narrative as representative of a life's history, to the continuous performance and achievement of one's self-identity (Van Langenhove & Harré, 1993), and as the narrative construction of meaning (Sluzki, 1992). As there are many different approaches and philosophies associated with narrative approaches, it is again important for researchers to ground their research in a specific epistemological and theoretical framework.

Finally, discourse analysis can refer to many different methodological approaches for analyzing texts and conversations. For example, sociolinguistics (Labov, 2001) considers how language achieves cultural norms and power relationships, while discursive psychology (Edwards & Potter, 1992; Gale, 2010) examines cognitions and emotions as discursive social events, rather than as an intrapsychic state. Conversation analysis (Gale, 1991; Gale & Newfield, 1992) examines how participants themselves make sense of each other's communication. Critical discourse analysis (CDA; Fairclough, 1995) examines how texts and conversations, as embedded in cultural contexts, produce power inequities.

Types of Qualitative Data

Just as multiple epistemological frameworks and methodological approaches can be used within qualitative family therapy studies, qualitative inquiry includes many different types of data, such as video/audio recordings of sessions or interviews (Gale, 1993), transcripts of video/audio recordings (Charlés, 2012), photos, physical structure and space, field notes, and life stories (Brimhall & Engblom-Deglmann, 2011), current and historical documents, and art products and performances (Piercy & Benson, 2005), among many others. Information gathered from participants may include self-reports (Hunter, 2012), observational descriptions, attributions about self or others (Falicov, 2010), dyadic information (e.g., interviewing a couple together or interviewing them separately; Beitin, 2008), group information (e.g., a family interview), introspective memories and feelings (Yap & Tan, 2011), and self-reflection of participants (Knoble & Linville, 2012) or the researcher (Allen & Piercy, 2005). Researchers may choose to study the talk itself (discourse analysis of the talk-in-therapy[9]; Gale, 1991; Gale & Newfield, 1992, 2011; Singh, 2009) or the talk-about-the-talk (video recording playback interviewing participants about

---

9 This is different than when we ask participants what they intended or attributed in their talk, and considers the talk itself as achieving individual and institutional psychological and moral characterization (Gale, 1991, 2011).

a session; Gale, Odell, & Nagireddy, 1995) or narrative constructions (Fiese & Wamboldt, 2003). Depending on the research questions, the guiding epistemology, and the qualitative approach, the number of participants in a study may range from between one and four (e.g., case study or phenomenology), to several dozen (e.g., grounded theory), to a community (e.g., ethnography), to multiple exemplars of a particular type of talk (e.g., conversation analysis).

Perspectives, Points of View, and Relationships

Another consideration for qualitative family therapy researchers is whose perspective is being studied. From a systemic perspective, the researcher might study the (a) individual (client); (b) client system; (c) expanded context of other family members or social networks; (d) clinician; (e) clinical team; (f) researcher(s); (g) community; and (h) cultural discourses. From each of these perspectives, data can be based on events in the moment (e.g., video/audio of the talk-in-sessions), retrospective (e.g., interviews that talk about the talk-in-sessions), or longitudinal (e.g., multiple points of time based on the talk-in-session and/or the talk about the talk-in-sessions, e.g., Gale et al., 1995). Thus, when designing a qualitative study of family therapy, researchers must decide who their participants and data sources should be by asking themselves the question "Whose points of views do I want to study and from which point of time?"

When considering multiple individuals as sources of data, qualitative family therapy researchers must consider how decisions are made to interview a couple or family individually, together, or a combination of both (Ashborne & Daley, 2010; Beitin, 2008; Gale, n.d.). If data are collected over the course of clinical treatment, researchers must also ask themselves about the timing of the data collection and the impact the research has on treatment or the relationship between the client and the therapist. Other relevant considerations include the implications when the therapist is also the researcher. Additionally, the researcher her/himself can also be a source of data. This is true in autoethnography (Allen & Piercy, 2005) and heuristic inquiry (Moustakas, 1990). Finally, one can also consider the larger cultural perspectives on clinical practices that might influence the design of a research study. For example, society's dominant discourses might influence the definitions of health, dysfunction, pathology, diagnoses, practitioner/healer, and responsible treatment.

In addition to attending to these issues, qualitative family therapy researchers must reflect on and make decisions about the researcher/participant relationship. While so far we have used the term "participant" in the chapter to describe the person or people being studied, this word is not always the best descriptor. How researchers conceptualize and conduct their research with the people in the study can vary. For instance, if the researcher considers participants to be "co-researchers," they will likely involve them in all aspects of the research (design, implementation, analysis, and presentation), and they would participate in and initiate research decisions. Considering participants as "collaborators," in contrast, tends to lead to research transparency and inviting their active participation in many of the research steps, but often not the power to have a voice in final research decisions. Considering participants as "participants" tends to maintain a power relation that keeps the researcher responsible for the entire research project, while the participant has the informed ability to participate or not. Embedded in these three aspects of researcher/participant relationships is the question of relational power. How power is distributed between the researcher and the people who participate in the study has implications for the entire research venture and contributes to different degrees of researcher transparency and self-reflectivity. The nature of this relationship also has implications for how findings are presented (whose voice shapes the findings), as well as how convergent and divergent views are presented. Qualitative family therapy researchers must be explicit about the approach that they are taking and design their studies to be congruent with this approach.

Trustworthiness

Lincoln and Guba (1985) coined a number of terms to reconceptualize validity and reliability within the context of qualitative research. Collectively, these terms are often described as being indicators of a study's trustworthiness, or the degree to which its processes and conclusions are rigorous. Specific terms associated with trustworthiness include credibility, which asks if the research findings are credibly drawn from the original data. Transferability refers to the degree to which findings can apply to other projects or contexts. Dependability involves having coherent data collection, analysis, and theory generation. Confirmability reflects how well the findings are supported by the data. Qualitative family therapy researchers should strive to achieve as many of these indicators of trustworthiness as possible. A good chapter on this topic is in Creswell's (2013) chapter on standards of validation and evaluation, which covers many of the terms noted below.

There are a number of practices used in qualitative inquiry to demonstrate the trustworthiness of one's study. One example is the use of rich and thick descriptions in order to provide detailed representations of the participants, the data, and the setting. This allows readers to determine for themselves the transferability of findings. Conducting external audits is another method for enhancing trustworthiness, and in this case, an external research consultant examines the research processes, the data, and the preliminary analysis to assess credibility, dependability, and confirmability. A third method is the use of researcher subjectivity statements, which can help establish credibility and confirmability. In these statements, researchers note past experiences and values that have shaped their approach to a study and their interpretations of the data. Triangulation (objectivist epistemology) or crystallization (constructionist epistemology) is another approach to enhancing trustworthiness and involves using multiple methods of data collection, multiple data sources, and more than one data analyst to discuss and compare findings. Many qualitative researchers also use member checking as a means of demonstrating the trustworthiness of their studies. This involves having participants review transcripts of their interviews to assess the accuracy of what they said or to review findings of the study to present their views of these results. Field notes are also very important to trustworthiness, as they note details about the study that might not be in a recorded interview and help researchers document their analytical thoughts throughout the research process. In preparing to do interviews, the rigor of a qualitative study can be improved by pretesting interview questions and avoiding the use of closed-ended or ambiguous interview questions. Law and colleagues (1998) also provide an excellent resource on systematically reviewing a qualitative study for the purposes of determining its trustworthiness and rigor.

Clinical Qualitative Research with Couples and Families

The previous section of this chapter outlined conceptual and design considerations that are applicable to all types of qualitative inquiry. However, for family therapy researchers, there may be additional, specific considerations related to studying clinical processes with couples and families. In this section, we outline some of these considerations and highlight strategies that family therapy researchers may want to incorporate.

Interview Constellation

For qualitative researchers interested in interviewing couples and families, it is important to give careful consideration to the constellation of the interviews. Do you interview family members individually? Together? Or both? If you are doing both individual and family interviews, does the order matter? These questions require careful consideration, as they can influence both the quality and interpretation of the data. Epistemological factors, the purpose of the research, and the overall research question have bearing on this issue. For instance, if the goal of the research is to uncover facts about the couple and their relationship (objectivist epistemology), this has specific implications on how the data are viewed when interviewing a couple together and/or separately. That is, if the researcher is seeking to find underlying facts about the couple, then there is the agenda of finding out what really happened, how the couple discerns different accounts, and using triangulation to get to the truth. Data that present different accounts and an individual presenting contradictory narratives can be problematic for this approach. In contrast, if the researcher views truths as always in negotiation (constructionism), there are different implications for the researcher's analysis of individual narratives and the co-constructed narratives of the couple, and contradictions and disagreements are not problematic.

The decision about the constellation of interviews also depends on whether the research question is individual or relational, because relational research questions may be best answered by some type of family or dyadic interview. The decision about the interview constellation also depends on the topic of the interview, and the particular population being studied. For example, in the second author's (M.L.D.-M.) work with grandparents raising adolescent grandchildren (Dolbin-MacNab & Keiley, 2006, 2009), important information about the circumstances surrounding the caregiving situation was obtained by interviewing the grandparents individually—had they been with their grandchildren, they would not have given this information for fear of upsetting the children. While the considerations regarding the constellation for interviews or data collection would be different for other populations and research questions, this example illustrates the need for couple and family qualitative researchers to think carefully about whom to interview and in what constellation.

Interviewers

Another consideration that is relevant to clinical qualitative research with couples and families is the question of who is the best person to interview participants. The answer to this question depends on a number of factors. First, is it necessary for the members of the research team to do the interviews? One specific benefit of the researcher(s) themselves doing the interviews is that ongoing analysis is achieved as one does an interview, and as a result, the researcher has the ability to adjust the interview questions as needed. There is a richness of understanding and description achieved by researchers when they do their own interviewing (and even transcribing). However, this can be problematic when there are an abundance of interviews to conduct. As such, for pragmatic reasons of time and resources, there is often value in training others to conduct the interviews. In this case, there is a critical need to have clear protocols for how to conduct the interviews, interviewers must keep good field notes, and researchers must receive prompt and concise data collection reports from their interviewers.

Second, researchers must consider the appropriate matching of interviewer to participant characteristics. In a recent study that the first author (J.G.) conducted (Aholou, Gale, & Slater; 2011), ministers at African American churches were interviewed about premarital counseling and HIV-AIDS. It was decided that two African American Christian students would be better interviewers, both in terms of connection with the respondents and in regard to getting detailed and personal information (versus J.G., an older, Caucasian, Jewish Buddhist). As illustrated by this example, depending on the population being interviewed (individually, as couples or families, or as groups), there may be benefits in having trained interviewers who, for various reasons, may have more access to and openness from the population being interviewed.

Gaining Entry and Building Trust

Qualitative family therapy researchers, by the nature of our work, are usually studying populations that are vulnerable, marginalized, or otherwise stressed. For this reason, it is important to give consideration to how to access clinical populations for the purposes of conducting a qualitative study. Specifically, researchers should consider strategies they can use to gain entry into their population of interest and to build their trust. Depending on the population, gaining entry may involve partnering with respected community leaders or other professionals, or making a connection with a gatekeeper for the population participating in the study. Being present and visible within the community of participants (particularly over a long period of time, if possible) is another strategy for gaining participants' trust and participation in a qualitative study.

Considering cultural influences and nuances is also critical to understanding how to effectively execute a qualitative study. To appreciate this aspect, it is useful to shift the Golden Rule from "treat others as you would like to be treated" to the perspective of "treat others like *they* want to be treated" (Adams et al., 2010). This is not necessarily an obvious awareness, and as a result, utilizing cultural consultants may be of great value, as is having members of the research team who are also from the cultural background of the community being studied (Fine, Wis, Wessen, & Wong, 2000). Qualitative family therapy researchers must understand how culture might intersect with and influence participants' ideas about informed consent, compensation, the interview constellation, appropriate types of data, and the relationship between the researcher and the participants. Without a thorough and careful consideration of these issues, researchers risk creating a situation where participants do not trust the researcher enough to participate in the study at all, or only participate superficially.

Research or Therapy?

In clinical family therapy research, an important distinction to negotiate is the difference between doing qualitative clinical interviews and therapy interviews. During qualitative interviews, participants may present information or interaction patterns that family therapists recognize as problematic. Participants may also become emotional, which may elicit concerns about the participants' overall well-being and ability to cope. Novice qualitative researchers (who are also family therapists) may be unsure of how to respond to these situations and may be tempted to assume a "helping professional" role with research participants. While qualitative interviewers require many of the same qualities as therapists, such as an empathic stance and excellent listening and observational skills, the two processes are distinct, have different purposes, and should not be confused (Rosenblatt, 1995). That said, qualitative interviews do have the potential to be therapeutic or to result in some type of change (e.g., viewing a situation in a new way; Gale et al., 1995; Laslett & Rapoport, 1975; Rosenblatt).

As suggested by Rosenblatt (1995), qualitative family therapy researchers can manage the lack of clarity between therapy and research by recognizing the therapeutic potential of qualitative interviewing, being willing to take an empathic and supportive stance with participants, but not engaging in therapeutic interventions designed to promote change. It may be useful for the therapist/interviewer to explain this stance to participants by saying, "This is not a clinical interview and I am not in the role of therapist. I am in the role of a researcher, and as such, you are the expert on your ideas. If a clinical issue were to arise, you should take it to your therapist" (see Gale et al., 1995). Nonetheless, some postmodern qualitative researchers, based on the premise that all interviews are fundamentally shaped by the interviewer's questions, still call for active interviewing, in which the researcher, through his or her questions and responses, pursues a discourse of empowerment and change (Gubrium & Holstein, 2001).

Ethical Considerations

Beyond making decisions about the underlying epistemology and design of a qualitative family therapy study as outlined above, family therapy researchers conducting qualitative clinical research must attend to a number of ethical issues. While many of these ethical considerations are applicable to all methodological approaches to research involving humans (e.g., autonomy, nonmaleficence, beneficence, justice), which are discussed in Chapter 5, some ethical issues take on additional significance or complexity when applied to clinical qualitative family research therapy. This is because, to a large degree, participation in qualitative research is confidential, not anonymous, and because of relationship and boundary issues between clients and therapists/researchers, participants may mistakenly perceive unintended benefits or risks to participation. To address some of these issues, researchers can employ "processual" consent by regularly assessing consent throughout data collection (Rosenblatt, 1995). In the case of couple or family interviews, potential coercion by one family member of another can be addressed via an individualized consent process and a number of other strategies (Wittenborn, Dolbin-MacNab, & Keiley, 2013). It is also relevant when working with participants from other cultures and countries to consider how individual informed consent might be problematic. For example, for clients from a communal or collective culture, it may not be appropriate for them to even sign an informed consent form without first getting approval from community elders or other family members.

A final ethical issue to consider that is unique to qualitative family therapy research is when the research involves studying therapists' experiences in therapy (or supervision). There may be dual role relationships between the researcher and therapists, and there may be perceived or implied benefits of participating in the research that may not be accurate.

Related to ethical considerations in qualitative research, a number of qualitative researchers have reported difficulty obtaining institutional review board (IRB) approval for their studies (Cheek, 2005; Lincoln, 2005). For instance, qualitative researchers may find themselves having to couch their work in quantitative terms, defend the scientific rigor of a qualitative approach, justify the need for research that cannot be widely generalized, or explain "unusual" methodological approaches and procedures, such as an emergent interview protocol or action research (Cheek; Lincoln). Cheek explains that these difficulties often arise because members of IRBs tend to be most experienced with the positivist traditions of medicine and science and do not understand rigorous qualitative research.

To overcome these obstacles, family therapy qualitative researchers can employ a number of strategies. Researchers may need to educate their IRBs about qualitative research. This could involve calling the IRB to discuss elements of research protocol that could be problematic, attending an IRB meeting for the purpose of responding to questions about the research design, and volunteering to serve on the IRB (Cheek, 2005; Lincoln, 2005). Other strategies include obtaining examples of successful research protocols and getting feedback on research protocols from successful qualitative researchers. Whatever the approach, when interacting with IRBs, it is important for the researcher to maintain the integrity of the qualitative design. There may be times when making an adaptation will satisfy the IRB and allow the project to move forward. However, there may be times when the IRB is asking for an adaptation that is counter to a study's epistemology or methods or is inappropriate for the population to be studied. As Cheek suggests, in these situations qualitative researchers should consider defending the integrity of their work.

Qualitative Research Case Example

This study was selected because it demonstrates the iterative nature of qualitative research (this study arose unexpectedly from a different study), the use of discourse analysis from a constructionist epistemology, the therapeutic aspect of research interviewing, and the relevance of qualitative methods in couple therapy. Gale, Odell, and Nagireddy (1995) conducted a discourse analysis of a couple's experience in therapy. What began as an exploratory study with multiple couples turned into a detailed analysis of multiple interviews with one couple when they reported that the research interview provided greater therapeutic gain than did their therapy sessions. The research procedure used Kagen's (1980) and Elliot's (1986) Interpersonal Process Recall (IPR) approach. Two days after their first therapy session, the couple watched a videotape playback of their session and was asked to independently identify on a rating sheet meaningful moments (positive and negative) in the session. After each event was identified, the couple was conjointly interviewed, with each being asked to explain why s/he selected that event as meaningful, and in turn, what the other person thought about the event as well. The therapist was interviewed on a separate occasion and was also asked to identify meaningful moments and explain why he selected them as meaningful.

The couple was interviewed again 4 months after their last therapy session. At this time, the transcripts of the first session, and the analysis of the two IPR interviews (couple's interview and therapist's interview) were also shared with the couple. The couple was then asked to conjointly reflect on their experiences of couple therapy, as well as their experiences of the research interview conducted after session 1. This interview was recorded and transcribed as well. Each conjoint interview conducted with the couple lasted over 2 hours.

Analysis of the four transcripts (i.e., the therapy session, two conjoint interviews with the couple, and the interview with the therapist) included discourse analysis (Potter & Wetherell, 1988) of the transcripts, the constant comparative method of looking at themes across the different interviews, reviewing field notes, and group discussion of the themes by the three authors. A benefit of analyzing the different transcripts is that different ways the couple talked about specific issues could be compared between the clinical and research contexts.

One of the results of this study, both reported by the couple, and seen in the transcripts, is that the husband and wife communicated differently about their issues in therapy versus the research interview. They reported that in therapy, they were both advocating their own position, seeking to have the therapist serve as a referee of their differences. In the research interviews, the husband and wife each presented their positions without trying to convince or change their partner's point of view. Part of the explanation of this difference is that in the research interview, the couple was told they were the expert of their own opinions and it was acceptable for them to have unique views. Also, if an issue were to arise in the research, they were told they should bring it to their therapist, as the researcher (who was a therapist) was not there for therapy, but to understand each of their experiences. The couple reported that the researcher's positive regard for them, and their ability to talk to one another without judgment or seeking to change the other, was very "therapeutic" and different than the type of conversation that occurred in their therapy sessions, where the focus was on trying to resolve their problems. The couple reported they were better able to understand and appreciate each other from the research interview.

Some of the implications of this research project demonstrate that what clients say and present is not independent of the context (nor strictly an intrapsychic report), but is shaped by how an interaction is framed (as research or as therapy), and that the explicit goal (intention) of the conversation has influence on what is said and what is meaningful.

Summary and Conclusions

Qualitative research can provide family therapy researchers with the opportunity to learn valuable information about clinical processes and about how clients, therapists, or supervisors experience therapy. We have highlighted a number of factors that family therapy researchers should consider when conceptualizing and designing rigorous qualitative family therapy research. In particular, qualitative family therapy research stresses the importance of the researcher(s) presenting their epistemological stance and that this stance should be logically coherent with all other aspects of the study. Additionally, qualitative family therapy researchers need to make decisions about the focus of the study, and the type of data that are needed to address a given research question. In the context of clinical research with couples and families, there is value in placing attention on the interview constellations, the distinction between therapy and research, and a variety of unique ethical considerations. As in all research inquiry, decisions related to qualitative family therapy research should maintain a focus on rigor, so as ensure that the study has a high level of trustworthiness. When this occurs, qualitative family therapy research can move the field forward in terms of promoting greater understanding of the therapy experiences of both clients and therapists, as well as offering insight into the processes that underlie successful intervention and change.

References

Adams, M., Blumenfeld, W. J., Castaneda, C., Hackman, H. W., Peters, M. L., and Zuniga, X. (Eds.). (2010). *Readings for diversity and social justice* (2nd ed.). New York: Routledge/Taylor & Francis.

Aholou, T.M.C., Gale, J.E., & Slater, L.M. (2011). African American clergies perspectives on addressing sexual health and HIV prevention in premarital counseling settings: A pilot study. *Journal of Religion and Health, 50,* 330–347. doi: 10.1007/s10943-009-9257-7. http://www.springerlink.com/content/y124739374v7k536/fulltext.pdf

Allen, K.A., & Piercy, F.P. (2005). Feminist autoethnography. In D.H. Sprenkle & F.P. Piercy (Eds.), *Research methods in family therapy* (2nd ed.; pp. 155–169). New York: Guilford.

Ashbourne, L.M., & Daly, K.J. (2010). Parents and adolescents making time choices: Choosing a relationship. *Journal of Family Issues, 31,* 1419–1441. doi: 10.1177/0192513X10365303

Atkinson, P., & Delamont, S. (2005). Analytic perspectives. In N.K. Denzin & Y.S. Lincoln (Eds.), *The Sage handbook of qualitative research* (3rd ed.; pp. 821–840). Thousand Oaks, CA: Sage.

Beitin, B. (2008). Qualitative research in marriage and family therapy: Who is in the interview? *Contemporary Family Therapy: An International Journal, 30,* 48–58. doi: 10.1007/s10591-007-9054-y

Brimhall, A.S., & Engblom-Deglmann, M.L. (2011). Starting over: A tentative theory exploring the effects of past relationships on postbereavement remarried couples. *Family Process, 50,* 47–62. doi: 10.1111/j.1545-5300.2010.01345.x.

Brunner, J. (1986). *Actual mind, possible worlds.* Boston: Harvard University Press.

Charlés, L.L. (2012). Producing evidence of a miracle: Exemplars of therapy conversation with a survivor of torture. *Family Process, 51,* 25–42. doi: 10.1111/j.1545-5300.2012.01381.x

Charmaz, K. (2006).*Constructing grounded theory: A practical guide to qualitative analysis.* New York: Sage.

Cheek, J. (2005). The practice and politics of funded qualitative research. In N.K. Denzin & Y.S. Lincoln (Eds.), *Handbook of qualitative research* (3rd ed., pp. 387–410). Thousand Oaks, CA: Sage.

Clarke, A. E. (2005). *Situational analysis: Grounded theory after the postmodern turn*: London: Sage.

Creswell, J. W. (2013). *Qualitative inquiry and research design: Choosing among five approaches.* Thousand Oaks, CA: Sage.

Crotty, M. (1998). *The foundations of social research: Meaning and perspective in the research process.* London: Sage.

Denzin, N. K. (2003). *Performance ethnography: Critical pedagogy and the politics of culture.* London: Sage.

Denzin, N. K., & Lincoln, Y. S. (2005). Introduction: The discipline and practice of qualitative research. In N. K. Denzin & Y. S. Lincoln (Eds.), *The handbook of qualitative research* (3rd ed.; pp. 1–32). Thousand Oaks, CA: Sage.

Dolbin-MacNab, M. L. (2006). Just like raising your own? Grandmothers' perceptions of parenting a second time around. *Family Relations, 55,* 564–575. doi: 10.1111/j.1741-3729.2006.00426.x

Dolbin-MacNab, M. L., & Keiley, M. K. (2006). A systemic examination of grandparents' emotional closeness with their custodial grandchildren. *Research in Human Development, 3,* 59–71. doi:10.1207/s15427617rhd0301_6

Dolbin-MacNab, M. L., & Keiley, M. K. (2009). Navigating interdependence: How adolescents raised solely by grandparents experience their family relationships. *Family Relations, 58,* 162–175. doi: 10.1111/j.1741-3729.2008.00544.x

Edwards, D., & Potter, J. (1992). *Discursive psychology.* London: Sage.

Elliott, R. (1986). Interpersonal process recall (IPR) as a psychotherapy process research method. In L. Greenberg & W. Pinsoff (Eds.), *The psychotherapy process: A research handbook* (pp. 503–527). New York: Guilford.

Fairclough, N. (1995). *Critical discourse analysis.* Boston: Addison Wesley.

Falicov, C. J. (2010). Changing constructions of machismo for Latino men in therapy: "The devil never sleeps." *Family Process, 49,* 309–329. doi: 10.1111/j.1545-5300.2010.01325.x

Fiese, B. H., & Wamboldt, F. S. (2003). Coherent accounts of coping with chronic illness: Convergences and divergences in family measurement using a narrative analysis. *Family Process, 42,* 439–451. doi: 10.1111/j.1545-5300.2003.00439.x

Fine, M., Wis, L., Wessen, S., & Wong, L. (2000). For whom? Qualitative research, representations and social responsibilities. In N. K. Denzin & Y. S. Lincoln (Eds.), *The handbook of qualitative research* (2nd ed., pp. 107–131). Thousand Oaks, CA: Sage.

Gale, J. (1993). A field guide to qualitative research and its clinical relevance. *Contemporary Family Therapy: An International Journal, 15,* 73–91.

Gale, J. (2010). Discursive analysis: A research approach for studying the moment-to-moment construction of meaning in systemic practice. *Human Systems: The Journal of Systemic Consultation and Management, 21,* 2 7–37.

Gale, J. (n.d., unpublished paper). Dyadic interviews: A review of literature and methodological considerations.

Gale, J., & Newfield, N. (1992). A conversation analysis of a solution-focused marital therapy session. *Journal of Marital and Family Therapy, 18,* 153–165. doi: 10.1111/j.1752-0606.1992.tb00926.x

Gale, J., Odell, M., & Nagireddy, C. (1995). Marital therapy and self-reflexive research: Research and/as intervention. In G. H. Morris & R. Chenail (Eds.), *The talk of the clinic* (pp. 105–130). Hillsdale, NJ: Lawrence Erlbaum.

Gale, J. E. (1991). *Conversation analysis of therapeutic discourse: Pursuit of a therapeutic agenda*. Norwood, NJ: Ablex Publishing.

Glaser, B. G., & Strauss, A. L. (1967). *The discovery of grounded theory: Strategies for qualitative research*. Chicago: Aldine.

Glesne, C. (2011). *Becoming qualitative researchers: An introduction* (4th ed.). Boston: Pearson. doi: 0-13-704797-5

Gubrium, J. E., & Holstein, J. A. (2001). From the individual interview to the interview society. In J. E. Gubrium & J. A. Holstein (Eds.), *Handbook of interview research: Context and method* (pp. 3–32). Thousand Oaks, CA: Sage.

Guilfoyle, M. (2003). Dialogue and power: A critical analysis of power in dialogical therapy. *Family Process, 42*, 331–343. doi: 10.1111/j.1545-5300.2003.00331.x

Hunter, S. V. (2012). Walking in sacred spaces in the therapeutic bond: Therapists' experiences of compassion satisfaction coupled with the potential for vicarious traumatization. *Family Process, 51*, 179–192. doi: 10.1111/j.1545-5300.2012.01393.x

Kagen, N. I. (1980). Influencing human interaction: Eighteen years with IPR. In A. K. Hess (Ed.), *Psychotherapy supervision: Theory, research and practice* (pp. 262–283). New York: Wiley.

Knoble, N. B., & Linville, D. (2012). Outness and relationship satisfaction in same-gender couples. *Journal of Marital and Family Therapy, 38*, 330–339. doi: 10.1111/j.1752-0606.2010.00206.x

Labov, W. (2001). *Principles of linguistic change: Social factors*. New York: Wiley.

Laslett, B., & Rapoport, R. (1975). Collaborative interviewing and interactive research. *Journal of Marriage and Family, 37*, 968–977.

Lather, P. (2007). *Getting lost: Feminist efforts toward a double(d) science*. Albany, NY: SUNY Press.

Law, M., Stewart, D., Letts, L., Pollock, N., Bosch, J., & Westmorland, M. (1998). *Guidelines for critical review of qualitative studies*. Retrieved from http://www.usc.edu/hsc/ebnet/res/Guidelines.pdf

Lincoln, Y. S. (2005). Institutional review boards and methodological conservatism: The challenge to and from phenomenological paradigms. In N. K. Denzin & Y. S. Lincoln (Eds.), *The Sage handbook for qualitative research* (3rd ed.; pp. 165–181). Thousand Oaks, CA: Sage.

Lincoln, Y. S., & Guba, E. (1985). *Naturalistic inquiry*. Beverly Hills, CA: Sage Publications.

Lock, A., & Strong, T. (2010). *Social constructionism: Sources and stirrings in theory and practice*. Cambridge, UK: Cambridge University Press.

Moustakas, C. (1990). *Heuristic research: Design, methodology and applications*. London: Sage.

Piercy, F. P., & Benson, K. (2005). Aesthetic forms of data representation in qualitative family therapy research. *Journal of Marital and Family Therapy, 31*, 107–119. doi: 10.1111/j.1752-0606.2005.tb01547.x

Potter, J., & Wetherall, M. (1987). *Discourse and social psychology: Beyond attitudes and behaviors*. London: Sage.

Reason, P., & Bradbury, H. (Eds.). (2008). *Sage handbook of action research: Participative inquiry and practice* (2nd ed.). London: Sage.

Rosenblatt, P. C. (1995). Ethics of qualitative interviewing with grieving families. *Death Studies, 19*, 139–155.

Roulston, K. (2010). *Reflective interviewing: A guide to theory and practice.* Los Angeles: Sage.

Sarbin, T. R. (Ed.). (1986). *Narrative psychology: The storied nature of human conduct.* New York: Praeger.

Silverman, D., & Marvasti, A. (2008). *Doing qualitative research: A comprehensive guide.* Thousand Oaks, CA: Sage.

Singh, R. (2009). Constructing 'the family' across culture. *Journal of Family Therapy, 31*, 359–383. doi: 10.1111/j.1467-6427.2009.00473.x

Sluzki, C. E. (1992). Transformations: A blueprint for narrative changes in therapy. *Family Process, 31*, 217–230. doi: 10.1111/j.1545-5300.1992.00217.x

Strong, T., & Gale, J. (in press). Postmodern clinical research: In and out of the margins. *Journal of Systemic Therapies.*

Tudge, J. R. H., Mokrova, I., Hatfield, B. E., & Karnik, R. B. (2009). Uses and misuses of Bronfenbrenner's bioecological theory of human development. *Journal of Family Theory & Review, 1*, 198–210. doi: 10.1111/j.1756-2589.2009.00026.x

Van Langenhove, L., & Harré, R. (1993). Positioning and autobiography: Telling your life. In N. Coupland & J. F. Nussbaum (Eds.), *Discourse and lifespan identity* (pp. 81–99). London: Sage.

van Maanen, J. (1995). *Representation in ethnography.* Thousand Oaks, CA: Sage.

Wittenborn, A. K., Dolbin-MacNab, M. L., & Keiley, M. K. (2012). Dyadic research in marriage and family therapy: Methodological considerations. *Journal of Marital and Family Therapy.* doi: 10.1111/j.1752-0606.2012.00306.x

Yap, P. M. E. H., & Tan, B. H. (2011). Families' experience of harmony and disharmony in systemic psychotherapy and its effects on family life. *Journal of Family Therapy, 33*, 302–331. doi: 10.1111/j.1467-6427.2011.00543.x

265

17

MIXED METHODS CLINICAL RESEARCH WITH COUPLES AND FAMILIES

Megan L. Dolbin-MacNab, José Rubén Parra-Cardona, and Jerry E. Gale

A family therapy researcher is conducting a randomized clinical trial to examine the impact of a family therapy model on distressed couples' conflict and relationship satisfaction. At the end of the trial, analyses of the survey data revealed that while the couples who received the intervention reported significant decreases in their conflict, there were no significant changes in their relationship satisfaction, nor did their relationship satisfaction differ significantly from the couples in the control group. At the 12-month follow-up, the researcher discovered that in comparison with those couples who were part of the control group, the couples who received the intervention maintained their decreased levels of conflict. However, both groups of couples continued to report problematic levels of relationship satisfaction. The family therapy researcher is confused. Why didn't the decrease in conflict result in a corresponding decrease in relationship satisfaction? Why was there no difference between the two groups of couples?

In clinical research with couples and families, it is not uncommon for family therapy researchers to have unexpected, unusual, or less than ideal findings. Even if the study outcomes are positive or as expected, there may still be questions about the processes that contributed to the assessed outcomes or about how the intervention was received by the participant therapists and/or clients. Moreover, in effectiveness studies, researchers might want to understand the issues involved in implementing an intervention in a real-world setting or with diverse populations. To address these and other complex questions about clinical processes and outcomes, family therapy researchers may find that the most appropriate approach to answering their research questions requires both quantitative and qualitative data. Mixed methods research, which is defined as "a set of designs and procedures in which both quantitative and qualitative data are collected, analyzed, and mixed in a single study or series of studies" (Creswell & Plano Clark, 2010; Plano Clark, Huddleston-Casas, Churchill, Green, & Garrett, 2008,

p. 1546), holds great potential for helping family therapy researchers enhance their clinical studies.

Despite its potential utility to clinical research with couples and families, family therapy researchers have been slow to engage in mixed methods research (Gambrel & Butler, 2013). While some have used these methods to study couple relationships and training issues (e.g., Blow et al., 2009; Olson & Russell, 2004; Russell, DuPree, Beggs, Peterson, & Anderson, 2007; Ward, 2007), in a content analysis of 10 years of empirical articles in eight marriage and family therapy journals, Gambrel and Butler (2013) found that only 1.3% were studies that used both quantitative and qualitative methods, and only 0.6% were true mixed methods studies. Of the mixed methods studies, an even smaller number focused on clinical research. Generally, the mixed methods studies tended to lack an explicit theory or rationale for combining the two types of data. Additionally, the studies demonstrated little methodological diversity—most used surveys for the quantitative strand and interviews for the qualitative strand (Gambrel & Butler). Similar critiques, along with a lack of analytical sophistication, have been noted in mixed methods content analyses of family science (Plano Clark et al., 2008) and counseling psychology research (Hanson, Creswell, Plano Clark, Petska, & Creswell, 2005).

In this chapter, we argue that despite being underutilized, rigorous mixed methods research has great potential for clinical research with couples and families. We outline ways that this type of research can enhance family therapy research, provide guidelines and considerations for designing rigorous and valid mixed methods studies, and offer some practical considerations. As mixed methods research is a well-developed area of scholarship with many excellent resources (e.g., Creswell & Plano Clark, 2010; Tashakkori & Teddlie, 2010), we acknowledge that this chapter cannot fully address all of the intricacies of mixed methods research in sufficient detail. Therefore, interested readers will want to seek additional information in order to expand their understanding and knowledge of this approach.

A Definition of Mixed Methods Research

There have been numerous recommendations for greater diversity of research methods in the social sciences (Hanson et al., 2005; Plano Clark et al., 2008; Sprenkle & Piercy, 2005). According to Plano Clark and colleagues (2008), this is due to critiques about the incongruence of many researchers' theories and methods (O'Brien, 2005), a tendency to prioritize methods over questions (Handel, 1996), and methodological hierarchies (Hendrickson Christensen & Dahl, 1997). Combining quantitative and qualitative research methods for the purpose of answering a given research question is one means of increasing methodological diversity.

Mixed methods research, which has been described as a "legitimate, stand-alone research design" (Hanson et al., 2005, p. 224), is "the collection or analysis of both quantitative or qualitative data in a single study in which the data are collected concurrently or sequentially, are given a priority, and involve the integration of the data at one or more stages in the process of research" (Creswell, Plano Clark, Gutmann, & Hanson, 2003, p. 212). Mixed methods research could be viewed as a methodology, as well as a method (Creswell & Plano Clark, 2010; Plano Clark et al., 2008). As a methodology, mixed methods research has a theoretical or epistemological basis that guides the entire design and execution of a study, from study conceptualization through data collection, analysis, and interpretation (Creswell & Plano Clark). When it is viewed as a method, mixed methods research emphasizes the procedures associated with how "both quantitative and qualitative data are collected, analyzed, and mixed in a single study or series of studies" (Plano Clark et al., p. 1546).

This approach is not equivalent to simply gathering quantitative and qualitative data in the same study or in a series of related studies. When the quantitative and qualitative components of a study do not interact, or are combined without a theoretical or epistemological basis, the study would be considered multimethod. For a study to be considered truly mixed methods, the researcher would need to intentionally combine or mix the qualitative and quantitative data in some way (Creswell & Plano Cark, 2010). However, rigorous mixed methods research involves more than just intentionality—there should also be a theoretical or epistemological framework that guides the mixing of the two approaches (Crotty, 1998; Flyvbjerg, 2001; Hanson et al., 2005) and that permeates all aspects of the study. This would include the study design, data collection, data analysis, and/or data interpretation (Creswell & Plano Clark).

A Philosophical Perspective on Mixed Methods Research

While a complete discussion of the historical and philosophical underpinnings of mixed methods research is beyond the scope of this chapter, there are many resources related to this topic (e.g., Greene, 2007 and Tashakkori & Teddlie, 2010). Broadly, these discussions highlight the long history of this approach and the recent growth in the scholarship of mixed methods research (Hanson et al., 2005). They also highlight current and ongoing controversies and points of discussion related to mixed methods research. Some of these include the marginalization of qualitative components of mixed methods studies, uncritical adoption of a mixed methods approach because of its appeal to funders and other stakeholders, and questions about the value that is added by gathering both quantitative and qualitative data (Creswell, 2011).

A common point of discussion related to mixed methods research is the paradigmatic or philosophical mixing that occurs in these studies (Greene & Hall, 2010). Some scholars have argued that mixed methods research is an impossible approach due to the inherent conflict between the positivist assumptions associated with quantitative research and the postpositivist, constructivist, or postmodern assumptions often associated with qualitative research (Howe, 1988;

Sale, Lohfeld, & Brazil, 2002). Less extreme than this "incompatibility thesis," a related stance is that qualitative and quantitative approaches should "remain separate so that paradigmatic and methodological integrity can be maintained" (Greene & Hall, p. 123).

Scholars have addressed these concerns by proposing two main paradigmatic stances for mixed methods research—dialectic and pragmatism. The dialectic stance values all approaches and proposes that more than one paradigm and methodology can be meaningfully combined in the same study (Greene & Hall, 2010). While paradigmatic assumptions are important and central in guiding a study, mixed methods researchers who take a dialectic stance assume that the dialogue that arises in their studies from the two different approaches results in valuable information about difference, dissonance, and divergence (Greene, 2007; Greene & Hall, 2010). In contrast, pragmatism focuses on selecting methods that are most appropriate for a given research question, which allows for a multitude of methods and mixtures of quantitative and qualitative approaches (Biesta, 2010; Greene & Hall, 2010; Johnson & Onwuegbuzie, 2004). This stance does not reject the importance of paradigmatic assumptions but focuses on the practical value of different types of data as they relate to addressing a research problem (Greene & Hall, 2010). The pragmatic stance may be particularly useful to family therapy scientist-practitioners, given its emphasis on finding solutions to real-world problems and generating "actionable knowledge" (Gambrel & Butler, 2013; Greene & Hall, 2010, p. 140; Morgan, 2007). While these stances may be the most common, other mixed methods scholars have linked mixed methods research to realism, feminism, and transformative or action perspectives (see Tashakkori & Teddlie, 2010 for excellent chapters on these topics).

Mixed Methods for Clinical Research with Couples and Families

Regardless of the paradigmatic stance adopted by the researcher, mixed methods research may be valuable to family therapy clinical research for a number of reasons. First, by combining quantitative and qualitative data, researchers may be able to arrive at a more complete and valid understanding of complex phenomena, such as therapist-client relationships, the process of change, and family system interactions (Gambrel & Butler, 2013). Similarly, by comparing the data obtained from the quantitative and qualitative approaches, researchers can confirm their findings and build support for the validity of their theories (Hanson et al., 2005; Plano Clark et al., 2008). Relatedly, researchers can use mixed methods to develop and validate measures. Though using mixed methods to validate findings or measures is beneficial, mixed methods can also be used to explore contradictory or divergent data (Greene, 2005; Perlesz & Lindsay, 2003; Plano Clark et al., 2008), which may be useful in uncovering new ways of understanding clinical processes and exploring new ideas about "what works" in therapy.

Specific to clinical research with couples and families, including randomized clinical trials, mixed methods research can be used to evaluate an intervention and its delivery, explain diverse study outcomes, and confirm the impact of an intervention on a given outcome (Sandelowski, 1996). For instance, the data derived from a mixed methods approach can provide valuable information about the extent to which an intervention was delivered as intended and how participants (e.g., clients, clinicians, supervisors) experienced the intervention (Sandelowski). Additionally, the data obtained from a mixed methods clinical study could provide family therapy researchers with insights about the clinical or practical significance of statistically significant findings (LeFort, 1993; Sandelowski). The qualitative data can also provide additional relevant contextual information that might not be assessed elsewhere. For example, there could be instances where an intervention is demonstrated to result in a statistically significant change in some outcome, such as a reduction in adolescent behavior problems, but the parents are still reporting that their adolescent is defiant and difficult to manage. Without a qualitative component, this information could be difficult to capture, and the researchers would be at risk for drawing false conclusions about the ability of their intervention to create meaningful change in clients' lives. Similarly, it is possible that a quantitative measure could fail to capture the nuances of change in an outcome variable or not detect change altogether (Sandelowski; Stewart & Archbold, 1992, 1993). Finally, even if there is no significant change in the outcome of interest, participants may have practically experienced meaningful change (Sandelowski). By using mixed methods research, family therapy clinical researchers would have the ability to obtain this valuable and nuanced information.

Finally, family therapy clinical researchers may also appreciate that mixed methods research is a flexible and practical approach (Greene & Caracelli, 2003) that can help bridge the scientist-practitioner gap (Sandelowski, 1996). However, there are also epistemological and philosophical reasons that mixed methods research may be appealing to family therapy clinical researchers. By capitalizing on the advantages of quantitative and qualitative approaches, mixed methods can capture or describe both process and content (Mangen, 1995; Plano Clark et al., 2008), which is congruent with family therapy's historical grounding in systemic theories. Additionally, given family therapy clinical researchers' interest in attending to diversity and understanding how culture and context shape couples' and families' lives and the experience of therapy, mixed methods research may be ideal for reporting this information and for remaining congruent with the underlying assumptions of the field.

Mixed Methods Research Problems and Questions

Creswell and Plano Clark (2010) describe mixed methods research as being applicable to any number of research topics but stress that not all studies require the use of mixed methods. Mixed methods research may be most applicable when one type of data is inadequate for fully addressing a research problem, when findings from an initial study require further explanation, or when researchers want to generalize their findings or emerging theory to a larger population (Creswell & Plano Clark, 2010). They may also be useful when a research project is large and requires multiple studies to meet the overall research goals (Creswell & Plano Clark).

Regardless of the specific research problem, to enhance the validity of any mixed methods study, there should be an explicit and clear justification for combining the qualitative and quantitative approaches (Creswell & Plano Clark, 2010). There are a variety of important reasons for mixing data, ranging from triangulating findings to examining unexpected results to improving the practical utility of the findings (Creswell & Plano Clark, 2010; for a more detailed discussion of the multiple rationales for selecting a mixed methods approach, see Bryman, 2006 and Greene, Caracelli, & Graham, 1989). In the context of clearly justifying a mixed methods approach, family therapy clinical researchers can establish the rigor and validity of their studies by drawing an explicit connection between the theoretical and empirical need for the study and the choice of a mixed methods approach (Creswell & Plano Clark). They should also be clear about the epistemological or paradigmatic stance they are taking for the study, as this will impact all other elements of data collection and design (Hanson et al., 2005).

In preparing research questions for a mixed methods study, there should be qualitative research question(s), quantitative research question(s) and associated hypotheses, and a mixed methods research question (Creswell & Plano Clark, 2010). The mixed methods research question explicates how the quantitative and qualitative data will be combined and analyzed (Creswell & Plano Clark). Some researchers also include a broader, methodologically nonspecific research question that captures the larger purpose of the study (Plano Clark & Badiee, 2010). Depending on the study design, research questions in a mixed methods study may be prepared ahead of time or developed as data are collected and analyzed. Similarly, one research question may be primary, depending on the focus of the study and its approach to mixing the quantitative and qualitative data (Creswell & Plano Clark; Plano Clark & Badiee).

Though the quantitative and qualitative research questions in a mixed methods study are similar to those in traditional studies, as mentioned, mixed methods research questions relate to how the data are mixed or integrated (Creswell & Plano Clark, 2010; Plano Clark & Badiee, 2010). Creswell and Plano Clark (2010) outline three types of mixed methods research questions—content-focused, methods-focused, and combination. Content-focused questions make it clear that the study takes a mixed methods approach but emphasize the content of the study (e.g., "How does participating in a couple therapy intervention impact male depression, given couples' perceptions that male depression is a couples problem?"). Methods-focused mixed methods research questions address the methodological aspects of the study (e.g., "To what degree do the results of the quantitative study validate the theoretical model described in the qualitative study?"). Combination mixed methods questions combine the methods- and content-focused questions into a single question. Creswell and Plano (2010) recommend using this type of question due to its completeness and clear explication of how the quantitative and qualitative data are integrated. An example of this type of question might be, "How do the findings from the quantitative survey of male depression following a couples therapy intervention compare with the qualitative model of treating male depression?"

Designing Mixed Methods Clinical Research

Assuming that a mixed methods study is needed and well justified, family therapy researchers must make a number of decisions about how they will conduct their studies (Creswell & Plano Clark, 2010; Teddlie & Tashakkori, 2009). In order to enhance the validity of the overall study, each of these decisions should fit logically and coherently with all other aspects of the study. That is, the guiding paradigm, theoretical orientation, research problem, research questions, and approach to the study should all be coherent. Additionally, researchers must be explicit about what has informed each of their choices (Gale & Bermudez, 2008).

Specific to validity, mixed methods researchers should employ strategies to enhance validity during all phases of the study, from study design to data interpretation (Creswell & Plano Clark, 2010; Onwuegbuzie & Johnson, 2006; Teddlie & Tashakkori, 2009). These strategies are often those traditionally associated with quantitative and qualitative research, but mixed methods researchers must also consider the validity issues associated with mixing the two types of data (Creswell & Plano Clark). Creswell and Plano Clark (2010) outline a number of threats to validity that are specific to mixed methods studies and potential solutions to these threats. For instance, they highlight validity problems that can arise when discrepancies in findings are not resolved, or when strands of data are unrelated (Creswell & Plano Clark).

With these validity issues in mind, Creswell and Plano Clark (2010) suggest that researchers first decide the degree of interaction that will occur between the qualitative and quantitative strands and when each strand will be collected. They must also determine how to prioritize the qualitative and quantitative strands relative to one another and clarify how the strands will be mixed or integrated. The combination of each of these decisions results in a multitude of possible designs for any given mixed methods study.

Of the multiple design decisions that must be made, delineating the degree of interaction between the qualitative and quantitative strands is among the most important (Creswell & Plano Clark, 2010; Greene, 2007). In mixed methods research, strands can be independent or interactive. When the level of interaction is independent, all phases of the qualitative and quantitative strands are executed separately and are only mixed at the end of the study during data interpretation. Interactive mixed methods studies involve mixing of the quantitative and qualitative strands at some point in the research process (Creswell & Plano Clark, 2010).

With regard to timing, mixed methods researchers must decide the temporal order of the quantitative and qualitative strands (Plano Clark et al., 2008). Timing can be concurrent, with the quantitative and qualitative portions of the study occurring simultaneously, or sequential. In sequential studies, data collection and analysis of one strand is completed before beginning the other (Creswell & Plano Clark, 2010; Plano Clark et al.). In multiphase projects, it is possible that both concurrent and sequential approaches could be employed.

Another key decision is how the qualitative and quantitative data will be weighted or prioritized (Plano Clark et al., 2008). Ultimately, this decision depends on the overall purpose of the study and its theoretical and epistemological basis (Morgan, 1998; Plano Clark et al.). In some cases, the purpose of the study might call for an equal weighting of the two approaches. In other cases, the weighting would be unequal. Researchers use unequal weighting to prioritize or emphasize one strand of the data and use the other in a supportive or secondary role (Creswell & Plano Clark, 2010; Hanson et al., 2005; Morgan).

Finally, in conceptualizing a mixed methods study, researchers must determine when and how the quantitative and qualitative data will be mixed or integrated. Depending on the guiding theoretical and paradigmatic orientation and the purpose of the study, mixing can occur during the design of the study, data collection, data analysis, or data interpretation (Creswell & Plano Clark, 2010). For instance, the two strands can be combined by (1) merging the two sets of findings during data analysis or data interpretation, (2) connecting the two strands during data collection by having the findings from one strand inform the design and execution of the other strand, and (3) embedding one strand within the other at the level of design (Creswell & Plano Clark; Plano Clark et al., 2008). Specific to data analysis, mixing can occur by analyzing the two strands of data independently and then comparing and contrasting the findings. Other options would be transforming data (e.g., transforming qualitative data into categories with frequencies) to facilitate mixing, or connecting the data during analysis (e.g., using qualitative findings as the basis for selecting quantitative measures) (Hanson et al., 2005; Onwuegbuzie & Teddlie, 2003; Plano Clark et al.). Given critiques that many mixed methods studies have an inadequate amount of mixing (O'Cathain, Murphy, & Nicoll, 2007; Plano Clark et al.), to enhance the validity of their studies and the associated conclusions, mixed methods researchers will want to ensure that their designs involve sufficient integration of the qualitative and quantitative data.

Together, all of the decisions that are made about constructing a mixed methods study result in multiple design combinations. For example, a study could be interactive and concurrent, with unequal weighting in favor of the quantitative strand. This type of study might involve gathering survey data from therapists about their adherence to a particular treatment model while concurrently conducting short interviews with their supervisors in order to support the survey findings. Alternatively, a mixed methods study could be interactive and sequential and equally prioritize the quantitative and qualitative strands. An illustration of this type of study would be use of the findings from the observations of family members who participated in a parenting intervention to guide the development of open-ended questions for follow-up focus groups about how the participant families believe they changed as a result of the intervention.

Types of Mixed Methods Designs

To organize the multitude of options for designing a mixed methods study, numerous scholars have developed typologies of mixed methods research designs (for an excellent summary, see Nastasi, Hitchcock, & Brown, 2010). Typologies are thought to be useful in facilitating communication and in promoting the organization and legitimacy of mixed methods research (Nastasi et al.; Teddlie & Tashakkori, 2003). However, some have called for greater innovation in mixed methods typologies so that they have the ability to capture the iterative nature of mixed methods research and have more relevance and applicability to real-world research problems and community partners (Nastasi et al.).

Given the utility of typologies, particularly for researchers who are new to mixed methods designs, for this chapter we provide an overview of the typologies originally delineated by Creswell and colleagues (2003). This particular typology was selected due to its use among family science researchers. The typology, in its latest iteration, includes six designs (Creswell & Plano Clark, 2010). Due to space limitations, detailed discussions of each design type are not offered, but readers are referred to a number of valuable resources related to these mixed methods designs (e.g., Creswell & Plano Clark; Hanson et al., 2005; Plano Clark et al., 2008).

Convergent parallel design. This design equally prioritizes the qualitative and quantitative components of the study, and data for both strands are collected concurrently (Creswell & Plano Clark, 2010). Data from the two strands are generally independent, such that the findings from each strand are usually mixed at the conclusion of the study. Researchers use this design to build understanding of a topic or validate findings (Hanson et al., 2005; Plano Clark et al., 2008). An example of this type of study would be observation of therapist-client interactions and comparing those findings to the conclusions drawn from qualitative interviews conducted with the therapists and their clients.

Exploratory sequential design. This design, which involves collecting qualitative data followed by quantitative data, is interactive and sequential (Creswell & Plano Clark, 2010). The results of the qualitative study, which is the strand that is prioritized, are used to develop the quantitative study, usually for the purposes of testing theory, exploring relationships among variables, instrument development, or generalizing findings (Hanson et al., 2005). These designs are particularly useful for topics that have received limited empirical exploration (Creswell et al., 2003). For instance, a study using this design could examine whether a grounded theory of engaging court-mandated families in family therapy could be confirmed in a larger-scale survey.

Explanatory sequential design. In this interactive, sequential design, the quantitative strand is collected first (Creswell & Plano Clark, 2010). The quantitative data are prioritized and these findings form the basis for the design and execution of qualitative study. The qualitative findings are typically used to elaborate on the quantitative findings (Plano Clark et al., 2008). Often, but not always, the sample for the qualitative strand is derived from the quantitative strand. When this is the case, researchers will want to think carefully about how they approach participant selection (e.g., examining negative cases, random selection of participants, successful outcomes). An example of this type of study would be following a survey assessing predictors of client satisfaction with therapy, interviewing a selection of the survey participants to explore the factors that shaped their satisfaction.

Embedded design. Given their use in randomized clinical trials, embedded designs might be especially relevant to family therapy researchers. Embedded designs can be sequential or concurrent. The hallmark of this design is that one strand is given priority and viewed as the major design of the study, with the other strand/ data fulfilling a more supplementary role (Plano Clark et al., 2008). The embedded design is valuable when researchers want to gather preliminary data prior to an intervention, need to explain intervention outcomes, or want to understand the intervention process (Creswell et al., 2003; Creswell & Plano Clark, 2010). The example given at the beginning of this chapter, with the addition of open-ended interviews at the follow-up assessments, would be an example of an embedded design.

Multiphase design. This design is typically implemented over a long-term or multiphase study, in the service of a larger study goal or research agenda (Creswell & Plano Clark, 2010). With this approach, the collection of the quantitative and qualitative data may occur repeatedly over multiple phases of the study. Within each phase, the approach can be concurrent or sequential and may use any of the designs already addressed. In family therapy research, multiphase designs might be seen across the various phases of randomized clinical trials or within a larger program of research examining the effectiveness and efficacy of an intervention.

Transformative design. Unlike some of the other designs, the transformative design uses an "explicit advocacy lens," such as feminism or critical theory (Hanson et al., 2005, p. 229). This lens underlies all design decisions. Studies using transformative designs may look like any of the other design typologies already reviewed. However, transformative studies focus on "giving voice to diverse or alternative perspectives, advocating for research participants, and better understanding a phenomenon that may be changing as a result of being studied" (Hanson et al., 2005, p. 229). An illustration of this design would be an explanatory sequential design that serves the larger purpose of advocating for family therapy interventions with homeless families.

Case Example of Mixed Methods Clinical Research

Parra-Cardona and colleagues have implemented a mixed methods and long-term program of cultural adaptation research with Latino immigrant parents that involves empirically testing the impact of a culturally adapted, evidence-based parenting intervention originally developed with a majority of Euro-American participants.[1] A detailed description of this study is presented elsewhere in this book (see Chapter 11). However, in this chapter, we utilize this investigation to illustrate how a mixed methods approach characterized by rigorous assessments and intervention delivery can be applied with an underserved population.

To meet their larger project objectives, Parra-Cardona and colleagues selected a sequential, embedded mixed methods design with a transformative focus. In an effort to culturally inform the research, researchers initiated the investigation by implementing focus groups with members of the targeted Latino community (Parra-Cardona et al., 2009). The benefits of beginning with a qualitative strand were multiple, as the findings helped the researchers (a) obtain feedback from potential participants related to barriers to participation in a parenting intervention, (b) explore the cultural appropriateness of the intervention and study procedures, (c) examine details regarding culturally relevant methods of intervention delivery, and (d) gain specificity regarding the culturally focused themes that parents wanted to address in the intervention (for more details, see Parra-Cardona et al.). In addition to this information, the focus groups also facilitated the implementation of the community-based participatory research (CBPR) approach. By embracing this approach, the researchers learned from the participants' life experiences, understood the history of the community, and established strong alliances with community leaders—all of which were essential to the success of the later phases of the project.

Following the qualitative phase, a mixed methods pilot study (12 two-parent families, $n = 24$ parents) was implemented in which parents participated in one of two culturally adapted parenting interventions (Parra-Cardona et al., 2012). The primary goal of the pilot study was to refine research procedures and increase implementation feasibility. All participants were exposed to a rigorous quantitative assessment procedure consisting of self-report and observation-based measures. Because parents were not randomized into any intervention condition, these data were not used for statistical outcome analyses. However, the qualitative data collected at intervention completion was critical to improving research procedures and the intervention. For example, parents asserted that the active participation of research staff was essential because they offered a level of trust that graduate students could not provide (see Parra-Cardona et al., 2012).

1 Funding for this study has been provided by the National Institute of Mental Health, grant #5R34MH087678-02, the Michigan State University (MSU) Office of the Vice-President for Research and Graduate Studies, the MSU College of Social Science, and the MSU Department of Human Development and Family Studies.

Currently, the researchers are implementing a mixed methods (qualitative data supplementing quantitative data) randomized controlled trial (RCT). The study sample size ($n = 90$ families, 160 individual parents) will facilitate the qualitative examination of participant satisfaction with the intervention once parents complete their parenting groups. With regard to the quantitative strand, the core analytical procedures will consist of multilevel analyses, which will be assessed at the level of individual parents nested within families. These analyses will be critical to thoroughly assessing the initial efficacy of the intervention.

Despite the fact that the design of the RCT involves a rigorous assessment protocol and an extended intervention delivery period (12 weekly parent training sessions), researchers consider that the qualitative focus groups, followed by the rigorous mixed methods pilot study, provided key information necessary for the success of the larger RCT. Through the use of mixed methods throughout this program of research, and a CBPR focus, essential cultural information was incorporated into the RCT. This has helped overcome common barriers associated with implementing community-based trials with Latinos and is improving the likelihood of participant satisfaction and retention (which is currently 94%).

Considerations for Clinical Research with Couples and Families

Conducting mixed methods clinical research with couples and families requires a number of special considerations. First, mixed methods research can be time consuming. It takes time to develop trust with participants, establish research collaborations, implement interventions, and collect and fully analyze both quantitative and qualitative data (Creswell & Plano Clark, 2010). Mixed methods studies can also be resource intensive due to the financial costs associated with personnel, training, and data collection and analysis. Specific to personnel, since research staff must be skilled with both quantitative and qualitative methods, training can be expensive and time consuming (Creswell & Plano Clark; Miall & March, 2005; Plano Clark et al., 2008). Principal investigators, too, must have expertise in quantitative, qualitative, and mixed methods or work in collaborative teams (Creswell & Plano Clark; Hanson et al., 2005).

When considering clinical mixed methods research with couples and families, family therapy researchers should think carefully about the design of their studies and how the study activities might intersect with the interventions under investigation. This is because, as Sandelowski (1996) notes, it is possible that research activities may serve as interventions or be therapeutic. For example, it is possible that telling an interviewer about how therapy has been helpful might cause parents to feel more hopeful about their child's behavior, an outcome that might be more related to the interview process than the actual intervention. Additionally, family therapy researchers considering mixed methods studies should examine how the research design will impact participant burden. Mixed methods studies, depending on how they are designed and executed, may also give negative feedback about an intervention or client outcomes prior to the completion of the study (Sandelowski, 1996). Thus, family therapy researchers planning a mixed methods design must consider their protocols for responding to this type of information and determine how they will balance scientific rigor with participant (therapist and/or client) needs. Finally, researchers should always be attentive to the possibility of other emerging ethical issues.

A final consideration for family therapy researchers interested in conducting mixed methods studies relates to presenting mixed methods research to others. There are a number of challenges associated with getting mixed methods research published and funded (Committee on Facilitating Interdisciplinary Research, 2004; Creswell & Plano Clark, 2010; Dahlberg, Wittink, & Gallo, 2010). For example, Plano Clark and colleagues (2008) discuss the lack of clear guidelines for publishing mixed methods findings, including whether to present them in one or multiple manuscripts, how to report the findings and demonstrate the mixing, and how to present the studies within space limitations. Funders may also fail to see the scientific and practical value of mixed methods research for a particular research problem, particularly in light of the increased time and resource demands. These challenges, however, are not insurmountable. In a very useful chapter, Dahlberg and colleagues (2010) provide detailed, practical guidelines for preparing mixed methods manuscripts for publication and developing fundable grant proposals.

Summary and Conclusions

Mixed methods research holds great potential for clinical research with couples and families. It can enhance the validity of a study and provide family therapy researchers with valuable deductive and inductive perspectives on clinical problems and their treatment (Dahlberg et al., 2010). Rigorous and valid mixed methods research can also offer important guidance for developing and delivering effective interventions in real-world settings (Sandelowski, 1996). Despite these benefits, mixed methods approaches are not without challenges and may not be suited for every research problem. Nevertheless, mixed methods protocols constitute a key alternative to expanding the understanding of family therapy interventions, as well as to extending the benefits of family therapy practice to couples and families.

References

Biesta, G. (2010). Pragmatism and the philosophical foundations of mixed methods research. In A. Tashakkori & C. Teddlie (Eds.), *Mixed methods in social and behavioral research* (2nd ed.; pp. 95–118). Thousand Oaks, CA: Sage.

Blow, A. J., Morrison, N. C., Tamaren, L., Wright, K., Schaafsma, M., & Nadaud, A. (2009). Change processes in couple therapy: An intensive case analysis of one couple using a common factors lens. *Journal of Marital and Family Therapy, 35,* 350–368. doi:10.1111/j.1752-0606.2009.00122.x

Bryman, A. (2006). Integrating quantitative and qualitative research: How is it done? *Qualitative Research, 6,* 119–136. doi:10.1177/1468794106058877

Committee on Facilitating Interdisciplinary Research. (2004). *Facilitating interdisciplinary research.* Washington DC: National Academic Press.

Creswell, J.W. (2011). Controversies in mixed methods research. In N.K. Denzin & Y.S. Lincoln (Eds.), *The handbook of qualitative research* (4th ed.; pp. 269–284). Thousand Oaks, CA: Sage.

Creswell, J.W., & Plano Clark, V.L. (2010). *Designing and conducting mixed method research* (2nd ed.). Thousand Oaks, CA: Sage.

Creswell, J.W., Plano Clark, V.L., Gutmann, M.L., & Hanson, W.E. (2003). Advanced mixed methods research designs. In A. Tashakkori & C. Teddlie (Eds.), *Handbook of mixed methods in social and behavioral research* (pp. 209–240). Thousand Oaks, CA: Sage.

Crotty, M. (1998). *The foundations of social research: Meaning and perspective in the research process.* London: Sage.

Dahlberg, B., Wittink, M.N., & Gallo, J.J. (2010). Funding and publishing integrated studies: Writing effective mixed methods manuscripts and grant proposals. In A. Tashakkori & C. Teddlie (Eds.), *Mixed methods in social and behavioral research* (2nd ed.; pp. 775–802). Thousand Oaks, CA: Sage.

Flyvbjerg, B. (2001). *Making social science matter: Why social inquiry fails and how it can succeed again.* Cambridge, UK: Cambridge University Press.

Gale, J., & Bermudez, J.M. (2008). Clinical research. In L.M. Given (Ed.), *The Sage encyclopedia of qualitative research methods* (pp. 79–84). Thousand Oaks, CA: Sage.

Gambrel, L.E., & Butler, J.L. (2013). Mixed methods in research in marriage and family therapy: A content analysis. *Journal of Marital and Family Therapy, 39,* 163–181. doi:10.1111/j.1752–0606.2011.00260.x

Greene, J.C. (2005). Synthesis: A reprise on mixing methods. In T.S. Weisner (Ed.), *Discovering successful pathways in children's development: Mixed methods in the study of childhood and family life* (pp. 405–419). Chicago: Chicago University Press.

Greene, J.C. (2007). *Mixed methods in social inquiry.* San Francisco: Jossey-Bass.

Greene, J.C., & Caracelli, V.J. (2003). Making paradigmatic sense of mixed methods practice. In A. Tashakkori & C. Teddlie (Eds.), *Handbook of mixed methods in social and behavioral research* (pp. 91–110). Thousand Oaks, CA: Sage.

Greene, J.C., Caracelli, V.J., & Graham, W.F. (1989). Toward a conceptual framework for mixed-method evaluation designs. *Educational Evaluation and Policy Analysis, 11,* 255–274.

Greene, J.C., & Hall, J.N. (2010). Dialectics and pragmatism: Being of consequence. In A. Tashakkori & C. Teddlie (Eds.), *Mixed methods in social and behavioral research* (2nd ed.; pp. 119–144). Thousand Oaks, CA: Sage.

Handel, G. (1996). Family worlds and qualitative family research: Emergence and prospects of whole-family methodology. In M.S. Sussman & J.E. Gilgun (Eds.), *The methods and methodologies of qualitative family research* (pp. 335–348). Binghamton, NY: Haworth.

Hanson, W.E., Creswell, J.W., Plano Clark, V.L., Petska, K.S., & Creswell, J.D. (2005). Mixed methods research designs in counseling psychology. *Journal of Counseling Psychology, 52,* 224–235. doi:10.1037/0022–0167.52.2.224

Hendrickson Christensen, D., & Dahl, C.M. (1997). Rethinking research dichotomies. *Family and Consumer Sciences Research Journal, 25,* 269–285. doi: 10.1177/1077727X9702530 02

Howe, K.R. (1988). Against the quantitative-qualitative incompatibility thesis (or dogmas die hard). *Educational Researcher, 18,* 10–16.

Johnson, R.B., & Onwuegbuzie, A.J. (2004). Mixed methods research: A research paradigm whose time has come. *Educational Researcher, 33,* 14–26.

LeFort, S.M. (1993). The statistical versus clinical significance debate. *Image: Journal of Nursing Scholarship, 25,* 57–62.

Mangen, D.J. (1995). Methods and analysis of family data. In R. Blieszner & V. Hilkevitch Bedford (Eds.), *Handbook of aging and the family* (pp. 148–178). Westport, CT: Greenwood.

Miall, C.E., & March, K. (2005). Community attitudes toward birth fathers' motives for adoption placement and single parenting. *Family Relations, 54,* 535–546. doi:10.1111/j.1741–3729.2005.00341.x

Morgan, D.L. (1998). Practical strategies for combining qualitative and quantitative methods: Applications to health research. *Qualitative Health Research, 8,* 362–376. doi: 10.1177/104973239800800307

Morgan, D.L. (2007). Paradigms lost and pragmatism regained: Methodological implications of combining qualitative and quantitative methods. *Journal of Mixed Methods Research, 1,* 48–76.

Nastasi, B.K., Hitchcock, J.H., & Brown, L.M. (2010). An inclusive framework for conceptualizing mixed methods design typologies: Moving toward fully integrated synergistic research models. In A. Tashakkori & C. Teddlie (Eds.), *Mixed methods in social and behavioral research* (2nd ed., pp. 305–338). Thousand Oaks, CA: Sage.

O'Brien, M. (2005). Studying individual and family development: Linking theory and research. *Journal of Marriage and Family, 67,* 880–890. doi:10.1111/j.1741–3737.2005.00181.x

O'Cathain, A., Murphy, E., & Nicoll, J. (2007). Integration and publications as indicators of "yield" from mixed methods studies. *Journal of Mixed Methods Research, 1,* 147–163.

Olson, M.M., & Russell, C.S. (2004). Understanding change in conjoint psychotherapy: Inviting clients to comment upon the validity of standardized change scores. *Contemporary Family Therapy, 26,* 261–278. doi:10.1023/B:COFT.0000037914.58558.58

Onwuegbuzie, A.J., & Johnson, R.B. (2006). The validity issue in mixed research. *Research in the Schools 12,* 48–63.

Onwuegbuzie, A.J., & Teddlie, C. (2003). A framework for analyzing data in mixed methods research. In A. Tashakkori & C. Teddlie (Eds.), *Handbook of mixed methods in social and behavioral research* (pp. 351–383). Thousand Oaks, CA: Sage.

Parra-Cardona, J.R., Domenech Rodríguez, M., Forgatch, M.S., Sullivan, C., Bybee, D., Tams, L.,...Dates, B. (2012). Culturally adapting an evidence-based parenting intervention for Latino immigrants: The need to integrate fidelity and cultural relevance. *Family Process, 51,* 56–72. doi:10.1111/j.1545–5300.2012.01386.x

Parra-Cardona, J.R., Holtrop, K., Córdova, D., Escobar-Chew, A.R., Tams, L., Horsford, S.,...Fitzgerald, H.E. (2009). "Queremos aprender": Latino immigrants call to integrate cultural adaptation with best practice knowledge in a parenting intervention. *Family Process, 48,* 211–231. doi:10.1111/j.1545–5300.2009.01278.x

Perlesz, A. L., & Lindsay, J. (2003). Methodological triangulation in researching families: Making sense of dissonant data. *International Journal of Social Research Methodology, 6,* 25–40. doi:10.1080/13645570305056

Plano Clark, V. L., & Badiee, M. (2010). Research questions in mixed methods research. In A. Tashakkori & C. Teddlie (Eds.), *Mixed methods in social and behavioral research* (2nd ed., pp. 275–304). Thousand Oaks, CA: Sage.

Plano Clark, V. L., Huddleston-Casas, C. A., Churchill, S. L., Green, D. O., & Garrett, A. L. (2008). Mixed methods approaches in family science research. *Journal of Family Issues, 29,* 1543–1566. doi:10.1177/0192513X08318251

Russell, C. S., DuPree, W. J., Beggs, M. A., Peterson, C. M., & Anderson, M. P. (2007). Responding to remediation and gatekeeping challenges in supervision. *Journal of Marital and Family Therapy, 33,* 227–244. doi:10.1111/j.1752–0606.2007.00018.x

Sale, J. E., Lohfeld, L. H., & Brazil, K. (2002). Revisiting the quantitative-qualitative debate: Implications for mixed methods research. *Quality and Quantity, 36,* 43–53.

Sandelowski, M. (1996). Using qualitative methods in intervention studies. *Research in Nursing and Health, 19,* 359–364.

Sprenkle, D. H., & Piercy, F. P. (2005). Pluralism, diversity, and sophistication in family therapy research. In D. H. Sprenkle & F. P. Piercy (Eds.), *Research methods in family therapy* (2nd ed., pp. 3–18). New York: Guilford.

Stewart, B. J., & Archbold, P. G. (1992). Nursing intervention studies require outcome measures that are sensitive to change: Part one. *Research in Nursing and Health, 15,* 477–481.

Stewart, B. J., & Archbold, P. G. (1993). Nursing intervention studies require outcome measures that are sensitive to change: Part two. *Research in Nursing and Health, 16,* 77–81. doi:10.1002/nur.4770160110

Tashakkori, A., & Teddlie, C. (2010). *Mixed methods in social and behavioral research* (2nd ed.). Thousand Oaks, CA: Sage.

Teddlie, C., & Tashakkori, A. (2003). Major issues and controversies in the use of mixed methods in the social and behavioral sciences. In A. Tashakkori & C. Teddlie (Eds.), *Handbook of mixed methods in social and behavioral research* (pp. 3–50). Thousand Oaks, CA: Sage.

Teddlie, C., & Tashakkori, A. (2009). *Foundations of mixed methods research: Integrating quantitative and qualitative approaches in the social and behavioral sciences.* Thousand Oaks, CA: Sage.

Ward, M. R. (2007). Clients' perceptions of the therapeutic process: A common factors approach. *Journal of Couple and Relationship Therapy, 6,* 25–43.

18

COMMUNITY-BASED PARTICIPATORY RESEARCH
Where Family Therapists Can Make a Difference

Dave Robinson, Michael M. Olson, Richard Bischoff, Paul Springer, and Jenenne Geske

Community-based participatory research (CBPR) is a research paradigm and approach that can be used to engage research participants as collaborators in the research process. CBPR was created to address criticisms of traditional research, which often left subjects feeling used by the researcher, without getting much in return for their participation. This approach maximizes the benefit to the community through full participation in the research process, including formulation of the problem, identification of the data to be gathered, and how results will be used (O'Fallon & Dearry, 2002). Consequently, CBPR requires researchers to reevaluate and expand their perception of expertise and to suspend their ownership of the research process. Researchers become partners in the research endeavor with the very people who are being studied. In this chapter we will describe the key components, tasks, and processes of CBPR and how it can be used to maximize the impact of research for individuals, couples, families, and communities. Finally, we will discuss common ethical issues related to CBPR and strategies for overcoming these issues when using this approach.

An "Insurmountable" Problem: Mental Health Disparities

The rural town of Clearwater (fictional name), with a population of 2,290, had a problem: Too many people in the community were experiencing mental health problems that were not being adequately addressed by existing community resources. Patients and family members were frustrated because of the limited resources in the community, which made them not able to get the help they needed. Medical providers in the community were also frustrated because they were unable to find mental health providers that could offer the level of care their

282

COMMUNITY-BASED PARTICIPATORY RESEARCH

patients needed. The town had a state-of-the-art, critical access hospital and clinic with six medical providers serving the surrounding communities. Many of these medical providers had received some mental health care training, and several new hires were particularly attuned to patient and family member mental health. Three mental health care therapists (MHTs) were practicing in the Clearwater community. There was also a town with a population of 48,000 only 25–30 miles away. Still, the mental health care needs of community members were not being met. As a result, patients and providers felt isolated, alone, and overwhelmed in their efforts to address the mental health needs they were facing.

The Origins of CBPR

CBPR is a type of *participatory action research* (PAR). PAR is a form of experimental disciplined inquiry that focuses on understanding improvement in group performance over time. PAR is unique compared with other types of research because it is iterative, with changes in assessment and intervention made with each cycle of the process (Reason & Bradbury, 2008).

American psychologist Kurt Lewin (1948, 1997) is credited with developing the PAR methodology. He described his approach as consisting of four steps: plan, act, observe, and reflect. Wallerstein and Duran (2008) explained that Lewin developed PAR because he "rejected the positivist belief that researchers study an objective world separate from the meanings understood by the participants as they act in their world" (p. 27). CBPR and PAR have similar philosophical underpinnings, but what distinguishes CBPR from PAR is the focus on community-level impact and community involvement in the research process.

CBPR Is a Meta-research Strategy

Cornwall and Jewkes (1995) have explained that CBPR is not so much a methodology as an orientation to research. The CBPR process can best be thought of as a meta-research strategy because researchers and community members contrast and combine a variety of existing research methodologies with the goal of affecting change within the community. Researchers will often use focus groups, community needs analysis, survey, pre- and posttest program evaluation, and other research methodologies within the CBPR framework.

Organizing and facilitating focus groups is a key part of this research strategy. Due to the multiple informants at a variety of levels, researchers using CBPR should have a clear data management strategy and employ specific ways to organize the data. Keeping field notes is one way of making the data more manageable. Because of the great needs for the community of interest, researchers must also be skilled in quantitative data and be able to find existing data sources that can help show the effectiveness of these groups (e.g., emergency room crisis visits, law enforcement mental health crisis events, change in utilization of noncrisis mental health services). When previous data are not available, researchers must be skilled in using the community as a unit of analysis to implement a needs assessment that can capture the nature and extent of the community's problem (Center for Urban Research and Learning, 2012; McAllister, Green, Terry, Herman, & Mulvey, 2003). These results are then used by the CBPR group to develop interventions and are measured for their effectiveness.

Using CBPR requires investigators to be adept at bringing together multiple sources of information/data and a team that will support community needs. Some of the skills requisite for success include knowledge of qualitative methods (focus group interviewing, collecting field memos, thematic analysis and coding strategies, needs/resource analysis, etc.) and of quantitative approaches (identifying database resources, survey construction, evaluative tools to measure impact/outcome of programs/interventions, etc.).

Using CBPR to Address Presumably Insurmountable Problems

CBPR can address the kinds of problems experienced by communities like Clearwater. Specifically, in Clearwater: (a) there was a problem—mental health disparities—that directly and indirectly impacted a significant number of people from various walks of life (individuals with mental health problems, family members and caregivers, school teachers, law enforcement officers, medical providers, mental health therapists, etc.); (b) the attempts to solve the problem by any one person or any one segment of the helping community met with limited success, and in many cases attempts to solve the problem just added to the frustration; and (c) there were community leaders from a variety of professions who wanted to do something about it. The research team using a CBPR approach can begin to address these kinds of problems by creating a partnership with members and key stakeholders in the community. Through this collaborative process and relationship, the team can begin to identify collective strategies/efforts to generate local solutions specific to their needs.

A key difference in this approach to research includes a focus on situating existing empirical/scientific knowledge within the community context such that the idiosyncratic needs, challenges, and solutions can be mobilized to affect outcomes. This distinction is important, as evidenced by recent efforts by federal institutes of health to promote "multidisciplinary" and "translational" research, recognizing that there is a significant gap between traditional scientific methods and findings generated by these studies and the penetration of rural underserved populations. Consequently, CBPR is a research method that has been recognized by the National Institutes of Health (NIH) in the United States, because it is an approach that maximizes the local impact of social science research. Through CBPR, research efforts can be translated immediately into solutions that make a difference in local communities. According to the NIH, CBPR (a) promotes active collaboration between trained researchers and community members and participation by both at every stage of research, (b) fosters co-learning (by both researchers and community members), (c) ensures that projects are community driven to meet community needs, (d) disseminates results in terms useful to the participants, (e) ensures that research and intervention strategies are culturally appropriate, and (f) defines community as a unit of analysis (O'Fallon & Dearry, 2002).

CBPR promotes active collaboration. CBPR fosters partnerships between researchers and community members. Community members, who are normally the passive subjects of research investigation, are brought together as co-investigators and team members. They help to define the problem to be studied and are co-leaders in the development of the methodology that leads to data collection. Their active participation in the research process ensures that results are relevant and have an impact in the community.

CBPR fosters co-learning. As co-investigators, members of the community learn from participation in the study, as does the academic team. Community members are involved in determining the research questions and hypotheses, what data should be gathered and how it should be gathered, and in data collection and analysis. The knowledge community participants acquire and how they put that learning to use to make a difference in their community is considered one of the key indicators of a successful CBPR investigation/method (Bradbury & Reason, 2008).

CBPR ensures that projects are community driven. As key stakeholders and community members invest themselves, the CBPR process becomes more effective and more likely to have an impact that will meet the proximal and distal needs of the community. As the members of the community come together, they can identify what research would be relevant to the local community, including the development of solutions to local problems and the advancement of local initiatives.

CBPR disseminates results in terms useful to participants. CBPR is conducted not to generate knowledge for knowledge sake, but rather for the express purpose that the results will be able to be used to influence change within the community. The results of the CBPR process are jointly "owned" by researchers and community participants. Consequently, researchers and community members work together to disseminate the results that contribute to the professional literature, and to the community as a whole.

CBPR ensures that research and intervention strategies are culturally appropriate. Because of the symbiotic involvement of the community stakeholders in each step of the research process, outcomes are directly relevant and grounded in the context and culture of the local community.

CBPR defines community as the unit of analysis. The unit of analysis in CBPR is the community, rather than the individual. Data are assimilated from a variety of sources (e.g., individuals, couples, families, organizations, professionals, leaders) to understand the community as a whole. So, while a variety of data collection methods are used (see below), the focus is always at the community level.

The CBPR Process

CBPR is an iterative process of engagement, problem identification, solution generation, planning, implementation, and feedback (Figure 18.1) (Robinson, Carroll, & Watson, 2005). Each iteration builds upon the previous one in a developmental fashion so that motivation for and investment in change is built to the point that participants are ready to implement solutions. Thus, rather than the participants being passive contributors of data (e.g., filling out surveys developed by the researchers), they are active collaborators with the researchers in gathering data, conducting analyses, developing solutions, and following through with implementation strategies.

While it can be argued that participation in research changes participants, most research methods either downplay or attempt to minimize this impact. Researchers using CBPR both acknowledge it and embrace it. In fact, it is an expected result of the CBPR process and is actively encouraged as a means to create sustainable changes that make a difference in the community (Israel, Schulz, Parker, & Becker, 1998). As a result, change is encouraged and expected at both the individual and community levels. So, while CBPR is a form of disciplined inquiry, it is also an intervention.

Core CBPR Tasks and Examples

The following are core CBPR tasks that must be accomplished when employing this approach. Case examples are given to show how each task was implemented in the community of Clearwater.

Task 1: Community engagement and problem identification. In identifying a community that is a good fit for CBPR, we spoke with a rural physician who, on a

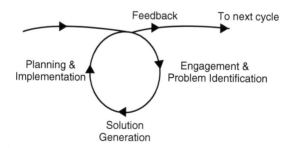

Figure 18.1 CBPR iterative cycle.

previous occasion, had lamented about mental health disparities in her community. She acknowledged that there were many caring professionals doing their best, but it still was not enough. Because of her interest in making this problem better, and after being educated about the CBPR process, she invited 25 members from her community to learn more about CBPR and to participate in a focus group about the challenges of mental health care in the community. In preparation for this meeting, we collected community assessment data by conducting a focus group with patients and caregivers challenged with mental health problems. These patients and caregivers were invited to participate in a focus group by local physicians who felt that they would be able to provide a useful assessment of the state of mental health care in the community. A few members of this group were then invited to the first CBPR meeting to represent results of the focus group and to participate in the grassroots effort to improve mental health outcomes. In this way, the results of research conducted locally were fed back into the community. Professionals and patients/caregivers were able to see immediately how research could be used to help them formulate problems and solutions.

Community needs assessments typically used by CBPR groups can be broadly categorized into two main types: (1) assessments that aim to discover strengths and weaknesses within the community, (2) assessments that are structured around already known or potential problems in the community (Center for Urban Research and Learning, 2012). Both types of assessments, while targeted, are structured around how to best get information, opinions, and input from the community and key stakeholders that can contribute to the community.

There are several strategies that should be used when doing these assessments in general and within the CBPR process. First, a useful needs assessment must focus on identifying needs first, and solutions second (Watkins, Meiers, & Visser, 2012). Focusing on identifying strengths, weaknesses, and needs ensures that interventions are not only purposeful but relevant to the community. It prevents community members from being tempted to put the "cart before the horse" by making decisions based on assumptions or anecdotal data. Second, it is important to determine what data are required to identify the needs, as well as who the potential sources of data are (e.g., community members, groups). Third, the collection of the data can utilize a variety of tools and techniques (Watkins et al.) that represent a variety of perspectives. This can include focus groups, interviews, and surveys. Finally, the needs of the community are identified based on the data that are analyzed.

The outcome of this first task is initial problem identification and the formulation of a CBPR team composed of academically trained researchers; medical, mental health, and other professionals serving the community; and patients and caregivers.

Task 2: Establishing the CBPR goals and identity. Informed by the results of focus groups conducted in their own community, the CBPR team was able to meet and discuss the mental health needs of the town. This discussion was enriched because of the multidisciplinary nature of this group (mental health professionals, law enforcement, individuals and families struggling with mental health concerns, etc.). The group decided to focus solution building in three areas: (1) community education, (2) development of a professional resource list, and (3) community funding opportunities. The CBPR group then created a task force for each of these topics. From these task forces emerged additional leaders who rallied around the community champion in conducting meetings, taking notes, and recruiting community participants. As leadership within the group strengthened and shared goals were developed, the CBPR team was able to identify a team name they could all be associated with.

Task 3: Establishing work groups and working on team goals. In Clearwater, the CBPR team began to meet within their selected task forces, independently of the academic team. This allowed the group the flexibility to move the agenda forward, and the time to complete the necessary tasks before reporting back to the entire team. During these meetings, the team would report on their successes in accomplishing their tasks, as well as make recommendations for community members who needed to be contacted or invited to the group.

Task 4: Reviewing team goals and accomplishments. The CBPR team followed an iterative process in which they reviewed, altered, organized, and celebrated their accomplishments in each task area. The CBPR champion (community member and point person) and academic team played a critical role in ensuring that each task force established achievable goals and that key community stakeholders were involved to utilize their expertise so as to lessen discouragement and avoid burnout. As each task force began to present its successes, the CBPR group began to see the vision of what they could accomplish. They were working more fluidly with each other and were critically looking at all aspects of mental health problems in their community. A by-product of this success was that they were feeling less alone and isolated and that they could make a difference in their community.

Tasks 5 and 6: Revising team goals, celebrating successes, and establishing an independent CBPR team. In Clearwater, the CBPR team began to function more independently from the academic team and take more of a leadership role in managing the group. In this way, the academic team could function more as a resource to each task force in ensuring that quality and targeted surveys, questionnaires, and evaluative measures could be developed and implemented. Unlike traditional research, where standardized measurements are utilized to determine outcome and success, CBPR evaluative measures are typically developed based on needs of the community and the unique interventions implemented to address them. These measurements are developed in conjunction with community members and are utilized to determine effectiveness of interventions, how knowledge has changed, and how resources are utilized. Typically, CBPR teams focus their work on clear, small, achievable goals that in time result in measurable outcomes for the group. Two of these outcomes in Clearwater included publishing a professional resource list for the community and professionals and establishing a website (created by a class at the local high school) to facilitate community education and publicize group events. Utilization of these resources was tracked, resulting in quantitative data that demonstrated their impact on the community. Finally, the group began to organize educational seminars that were open to the community as a means to meet its needs. Pretest and posttest surveys were administered that evaluated the effectiveness of the information provided, collecting additional demographic information, as well as areas of future needs.

Bringing Forward the Issue at Multiple Levels: Seeing the Big Picture

A major goal of the whole CBPR process is "seeing the big picture." Marriage and family therapy (MFT) researchers are uniquely trained to see the big picture. A fundamental characteristic that situates MFT to conduct CBPR is MFT's extensive training in systemic theory and clinical practice models. This systemic lens allows MFT researchers to "see" the community as the principal unit of research and action, rather than a single unit/individual independent from the parts. Further, the basic systems tenet that the whole is above and greater than the sum of its parts (Aristotle, 350 B.C.E./1966) embodies the spirit of an approach that recognizes the synergistic and cumulative effects of researchers partnering with communities, families, patients, and key stakeholders. MFT professionals also possess unique skills to join complex systems and manage multiple levels of relationships. CBPR researchers must be adept at joining communities as a democratic partner and navigating/facilitating important relationships and dynamics/processes to meet collective goals. The assumption that pathology exists primarily as a function of relationships between and/or among parts, rather than within an individual unit, is also congruent with the CBPR principle that resources, strengths, and solutions lie within relationships and levels of systems working together.

Questions to Ponder as You Create Your CBPR Project

- What is your community of interest?
- What are the community-based issues and concerns?
- What are your goals/objectives? How might the goals/objectives of the community differ from yours? How will you reconcile these differences?
- How would you go about gaining entry into the community and recruiting participants?
- What format and procedures will you use for the CBPR group meetings?
- What data will you collect?
- How will data be collected?
- How will you measure outcomes/success?
- How will you work with the group to establish community-based leadership?
- If long-term commitment by you is not feasible, what will you do to prepare the community for your departure?

Roles of the CBPR Team

Researchers. Members of the CBPR team assume various roles. Researchers are those having received graduate-level training in research methods generally and in CBPR specifically. Because of the complexity and time-intensive nature of CBPR, researchers rarely work alone, but rather as part of a trained academic team. This team may include the following members:

(a) *Principal investigator/project director.* The project director coordinates efforts of the team and ensures that all activities are performed according to protocol and that principles of CBPR are followed. He/she is usually responsible for reporting results to funders of the research.
(b) *Co-investigators/focus group facilitators/interviewers.* This individual or group is responsible for data collection efforts, which include efforts to elevate community members to the role of co-investigators.
(c) *Methodologist.* It is critically important that there be individuals on the research team who have expertise in survey development, sampling, survey administration, and data analysis. Because surveys are developed in collaboration with all members of the CBPR team (including community members), it is important that there be someone who can assist in the development of these instruments and in thinking through the best ways for collecting useful data. This person also assists with analysis of data obtained from focus groups and other interviews.

Community members. Community members include individuals, couples, families, and key stakeholders who live within the community or who have a vested interest in it (state health department, state lawmakers) and have a desire to improve the quality of the issue deemed important in the community. These community members can come from a variety of walks of life and should not only include providers and government and civic leaders, but especially community members and consumers directly affected by the problem identified. Within the group of community members participating in the project, the following may be identified:

(a) *Key informants.* These are individuals who are directly impacted by the problem facing the community but who are not participating in the CBPR group. In Clearwater, the key informants were consumers of mental health care.
(b) *Participants.* These are members of the community who respond to community assessment surveys and contribute other data. In Clearwater, this group included those who participated in educational programming designed to increase awareness of mental health problems in the community. These were community members who attended these community events and completed satisfaction surveys afterward.

(c) *Community champions.* These are individuals who have motivation to make a difference in the community with the problem identified. They are usually people who have a position of status or prestige in the community. For example, in Clearwater, three community champions emerged: a family practice physician, a physician's assistant, and a mental health provider. Without community champions, the CBPR process will never gain the traction it needs to produce results. The champions provide a local leadership role in the CBPR group.

(d) *Community members of the CBPR group.* These are community members who are interested in making a difference in their community. Community members of the CBPR group include others who may not be in the champion role, but who are no less important to achieving successful outcomes. These are people from multiple professions and disciplines. The CBPR group should also include some who are directly affected by the problem. For example, in Clearwater, the CBPR group members who are consumers of mental health services provide a valuable perspective and contribution to the changes in performance that we have observed there.

(e) *Silent partners.* These are community members who occupy positions of influence within the community and who are not directly involved in the CBPR group but are aware of what the group is doing and provide support (financial or otherwise) to the CBPR group. Clearwater has a number of silent partners. For example, the hospital CEO has never attended a group meeting, yet he is supportive of what the group is attempting to accomplish, so he makes space available for monthly meetings, occasionally provides meals for group meetings, and provides some financial assistance to support some group activities, such as community education programs. The high school principal is another silent partner. He has approved the use of the high school as a location for community education events and has even approved the use of students to create a website for the group.

Data Collection

One of the challenges of successfully implementing community-based research efforts is in gathering data in such a way that the process of CBPR is not lost. As a result, community partners can help in identifying problems, developing solutions, tailoring the data collection process, giving advice when problems arise, promoting the study in the community, and aiding in the collection of community responses. This iterative process helps generate rich data that not only guide further research but can lead to the development of culturally appropriate measures that enhance the quantity and quality of data collected (Schultz et al., 1997; Cousins & Earl, 1995). There are several data gathering strategies that are helpful for CBPR researchers.

Interviews. It is important that CBPR researchers have expertise in designing and conducting a wide variety of research interviews. Interviews have a dual purpose: data collection and participant buy-in. We have found that while the administration of a mail or telephone survey is often a good vehicle for collecting data, it is a poor substitute for an interview in helping develop collaborative relationships with participants. Interviews can occur in a variety of formats and follow the literature that is well established in the field by qualitative researchers (Creswell, 2007; Strauss & Corbin, 1998). This methodology provides in-depth context, stories, and discussions related to the data collection process or needs assessment (Watkins, Meiers, & Visser, 2012). Several advantages of this methodology include more focused discussions and follow-up questions, and a context where individuals may offer information that they otherwise wouldn't offer in a group context (Watkins et al.).

Focus group interviews are particularly useful in CBPR. It is through focus group interviews that assessment at the community level can occur. In fact, focus groups provide an opportunity to gain valuable information related to both identifying needs and desired results. This methodology relies on group dynamics to elicit individual perceptions, stimulate self-reflection, generate new ideas, and reach consensus (Breen, 2007 Creswell, 2007; Robinson, Springer, Bischoff, Geske, & Olson, 2012). During focus groups, it is critical to maintain focus on the collection of information that will help you identify (a) gaps between current and desired results, (b) evidence to support those needs, and (c) information that will allow you to prioritize needs before selecting solutions or a course action (Watkins et al., 2012).

The methodology for focus groups in CBPR research follows that suggested by Creswell (2007) and Watkins, Meiers, and Visser (2012), in which facilitators guide each focus group. Consistent with best practices (Breen, 2006), the moderator(s) should be skilled in facilitating focused discussions by using thoughtful questions and active listening skills that will allow participants to explore their own personal experiences in light of those of others. One strength of this methodology is that discussions result not only in the formulation of new ideas but in consensus building among participants (Stewart, Shamdasini, & Rook, 2007).

It is our belief that when community members from multiple disciplines come together to discuss an issue relevant to their community, their perspectives inform one another, allowing for a multidimensional assessment of the problem at hand. This also contributes to participants learning, as they are able to learn from one another and their varied points of view. Our experience is that focus group interviewing also leads to problem solving as participants begin to see possibilities for solutions that they had not previously seen.

Video and audio recordings. Similar to other qualitative data collection procedures, such as focus group methodology (Piercy & Hertlein 2005), the use of videotaping and/or audio recording is highly encouraged. This ensures that group discussions can be captured accurately so that nothing is lost, and it allows researchers and community partners to return to the data at any time. We have found that it is particularly helpful to transcribe the group discussions and review the results of these discussions in subsequent meetings. It also serves as an opportunity for the researchers to evaluate their roles as facilitators and partners in this process in order to ensure that they are not treating the community participants as research subjects (Walsh, Hewson, Shier, & Morales, 2008).

Field notes and journals. The research facilitators of CBPR groups are encouraged to maintain ongoing case notes or journals during and immediately after each meeting. The purpose of the field notes/journals is to allow members of the research team to each further evaluate their impressions, ideas, and concerns about the CBPR process and to have an avenue to discuss these issues with other team members. These notes and journals help the research team remain objective in the CBPR process and allow them to identify ways they can better collaborate and facilitate the groups toward their identified goals.

Surveys. Targeted community assessment surveys (determined by the needs identified by the CBPR group) are often at the heart of CBPR work and are important in assessing the strengths and weaknesses of a community (Watkins et al., 2012). These assessments are critical and provide a systematic process for determining and identifying the strengths and weaknesses within a community. It is particularly an effective tool in clarifying problems and identifying appropriate interventions (Watkins et al.). These assessments need to be conducted early in the CBPR process and should be constructed through the collaborative work of the CBPR team. Working together helps identify the most pressing issues to consider and ensures that the individual items and the overall survey are culturally sensitive and that the survey is administered to those who are in the best position to contribute data useful to the purposes of the study.

Ethics and the CBPR Process

While CBPR is a methodology that attempts to address many of the common problems experienced by traditional community inquiry (Flicker, Travers, Guta, McDonal, & Meagher, 2007; Israel et al., 1998), researchers need to be aware of the unique ethical issues that may emerge when doing this research.

Institutional review board dilemmas. The unique nature of the CBPR process/methodology requires researchers and community participants to come together and jointly promote an initiative or initiatives that will address identified community problems. Because these problems and subsequent solutions are developed through an iterative process, it can create several challenges for researchers in working with institutional review boards (IRBs). For example, subject recruitment, data collection protocols, and the development of appropriate and sensitive instruments can change with each iteration as community members shift their focus and intervention to meet the ever-changing needs of their community. Many IRBs, when informed, are sensitive to this methodology and will work with researchers to expedite this process.

Informed consent. Unlike clinical research in which the process of acquiring informed consent is straightforward (Buchanan, Miller, & Wallerstein, 2006), the CBPR process is often more complex. First, the problem of securing informed consent can be challenging due to the open dynamic system of CBPR groups, in which new participants and stakeholders are always being recruited. As a result, acquiring informed consent of participants is an ongoing process that can occur during every meeting. Second, the informed consent document needs to demonstrate respect for community autonomy. Unlike individual research, where the methods and risks and benefits are explained, true CBPR research should clearly specify how respect for community autonomy is met (Buchanan et al.).

Determination of roles. The CBPR methodology clearly places a high value on elevating community members as equal partners in the decision-making process. While this is a strength of CBPR, it does have the danger of blurring the roles between the researchers and community participants.

Issues of confidentiality. Issues of confidentiality, anonymity, and privacy are common in all social research. Examples of issues of confidentiality include how data are maintained and stored, who has access to information, how information is released, and the use of audio in presenting findings. While much of this is addressed in the informed consent form, there are other unique challenges inherent in the CBPR process in relation to these principles. For example, protecting the privacy and confidentiality of research participants is challenging when community members are elevated to co-investigators.

Ethics regarding existing data. One of the roles as a researcher in the CBPR process is to assist community professionals to ethically access existing data to identify community issues and concerns. This is an important component of the CBPR process. However, when doing so, it is important to make sure that community participants follow ethical principles in the dissemination of these data to the CBPR group and that they are utilized in an appropriate way. The dissemination of the data or summaries of results should not compromise the privacy and confidentiality of community members.

Funded research and CBPR. One of the ethical challenges that researchers may experience when receiving funding for CBPR work is meeting the demands of the funders. Often funding agencies expect outcomes that are paradoxical in nature to the CBPR process. In fact, researchers may struggle with balancing the stress associated with state and federal funders demanding specific outcomes (e.g., improving mental health) and listening and collaborating with local communities and providers who are not scientifically trained but have identified specific needs they want to address in their communities.

Disseminating findings. Another ethical issue that may arise when doing CBPR relates to how information is disseminated upon completion of the study. This is especially problematic when results are potentially unflattering for a given community (Grossman, Agarwal, Biggs, & Brenneman, 2004). Researchers and community members need to be transparent from the beginning regarding how research results should get presented and whose voice is heard or represented in this process. Ultimately, community partners should have a voice in this process, and researchers should allow these participants to see the results and manuscripts that will be submitted.

Conclusion

CBPR is a dynamic research strategy that allows researchers and communities to work together to make meaningful changes. Systems trained researchers and clinicians are particularly well equipped to conduct this type of research, as they are capable of evaluating, engaging, and working with the community system of interest. Community engagement and careful selection of key research and community players creates a dynamic environment where the CBPR process can be most effective. Through the use of the strategies discussed in this chapter, researchers and communities alike will be able to create their own CBPR groups within their own communities of interest.

References

Aristotle. (1966). *Aristotle's metaphysics* (H. G. Apostle, Trans.). Bloomington: Indiana University Press. (Original work published 350 B.C.E.)

Bradbury, H., & Reason, P. (2008). Issues and choice points for improving the quality of action research. In M. Minkler & N. Wallerstein (Eds.), *Community-based participatory research for health from process to outcomes* (2nd ed., pp. 225–242). San Francisco: Jossey-Bass.

Breen, R. (2007). A practical guide to focus-group research. *Journal of Geography in Higher Education, 30(3)*, 463–475.

Buchanan, D. R., Miller, F. G., & Wallerstein, N. (2006). Ethical issues in community-based participatory research: Balancing rigorous research with community participation in community intervention studies. *Progress in Community Health Partnerships: Research, Education and Action, 1.2*, 153–160.

Center for Urban Research and Learning. A Community Needs Assessment Guide. Retrieved from http://loyolacurl.squarespace.com/storage/pdf/square-space-projects/community-needs-assessment-guide-a-brief-guide-on-how-to-con/A_Community_Needs_Assessment_Guide_.pdf

Cornwall, A., & Jewkes, R. (1995). What is participatory research? Social *Science and Medicine, 41,* 1667–1676.

Cousins, J. B., & Earl, L. M. (1995). *Partcipatory evaluation: Studies in evaluation use and organization learning.* London: Falmer.

Creswell, J. W. (2007). *Qualitative inquiry and research design: Choosing among five approaches* (2nd ed.). Thousand Oaks, CA: Sage.

Flicker, S., Travers, R., Guta, A., McDonal, S., & Meagher. (2007). Ethical dilemmas in community-based participatory research: Recommendations for institutional review boards. *Journal of Urban Health: Bulletin of the New York Academy of Medicine, 84,* 478–493.

Grossman, D., Agarwal, I., Biggs, V., & Brenneman, G. (2004). Ethical considerations in research with socially identifiable population. *Pediatrics, 113,* 148–151.

Israel, B., Schulz, A., Parker, E., & Becker, A. (1998). Review of community-based research: Assessing partnership approaches to improve public health. *Annual Review of Public Health, 19,* 173–194.

Lewin, K. (1948). Action research and minority problems. In G. W. Lewin (Ed.), *Resolving social conflicts* (pp. 143–152). New York: Harper.

Lewin, K. (1997). *Resolving social conflicts and field theory in social science.* Washington, DC: American Psychological Association. (Original work published in 1948.)

McAllister, C. L., Green, B. L., Terry, M., Herman, V., & Mulvey, L. (2003). Parents, practitioners, and researchers: Community-based participatory research with Early Head Start. *American Journal Of Public Health, 93,* 1672–1679.

O'Fallon, L. R., & Dearry, A. (2002). Community-based participatory research as a tool to advance environmental health sciences. *Environmental Health Perspectives, 110* (suppl 2), 155–159.

Piercy, F. P., & Hertlein, K. M. (2005). Focus groups in family therapy research. In D. H. Sprenkle & F. P. Piercy (Ed.), *Research methods in family therapy* (pp. 85–99). New York: Guilford Press.

Reason, P., & Bradbury, H. (2008). *The Sage handbook of action research* (2nd ed.). Los Angeles: Sage.

Robinson, W. D., Carroll, J., & Watson, W. (2005). Shared experience building around the family crucible of cancer. *Families, Systems, and Health, 23,* 131–147.

Robinson, W. D., Springer, P. R., Bischoff, R. J., Geske, J., & Olson, M. M. (2012). Rural experiences with mental illness: Through the eyes of patients and their families. *Families, Systems, and Health, 30,* 308–321.

Schultz, A. J., Parker, E. A., Israel, B. A., Becker, A. B., Maciak, B. J., & Hollis, R. (1997). Conducting a participatory community-based survey: Collecting and interpreting data from a community health intervention on Detroit's East Side. *Journal of Public Health Management Practice, 4,* 10–24.

Steward, D. W., Shamdasani, P. N., & Rook, D. W. (2007). *Focus Groups: Theory and Practice* (2nd ed.). Thousand Oaks, CA: Sage.

Strauss, A., & Corbin, J. (1998). *Basics of qualitative research: Techniques and procedures for developing grounded theory* (2nd ed.). Thousand Oaks, CA: Sage.

Wallerstein, N., & Duran, B. (2008). The theoretical, historical, and practical roots of CBPR. In M. Minkler & N. Wallerstein (Eds.), *Community-based participatory research for health: From process to outcomes* (2nd ed., pp. 25–46). San Francisco: Jossey-Bass.

Walsh, C.A., Hewson, J., Shier, M., & Morales, E. (2008). Unraveling ethics: Reflections from a community-based participatory research project with youth. The Qualitative Report, 13(3), 379–393.Watkins, R., Meiers, M.W., & Visser, Y.L. (2012). *A guide to assessing needs: Essential tools for collecting information, making decisions and achieving developmental results.* Washington DC: The World Bank.

19

HEALTH SERVICES RESEARCH
Optimizing Delivery of Care

Adrian Blow and Chris Marchiondo

Imagine that you are the clinical director of a small nonprofit agency that provides therapeutic services to families in your community. You have just been called to the executive director's office. As is often the case, your agency is experiencing significant pressure to reduce costs while increasing the effectiveness of the services offered. The director asks you to develop a report for the board of directors detailing the interventions that family therapists are using in the agency, the existing evidence to support their use, the evidence that your staff are effectively delivering them, whether they are the best interventions given financial constraints, and what changes you suggest be made. Implicit in these questions are perhaps dozens of other questions about your agency's mission, the therapists, the families they serve, the budget, time constraints, measures of effectiveness, and alternative therapies available. The director concludes by stating that you will need to develop a protocol for future monitoring of clinical effectiveness. You have no idea where to begin. As you walk out of the director's office with your head still spinning, you realize that you have a very challenging and complex task ahead of you. You vaguely recall a conversation with a friend who mentioned that she is now working in something she called health services research; you do not know what she does, but you recognize that it will be very helpful for you to learn about the kind of research she does.

Health services research (HSR) is a growing field created specifically to answer complex health care questions such as those posed by the agency director. For instance, what tools are most effective for enhancing communication between patients, family members, and health care providers? How can providers most efficiently reach rural clients who lack transportation? What needs to change in the health care system to connect military service members and their families to competent mental health and family providers? How many sessions are optimal for couples struggling with infidelity? What barriers to implementation exist in an agency seeking to increase the role of family therapy in its programs? These are just a few of the questions that typify the field of HSR, a research approach often conducted with clients, their families, and the providers who serve them, all in settings ranging from small practices to nationwide health care systems. In short, health services researchers seek to answer these questions: What works? For whom? At what cost? Under what circumstances? (Academy Health, n.d.).

While many groups that conduct this important research are composed of scientists from a wide range of specializations, family therapists are increasingly sought for their expertise in relational matters and interventions. In this chapter, we provide a brief overview of the nature of research conducted by HSR teams and the roles often filled by family researchers within them. The sheer size and scope of the health care industry and the problems under study in HSR preclude a comprehensive review of each aspect of this research. However, we hope the reader will become acquainted with this growing field that is rich with opportunities for MFT clinicians and scientists to contribute in unique and valuable ways. We will provide an overview of the methods commonly used in HSR, focusing, in particular, on important approaches used in this research. First, we will discuss a comprehensive research framework: Reach Effectiveness–Adoption Implementation Maintenance (RE-AIM), which is increasingly used in HSR to help ensure that interventions are a good fit for recipients and to assess what changes need to be made to improve their delivery and effectiveness. Next, we will provide a brief overview of survey methodologies, a common research method in HSR, along with a brief discussion of qualitative methods. We will talk about some of the unique challenges inherent in this research, as well as ways in which MFT scholars, in particular, can contribute most effectively. Finally, we will provide an example that illustrates how MFT researchers can conduct HSR studies.

The Need for Health Services Research

The goals of HSR are challenging. Health services researchers in both the public and private sectors actively seek to improve the quality, efficiency, safety, and effectiveness of health care ("AHRQ at a Glance: Mission, Focus, and Goals," n.d.). The website of *Academy Health*, a key organization in HSR, further defines HSR as:

The multidisciplinary field of scientific investigation that studies how social factors, financing systems, organizational structures and processes, health technologies, and personal behaviors affect access to health care, the quality and cost of health care, and ultimately our health and well-being. Its research domains are individuals, families, organizations, institutions, communities, and populations (Academy Health, n.d.).

As health care spending in the United States approaches three trillion dollars per year, or nearly one fifth of the gross national product (National Health Statistics Group, n.d.), increasing demands for accountability have spurred the development of research methods that examine the quality, safety, efficiency, and effectiveness of health care provision (U.S. GAO, 2011). Moreover, as the nation's roughly 76 million "baby boomers" retire and enter older age, the higher health care costs associated with adults older than 65 (5.6 times higher per person than children, and 3.3 times higher than younger adults [Centers for Medicare & Medicaid Services, 2013]) suggest that costs will only continue to rise. While issues such as cost and efficiency loom large as economic constraints grow, the most important goal of health services research is, quite simply, to improve the quality and duration of patients' lives through improvements in health care.

While the federal government is a key proponent of HSR, the principles, methods, and goals of this research are both useful and in high demand across the spectrum of health care, including among small agencies and clinics. MFT clinicians and researchers are thus likely to encounter and potentially contribute to HSR at many times throughout their careers.

The Role of Family Therapists in HSR: Comfort with Complexity

The complexity of modern health care demands researchers who are innovative and able to employ complex research designs in order to understand the interactions among multiple, overlapping systems. Family therapy researchers are particularly well trained for this type of research, given their abilities to think systemically and live with the inherent ambiguity of multiple interlocking systems. Historically, however, the field of marriage and family therapy has not had a strong presence in HSR, due, in part, to the smaller size of the field compared with medicine, social work, psychology, and other disciplines, but also because marriage and family therapy researchers have not been well integrated into health delivery systems. Given that the majority of patients receiving health care are supported by family members, both during and after care, the shortage of MFT-trained researchers and clinicians in health services research is unfortunate. For example, in some health care settings, patients may benefit from the presence of helpful, supportive family members; or conversely, patients may just as quickly decline when experiencing stress and strain from family discord. Studying the presence of family members alone in health care settings may be a niche that MFT researchers could contribute to HSR studies for years to come, especially as patients face challenging health-related decisions and outcomes.

While the systems studied by HSR are complex, even at the level of small agencies, many of the basic methods used to study such systems are likely familiar to most family therapy researchers. Observational designs, qualitative interviews, secondary data analysis, surveys, longitudinal analysis, health records reviews, and market analysis are just some of the many methods used to generate data and improve patient outcomes. Traditional research methods and validity approaches are used in all cases, but HSR researchers must also be familiar with a wide range of methodologies or have members on their teams who are competent in specific methodological approaches.

While many researchers choose to specialize in one methodology (e.g., secondary data analysis), health systems have become so complex that studies must incorporate multiple methods, while realizing that effective studies in HSR rely on competent researchers able to draw from multiple perspectives and working effectively with other partners and stakeholders.

The RE-AIM Approach Framework for HSR Studies: Taming Complexity

The variety of research methods used in HSR hint at the scope of the complexity of HSR research. The types of questions can be bewildering in their complexity; the direct impact on patient populations that their findings often have mean that valid and useful findings are critical. In an effort to assist researchers who conduct translational research, program evaluation, and implementation studies, the RE-AIM framework (http://www.re-aim.org) is a popular and helpful system that has been developed to use when planning and conducting HSR. RE-AIM is a change-oriented evaluation approach that is especially attuned to assessing, in an ongoing way, any discrepancies between the expected direction and outputs of the program/intervention and what is really happening. This generates feedback allowing the evaluation team to understand the methods that will enhance program implementation. In discussing the RE-AIM approach, we will use an example of a 10-week multifamily group (MFG) implemented with military service members and their parents after the service members returned from a deployment in Afghanistan. (Note, this example is a composite of work we have conducted.) The MFG is implemented in a service agency that serves veterans primarily, but this is the first time this family therapy group approach has been implemented in the agency. The agency is made up of two administrators (a CEO and a deputy CEO), 16 therapists, a receptionist, and four support staff that assist in therapy activities. The RE-AIM approach is used to establish whether the MFG is helping the reintegration of service members, whether therapists believe in the approach, whether the approach is cost-effective, and whether there is a different group format that would better serve the needs of these families.

The RE-AIM framework is particularly well suited to translational research and is designed to enhance the quality, speed, and public health impact of efforts to translate research into practice in a series of five steps. These five steps include: reach, effectiveness, adoption, implementation, and maintenance (Glasgow, Nelson, Strycker, & King, 2006). Assessment in each of these areas ensures that the HSR will thoroughly evaluate key aspects of the implemented program from multiple data points (usually brief surveys, interviews of key stakeholders in the implementation, and interviews of recipients of the program). In particular, RE-AIM has been widely used to assess how well interventions were implemented and what changes need to be made in the implementation process to ensure that programs are functioning well. Through the use of RE-AIM, researchers are able to look beyond simply determining whether interventions are efficacious (i.e., client outcomes). By measuring implementation processes, using this information to develop interventions effective at the individual level (i.e., are programs meaningful?), and evaluating organizational promotion, support, and sustainment,

HSR can maximize an organization's service delivery when it comes to specific programs.

RE-AIM involves a formative evaluation, which is a method of judging the worth of a program as the program activities are developing and making changes based upon the feedback obtained during the process. In this way, important midcourse shifts in direction can occur, improving the program and increasing its chance of sustainability. Among other things, the formative evaluation assesses the delivery of the program, the quality of its implementation, and relevant contextual factors that may influence the program, including organizational features, personnel, programmatic issues, and procedures. Evaluators conducting a formative evaluation ask many different kinds of questions that are commonly open-ended and exploratory and are aimed at uncovering the processes of program development, establishing what has changed from the original plan of action and why, and assessing aspects of the program, such as "buy-in" by program participants and organizational staff. Usually, program participants are part of the evaluation process and provide feedback about what is working and not working, and then changes are made based upon this feedback. It is important to incorporate decision-making points and processes that allow for changes in the program along the way.

Reach

When examining a complex health care initiative, an important consideration is the extent to which the program reaches the population intended. Under the RE-AIM framework, evaluating the *reach* of a program requires determining the number of individuals receiving care, the proportion of those in need who are receiving it, the degree to which the patients are in fact representative of the population who would participate in and benefit from the program, and the engagement of these individuals in the program.

In the RE-AIM assessment of the MFG treatment program, the study team kept careful records of all participants attending the groups. These records served to help the team answer questions related to how many service members attended the groups and how often they did so, whether parents of service members attended the groups, and whether those attending were representative of those in need of services. The answer to these questions were fed back to the HSR team, who were able to adjust outreach efforts related to advertising the group, as well as starting groups in other locations in the city whose meetings would be more convenient for service members to attend.

Effectiveness

Effectiveness refers to the degree to which a program or intervention has its intended positive effects outside of controlled settings (e.g., placebo-controlled, double-blind studies), that is, in the communities in which it will be delivered, especially related to targeted outcomes and quality of life of participants. For instance, a program can be evaluated on the percentage of patients who remain compliant with medications prescribed relative to those not involved in a given intervention. HSR teams frequently conduct research in community or hospital settings to evaluate the effectiveness of an intervention in natural service delivery settings, as well as the rates of dropout encountered, and to obtain both qualitative and quantitative data describing patient outcomes. This type of research draws on the wide range of metrics, including health records, provider feedback, patient reports about their health and quality of life, adverse events, and economic considerations. Comparisons to nontreatment groups could include a randomized controlled trial.

In the MFG under evaluation, of primary concern was whether or not the treatment group realized a better postdeployment reintegration experience and quality of life for participants. The team had participants complete several surveys related to key indicators of postdeployment adjustment, including measures of overall reintegration adjustment, mental well-being (e.g., depression, alcohol misuse), quality of life measures, and work stability. In addition, focus groups were held with a randomized selection of participants to allow for feedback on their adjustment processes, as well as their perceptions of the helpfulness of the services. These items were fed back to the evaluation team.

Adoption by Target Staff, Settings, or Institutions

Adoption refers to both the setting of the study and the staff involved. Consideration of the setting includes examining the percentage of settings that agreed to participate and the characteristics of those settings. Consideration of staff examines the number of providers (e.g., physicians, psychologists, family therapists, social workers) who are willing and able to implement the program and the degree to which they represent the broader population of providers. A critical concern of those who seek to develop, implement, and evaluate a program of care is how to go about generating support and commitment among providers to ensure adequate and effective implementation of the program. This can be a considerable challenge, given that researchers and developers of interventions are typically excited by their work, while health care providers may have different interests and agendas. In fact, a new program can create substantial burdens for providers who may already perceive themselves as overloaded. A deliberate investigation of the characteristics of settings and providers who adopt or do not adopt a program is valuable.

Some of the more common problems in adoption include insufficient allegiance to the approach by the program implementers, especially when program decisions are heavily "top down," as well as insufficient training, which leads to inadequate use of key change mechanisms in the treatment (Klein & Sorra, 1996). It is also essential to ensure that the program is congruent with the values of the culture of the organization (Mancini & Marek, 2004). Key considerations

in the organization include leadership styles, plans for sustainability, and allocation of resources. Fixen et al. (2005) suggest that for adoption to be successful
from an organizational perspective, there need to be key processes in place. These
include a clear model of change, an adequate funding stream, and an agency
champion who serves as a "cheerleader," promoting the approach and motivating the team. This champion needs to be someone who can help overcome the
resistance that will almost inevitably arise when something new is brought into a
system. The organizational staff needs to be able to tolerate changes during the
implementation and cope with the various tensions that will undoubtedly arise
(Mancini & Marek). The pull to go back to the way things were will be strong at
the implementation outset. For a full and sustained implementation to occur, the
new way of providing treatment needs to be integrated into the practices, policies, and procedures of the organization. This is difficult to ensure, as key individuals may leave the organization and be replaced with other leaders and staff
who do not have the same training or vision. In addition, leaders may lose interest because of changes in funding, political pressures, or organizational crises.

In evaluating the MFG, the research team conducted two focus groups of the
therapists delivering the program. These focus groups targeted the therapists'
perception of the intervention, their level of satisfaction with the protocol, and
changes they would recommend. In addition, the two CEOs were also interviewed individually about their views on the program adoption. As a result of
these focus groups and interviews, recommendations were made to the agency,
and changes were made to the program. This process ensures that a program is
refined to suit therapist needs, tailored to a specific setting, and that the program
itself is more rigorous and, through this process, more transportable to other
settings.

Implementation

Similarly, the issue of *implementation* is critical in HSR research. The consistency
and skill with which key program elements are delivered, or fidelity, are critical to
ensure that the program is delivered as intended. Simply put, a magnificent intervention may be worthless, or even harmful, if it is poorly or improperly implemented with actual patients. To protect against this potential threat to internal
and conclusion validity, researchers develop thorough and detailed protocols
describing how to consistently and skillfully implement the program or intervention. Clinicians or staff may be trained to supervise providers and maintain
fidelity of the model.

Implementation of programs in existing systems is not easy; every step of the
implementation process is fraught with difficulties, from system transformation,
to changing business as usual, to restructuring organizational contexts (Fixen,
2005). Lipsey (2003) suggests that when programs are implemented in organizational settings, the process of implementation is *as important* as the efficacy data
of the approach that is implemented. It is essential to ensure a good fit with the

community/organization without compromising the core features of the treatment approach that benefit the individual, couple, or family. Implementation of a new treatment cannot be seen within the agency as a one-time, short-term process. Instead, it is best for researchers, administrators, and clinicians to view implementation as a long-term process with multiple decisions and choice points. In any successful implementation, these choice points need to be negotiated by all stakeholders if the agency hopes to successfully change.

In evaluating the MFG, a select number of therapy groups were videotaped. These videos were viewed by the team implementing the intervention. While not on the same scale as a large clinical trial, the reviewers used a fidelity scoring sheet to evaluate whether key program elements were included and whether they were implemented effectively. The team met to talk about their ratings of the treatment, and recognizing that the program as delivered was not meeting expectations in terms of fidelity of treatment delivery, a decision was made to provide additional supervision to the therapists to ensure that they were implementing the program as expected.

Maintenance

Finally, this framework encourages researchers to examine program *maintenance*, or the degree to which the program has become a part of standard operating procedures of the organization where it was implemented. This dimension of the framework provides consideration for both individual- and setting-level concerns. According to the RE-AIM framework, a program is considered to be adequately maintained if it remains running for 6 months after the last contact with the developer. This time frame allows the research team to make valid and informed conclusions regarding the long-term effects of the program.

In terms of the MFG, the research team did a 6-month evaluation of the status of the program. This evaluation involved interviews with key agency-level administrators (executive director and clinical coordinator), as well as therapists involved in the program. In addition, these individuals, as well as a random sample of new clients, completed brief satisfaction surveys about their experiences in the program. Conclusions were that the program was in good condition because the executive director continued to commit funds to the work. In addition, the clinical coordinator and therapists reported that there was still a high demand for the program and that they continued to provide services in accordance with the treatment protocol.

RE-AIM Summary

The RE-AIM framework was developed to provide a consistent method of examining programs and their implementation processes, as well as providing quick and efficient ways of reporting the findings about those programs and making rapid changes to enhance their effectiveness. Importantly, RE-AIM evaluates a program impact at two levels: the individual and the organizational. At the individual level, the focus is on reach and efficacy dimensions, while adoption and implementation are most relevant to the organizational level. It is of high value to evaluate both individual and institutional levels because each provides valuable independent information of intervention impact, and attaining buy-in from both levels is critical to programmatic sustainability (Glasgow, McKay, Piette, & Reynolds, 2001; Glasgow, Vogt, & Boles, 1999).

The RE-AIM framework just described provides one example of a comprehensive format for evaluating complex and dynamic health care programs, settings, and providers as they interact in providing care for clients. HSR teams must make decisions related to the specific methodologies that they use.

Data Collection Methodologies in HRS

Surveys are vitally important research tools in HSR. Advancements in survey design, delivery, tracking, and analysis have significantly changed with the evolution of technology. For example, with computerized surveys, smartphones, and tablets, data collection and entry are easier than ever before.

Well-designed surveys are often far more complex and refined than their clear and concise questions might lead a respondent (or researcher) to believe. The interdisciplinary composition of research teams in HSR, as well as the complex problems they tackle, means that survey development can be a lengthy process. The divergent perspectives of HSR team members often lead to competing ideas regarding issues such as the best measures to include, the order in which to present them, the allocation of limited print space, and survey completion time. These decisions require close collaboration among team members. Individual instrument factors, such as relevance to the study, analysis constraints, item length and clarity, cognitive demands, recognition and prior use in the literature, and perhaps most importantly, validity, all demand the attention of the team. Through a process of careful refinements and compromises, HSR teams can produce surveys high in construct validity and usefulness. These measures are usually pilot tested and refined before they are used in the main study. It cannot be overstated how important it is for there to be a collegial and collaborative working relationship among members of these often large interdisciplinary teams.

In order for the survey to be effective, HSR teams must focus on identifying samples in the population to maximize response rates and, thereby, improve external validity. In some cases, the groups to be surveyed are clear—for instance, every client of a given clinic in a given time frame. Other studies require seeking representative samples of the population. Adding to the challenge, populations studied by HSR teams may be very difficult to reach, such as transient populations (e.g., homeless, deployed military units), which often require the use of innovative sampling methods. It is usually critical to forge meaningful relationships with members of the groups under study and seek their input on how to overcome these challenges.

Other Data Collection Methods

Researchers in HSR rely on a variety of other methods as they study health care implementation and patient outcomes. Technology has provided the opportunity to collect large data sets on health services, and with the increased use of electronic health records, these opportunities will continue to grow. When using such methods, researchers typically develop a list of elements or events that the team has decided are of particular relevance to the questions under consideration. The Veterans Administration (VA), for example, has a wide availability of electronic health records that researchers are mining daily (see below).

Researchers may also use qualitative interviews to glean information from stakeholders, organizational leaders, patients, or workers. These interviews can enable decisions about whether to conduct future studies, as well as about which individuals to target using quantitative methods. Prior to conducting such interviews, teams consider which persons might be in the best position to provide useful information about a program, treatment, or problem. Quite often this entails interviewing multiple participants at varying organizational levels using interview guides specifically tailored to each participant. Focus groups are also widely used in collecting qualitative data. These groups usually include 6–12 individuals who are connected to a specific topic of interest related to the health services under evaluation. In evaluating programs, focus groups are useful *before* a project begins in order to understand more fully the needs the program will address. Focus groups are also used *during* a program's delivery to help assess whether the program is achieving the goals it set out to achieve. Finally, focus groups are also used after a program has been implemented in order to assess program strengths and limitations (Piercy & Hertlein, 2005).

HSR studies frequently rely on patient health records for additional data on study participants. Patients must consent to release their health records and can, at any time, revoke their consent. In some cases, health record data exist in large deidentified data sets—such as at the VA, but access to these data is governed by the VA. Precautions to safeguard the privacy and security of health records generally require additional training and certification. Regulatory oversight and audits of research studies can be a significant added cost of this type of research. However, the value of this information more than offsets these challenges. For example, researchers can compare outcomes among groups of patients who received a particular intervention and those who did not, thereby in effect creating a comparison group. Agencies with health records can also conduct internal studies with consenting patients and, in the process, obtain very rich health data.

All of these different methods of data collection present risks for the validity of the study that are similar to those affecting other studies that use survey or qualitative methodologies. What is different about HSR, however, is its use of multiple methods and assessment of different samples. In addition, continuous developments in health care technology, training, provision of care, funding, and knowledge of best practices mean that study-based guidelines in health care may be valid for only a few short years before needing reassessment (Shekelle et al., 2001). Thus, researchers in HSR face constant threats to validity, both while conducting studies and in making recommendations based upon their findings. This is because of the complex contexts involved in conducting this research and the many moving parts of organizations that do health care delivery. This research is usually conducted in real-world contexts, meaning that the controlling of all nuisance factors is impossible. An advantage, though, of the complexity of HSR is that there are opportunities to triangulate data in order to enhance internal and conclusion validity. For example, triangulating the results of qualitative interviews on patients, service providers, and administrators can increase the confidence that researchers have in their findings.

There are a number of significant threats to the internal and external validity of studies conducted in HSR. Developing a valid sample presents a variety of challenges in HSR, beginning with the requirement to minimize bias in sampling. Bias in HSR studies is typically evident when an error in the study's design, implementation, or analysis systematically misrepresents the effects of treatments, interventions, and policies on the health care–related question under consideration. For example, a study of treatment dropouts that only obtains data through an Internet-administered survey is quite likely to bias the data toward respondents who have ready access to a computer and the Internet. In so doing, lower-income treatment dropouts may never receive the opportunity to provide feedback or describe the unique circumstances that may have led to their decision to withdraw from treatment. Similarly, a study of outpatient care for diabetes relying on a convenience sample of mostly older, primarily male patients contains obvious biases that substantially constrain the validity of the findings. Some degree of selection bias in sampling is often unavoidable; however, it is possible to minimize the effects through careful, collaborative consideration of the population under study.

Temporal changes in patients studied using longitudinal designs represent another significant threat to validity. Given that many health care treatments may require years to completion or even lifelong care, it is important to consider the developmental changes occurring in subjects during the study. Similarly, subjects who have experienced significant, life-altering events, such as war, can reasonably be expected to have changed in somewhat systematic ways relative to similar samples of peers who did not experience such an event. Thus, any attempt to better understand suicide among military populations, for example, must include careful consideration of temporal factors that may make it impossible to differentiate the effects of an intervention or policy from the effects of growth and experiences. Similarly, HSR researchers should attempt to use the same measures of a given construct at different time points when conducting longitudinal studies of patients. This can be a challenge, particularly as team compositions change during extended studies or as new and improved measures emerge in the literature.

Measurement error is another challenge facing HSR scientists. Errors in classifying patients, whether by diagnostic category, demographic variables, treatments received, or a wide range of confounding variables not accounted for in a study, present serious threats to construct and internal validity. A physician who fails to adhere to a complex treatment protocol potentially introduces systematic errors in the data collected. This, in turn, may lead to either a stronger or weaker link between the treatment protocol and patient outcomes. A study relying on medical record reviews of patients may be similarly flawed if subjects who are simultaneously receiving care in another health care system have not been asked to provide those medical records. A study that relies exclusively on a single measure known to be reactive to one subtype of a disorder but not another will likely lead to skewed data as a result.

In many cases, it is impossible to study an entire population in order to answer a research question stemming from a health care need or problem experienced by the population. Thus, HSR scientists rely on a variety of research methods to carefully construct a representative sample of the population under study. As noted previously, this challenging task is critical if the results of the study are to be generalized to the broader population. External validity is obviously of critical importance in HSR. A study whose results scientists have derived from a sample that is later shown to poorly represent the population as a whole should not be used to change health care practice, policy, and guidelines. More seriously, implementation of such changes based upon a study with inadequate external validity can potentially lead to worse outcomes among patients. Clearly this is a significant concern in HSR, and extensive efforts are made to ensure that samples and conditions are representative and findings are generalizable. Researchers must constantly walk the line between internal and external validity. Increasing the internal validity by, for instance, increasing the stringency of inclusion criteria of patients carries with it the possible side effect of creating a sample that is nonrepresentative of the population, and data are not generalizable.

Contributions of Marriage and Family Therapy Scholars

Research scientists who are also trained as marriage and family therapists bring unique knowledge, skills, and abilities to HSR teams. The ability of these teams to solve challenging and complex problems is in large part a result of their interdisciplinary composition and the often well-honed research specializations of individual members. MFT scholars are no different in this regard, having acquired rigorous training and experience in research. In addition to research skills, MFT scholars bring an ability to think systematically, in terms of both family systems and organizational systems.

In many HSR studies, patients receiving care are studied at the individual level, with little interest in or consideration of the impact of family members, close friends, and broader social support networks. This trend will change as researchers include in their studies spouses, parents, children, and other significant persons in a patient's life.

Improvements in research methodology and data analysis have enabled broader and more rigorous consideration of the roles of family. Dyadic data analysis, for instance, has provided researchers with powerful tools to consider the influences of spouses or significant others on patients in studies (Kenny, Kashy, & Cook, 2006). The absence of an MFT scholar on a team means that the measures and data collection methods necessary to obtain and examine dyadic data may not be included. MFT scholars regularly advocate for the consideration of the family or other key system players in these studies, realizing the critical importance of close relationships—particularly among those who are ill and seeking care.

While HSR is not unique in benefiting from team members with excellent social skills, the size and scope of these studies often means navigating the challenging interpersonal waters encountered when working with diverse individuals. As noted earlier, maintaining buy-in and open communication between groups is critical to ensuring the success of a study. Under the pressures of tight timelines, financial constraints, staffing difficulties, challenging study populations, and the necessity of achieving study requirements, the presence of a team member who is capable of forging and maintaining positive interdisciplinary professional relationships under such conditions is truly valuable.

Medical family therapy has increasingly done an excellent job of integrating family therapists into health care settings (McDaniel, Hepworth, & Doherty, 1992). The role of the family therapist in these circumstances is to improve the quality of life of patients and their loved ones, improve communication between patients and physicians, decrease emotional stressors that come with illness, and increase familial support for the patient. An effective family therapist working in this setting should ideally increase positive outcomes for families and decrease the burden on other parts of the health care system. It is important for the sustainability of the family therapist in medical settings that research that studies these processes continue to establish how medical family therapists reduce costs of health care and improve the quality of health care by enhancing existing services and how patient lives overall can be enhanced by these services. In particular, family therapy researchers using an HSR perspective are well situated to answer the questions of what works, for whom, at what costs, and under what circumstances.

The Unique Opportunities and Challenges of Health Services Research

HSR is often fast-paced, exciting work driven by the awareness that studies and the data they provide can directly influence health care policy and delivery and, in the process, improve outcomes for real-world patients. By the same token, this type of research presents obstacles that demand creativity, skillfulness, persistence, and the collaborative abilities of team members. HSR researchers frequently must contend with the challenges of interdisciplinary teams, inter-university and inter-agency collaborations, multiple institutional review boards, intense competition for grant funding, stringent requirements for the safeguarding of patients and their sensitive health care information, obtaining buy-in from health care professionals and patients alike, adequately training providers and research staff, minimizing patient dropout, and publishing results under tight deadlines. Moreover, many studies operate across multiple states in order to compare different programs and to obtain representative samples. These, and many other challenges, are part of the daily realities of HSR teams and require a great deal of personal investment. For readers who wish to learn more about HSR studies, there are several resources available. For example, there is a journal devoted exclusively to HSR research (*Health Services Research*), an HSR-oriented website (https://www.academyhealth.org/index.cfm), and the website, as previously noted, that provides comprehensive discussions and links related to RE-AIM (http://www.re-aim.org).

References

Academy Health. (n.d.) What Is HSR. Retrieved from http://www.academyhealth.org/About/content.cfm?ItemNumber=831&navItemNumber=514

"AHRQ at a Glance: Mission, Focus, and Goals." (n.d.). Retrieved from http://www.ahrq.gov/about/ataglance.htm

Centers for Medicare & Medicaid Services. (2013, January 9). NHE fact sheet. Retrieved from https://www.cms.gov/Research-Statistics-Data-and-Systems/Statistics-Trends-and-Reports/NationalHealthExpendData/NHE-Fact-Sheet.html

Fixen, D. L. (2005). *Implementation research: A synthesis of the literature*. Tampa: University of South Florida.

Glasgow, R. E., McKay, H. G., Piette, J. D., & Reynolds, K. D. (2001). The RE-AIM framework for evaluating interventions: What can it tell us about approaches to chronic illness management? *Patient Education and Counseling, 44*, 119–127.

Glasgow, R. E., Nelson, C. C., Strycker, L. A., & King, D. K. (2006). Using RE-AIM metrics to evaluate diabetes self-management support interventions. *American Journal of Preventive Medicine, 30*, 67–73.

Glasgow, R. E., Vogt, T. M., & Boles, S. M. (1999). Evaluating the public health impact of health promotion interventions: The RE-AIM framework. *American Journal of Public Health, 89*, 1322–1327.

Kenny, D. A., Kashy, D. A., & Cook, W. L. (2006). *Dyadic data analysis*. New York: Guilford Press.

Klein, K. J., & Sorra, J. S. (1996). The challenge of innovation implementation. *Academy of Management Review, 21*, 1055–1080.

Lipsey, M. W. (2003). Those confounded moderators in meta-analysis: Good, bad, and ugly. *Annals of the American Academy of Political and Social Science, 587*, 69–81.

Mancini, J. A., & Marek, L. I. (2004). Feature article: Sustaining community-based programs for families: Conceptualization and measurement. *Family Relations, 53*(4), 339–347.

McDaniel, S. H., Hepworth, J., & Doherty, W. J. (1992). *Medical family therapy: A biopsychosocial approach to families with health problems*. New York: Basic Books.

National Health Statistics Group. (n.d.). National health expenditures. Retrieved from https://www.cms.gov/Research-Statistics-Data-and-Systems/Statistics-Trends-and-Reports/NationalHealthExpendData/downloads/tables.pdf

Piercy, F. P., & Hertlein, K. (2005). Focus groups. In D. S. Sprenkle & F. P. Piercy (Eds.), *Research methods in family therapy* (pp. 85–99). New York: Guilford.

Shekelle, P. G., Ortiz, E., Rhodes, S., Morton, S. C., Eccles, M. P., Grimshaw, J. M., Woolf, S. H. (2001). Validity of the Agency for Healthcare Research and Quality clinical practice guidelines: How quickly do guidelines become outdated? *JAMA*, *286*(12), 1461–1467.

U.S. GAO. (2011, September 23). Health care price transparency: Meaningful price information is difficult for consumers to obtain prior to receiving care. Retrieved from http://www.gao.gov/products/GAO-11-791

Section IV

ANALYSIS

20

APPLIED STATISTICAL ANALYSIS AND INTERPRETATION

Lee N. Johnson and Richard B Miller

Why do we need a chapter on basic statistics in an advanced research methods book? In our many years of teaching graduate and undergraduate research methods, conducting clinical research, and serving as journal reviewers, there have been three research problems that we have seen repeatedly. First, we have been amazed at the number of people who do not understand the use and interpretation of basic statistics (*t*-test, ANOVA, chi-square, regression, correlation, etc.). This is largely due to the fact that marriage and family therapists (MFTs) learning statistics typically have the goal of learning advanced statistical strategies, such as structural equation modeling and multilevel modeling. As a result, they don't focus on mastering more elementary statistical analyses. In addition, with the emphasis on advanced statistics being the "gold standard" of statistical analysis, researchers tend to undervalue the utility of simpler statistical tests. Thus, the goal is often to use the most sophisticated analysis, rather than the most appropriate analysis, for the particular research question and type of data.

Second, there tends to be confusion surrounding statistical significance, clinical significance, and the magnitude or importance of results (Cohen, 1994; Haase, Ellis, & Ladany, 1989; Murray & Dosser, 1987). Although it is important to know what level of possibility there is that our results were not found by chance (e.g., statistical significance), we repeatedly observe that the idea of a statistically significant finding is usually interpreted as important or meaningful. Additionally, many clinical researchers have heard the concept of clinical significance (Jacobson & Truax, 1991; Kazdin, 2003), but they do not use the recommendations for determining clinical significance in their research.

Third, we repeatedly hear people confuse correlation and causation. Although experimental research is important in marriage and family therapy (MFT) outcome research, much of MFT research is correlational. We believe that most researchers know the difference between the two, but they confuse increasingly sophisticated statistical tests as showing relationships as being more casual than the research design and data can justify. This mistake is most common in the

315

discussion or conclusion sections, where correlation findings are interpreted as being much stronger than an association between variables.

We acknowledge that these three issues are not new or innovative in the research methodology and statistical literature. Our hope is that this chapter will provide a description of these three issues, a review for experienced researchers, and a basic foundation for beginning researchers.

Review of Basic Statistics: What to Use When

The use of statistics among researchers has become greatly simplified over the past few decades. In years past, the most difficult part of doing statistical analysis was to know the specific formulas, as well as how to apply them. Today, however, statistical software, such as SPSS, is able to perform analyses with dropdown menus, thereby relieving researchers of the burden of knowing and understanding complicated formulas. Books are available that have step-by-step instructions for conducting each statistical test using the software (see Acock, 2012; Field, 2013; Leech, Barrett, & Morgan, 2011). There are videos on YouTube that demonstrate how to perform statistical analyses using SPSS.

With computer software doing the "hard work," the most important responsibilities for researchers are to know which statistical test to use and how to appropriately interpret the output. Indeed, knowing which statistical test to use may seem like one of the "mysteries" of doing statistical analysis. The truth, though, is that the process of figuring out the appropriate statistical test is pretty straightforward. The key to using the correct statistical test is to know what type of variables you are using.

You will recall from research-methods classes or basic research-methods books that variables can be divided into two major categories: categorical and continuous (Babbie, 2008). Examples of categorical variables include race (White, African American, Hispanic, etc.), employment status (full-time, part-time, unemployed, retired), or sex (female, male). These types of variables are also called nominal level variables because they cannot be rank ordered (Trochim, 2005).

Continuous variables, on the other hand, are variables that can be rank ordered, and the differences between numbers are meaningful. Most research-methods texts divide continuous variables into interval and ratio variables. Ordinal variables, on the other hand, are categorical variables that take on some of the properties of continuous variables because the values can be rank ordered (education achievement: high school, associate's degree, bachelor's degree, etc.). In this example the variables can be rank ordered, but where ordinal variables differ from continuous variables is that there is no math operation that can tell you meaningful differences between two of the categories (Frankfort-Nachmias & Leon-Guerrero, 2009). Where ordinal variables become more like continuous variables is when one is using Likert-type scales that include the response options *strongly agree, agree, disagree,* and *strongly disagree,* assigned values of 1 to 4. In cases where these variables are treated as continuous, the assumption being made, but often not true, is that the distance between *strongly agree* and *agree* is the same as the distance between *disagree* and *strongly disagree*. So, while most statistical software programs are able to treat ordinal variables as interval variables and therefore as continuous, researchers need to understand that the computer software is "forcing" the data points to be equidistant.

Interval variables, on the other hand, have an actual, uniform distance between the response options, such as income (reported in actual dollars and not categories), age, or summed or averaged items on a Likert-type scale (e.g., score on a standardized assessment). Ratio variables are continuous variables that have a meaningful zero (e.g., Kelvin temperature has an absolute zero, where the Fahrenheit scale does not).

Once researchers are able to determine the type of variables they are using in their statistical analysis, they can choose the appropriate statistical test. The various statistical tests and the types of variables that are used for each can be found in Table 20.1.

t-Tests

An independent *t*-test is used to compare the means of a variable between two groups (Roberts & Russo, 1999). For example, do doctoral-level licensed MFTs, on average, charge a higher session fee than master's-level MFTs? The independent categorical variable is dichotomous (master's- and doctoral-level MFTs), and the dependent variable is continuous (number of dollars charged per session). If the independent variable has more than two categories, an independent *t*-test may not be used. (In the case of three or more groups, an analysis of variance [ANOVA] is usually the statistic of choice.)

Paired *t*-tests are different because they determine whether two means that are linked, paired, or have some issues with nonindependence are different. For example, if you want to see whether parents and children have the same level of relationship quality, you conduct a paired *t*-test because the two participants are linked in the dataset. Paired *t*-tests can also be used to determine change over time between two data points. In essence, a paired *t*-test determines whether or not the difference between the two scores (parent's score minus child's score) is zero. If, over the entire sample, the average value is not statistically different from zero, researchers will conclude that the mean score of the parents and the mean score of their children are not statistically different.

Correlations

Bivariate correlations are conducted to determine whether two continuous variables (e.g., age and marital quality) are associated (e.g., covary with each other). Correlations can also be used to look at relationships between two identical variables measured for two different people (e.g., the relationship between a wife's marital satisfaction score and her husband's marital satisfaction score).

Table 20.1 Statistical Tests as Determined by Types of Variables

Statistical Procedure	Independent Variable (IV)	Dependent Variable (DV)	Example
Independent *t*-test	Dichotomous	Continuous	Do males and females (IV) have different levels of marital quality (DV)?
Paired *t*-test	None	Two paired continuous variables	Does marital quality change from pretest (DV 1) to posttest (DV 2)?
Bivariate correlation	Continuous	Continuous	Is the therapeutic alliance (IV) associated with posttherapy marital quality (DV)?
Chi-square	Categorical	Categorical	Is therapist's gender (IV) associated with whether or not a family drops out of therapy (DV)?
Multiple regression	Multiple; can be categorical or continuous	Continuous	Are therapeutic alliance (IV 1) and level of marital distress (IV 2) associated with posttest marital quality (DV)?
Logistical regression	Multiple; can be categorical or continuous	Dichotomous	Does therapeutic alliance (IV) and level of marital distress (IV) predict couples dropping out of therapy?
One-way ANOVA	1 categorical variable (1 Factor)	Continuous	Is type of therapy (EFT, CBT, and wait list) (IV or factor) associated with posttest marital quality (DV)?
Two-way ANOVA	2 categorical variables (2 Factors)	Continuous	Is type of therapy (EFT, CBT, and wait list) (factor 1) and therapist's gender (factor 2) (and their interaction) associated with posttest marital quality (DV)?
ANCOVA	Categorical IV, with covariate variable(s)	Continuous	Is type of therapy (EFT, CBT, and wait list) (IV or factor) associated with posttest marital quality (DV) while controlling for years married (covariate)?
MANOVA	Categorical	Multiple continuous variables	Is type of therapy (EFT, CBT, and wait list) (IV or factor) associated with posttest levels of marital quality (DV 1), sexual satisfaction (DV 2), and conflict (DV 3)?
Repeated measures ANOVA	None; covariate variable(s) can be included	The same continuous variable measured at different points of time	Does marital quality (DV) in couples therapy change from pretest to posttest to 6-month follow-up while controlling for years married (covariate)?

Note: EFT = emotionally focused therapy; CBT = cognitive-behavioral therapy.

Chi-Square (χ^2)

The chi-square test is used to determine the association between two categorical variables. Each variable must have two or more levels, but variables with multiple categories require a larger number of participants. The test determines the level of association by comparing the actual count in each cell to what the expected count in each cell should be, based on chance. For example, if we want to know whether males and females differ in their employment status, we would use a chi-square test because both variables are categorical. Likewise, we would use the chi-square statistic to determine whether therapists' level of education (master's or doctoral) is associated with whether or not a family drops out of therapy (dropouts or completers of therapy).

Regression

Multiple regression is an extension of the correlation statistic. Both are based on finding the best fitting a line to the data. The correlation statistic determines whether or not two continuous variables are statistically significantly associated. For example, a correlation analysis may demonstrate that the level of in-session activity of the therapist is associated with positive therapy outcome. However, is that association true regardless of the level of distress of the "identified patient"? Also, is the association true regardless of the gender of the therapist? It may be helpful to think of the algebra equation $y = mx + b$. You may recall from algebra class that with this equation, you can plot any line. Regression analysis is the same equation written in a different order.

Multiple regression allows the researcher to include additional variables in the statistical analysis (Lewis-Beck, 1980; Schroeder, Sjoquist, & Stephan, 1986). Thus, level of therapists' in-session activity is the main independent variable, but level of distress and therapists' gender are included as "control variables," which demonstrates that the association between therapists' in-session activity and therapy outcome remains significant regardless of the level of distress and therapists' gender (e.g., "level of therapists' in-session activity is significantly associated with positive therapy outcome, *while controlling for level of distress and therapists' gender*"). Therapy outcome (such as relationship quality) is the dependent variable. In multiple regression, the independent variables can be either categorical or continuous, but the dependent variable must be continuous.

Logistical regression is used in situations when the dependent variable is dichotomous (Pampel, 2000). For example, the dependent variable may be whether or not fathers come to the first session of family therapy, and the researchers want to know what factors might predict fathers' attendance. Logistical regression can have more than one independent variable, so father's employment status, father's education, and the quality of the relationship between the mother and father might be included as independent variables in order to determine whether any of these variables are significant predictors of fathers' attendance.

319

Analysis of Variance

ANOVA is used to determine whether the means of two or more groups are the same or statistically different (Roberts & Russo, 1999). ANOVA is the most common statistic used with experimental designs (Brown & Melamed, 1990). The simplest type of ANOVA is a one-way ANOVA, which compares a continuous dependent variable, such as scores on a depression scale, across a categorical variable, such as treatment groups that include individual therapy, couples therapy, and a wait-list group. If the overall F-score is statistically significant, it informs the researchers that the means across the three groups are not equal. In that case, a post-hoc test, such as the Tukey, is conducted to determine which group has a significantly different mean, compared with the groups (Roberts & Russo).

The basic ANOVA procedure or model can be expanded to address different research questions. One expansion is the inclusion of more than one factor in the model. When there are two factors in the model, it becomes a two-way ANOVA (Iversen & Norpoth, 1987). Thus, gender of the therapist can be added to the model to see what effect therapists' gender has on depression scores at the end of therapy. In this model, there are two possible "main effects": the effect of treatment group and the effect of therapists' gender. The advantage of conducting a two-way ANOVA, rather than two one-way ANOVAs (with one having a factor for treatment group and the other having a factor for therapists' gender), is that researchers can test for an "interaction effect" by examining the effect of gender *and* treatment group on depression scores.

Covariates can be added to the basic ANOVA model, making it an analysis of covariance (ANCOVA; Huitema, 2011). Covariates act as control variables, similar to control variables in multiple regression. Thus, the model that examines the effect of individual therapy, marital therapy, and a waitlist group on depression could add severity of depressive symptoms at intake as a covariate.

Multiple dependent variables can be simultaneously analyzed within the ANOVA framework by conducting a multiple analysis of variance (MANOVA; Bray & Maxwell, 1985). Consequently, instead of just testing for the effect of treatment on depressive symptoms, relationship satisfaction and sexual satisfaction can be added as dependent variables. An advantage of conducting a MANOVA, rather than a series of ANOVAs, is that it reduces the chance of a type I error (a false positive) (Bray & Maxwell). Covariates can be included in the model to create a MANCOVA.

Finally, a repeated measures ANOVA is used to test for change in a continuous dependent variable over multiple waves of data collection (Girden, 1992). These are also called within-subjects designs because they are comparing means that are associated with individual people, rather than between people (Roberts & Russo, 1999). If researchers have depression scores that were collected at pretest, posttest, and 6-month follow-up, they would conduct a repeated measures ANOVA to determine whether or not the mean level of depression is the same or changes across waves of data collection.

Thus, the type of variable that you are analyzing provides an important key to what statistical test you should use. However, type of variables used for each statistical test is only one assumption that needs to be met. Once researchers have determined which test to use, they must make sure that they are meeting the assumptions of each statistical test. (The other assumptions associated with basic statistics are beyond the scope of this chapter.) For a review of statistical assumptions for basic statistics, see the studies by Frankfort-Nachmias and Leon-Guerrero (2009), Berry (1993), and Roberts and Russo (1999).

Review of Basic Statistics: Interpretation

t-Tests

The t-test uses a significance test to determine the probability that the findings were not by chance. Magnitude of the findings can be determined by applying the findings and means from each group to the metric from which they were measured, which is true for both types of t-tests previously discussed. For example, let's say we are trying to determine the difference between scores on the Couple Satisfaction Index (CSI; Funk & Rogge, 2007) of clients who drop out of therapy versus clients who remain in therapy. Scores on the CSI-16 range from 0 to 80, with lower scores showing more relationship distress. The t-test results show that the people who dropped out of treatment had statistically significant lower couple satisfaction scores (dropouts, $M = 55$; nondropouts, $M = 45$). Thus, we have a mean difference of 10 points, and depending on the sample size, this could be statistically significant. However, a mean change of 10 points is not very large compared with the total range of possible values on the CSI. However, it is also important to note that the CSI-16 has a clinical cutoff score of 51.5 (Funk & Rogge), so the fact that the mean difference is across the clinical cutoff score adds some importance to the findings. Finally, to determine the magnitude of findings, we recommend the procedures described below in the "Statistical Significance, Magnitude, and Clinical Significance" section.

Correlations

Correlation analysis uses a significance test to determine the probability that the findings were not by chance. The magnitude of a correlation can be determined by looking at the absolute value of the correlation. It is obvious that a correlation of 0.54 is stronger than a correlation of 0.22. Also, you can square any correlation coefficient to turn it into an R^2 and determine the amount of variability explained by the correlation. For example, $0.54 \times 0.54 = 0.29$, meaning that 29% of the variability is explained between these two variables.

Chi-Square

The chi-square test uses a significance test to determine the probability that the findings were not by chance. Magnitude of the findings from a chi-square

---

Table 20.2 Chi-Square Results of the Association Between Trying Something From Therapy and Having an Argument

Try Something		Argue	
		No	Yes
No	observed	168	35
	expected	153	50
Yes	observed	82	46
	expected	97	31
$X^2 = 14.85; \phi = 0.21$		$p < .001$	

test can be determined in one of two ways: (1) Calculate a *phi* (ϕ) coefficient or (2) examine the actual difference between the expected and observed counts in the cells. To demonstrate this, we will use an example from my (L.J.) research. These results are from a daily diary study, and the test is trying to determine whether there is an association between trying something learned from therapy and having an argument on any given day. Table 20.2 contains preliminary results. The chi-square is highly significant, indicating that these results are not by chance. The first method of examining magnitude is to calculate a *phi* coefficient. *Phi* ranges from 0 to 1.00 and tells you the amount of shared variability or explained variance between the two variables; this is similar to an R^2 in a regression equation. In the example below, $\phi = 0.21$; thus, we can say that we are explaining 21% of the variability between having an argument and trying something from therapy on any given day. The second way to determine magnitude is to compare the expected counts with the observed counts. In the lower quadrant, you can see that it is expected that 31 people would try something from therapy and have an argument the same day. However, the actual count is 46, which is 15 days higher than expected. Thus, trying something from therapy is associated with having an argument 15 days more than expected. It is important to remember that chi-square is about associations and does not imply any direction in association, so the inverse may also be true, that having an argument is associated with trying something from therapy, and this occurs on 15 more days than would be expected by chance. As a clinical researcher or consumer, you need to make a determination of whether 15 days is a meaningful finding, but this examination gives you more information than a simple statistically significant finding.

Regression

Regression uses two significance tests to determine the probability that the findings were not by chance. The first significance test is an *F*-test. This test tells you whether the slope of the regression line is significantly different from zero. It is important to look at this test first because this test determines whether you need to look at each of the independent variables. If the F-test is nonsignificant, you do not need to look at the independent variable t-tests; basically, the regression line is not different from a flat line. If the F-test is significant, then the independent variable t-tests tell you which independent variables make a statistically significant contribution to the slope of the overall regression line.

Magnitude in regression analysis can be demonstrated in two ways: (1) by looking at the overall R^2 of the regression model, where higher numbers show that more of the variability is explained; and (2) by taking the slope or b values in the regression equation back to the original metric. Allison (1999) did a great job of showing how this is done with a regression coefficient of $b = 0.076$ for education predicting self-rated health (this coefficient was statistically significant). He said:

> To get a better idea of what the coefficient of .076 for education means, it's essential to have clear understanding of the units of measurement for the dependent and independent variables. Recall that self-rated health is measured on a 5-point scale and education is measured in years of schooling. We say, then, that each 1-year increase in schooling is associated with an increase of 0.76 in self-rated health. This implies that it would take $13 = 1/.076$ additional years of schooling to achieve a 1-point increase in self-rated health (e.g., moving from "satisfactory" to "good"). This to me does not seem like a very large effect. (p. 28)

We agree with Allison (1999) that this process should be done and reported when regression analysis is used.

Analysis of Variance

ANOVA uses a significance test to determine the probability that the findings were not by chance. To determine whether there is a mean difference somewhere among the groups in an ANOVA, this procedure uses an F-test. If the F-test is significant, it means that there are group mean differences somewhere between the groups (Frankfort-Nachmias & Leon-Guerrero, 2009). The magnitude of the differences in means can be determined in two ways. One way requires you to be familiar with the metric used to measure the variables; similar to a t-test, you can compare the means between groups to make a determination of the size of the difference relative to the measurement metric. The second method is to calculate an eta^2 (η^2) coefficient. Eta^2 is interpreted the same as an R^2 in regression analysis and will tell you the overall percentage of explained variance.

323

Statistical Significance, Magnitude, and Clinical Significance

Statistical significance is an important part of research. When we find that one of the results of our analysis is significant, we have found that at some level of alpha (traditionally 0.05); the relationship is not by chance. For example, if we are conducting a t-test and our results show that $t = 2.94$ and $p < .05$, then we can be 95% sure that we did not find the difference by chance. It also means there is a 5% possibility that our finding is by chance. Significance tests do not tell us anything about how true, correct, or important our results are. This is the reason so many people have written about the problems associated with significance testing (Cohen, 1994; Haase, Ellis, & Ladany, 1989; Murray & Dosser, 1987).

An additional problem associated with significance testing is that the process is highly influenced by sample size (Kelly & Maxwell, 2003; Wiley, 2009). In fact, as early as 1968, Lykken stated: "Statistical significance is perhaps the least important attribute of a good experiment" (p. 151). Sample size and significance tests are correlated, with larger sample sizes more likely to show statistically significant results, even when mean differences are small. Thus, as a researcher, if you are looking for only statistical significance and you run your analyses and come up just shy of a significant finding at the .05 level, you can reach statistical significance simply by gathering data from additional people. So in summary, statistical significance tells us the likelihood of our findings being by chance and does not tell us about importance or practical significance (Cooper, 1981; Sun, Pan, & Wang, 2010).

One way that has been discussed extensively in the literature for describing the magnitude of a statistical result is an effect size (Cohen, 1992; Fritz, Morris, & Richler, 2012; Kelley & Preacher, 2012). There are many subtly different definitions of an effect size, but the definition that best describes an effect size is "a quantitative reflection of the magnitude of some phenomenon that is used for the purpose of addressing a question of interest" (Kelley & Preacher, p. 2). There are also many ways to calculate an effect size based on what statistical analysis you are using. The basic idea behind an effect size is that it is the difference between two means divided by the standard deviation. This provides a standardized measure of the magnitude of the effect. Cohen (1992) provides guidelines for interpreting a small, medium, and large effect size based on the statistics used.

Clinical significance (Jacobson, Roberts, Berns, & McGlinchey, 1999; Jacobson & Truax, 1991) is one method that has been developed to assess the importance of findings in clinical research. Clinical significance has been defined in various ways, but most focus on some combination of participants returning to normal functioning and whether they have had a change that is not attributable to chance or measurement error (Jacobson et al.). For clinically significant change to occur, both criteria must be met. Jacobson and Truax developed a reliable change index that takes these factors into account and establishes how much change is necessary to accomplish this. Jacobson et al. state: "When used alone, the RCI [reliable change index] tells one only if the change was real, not if it was clinically significant" (p. 302). It is interesting to note that the whole idea of clinical significance started during Jacobson and colleagues' work on couple therapy outcome research, but subsequently few outcome studies on couple therapy report findings related to clinical significance.

For a basic illustration, consider the following example. You have participants in a depression couple therapy study whose depression levels you take at pretest and at posttest. The hypothetical depression measure we are using has possible scores that range from 0 to 30, and the cutoff for being depressed is a score higher than 15, with a higher score representing higher symptoms of depression. Using Jacobson and Truax's (1991) method of the RCI, we calculate a hypothetical RCI of 7.9. Participants in our hypothetical study are 10 couples, with at least one member of each couple having a depression score higher than 15 on our measure. You can find the difference in the means between the two time points. Let's say that the mean depression level at time −1 is 10 and that the mean depression level at time −2 is 15. Table 20.3 contains hypothetical results and the classification of clinically significant change for each depressed person in the couple. From looking at the table, you can see that the depressed person within couple 7 met the criteria for reliable change (this person reduced his/her depression by 11 points, which is greater than 7.9, but is still scoring in the range of depression). The depressed person who is part of couple 5 has the opposite result: He/she is no longer scoring in the range of depression but experiences a change of only 4 points, which is not large enough to be considered reliable. Based on the data presented in Table 20.3, 20% of the depressed individuals experienced clinically significant change, 70% improved but did not meet both criteria, 60% scored lower than the clinical cutoff, and 10% (the individual in couple 9) got worse.

Table 20.3 Hypothetical Results in Determining Clinical Significance

Couple #	Pretest Score	Posttest Score	Change to Within Range of Normal Population (score ≤15)	Change > RCI (7.9)	Clinically Significant Change
1	20	15	Yes	No	No
2	23	20	No	No	No
3	28	14	Yes	No	No
4	18	10	Yes	Yes	Yes
5	17	13	Yes	No	No
6	22	20	No	No	No
7	27	16	No	Yes	No
8	26	10	Yes	No	No
9	17	20	No	No	No
10	19	8	Yes	Yes	Yes

The mean pretest depression score is $M = 21.7$, and the mean posttest depression score is $M = 14.6$. Using a paired t-test, we get the following result: $t(9) = 3.78$, $p = .004$. In terms of statistical significance, the difference between pretest and posttest is highly significant. However, only 20% meet both criteria for clinical significance.

We recommend that clinical research in MFT, in addition to reporting statistical significance, should also report the following, which requires the calculation of an RCI (Jacobson & Truax, 1991):

(1) Report the percentage of individuals, couples, or families that move from a distressed to a nondistressed range on the scale.
(2) Report the percentage of individuals, couples, or families that change at a level greater than the RCI value.
(3) Report the percentage of individuals, couples, or families that meet both criteria.

Association and Causation

The goal of research, where possible, is to show that some independent variable causes some effect on a dependent variable. We want to be able to say that our treatment, in-session intervention, or some other independent variable caused the change in our dependent variable. With increasing accessibility of powerful statistics that allow us to model relationships among variables while accounting for measurement error, control confounding variables, and account for issues like nonindependence, it is easy to forget one basic research principle: Determining causal relationships has nothing to do with statistics and everything to do with research design. Trochim (2005) described three criteria necessary to show causal relationships: (1) the cause (independent variable) precedes the outcome (dependent variable); (2) the cause (independent variable) is present when the dependent variable changes, but when the independent variable is not present, the dependent variable does not change; and finally (3) alternative explanations have been ruled out. These criteria are all design issues, not statistical issues, and are the main reason that randomized controlled trials and single case research designs are recommended for determining causal relationships (see Chapters 12 and 13).

Conclusions

Given the power of statistical software programs to calculate basic statistical tests, researchers are able to focus their attention on choosing the appropriate statistical test, as well as accurately interpreting the output from the tests. Choosing the appropriate statistical test depends largely on researchers correctly identifying the type of variables involved in the analysis, as well as the basic design of the study. Rather than relying simply on significance tests, we remind researchers to test for the clinical significance of their results. Finally, we remind researchers to be cautious in their attribution of causality to their findings.

References

Acock, A. (2012). *A gentle introduction to Stata* (3rd ed.). College Station, TX: Stata Press.

Allison, P. D. (1999). *Multiple regression: A primer*. Thousand Oaks, CA: Pine Forge Press.

Babbie, E. (2008). *The basics of social research* (4th ed.). Belmont, CA: Thomson.

Berry, W. D. (1993). *Understanding regression assumptions*. Thousand Oaks, CA: Sage.

Bray, J. H., & Maxwell, S. E. (1985). *Multivariate analysis of variance*. Thousand Oaks, CA: Sage.

Brown, S. R., & Melamed, L. E. (1990). *Experimental design and analysis*. Thousand Oaks, CA: Sage.

Cohen, J. (1992). A power primer. *Psychological Bulletin, 112*, 155–159.

Cohen, J. (1994). The earth is round ($p < .05$). *American Psychologist, 49*(12), 997–1003.

Cooper, H. M. (1981). On the significance of effects and the effects of significance. *Journal of Personality and Social Psychology, 41*(5), 1013–1018.

Field, A. (2013). *Discovering statistics using IBM SPSS Statistics*. Thousand Oaks, CA: Sage.

Frankfort-Nachmias, G., & Leon-Guerrero, A. (2009). *Social statistics for a diverse society* (5th ed.). Thousand Oaks, CA: Pine Forge Press.

Fritz, C. O., Morris, P. E., & Richler, J. J. (2012). Effect size estimates: Current use, calculations, and interpretations. *Journal of Experimental Psychology: General, 141*(1), 2–18. doi: 10.1037/a0024338

Funk, J. L., & Rogge, R. D. (2007). Testing the ruler with item response theory: Increasing precision of measurement for relationship satisfaction with the Couples Satisfaction Index. *Journal of Family Psychology, 21*(4), 572–583. doi: 10.1037/0893-3200.21.4.572

Girden, E. R. (1992). *ANOVA: Repeated measures*. Thousand Oaks, CA: Sage.

Haase, R. F., Ellis, M. V., & Ladany, N. (1989). Multiple criteria for evaluating the magnitude of experimental effects. *Journal of Counseling Psychology, 36*(4), 511–516.

Huitema, B. (2011). *The analysis of covariance and alternatives*. Hoboken, NJ: John Wiley & Sons.

Iversen, G. R., & Norpoth, H. (1987). *Analysis of variance*. Thousand Oaks, CA: Sage.

Jacobson, N. S., Roberts, L. J., Berns, S. B., & McGlinchey, J. B. (1999). Methods for defining and determining the clinical significance of treatment effects: Description, application, and alternatives. *Journal of Consulting and Clinical Psychology, 67*(3), 300–307.

Jacobson, N. S., & Truax, P. (1991). Clinical significance: A statistical approach to defining meaningful change in psychotherapy research. *Journal of Consulting and Clinical Psychology, 59*(1), 12–19.

Kazdin, A. E. (2003). Clinical significance: Measuring whether interventions make a difference. In A. E. Kazdin (Ed.), *Methodological issues and strategies in clinical research* (3rd ed., pp. 691–710). Washington, DC: American Psychological Association.

Kelley, K., & Maxwell, S. E. (2003). Sample size for multiple regression: Obtaining regression coefficients that are accurate, not simply significant. *Psychological Methods, 8*(3), 305–321. doi: 10.1037/1082-989X.8.3.305

Kelley, K. & Preacher, K. J. (2012). On effect size. *Psychological Methods, 17, 137–152.*

Leech, N. L., Barrett, K. C., & Morgan, G. A. (2011). *IBM SPSS for intermediate statistics: Use and interpretation* (4th ed.). New York: Routledge.

Lewis-Beck, M. S. (1980). *Applied regression: An introduction.* Thousand Oaks, CA: Sage Publications.

Lykken, D. T. (1968). Statistical significance in psychological research. *Psychological Bulletin, 70*(3), 151–159.

Murray, L. W., & Dosser, D. A. (1987). How significant is a significant difference? Problems with the measurement of magnitude of effect. *Journal of Counseling Psychology, 34*(1), 68–72.

Pampel, F. C. (2000). *Logistic regression: A primer.* Thousand Oaks, CA: Sage.

Roberts, M. J., & Russo, R. (1999). *A student's guide to analysis of variance.* New York: Routledge.

Schroeder, L. D., Sjoquist, D. L., & Stephan, P. E. (1986) *Understanding regression analysis: An introductory guide.* Thousand Oaks, CA: Sage.

Sun, S., Pan, W., & Wang, L. L. (2010). A comprehensive review of effect size reporting and interpreting practices in academic journals in education and psychology. *Journal of Educational Psychology, 102*(4), 989–1004. doi: 10.1037/a001950

Trochim, W. M. K. (2005). *Research methods: The concise knowledge base.* Cincinnati, OH: Atomic Dog Publishing.

Wiley, R. H. (2009). Trade-offs in the design of experiments. *Journal of Comparative Psychology, 123*(4), 447–449. doi: 10.1037/a0016094

21

MISSING DATA

Colwick M. Wilson, Ruth Houston Barrett,
and Sarah C. Stuchell

One of the challenges that often confront family scientists and clinicians is the issue of missing data (MD). It is not uncommon for values to be missing on a number of variables in an empirical study. Thus, marriage and family therapists who adopt a quantitative approach are often forced to respond to the incompleteness of the collected data in their efforts to ensure fidelity of the information provided by the participants. While there has been a steady growth in empirical studies of MD, marriage and family therapy (MFT) research has not emphasized current advancements, as evidenced in the field's flagship journals.

We reviewed all articles published from 2003 to 2012 in the *Journal of Marriage and Family Therapy* (*JMFT*), *Contemporary Family Therapy* (*CFT*), and the *American Journal of Family Therapy* (*AJFT*) to examine whether quantitative studies explicitly reported MD and what MD techniques were used (if any). During this period, 303 articles were identified as quantitative or having a quantitative component (i.e., mixed methods study). Of these, 41% discussed MD, while 59% made no mention of missingness. Less than a third of studies provided the response rate (31%) and/or the attrition rate (16%); we consider those that mentioned only the response rate with no further MD description (15%) as not reporting MD (i.e., MD applies only to cases with some data). Some studies (34%) provided description of MD but did not describe using a method to account for MD. Overall, only 66 studies (22%) described using an MD method; the vast majority (88% of those using any MD technique, 19% overall) used case deletion to handle incomplete cases. The remaining 8 studies used the following strategies: manual recoding scheme (4), mean substitution (2), full-information maximum likelihood (FIML) (1), and expectation maximization (1). Thus, only 2 (0.7%) of the 303 studies published in *JMFT*, *CFT*, and *AJFT* over the last decade used an advanced modern missing data strategy.

This chapter provides information on the definition of MD, its sources and context, and the analytical approaches available in response to MD when conducting MFT research.

Table 21.1 Reports on Missing Data in the Quantitative/Mixed Methods Studies Published 2003–2012 in *JMFT, CFT,* and *AJFT* (#: number of studies, %: proportion of studies)

	Studies in JMFT		Studies in CFT		Studies in AJFT		Studies in the Three Journals	
	#	%	#	%	#	%	#	%
No mention of MD	63	48.1	65	71.4	51	63.0	179	59.1
Identified MD as present, but no MD method	35	26.7	8	8.8	15	18.5	58	19.1
No MD method was used	98	74.8	73	80.2	66	81.5	237	78.2
Deletion: Case or listwise	27	20.6	16	17.6	15	18.5	58	19.1
Mean substitution	1	0.8	1	1.1	0	0	2	0.7
Logical recoding scheme	3	2.3	1	1.1	0	0	4	1.3
Traditional MD methods, all	31	23.7	18	19.8	15	18.5	64	21.1
Full-information maximum likelihood (FIML)	1	0.8	0	0	0	0	1	0.3
Expectation maximization	1	0.8	0	0	0	0	1	0.3
Multiple imputation (MI)	0	0	0	0	0	0	0	0
Advanced MD methods, all	2	1.5	0	0	0	0	2	0.7
	131	100	91	100	81	100	303	100

What Are Missing Data?

Having MD means that there is incomplete information about a particular phenomenon under study. Data are collected in an effort to accurately represent the views of the respondents, and missing information on the characteristics of the participants could significantly influence the results (McKnight, McKnight,

Sidani, & Figueredo, 2007). In survey research, *unit nonresponse* occurs when the data collection procedure fails for a particular case—for example, because the sampled person cannot be located or refuses to participate. This has traditionally been distinguished from *item nonresponse*, in which at least partial data are available (Schafer & Graham, 2002). In longitudinal studies, participants may provide data for some waves but be not for others; this phenomenon is called *wave nonresponse*. Attrition is an example of this form of missingness, when participants may drop out of the study and fail to return for a variety of reasons (Schafer & Graham). Clinical examples of MD include cases in which a family member is absent from a particular session. Missing values may also be a function of the analytical process, such as when numbers have been grouped, censored, rounded, aggregated, truncated, or scaled, thus obscuring or partially losing information (Schafer & Graham).

An MD approach includes much more than an understanding of the available statistical strategies that may be used to accurately and appropriately respond to missingness. Intentionality about minimizing the prevalence of MD by thoughtful consideration of the presence of missingness in the conceptualization and implementation of the study is critical; it reduces both the occurrence and the impact of incomplete data. While this chapter seeks to provide a thorough overview of the established and emerging analytical strategies for dealing with missingness in quantitative studies, we do recommend careful attention to study design and implementation to prevent or limit the presence of MD (see McKnight et al., 2007). Planning ahead to *minimize* MD is an effective way to deal with the challenges of unplanned missingness. In research with couple and family therapy, a study protocol could reduce missingness by specifying that therapy occurs only when all family members are present, incorporating techniques to increase engagement and attendance, or contacting missing participants via follow-up phone calls to obtain certain data.

The complexities of MD are often heightened by their relationship to variables that are not in the study, and a researcher may theorize that the mechanism responsible for the presence of MD was not available. For example, it may be plausible to contend that MD are a function of depression and the associated malaise of selected participants. However, if the investigator has no information about the mental status of the individuals who did not respond to certain items, imputation strategies are difficult to utilize. Data may also be missing as a result of the question or item itself. For instance, people with higher and lower levels of income are less likely to answer questions about income (Pleis, Dahlhamer, & Meyer, 2007).

The Pattern of Missing Data

A *pattern* in MD relates to how and why the data are missing, such as a systematic relationship between the presence of missing values and other variables. Data missing at random are commonly considered the least problematic pattern.

For example, MD values for a test of marital quality are less troublesome if they do not depend on the marital quality score (e.g., one does not lose higher or lower scores) or any other scores in the model, such as the marital conflict scores. However, when MD on one variable are related to another, this pattern poses a potentially serious problem. For instance, in studying the relationship between maternal employment and children's outcomes, one might find that individuals with greater hours of employment are more likely to have missing interview scores. In other words, the interview was subject to "censoring" by the related variable of employment hours. This mechanism may lead to bias in estimating parameters, such as biasing correlation coefficients downward (Roth, 1994), because variation (values that are further from the mean) has been lost from interview scores. Thus, the *pattern* of missingness is salient and at times even more critical than the amount of MD.

Problems with Missing Data

MD can impact the overall validity of research studies in several meaningful ways (Roth, 1994), affecting analysis, interpretations, and conclusions and reducing internal, external, and conclusion validity of study results. Fidelity of the collected data is also largely a function of construct validity for the measured variables, which of necessity affects the reliability of the measures used over time (McKnight et al., 2007). Specifically, MD can diminish sample size, statistical power, and the ability of a statistical test to detect relationships among variables (Ward & Clark, 1991), thereby reducing internal and conclusion validity. This is a particularly crucial issue in clinical research, in which sample sizes tend to be small, and loss of data can severely compromise study results. In general, MD have the potential to create biased parameter estimates, inflate the rates of type I and type II errors, and degrade the accuracy of confidence intervals (Collins, Schafer, & Kam, 2001). That is, depending on how MD are handled, not only can loss of information bias correlation coefficients downward, MD may affect measures of central tendency and dispersion, since they may fluctuate upward or downward in concert, "depending upon where in the distribution the missing data appear" (Roth, 1994, p. 539). For example, the mean score and variance are biased downward if data are disproportionately unavailable at the high end of a distribution. This could occur in a clinical outcome study if, for example, the most conflictual couples in a wait-list control group were more likely to drop out, reducing the mean and variance for conflict: This could falsely obscure the effectiveness of treatment by artificially decreasing the difference between the treatment and control group outcomes. Thus, to counteract this known effect of missing values and to increase conclusion validity, investigators might choose to oversample among populations that are less likely to respond or remain in a study, particularly if they theorize that such individuals are more likely to provide especially high or low values on variables of interest.

The problematic effects of MD in analysis and research depend on why the data are lost and what MD strategy is employed to deal with them in the analysis.

In general, researchers tend to use the rule of thumb that if only a few data points (5% or less) are missing in a random pattern from a large dataset, the problems are less serious, and almost any procedure for handling missing values yields similar results (Graham, 2009; Olinsky, Chen, & Harlow, 2003). If, however, a substantial proportion of data are missing from a small to moderately sized dataset, the effects can be very serious. Some evidence suggests that parameter estimates and answers to research questions are often only negligibly affected when less than 10% of the data are missing, but the strategy a researcher chooses for handling MD becomes increasingly important as the amount of MD approaches 15–20%, and critical when the MD exceed 30% (Malhotra, 1987).

Approaches to Addressing Missing Data

The three main strategies for dealing with MD are deletion, substitution, and imputation. Selecting the optimal technique is dependent on a number of factors, such as study's aims, researcher's interpretation of the data with respect to theory, and the nature and meaning of the MD. In this section, we describe current strategies for dealing with MD, along with the ramifications for their use. First, we describe how and why to perform MD analysis as a basis for determining an appropriate and practical strategy for dealing with MD. Then we explore how various techniques work for differing data characteristics, study approaches, and research goals.

Missing Values Analysis

Determining the nature or pattern of the "missingness" of the MD is an essential early step in determining appropriate, information-preserving ways to deal with it. For example, in longitudinal studies, some amount of participant dropout is almost inevitable over time, so it is important to examine trends in the resultant MD (Enders, 2010). In fact, being married, older, White, educated, or female tends to increase the likelihood of remaining in a longitudinal study (Goodman & Blum, 1996). In clinical data, family members are highly likely to be absent at some sessions, providing valuable insight into family functioning (i.e., the fact of missingness is itself a datum). In survey research, individuals may refuse to answer questions that are highly emotional, so a missing value may have significant impact on the validity of the study results. In MFT research on couples, data may be lost as a couple divorce or separate, or if one spouse dies. In other conditions, data may be missing randomly, with no relationship between the missingness and the variables of interest. Clearly, whatever form it takes, the pattern of missingness is strongly tied to the investigation. Thus, it is important to conduct an MD analysis to test whether there is a pattern to the missingness, indicating a relationship between absence of data and variables' values and variances that should be noted in further analysis (Little & Rubin, 1987).

SPSS and other software provide tools to conduct missing values analysis (MVA), which examines whether there are significant trends in the data such that there are patterns to the missingness. For data that are *missing completely at random* (MCAR), the distribution of missingness is related to neither the observed data nor the MD (Rubin, 1976). SPSS MVA performs Little's (1988) MCAR test; a result of nonsignificance indicates that the data are MCAR, suggesting that there is no significant relationship between the values of the data and the distribution of MD. A less stringent condition of missingness is called *missing at random* (MAR) or *ignorable nonresponse*, which indicates that the distribution of missingness depends on the observed data, but not on the MD (Rubin). MCAR is a special, more stringent, type of MAR.

If there is a pattern to the missingness, however, the researcher must interpret it in conjunction with pronounced familiarity with the practical and theoretical aspects of the study in order to select an appropriate MD strategy. This kind of missingness is called *missing not at random* (MNAR) or *non-ignorable nonresponse*. In this case, newer methods that account for patterns in missingness are available. However, erroneous assumptions of MAR in many realistic cases have only a minor impact on estimates and standard errors (Collins et al., 2001), and in most psychological research, departures from MAR are probably not serious (Schafer & Graham, 2002). For example, this would mean that a clinical study might ignore the relationship (i.e., assume MAR) between frequency of absence of a family member and outcomes (say, moderated by engagement in therapy), and although there may actually be a nonnegligible relationship between missingness and outcomes (i.e., MNAR), it may nonetheless be reasonable to assume that this MD will not greatly affect the relationships among study variables. However, in many realistic cases, as missingness moves from MCAR to MAR to MNAR, it becomes increasingly more likely that the observed data are selective relative to the population (Schafer & Graham), affecting external validity.

Planned Missingness and Missing Values that Are Out of Scope

In some cases, data are missing because they were never intended to be collected. In fact, building planned missingness into the research design is one way to make the best use of limited resources (Enders, 2010). Scenarios of planned missingness include cohort-sequential designs for longitudinal studies and studies that use multiple versions of questionnaires with different subsets of items (Schafer & Graham, 2002). Generally, this kind of missingness is MCAR, although there are some cases in which it is MAR, such as when the missingness in some items is decided based on a participants' other scores. Missingness can also occur when values are out of scope, such as when a survey question is not applicable for the respondent. This type of missingness can safely be treated as MAR for analysis purposes (Schafer & Graham).

MD are not always bad news, and in fact strategies of planned missingness, followed by well-selected imputation strategies, can be used to best utilize finite resources to collect data strategically (Enders, 2010). For example, the three-form design can increase the number of questions in a survey by 33% by asking different specific sets of questions of different respondents (Graham, Taylor, Olchowski, & Cumsille, 2006). That is, each participant completes one of three versions, each version being two thirds of the full questionnaire. Such planned missing designs produce MCAR data and make possible the inclusion of additional variables, with the only design tradeoff being a loss of statistical power (Enders). That is, a given sample size has the power to effectively examine a finite number of variables. However, by employing this three-form design along with imputation methods described later in this chapter, we can *stretch* the utilization of a sample to effectively include 50% more variables. For example, if each survey addresses 10 variables, the three versions would address 15 variables.

Another planned missingness design employs two-method measurement for latent variables in structural equation modeling (SEM). Complete data are collected with an inexpensive measure, and incomplete data (for a random subsample) are collected on a superior, more expensive measure, providing higher statistical power than if all resources were used for the more expensive measure. This leads to greater construct validity than if only the inexpensive measure were used (Graham, 2009). For example, in a clinical study on attachment, most parents might be asked to complete relatively short surveys on current parent–child functioning, while extensive historical questionnaires might be added for a subset of participants.

Eliminating Missingness by Averaging the Available Items

A method that can account for MD almost invisibly is for the researcher to define a variable as the mean of a set of items. For example, if a latent variable called *joy* is defined as the average of five items, a score can be obtained for *joy* as long as at least one of those items has a nonmissing value. In this (sleight-of-hand) way, the number of missing values can be greatly reduced for that composite variable. The implementation must be well conceived, based on the researcher's strong familiarity with the concepts involved. Even then, it is theoretically problematic in that the variable is defined as the average of the available items, rather than the average of a complete set of items, and thus the definition can differ from participant to participant, making it an artifact of the dataset, rather than a well-defined parameter of the population (Schafer & Graham, 2002). Theoretically, a preferable strategy would be to employ a multiple imputation (MI) technique for MD on individual items prior to forming the variable. However, studies have shown that the items-averaging approach can work reasonably well, particularly under the following conditions: if the grouped items to be averaged are highly and similarly correlated, if the reliability is high (i.e., alpha > 0.70), and if the items seem to indicate a single construct (Schafer & Graham). These are the qualities of a good scale. Also, it has been shown that forming a scale score equal to the average of its items comprised can be acceptable if at least half of the items have nonmissing values in each case (Graham, 2009).

For scales used by MFT researchers, this set of circumstances frequently exists, and so items can be a useful, simple technique to handle missing values. For example, a set of items might be used to indicate a construct of relationship quality. If these items meet the above criteria for a good scale, then an average score rather than a summation score could legitimately be used. This would likely reduce the effects of MD and preserve the statistical power by including cases with some missing responses while preserving the information actually present in the data. However, as described later, more sophisticated and rigorous techniques are available to handle MD.

The following sections describe a number of well-known strategies for handling MD. The presentations generally progress from the simplest and most bias-producing techniques to more reasonable techniques for specific circumstances to the most sophisticated, information-preserving, and recommended modern approaches. We make the case that the effort required to employ the more advanced strategies of imputation is highly worthwhile, because they best preserve the information and power of a dataset, including the variability, correlations, and statistical uncertainty due to MD that are present in the data. Thus, they maximize the validity of our analyses and interpretations (conclusion validity), allowing rich, realistic, and meaningful inferences to be achieved.

Casewise Deletion for Missing Data

This limited strategy of employing deletion for MD is one of the earliest, most popular, and easiest techniques to implement. Until the 1970s, deleting or logically editing in values were the principal methods of handling MD (Schafer & Graham, 2002). In the deletion approach, entire cases are removed from the analysis if they have any missing values for any of the variables being considered. This is called *case deletion* or *listwise deletion*, and the resulting analysis is called *complete cases analysis*. A similar strategy uses *pairwise deletion*, deleting cases that have missing values for each particular variable. This preserves more data, but since different variables are based on different sets of cases, subsequent analyses can be troublesome (Schafer & Graham). In a related strategy, complete cases are weighted to better represent the entire sample; this is called *weighted casewise deletion* (Brick & Kalton, 1996).

The greatest advantage to casewise deletion is its simplicity. However, this initially straightforward approach has a number of inherent disadvantages. In most studies, data are not so overabundant that the loss of sample size and statistical power resulting from deleting incomplete cases is of no import, and this strategy can lead to the loss of a large amount of data for even a small amount of missing values (Roth, 1994; Roth, Switzer, & Switzer, 1999). The time and expense of gathering data behooves the researcher to seek a method of preserving data. Also, if there is a relationship between the absence of data from certain cases and variables in the study, then meaningful information is lost when those cases are deleted. Then, removing these cases can introduce bias into the analysis that is conducted with the other cases, and conclusions and interpretations may miss or misinterpret significant aspects of what is actually occurring in the study. For these reasons, the case-deletion strategy is best used for data that are MCAR with small proportions of missing values. Additionally, even for this kind of data, it is important to scrutinize the cases with missing values to determine whether they represent an important subpopulation of interest.

Single Imputation: Mean Substitution

Rather than discarding all cases with any MD, the information that is present in the data can be used to construct representations of what is missing. The simplest of such imputation approaches is to employ mean substitution. In this coarse single-imputation method, the mean is calculated based on all present values for a particular variable and then used to replace the missing values. Note that the mean of the resulting dataset is then unchanged, remaining a reasonable representation of what would theoretically be present if there were no MD. However, by replacing missing values with the mean, the distribution of values is made to cluster more centrally, narrowing the distribution and reducing variation such that the standard deviation, variance, covariance, and correlations among variables are reduced from what would theoretically be present if there were no MD and what is likely present in the population. The degree of this artificial reduction in variability is related to the number of substitutions, that is, the amount of MD. This reduction is particularly problematic if the missingness is related to more extreme values (thus MNAR), because the most interesting cases of difference are then replaced by the most conforming of values. This effect makes MVA and the researcher's knowledge paramount considerations in selecting this strategy.

This simple-to-execute approach does have the positive consequence of preserving sample size and statistical power, which are important improvements over using case deletion. However, even in the best scenario of MCAR data and low proportions of MD, this technique inherently imposes loss of information—thus, validity of conclusions and inferences are compromised (Little, 1992). Further, it tends to underestimate the standard errors and confidence intervals, leading to rejecting the null hypothesis too often (Paul, Mason, McCaffrey, & Fox, 2008), and the possibility of increasing type I error. In clinical research, this leads to being inaccurately optimistic about treatment effectiveness. Thus, ironically, while the statistical power to find significant relationships is preserved in one sense, the accuracy of calculated relationships is artificially reduced in another, degrading the ability to discern what is present in the data. That is, the artificial, introduced loss of variance and covariance may result in the obfuscation of existing relationships present in the original data. A number of investigations have shown that mean substitution yields biased estimates and incorrect standard errors (e.g., Allison, 2001; Raghunathan, 2004). We therefore recommend more sophisticated, information-preserving approaches to handling MD.

Single Imputation: Hot Deck Imputation

Hot deck imputation is another ad hoc single imputation method that, unlike mean substitution, seeks to preserve the characteristics of the data distribution. It replaces each missing value (recipient) with an observed response from a similar unit (donor): Donor selection can be *random* or based on researcher-supplied metric(s), i.e., *deterministic* (Brick & Kalton, 1996). In couple or family therapy research, the donor might be a similar couple or family in the study. To balance tractability and effectiveness, three to five imputation classes (categories/values for an imputed variable, such as high-medium-low) have been suggested (Little & Rubin, 2002). This strategy was originally devised when lines of code and data were entered via computer punch cards; when a missing card was encountered, another from that current ("hot") deck was used in its place (Andridge & Little, 2010). A recent review found no consensus for how to use hot deck imputation or interpret analysis results based on the created dataset, although it continues to be used by, for instance, the U.S. Census Bureau (Andridge & Little). Further refinements include using sampling weights to reduce bias, partitioned hot decks to better preserve associations (Andridge & Little), a jackknife estimator to improve variance estimation with stratified multistage surveys (Rao & Shao, 1992), and multiple weighted imputed values in fractional hot deck imputation to improve variance and other parameter estimations (Kim & Fuller, 2004).

Its strengths are that it imputes real (and hence realistic) values, avoids strong parametric assumptions, can incorporate covariate information, and can provide good inferences for both linear and nonlinear statistics if appropriate attention is paid to imputation uncertainty (Andridge & Little, 2010). But while it maintains data variability, it reduces correlation and other measures of association among items (Schafer & Graham, 2002), increasing type II error, and does not account for the fact that imputed values are resampled, rather than there being new observations (Paul et al., 2008). Thus, it tends to underestimate true variance (Rao & Shao, 1992). Another challenge is that it requires good matches of donors to recipients, more likely in larger samples (Andridge & Little). Since MFT clinical research typically works with fairly small samples, hot deck is not likely to be an effective MD strategy, and further, it is philosophically problematic given that MFT research seeks to understand difference in a clinical population, not impute from one family, couple, or individual to another.

Single Imputation: Conditional Mean Imputation Using Regression

A more information-preserving single imputation method is to construct a regression equation for each item Y from the nonmissing (observed) values in the data, which is then used to impute a value for each case with a missing value for that item (Schafer & Graham, 2002). In a regression equation, the calculated value for Y is a function of its predictors $(X_1, X_2, \ldots)$; so for each case, the missing value for Y can be estimated from the observed values for $X_1, X_2, \ldots$. This is called *conditional mean imputation* because the imputed value is conditioned on the observed values for that case. A dummy variable that represents missingness among the variables in the analysis is sometimes included in the covariate list for the generalized regression analysis as an indicator of MCAR; if its coefficient is significant, then the data are not MCAR (Paul et al., 2008).

Conditional mean imputation assumes MAR (missingness may depend on observed data but not on MD), which is clearly required because in this method the *missing* Y data are portrayed as having the same relationship with the observed X data that the *observed* Y data have (Schafer & Graham, 2002). This is often a reasonable assumption, and analysis has shown that with appropriate corrections for standard errors, conditional mean imputation can be very accurate for certain types of estimation problems (Schafer & Schenker, 2000). However, because the imputed data are of course 100% consistent with the regression equations used ($R^2 = 1.00$ among the imputed values), the imputed dataset shows an *artificially increased strength of relationship* between Y and X_1, X_2, . . ., which makes this method *unsuited to analyses of covariances and correlations* (Schafer & Graham). This makes it an undesirable technique for a large proportion of MFT research.

Single Imputation: Unconditional Mean Imputation Using Regression

Unconditional mean imputation can also use regression to create estimating equations for missing values, but the imputed value is then randomly selected from a conditional distribution of Y, given X. For linear models, this is done by adding to the estimated Y value an error value that is randomly selected from the residual error distribution (Schafer & Graham, 2002). This strategy eliminates the distortion of covariances created by the methods described above, and it provides estimates with very little bias, *if* the model is correctly specified, and *if* the MD are MAR. Imputations are relatively simple for univariate MD patterns and are manageable for monotone patterns (variables either increase together or vary inversely, including linear but not u-shaped relationships), but they are very complex for arbitrary patterns (Schafer & Graham). In the latter case, imputation with this method can require as much effort as using MI, which has superior properties (Schafer & Graham). Of the simple methods presented thus far, this one is likely to yield the best results for many MFT researchers. However, as the ensuing discussion will demonstrate, there are more precise ways of dealing with MD.

Simple "Traditional" Versus Advanced "Modern" Imputation Strategies

As single imputation methods increase in sophistication, they tend to produce less biased results. Except under restrictive conditions, deletion and single imputation methods have been shown conclusively to perform poorly, yielding biased estimates and incorrect standard errors (Raghunathan, 2004). Using mean substitution or hot deck imputation produces imputed datasets that are biased for any kind of missingness; conditional mean imputation yields slightly less biased datasets under MCAR or MAR; and unconditional mean imputation can be unbiased under MCAR or MAR (Schafer & Graham, 2002). Also, and quite importantly, single imputation methods underestimate the statistical uncertainty of data.

For these reasons, we recommend MI and FIML because they are more proficient ways to deal with MD. These techniques are based on sound theory and produce efficient estimates of means, variances, regression coefficients, and correlations, and include accurate representations of statistical uncertainty (Johnson & Young, 2010). Both of these methods regard MD as a source of random variation to be averaged over, in contrast to the aforementioned editing methods that create complete, although problematic, datasets (Collins et al., 2001).

MI and FIML share the property of relying on joint probabilistic models for the observed data and MD that must be specified by the researcher (Collins et al., 2001). Thus, the variables to be included in the models must be selected for each analysis. While these strategies have excellent performance when thoughtfully implemented, they may not be accurate if the models are poorly specified or if underlying assumptions for the observed or unobserved values are not met (Collins et al.). However, the consensus is that the advanced approaches of FIML and MI produce superior results (Johnson & Young, 2010). In fact, these modern approaches, made possible by recent advances in software, represent such a new perspective on MD that Graham (2009) called it "the missing data revolution" (p. 552).

In one study of specific interest to MFT researchers, Johnson and Young (2010) demonstrated how various approaches to handling MD worked on data from the National Survey of Families and Households ($N = 2,000$). With marital happiness as the dependent variable, 13 predictor variables, and one interaction term, they compared three "traditional" deletion and substitution methods and the two modern approaches of FIML and MI (with 25 imputed datasets), finding that the modern methods were superior in terms of improved accuracy of standard errors, increased statistical power to detect a larger number of significant relationships among variables, and more accurate coefficient estimates. Further, Johnson and Young argued that while substantive interpretations using older methods to handle MD are not extremely dissimilar to those obtained via modern approaches, "the differences in the patterns of significant effects and the size and direction of the coefficients raise serious concerns about the validity of continued use of these approaches by family researchers" (p. 932).

Modern Approaches to Missing Data

Current state-of-the-art techniques for handling MD have developed from one of two directions: imputing MD to create complete datasets or using a maximum likelihood procedure to estimate the joint distribution of variables in the model

(Johnson & Young, 2010). These two paths have led to the two most widely used modern MD methods: MI and FIML. In fact, for a large enough number of imputations in MI, these methods produce equivalent results when used on the same model (Graham, 2009). The following sections provide an overview of these techniques; however, more complete reviews can be found elsewhere (e.g., Graham; Johnson & Young).

Multiple Imputation

The MI technique performs M independent imputations to create M complete datasets, each with the same nonmissing values but potentially different imputed values (Johnson & Young, 2010). Each dataset reflects the degree of uncertainty for the imputations by including a random error component inversely proportional to the degree that the other variables in the imputation model can predict its value accurately: Imputations on variables that are strongly (weakly) related to other variables in the model have small (large) random error components (Johnson & Young). The purpose is to increase the estimation precision while incorporating variability from the imputation process into assessments of how accurately the substantive model's coefficients and parameters are estimated (Rubin, 1987).

The analyst estimates the substantive model for each dataset—M times—then obtains the final estimate for the statistical parameters and coefficients by averaging over the M regressions (Rubin, 1987), either manually or by using automated procedures such as found in SPSS, SAS, and Stata. This creates a single set of pooled estimates. The resulting estimate for standard errors of each coefficient is a combination of the average within-replicate uncertainty and between-replicate uncertainty or difference across the M regressions (Paul et al., 2008). Averaging over the M imputed datasets improves the precision of the estimate and makes it easy to estimate variances, means, and totals for sample parameters (Andridge & Little, 2010).

MI is viewed as one of the most respectable strategies for dealing with MD (Johnson & Young, 2010). Imputing data in this way fully utilizes and preserves the information contained in the dataset, allowing meaningful analysis. For example, the MI method in SPSS uses linear regression to predict MD in a multistage process that uses the values present in the incomplete dataset to construct full datasets (i.e., with no missing values) while preserving the meaningful aspects of the original data. This approach for imputing MD maintains *variability* of the missing data, preserves *relationships* among variables, and incorporates appropriate *uncertainty* by observing the variability of the multiple imputed datasets (Tabachnick & Fidell, 2006).

To perform MI using the SPSS Missing Values add-on module, the basic steps are: (1) Perform MI to create the MI dataset, (2) activate the MI dataset for analysis by splitting it on the new variable *Imputation*, (3) perform analysis using SPSS procedures that work with MI data, and (4) use pooled outcomes as final analysis results. These steps are expanded somewhat below, and detailed descriptions can be found in the IBM SPSS Missing Values 20 manual at ftp://public.dhe.ibm.com/software/analytics/spss/documentation/statistics/20.0/en/client/Manuals/IBM_SPSS_Missing_Values.pdf

First, perform multiple imputations by clicking "Analyze>Multiple>Imputation>Impute Missing Data Values" from the menu at the top of the screen. Then select at least two variables and up to all variables for the imputations; select the number of imputations, i.e., the number of imputed datasets to be created (the default is 5); and specify the output file. Use the "Method" tab to specify how data are to be imputed. The created dataset will consist of the original dataset with missing values plus one imputed dataset for each selected number of imputations, each with the same cases and variables as defined in the original dataset plus a variable called *Imputation_*.

Second, for analysis, the dataset created by MI must be "split" using the *Imputation_* variable. This can be done by choosing "Data > Split File," then selecting "Compare groups" and selecting *Imputation_* as the variable to group cases on. Alternatively, the file is split on *Imputation_* when "markings" is turned on. This also causes an icon to display next to each type of procedure that works with MI datasets and supports pooling of outcomes.

Third, employ the SPSS analytic procedures that work with MI datasets; these produce an output for each imputed dataset and a pooled output that takes into account variations across the imputations. MI output is controlled using a new tab on the Options dialog. The specific statistics pooled varies by analysis procedure. Pooled outputs are either "naïve" (only the pooled parameter is available) or "univariate" (the pooled parameter and various related statistics are provided, such as its standard error, *p*-value, confidence interval, effective degrees of freedom, and pooling diagnostics, e.g., relative increase in variance). Finally, use the pooled outputs as the analysis results.

A description of the mathematics involved in the generation of imputed data in statistical software is beyond the scope of this chapter. However, MI provides adequate results even in the presence of low sample sizes or high rates of MD (Schafer & Graham, 2002). Therefore, MI is a highly effective strategy for MFT clinical research. The number of imputations needed for good estimations have been suggested to be as low as 3 to 5 (Rubin, 1996), but more recent investigations suggest 25 or more (Johnson & Young, 2010), with more imputations, on the order of 100, required for large proportions of MD (Graham, Olchowski, & Gilreath, 2007). Thus, MFT researchers might want to consider 25 as a typical effective choice.

Note that the investigator should not just enter values in imputed datasets to recode out-of-range values or to round fractional values to whole numbers, largely because this can bias the estimates (Horton, Lipsitz, & Parzen, 2003). The imputation model assigns values based on the covariance matrix, and altering these values will create inaccuracies in imputed data values that *cannot be viewed as equivalent to observed data*, but rather as values to facilitate the covariance-based analyses (Johnson & Young, 2010).

It is also important to include dependent variables in the imputation model—while it may seem like some form of cheating to impute missing outcomes, MD algorithms do not make a distinction between dependent and independent variables. Thus, all variables in the model should be included in the imputation (Graham, 2009). Any variables not included in the imputation are set to have zero correlation with the other variables in the model, so excluding the dependent variable would mean that the imputations are conducted under the assumption that the outcome is not related to the independent variable (Johnson & Young, 2010), biasing that relationship to be smaller than it truly is (Graham). Thus, after imputation, it may be desirable to omit cases with missing values for the dependent variable (MI then deletion, or MID), especially if the number of such cases is as large as 20% to 50% (von Hippel, 2007). However, analysis has demonstrated that for large numbers of imputed datasets, such as 25, MI and MID yield very similar results, even with high levels of MD (Johnson & Young).

Full Information Maximum Likelihood Estimation

The maximum likelihood approach does not impute datasets. Instead, it provides parameter estimates and standard errors based on the complete and incomplete cases (Collins et al., 2001). ML estimation selects parameter values that maximize the probability that the observed data would occur; this complicated computation is generally performed by expectation maximization algorithms (Johnson & Young, 2010). FIML has evolved for use in SEM software to maximize the likelihood of a specified model (Johnson & Young). Since *MI is data based* and *FIML is model based*, parameter estimates may vary for different models in FIML, whereas they are consistent for MI, making MI more attractive for use by multiple researchers (Olinsky et al., 2003).

FIML has the advantage that it handles MD and provides parameter estimates and standard errors in a single step, with accuracies similar to MI with a large number of imputations (Graham, 2009). But FIML has the disadvantage that to use it, current software written for complete-cases scenarios will have to be completely rewritten to handle MD; currently, FIML is most commonly available in SEM software (Graham). Since MFT clinical research typically uses samples that are often not large enough to employ SEM effectively, MI would more often be the technique of choice. Also, FIML does not easily allow the inclusion of auxiliary variables that can substantially improve imputation models (Collins et al., 2001), as described in the following section.

Adding Auxiliary Variables to Improve Imputation

Modeling of missing values can be improved substantially by thoughtful inclusion of auxiliary variables, which are variables that are related to, but not one of, the variables in the central analysis (Collins et al., 2001). Appropriate selection of auxiliary variables is determined by the researcher's knowledge of the subject area. When these variables are highly correlated ($r > .50$) with those in the central analysis that contain MD, they can add substantially to the accuracy of imputation (Graham, 2009). Also, note that any variables *not* included in the imputation model are assumed in the analysis to have zero correlation with those in the model; this clearly impacts subsequent analyses if omitted variables are actually highly correlated with those under imputation (Graham). On the other hand, auxiliary variables are not always crucial (Johnson & Young, 2010). Including them in the imputation model does no harm but may help substantially (Collins et al.). With current software, it is a much simpler matter to include auxiliary variables with MI, in which imputation is done before analysis, than with FIML, in which it is done in a single step (Graham et al., 2007).

Considerations for Missingness that Is MNAR

For MNAR MD, the pattern of missingness is related to the values that are missing. Thus, one way to deal with this type of MD is to incorporate a model of that relationship. Models such as a logical decision process and a mathematical expression relate the presence of missingness to likely missing values, possibly using other observed variables. A number of models propose to do this (see Schafer & Graham, 2002). The best models employ expert knowledge of how the missingness is related to the values that are missing. Say that a researcher knows that noncompleters of a set of therapy sessions usually fall into one of two categories: doing very well or doing very poorly in meeting goals of therapy. If a variable in the data, such as improvement by the third session, indicates the more likely of these outcomes, then investigators could model the relationship to logically impute missing outcome values, which could be particularly useful if examining relationships between outcomes and early treatment strategies.

Reporting Missing Data and the Strategies Used to Account for Them

Current reports of research in the family science literature tend to include scanty, if any, information about MD. In response to the call for evidence-based therapy, researchers should describe the nature of MD in their study and the steps employed to account for them. We recommend that the methods section of a published paper should detail the MD in each variable, the MD method and software used, the imputation model, and the number of imputations (if using MI).

Conclusions

As scientists attend to the conceptual and practical implications of missingness in quantitative studies, marriage and family therapists will continue to grapple with ways to appropriately respond to the impact that MD may have on the understanding and interpretation of the phenomenon being evaluated. Clinicians can also benefit from considering the role that missingness may play in employing a systemic approach to helping families respond to the challenges of daily living.

References

Allison, P. D. (2001). *Missing data*. Thousand Oaks, CA: Sage.

Andridge, R. R., & Little, R. J. A. (2010). A review of hot deck imputation for survey non-response. *International Statistical Review, 78*, 40–64.

Brick, J. M., & Kalton, G. (1996). Handling missing data in survey research. *Statistical Methods in Medical Research 5*, 215–238.

Collins, L. M., Schafer, J. L., & Kam, C. M. (2001). A comparison of inclusive and restrictive strategies in modern missing-data procedures. *Psychological Methods, 6*, 330–351.

Enders, C. K. (2010). *Applied missing data analysis*. New York: Guilford Press.

Goodman, J. S., & Blum, T. C. (1996). Assessing the non-random effects of subject attrition in longitudinal research. *Journal of Management-Research Methods & Analysis, 22*, 627–652.

Graham, J. W. (2009). Missing data analysis: Making it work in the real world. *Annual Review of Psychology, 60*, 549–576.

Graham, J. W., Olchowski, A. E., & Gilreath, T. D. (2007). How many imputations are really needed? Some practical clarifications of multiple imputation theory. *Prevention Science, 8*, 206–213.

Graham, J. W., Taylor, B. J., Olchowski, A. E., & Cumsille, P. E. (2006). Planned missing data designs in psychological research. *Psychological Methods, 11*, 323–343.

Horton, N. J., Lipsitz, S. R., & Parzen, M. (2003). A potential for bias when rounding in multiple imputation. *American Statistician, 57*, 229–232.

Johnson, D. R., & Young, R. (2010). Toward best practices in analyzing datasets with missing data: Comparisons and recommendations. *Journal of Marriage and Family, 73*, 926–945.

Kim, J. K., & Fuller, W. (2004). Fractional hot deck imputation. *Biometrika, 91*, 559–578. doi: 10.1093/biomet/91.3.559

Little, R. J. A. (1988). A test of missing completely at random for multivariate data with missing values. *Journal of the American Statistical Association, 83*, 1198–1202.

Little, R. J. A. (1992). Regression with missing X's: A review. *Journal of the American Statistical Association, 87*, 1227–1238.

Little, R. J. A., & Rubin, D. B. (1987). *Statistical analysis with missing data*. New York: Wiley.

Little, R. J. A., & Rubin, D. B. (2002). *Statistical analysis with missing data* (2nd ed.). New York: Wiley.

Malhotra, N. K. (1987). Analyzing marketing research data with incomplete information on the dependent variable. *Journal of Marketing Research, 24*, 74–84.

McKnight, P. E., McKnight, K. M., Sidani, S., & Figueredo, A. J. (2007). *Missing data: A gentle introduction*. New York: Guilford Press.

Olinsky, A., Chen, S., & Harlow, L. (2003). The comparative efficacy of imputation methods for missing data in structural equation modeling. European Journal of Operational Research, 151, 53–79.

Paul, C., Mason, W., McCaffrey, D., & Fox, S. (2008). A cautionary case study of approaches to the treatment of missing data. *Statistical Methods and Applications, 17,* 351–372.

Pleis, J., R., Dahlhamer, J. M., & Meyer, P. S. (2007, August). Unfolding the answers? Income nonresponse and income brackets in the National Health Interview Survey. Proceedings of the 2006 Joint Statistical Meetings [CD-ROM]. American Statistical Association, Alexandria, Virginia.

Raghunathan, T. E. (2004). What do we do with missing data? Some options for analysis of incomplete data. *Annual Review of Public Health, 25,* 99–117.

Rao, J. N. K., & Shao, J. (1992). Jackknife variance estimation with survey data under hot deck imputation. *Biometrika, 79,* 811–822.

Roth, P. L. (1994). Missing data: A conceptual review for applied psychologists. *Personnel Psychology, 47,* 537–560.

Roth, P. L., Switzer, F. S., & Switzer, D. M. (1999). Missing data in multiple item scales: A Monte Carlo analysis of missing data techniques. *Organizational Research Methods, 2,* 211–232.

Rubin, D. B. (1976). Inference and missing data. *Biometrika, 63,* 581–592.

Rubin, D. B. (1987). *Multiple imputation for nonresponse in surveys.* New York: Wiley.

Rubin, D. B. (1996). Multiple imputation after 18+ years. *Journal of the American Statistical Association, 91,* 473–489.

Schafer, J. L., & Graham, J. W. (2002). Missing data: Our view of the state of the art. *Psychological Methods, 7,* 147–177.

Schafer, J. L., & Schenker, N. (2000). Inference with imputed conditional means. *Journal of the American Statistical Association, 95,* 144–154.

Tabachnick, B. G., & Fidell, L. S. (2006). *Using multivariate statistics* (5th ed.). Boston: Allyn and Bacon.

von Hippel, P. (2007). Regression with missing Ys: An improved strategy for analyzing multiply imputed data. *Sociological Methodology, 37,* 83–117.

Ward, T. J., & Clark, H. T. (1991). A reexamination of public-versus-private-school achievement: The case for missing data. *Journal for Educational Research, 84,* 153–163.

22

MEDIATION AND MODERATION

Conceptual Foundations and Analytical Applications

Jared R. Anderson, Jared A. Durtschi, Kristy L. Soloski, and Matthew D. Johnson

Imagine that a colleague asks you to define what a mediator variable and a moderator variable are. Would you know what to say? Now imagine that this same person asks you to provide a detailed explanation of how to test both mediation and moderation models in a way that is in keeping with the most current and advanced recommendations by experts on the topic. Would you feel comfortable answering the question, or would you attempt to somehow defer? It is clear that there is quite a bit of confusion about tests of mediation and moderation among researchers (Baron & Kenny, 1986; Frazier, Tix, & Barron, 2004; Holmbeck, 1997; Whisman & McClelland, 2005), including those studying couples and families. It is unfortunate that mediation and moderation continue to remain so obscure because these tests have so much to offer in advancing current knowledge, theory, intervention, and policy. Our purpose in writing this chapter is to clarify conceptually what these tests are, provide examples of their use, and provide detailed information on how to conduct these tests.

In order to further advance the study of couples and families, it is very important to understand processes, mechanisms, and conditions that impact the outcomes of interest to couples and families. Family therapy researchers should no longer be satisfied with just knowing that variable X (e.g., negative behavior) is associated with variable Y (e.g., relationship satisfaction). We need to know more about how this happens and under what circumstances. It is less helpful to do a study on *whether* negative behaviors influence relationship satisfaction, but more helpful to understand *under what conditions* negative behaviors may actually help a relationship (i.e., moderation) or the underlying process of *how* negative behaviors impact relationship satisfaction (i.e., mediation). Further advancements in understanding mediators and moderators will help our field become increasingly mature and sophisticated, and it will help us make meaningful advances in theory (Aguinis, Boik, & Pierce, 2001). These tests of mediation and moderation are relatively simple, both conceptually and analytically, and allow further insight and depth to understanding outcomes of interest. Whatever your research area, it is probable that you are interested in predicting an outcome, knowing the process for how this outcome is affected, and understanding when and for whom it has the strongest prediction. Although mediation and moderation have existed as methodologies for quite some time, there have been important recent advances in how to test them that should be reviewed, understood, and used in future research. These advances, as well as definitions and best practices in conducting tests of mediation and moderation, are the focus of this chapter.

Overview of Mediation

Mediation provides insights into the mechanism(s) by which an independent variable (X) affects or causes the dependent variable (Y). The assumption inherent within this statement is that there is a *direct* relationship between the independent and dependent variables, that X predicts or causes Y. As researchers, we are interested in this direct relationship (X → Y), but often we are more interested in the *mechanism(s)* through which the independent variable (X) exerts its influence on the dependent variable (Y) *indirectly* through its relationship with one or more mediators (M). Mediation analysis is therefore interested in *quantifying and testing* these indirect effects. As we will see later, it is possible, and even recommended, that researchers test the *indirect effects* (X → M → Y) in their models even when their results show that the *direct effect* (X → Y) is nonsignificant. For this reason, there is some debate about the proper use of the term *mediation* versus *indirect effect* (see Mathieu & Taylor, 2006). Following research by Hayes, Preacher, and Myers (2011), we use the terms *mediation* and *indirect effects* more or less interchangeably in this chapter.

Researchers interested in the process of marriage and family therapy will want to become familiar with testing mediation. Although it is vitally important to know *that* a given approach is effective, it is also important to know *how* or *why* an approach is effective. Mediation analyses help us to understand the mechanisms or processes by which a given treatment approach influences positive client outcomes. The use of mediation analysis in clinical research is indispensable and can answer a key question of interest to marriage and family therapy researchers and practitioners: "How do our treatments work?"

Each clinical approach offers a specific protocol for ameliorating client distress. Each approach is likely successful in improving client outcomes, to some degree, but it is often empirically unclear what constitutes the key mechanisms of change for many approaches. In other words, what specifically is the treatment doing that helps? Progenitors of the various models have posited a variety of mechanisms responsible for therapeutic change, such as restructuring problematic interactions and discovering the solutions clients already possess. Mediation analysis allows for those mechanisms to be tested empirically. Uncovering the key mechanisms responsible for symptom relief allows for treatments to become more precise and effective, rendering them more useful to clients and practitioners alike. Mediation is a versatile tool that can be used in a variety of ways in clinical research. For example, a study sought to determine whether multisystemic therapy creates positive parenting changes that might lead to a reduction in adolescent externalizing behaviors (Dekovic, Asscher, Manders, Prins, & van der Laan, 2012). The results revealed that participating in multisystemic therapy led to increases in parental sense of competence, which predicted changes in positive discipline, which predicted decreases in externalizing behavior among adolescents. This model was able to link together multiple mediators between intervention and outcome.

Mediation analysis is also an important part of basic research. For example, Karney and Bradbury (1995) developed the vulnerability-stress-adaptation model as a way of understanding the mechanisms through which enduring vulnerabilities (e.g., early life experiences, mental health and personality factors) and stress influence marital quality and stability. They proposed that adaptive processes (e.g., communication, problem-solving skills, ways in which couples provide support to each other) mediate the relationship among enduring vulnerabilities, stress, and marital quality. Thus, their conceptual model provides a multitude of hypotheses that can be tested using mediation analysis. Figure 22.1 includes examples of both single and multiple mediator models that could be tested based on the vulnerability-stress-adaptation model. In Figure 22.1a, the independent variable, work stress, is thought to influence the dependent variable, marital quality. This is a simple, direct relationship. In Figures 22.1b and 22.1c, two mechanisms through which work stress influences

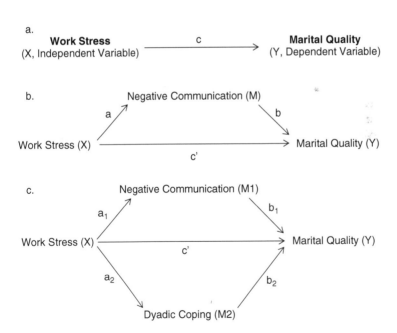

Figure 22.1 Single and multiple mediator models.

marital quality are proposed. In 22.1b, it is hypothesized that work stress leads to more negative communication and that therefore more negative communication is likely to lead to lower marital quality. Mediation analysis allows us to test whether the pathway from work stress to marital quality, through negative communication (an indirect path), is significant, but it also allows us to test whether the path from work stress to marital quality is also significant (a direct path).

Considerations in Designing a Mediation Study

By definition, mediation denotes a causal process. Because causality is the result of study design and not statistical analysis, researchers need to keep their study design in mind when interpreting their results. As Hayes and colleagues (2011) aptly put it, "Use your analysis to inform your thinking rather than as a substitute for thinking" (p. 436). Experimental designs provide the strongest designs for making causal inferences (see Shadish, Cook, & Campbell, 2002). In addition, longitudinal designs, in which each variable of interest is measured across at least three time points, taking into consideration the temporal relationship of the variables and not just their temporal measurement (Mathieu & Taylor, 2006), can also help to strengthen causal inference. Just as causality is determined by design and not statistical analysis, temporal ordering of variables should be directly linked to sound theory, as temporal measurement alone does not justify a sound rationale for temporal ordering. Although experimental designs and to some degree longitudinal designs are the strongest from which to make causal inferences, many other designs, including quasi-experimental designs, two-wave longitudinal designs, and cross-sectional designs, have been used to test for mediation. Researchers using these nonexperimental designs in tests of mediation need to be clear that they are testing *associations* between their X and Y variables rather than testing a causal pathway, given the design of their study. A good theoretical framework then becomes the strongest basis for proposing a particular ordering of the independent, mediating, and dependent variables.

Approaches for Testing Mediation

Mediation analyses can be performed using a number of analytical approaches, including multiple regression, structural equation modeling (SEM), and multi-level modeling (MLM). Although there are many other methods of mediation-analysis strategies available (MacKinnon, 2008; Preacher & Hayes, 2008), we focus on the three most common: the causal steps approach, the product of coefficients approach, and bootstrapping, with bootstrapping currently being the overwhelmingly preferred method for testing mediation (Hayes, 2013; Hayes et al., 2011; MacKinnon; Shrout & Bolger, 2002; Williams & MacKinnon, 2008). These three methods can be used with basic statistical programs such as SPSS and SAS.

Causal steps approach. The causal steps approach (Baron & Kenny, 1986) is the most common method for testing mediation in psychological research (MacKinnon, Fairchild, & Fritz, 2007; Rucker, Preacher, Tormala, & Petty, 2011). In this approach, mediation is established by the following four steps. First, there must be a statistically significant relationship between the independent (X) and dependent variables (Y) (path c in Figure 22.1). Second, the independent variable must be significantly related to the proposed mediator (path a in the model). Third, the mediator must be significantly related to the dependent variable (path b in the model). Fourth, when paths a and b are controlled in the model, the relationship between the independent and dependent variables, path c′, should be non-significant or at least attenuated. In a multiple regression framework, these steps are carried out through three separate regressions: regressing the mediator on the independent variable, regressing the dependent variable on the independent variable, and regressing the dependent variable on both the independent variable and the mediator (Baron & Kenny).

Despite its continued widespread use, the causal steps approach is *no longer recommended* (Hayes, 2009, 2013; Hayes et al., 2011; MacKinnon, 2008; Rucker et al., 2011; Zhao, Lynch, & Chen, 2010). At least three arguments have been made against using the causal steps approach when conducting mediation analyses. First, the causal steps approach requires the researcher to conduct a series of analyses on multiple hypotheses to determine whether mediation is a tenable assumption. After conducting these separate analyses, the researcher is left to decide whether there is mediation or no mediation, rather than being able to report an estimate of the indirect effect (i.e., the pathway through which the independent variable affects the dependent variable through one or more mediators). Thus, the causal steps approach "encourages researchers to not think about effect size, and it does not allow for the construction of a confidence interval for the indirect effect to acknowledge the uncertainty in the estimation process" (Hayes et al., 2011, p. 446). Second, simulation studies have shown the causal steps approach to be among the lowest in power of the available methods for testing mediation (Fritz & Mackinnon, 2007; MacKinnon, Lockwood, & Williams, 2004). Finally, the requirement of a significant X–Y relationship before testing for mediation has been found to be too stringent (Kenny, Kashy, & Bolger, 1998; MacKinnon, Lockwood, Hoffman, West, & Sheets, 2002) and should not preclude the researcher from testing for mediation in the absence of a significant direct effect. For example, significant indirect effects in the presence of a nonsignificant direct effect are more likely to occur when the sample size is small and when suppressor effects are present (see Rucker et al., 2011 for more details). This does not give researchers license for the indiscriminate testing of indirect effects, but where there is strong theory and/or prior empirical support for a relationship between your independent and dependent variables, especially in the presence of low(er) power, it is strongly recommended that researchers test the indirect relationships in their model. For these reasons, researchers should not employ the causal steps approach when conducting mediation, especially when more powerful alternatives exist.

Product of coefficients approach. The product of coefficients approach provides a point estimate of the indirect effect (*ab* pathway from Figure 22.1b) from which the standard error of this point estimate (e.g., the standard deviation of the sampling distribution of *ab*) can be estimated and used in hypothesis testing to determine whether the indirect effect is statistically significant. The most common from among these procedures is the Sobel test (1982), and it is generally considered a superior test of mediation than the causal steps approach. There are several different formulas available for estimating the standard error of *ab*, but in practice the differences between these approaches are small (Preacher & Hayes, 2004). Formulas are available for estimating the standard errors of simple and multiple mediator models, as well as specific indirect effects and total indirect effects. Although point estimates of the indirect effects and their standard errors can be calculated by hand, there are several online calculators (for example, www.danielsoper.com/ statcalc3/calc.aspx?id=31; http://quantpsy.org/sobel/sobel.htm) that have been developed that can quickly and easily test whether there is a significant indirect effect with some basic information from your regression models (*a*, *b*, and the standard error of *a* and *b*) inputted into the online calculator.

This approach, though more powerful than the causal steps approach, assumes that the indirect effect has a normally distributed sampling (Hayes, 2009; Preacher & Hayes, 2004). Unfortunately, this assumption is not justified in small samples, as the sampling distribution of the indirect effect tends to be skewed and kurtotic (Bollen & Stine, 1990). This distribution approaches normality as the sample size increases, though some have argued against using the Sobel test for sample sizes of less than 500. Therefore, in large samples (>500), results are similar to that of bootstrapping procedures; but in smaller samples, bootstrapping is the preferred method.

Bootstrapping. Bootstrapping is currently the method of choice when testing mediation, because unlike the product of coefficients approach, bootstrapping does not rely on the restrictive assumption that the sampling distribution of the indirect effect is normally distributed. Bootstrapping is referred to as a "nonparametric resampling procedure." (See Preacher & Hayes, 2008 for a more in-depth discussion of the merits of bootstrapping procedures.) So how does bootstrapping actually work? Say you have a sample of 200 clients in your data set and you request 2,000 bootstrap samples. You are in effect asking that your software program "create" 2,000 samples based on your original sample of 200. It does this by "sampling with replacement" in that it randomly selects someone from your sample, say client #45, then returns client #45 to the pool of 200 clients and selects another. Maybe client #132 is selected next and returned to the sample of 200, and another client is selected. This strategy is repeated until a sample of 200 clients is developed, of which clients #45 and #132 may be represented only once, but possibly twice, three times, or even more frequently. This process is repeated 2,000 times, so instead of one sample of 200 clients, you now have 2,000 samples of 200 clients. These 2,000 samples are then used to generate the point estimate of ab (indirect effect) by taking the mean ab of the 2,000 samples. Likewise, the estimated standard error (which is used to test the significance of the indirect effect) is the mean standard deviation of the 2,000 ab estimates. So, unlike the product of coefficients approach that assumes that the distribution of the standard error of the indirect effect is normally distributed, bootstrapping "eliminates the need for such assumptions about the shape of the sampling distribution because it relies on an empirical approximation of the sampling distribution by mimicking the sampling process" (Hayes et al., 2011, p. 450).

To make inferences about the significance of one or multiple indirect effects, it is generally suggested that bootstrap confidence intervals be utilized. This is accomplished by sorting the 2,000 bootstrap estimates that you have just generated from lowest to highest and then finding the estimates that represent the "lower level" (LL) confidence interval and the "upper level" (UL) confidence interval using the following formulas: LL = $(k/100)$ $(50 - €/2)$ and UL = $(k/100)$ $(50 + €/2) + 1$, where k equals the number of bootstraps and € equals the confidence interval level. In our example, the 95% confidence interval for 2,000 bootstraps would be the point estimate of the 50th and 1,951st scores in the sorted distribution of 2,000 estimates. This approach is called the percentile bootstrap. Given that the mean ab point estimate is not usually equidistant from these two percentile scores, it is often referred to as an asymmetric interval estimate. There is some evidence to suggest that bias corrected (BC) or bias corrected and accelerated (BCa) confidence intervals yield more accurate results than the percentile bootstrap, and either of these are generally recommended (Preacher & Hayes, 2008). If zero is not included in the 95% (or 99%, if preferred) BC or BCa bootstrapped confidence intervals, you can conclude that the indirect effect is significantly different from zero.

How to Test for Mediation

Thankfully, most software programs, including M*plus*, Amos, SPSS, SAS, and Stata, to name a few, now include bootstrapping procedures as part of their software packages. In addition, SPSS and SAS bootstrapping macros have been developed that can be downloaded for free (http://quantpsy.org/sobel/sobel.htm and www.afhayes.com/spss-sas-and-mplus-macros-and-code.html). Mediation analyses within MLM models are also advancing (Zhang, Zyphur, & Preacher, 2009), as are multilevel SEM approaches to mediation (Preacher, Zhang, & Zyphur, 2011; Preacher, Zyphur, & Zhang, 2010). The two websites given above are a treasure trove of information, examples, and various macros for conducting a variety of mediation analyses, including single and multiple mediator models; models including covariates; continuous, dichotomous, or multicategorical independent variables; multiple independent variables simultaneously; mediation models with nonlinear paths; moderated mediation and mediated moderation, among others. We limit our examples here to syntax related to a multiple mediator model (Figure 22.1c) for both SPSS and M*plus*. If you have a large enough sample size (most experts suggest at least 100 participants), an SEM framework is always preferable to a multiple regression framework (see Kline, 2011 for details). In our multiple mediator model, we are proposing that work stress exerts its influence on marital quality through two potential mediators, negative communication and dyadic coping. Theoretically, we hypothesize that higher levels of work stress will lead to higher levels of negative communication and, thus, lower levels of marital quality. Likewise, higher levels of work stress will lead to lower levels of dyadic coping, leading to lower levels of marital quality. In order to test this, we first need to download the "INDIRECT" macro from Hayes's website given above and use the following syntax for IBM SPSS (each macro is complemented by a set of instructions including related syntax as well as published and/or unpublished articles related to the procedure):

INDIRECT Y = mquality/X = wstress/M = ncomm dycoping /C = 0/ CONTRAST = 1/CONF = 95/PERCENT = 1/BC = 1/BCA = 1/BOOT = 5000.

The INDIRECT command specifies your test of mediation, followed by the variable names for your dependent (Y), independent (X), and mediating (M1, M2) variables. The C states that there are zero covariates, but they could easily be included in the model if desired and would be listed directly after the mediators. The "CONTRAST = 1" command signifies that you want to conduct a contrast between your two specific indirect effects (i.e., determine whether the pathway from wstress to mquality through ncomm is stronger than the pathway from wstress to mqual through dycoping). The CONF command sets the level of your confidence interval and the PERCENT, BC, and BCA allow you to see the percentile, bias corrected, and bias corrected and accelerated bootstrap confidence intervals. Finally, the BOOT command signifies the number of bootstrap samples you want to generate (typically the recommended minimum is 1,000, although Hayes, 2009 and Preacher & Hayes, 2008 recommend 5,000). The output file will provide you with information related to total effect of the independent variable (IV) on the dependent variable (DV) (c path), the direct effect of the IV on the DV (c' path), the IV to the mediators (a paths), the direct effects of the mediators on the DV (b paths), the indirect effects of the IV on the DV through the proposed mediators (ab paths), and the percentile, bias corrected, and bias corrected and accelerated confidence intervals. As discussed previously, mediation is assumed when the confidence intervals of each ab pathway does not include zero.

We could test this same mediation model within an SEM framework. However, bootstrapping procedures cannot be done at this time in Amos when there is missing data; *Mplus* can bootstrap with missing data. Sample syntax for *Mplus* could include:

TITLE: Two-mediator example with contrast
DATA: FILE IS example.dat;

```
VARIABLE:  NAMES ARE wstress ncomm dycoping mqual;
           USEVARIABLES wstress ncomm dycoping mqual;
ANALYSIS:  BOOTSTRAP = 5000;
MODEL:     ncomm ON wstress (a1); dycoping ON wstress (a2); mqual ON
           ncomm (b1); mqual ON dycoping (b2); mqual ON wstress; ncomm
           WITH dycoping;
MODEL INDIRECT: mqual IND ncomm wstress;
                mqual IND dycoping wstress;
MODEL CONSTRAINT: NEW (a1b1 a2b2 con);
     a1b1=a1*b1; a2b2=a2*b2; con=a1b1-a2b2;
OUTPUT: CINTERVAL (BCBOOTSTRAP);
```

Utilizing this syntax will provide the same test as above, including an estimation of the total, direct, and indirect pathways, as well as testing the contrast hypothesis that the two indirect effects are equal. In addition, just as in model testing within a regression or SEM framework, the statistical significance of a coefficient is not as meaningful as the effect size. Recent advances have provided ways to calculate the effect size of the indirect effects (see Preacher & Kelley, 2011), and best practice in mediation analysis reporting is moving toward the inclusion of effect size estimates. The research community is extraordinarily generous when it comes to sharing ideas and syntax. Therefore, when you get stuck, the two websites above are extremely helpful, and there are literally dozens of additional webpages with tutorials that can be searched for information related to mediation analyses in Amos, M*plus*, and hierarchical linear modeling (HLM) for a variety of model and data types. Finally, for more in-depth information on this topic, as well as information related to reporting results of mediation analyses, see the studies by Hayes (2013) and MacKinnon (2008).

Overview of Moderation

Moderation occurs when the magnitude of the relationship between two variables can be changed by including a moderator variable in the model. This is of great importance to researchers, clinicians, and those involved in making policies to know under what circumstances something may have a desired effect. The importance of research on moderation was underscored by Cohen, Cohen, West, and Aiken (2003), who said, "It is safe to say that the testing of interactions is at the very heart of theory testing in the social sciences" (p. 255). Perhaps, for example, it would be helpful to know, when working with couples, that teaching the speaker-listener technique might not benefit couples who already communicate well, but those couples with the poorest communication may benefit from this intervention (Braithwaite & Fincham, 2011). Our understanding of couples and couples therapy could improve dramatically with additional information about under what circumstances (e.g., gender, age, race, presenting problems) a given intervention may or may not be helpful.

It is a clear sign that the study of relationships is advancing when, after direct effects have been found, we then move on to explanation and theory testing regarding those relations (Frazier et al., 2004; Hoyle & Kenny, 1999). Let us examine a few recent findings related to moderation and couples' relationship satisfaction. There are a number of "positive processes" that most of us would consider helpful for couples from an intuitive standpoint but that actually do not help and in fact make things worse across time in studies of newlywed couples. For example, more positive expectations, more positive attributions, less negative behavior, and more forgiveness were only helpful in couples who faced infrequent and minor problems. In couples facing more frequent and severe problems, less positive expectations, less positive attributions, more negative behavior, and less forgiveness most effectively maintained satisfaction among spouses because those processes helped spouses acknowledge, address, and resolve their problems (McNulty, 2010). Before these moderators were identified, well-intentioned therapists could have guided couples to do something that was less effective for their particular circumstance. In this example, the predictors (expectations, attributions, negative behavior, and forgiveness) have an impact on relationship satisfaction, but that impact is changed contingent upon the moderators (frequency and severity of problems newlywed couples are facing). See Figure 22.2 for a visual depiction of this moderation example.

There are many potential tests of moderation that could be done in clinical research on couples and families in therapy. For example, do predictive relationships in clinical treatment work differentially based on clients' hope, race, gender, age, income, problem severity, relationship length, parental status, geographic location, religiosity, or family structure? Further, in clinical research, do predicted treatment outcomes vary by the clinicians' age, gender, clinical experience, theory, clinical training, expectations for treatment, or therapists' self-care? Tests of moderation can be conducted with any combination of categorical or continuous variables.

How to Test for Moderation

The estimation of moderation with continuous variables can be done in a similar way in a multiple regression, SEM, or MLM analysis: simply by multiplying the moderator variable by the predictor variable to create an interaction variable,

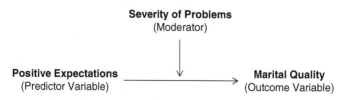

Figure 22.2 Severity of problems moderates the relationship between positive expectations and marital quality.

and then including the predictor, moderator, and interaction variables as three predictors of the outcome. In SEM, the moderator can be included within the model for any outcome of interest as long as the predictor variable, moderator variable, and the interaction variable are each included as predictors of that particular outcome variable (see Kline, 2011, pp. 327–333). Moderation can also be tested within MLM, also called HLM, by adding the predictor variable, moderator variable, and interaction variable as predictors of the same outcome, at the same level. However, because most of these tests of moderation are currently done in SPSS, we will give a more detailed account of how to do this in that framework, though most of these steps directly apply to tests of moderation in SEM and HLM as well. There are eight steps to performing a moderator analysis.

In *Step 1*, as in all research, we need to have a well-defined theory guiding why variable M will moderate variables X and Y. It is also important to specify the direction you believe this moderator will have on the relationship between X and Y. For example, will the moderator enhance and strengthen the relationship between X and Y, or weaken and buffer the relationship between X and Y?

Step 2 is to check that there is enough statistical power to detect the moderation effect. In tests of moderation, power is reduced by many things, including a smaller sample size, unequal sizes between different levels of the moderator (e.g., 10 males, 90 females), error variances across groups being unequal, small effect sizes in the population, measurement error, range restrictions among predictors and moderators (e.g., having more extreme values at the high and low end increases power), and the outcome variable having a smaller range than the range of the interaction variable (e.g., when the interaction term has a range of 50, and the outcome variable has a range of 5, power is reduced; Russell & Bobko, 1992). Measurement error is compounded in tests of moderation. For example, if variable X has a reliability of 0.7 and variable M has a reliability of 0.8, the reliability is 0.56 for the interaction term ($0.7 \times 0.8 = 0.56$). This is further compounded when the interaction is among three variables. The power for assessing an interaction is reduced by up to half when the reliabilities are 0.80 rather than 1.00 (Aiken & West, 1991). However, conducting tests of moderation in SEM has the advantage of accounting for measurement error in the model and reducing this weakness (e.g., Aguinis, 1995; Frazier et al., 2004; Holmbeck, 1997).

Step 3 is to appropriately code all categorical variables, such as gender and race. For example, consider a race variable with three possible responses (e.g., Asian American, African American, and European American) used as a predictor of relationship quality. Frazier et al. (2004) recommended using dummy codes (0, 1) when comparisons with a control or base group are desired (e.g., comparing differences in relationship quality between a reference race—African American—and the other two races). Frazier and colleagues recommended using effect codes (–1, 1) when comparisons with the grand mean are desired (e.g., testing whether Asian Americans' relationship quality was significantly different from the grand mean of relationship quality). Frazier and colleagues recommended the use of contrast codes (–½, ½) when comparisons between specific groups are desired (e.g., testing differences in relationship quality between African American and Asian American, Asian American and European American, and European American and African American). Depending on how many groups there are, there will be one less computed variable than the total number of groups. For example, if there are five races listed, there would be four coded variables for race, whereas gender would have one coded variable. All of these coded categorical variables would be included as predictors in the model. How these variables are coded has very important implications for interpreting the findings, and although dummy coding is most often used, it may not be the optimal coding scheme for your specific research question (Cohen et al., 2003).

Step 4 is to transform the variables to be used in the moderation model by mean centering or standardizing the continuous predictor and moderator variables. The purpose of mean centering or standardizing predictor and moderator variables is so that the mean of that variable will become zero. This is important for at least two reasons. First, when interpreting results from an interaction model, it is important that all other variables are understood to be at zero. Second, it is much easier to interpret the results of a significant interaction beta coefficient when the variables have a mean that equals zero. This is explained in greater detail below.

Mean centering is accomplished by simply subtracting the mean from the variable. Let's imagine we have a continuous variable, hope, with a mean score of 12.5. To create a new variable of hope that is mean centered in SPSS (i.e., mc_hope), the syntax would look like this: COMPUTE mc_hope = hope—12.5. However, standardizing by using z-score transformations makes it much simpler to create the figure that plots the interaction, covered in Step 8, and therefore this method is highly recommended. To create a new standardized variable using SPSS syntax, you could use the following formula for variable X: [(X—Mean of X)/standard deviation of X]. In SPSS, however, this is as easy as checking a box. Simply go to "Analyze," then to "Descriptive Statistics," then again to "Descriptives," then highlight and move the variables you want standardized to the Variable(s) column on the right and check the box "Save standardized values as variables" on the bottom left corner. It should be noted that you should not standardize or mean center any coded categorical variable, only continuous variables.

In *Step 5*, after the categorical variables have been coded and continuous variables have been centered or transformed into z-scores, these newly coded and transformed predictor and moderator variables will simply be multiplied together. This is done in SPSS by computing a new variable, multiplying the predictor variable by the moderator variable. If there are multiple coded categorical variables, such as 4 contrast coded race variables, there needs to be 4 interaction variables computed with each of these coded variables separately multiplied by the other predictor variable.

Step 6 is to conduct a hierarchical multiple regression, which analyzes the regression model in stages, which are called blocks. In SPSS, go to "Analyze," then "Regression," then "Linear." Next, enter the outcome variable in the box labeled "Dependent," followed by adding the transformed and coded predictor(s) and moderator variable(s) into the "Independent(s)" box. Then click on "Next" and enter the interaction(s) into the second block. Then click on "Statistics" and check the box for "R squared change," then click "Continue," and then click "OK." It is not acceptable to test moderation and not include the predictor and moderator variables in the same model with the interaction term because the products only represent the interaction when the other components (i.e., predictor and moderator) have been partialed out (Cohen, 1978). Thus, the predictor and moderator variables must always be included in the analysis prior to the interaction term.

Step 7 is to interpret the results. In evaluating the predictor and moderator variables, it is important to know that their interpretation is different than in a typical regression model that does not include an interaction term. The effects of predictors in this type of model are called "conditional effects" at the value of 0 for all the other variables in the model, and not as "main effects," as is inappropriately often done (Frazier et al., 2004; Judd, McClelland, & Culhane, 1995). In a regular regression, when interpreting any single predictor, that coefficient is understood while *holding all other variables constant.* In a regression model that includes an interaction term, when interpreting any single predictor, that coefficient is interpreted instead by understanding that *the other predictor variables in the model are at 0.* For example, imagine we want to conduct a process test of emotionally focused couples therapy that included the quality of enactments as a predictor of the outcome blamer-softening, and that this predictive relationship was proposed to be moderated by the therapeutic alliance. More specifically, let us imagine that the unstandardized regression coefficient for enactments was 0.35; we would interpret this as "For every one unit increase in enactments, scores on blamer-softening are expected to be 0.35 higher, *while therapeutic alliance is at zero.*" In a typical regression without an interaction term, the italicized portion of the previous sentence would instead read, "while holding therapeutic alliance constant." This is important to understand so we can interpret our moderation results accurately. When the predictor and moderator variables have been centered or standardized, understanding the other covariates being at 0 now has a meaning: specifically, that each beta coefficient is understood when the other covariates are at their average level. If a predictor was entered into the regression scaled 1 to 7, it does not make sense to interpret this variable at a value of 0 because that is outside of the range of this variable (Frazier et al., 2004). Because of the difference in how covariates are interpreted in a moderation model, in some cases it may be helpful to remove the interaction term when it is not significant, so other covariates are no longer conditional on being 0.

Predictor variables, or conditional effects, are interpreted by evaluating the unstandardized coefficients, never the standardized coefficients. The standardized beta coefficients in the regression output are not correctly standardized and do not generalize to moderator models, and thus should not be interpreted at all (Aiken & West, 1991; Frazier et al., 2004; Whisman & McClelland, 2005).

The benefit of conducting a hierarchical regression opposed to a normal regression is that it can test whether the addition of entering the interaction term to the equation explains significantly more variation beyond the variation accounted for by the model that only included the predictor variable and the moderator variables. In this example, block 1 included the predictor and moderator variable, and block 2 included the interaction term between them. It can be evaluated whether the interaction term explained significantly more variance in the outcome beyond the predictor and moderator variables. This can be evaluated by observing the R-square change value to see the amount of change in explained variance between the blocks, and the F-change value to determine whether this increase in explained variance was a significant increase beyond the previous block. If the interaction term is significant, it means that the moderator term had a significant effect or change on the relationship between the predictor and outcome variables.

Step 8 is to plot this interaction on a figure. A visual display of moderation can be especially helpful for understanding the interaction of two variables on an outcome variable, and to recognize the magnitude of the effect. A line or bar graph can depict the strength and direction of the interaction at various levels of the predictor and outcome variable by a function of the moderating variable. Various tools can be found online to aid with the process of creating this graph. Additionally, the slides that accompany this chapter include an Excel spreadsheet that requires you to enter the intercept, and unstandardized betas for the predictor, moderator, and interaction terms, and then the figure will be created for you. The predictor should be on the x-axis, and the outcome should be on the y-axis, and the effect of the moderator is represented by the different lines on the graph. The effect of the moderating variable is depicted within the graph as the distance between the lines at various levels of the predictor and outcome variable.

Other Types of Moderation Tests

Moderation can also be tested in a variety of ways through the flexible analysis of SEM. Moderation effects in SEM are commonly examined by testing for invariance between models. For example, a multiple-sample SEM can be conducted where the moderator (e.g., gender) is tested with an SEM that is run simultaneously for both men and women. This fully unconstrained model can then have constraints added, one at time, on path coefficients, factor loadings, means, or variance of variables constrained to be equal between men and women (Kline, 2011). Then a chi-square difference test can be conducted to determine whether the model fit became significantly worse after forcing the model to be the same between men and women. The unconstrained chi-square for model fit is then compared with the constrained model where, for example, a path coefficient is constrained to be equal for men and women. Adding one constraint adds 1 degree of freedom (df) to the SEM, and the critical ratio for a chi-square test with 1 df is 3.84. Thus, if after the constraint was added to the model, the chi-square for model fit increased more than 3.84, there is evidence that the parameter that was forced to be equal between men and women did not fit the data well because men and women significantly differ on the compared parameter. Imagine we wanted to test narrative therapy with couples to examine whether a higher frequency of externalizing conversations was related to higher scores on hope that the relationship could improve, and to test whether this relationship was moderated by gender. Let's say in a multiple-sample SEM, with male and female samples, that we tested a fully unconstrained model and obtained a model fit for chi-square of 10.0, with 6 *df.* Then we constrained the pathway from externalizing to hope to be equal between both male and female samples and obtained a model fit value for chi-square of 15, with 7 *df.* Because this chi-square value increased by more than 3.84 with 1 *df* (e.g., 15 – 10 = 5), we have evidence that this predictive pathway differs between genders. A nonsignificant chi-square value would indicate that the two paths are invariant, meaning that the two paths are not significantly different and that gender does not moderate the relationship between the predictor and outcome variables.

There is also another way to test moderation in SEM using the interaction term as a latent variable. This is explained in detail elsewhere (Kline, 2011, pp. 336–340). In short, this can be done by creating three latent variables (i.e., predictor, moderator, and interaction variables) predicting an outcome variable. The predictor and moderator variables will have their respective indicators loading onto those latent factors, as would typically be done in an SEM. The interaction latent variable is then specified by using interaction terms from among the indicators of the predictor and moderator (see Kline, 2011, p. 338 for a figure). For example, imagine that our predictor latent variable has indicators X_1 and X_2, our moderator latent variable has indicators W_1 and W_2. Then the interaction latent variable would have each of these possible interactions between factor loadings as the indicators of this latent variable, including X_1*W_1, X_1*W_2, X_2*W_1, and X_2*W_2. These interaction terms would be computed previously in SPSS. This type of model can be done in Amos by drawing such a model with these latent variables and indicators. It can also be done in M*plus* by specifying the following model syntax with outcome, Y:

MODEL: X by X_1 X_2; W by W_1 W_2; XW by X_1W_1 X_1W_2 X_2W_1 X_2W_2; Y on X W XW;

Advances in Mediation and Moderation Analyses

More advanced uses of mediation and moderation are being developed. Mediation and moderation can be tested within SEM frameworks, and they can be used in longitudinal analyses. As research on couples and families continues to progress, and the testing of MFT models in clinical settings become increasingly advanced, it will likely be much more common to see tests of mediators and moderators in the same model. Moderated mediation refers to models where the mediated relationship between X and Y varies across levels of a moderator, whereas mediated moderation refers to models where a mediator variable explains the relationship between an interaction term and the outcome (see Kline, 2011, pp. 333–335; Edwards & Lambert, 2007; Muller, Judd, & Yzerbyt, 2005; Preacher, Rucker, & Hayes, 2007). Hayes & Preacher (2013) refer to these models as conditional process models, and Hayes (2012) provides an in-depth discussion of these models, along with an overview of his SPSS and SAS macro for conducting these analyses. Moderation can also be tested in growth curve models to see whether the prediction of a trajectory is significantly changed by a moderator. This can also be done in dyadic growth curve models in SEM or HLM frameworks (see Chapter 23). In tests of dyadic models, such as the actor–partner interdependence models, moderation can also be tested as interactions between partners, or partners and treatment (Cook & Snyder, 2005). Likewise, mediation analyses in longitudinal models are common and important methods for understanding processes over time (Cheong, MacKinnon, & Khoo, 2003; Selig & Preacher, 2009).

Conclusion

Tests of mediation and moderation are vital to advancing theory and research and can help us better understand the underlying mechanism of our therapeutic approaches, as well as relationship processes that lead to human flourishing. This is an area that is rapidly advancing, but alongside this development are countless tools that will enable researchers to competently construct and test models of mediation, moderation, or both. We encourage you to stay abreast of these ongoing developments by accessing relevant literature and frequenting the very valuable websites, which often post new macros and white papers prior to publication.

References

Aguinis, H. (1995). Statistical power problems with moderated multiple regression in management research. *Journal of Management Research, 21,* 1141–1158.

Aguinis, H., Boik, R. J., & Pierce, C. A. (2001). A generalized solution for approximating the power to detect effects of categorical moderator variables using multiple regression. *Organizational Research Methods, 4,* 291–323.

Aiken, L. S., & West, S. G. (1991). *Multiple regression: Testing and interpreting interactions.* Newbury Park, CA: Sage.

Baron, R. M., & Kenny, D. A. (1986). The moderator-mediator variable distinction in social psychological research: Conceptual, strategic, and statistical considerations. *Journal of Personality and Social Psychology, 51,* 1173–1182.

Bollen, K. A., & Stine, R. (1990). Direct and indirect effects: Classical and bootstrap estimates of variability. *Sociological Methodology, 20,* 115–140.

Braithwaite, S. R., & Fincham, F. D. (2011). Computer-based dissemination: A randomized clinical trial of ePREP using the actor partner interdependence model. *Behaviour Research and Therapy, 49,* 126–131.

Cheong, J., MacKinnon, D. P., & Khoo, S. T. (2003). Investigation of mediational processes using parallel process latent growth modeling. *Structural Equation Modeling, 10,* 238–262.

Cohen, J. (1978). Partialed products *are* interactions; partialed vectors *are* curve components. *Psychological Bulletin, 85,* 858–866.

Cohen, J., Cohen, P., West, S. G., & Aiken, L. S. (2003). *Applied multiple regression/correlation analysis for the behavioral sciences* (3rd ed.). Mahwah, NJ: Erlbaum.

Cook, W. L., & Snyder, D. K. (2005). Analyzing nonindependent outcomes in couple therapy using the actor–partner interdependence model. *Journal of Family Psychology, 19,* 133–141.

Dekovic, M., Asscher, J. J., Manders, W. A., Prins, P. J. M., & van der Laan, P. (2012). Within-intervention change: Mediators of intervention effects during multisystemic therapy. *Journal of Consulting and Clinical Psychology, 80,* 574–587.

Edwards, J. R., & Lambert, L. S. (2007). Methods of integrating moderation and mediation: A general analytical framework using moderated path analysis. *Psychological Methods, 12,* 1–22.

Frazier, P. A., Tix, A. P., & Barron, K. E. (2004). Testing moderator and mediator effects in counseling psychology research. *Journal of Counseling Psychology, 51,* 115–134.

Fritz, M. S., & MacKinnon, D. P. (2007). Required sample size to detect the mediated effect. *Psychological Science, 47,* 556–572.

Hayes, A. F. (2009). Beyond Baron and Kenny: Statistical mediation analysis in the new millennium. *Communication Monographs, 76,* 408–420.

Hayes, A. F. (2012). PROCESS: A versatile computational tool for observed variable mediation, moderation, and conditional process modeling [White paper]. Retrieved from http://www.afhayes.com/public/process2012.pdf

Hayes, A. F. (2013). *Introduction to mediation, moderation, and conditional process analysis: A regression-based approach.* New York: Guilford.

Hayes, A. F., & Preacher, K. J. (2013). Conditional process modeling: Using structural equation modeling to examine contingent causal processes. In G. R. Hancock & R. O. Mueller (Eds.), *Structural equation modeling: A second course* (2nd ed.). Greenwich, CT: Information Age Publishing.

Hayes, A. F., Preacher, K. J., & Myers, T. A. (2011). Mediation and the estimation of indirect effects in political communication research. In E. P. Bucy & R. Lance Holbert (Eds.), *Sourcebook for political communication research: Methods, measures, and analytical techniques* (pp. 434–465). New York: Routledge.

Holmbeck, G. N. (1997). Toward terminological, conceptual, and statistical clarity in the study of mediators and moderators: Examples from the child-clinical and pediatric psychology literatures. *Journal of Consulting and Clinical Psychology, 65,* 599–610.

Hoyle, R. H., & Kenny, D. A. (1999). Sample size, reliability, and tests of statistical mediation. In R. Hoyle (Ed.), *Statistical strategies for small sample research* (pp. 195–222). Thousand Oaks, CA: Sage.

Judd, C. M., McClelland, G. H., & Culhane, S. E. (1995). Data analysis: Continuing issues in the everyday analysis of psychological data. *Annual Review of Psychology, 46,* 433–465.

Karney, B. R., & Bradbury, T. N. (1995). The longitudinal course of marital quality and stability: A review of research, theory, method, and research. *Psychological Bulletin, 118,* 3–34.

Kenny, D. A., Kashy, D. A., & Bolger, N. (1998). Data analysis in social psychology. In S. F. D. Gilbert & G. Lindzey (Eds)., *Handbook of social psychology* (4th ed., Vol. 1). Boston: McGraw-Hill.

Kline, R. B. (2011). *Principles and practice of structural equation modeling* (3rd ed.). New York: Guilford Press.

MacKinnon, D. P. (2008). *Introduction to statistical mediation analysis.* Mahwah, NJ: Lawrence Erlbaum Associates.

MacKinnon, D. P., Fairchild, A. J., & Fritz, M. S. (2007). Mediation analysis. *Annual Review of Psychology, 58,* 593–614.

MacKinnon, D. P., Lockwood, C. M., Hoffman, J. M., West, S. G., & Sheets, V. (2002). A comparison of methods to test the significance of the mediated effect. *Psychological Methods, 7,* 83–104.

MacKinnon, D. P., Lockwood, C. M., & Williams, J. (2004). Confidence limits for the indirect effect: Distribution of the product and resampling methods. *Multivariate Behavioral Research, 39,* 99–128.

Mathieu, J. E., & Taylor, S. R. (2006). Clarifying conditions and decision points for mediational type inferences in organizational behavior. *Journal of Organizational Behavior, 27,* 1031–1056.

McNulty, J. K. (2010). When positive processes hurt relationships. *Current Directions in Psychological Science, 19,* 167–171.

Muller, D., Judd, C. M., & Yzerbyt, V. Y. (2005). When moderation is mediated and mediation is moderated. *Journal of Personality and Social Psychology, 89,* 852–863.

Preacher, K. J., & Hayes, A. F. (2004). SPSS and SAS procedures for estimating indirect effects in simple mediation models. *Behavior Research Methods, Instruments, and Computers, 36,* 717–731.

Preacher, K. J., & Hayes, A. F. (2008). Asymptotic and resampling strategies for assessing and comparing indirect effects in multiple mediator models. *Behavior Research Methods, 40,* 879–891.

Preacher, K. J., & Kelley, K. (2011). Effect size measures for mediation models: Quantitative strategies for communicating indirect effects. *Psychological Methods, 16,* 93–115.

Preacher, K. J., Rucker, D. D., & Hayes, A. F. (2007). Addressing moderated mediation hypotheses: Theory, methods, and prescriptions. *Multivariate Behavioral Research, 42,* 185–227.

Preacher, K. J., Zhang, Z., & Zyphur, M. J. (2011). Alternative methods for assessing mediation in multilevel data: The advantages of multilevel SEM. *Structural Equation Modeling, 18,* 161–182.

Preacher, K. J., Zyphur, M. J., & Zhang, Z. (2010). A general multilevel SEM framework for assessing multilevel mediation. *Psychological Methods, 15,* 209–233.

Rucker, D. D., Preacher, K. J., Tormala, Z. L., & Petty, R. E. (2011). Mediation analysis in social psychology: Current practices and new recommendations. *Social and Personality Psychology Compass, 5/6,* 359–371.

Russell, C. J., & Bobko, P. (1992). Moderated regression analysis and Likert scales: Too coarse for comfort. *Journal of Applied Psychology, 77,* 336–342.

Selig, J. P., & Preacher, K. J. (2009). Mediation models for longitudinal data in developmental research. *Research in Human Development, 6,* 144–164.

Shadish, W. R., Cook, T. D., & Campbell, D. T. (2002). *Experimental and quasi-experimental designs for generalized causal inference.* Belmont, CA: Wadsworth.

Shrout, P. E., & Bolger, N. (2002). Mediation in experimental and nonexperimental studies: New procedures and recommendations. *Psychological Methods, 7,* 422–445.

Sobel, M. E. (1982). Asymptotic confidence intervals for indirect effects in structural equation models. In S. Leinhardt (Ed.), *Sociological methodology* (pp. 290–312). San Francisco: Jossey-Bass.

Whisman, M. A., & McClelland, G. H. (2005). Designing, testing, and interpreting interactions and moderator effects in family research. *Journal of Family Psychology, 19,* 111–120.

Williams, J., & MacKinnon, D. P. (2008). Resampling and distribution of the product methods for testing indirect effects in complex models. *Structural Equation Modeling, 15,* 23–51.

Zhang, Z., Zyphur, M. J., & Preacher, K. J. (2009). Testing multilevel mediation using hierarchichal linear models: Problems and solutions. *Organizational Research Methods, 12,* 695–719.

Zhao, X., Lynch, J. G., & Chen, Q. (2010). Reconsidering Barron and Kenny: Myths and truths about mediation analysis. *Journal of Consumer Research, 37,* 197–206.

23

DYADIC OR SYSTEMIC
DATA ANALYSIS

Suzanne Bartle-Haring, Lenore M. McWey,
and Jared A. Durtschi

Couple and family therapy (CFT) works. Yet, there is evidence that individual therapy also works. So what is the added value of using a CFT approach? From a systemic perspective, it is the system that changes, which in turn impacts the changes in symptomatic behavior. Few studies have included information about how other members of the system change in relation to a single individual. However, recent developments in quantitative methods now allow for tests of whether and how family members influence one another, which is more closely aligned with traditional CFT theory on relationships and change. There are probably several reasons for the great divide that has long existed between our theoretical orientation and our research, but one that we highlight here is that the more traditional forms of statistical methods do not allow for multiple members of the same system to be included in the same analysis.

That is, the more traditional methods of statistical analysis often used in clinical trials research (repeated measures analysis of variance [ANOVA], multiple regression, etc.) assume independence in the data. When that assumption is broken, the standard errors are biased, and thus significance testing is problematic (Kenny, Kashy, & Cook, 2006). It is also the case that in these more traditional forms of data analysis, only one dependent variable is allowed, and only one change process can be analyzed at a time. These types of analyses clearly limit what a CFT researcher can do when showing the effectiveness of CFT models.

More recently, however, an emerging field has been developing, known as dyadic data analysis, allowing for the statistical inclusion of multiple family members. In order to understand these methods, we provide an example of a research project that will allow us to take the reader through the steps of a dyadic data analysis and then expand on this design to include multiple members of the family. Suppose a CFT researcher has read the literature about depression and its impact on marital satisfaction. Being a CFT professional, this researcher conceptualizes the findings from the literature from a systemic frame but notes how few studies include data from both partners. This researcher decides that in order to really understand both the association between relationship satisfaction and depression and how changes in one can impact the other, he/she designs an intervention study that includes data collection from both members of a couple. Let's say the researcher randomly assigns participants to intervention and wait-list control groups. The treatment provided includes 10 sessions. Assessment includes both partners' levels of depressive symptoms, relationship satisfaction, and ability to experience intimacy before treatment (baseline), at session 5, session 10, and 6 months posttreatment. Thus, the researcher has four waves of data from both partners in the intervention group and control group.

From a systemic perspective, we would expect that both partners would show some sort of change due to the intervention, and we would expect that their changes would be related to each other in some way. Since we are in the business of psychotherapy more generally, and we hope that problem behaviors decrease during treatment, we would also hypothesize that (a) depressive symptoms would decrease more in the intervention group, (b) relationship satisfaction would increase more in the intervention group, and (c) hopefully, these gains would be maintained at the 6-month follow-up. Now that we have a theory, hypotheses, and a data set, what do we do with all that data? If both partners are changing, and their changes are related in some way, we have two "outcome (dependent) variables." However, we also have other variables that may be influencing those changes, and they are also changing based on the treatment. In other words, as couple and family therapists, it may be our goal to decrease depressive symptoms and increase intimacy between the partners in order for their relationship satisfaction to increase, rather than simply think about increasing satisfaction. How do we include all of that in one analysis?

The answer is pretty straightforward, but the analysis is slightly more complex. The answer is to treat the couple as the unit of analysis, instead of treating the individual as the unit of analysis. Then we can allow for each individual's scores to be included in the analysis. The complexity in the data analysis lies in the fact that the data from the two individuals are not independent. Thus, using traditional analyses (i.e., t-tests, ANOVA, and regression), which assume independence in the data, would be inappropriate. In the following sections, we outline the meaning of nonindependence in data, how to determine whether the nonindependence in the data is consequential, and provide several statistical strategies for the analysis of dyadic data.

Dyads: Nonindependence and Its Sources

As systems thinkers, we believe that members of a system will influence and be influenced by each other (von Bertalanffy, 1969). Therefore, when researching members of the same system, we may expect a higher correlation between members in the same system, relative to individuals not in the same system. The first chapter in the book discusses what nonindependence is; we briefly reiterate this here. Nonindependence is the degree to which scores from one partner are correlated with the scores of the other partner. From a statistical standpoint, nonindependence would mean that two points of data were not "independently" selected.

There are different types of nonindependence, including voluntary, kinship, experimental, and yoked linkages (Kenny et al., 2006). As the name implies, voluntary linkages are those, for instance, among friends and dating partners. Kinship linkages occur between family members. Experimental linkages are those created when members who do not initially know each other become acquainted with one another due to their participation in a study, for example. Yoked linkages occur between people who do not know each other but share the same stimuli, such as the same therapist. The same system may have a number of linkages. In our example study of relationship satisfaction, depression, and intimacy, couples may have voluntary, kinship, experimental (e.g., if the intervention is group therapy), and yoked linkages (e.g., if they share the same therapist).

There are a variety of sources that may be associated with nonindependence, including compositional effects, partner effects, mutual influence, and common fate (Grawitch & Munz, 2004). Couple members, for example, may share a number of similarities before beginning their relationship. They might have had the same level of educational attainment, socioeconomic status, and religious and political views before engaging in the relationship. This source of nonindependence is called a compositional effect (Kenny et al., 2006).

After dyads are formed, partner effects, mutual influence, and common fate also may affect nonindependence. Partner effects occur when one person's behaviors affect another. We may expect one partner's clinically significant depression to be correlated with the other partner's relationship satisfaction, for example. We also expect that both partners will affect one another. In our example, we anticipate that wives' depressive symptoms will predict husbands' depressive symptoms and that in turn husbands' depressive symptoms will predict wives' depressive symptoms, creating a bidirectional feedback loop of prediction between partners. This is called mutual influence. Common fate occurs when participants share the same environment (Grawitch & Munz, 2004). The couples in our example share the same study conditions, whether they are in the intervention or control group, or they may share the same therapist, and this sharing of an environment may also affect nonindependence.

Consequences of Ignoring Nonindependence

There are consequences when statistical assumptions of independence are broken. Specifically, ignoring nonindependence by using traditional statistical tests with nonindependent data results in biased variances (Kenny et al., 2006). Biased variances can produce inaccurate test statistics and degrees of freedom and biased p-values (Cook & Kenny, 2005; Kenny et al.). There are ways to compute the degree of bias in p-values caused by nonindependence (see Kenny, Kashy, & Bolger,

1998 for computational formulas). Ultimately, ignoring nonindependence can result in the increased potential for type I error when scores are negatively correlated or type II error when correlations are positive (Laursen, Popp, Burk, Kerr, & Stattin, 2008). This would impact conclusion validity. That is, if the standard errors are biased, p-values will be biased, and thus the researcher could suggest that something is significant when it is not, or vice versa. Given these issues, researchers have made efforts to avoid nonindependence, such as randomly selecting one member of a pair for analysis, or sampling only one member of a family, or averaging the scores between couple members to create a "couple" variable (Card, Little, & Selig, 2008). In the past, nonindependence has been considered a statistical nuisance to be avoided. Yet, the interdependencies of a system are precisely what we, as CFT professionals, are interested in! If a systems thinker made efforts to avoid the biases of nonindependence in order to analyze data, the internal validity of a study would, in essence, be questionable. That is, how would a researcher who believes that being part of a couple matters separate couple member data?

Distinguishability

Distinguishability is an important concept in dyadic data analysis. Distinguishability refers to whether or not there is a way to meaningfully differentiate the members of a dyad. There are two types of distinguishability: conceptual and empirical.

In our vignette, if the partners in our depression and relationships satisfaction study are heterosexual, gender can be a variable used to differentiate members of the couple; therefore, they would be a conceptually distinguishable dyad. If, however, they were a gay couple, the dyad members would be indistinguishable by gender. Other examples of conceptually distinguishable dyad members include parents and children, younger and older siblings, and therapists and clients. Conceptually indistinguishable dyads may include gay parents and same-sex twins, for example. Kenny and colleagues (2006) provide a number of examples of dyads with distinguishable and indistinguishable partners. Ultimately, the variable used to distinguish dyads should be meaningful both conceptually and empirically (Kenny et al.).

Empirical distinguishability refers to whether or not the dyad members come from the same population in statistical terms. Just because partners may be conceptually distinguishable does not necessarily mean they differ from each other statistically. That is, although sex may provide a conceptual distinction between heterosexual partners, do males and females differ enough on the variables of interest for them to be considered different populations? There are a few ways to test for empirical distinguishability. The I-SAT model (or the saturated model for indistinguishable dyads) is described by Kenny et al. (2006), and there is also a way to test the differences in fit between a model in which the means, variances, and covariances are free to vary and a model in which the means, variances, and covariances are constrained to be equal (Ackerman, Donnellan, & Kashy, 2011). If there is not a significant loss of fit between the two models, then the dyads are not empirically distinguishable. That is, if the means, variances, and covariances among your variables of interest are not different between the two sets of partners, then the dyads are empirically indistinguishable. If the means, variances, and covariances among the variables of interest do differ among the two sets of partners, then the dyads are distinguishable (i.e., they come from two separate statistical populations). Ackerman and colleagues caution social science researchers against assuming that gender is always a distinguishing variable. Thus, in our example we would need to test the means, variances, and covariances of depression, intimacy, and marital satisfaction between the male and female partners. If there is no loss of fit between the fully constrained model and the free-to-vary model, then we would have to treat the dyads as indistinguishable, or as having come from the same population, statistically speaking. Having performed this test on marital satisfaction in a small study of heterosexual relationships, there was evidence that the partners were empirically distinguishable based on gender, so we will make the assumption in our example that the couple members are distinguishable dyads. If that were not the case, we would constrain the means, variances, and covariances to be equal in all subsequent analyses, or perform the analyses in ways that would accommodate the fact that the dyads are indistinguishable (see Kenny et al.). Failure to do so could jeopardize the conclusion validity of our study.

Types of Dyadic Variables

One aspect of construct validity involves accurately identifying the type of variables in a study. There are different types of variables in dyadic research: between-dyads, within-dyads, and mixed variables (Kenny et al., 2006). With between-dyad variables, both members of a dyad have the same score; however, the value of the variable is not the same across dyads. In our example, we have couples in the intervention group and couples in a control group. If a couple is in the intervention group, both partners have the same score for the grouping variable, but their score differs from another couple's in the control group. Length of relationship, number of children in the household, and combined annual income are also examples of between-dyad variables for couples.

Within-dyad variables involve different values between two members of the same dyad, but when the two values are averaged, each dyad in the sample has the same score (Kenny et al., 2006). For the sake of illustrating within-dyad variables, let's say we limited our sample to couples in which only one member was clinically depressed but made no other restrictions regarding who that member was (it could be the husband, wife, girlfriend, boyfriend). The person diagnosed with depression will differ from couple to couple, but among all couples there is one person with the diagnosis. This is an example of a within-dyad variable.

370

Mixed variables occur when there is variation both between and within dyads (Kenny et al., 2006). In our example, relationship satisfaction scores will differ from couple to couple, but some couples will have higher scores than others, and the differences within couples will vary as well. Kenny and colleagues suggest that most outcome variables in dyadic research are mixed.

Analyses

Now that we have determined that we have a dyad (whether distinguishable or not) we turn to what to do with the data. Dyadic data can be analyzed with structural equation modeling (SEM) or multilevel modeling. These two methods are in many ways similar but require different data structures. There is also the question of sample size. How many couples would be enough to test the hypotheses in our example? Unfortunately, there is very little consensus on what is enough. We don't have Jacob Cohen, the early sample size pioneer, to help us with this problem. Kenny et al. (2006) suggest that in order to empirically verify noninde-pendence, you need at least 25 dyads. Beyond that, the power of a test is based on the degree of nonindependence of the dyads and effect size. Kenny et al. provide a table that compares the power of a test between 100 individuals and 50 dyads. With a moderate effect size (i.e., 0.4) the power of the test for the individuals is 0.51, while for the dyads it ranges from 0.37 to 0.68, with decreasing intraclass correlations. Thus, statistical power for dyadic research depends on the number of dyads and the degree of nonindependence of those dyads. The greatest power is with negative intraclass correlations. This is only for the case of one between-dyad variable. Other considerations include the number of between, within, and mixed dyad variables in the model. The power of a particular estimate in a dyadic data analysis, given a particular sample, depends on a complex set of equations outlined by Kenny et al. As always, more is better, but at least 25 dyads is a good start, depending on the complexity of the model.

Structural Equation Models

In SEM, data for the couple appear on the same line of data (i.e., couple is the unit of analysis) such that there is a score for male partner's depression, rela-tionship satisfaction, and intimacy and a score for female partner's depression, relationship satisfaction, and intimacy on the same line of data. This will enable us to understand not only relationships within the person, but across partners. Ultimately we would like to see all of this over time, but for now, let's focus on our baseline measures. Once the data are in place, the rest is fairly straight-forward. There is a specific model known as the actor–partner interdependence model (APIM; Kenny et al., 2006) that can be of use for us here. In this case, we will conjecture that depression is the "exogenous" variable (the one that is not predicted by anything within the model), which leads to intimacy, which then leads to relationship satisfaction. In Figure 23.1, the arrows going from the

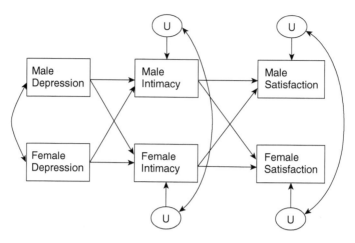

Figure 23.1 APIM for our example study at baseline.

male or female partner to his or her own intimacy and his or her own satisfaction are labeled actor effects. That is, if the male partner is depressed, that will impact his ability to experience intimacy, which in turn will impact his satisfaction in the relationship. On the other hand, as couple therapists, we also know that one partner's depression can impact the other partner. So, in Figure 23.1, we include the arrows (i.e., path coefficients) that cross over to the other partner, which are known as partner effects. In this hypothesized model, the female partner's depression impacts the male partner's ability to experience intimacy, which impacts not only his satisfaction, but her satisfaction as well. This is an APIM. It can be tested using common SEM software, such as Amos and M*plus*, to estimate the path coefficients for the actor and partner effects.

The actor and partner effects can also be tested for equivalence. That is, does female partner's depression have a stronger effect on her ability to experience intimacy than male partner's depression on his ability to experience intimacy? Another question that could be addressed is whether the partner effect from male to female is equivalent to the partner effect from female to male. It should also be noted that the "disturbance" terms for the "endogenous" variables are set to be correlated. This is another way of modeling or accounting for nonindependence. What this suggests is that any leftover variance for intimacy and satisfaction for both partners is related.

The APIM can also be tested in multilevel modeling (MLM). In essence, MLM was created to account for nonindependence in consecutively embedded units. That is, in educational research, MLM is used to account for the idea that students are embedded in classrooms, which are embedded in schools, which are embedded in school districts, etc. For our purposes, MLM allows us to account for nonindependence of the two individuals embedded in the couple. In order for MLM to be used for the APIM model, the data need to be structured differently

Table 23.1 Example of the Data Structure for an APIM Model in MLM

Dyad ID	Satisfaction	Spouse	Intimacy	Depression	Partner Intimacy	Partner Depression	Partner Satisfaction
001	5	−1	4	16	5	9	8
001	8	1	5	9	4	16	5
002	10	−1	10	4	4	16	5
002	5	1	4	16	10	4	10
003	7	−1	7	8	2	20	2
003	2	1	2	20	7	8	7

than in the SEM example above. The data structure is known as pairwise and double entry (Kenny et al., 2006), and can be seen in Table 23.1. So, each individual in the dyad has a line of data and the partner's data is also entered on that line. This is the data structure for hierarchical linear modeling; other statistics programs have different data structure requirements. To continue, each couple has two lines of data, and there is a variable that indicates which partner is which. Once the data structure is set, then a multilevel model is estimated with the individual at level 1 and the couple at level 2. Level 1 in our example would be satisfaction as the dependent variable, with actor's intimacy and depression, and partner's depression, intimacy, and satisfaction (we can have only one dependent variable in MLM), along with a variable that designates male or female partner. The level 1 equation would be the following:

$$\text{Satisfaction} = \beta_0(\text{Intercept}) + \beta_1(\text{Spouse}) + \beta_2(\text{Depression})$$
$$+ \beta_3(\text{Intimacy}) + \beta_4(\text{Partner Depression}) + \beta_5(\text{Partner Intimacy}) + \beta_6(\text{Partner Satisfaction}) + r$$

β_1 in this equation represents the difference in satisfaction between the partners. What distinguishes multilevel models from other models is their ability to partition variance into fixed and random effects. In essence, what multilevel models provide are the average influences (fixed effects) of predictor variables (what we normally see in ANOVA or regression or the βs in the equation above) and random influences (random effects) or variability around the average influence. With enough data, we can test the random effects of all variables in the model, in this instance; however, because we have only two data points per case, we cannot have random effects for all the fixed effects in the model. There are not enough degrees of freedom, so we would only have a random effect (variation across dyads) for the intercept (β_0) and the error (r). Thus, at level 2, there can only be a random effect for the intercept, but we can still use predictor variables to explain the fixed effects of the βs in the equations with dyad or couple level variables or mixed variables (i.e., length of relationship, past treatment, or other variables of interest). These variables would, in essence, be moderators, suggesting that with differences in these level 2 variables, there would be differences in the *relationships* between the level 1 variables and the outcome (i.e., the actor or partner effects might be different under different circumstances). The level 2 equation would be the following:

$$\beta_0 = \gamma_{00} + \gamma_{01}(\text{Relationship Length}) + u_0$$

$\beta_1 = \gamma_{10} + \gamma_{11}(\text{Relationship Length}) + u_1$ (we would continue to create the same equation for each of the βs in the level 1 equation).

The APIM is a special case of a dyadic model. Researchers can use dyadic data in many different ways, without including all the actor and partner effects suggested by the APIM. The most important part of these dyadic models would be the correlated disturbances for each outcome assessed for both partners.

Longitudinal Approaches

As couple and family therapists, however, we are less interested in the relationships among our variables of interest at baseline (i.e., intake) than we are about whether or not our variables of interest change over time, and how the change in one partner might impact change in the other. In order to construct a dyadic data analysis with data over time, we can use SEM or latent growth curve (LGC) models, or MLM that includes time as a variable at level 1. In the following sections, we provide examples of how to construct a longitudinal model for dyadic data.

Latent Growth Curve Modeling

Questions that can be addressed for our example with an LGC model include: How does relationship satisfaction change across time with and without treatment? What is the rate of change? Does the rate of change vary by level of depression or change in depression? Does the rate of change in relationship satisfaction vary by the rate of change in intimacy? Are the partners' rates of change associated? Is the rate of change in a variable related to its initial level? In LGC models, the variables that are modeled to be changing have two latent variables: an intercept (or initial level in most cases) and a slope or rate of change (cf. Duncan, Duncan, & Strycker, 2006). In our example, the intercept would be created by forcing all the "loadings" going to our four time points to be 1. The linear slope would be created by designating the loadings going to our four time points to be 0, 5, 10, and 34 weeks, with all time coded as weeks from baseline (see Figure 23.2). If we thought that change was not linear or that there may be an initial increase, then a decrease and leveling off, we could model that as well. If we think the change is curvilinear (a U shape), we could add a quadratic term, with loadings going to our four time points being the square of the linear slope loading (i.e., 0, 25, 100, and 1,156).

The MLM and SEM approaches to estimating growth models are equivalent in terms of the underlying statistical model (e.g., Curran, 2003; Kashy &

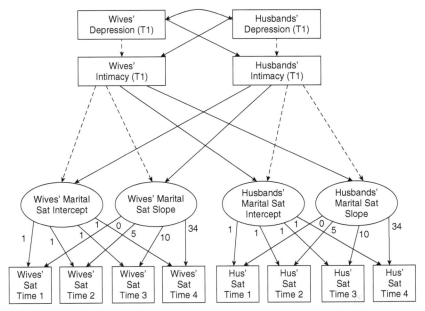

Note: In this model the dashed lines correspond to actor pathways, whereas the solid lines correspond to partner pathways. T1 = Time 1, Sat = Satisfaction, Hus' = Husbands'. To simplify the presentation of this model, the error terms are not shown (all variables in this model have an error term except for husbands' and wives' depression). In a dyadic model, these error terms between spouses on the same variables would also be correlated. For example, the error terms on both spouses' intimacy would be correlated, as would the error terms for each corresponding relationship satisfaction time point (e.g., wives' sat time 1 correlated with husbands' sat time 1).

Figure 23.2 Dyadic growth curve model with predictors of wives' and husbands' relationship satisfaction.

Donnellan, 2008). However, growth modeling in SEM has the unique advantage of testing how well the models and rates of change actually fit the data and may be more flexible in conducting dyadic and triadic growth models, as well as in ease of applying constraints to the model. See Karney and Bradbury's (1995) article for an overview of conducting growth curves from an MLM framework.

Different patterns of change. The first step in studying change is to identify what pattern of change is occurring. For example, change in relationship quality through couples therapy can be a linear improvement; a quadratic improvement (U-shaped), where relationship quality initially declines when talking about problems and then improves; a piecewise improvement, where there is a different rate of change for different parts of therapy (e.g., each of the three stages of emotionally focused therapy providing a different rate of change for couples); or more complex rates of change, such as polynomial, where relationship quality initially increases, then decreases, and then increases again. The pattern of change across time can be tested by specifying differing patterns of changes and evaluating which of the specified models is the best fit to the actual data. For example, if the true pattern of change across time is quadratic, but we specify the rate of change as linear, the linear model will have a worse fit than a quadratic model. For further information on interpreting model fit, there are a number of helpful sources in making these decisions (Hu & Bentler, 1999). Dependent on the complexity of the pattern of change tested, differing numbers of data points are required: at least three data points (or waves of data collection) are required to test a linear rate of change, four data points for a quadratic rate of change, five data points for a piece-wise rate of change, and even more data points for a polynomial rate of change.

Each individual participant measured across time has a single growth curve. For our example, at intake one partner may score fairly low on our relationship satisfaction scale, say 4 out of 10, while the other partner may score at a 6. If we use baseline as our "0" time, which conceptually makes sense, then partner 1 would have an intercept of 4, and partner 2 would have an intercept of 6. During the course of treatment, we may see a decline in satisfaction, or it may stay the same or increase (we hope). At session 5, partner 1 may have increased to an 8, at session 10 stayed at 8, and then at the 6-month follow-up scored a 7. At session 5, partner 2 may have had a score of 9, and at session 10 he/she was at a 10, and at the 6-month follow-up was at an 8. Now imagine these sorts of changes across a large sample and a fitting procedure that tries to "see" the common shape of the change. In essence that is the process of LGC models. Figure 23.3 provides some raw data for our example.

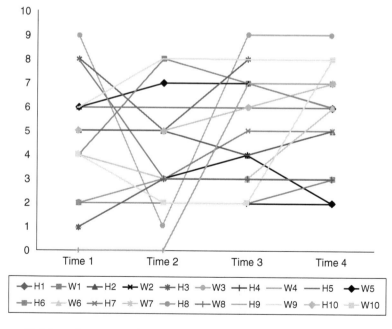

Figure 23.3 Raw data on satisfaction from 10 couples.

As can be seen, not all members of couples change in the same way; thus, there is variance in the shape of change, variance in where couple members start and where couple members end, as well as variance in the rate of change overall.

Dyadic Growth Curves

Dyadic researchers could then apply the APIM to growth curves. Growth curve analyses can be used to test the rate of change in relationship satisfaction for both husbands and wives simultaneously, in the same model. In a dyadic growth curve model, it is possible to then correlate the intercepts and slopes between husbands and wives. This can be useful to establish whether the initial level of marital satisfaction for husbands is correlated with wives' rate of change in relationship satisfaction. Also, the rate of change in wives' marital satisfaction can be correlated with the rate of change in husbands' marital satisfaction, to test interdependence between spouses across time.

After this baseline model is tested, it is then possible to also add predictors from both spouses to predict the intercept and slope of spouses' relationship quality (see Figure 23.2). For example, both spouses' reports of their initial levels of depression can be used to predict both spouses' rates of change in marital satisfaction. In the same way we conceptualized actor and partner effects at one time point, we can consider actor and partner effects predicting intercepts and slopes in LGC models.

Interlocked Dyadic Growth Curves

A further extension of the use of growth curves to study dyadic data is interlocked growth curves. Similar to the dyadic growth curves discussed above, two or more growth curves can be tested simultaneously, but now rates of change in one variable can also be used to predict rates of change in another variable. There are many useful applications of this methodology to scholars interested in dyads and families. As we theoretically believe in systemic change, interlocked growth curves are a method that can assess how the variation in change of trajectories of variable X can predict variation in the change of variable Y across time. For our example, we could estimate how the slopes in depression for both partners impact the slopes in intimacy for both partners (with actor and partner paths), which in turn impact the slopes in relationship satisfaction (with actor and partner paths). We could test the equivalences of the actor and partner effects in the same way we did above. This would tell us whether male partner's change is more influential than female partner's or vice versa. For examples of how dyadic data analyses have been conducted in the past using interlocked growth curve analyses to examine how changes in one family member relate to changes in another, see the studies by Cui, Conger, and Lorenz (2005) and Cui and Donnellan (2009). However, it should be noted that interlocked growth models are computationally complex and will require a large sample size to test (e.g., 10 cases per estimated parameter in the model).

Longitudinal Analysis with MLM

Constructing dyadic growth curves in an MLM framework is conceptually different but fundamentally equivalent to doing these tests in a SEM framework, as previously described. In MLM, growth models are still measuring an intercept (scaled at 1 for each time point) and slope (scaled at each measurement occasion: 0, 5, 10, and 34) for both partners that can be predicted by both partners, with actor and partner paths. In order to estimate change using MLM, a variable for time needs to be added to the data, in our case measured in weeks (e.g., 0, 5, 10, and 34). It should be noted that the assumption of these longitudinal models is that the time points are equidistant for each unit of analysis. That is why in our example we used weeks instead of sessions. If we wanted to use sessions as our "time" indicator, we need to be sure that everyone has the same interval of time between sessions. It should also be noted, however, that there is very little information about the impact that varying time intervals have on these analyses. In our example, we have four time points; thus, each partner would have four lines of data, for a total of eight lines for each couple. There would be a variable to designate time and partner. There are several options to determining data structure for MLM. If we are interested in examining both partners' slopes and intercepts, we would create a two-intercept, two-slope model. This requires that we have variables that designate partner 1 and partner 2, and then variables that designate partner 1 time and partner 2 time. Table 23.2 illustrates the data for two fictional dyads for this model. Thus for level 1, the equation would be:

Level 1:

Relationship Satisfaction = β_1(Partner 1 Intercept) + β_2(Partner 1 Slope) + β_3(Partner 2 Intercept) + β_4(Partner 2 Slope) + r

In this equation that there is no β_0, or "grand" intercept, but an intercept for both partners and a slope for both partners. In an unconditional model (one with no predictors), we could assess the correlations among the intercepts and slopes both within and between partners. If we determine that the intercepts are highly correlated and/or the slopes are highly correlated, we might decide to create a model with two intercepts but a single slope, or a model with a single intercept and two slopes, or even a single intercept and a single slope and a variable to designate partner and one that would designate partner by time. These options would provide us with the average difference in the intercepts between partners, as well as the variance in the difference, and the interaction would provide us with the average difference in the rate of change between partners as well as the variance in that difference. Because we have more degrees of freedom, we would be able to test the random effects of the slopes and intercepts.

MLM is limited, however, in that we can only predict change in satisfaction (albeit in two people in this example), and can only treat other variables that may

Table 23.2 Example of Data Structure for a Longitudinal Multilevel Model of Relationship Satisfaction for a Dyad

Dyad ID	Satisfaction	Partner 1	Partner 2	Partner 1 Time	Partner 2 Time
001	2	1	0	0	0
001	5	1	0	5	0
001	8	1	0	10	0
001	7	1	0	34	0
001	4	0	1	0	0
001	7	0	1	0	5
001	9	0	1	0	10
001	8	0	1	0	34
002	8	1	0	0	0
002	5	1	0	5	0
002	3	1	0	10	0
002	10	1	0	34	0
002	4	0	1	0	0
002	8	0	1	0	5
002	3	0	1	0	10
002	10	0	1	0	34

be changing as time-varying covariates. This is not the same as testing whether the rate of change in intimacy is related to the rate of change in satisfaction both within and across dyads, as can be done with LGC models. The results of a longitudinal MLM with time-varying covariates would only provide us with whether the score of our time-varying covariate at a particular time made a difference in the outcome variable (see Karney & Bradbury, 2000 for an MLM example), which could provide some clues to how change in one variable might effect change in another, but not as elegantly as the LGC models. Once you determine which model best fits the data (two intercepts, two slopes, or some other variation), the level 2 model looks the same as it did above. You use other variables of interest to predict your level 1 variance. Lyons and Sayer (2005) provide a good example of testing a two-intercept, two-slope model. For examples of variations on this model, see the studies by Bartle-Haring and Lal (2010) and Knerr and Bartle-Haring (2010).

Note About Validity

As a quantitative methodologist once said, "All models are flawed." Using more sophisticated statistical analyses will not help if the measures used are not internally consistent or valid (i.e., internal validity, conclusion validity). If the intervention that is used is not applied with fidelity, then the "experiment" we proposed here would not be valid and our results would not be useful (i.e., external validity, internal validity, conclusion validity). The statistical methods we have reviewed here, however, do provide a "better" approximation of our systemic theories than do the more traditional statistical methods we have used in the past, which provide more internal validity to our studies and allow us to increase our conclusion validity when discussing the findings from a dyadic perspective. With dyadic data analysis, and extensions to multiple perspectives beyond dyads, we can provide results that have the potential to validate our systemic hypotheses in ways that we have been unable to in the past. Since systems theory proposes circular causality and nonlinearity, it is difficult to fully test it with statistical procedures that assume linear relationships, so our statistical models are "flawed." As couple and family therapists, we have embraced systems theory as a valid way to represent "reality." Although dyadic data analysis procedures are "flawed" in many ways as a representation of systems theory, they are a more valid approximation than ANOVA, multiple regression, or any other analysis that assumes nonindependence of the data. In essence, using dyadic data analysis in CFT research has the potential to enhance the validity of our research.

Summary and Conclusions

The most important points to remember from this chapter are the issues of nonindependence in the data and unit of analysis. Once it is understood that typical or traditional statistical procedures cannot be used when data are nonindependent and that as couple and family therapists we believe that change in one person in the family will influence change in another, then the data analyses described in the chapter are conceptually easily applied. It is up to the reader to become familiar with the statistical procedures required to handle this sort of data. Once the basics and the models are understood, at least conceptually, the rest can fall into place.

Research clinicians need to become familiar with these types of quantitative methods in order for CFT as a field to move forward and to provide evidence that family therapy not only relieves symptoms, but effects change in all members of the family. Without these methods, we will be able to show only what individual therapy is able to show, that symptoms are reduced with treatment. However, if the CFT field is to stand out as providing an added value, then we need to look beyond symptom reduction and be able to show that symptom reduction is accompanied by change in other family members, through the use of variables salient to our field (differentiation, relational ethics, boundaries, etc.).

With these recent developments in quantitative methods, CFT researchers can now more closely match their analyses to the complex systemic theories that guide how we think about people, relationships, and change. For decades we theorized about how each person could affect him or herself and others in their system, how change in one person was related to change in another, and how these relationships were affected by differences in culture and context. During many of those same decades we were limited in our ability to test our theories because our statistical procedures were limiting. At present, a number of substantial advances have been made in quantitative statistics (SEM and MLM) that allow for tests of dyadic analyses, examining how family members affect one another, how change in one person is related to change in another, and how one environment might be different than another. The questions systems thinkers are passionate about can now be tested quantitatively, and there no longer remains the great divide between how we think and theorize about relationships and the type of research we are able to do.

References

Ackerman, R. A., Donnellan, B., & Kashy, D. (2011). Working with dyadic data in studies of emerging adulthood: Specific recommendations, general advice, and practical tips. In F. D. Fincham & M. Cui (Eds.), *Romantic relationships in emerging adulthood* (pp. 67–97). New York: Cambridge University Press.

Bartle-Haring, S., & Lal, A. (2010). Using Bowen theory to look at progress in couple therapy. *Family Journal, 18,* 106–115.

Card, N.A., Little, T.D., & Selig, J.P. (2008). Modeling dyadic and interdependent data in developmental research: An introduction. In N.A. Card, J.P. Selig, & T.D. Little (Eds.), *Modeling dyadic and interdependent data in the developmental and behavioral sciences* (pp. 1–10). New York: Routledge.

Cook, W.L. (2012). Foundational issues in nonindependent data analysis. In B.P. Laursen, T. D. Little, & N.A. Card (Eds.), *Handbook of developmental research methods* (pp. 521–536). New York: Guilford Press.

Cook, W.L., & Kenny, D.A. (2005). The actor–partner interdependence model: A model of bidirectional effects in developmental studies. *International Journal of Behavioral Development, 29,* 101–109.

Cui, M., Conger, R.D., & Lorenz, F.O. (2005). Predicting change in adolescent adjustment from change in marital problems. *Developmental Psychology, 41,* 812–823.

Cui, M., & Donnellan, M.B. (2009). Trajectories of conflict over raising adolescent children and marital satisfaction. *Journal of Marriage and Family, 71,* 478–494.

Curran, P.J. (2003). Have multilevel models been structural equation models all along? *Multivariate Behavioral Research, 38,* 529–569.

Duncan, T.E., Duncan, S.C., & Strycker, L.A. (2006). *An introduction to latent variable growth curve modeling: Concepts, issues, and applications* (2nd ed.). Mahwah, NJ: Lawrence Erlbaum Associates.

Grawitch, M. J. & Munz, D. A. (2004). Aare you data nonindependent? A practical guide to evaluating nonindependence and within-group agreement. *Understanding Statistics, 3,* 231–257.

Hu, L., & Bentler, P. M. (1999). Cutoff criteria for fit indexes in covariance structure analysis: Conventional criteria versus new alternatives. *Structural Equation Modeling, 6,* 1–55.

Karney, B. R., & Bradbury, T. N. (1995). Assessing longitudinal change in marriage: An introduction to the analysis of growth curves. *Journal of Marriage and Family, 57,* 1091–1108.

Karney, B. R. & Bradbury, T. N. (2000). Attributions in marriage: State or trait? A growth curve analysis. *Journal of Personality and Social Psychology, 78,* 295-309.

Kashy, D. K., & Donnellan, M. B. (2008). Comparing MLM and SEM approaches to analyzing developmental dyadic data: Growth curve modeling of hostility in families. In N. A. Card, J. P. Selig, & T. D. Little (Eds.), *Modeling dyadic and interdependent data in the developmental and behavioral sciences* (pp. 165–190). New York: Routledge.

Kenny, D. A., Kashy, D., & Bolger, N. (1998). Data analysis in social psychology. In D. Gilbert, S. Fiske, & G. Lindzey (Eds.), *Handbook of Social Psychology (4th ed., pp. 233–265)*. New York: McGraw-Hill.

Kenny, D. A., Kashy, D. A., & Cook, W. L. (2006). *Dyadic data analysis*. New York: Routledge.

Knerr, M., & Bartle-Haring, S. (2010). Differentiation, perceived stress and therapeutic alliance as key factors in the early stage of couple therapy. *Journal of Family Therapy, 32*, 94–118.

Laursen, B., Popp, D., Burk, W. J., Kerr, M., & Stattin, H. (2008). Incorporating interdependence into developmental research: Examples from the study of homophily and homogeneity. In N. A. Card, J. P. Selig, & T. D. Little (Eds.), *Modeling dyadic and interdependent data in the developmental and behavioral sciences* (pp. 11–37). New York: Routledge.

Lyons, K. S., & Sayer, A. (2005). Longitudinal dyad models in family research. *Journal of Marriage and Family, 67*, 1048–1060.

Von Bertalanffy, L. (1969) General System Theory: Foundations, Development, Applications (Revised Edition), NY: George Braziller, Inc.

24

OBSERVING COUPLE AND FAMILY RELATIONSHIPS

Data Management and Analysis

Ryan B. Seedall

Introduction

As highlighted by Wampler and Harper (Chapter 25), observational research represents a particularly useful way of addressing questions germane to clinical work with couples and families. Observational research operationalizes what marriage and family therapists actually do, including focusing on both the content and process elements of couple and therapeutic relationships that inform intervention strategies and influence outcome. Despite its high relevance to clinical work with couples and families, the complexity of observational research and the time, personnel, and technology resources typically required have led to relatively little observational research being done in marriage and family therapy (MFT). Although some excellent research from non-MFT researchers has ultimately benefited work with couples and families, our specialized and intensive training in observing and understanding relationships makes us uniquely qualified to conduct research in this area.

Wampler and Harper (Chapter 15) provide an excellent overview of the process of planning and executing the coding process. After the coding has taken place, the researcher is often left with a large amount of data to manage and analyze. In fact, data management/analysis may be one of the most overwhelming aspects of observational research and a major factor in the relative lack of these observational studies in MFT. The goal of this chapter is to demystify the management and analysis of observational data by providing a conceptual framework for the decision-making process. Because of the numerous decisions associated with this type of research, as well as its overall complexity, this chapter will focus on four questions relating to the core considerations, principles, and options for researchers to make data management and analysis decisions. Although this chapter is not exhaustive, readers will gain an understanding of relevant issues and the specific analysis techniques that may be used to address them.

Question 1: What Are Your Unit of Analysis and Sampling Strategy?

In order to make appropriate data management and analytic decisions, observational researchers need to clearly understand the unit of analysis and the sampling strategy. It might be useful to think of the unit of analysis as *whom* and *what* make up your sample, and the sampling strategy as *how* you actually obtained the data. These questions may seem fairly simple and straightforward, but with the number of options and potential complexity of observing behavior and interaction, it can be a challenge. Clarity in both of these areas will help to inform the decisions you make regarding your statistical analyses. The following sections will illustrate some of the core considerations for identifying your unit of analysis and sampling strategy.

What Is the Focus of Your Observation?

This is a rather simple albeit important question to understanding your unit of analysis. You will need to decide whether you are coding the behavior of one person (individual coding) or multiple people (dyadic or triadic coding). It might seem counterintuitive not to code as much and as many people as possible in an effort to gather more data. Although it can at times be useful to code more people in greater detail in order to expand later data options (Bakeman & Quera, 2011), it is important to make decisions based upon available resources as well as your theoretical framework. For example, Mary Ainsworth moved forward the empirical study of attachment theory by developing a laboratory procedure known as the Strange Situation (SS), designed to be mildly distressing for the infant and thereby promote attachment-seeking behaviors. Interestingly, Ainsworth and her colleagues found that the child's response when the caregiver returned from being separated was the primary predictor of the infant–caregiver relationship. As a result, the SS rates only the child's behavior on four levels, without rating the caregiver's behaviors (Ainsworth, Blehar, Waters, & Wall, 1978).

What Are the Level of Your Coding and the Nature of Your Codes?

When thinking about your research questions and hypotheses within your research framework, you must decide what data are needed to adequately address them. To answer this question, it is important to understand (a) the level of your coding and (b) the nature of your codes, each of which has some relation to the amount of inference involved in the coding. Level of coding refers to whether you are attending to synthesized, global behaviors or very specific behaviors and more fine-grained coding units (Lindahl, 2001; Margolin et al., 1998). For example, you may be coding behaviors globally as positive or negative, or you may code more specific behaviors that represent specific positive and negative behaviors (e.g., humor, criticism). Level of coding also refers to whether observed behaviors are at the individual or relationship level. In other words, each partner's behavior may be coded separately (individual level), or the overall couple or family behavior might be coded (relationship level). Coding sequences of individual behaviors occurring between two or more people (e.g., coding one person's behavior and then coding how the other responds) also yields relationship-level data.

Another consideration is whether codes are based upon time or events. If based upon time, a code will be assigned for a specific time period. For example, you could globally code an entire 10-minute interaction, but you could also code each second of an interaction. Codes can also be based upon a specific event by coding client behaviors that occur after a particular therapeutic intervention or after each talk-turn. Nature of codes refers to your use of continuous ratings versus categorical labels. Specifically, this issue addresses whether you are primarily interested in coding and then rating the nature, quality, and intensity of particular behaviors (continuous rating) or in coding the frequency, duration, and sequencing of behaviors (categorical labeling; Margolin et al., 1998).

To further illustrate these issues, please compare Tables 24.1 and 24.2. Table 24.1 reflects hypothetical data obtained from a global Likert rating scale (1–7, low to high) of a 10-minute interaction. Positive and negative behaviors are broken down into three subcomponent behaviors. One of the decisions a researcher could make would be whether to maintain each subcomponent behavior or to average them to get a global score of positive and negative behavior for each participant. The researcher could also rate these behaviors more regularly within the 10-minute interaction and then calculate a composite score or analyze the behaviors over time.

Table 24.2 represents an alternative example of coding a 60-second interaction using the same six codes shown in Table 24.1. The primary difference is that behaviors are coded much more regularly, thereby decreasing the amount of inference involved by assigning a code to a 5-second segment rather than rating a 10-minute interaction. There are also a number of options for compiling these

Table 24.1 Example of Global Coding Using Continuous Ratings

Couple ID	Partner Number	Positive Behaviors			Negative Behaviors		
		Compliment	Humor	Smiling	Criticism	Sarcasm	Anger
001	−1	3.0	1.0	1.0	4.0	6.0	7.0
001	1	2.0	4.0	1.0	5.0	7.0	6.0
002	−1	5.0	4.0	7.0	2.0	1.0	2.0
002	1	1.0	2.0	4.0	5.0	5.0	3.0
003	−1	6.0	4.0	6.0	3.0	4.0	2.0
003	1	5.0	7.0	5.0	1.0	2.0	4.0

Table 24.2 Example of Fine-Grained Coding Using Categorical Labels

	5	10	15	20	25	30	35	40	45	50	55	60
001												
P1:			Crit	→		Ang				Sarc		
P2:	Hum	→			Sarc		Crit	→	→		Ang	→
002												
P1:	Com	→			Hum	Com				Cr	→	
P2:		Smi	Crit	→			Smi	Sar	→			Ang
003												
P1:	Com	→			Smi	Hum		Crit		Sar	→	
P2:			Smi	Com			Hum		Ang			Ang

data. One straightforward way is to focus on the frequency of each behavior. Including time with frequencies would make it possible to analyze the probability of a particular event or behavior occurring (i.e., conditional probability). In addition, a fine-grained approach that categorically labels behaviors would allow you to analyze the sequencing of particular behaviors and the probability of one behavior following another (i.e., behavioral contingency).

In sum, observational research in any form is complex and requires large amounts of time and resources. However, conceptually addressing both the level of coding and the nature of your codes will aid understanding and prepare you for data management and analysis, which vary greatly across these issues.

Question 2: How Will You Address Issues of Validity?

One of our challenges as researchers is to accurately operationalize the constructs we wish to study. In fact, operationalizing constructs is one of the primary reasons that more clinically based research is not available. For example, the challenge of operationalizing important theoretical concepts like multidirected partiality (contextual family therapy) or triangulation (Bowen family systems) has led to a lack of empirical research and additional understanding in these areas. Yet accurately operationalizing constructs is a core component of construct validity. There are a number of ways to demonstrate construct validity, including demonstrating that your operationalization predicts (predictive validity), aligns with (convergent validity), and is different from (divergent validity) constructs in ways that make sense according to your theoretical framework. One other way is to demonstrate that your operationalization appropriately distinguishes between groups (discriminant validity), such as distinguishing between distressed and nondistressed couples (cf. Sechrest, 1984).

It is the responsibility of the researcher to provide evidence of the validity of his/her observational codes. The easiest and most efficient way to do this is to use established coding systems. Margolin and colleagues (1998) note that "using a system already developed generally means that the reliability [and construct validity] of the system is established, and that data from the new study can be understood more readily in the context of previous findings" (p. 201). However, even if the coding system has been shown to be valid and reliable in previous studies, the high degree of inference involved in observational coding makes it important to provide evidence that validity and reliability transfer across studies and researchers by demonstrating that coding results converge or diverge in expected ways with other measured constructs.

In the case of newly developed coding systems, researchers must provide evidence of validity. To illustrate, one study (Crowell et al., 2002) sought to validate an attachment-based, observational rating system, the Secure Base Scoring System (SBSS). The researchers provided evidence for validity by comparing SBSS results with (a) self-reported relationship functioning (using the Family Behavior Survey; Posada & Waters, 1988), (b) a well-established measure of adult attachment (Adult Attachment Interview [AAI]; George, Kaplan, & Main, 2002), and (c) a well-established observational coding system (Rapid Marital Interaction Coding System; RMICS; Heyman & Vivian, 1993). These comparisons provided information regarding both the similarities and differences among the SBSS, the AAI, and the RMICS and represent a useful way of demonstrating the validity of a newly developed system (see Wampler, Riggs, & Kimball, 2004 for another example).

Factor analysis is one other statistical method that offers relatively unique evidence of validity in observational research. For some coding systems (especially more fine-grained systems), factor analysis can provide an empirical analysis of the constructs underlying all of the codes (see Heyman, Eddy, Weiss, & Vivian, 1995 for one example). It can also provide empirical confirmation of previously theorized categories (see Remen, Chambless, Steketee, & Renneberg, 2000 for this kind of example). Overall, the various forms of factor analysis (exploratory, confirmatory, and exploratory structural equation modeling) can provide understanding, as well as additional evidence, for construct validity of a newer coding system.

Question 3: Which Reliability Analysis
Is Most Appropriate?

It is also important for researchers to demonstrate the reliability of their constructs and codes. Reliability primarily refers to consistency and stability, including consistency across observers (interrater agreement) as well as stability across time (temporal stability; Heyman, 2001). Interrater agreement is by far the most common method of demonstrating reliability, meaning that the results are consistent across coders, and it is standard practice to report it in research reports. My review of literature revealed no commonly accepted benchmark for what percentage of the sample should be double-coded for reliability. As a result, the burden of proof is on the researcher to justify why the amount coded for reliability was sufficient.

Interrater Agreement

Cohen's kappa. For the most part, there are two approaches to analyzing case-by-case interrater agreement: Cohen's kappa and intraclass correlation. Both are well-utilized measures of reliability that go beyond simply reporting the percentage that coders agree upon, which can be problematic in accurately assessing interrater agreement (Bakeman & Quera, 2011). However, they typically serve different purposes. Cohen's kappa measures point-by-point agreement of categorical (nominal and ordinal) data and therefore "focuses on whether observers agree with respect to the successive intervals or events coded" (Bakeman & Quera, p. 58). Cohen's kappa corrects for chance agreement and is also not affected by sample size (Bakeman & Casey, 1995; Bakeman & Quera). In other words, Cohen's kappa goes beyond the percentage of agreement to take into account the potential for coders to agree simply by chance. In the range from −1 to +1, a negative value indicates poorer than chance agreement, zero indicates chance agreement, and a positive value indicates better than chance agreement (Fleiss & Cohen, 1973).

To illustrate, Table 24.3 is a frequency table that depicts point-by-point agreement using three possible codes (humor, compliment, and smiling) from two different coders (Coder A and Coder B). Exact agreement is demonstrated in the diagonal, with Coder A and Coder B agreeing on the humor code 25 times, the compliment code 12 times, and the smiling code 17 times. The other cells depict the frequency of coder disagreement. For example, the number of times that Coder A coded a segment as humor while coder B coded it as smiling is 10. Table 24.4 depicts how data from the frequency table are input into a statistical program such as SPSS. The total number of rows represents the different possible code combinations from each coder. Notice that there is the same number of rows in Table 24.4 as there are cells in Table 24.3. The *count* column represents the number of times that each combination occurred. Again, the values in the *count* column in Table 24.4 are the same as the cell values in Table 24.3. For the data in Table 24.4, kappa equals 0.44 ($p < .001$). According to Landis and Koch (1977), that is only moderate agreement (poor = 0; slight = .01 − .20; fair = .21 − .40; moderate = .41 − .60; substantial = .61 − .80; and nearly perfect = .81 − 1.0.).

In SPSS, select **Analyze → Descriptive Statistics → Crosstabs**. Enter one coder as the row, the other as the column. Click on *Statistics* and select *Kappa*.

388

Table 24.3 Frequency Table for Cohen's Kappa Reliability Analysis

		Coder B		
		Humor (1)	Compliment (2)	Smiling (3)
	Humor (1)	25	2	10
Coder A	Compliment (2)	3	12	4
	Smiling (3)	7	5	17

Table 24.4 Formatting the Frequency Table from Table 3 for Statistical Analysis

	Coder A	Coder B	Count
1	1	1	25
2	1	2	2
3	1	3	10
4	2	1	3
5	2	2	12
6	2	3	4
7	3	1	7
8	3	2	5
9	3	3	17

Intraclass correlation. When the data are continuous (typically interval or ratio, but sometimes ordinal), intraclass correlation is the most appropriate method of estimating case-by-case interrater agreement (Margolin et al., 1998). For example, Table 24.5 provides hypothetical ratings (ranging from 1 to 7) of a 10-minute couple interaction from two coders on an 8-item measure. Margolin and colleagues (1998) point out that "high intraclass correlations indicate that variation due to coders is low relative to the variance due to differences among participants on a measured behavior" (p. 209). The intraclass correlation coefficient ranges from 0 to 1.0.

When estimating reliability of continuous data, intraclass correlation is preferable over Pearson's *r*. Whereas Pearson's *r* estimates *relative* agreement, intraclass correlation estimates *absolute* agreement (Bakeman & Quera, 2011) by taking into account "overall mean levels of behavior" (Margolin et al., 1998, p. 209). In other words, Pearson's *r* might tell you whether coders agree as to the ranking of

> In SPSS, select **Analyze → Scale → Reliability Analysis**. Select data from each coder and move it to *Items*. Click on *Statistics* and select *Intraclass Correlation Coefficient*. Then select the *Model* and *Type* you want in your analysis.

Table 24.5 Contrasting the Results of Pearson's *r* and
the Intraclass Correlation Coefficient

	Coder A	Coder B
Item 1	7	4
Item 2	6	3
Item 3	5	2
Item 4	4	1
Item 5	7	4
Item 6	6	3
Item 7	5	2
Item 8	4	1

couple negativity (i.e., which couples are more negative than others), but it will not provide information on whether coders agree on the overall level of negativity. Intraclass correlation, as a measure of reliability, accounts for whether coders agree on relative rank and absolute values. To illustrate, Table 24.5 depicts the ratings of two coders on a 1–7 Likert rating scale. Because the relative ranking remains constant, Pearson's *r* equals a perfect 1.0. However, the intraclass correlation shows the absolute agreement to be only .23.

Intraclass correlations can also supplement Cohen's kappa estimates in observational studies involving categorical labeling of behaviors. In this manner, it can be used with summary scores as an estimate of global agreement (Bakeman & Quera, 2011). For example, imagine that two coders generated data similar to Table 24.2 for all couples in a sample. One couple at a time (i.e., case by case), I could estimate interrater reliability using Cohen's kappa by generating data similar to Tables 24.3 and 24.4. However, to give a more global estimate of reliability, I might generate data similar to Table 24.6. These hypothetical data show the comparison of two coders (A and B) on two variable frequencies (positive behaviors and sequence of a negative partner behavior followed by a positive response) for five couples. Whereas Cohen's kappa can be used to estimate interrater reliability for each couple across multiple behaviors or variables, intraclass correlation may be used to compare interrater reliability for one variable at a time across multiple couples. In this manner, both can be useful when working with sequential data.

One other point relevant to both Cohen's kappa and intraclass correlation is worth noting. Although kappa is most appropriate for categorical and intraclass correlation for continuous data, for ordinal data either weighted kappa or intraclass correlation (Fleiss & Cohen, 1973) may be used and yield identical results. Weighted kappa allows the researcher to distinguish the level of seriousness for different kinds of disagreement (Fleiss & Cohen). Linear or quadratic

Table 24.6 Intraclass Correlation of Summary Statistics

Dyad ID	Partner ID	Frequencies			
		Positive— Coder A	Positive— Coder B	Negative-Positive Sequence—Coder A	Negative-Positive Sequence—Coder B
1	1	15	12	7	7
1	2	17	18	9	5
2	1	9	7	5	8
2	2	14	7	9	12
3	1	20	21	7	7
3	2	11	8	8	10
4	1	17	15	9	10
4	2	16	16	9	6
5	1	21	23	12	11
5	2	19	18	10	10

weights may be used when specifying the weight given to each level of disagreement, with quadratic weights treating larger disagreements as even more serious (Bakeman & Quera, 2011). Although a potentially useful statistic, weighted kappa cannot be calculated in SPSS, and Bakeman and Quera (2011) point out that if you use weighted kappa, you must be "ready with convincing reasons for your different weights" (p. 82).

Question 4: What Analytic Technique Is Most Appropriate for Your Coding Strategy?

When analyzing observational data, a wide array of options exist, many of which depend upon your research questions/hypotheses and the nature of your data. In this section, I will highlight the two most important analytic strategies with great relevance to observational research: dyadic analysis with continuous, individual-level data, and sequential analysis with categorical, relationship-level data.

Dyadic Data Analysis

When your observational data (of more than one person at a time) are continuous and collected at the individual level, dyadic data analysis is the most appropriate analytic strategy. McWey, Bartle-Haring, and Durtschi (Chapter 23) provide a much more comprehensive treatment of this topic. However, I do want to highlight a few of the most important considerations regarding dyadic analysis with observational data. The overarching purpose of dyadic data analysis is to recognize that your data are nonindependent and that you must treat the dyad, rather than the individual, as the unit of analysis (Kenny, Kashy, & Cook, 2006). For example, if I am studying couples, and I count the number of positive and negative statements made by each partner, the results from partner 1 (in couple A) will be more similar to results from partner 2 (in couple A) than from other participants because they share the same relationship and couple interaction.

Within dyadic analysis, there are several approaches with potential utility for observational research: the Social Relations Model, the One-With-Many design, and the Actor–Partner Interdependence Model. Although data management is an extremely important part of dyadic analyses, these issues have been discussed in substantial detail elsewhere (see Kenny et al., 2006).

Social Relations Model (SRM). The SRM, although widely used, has been almost exclusively used to measure self-reported perceptions of relationships, rather than coded observations. In order to use the SRM within the context of family interaction, scores need to be generated for each person with each family member (i.e., for each possible dyadic relationship). As a result, a family of three would have six scores ($n^*(n-1)$), forming four analytic factors: an average across all family members (family mean effect), a person's average behavior across family members (actor effect), family members' average behavior across one person (partner effect), and the unique aspect of each dyadic relationship after removing the family mean, actor, and partner effects (relationship effect). For more information regarding these factors, and for an excellent example of using SRM with observational data within a longitudinal framework, see the study by Ackerman, Kashy, Donnellan, and Conger (2011).

One-With-Many (OWM) design. The OWM design holds particular promise for observations of the therapeutic process. In this design, there is one focal person (e.g., the therapist) and multiple individuals (e.g., clients; Kenny et al., 2006) nested within each focal person. Typically, the OWM design compares the perceptions of the focal person with the perceptions of the partners (Kashy & Donnellan, 2012). However, an observational study makes it possible to compare the focal person's perceptions with those of trained coders. Although it has not yet been used within the process of relationship therapy, it is possible to use OWM in the context of structural equation modeling by treating the therapy-couple triads as distinguishable and examining the relationships in a manner similar to SRM (D. Kashy, personal communication, July 2, 2012; see also Kenny et al., 2006). This would make it possible to account for the nonindependence between therapists and their clients as well as the nonindependence between partners. However, approximately 30 therapists would be needed to have sufficient power to detect therapist effects (D. Kashy, personal communication, July 2, 2012).

Actor–Partner Interdependence Model (APIM). The APIM (discussed at length by McWey, Bartle-Haring, and Durtschi, Chapter 23) is perhaps the most recognized dyadic model. Within the APIM, individual data are nested within couple-level data, and differences are estimated within dyads, between dyads, or both (i.e., mixed; Kenny et al., 2006). The APIM provides valuable information regarding mutual influence. In other words, it provides information regarding an individual's effect on his/her own outcomes (i.e., actor effects), as well as on his/her partner's outcomes (i.e., partner effects),. Within observational research, the APIM may be used to understand how the quality of specific individual behaviors influences individual and partner outcomes (see Humbad, Donnellan, Klump, & Burt, 2011 for one example of using APIM with observational data). The APIM also may be used for families, with the partner effects (i.e., cross-loadings) defined as "the effect of the average of the other group [or family] members' inputs on the person's outcomes" (Kashy & Donnellan, 2012, p. 231).

Sequential Analysis

When observational data are categorical and consist of interdependent sequences at the relationship level (i.e., partner behaviors and responses are linked together in the coding process), sequential analysis is the most appropriate analytic strategy. Sequential data analysis is used most commonly with more fine-grained coding systems that generate nominal data and for which order, time, and probability are factors. Sequential analyses allow researchers to examine behavioral reciprocity and common interaction patterns within couples and families, as well as between therapists and clients. Sayers and McGrath (2004) explain that the fundamental question of sequential analysis is: "Given that behavior A just occurred, does behavior B occur more often than expected?" (pp. 49–50).

For this reason, much of sequential analysis has a basis in contingency tables, which are used to illustrate and compute sequential association between variables (Bakeman & Quera, 2011; Yoder & Symons, 2010). Within sequential coding, behavior is divided into given behaviors (also referred to as antecedent behaviors) and target behaviors (Bakeman & Quera; Yoder & Symons). A given behavior is the hypothesized stimulus behavior, and a target behavior is one that has been hypothesized to follow the given behavior. Yoder and Symons (2010) highlight three types of sequential analysis, each of which varies in the way that the potential sequences are identified. Specifically, sequential codes specify whether a target behavior occurs after a specific number of behaviors (event-lag), after an exact time period (time-lag), or within a window of time (time-window) after a given behavior.

To illustrate, suppose that a researcher is interested in times when, in the context of a couple enactment, a therapist attempts to help facilitate a more softened couple interaction by offering a tentative expression on behalf of one partner that highlights his/her attachment needs and longings (i.e., proxy voice; see Seedall & Butler, 2006). The use of proxy voice by the therapist would be the given behavior, and the researcher would then identify specific target behaviors (verbal and nonverbal) of interest in both partners as well as the frame in which the coding would occur. If the target behavior was a softened response by the listening partner, the behavior of the listening partner immediately after the proxy voice intervention could be coded (event-lag). The researcher could also code whether the behavior occurred within 30 seconds of the intervention (time-window) or at a specific time (at 1 second, 30 seconds, etc.) following the intervention (time-lag). Ultimately, these decisions will be guided by theory and the researcher's specific hypotheses.

More advanced sequential analyses can involve very long and complex behavioral sequences, and a variety of computer-based programs have been developed to deal with that complexity. However, it is useful to begin with a two-event sequence in order to develop a conceptual understanding of this process and the steps involved. For this hypothetical example, your sample consists of heterosexual couples talking about a recent, moderately distressing issue of conflict. Your coding system focuses on three behaviors: anger, blaming, and avoidance. You are especially interested in understanding the potential contingency between blaming and avoidance, with blaming in one partner followed by avoidance in the other. Your coding will generate data similar to Table 24.2, with nominal labels marking specific events and/or times.

The next step is to generate a data set of summary statistics that includes separate data for each partner. According to Bakeman and Quera (2011), six of the most common and relevant summary statistics are frequency (how many times an event occurs), relative frequency (frequency of one code in relation to total number of codes), rate (how many times an event occurs over a specific time period), duration (how long a code lasts), relative duration (length of one code in relation to total length of codes), and probability (length of one code in relation to the session's duration). Depending on your research questions, these can provide important information and set the stage for your primary analyses (see Bakeman & Quera, 2011 for a more detailed description and overview of how to calculate each). Table 24.7 shows the data layout of blaming and avoidance code frequencies.

After generating summary statistics, you will need to generate a new data set that includes behavioral sequences. The first step is to tally the frequencies

Table 24.7 Data Layout for Avoidance and Blaming Frequencies

	Frequencies					
Couple #	Total Codes, Man	Total Codes, Woman	Blaming, Man	Blaming, Woman	Avoidance, Man	Avoidance, Woman
101	49	46	34	34	15	12
102	32	41	12	27	20	14
103	26	20	17	12	9	8
104	27	27	22	20	5	7
105	49	51	37	41	12	10

of each given code (i.e., blaming) and then look for the occurrence of a target code (i.e., avoidance; Bakeman & Quera, 2011; Sayers & McGrath, 2004). At this point, the complexity increases, as you are generating a data set that provides information about sequences rather than isolated behaviors. As a result, it is important to be able to justify your selection criteria for the tallying process, especially for more complicated code sequences. Some sequential programs exist to help with many of the intermediate steps we have been discussing (one example is the Generalized Sequential Querier program described by Bakeman and Quera, 2011).

For our simplified example, we would generate a data set with frequencies for each of the sequences of interest, which include any sequences involving our given or target codes (i.e., blaming as a given code and avoidance as a target code). Table 24.8 contains an example of what the data set might look like. For the sake of space, the data for men and women have been combined, but it would likely be useful to keep them separate in this data set.

The next step is to generate a 2 × 2, event-based contingency table (see Table 24.9). In our table, four cells depict each of the possible relationships between blaming and avoidance (and correspond with the columns in Table 24.8). Cell A represents those times when blaming was followed by avoidance. Cell B refers to those times when blaming occurred but was not followed by avoidance (e.g., blaming followed by anger). In cell C, we see the number of times that avoidance followed a code that was not blaming (e.g., anger followed by avoidance). Lastly, in cell D, we see the frequency that the given and target codes did not involve blaming as the given code or avoidance as the target code (e.g., anger followed by blaming). The conditional probabilities are calculated by dividing the value of each cell by the row total. It is important to note that the values in each cell should be independent of values in other cells, meaning that there is no overlap (Bakeman & Quera, 2011). This is extremely important and one of the most common errors that arise in the construction of contingency tables.

Table 24.8 Data Set Depicting Given (g) and Target (t) Behaviors for Men and Women

	Frequencies			
	a	*b*	*c*	*d*
Couple #	*Blaming (g)* *Avoidance (t)*	*Blaming (g)* *Anger (t)*	*Anger (g)* *Avoidance (t)*	*Anger (g)* *Blaming (t)*
101	3	4	2	6
102	5	0	0	2
103	5	1	0	5
104	3	3	2	4
105	4	2	1	3

After generating a contingency table, several straightforward options exist for examining contingency effect sizes: the odds ratio, Yule's Q, and log odds. The information provided by each is similar, and choosing which you will use is based more on which you feel offers more straightforward interpretation (Bakeman & Quera, 2011). The odds ratio is calculated by multiplying the frequencies in cells A and D and then dividing by the product of cells B and C (i.e., ad / bc). Values range from 0 to infinity, with 1 being no effect. The log odds is calculated by taking the logarithm of the odds ratio. Unlike the odds ratio, it ranges from negative infinity to positive infinity, with 0 indicating no effect. Yule's Q ranges from −1 to +1, with 0 also indicating no effect. It is calculated by subtracting the product of cells B and C from the product of cells A and D and then dividing by the sum of each of those products (ad − bc/ad + bc). For our example in Table 24.9, the odds ratio is 6.8, the log odds is 1.92, and Yule's Q is 0.74. An odds ratio of between 2.0 and 3.0 is considered moderate (0.33 – 0.50 for negative relationships), with an

> To calculate the odds ratio in SPSS, organize the contingency table from Table 24.9 in the following way:
>
> | Frequency | Blaming (g) | Avoidance (t) |
> |-----------|-------------|---------------|
> | 17 | Yes | Yes |
> | 10 | Yes | No |
> | 5 | No | Yes |
> | 20 | No | No |
>
> **Step 1:** Select **Data → Weight Cases.** Weight the cases by the frequency variable
>
> **Step 2:** Select **Descriptive Statistics → Crosstabs.** Select the *row* as the variable referring to the given behavior. Select the *column* as the variable referring to the target behavior.
>
> **Step 3:** Select **Statistics.** Mark *Chi-Square* and *Risk*
>
> Your outcome will show the significance of the chi-square test, provide the odds ratio, and indicate whether any cells have an expected count below the standard of 5 (Yoder & Symons, 2010).
>
> *Note:* SPSS does not calculate Yule's Q.

Table 24.9 Example of a 2 × 2 Contingency Table in Sequential Analysis

					Target Codes		Conditional Probabilities	
					Avoid	*Not avoid*	*Avoid*	*Not avoid*
Given Codes								
Blaming	a	17	b	10		27	.63	.37
Not blaming	c	5	d	20		25	.20	.80
		22		30		52	.42	.58

odds ratio of over 3.0 considered strong (<0.33 for negative relationships). For the Yule's Q, common values for small, moderate, and large effect sizes are 0.20, 0.43, and 0.60 (Rosenthal, 1996). Bakeman and Quera (2011) provide more information on these statistical tests and guidelines. The results from our hypothetical example indicate a large effect size for the blaming-avoidance sequence, where avoidance is 6.8 times more likely to occur after blaming occurs than after other behaviors.

The foregoing hypothetical example provides a conceptual foundation analyzing sequential behavior. However, codes and sequences can be much more complex. For example, we found evidence for a sequential pattern involving blaming and avoidance. However, we may want to look at a more elaborate sequence to understand what is likely to happen after blaming and then avoiding. We might also be interested in comparing blaming-avoidance sequential patterns in heterosexual couples when the male partner blames and the female partner avoids versus when the female partner blames and the male partner avoids.

Log-linear analysis. Log-linear analysis is a well-established approach for addressing a number of more complex sequential analyses that build upon the analysis of 2 × 2 contingency tables (Bakeman & Quera, 2011; Sayers & McGrath, 2004). Although a detailed explanation is beyond the scope of this chapter, there are several excellent resources that provide a more in-depth treatment of log-linear analysis (Bakeman & Robinson, 1994; Field, 2009; Kennedy, 1992). Nonetheless, it is important to understand that the conceptual framework for log-linear analysis is the same as for analyzing two behavioral sequences (Field). As with a 2 × 2 contingency table, the expected cell count must reach the appropriate level to conduct the analysis. However, with log-linear analysis, the expected cell count for all cells must be above 1, and no more than 20% of cells should have an expected cell count of less than 5 (Field).

With log-linear analysis, you can analyze your sequences using a hierarchical, backward elimination process. In other words, if our hypothesized three-way sequence was blaming-anger-avoidance, it would allow us to test the significance of the highest-order sequence (i.e., blaming-anger-avoidance), and then test the significance of lower-order sequences (i.e., blaming-anger, blaming-avoidance, anger-avoidance) in terms of the overall model. It is also possible for you to specify your own, nonsaturated model (i.e., you can specify that it not test all lower-order sequence combinations) within log-linear analysis (Field, 2009).

Analyzing sequential data across multiple observation episodes is also possible. This is especially valuable because of the greater impetus being given to gaining a more comprehensive view of relationship functioning by observing interactions across time and topics (Heyman, 2001). Howe, Dagne, and Brown (2005) introduce a "multilevel log-linear model" (p. 72) that uses multilinear modeling to nest observations within multiple episodes and then makes it possible to examine sequential patterns. Overall, analyzing sequences of multiple behaviors can be an extremely complex process. However, an understanding of sequential analysis using a 2 × 2 contingency table provides the conceptual foundation for more complex sequence analysis.

Conclusion: A Call for Research

Observational research naturally lends itself to many of the issues and questions that are most relevant to clinicians, and it provides additional meaning and understanding to intervention efforts. Existing observational research has provided a valuable foundation upon which to build. In addition to continuing to understand patterns or styles of conflict (Bradbury & Karney, 1993), we can examine "what happy couples do when they are not fighting" and how to "promote the various forms of love" (Heyman, 2001, p. 7). Existing research in the area of social support (see Sullivan, Pasch, Johnson, & Bradbury, 2010 for an example) is one area of research that has begun to look at more positive elements of couple interaction.

There is an especially great need to expand the use of observational research in MFT process research. Although there is significant evidence that MFT, as a field, is an effective modality of psychotherapy, we are still in the infancy stages of understanding *how* and *why* MFT models work. Observational research in clinical settings offers the opportunity to examine the behaviors of therapists and the couples and families that they treat to determine interactions that are therapeutic and are predictive of successful outcome. Such information will help MFT scholars better understand the therapeutic process and help therapists refine and adapt our approach with specific couple characteristics and interactional styles and thereby enact more effective and transformative interventions for our clients.

Despite the clear utility of and glaring need for observational research, the time and resources required are great, and the analyses are often complicated. The purpose of this chapter has been to demystify the process of analyzing observational data. It is by no means exhaustive. In fact, by focusing exclusively on observational data management and analysis, it may seem that I have de-emphasized more inductive approaches such as task analysis. Indeed, task analysis, with its focus on process, patterns, and mechanisms of change (see Bradley & Johnson, 2005; Greenberg, 2007; Pascual-Leone, Greenberg, & Pascual-Leone, 2009), represents an important part of a pluralistic approach to observation and analysis. By increasing the quality and quantity of observational research in MFT, we can enhance the meaningfulness of our research, increase our understanding of clinical process, and ultimately move the field of MFT forward.

Acknowledgment: I would like to thank Drs. Karen Wampler, Jim Harper, and Megan Oka for providing ideas and resources that helped in the development of this chapter.

References

Ackerman, R. A., Kashy, D. A., Donnellan, M. B., & Conger, R. D. (2011). Positive-engagement behaviors in observed family interactions: A social relations perspective. *Journal of Family Psychology, 25,* 719–730.

Ainsworth, M. D. S., Blehar, M. C., Waters, E., & Wall, S. (1978). *Patterns of attachment: A psychological study of the Strange Situation.* Hillsdale, NJ: Erlbaum.

Bakeman, R., & Casey, R. L. (1995). Analyzing family interaction: Taking time into account. *Journal of Family Psychology, 9,* 131–143.

Bakeman, R., & Quera, V. (2011). *Sequential analysis and observational methods for the behavioral sciences.* Cambridge, UK: Cambridge University Press.

Bakeman, R., & Robinson, B. F. (1994). *Understanding log-linear analysis with Ilog: An interactive approach.* Hillsdale, NJ: Erlbaum.

Bradbury, T. N., & Karney, B. R. (1993). Longitudinal study of marital interaction and dysfunction: Review and analysis. *Clinical Psychology Review, 13,* 15–27.

Bradley, B., & Johnson, S. (2005). Task analysis in family therapy: Reaching the clinician. In D. Sprenkle and F. Piercy (Eds.), *Research methods in family therapy* (2nd ed.). New York: Guilford Press.

Crowell, J. A., Treboux, D., Gao, Y., Fyffe, C., Pan, H., & Waters, E. (2002). Assessing secure base behavior in adulthood: Development of a measure, links to adult attachment representations, and relations to couples' communication and reports of relationships. *Developmental Psychology, 38,* 679–693.

Field, A. (2009). *Discovering statistics using SPSS* (3rd ed.). Thousand Oaks, CA: Sage.

Fleiss, J. L., & Cohen, J. (1973). The equivalence of weighted kappa and the intraclass correlation coefficient as measures of reliability. *Educational and Psychological Measurement, 33,* 613–619.

George, C., Kaplan, N., & Main, M. (2002). *The Adult Attachment Interview* (3rd ed.). Unpublished manuscript, University of California, Berkeley.

Greenberg, L. S. (2007). A guide to conducting a task analysis of psychotherapeutic change. *Psychotherapy Research, 17,* 15–30.

Heyman, R. E. (2001). Observation of couple conflicts: Clinical assessment applications, stubborn truths, and shaky foundations. *Psychological Assessment, 13,* 5–35.

Heyman, R. E., Eddy, J. M., Weiss, R. L., & Vivian, D. (1995). Factor analysis of the Marital Interaction Coding System (MICS). *Journal of Family Psychology, 9,* 209–215.

Heyman, R. E., & Vivian, D. (1993). *RMICS: Rapid Marital Interaction Coding System—training manual for coders.* Unpublished manuscript, State University of New York at Stony Brook.

Howe, G. W., Dagne, G., & Brown, C. H. (2005). Multilevel methods for modeling observed sequences of family interaction. *Journal of Family Psychology, 19,* 72–85.

Humbad, M. N., Donnellan, M. B., Klump, K. L., & Burt, S. A. (2011). Development of the Brief Romantic Relationship Interaction Coding Scheme (BRRICS). *Journal of Family Psychology, 25,* 759–769.

Kashy, D. A., & Donnellan, M. B. (2012). Conceptual and methodological issues in the analysis of data from dyads and groups. In K. Deaux & M. Snyder (Eds.), *The Oxford handbook of personality and social psychology* (pp. 209–238). New York: Oxford University Press.

Kennedy, J. (1992). *Analyzing qualitative data: Log-linear analysis for behavioral research* (2nd ed.). Westport, CT: Praeger.

Kenny, D.A., Kashy, D.A., & Cook, W.L. (2006). *Dyadic data analysis.* New York: Guilford Press.

Landis, J.R., & Koch, G.G. (1977). The measurement of observer agreement for categorical data. *Biometrics, 33,* 159–174.

Lindahl, K.M. (2001). Methodological issues in family observational research. In P.K. Kerig & K.M. Lindahl (Eds.), *Family observational coding systems: Resources for systemic research* (pp. 23–32). Mahwah, NJ: Lawrence Erlbaum Associates.

Margolin, G., Oliver, P.H., Gordis, E.B., O'Hearn, H.G., Medina, A.M., Ghosh, C.M., & Morland, L. (1998). The nuts and bolts of behavioral observation of marital and family interaction. *Clinical Child and Family Psychology Review, 1,* 195–213.

Pascual-Leone, A., Greenberg, L.S., & Pascual-Leone, J. (2009). Developments in task analysis: New methods to study change. *Psychotherapy Research, 19,* 527–542.

Posada, G., & Waters, E. (1988). *The Family Behavior Survey.* Unpublished manuscript, State University of New York at Stony Brook.

Remen, A.L., Chambless, D.L., Steketee, G., & Renneberg, B. (2000). Factor analysis of the English version of the Kategorien system fur Partnerschaftliche Interaktion [Interaction Coding System]. *Behaviour Research and Therapy, 38,* 73–81.

Rosenthal, J.A. (1996). Qualitative descriptors of strength association and effect size. *Journal of Social Science Research, 21,* 37–59.

Sayers, S.L., & McGrath, K. (2004). Data analytic strategies for couple observational coding systems. In P.K. Kerig & K.M. Lindahl (Eds.), *Couple observational coding systems* (pp. 43–63). Mahwah, NJ: Lawrence Erlbaum Associates.

Sechrest, L. (1984). Reliability and validity. In A.S. Bellack & M. Hersen (Eds.), *Research methods in clinical psychology* (pp. 24–54). New York: Pergamon Press.

Seedall, R.B., & Butler, M.H. (2006). The effect of proxy-voice intervention on couple softening in the context of enactments. *Journal of Marital and Family Therapy, 32,* 421–437.

Sullivan, K.T., Pasch, L.A., Johnson, M.D., & Bradbury, T.N. (2010). Social support, problem solving, and the longitudinal course of newlywed marriage. *Journal of Personality and Social Psychology, 98,* 631–644.

Wampler, K.S., Riggs, B., & Kimball, T.G. (2004). Observing attachment behavior in couples: The Adult Attachment Behavior Q-set (AABQ). *Family Process, 43,* 315–335.

Yoder, P., & Symons, F. (2010). *Observational measurement of behavior.* New York: Springer.

25

STATISTICAL ANALYSIS WITH SMALL SAMPLES

Rachel B. Tambling and Shayne R. Anderson

Introduction

In my doctoral research methods class, I (S.R.A.) was assigned the task of design-ing a research study to test the efficacy of couple therapy. I designed a randomized controlled trial in which both therapists and clients were randomly assigned to one of two treatment conditions or a wait-list control. To avoid mono-method bias, the outcome variable was rated by the client, the therapist, and indepen-dent observers. All participants were blinded to the purpose of the study. Treat-ment fidelity and competence would be closely monitored throughout the study. Measurements would be taken pretreatment, posttreatment and at 6-month and 12-month follow-ups. I had designed a study that would maximize internal valid-ity. The one element missing from this plan? Feasibility. The study I designed was not practical for at least two reasons. First, clinical samples are often difficult to obtain and retain. Ask anyone who does clinical research about her/his efforts to recruit and retain participants and you will undoubtedly hear tales of wonder-ful studies that were derailed by low participant engagement (see Chapter 6). Further, there are many client populations that are especially difficult to access for reasons of privacy, scheduling, or lack of interest in research. Yet, many of these difficult-to-engage groups are among the most interesting to clinical researchers. When working with clinical samples, it may be difficult to access large samples of clients. The second reason a study like the one mentioned above is rarely feasible is that such studies are often cost prohibitive. There are substantial costs involved in training research assistants, therapists, and coders, monitoring treatment adher-ence, compensating clients, etc. The time and consequently money invested in conducting such a study make it cost prohibitive for all but a select few.

Conducting strong clinical research requires great balance. Researchers must balance internal and external validity, the dialectic between committing type I and type II errors, and complexity with feasibility. To accomplish this balance, many researchers choose to increase sample size. Large samples are often highly valued, and in many fields, such as family studies, where large, national prob-ability samples are common, strong research has become synonymous with large samples. The October 2012 issue of the flagship journal of family studies, the *Journal of Marriage and Family*, for example, has a median sample size of 1,469 (range = 188–36,889) across the 16 quantitative studies in the issue. It is our contention that strong research comes in many sample sizes. What defines research as strong is not the size of the sample, but rather the rigor with which the study was designed and conducted. Small-sample studies not only are more feasible than large-scale studies, particularly for students conducting theses and dissertations, but can provide useful contributions to the literature if they are conducted well.

This chapter seeks to dispel myths about small-sample research and to offer suggestions to the researcher in hopes of improving the overall quality and rigor of studies with smaller samples. As proponents of high-quality research, regardless of sample size, we hope to convey the message that small-sample studies can be useful and should not be seen as either inferior to larger studies or the solution to a failed larger study. Small studies that are undertaken with attention to detail, sound methodology, and use of appropriate analysis techniques have the potential to offer unique and valid insights into a variety of clinical phenomena. In an effort to promote high-quality research with smaller sample sizes, we will first dispel some misconceptions about small samples. We will then briefly discuss strategies for maximizing power in small-sample studies and address the problem of missing data in small samples, a frequent problem in power analyses. Finally, we will discuss various analytic strategies appropriate for use with small samples.

Common Myths Related to Sample Size

Strong research is not synonymous with large-scale, large-sample research. Sound methodology, innovative design, and appropriate statistical analyses that lead to strong validity and sound conclusions can be present in studies of any sample size. In this section, we address common myths associated with small-sample studies and offer suggestions for managing risks associated with small sample sizes.

Myth #1: Size of Contribution Is Associated with Size of Sample

There is no direct association between the size of the sample and the rigor of the research or the impact of the study on the field. In other words, a large sample does not make up for weak methodology, nor does a large sample cover up a poorly contrived research question. While larger samples may enable the modeling of more complex phenomena, more complexity does not always lead to better validity. For example, as sample size increases, the probability of committing a type I error also increases, and the statistical conclusion validity of the study is compromised. With an extremely large sample size, any difference between the means of two samples will be statistically significant whether or not this difference corresponds to an actual difference between the two populations of interest. Further, a large sample does not necessarily indicate strong research. Consider, however, some small studies that have made a significant impact. John Watson's research on classical conditioning with "Little Albert" (Watson & Rayner, 1920) is among the best-known studies in psychology. This single-case study in which Watson conditioned a young boy to fear furry objects laid the groundwork for understanding conditioned responses in humans and has had a profound impact well beyond the field of psychology. It was well grounded in theory and useful and had important implications for the field. In short, it was well designed, thoughtfully conducted research. Likewise, Bradley and Furrow (2004) performed a task analysis of four videotaped sessions of emotionally focused therapy with couples to identify the process by which blamer softening occurs. This small-sample study answers an important question and does so with the appropriate methodology, including an attention to the dependence inherent in data collected from couples. Sound research occurs when the research question is important, the design and sample are selected to answer the research question in meaningful ways, and the analysis is well suited to the characteristics of the data.

Myth #2: Good Studies Use HLM or SEM or APIM (or the Most Sophisticated New Method)

The authors are strong proponents of knowing and being able to appropriately apply the most recent analytic advances in our field. In fact, we have each employed sophisticated analytic strategies in recent studies; however, a study is not of value because of the analytic strategy. The selection of an analytic strategy should be driven by the desire to use the strategy most appropriate for the question and sample, not the desire to demonstrate one's statistical knowledge. A great deal of useful information can be obtained from relatively simple analytic strategies, particularly when they are appropriate for the structure of the data and the research questions. This is particularly true when data are nonindependent in nature, as are data from couples and families. Often, researchers seek to manage nonindependence in the data through structural equation modeling (SEM) or hierarchical linear modeling (HLM). While this is acceptable, the methodology may not fit the question. Later in this chapter, we highlight several methods by which data from small samples can be analyzed, many of which manage nonindependence well.

It is worth noting that there have been a number of useful advances in data analytic strategies for studies with samples of all sizes. Many such advances are described elsewhere in this volume.

Myth #3: Small Samples Will Have Insufficient Power for Hypothesis Testing

A critical question in small-sample research is not size of the sample, but: What is the expected statistical power? Power refers to the probability that a test will reject the null hypothesis when the null hypothesis is false. Power is directly related to type II errors (the likelihood of failing to reject the null hypothesis when the null hypothesis is true). If the probability of committing a type II error is b, power is denoted as $1 - b$. Statistical power is more important than sample size. An example will illustrate this fundamental difference. Imagine a study with a sample of 10 therapists. Five are novice therapists and 5 are expert therapists. The research question is related to differences between novice and expert therapists in clinical outcomes. Whether or not this sample is small is irrelevant. The question we really care about is, "Does a sample of 10 therapists allow us to answer the question we care about?" Let's assume that among the population of therapists, there is a very large difference between novice and expert therapists' level of some variable (for the purpose of illustrating the point, we'll assume an effect size of $d = 2.0$, even though this large of an effect is rare in our field). If we set our p-value at .05, a one-tailed independent samples t-test will have a power estimate of .89[1] to detect differences between the experienced and novice therapists. Under these conditions, a sample of 10 therapists is quite large. In fact, we need only 8 therapists to achieve a power of .80, which is sufficient power to test the hypothesis (Faul, Erdfelder, Lang, & Buchner, 2007). However, if we assume a medium effect size ($d = .50$), our sample of 10 therapists is dreadfully small and results in a power of only .18. Under these conditions, we are very likely to commit a type II error (i.e., say there is no difference between the therapists when there really is a difference). To achieve the same level of power, we would need 134 therapists—which would likely require cost- and time-prohibitive recruitment strategies. Power must be considered quite carefully in studies in which the unit of analysis is the couple or family, rather than the individual. The reduction of data points in the form of grouping can obscure differences, requiring a larger sample to achieve the requisite level of power. In short, what we care about is statistical power, not the number of participants. While it is true that number of participants is one factor in computing statistical power, other elements must be taken into consideration as well.

Myth #4: Large Samples Are the Only Way to Demonstrate that Change Has Occurred in a Sample

One common misconception in our field is that change must be demonstrated across a large number of people for it to be "real" change. This is simply not true. Large samples are not needed to demonstrate either clinical significant or statistically significant change. Like most research questions, the evidence that change has occurred depends primarily on the research question and analytic strategy. For example, researchers can use information about the measurement properties of an instrument and previous knowledge about community and

---

1 Power analyses in this chapter were conducted with Faul, Erdfelder, Lang, and Buchner's (2007) program G*Power 3. This is a wonderful tool developed to assist researchers conduct power analyses that is available for free at: http://www.psycho.uni-duesseldorf.de/abteilungen/aap/gpower3/

clinical samples to know whether change has occurred with regard to scores on an instrument. One common way to do this is through the use of an established cutoff score or index (derived from the samples) that indicates that change has happened. Jacobson and Truax (1991) explain one common way to develop a reliable change index for a measure. The reliable change index is the degree to which a score on a given measure has to change to confidently state that a reliable change, or change that exceeds the measurement error of the instrument, has occurred. Researchers may also use cutoff scores on an instrument to determine whether research participants are more like community or clinical samples, or have experienced changes in scores. Finally, researchers may wish to use assessments of clinically significant change as markers of change occurring. Such methods offer a variety of meaningful ways to determine that change has occurred in samples as small as one individual, one couple, or one family.

Myth #5: The Sample Size Is the Number of Participants in the Study

A final common misconception about small-sample studies is that the sample size in question is always the number of participants. Many researchers choose to increase the number of people recruited into a study in an effort to increase the sample size and, consequently, the power. While this may be true for some research designs, an appropriate approach, depending on the research question, is to collect more observations from a smaller pool of participants. Depending on the research question, the sample may be observations, moments, or something similar, not participants. Many data analytic strategies are able to capture such an arrangement within people, organizing data as observations within subjects and subjects within families or couples, if desired. The sample size is relevant to the research question and the analytic strategy and may not always reference individual human subjects.

Consider the following example from John Gottman's early work. In one study, Levenson and Gottman (1983) gathered thousands of physiological observations from 15 distressed couples and compared them with those obtained from 15 non-distressed couples. In this case, the sample of interest consisted of observations, not participants. The research questions revolved around the characteristics of these observations, rather than the humans to which they were attributed. This study laid the groundwork for much of Gottman's future research and is an example of sound research design and implementation. While the number of human participants was relatively small, the sample (i.e., the number of observations) was quite large. There are a number of methods of data analysis for use in studies in which the unit of analysis is not a person, but rather an observation or some other phenomenon.

In conclusion, there are a number of misconceptions about small-sample studies, many related to the relative importance or usefulness of small-sample studies. While small-sample studies can be valuable, practical, feasible, and useful, a number of questions remain. Among those, the ways in which power is impacted by sample size, and the ways in which missing data impact samples, must be examined.

Power in Small-Sample Studies

The best planned research strategy is generally the one that has been developed to maximize power. First, sufficient statistical power is a necessary prerequisite to hypothesis testing. Insufficient power results in an increased risk of type II errors, or errors that occur when a false null hypothesis is confirmed. Sufficient power is also necessary to detect other effects, such as interaction effects, as in gender interactions between couple members, or other complex effects like mediation and moderation. Finally, sufficient power is necessary to ensure that data analysis can proceed with the selected analytic strategy, as some strategies are able to detect smaller effects than others.

Statistical power is determined by sample size, p-value, the alpha level, and the effect size of the phenomenon of interest. Of these, researchers often think of sample size as the most accessible to experimenter manipulation. However, if one is planning a small-sample study, statistical power can be enhanced by changing other determinants of power. Strategies that increase power without increasing sample size include focusing on large effects, selecting reliable measures, using balanced groups, limiting predictors, and adjusting the p-value.

Strategy 1: Select a research question in which the hypothesized effect size is large and directional. If a researcher knows that her funding will permit only a small sample, she can increase power by selecting a research question that posits a large effect size. Large effect sizes directly, and often drastically, impact the power of a study even when sample sizes are equal. The hypothesized effect size can be derived from theory, past qualitative work in the area, or clinical experience. Using past research and collected wisdom as a guide, researchers make estimates about the potential effect size of constructs in a given study. An example of the difference increasing the effect size has on power was presented earlier in this chapter. The larger the potential change, or effect size, all else being equal, the greater the effect size and fewer participants needed.

Directional hypotheses, in which the researcher specifies the nature of the hypothesized relationship between the variables, can also increase the power of many analyses. Consider the t-test with an alpha level of $p = .05$. t-Scores follow the t-distribution, which approximates a normal distribution. In a two-tailed significance test, for a t-score to be significant, it must fall within 2.5% of *either* the upper or the lower tail of the distribution. A one-tailed test specifies which side of the distribution the hypothesized result should fall. If the result falls within 5% of the tail in the hypothesized direction, it is considered significant. By specifying the direction of effect, we gain power to detect those effects.

Strategy 2: Select a reliable measure. The reliability of a measure impacts power through changes to the effect size. By minimizing the "noise" in a measure, the variability of scores within the sample due to measurement error is minimized. By decreasing variability in scores due to error, true differences in scores emerge and effect size is increased. Cohen's d, for example, is calculated by dividing the difference between the mean scores of two groups by the pooled standard deviation.

$$d = \frac{\bar{x}_1 - \bar{x}_2}{S_{pooled}} \tag{1}$$

By decreasing the variability within the sample, the value in the denominator is decreased, leading to a larger effect size and greater power.

Strategy 3: Balance the design. Generally speaking, the power of a test increases when all groups have the same number of participants (Keppel, 1991).[2] That is, when comparing across groups, having the same number of participants in each group increases the sensitivity of the test. Consider, for example, a one-way fixed effects analysis of variance (ANOVA) in which three groups have means of 6, 7, and 8 on the measure of interest. To simplify the analysis, assume that the standard deviations are the same across groups (SD = 1). The total sample consists of 21 participants. If the design is balanced, each group will consist of 7 participants and the effect size (f) of this mean difference will be 0.82. If we unbalance the n in each group to 4, 13, and 4 participants, respectively, the effect size of the mean difference is reduced to $f = 0.62$ and the power is reduced to .64. This occurs because the block effects do not cancel out as they would in a balanced design. To account for the block effects, the sum of squares is adjusted with an accompanying loss of power. In other words, without adding a single participant, a researcher can increase the power to optimal levels merely by ensuring that the design is balanced. Careful consideration of the optimal number of subjects in each group, condition, or category can increase power. Researchers can accomplish this before a study begins using a power analysis tool such as G*Power.

Strategy 4: Adjust the p-value. Many of the readers of this chapter (and perhaps some journal editors as well) are screaming, "Heresy!" at this strategy. This response confounds us. Despite the arbitrary nature of a p-value of .05 and the significant critique of this in the literature (Cohen, 1994; Cowles & Davis, 1982), most researchers consider $p = .05$ sacrosanct. However, researchers often adjust the significance level to account for type I error inflation. It is common practice to use a Bonferroni adjustment to control for the family-wise error rate involved in testing multiple hypotheses with the same data. Yet similar adjustments are not seen as acceptable when confronting inflated type II error rates. Small samples increase the type II error rate. Increasing the p-value for our hypothesis test is a logical way to

---

2 The exception to this general rule is when the different groups in the study have differing levels of cost and there is a fixed budget for the study. In this case, the gain in power from the increased n of the lower-cost group offsets the decrease in power from the unbalanced design. Hsu (1994) provides specific guidance for achieving optimal power under these conditions.

compensate for the inflated type II error rate associated with small samples. To see the difference that adjustments in the *p*-value make to sample size requirements, consider a study in which the researcher wants to examine mean difference between male and female adolescents' relationship with their parents. The researcher has $100 to spend on reimbursing participants for their time and she estimates that she will need an incentive of at least $2/participant to successfully recruit. As she sits to do her power analysis, she believes that there will be a medium effect size and wants a power of .80 and an alpha of .05. Upon running her analysis, she is saddened to see that she will need a total of 102 participants, well beyond the 50 she can afford. With a sample of 50 and an alpha of .05, her power will be only .54, much lower than she would like for her initial research in this area. By increasing her alpha level to .10, a sample of 50 participants will result in power of .68. While neither the alpha level nor the power level is ideal, it represents a better balance, and she sets her alpha level at .10. While this approach may be seldom used, from a methodological standpoint it is not only appropriate, but perfectly acceptable.

Strategy 5: Keep it simple. Jacob Cohen (1990) wrote a wonderful article for *American Psychologist* in which he outlined some of the lessons he had learned over his remarkable career. In this paper, he devotes an entire section to the idea that "Less Is More" (p. 1304). In describing researchers who design complex studies and thereby limit their power, he says, "The irony is that people who do studies like this often start off with some useful central idea that, if pursued modestly by means of a few highly targeted variables and hypotheses, would likely produce significant results" (p. 1305). A well-designed study that tests few predictors and answers a simple question well is preferred over a study that answers a complex question poorly or fails to answer any questions at all due to insufficient power. Decreasing the complexity of the planned analyses becomes necessary for a variety of reasons, most often due to low enrollment, participant attrition, or study discontinuance. Decreasing the complexity of the model—for example, by limiting the number of predictors or selecting a method of analysis more appropriate for smaller samples— can increase the power of the analyses and preserve the usefulness of the data. In making such concessions, a critical question must be answered: Will the modifications appropriately address my research question? We think it is preferable to answer a simple question well than a complex question with less precision. Answers to seemingly modest questions often move the field forward in significant ways.

A discussion of power in small-sample studies cannot be complete without mention of missing data in small samples. Missing data are a problem in most clinical research, and the problems posed by missing data are amplified when samples are small.

Missing Data in Small-Sample Studies

Missing data are a common source of frustration among researchers, as missing data impact power (see Chapter 21). Researchers may choose to delete cases with missing data. This results in reduced power, inaccurate confidence intervals, and a potential biasing of parameter estimates, particularly when using statistical methods that are sensitive to missing data, as many methods for use with small samples are (Collins, Schafer, & Kam, 2001). Studies with small samples and missing data are doubly burdened. Many researchers handle missing data by deleting cases listwise, also referred to as complete case analysis (Schafer & Graham, 2002). Listwise deletion is the elimination of any cases in which data are missing. This is the default method of handling missing data in many statistical software packages. In the case of small samples and data missing at random or completely at random, listwise deletion can result in the deletion of so many cases that there are too few observations with which to conduct the desired analyses or insufficient power to detect results. Worse, when data are non-ignorable missing and the sample is small, the deletion of cases listwise will likely result in systematic biases in the results (Malhotra, 1987; Roth, 1994).

Several methods for handling missing data statistically have been proposed. Two of the most popular methods are maximum likelihood (Little & Rubin, 1987) and multiple imputation (Enders, 2010; Rubin, 1977; Schafer, 1999). Both methods use sophisticated techniques to capture the data in the best possible way. Unfortunately, both were designed for use in very large samples and, thus, will not be described in this chapter. Instead, we focus on several emerging techniques that have been suggested for use with small samples: mean substitution, expectation maximization, and regression imputation.

Mean substitution is a single imputation technique in which missing data on one variable are replaced with the mean of the observed data on that same variable. Mean substitution, while preserving the mean of the variable, impacts the distribution in other ways. Often, the variance and median are affected (Little & Rubin, 1989), and the range of the variable is restricted, peaking the distribution at the mean point (Allison, 2002).

Regression-based methods refer to both single and multiple imputation methods and are also referred to as regression imputation or conditional mean imputation methods. All regression-based methods involve imputing missing data from either a single other variable, as in the case of single imputation, or multiple variables, as in the case of multiple imputation, by replacing the missing data with the result of a regression equation in which observed variable(s) with present data are utilized to predict the missing data (see Little & Rubin, 1989 for a detailed description). There are a variety of methods of multiple imputation regression (see Barnes, Lindbord, & Seaman, 2006 for an accessible explanation of each), though most methods generate multiple datasets with different values of the missing data and estimate parameters based on the combination of estimates from the generated datasets. Though regression-based methods are more sophisticated than mean substitution, the approach assumes that the variation in the missing data are completely explained by the observed data, thus restricting the range in the missing data (Enders, 2001) and, potentially, overestimating the relationship between predictors and outcomes (Schafer & Graham, 2002). It is worth noting that the accuracy of regression-based methods in estimating data is dependent upon the quality of the predictors selected for the regression equation (Rubin et al., 2007). Thus, strong associations between variables are essential, and multiple imputation is preferable to single imputation, meaning that more than one variable are used as predictors.

Expectation maximization is a catch-all term for a variety of different algorithms in which maximum likelihood estimated are produced in two steps. First, missing data are estimated using a regression-based method in which other variables are used as predictors, then the suggested values are modified based on statistics generated in the regression step (Enders & Peugh, 2002; Little & Rubin, 2002; Schafer, 1999). This process continues for a user-specified number of iterations or until the values stop changing. Unfortunately, there is uncertainty about the necessary sample size, and amount of missing data, for successful expectation maximization. Given that the method uses a complex imputation strategy, larger samples are suggested (see Enders & Peugh or Choi et al., 2004 for more information). As always, *larger* is in the eye of the beholder, so firm estimates of what is "large" are not available. Though expectation maximization, like regression-based approaches, uses researcher-selected predictors in the regression equation, the iterative nature of the procedure reduces the impact of marginal predictors in the estimation of missing data (Rubin et al., 2007).

In comparisons of the missing data approaches, results vary but tend to favor multiple implicate approaches, such as multiple imputation and expectation maximization. Saunders and colleagues (2006), in a study using samples of moderate and large size, suggested that multiple implicate methods, such as expectation maximization, be used for small to moderate amounts (1–10%) of missing data. Graham and Schafer (2009) found that multiple imputation performs well in samples as small as 50 cases and with as much as 50% missing data in the dependent variables. Further, Graham and Schafer suggested that multiple imputation can perform well with nonnormal data. Barnes, Lindborg, and Seaman (2006) examined a number of methods of multiple imputation and found good results in clinical research and biostatistics examples. Rubin and colleagues (2007) examined missing data in a very small sample with a repeated measures design. In a sample with 17 cases, the researchers found that listwise deletion was the worst performing strategy (Rubin et al., 2007). With low levels of missing data, around 1–2%, mean substitution, regression-based methods, and expectation maximization fared equally well. At higher levels of missing data, up to 10%, expectation maximization was the preferred method. The expectation maximization algorithm can be applied using freeware called NORM (Schafer, 1999). The NORM program can also be used for multiple imputation.

Analytical Techniques for Small-Sample Studies

Nonparametric Statistics

Nonparametric statistics is a branch of statistics that has not gained sufficient respect in the social sciences despite its widespread acceptance in the field of statistics (Hollander & Wolfe, 1999). Recently, one prominent MFT researcher shared his surprise when a statistician he had consulted with on a project recommended he use a chi-square test to test his hypothesis. Unlike many researchers, statisticians do not seem to worry about whether or not a test is in style, but rather focus on whether the test is appropriate for the data. While nonparametric procedures may not be as flashy as many other methods, they should be considered for small-sample studies for at least three reasons. First, they allow researchers to carry out hypothesis testing that is more robust than it is when utilizing the parametric counterparts. Second, when assumptions of normality are not met, nonparametric statistics have more statistical power than their parametric counterparts; and, third, nonparametric procedures are relatively insensitive to outliers, a common problem in smaller samples (Hollander & Wolfe).

It is clear that statistical conclusion validity is influenced by power in that insufficient power leads to decreased statistical conclusion validity. Statistical conclusion validity, however, also relies on the assumptions of statistical analysis having been met. Parametric statistical analyses (e.g., t-tests, ANOVAs, regression) assume that observations are independent, that the observations are drawn from a normally distributed population, and that variances are uniform across groups. These assumptions, particularly the assumption of normality and equality of variances, are often violated in small samples and are uniformly violated in research with couples and families. The assumption of independence inherent in all parametric statistical procedures is uniformly violated by samples of couples or families. As sample size increases, the parametric tests become more robust against violations of these assumptions, but with small samples, violations can have a significant impact on parametric hypothesis testing. While it is true that various parametric tests are more or less robust against violations of these assumptions, a better practice is to use nonparametric procedures that make no assumption regarding the distribution of the parameter in the population, particularly when the sample is small and may not be representative of the population parameter in question.

If the shape of the distribution of a parameter in the population and the normality of the distribution within the sample are clear, parametric procedures will be more powerful, and fewer type I errors will be committed. However, if the sample is small and nonnormally distributed or if the distribution of the parameter within the population is uncertain, greater power will be achieved by conducting hypothesis testing with nonparametric procedures.

Finally, because nonparametric procedures are often rank based (i.e., use the median rather than the mean), they are less susceptible to the influence of outliers. In large samples, researchers often apply a "data treatment" to outliers. That is, researchers often either delete the outlier or retain the outlier, knowing that its influence on the sample statistics, as a whole, will be minimal, given the large sample. When the sample is small, having outliers not only is likely, but poses problems for data analysis. Neither treatment typically used in parametric procedures—retaining the outlier in the dataset knowing this may influence the mean or deleting the outlier and losing a precious data point—is desirable.

Table 25.1 Common Parametric Procedures and Their Counterparts

Parametric Procedures	*Nonparametric Procedures*
Differences between independent groups	
Independent samples *t*-test	Mann–Whitney *U*-test
ANOVA	Kruskal–Wallis analysis
Differences between dependent groups	
Paired samples *t*-test	Wilcoxon's signed-rank test
	Sign test
Repeated-measures ANOVA	Friedman's two-way ANOVA by ranks
	Cochran Q
Relationship between variables	
Pearson product moment Correlation	Spearman *R*
	Kendall tau
	Gamma
	Chi-square (nominal)

Nonparametric hypothesis testing, because of its reliance on rank rather than mean, is less sensitive to outliers in the data.

By now, we have hopefully convinced you of the merits of nonparametric tests. Table 25.1 lists common parametric tests and their nonparametric equivalents. These nonparametric procedures are easily accessible in SPSS and other statistical packages. Space does not allow for a full presentation of all the appropriate nonparametric procedures. For a detailed explanation of nonparametric hypothesis testing, consult Hollander and Wolfe's (1999) useful volume on the subject.

In conclusion, nonparametric procedures are ideally suited for small samples in which the assumptions of normality and equality of variance are often violated. Under the conditions of nonnormality, they have greater power than do parametric procedures and are not as influenced by outliers. In short, nonparametric procedures should be among researchers' first choices when determining how to analyze data from small samples, particularly if those data are from couples or families.

Bootstrapping

Bootstrapping is a resampling technique that allows researchers to draw more accurate inferences about the population parameters using statistics from a sample (Efron & Tibshirani, 1993). Bootstrapping is particularly useful with small samples when the researchers are not sure whether the assumptions of parametric tests are met. In parametric statistics, researchers make assumptions about the population parameter of interest based on sample statistics. Unfortunately, any estimate derived from any sample, particularly a small sample, may differ from the corresponding population parameter because the sample is only one of an infinite number of samples that could have been drawn from the population's sampling distribution. Bootstrapping enables researchers to provide a measure of the accuracy of the sample estimates and confidence intervals without knowing anything about the shape of the distribution of that parameter in the population. This is done through a process of resampling data multiple times to approximate replication of a small study. For example, if a researcher were interested in determining the average level of couple satisfaction in the United States, she could use a random sample of 30 individuals, administer a measure of dyadic satisfaction, and compute the mean. If this study were replicated 1,000 times, one would notice that there is variability in the sample means. If those means were plotted, the researcher could better understand the distribution of marital satisfaction in the United States across the 1,000 samples of 30 individuals. Since replicating a study 1,000 times is impractical, bootstrapping is used to approximate this process by treating the data from a small sample as the population and randomly resampling and replacing values with values from the existing data to determine an approximate distribution.

To illustrate this concept, examine the process in a sample of five individuals with the following scores on an imaginary measure of satisfaction that ranges from 1–10: 7, 7, 3, 2, and 10. During the bootstrapping process, these data are randomly resampled. At each random resampling, the data from these five cases are used to create a new possible sample. For example, one sample might consist of the values 7, 7, 7, 7, and 2, while another might consist of the values 3, 2, 10, 3, 2, and so on. Each sampling results in a mean of marital satisfaction for that sampling. The resulting distribution approximates the sampling distribution in the population and allows us to provide more accurate inferences about the population parameters that are important to us. Bootstrapping does not impact the estimates of the original sample in any meaningful way, but it will provide more accurate standard errors and confidence intervals of the estimate, thus leading to more accurate calculation of effect sizes and improving the statistical conclusion validity of the study. Bootstrapping can be applied to parametric statistics from analyses ranging from t-tests to time-series analyses. Bootstrapping procedures are available in SPSS with the purchase of the bootstrapping add-on. After purchasing the bootstrapping add-on, a "bootstrap" button will appear in the main dialog box of the procedures in SPSS that support bootstrapping. Bootstrapping is also possible in SPSS without the add-on by creating syntax to resample the dataset. We have provided sample syntax for bootstrapped regression coefficients in Appendix A.

As researchers supplement their traditional small-sample analyses such as t-tests and ANOVAs with bootstrapping procedures, they will greatly improve the accuracy of their estimates. This improved accuracy is particularly important in improving the statistical conclusion validity of small sample research. Those interested in learning more about bootstrapping procedures are encouraged to consult Efron and Tibshirani's (1993) work on the subject.

Pooled Regression for Modeling Interdependence

The actor–partner interdependence model (APIM; Cook & Kenny, 2005) was developed to explicitly model interdependence among observations. In this model, individual data are retained, allowing for the estimation of both individual and dyadic features of data (Kenny, 1995). The APIM is the model of choice for many researchers who have couple data and wish to learn more about the dependence within the data. While the APIM can be estimated in several different ways, many of the most common estimation methods (SEM, HLM) require the use of larger samples than may be available to many clinical researchers. However, there is one approach to the estimation of the APIM that is suitable for small samples, a pooled regression approach that is based on ordinary least squares regression analyses (Kenny; Tambling, Johnson, & Johnson, 2011) and is suitable for couple research with small samples. In this method, two regression equations are estimated and the results are pooled together using simple mathematical procedures to obtain the parameters of interest (Kashy & Kenny, 2000; Kenny et al., 2006; Tambling et al.). The pooled regression approach is quite appealing, as it can be used to analyze data from samples that are quite small, as few as 10 to 20 individuals, depending on the reliability of the measures and the hypothesized effect size of the phenomenon of interest. Because the pooled regression approach is based on ordinary least squares regression, the sample sizes required for adequate power for single-predictor regression equations are the same sample sizes required to estimate the APIM using pooled regression.

For distinguishable dyads, as in the case of male-female couples, the statistical analysis of the APIM is straightforward. Two regression equations are computed, each with a single predictor. In the within-dyads regression, the difference between each partner's scores on the predictor variable $(X_1 - X_2)$ is regressed on the difference between each partner's scores on the outcome variable $(Y_1 - Y_2)$. The direction of the difference between Xs and Ys is arbitrary. Because of this, the intercept should not be estimated in the within-dyads regression (Kenny et al., 2006). This results in a within-dyads regression equation, shown in equation 2 below.

$$Y_{1i} - Y_{2i} = b_w(X_{1i} - X_{2i}) + E_{wi} \tag{2}$$

The between-dyads regression involves predicting the dyad mean of the outcome variable using the dyad mean of the predictor variable as a single predictor. This results in a between-dyads regression equation, shown in equation 3 below.

$$\frac{Y_{1i} + Y_{2i}}{2} = b_0 + b_b \frac{X_{1i} + X_{2i}}{2} + E_{bi} \tag{3}$$

The regression coefficients from these two equations (b_b and b_w), then, are used to estimate the actor and partner effects (Kenny et al., 2006), shown in equation 4.

$$actor = \frac{(b_b + b_w)}{2} \quad partner = \frac{(b_b - b_w)}{2} \tag{4}$$

Actor and partner effects can be interpreted as unstandardized regression coefficients. To determine whether these effects differ significantly from zero, a t-statistic is calculated using the pooled standard error as derived from equation 5 (Kenny et al., 2006).

$$SE_p = \sqrt{\frac{(s_b^2 + s_w^2)}{4}} \tag{5}$$

The estimate of the effect is divided by the standard error to obtain a t-statistic. The degrees of freedom for the t-tests can be calculated as follows in equation 6 (Kenny et al., 2006).

$$df = \frac{(s_b^2 + s_w^2)^2}{\dfrac{s_b^4}{df_b} + \dfrac{s_w^4}{df_w}} \tag{6}$$

To test the statistical significance of the t-statistic, examine a t-table and locate the cutoff value for the desired level of significance with the correct number of degrees of freedom. Readers who wish to learn more about this method or review an example of the process using data are encouraged to consult the study by Tambling, Johnson, and Johnson (2011).

Conclusion

It is clear that conducting strong clinical research requires great balance, finesse, and attention to detail. Researchers must balance internal and external validity, comfort with committing type I and type II errors, and complexity with feasibility. Sound research must maximize the rigor with which the study is designed and conducted. Small-sample studies are not inferior to larger studies, as some may believe, but can be well designed, grounded in theory, and highly rigorous. This chapter presented truths and myths about small-sample research, offered suggestions for the researcher, and addressed typical concerns in small-sample research such as power, missing data, and statistical analyses. In sum, rigorously conducted small-sample studies can not only make valuable contributions to the literature, but may be the most appropriate way to answer questions of research interest.

References

Allison, P. D. (2002) *Missing data*. Thousand Oaks, CA: Sage Publication.
Barnes, S. A., Lindbord, S. R., & Seaman, J. W. (2006). Multiple imputation techniques in small sample clinical trials. *Statistics in Medicine*, 25, 233–245.

Bradley, B. & Furrow, J. L. (2004). Toward a Mini-Theory of the Blamer Softening Event: Tracking the Moment-by-Moment Process. *Journal of Marital & Family Therapy, 30*(2), 233–246. doi: 10.1111/j.1752-0606.2004.tb01236.x

Choi Y. J., Nam C. M., Kwak M. J. (2004) Multiple imputation technique applied to appropriateness ratings in cataract surgery. *Yonsei Med J,* 45:829–837.

Cohen, J. (1990). Things I have learned (so far). *American Psychologist, 45,* 1304–1312. doi:10.1037/0003–066X.45.12.1304

Cohen, J. (1994). The earth is round (*p* <.05). *American Psychologist, 49,* 997–1003.

Collins, L. M., Schafer, J. L., & Kam, C. M. (2001). A comparison of inclusive and restrictive strategies in modern missing-data procedures. *Psychological Methods, 6,* 330–351.

Cook, William L., & Kenny, David A. (2005). The Actor-Partner Interdependence Model: A model of bidirectional effects in developmental studies. *International Journal of Behavioral Development, 29*(2), 101–109. doi: 10.1080/01650250444000405

Cowles, M., & Davis, C. (1982). On the origins of the .05 level of statistical significance. *American Psychologist, 37,* 553–558. doi:10.1037/0003–066X.37.5.553

Efron, B., & Tibshirani, R. J. (1993). *An introduction to the bootstrap.* New York: Chapman & Hall.

Enders, C. K. (2010). *Applied missing data analysis.* New York: Guilford Press.

Enders C. K. (2001) A primer on maximum likelihood algorithms available for use with missing data. *Structural Equation Modeling: A Multidisciplinary Journal* 8:128–141.

Enders C., Peugh J. (2004) Using an EM covariance matrix to estimate structural equation models with missing data: Choosing an adjusted sample size to improve the accuracy of inferences. *Structural Equation Modeling: A Multidisciplinary Journal* 11:1–19.

Faul, F., Erdfelder, E., Lang, A. G., & Buchner, A. (2007). G*Power 3: A flexible statistical power analysis program for the social, behavioral, and biomedical sciences. *Behavior Research Methods, 39,* 175–191.

Graham, J. W., Schafer, J. L. On the performance of multiple imputation for multivariate data with small sample size. In R. H. Hoyle (Ed.) *Statistical Strategies For Small Sample Research.* 1999. Sage Publications: Thousand Oaks: CA.

Hollander, M., & Wolfe, D. A. (1999). *Nonparametric statistical methods.* New York: J. Wiley.

Hsu, L. (1994). Unbalanced designs to maximize statistical power in psychotherapy efficacy studies. *Psychotherapy Research, 4,* 95–106. DOI: 10.1080/10503309412331333932

Jacobson, N. S. and P. Truax (1991). Clinical significance: A statistical approach to defining meaningful change in psychotherapy research. *Journal of Consulting and Clinical Psychology 59, 12–19.*

Kashy, D. A., & Kenny, D. A. (2000). The analysis of data from dyads and groups. In H. T. Reis & C. M. Judd (Eds.), *Handbook of research methods in social psychology.* New York: Cambridge University Press.

Kenny, David A. (1995). The effect of nonindependence on significance testing in dyadic research. *Personal Relationships, 2,* 67–75.

Kenny, David A., Kashy, Deborah A., & Cook, William L. (2006). *Dyadic data analysis.* New York: Guilford Press.

Keppel, G. (1991). *Design and analysis: A researcher's handbook* (3rd ed.). Upper Saddle River, NJ: Prentice Hall.

Levenson, R.W., & Gottman, J.M. (1983). Marital interaction: Physiological linkage and affective exchange. *Journal of Personality and Social Psychology, 45*, 587–597. doi:10.1037/0022-3514.45.3.587

Little, R.J.A., Rubin, D. B. (1989) The analysis of social science data with missing values. *Sociol Methods Res,* 18: 292–326.

Little, R.J.A., Rubin D. B. (2002). *Statistical analysis with missing data* (2nd ed.). New York: Wiley.

Little, R.J.A., Rubin, D. B. (1987) *Statistical analysis with missing data.* New York: Wiley.

Malhotra, N. K. (1987). Analyzing marketing research data with incomplete information on the dependent variable. *Journal of Marketing Research, 24,* 74–84.

Roth, P.L. (1994). Missing data: A conceptual review for applied psychologists. *Personnel Psychology, 47,* 537–560.

Rubin, D. B. (1977) Formalizing subjective notion about the effect of nonrespondents in sample surveys. *J Am Stat Assoc,* 72: 538–543.

Rubin, L. H., Witkiewitz, K., St. Andre, J., & Reilly, S. (2007). Methods for handling missing data in the behavioral neurosciences: Don't throw the baby rat out with the bath water. *The Journal of Undergraduate Neuroscience Education, 5*(2): A71–A77.

Saunders, J. A., Morrow-Howell, N., Spitznagel, E., Dort, P., Proctor, E. K., & Pescarino, R. (2006). Imputing missing data: A comparison of methods for social work researchers. *Social Work Research, 30*(1), 19–31.

Schafer, J.L. (1999). *NORM user's guide: Multiple imputation of incomplete multivariate data under a normal model.* http:// methodology.psu.edu/webfm_send/132

Schafer, J. L. (1999) Multiple imputation: A primer. Stat Methods Med Res 8: 3–15.

Schafer, J.L., & Graham, J.W. (2002). Missing data: Our view of the state of the art. *Psychological Methods, 7,* 147–177.

Tambling, R.B., Johnson, S.K., & Johnson, L.N. (2011). Analyzing dyadic data from small samples: A pooled regression actor–partner interdependence model approach. *Counseling Outcome Research and Evaluation, 2,* 101–114. doi: 10.1177/2150137811422901

Watson, J.B., & Rayner, R. (1920). Conditioned emotional reactions. *Journal of Experimental Psychology, 3,* 1–14.

APPENDIX A

Bootstrapping Syntax for Regression Coefficients

The following syntax is presented with permission of its author, Raynald Levesque. His website (www.spsstools.net) provides useful code for accomplishing a wide variety of tasks in SPSS. This syntax was retrieved from: http://www.spsstools. net/Syntax/Bootstrap/oms_bootstrapping.txt.

```
***oms_bootstrapping.sps***.
***if c:\temp is not a valid drive\path, replace all instances of c:\tempwith a
   valid drive\path.

PRESERVE.
SET TVARS NAMES.

*first OMS command just suppresses Viewer output.
OMS /DESTINATION VIEWER = NO /TAG ='suppressall'.

*select regression coefficients tables and write to data file.
OMS /SELECT TABLES
   /IF COMMANDS = ['Regression'] SUBTYPES = ['Coefficients']
   /DESTINATION FORMAT = SAV OUTFILE ='c:\temp\temp.sav'
   /COLUMNS DIMNAMES = ['Variables''Statistics']
   /TAG ='reg_coeff'.

*define a macro to draw samples with replacement and
run Regression commands.
DEFINE regression_bootstrap (samples = !TOKENS(1)
                            /depvar = !TOKENS(1)
                            /indvars = !CMDEND)

COMPUTE dummyvar = 1.
AGGREGATE
   /OUTFILE ='c:\temp\aggrtemp.sav'
   /BREAK = dummyvar
   /filesize = N.
MATCH FILES FILE = * /TABLE ='c:\temp\aggrtemp.sav'
   /BY dummyvar.
```

```
!DO !other = 1 !TO !samples
SET SEED RANDOM.
WEIGHT OFF.
FILTER OFF.
DO IF $casenum = 1.
- COMPUTE #samplesize = filesize.
- COMPUTE #filesize = filesize.
END IF.
DO IF (#samplesize>0 and #filesize>0).
- COMPUTE sampleWeight = rv.binom(#samplesize, 1/#filesize).
- COMPUTE #samplesize = #samplesize-sampleWeight.
- COMPUTE #filesize = #filesize-1.
ELSE.
- COMPUTE sampleWeight = 0.
END IF.
WEIGHT BY sampleWeight.
FILTER BY sampleWeight.
REGRESSION
  /STATISTICS COEFF
  /DEPENDENT !depvar
  /METHOD = ENTER !indvars.
!DOEND
!ENDDEFINE.

***insert any valid path\data file name***.
GET FILE ='c:\Program Files\SPSS\Employee data.sav'.

***Call the macro, and specify number of samples,
  dependent variable, and independent variables.
regression_bootstrap
  samples = 100
  depvar = salary
  indvars = salbegin jobtime .

OMSEND.

GET FILE 'c:\temp\temp.sav'.

FREQUENCIES
  VARIABLES = salbegin_B salbegin_Beta jobtime_B jobtime_Beta
  /FORMAT NOTABLE
  /PERCENTILES = 2.5 97.5
  /HISTOGRAM NORMAL.

RESTORE.
```

26

INTEGRATING COSTS INTO MARRIAGE AND FAMILY THERAPY RESEARCH

Jacob D. Christenson and D. Russell Crane

Introduction

Cost evaluations, such as cost-effectiveness, are nothing new. Even as early as 1971 E. S. Quade quipped that "the practice of cost-effectiveness started when [humans] first realized that [their] resources were limited. For one Congressional Committee, this took place in the Garden of Eden with the decision to eat or not to eat the apple" (Quade, 1971, p. 1). For a number of years, proponents of individually oriented mental health services have successfully embraced and used cost evaluation results to increase market share for their services, leading to calls from some within the field of marriage and family therapy (MFT) to follow their lead (e.g., Pinsof & Wynn, 1995). Despite the recognized need to include costs in MFT research, there continues to be significant inattention to costs in the MFT literature (e.g., Sprenkle, 2012). Indeed, one could well argue that clinical effectiveness (i.e., decrease of symptoms) is necessary but no longer sufficient evidence for a clinical treatment. Instead, consideration of the costs and benefits of clinical treatments are becoming vital in the competitive world of mental health services.

Among the factors influencing cost evaluation research in MFT are that researchers may be resistant to "monetizing" their interventions, unfamiliar with cost evaluation methods, or feel uncomfortable with the complexity of some of the calculations (e.g., Yates, 1994). Accordingly, the purpose of this chapter is to elucidate cost evaluations by discussing and demonstrating application of some of the methods for including costs in research, starting with the more simple methods (i.e., cost-effectiveness) and then moving to the more complex (i.e., cost-benefit analysis). Attention will also be given to discussing the construct and conclusion validity of cost analyses, as well as special considerations for conducting this type of research within the field of MFT. The chapter will conclude with a discussion of how marriage and family therapists (MFTs) can use findings from cost evaluations to effectively promote their profession.

Controversy, Purpose, and Importance

Before describing and outlining the methods for conducting cost evaluations, it is essential to first consider some of the reasons why researchers might resist this type of investigation in the first place. According to Yates (1994), among the most commonly heard arguments against cost-benefit and cost-effectiveness analyses are that it is concerned with a simplistic analysis considering only money. The argument is that these analyses ignore the quality of clinical interventions and are only used to justify inadequate funding for mental health psychological services. Notwithstanding this criticism, Yates goes on to point out that cost-benefit analysis has been used to show that the overall benefits of a particular treatment far outweigh the cost of providing the treatment.

Recent research has shown that this is true even for programs that are more expensive to implement than treatment as usual (e.g., Klietz, Borduin, & Schaeffer, 2010). It is also important to note that cost evaluations are often most useful when a particular treatment has already been found to be clinically effective, and the researcher is attempting to justify wider distribution (Klarreich, DiGiuseppe, & DiMattia, 1987). Essentially, if a treatment isn't effective, then it doesn't matter that it costs less because cost evaluations factor effectiveness into the calculations. Furthermore, cost-effectiveness research has been used efficiently and successfully by psychologists to argue for the inclusion of their services within various practice settings and insurance programs (e.g., Kessler, 2008), which is in direct contrast to the assumption that cost evaluation is only used to determine which programs to cut.

The utility of highlighting costs, in addition to demonstrating improved clinical outcomes, is especially apparent in the current health care market. After discussing the almost exclusive focus on clinical outcomes in MFT research, Fals-Stewart, Yates, and Klostermann (2005) point out: "In many respects, this nearly myopic focus on clinical outcomes in therapy research trials implicitly ignores a long-standing national apprehension about the economic profile of health care in the United States, including that related to mental health" (p. 28). Similarly, Crane and Christenson (2012) argue: "Unless there is a . . . concerted effort to likewise show that MFT services are cost-effective, MFTs risk at best becoming marginalized in the health care market, and at worst becoming irrelevant" (p. 212). Indeed, it can be argued that in a competitive marketplace, if a product has been not demonstrated to be cost-effective, it will wane in the presence of the product that has demonstrated cost-effectiveness. Further, even if one product has been shown to be cost-effective, it needs to be able to compete well (in price and quality) against other potentially comparable products because the most costly product could soon disappear. Following this line of thinking, Pinsof and Wynn (1995), in a review of the MFT literature, made a plea for more cost research to address the lack of MFT-specific studies. Seventeen years later, in an update of Pinsof and Wynn, Sprenkle (2012) laments: "Sadly, in the first [*Journal of Marital and Family Therapy*] review, [they] called for more attention

421

to this kind of research . . ., and I must repeat that call now. It is hard to over-emphasize the value of cost research for CFT in a cost conscious culture" (p. 9).

The remainder of this chapter will focus on helping bridge the gap between clinical outcomes research and cost research by introducing and highlighting common methods of analyzing costs. Before moving into this discussion, it is important to note that some of the methods can be complex and difficult to apply in research, and in an effort to provide the information in a digestible manner, some of the calculations have been simplified. Accordingly, researchers who wish to integrate cost evaluations into their research should consult additional resources beyond what is contained in this chapter.

Components of Cost Evaluation

Cost evaluations require the consideration of three core elements: costs, effectiveness, and benefits (Fals-Stewart et al., 2005). The specific subtype of cost evaluation is determined by how the researcher employs one or more of these core elements. A list of the common cost evaluation methods discussed in this chapter and their descriptions is provided in Table 26.1. Not surprisingly, defining and determining "costs" is the first task in any type of research that includes cost considerations. Although this may seem a straightforward proposition, there are at least three types of costs that could be included. Lazar (2010) used the perspective of (a) management, (b) an accountant, and (c) an economist to delineate these levels. The management level includes costs related to psychotherapist pay, facility expenses, and administrative and insurance costs. An accountant would add in additional costs (e.g., indirect costs such as parking, security force), and the economist adds in even more abstract costs (i.e., impact on society). Ideally, all three levels would be monetized and included in the calculation of

Table 26.1 Types and Descriptions of Common Cost Evaluation Methods

Method	Description
Cost allocation	Tracking and totaling the costs of delivering a program, treatment, or specific intervention
Cost-effectiveness	Used to determine the cost of achieving a particular outcome. A common method is to calculate the incremental cost-effectiveness ratio
Cost-unit analysis	Similar to cost-effectiveness, but uses a common metric (e.g., quality adjusted life years) to compare programs
Cost-benefit analysis	Used to determine the fiscal benefits of a treatment beyond the costs of delivery. Usually includes a calculation of the present value and net present value of the treatment

cost. However, since many researchers have limited resources for cost evaluation (and often find this process daunting in the first place), we recommend that all researchers start with at least gathering data for the management level. This would include costs within three broad categories: (a) time (e.g., therapist pay, training, supervision), (b) materials (paper assessments, heart rate monitors, electroencephalograph), and (c) overhead (office space rent, utility costs, related office equipment, etc.).

Effectiveness, often referred to as the "clinical outcome, is viewed as changes in clients' behaviors, thoughts, feelings, or health" (Fals-Stewart et al., 2005, p. 30). Unlike costs and benefits, effectiveness is not directly monetized, but instead serves as the constant between treatments that are being evaluated. Without a common measure of effectiveness, it is impossible to compare the costs and benefits of two treatments because it would be like comparing "apples and oranges" with regard to outcomes. In some cases, effectiveness can simply be determined using the effect sizes of two comparable treatments in a clinical trial or other outcome study. This is most useful when calculated effect sizes show that two treatments result in basically the same amount of change on a particular measure, as evidenced by effect sizes that are very close (Hunsley, 2003). Some other possible indicators of effectiveness might be number of days sober in a year, years lived after a heart attack, recidivism rate, pounds lost in a weight loss program, unit change in scores on a depression/anxiety measure, etc.

While some basic cost-effectiveness analyses can be completed with only information about the cost of treatment delivery, benefits such as generalization of improvement across family members, decreased illness, or fewer employee absences should also be included whenever possible. This is especially true when one program is thought to be superior but also costs much more to deliver than the alternate treatment or treatment as usual. Benefits are usually tangible and intangible outcomes that can be monetized according to an accepted standard. For example, a particular treatment program may be associated with fewer on-the-job accidents or injuries. The research could then ask the human resources department how much the company loses per accident or injury and use that information to calculate the savings associated with treatment.

The potential benefits of a particular intervention can be wide and far reaching. In considering costs associated with the juvenile justice system, Lee and Aos (2011) included savings associated with avoided jail/prison, court costs, medical costs, and law enforcement, as well as increased wages, tax revenue, and quality of life as potential "benefits" of intervention. The potential benefits of treatment program are only limited by the resourcefulness of researchers and their ability to monetize the outcome according to an accepted standard. Although researchers may need to derive some of the dollar amounts from the data in their study, there are some figures that have been precalculated. For example, the U.S. National Library of Medicine provides links to numerous websites with data related to health economics that can aid the effort to quantify costs and benefits (http://www.nlm.nih.gov/nichsr/edu/healthecon/websites.html).

Cost-Effectiveness Analysis

Cost-effectiveness is the least complex set of analyses for evaluating costs, as well as the most accessible for clinical researchers. In the general sense, "cost-effectiveness [simply] refers to the value returned per dollar spent" (Lazar, 2010, p. 13). Even without extensive data concerning effectiveness (as defined above), cost-effectiveness calculations can be employed. The simplest method for evaluating costs is to take two treatments with nearly identical effect sizes and compare the costs of the intervention directly. Gould, Otto, and Pollack (1995) used this method to show that cognitive behavioral therapy (CBT) alone was more cost-effective than medication management alone in the treatment of panic disorder. In their analysis, they found that treatment with CBT over 2 years had average per patient direct costs of $1,650, while medication management had direct costs of approximately $3,000 across the same time period. Using similar effect sizes as the basis for their argument, Gould et al. were able to successfully demonstrate that CBT alone produced similar outcomes to medication management while also consuming fewer resources. Similar studies could be completed for competing treatments in MFT that have similar effect sizes (e.g., emotion focused therapy vs. behavioral marital therapy).

When it comes to evaluating cost-effectiveness for comparable treatments that do not have equal outcomes, the most common tool used is the incremental cost-effectiveness ratio (ICER), which is represented by the following formula:

$$ICER = (C_a - C_b) / (E_a - E_b).$$

In this formula C_a is the cost of Treatment A (the new or preferred treatment) and C_b is the cost of Treatment B (treatment as usual), while E_a equals the effect of Treatment A and E_b equals the effect of Treatment B (e.g., Briggs, O'Brien, & Blackhouse, 2002). The "effect" can be any equivalent measure of outcomes employed across studies. For example, if two studies used the same measure (e.g., the Revised Dyadic Adjustment Scale), change scores can be used. Furthermore, in the case where different measures are employed, scores can be converted to effect sizes. The ICER is most often used when the research wants to show that one particular treatment produces better outcomes with similar or fewer costs (e.g., Detsky & Naglie, 1990).

As described above, in order to avoid the problem of comparing apples and oranges, the outcome, or effectiveness measure, must be represented by a common metric. For example, two different interventions for alcohol abuse can be compared based on the number of days sober that the treatment produced in a 12-month period (e.g., Dennis et al., 2004). In this example, we'll say a course of couples therapy (i.e., Treatment A) costs $15,000 per couple and results in 93 days sober, while a course of individual therapy (i.e., Treatment B) costs $12,000 per individual and results in 75 days sober. The dollar amount for the treatment would be expected to include the sum of costs associated with therapist fees, treatment manuals, urinalysis, pen and paper measures, test scoring, a proportion of overhead expenses, transportation to/from the sessions, etc. When these data are entered into the ICER formula, a result of $166 is produced.

$$ICER = (\$15,000 - \$12,000) / (93 \ days - 75 \ days) = \$166.$$

This shows that the 18 extra days of sobriety gained with Treatment A (compared with Treatment B) were obtained at an additional cost of about $166 per day. In this case the two programs would be considered equally cost-effective, since both produce 1 day of sobriety for approximately $160 (Treatment B cost per day sober: *$12,000 / 75 days* = *$160*). Although this result does not support the conclusion that Treatment A is less costly, it does at least show that you are getting about the same return for each dollar put in, which is often enough to convince stakeholders that there is no fiscal "harm" in providing the alternative treatment and that any additional money is "well spent." Taking this example further, the ICER can also be used to demonstrate that a particular intervention results in better clinical outcomes at a lower cost. In this scenario, suppose that the cost of Treatment A was $10,000 and produced 90 days of sobriety, while Treatment B cost $12,500 and produced 63 day of sobriety. Applying the ICER formula returns a result of negative $89, which indicates Treatment A is actually associated with cost savings for each additional day of sobriety produced compared with Treatment B.

A related method, similar to cost-effectiveness analysis, is cost-unit analysis. In contrast to cost-effectiveness analysis, where the outcome of interest is determined by the researcher, in cost-utility analysis a common outcome is calculated and used to compare treatments. The most common outcome in this type of analysis is quality-adjusted life years (QALY). QALY is derived by combining data regarding two health indicators affected by the treatment, life expectancy and quality of life (e.g., Noyes & Holloway, 2004). Although a complete discussion of cost-utility analysis and QALY calculations is beyond the scope of this chapter, it is useful to note that cost-utility analysis can be applied to mental health concerns (e.g., depression management). Additionally, using QALY as the outcome allows for a comparison of costs between two competing treatments, as well as between a particular treatment with different presenting problems, which has led to some governmental agencies using cost-utility analysis as the "gold standard" for evaluating programs (Pirraglia, Rosen, Hermann, Olchanski, & Neumann, 2004).

MFT Cost-Effectiveness Illustration

As an example of MFT cost-effectiveness research, Crane and Payne (2011) examined mental health care claims from 490,000 individuals covered by Cigna to determine what modality of therapy (e.g., individual and family therapy) and what provider type (e.g., MFTs) were the most cost-effective. The authors developed and employed the following formula as a way to compare cost of treatment between different treatment modalities:

$$ECE = \textit{1st EoC Average Cost} + (\textit{1st EoC Average Cost} \times \textit{Recidivism Rate}).$$

In this formula *ECE* is the estimated cost-effectiveness, while *EoC* (i.e., episode of care) was defined as a string of services using a particular modality and ending when no psychotherapy claims were filed for 90 days. Recidivism rate served as the common metric for comparing modalities and was defined by the percentage of clients who returned for a second *EoC* using the same modality after termination. The *1st EoC Average Cost* is the amount paid by Cigna for the first episode of care.

Using this formula, Crane and Payne (2011) were able to show that family therapy was the most cost-effective form of treatment. For family therapy as a modality of care, the *1st EoC Average Cost* was $216.30 and the recidivism rate was 15.4%, so in this case *ECE* = $216.30 + ($216.30 × .154) = $249.61, where $249.61 is the estimated cost-effectiveness for family therapy, which can be interpreted as the expected cost of care for each new case seen exclusively in a family therapy format. Individual therapy, on the other hand, had an average cost of $333.63 for the first EoC, with a recidivism rate of 14.9%. Here *ECE* = $333.63 + ($333.63 × .149), which produced $383.34 as the estimated cost of care for each new case seen exclusively in individual therapy. Using similar methods, Crane and Payne were also able to demonstrate that professional counselors were the most cost-effective provider type in their sample, followed by MFTs.

Cost-Benefit Analysis

Even though cost-effectiveness research provides a solid foundation for integrating cost data into research, there may be times when a particular treatment is felt to be superior over another, even though it costs more to implement and does not appear to have significantly different outcomes at first glance. In such a case, researchers can incorporate more broadly interpreted benefits of treatment into their calculations, which has the effect of extending the fiscal impact beyond just the particular individual. In cost-benefit analysis, the researcher attempts to quantify all possible benefits, as well as all possible costs to determine the overall impact of an intervention. To illustrate the extent to which researchers may go in their analysis, Table 26.2 provides a list of the benefits and costs that Lee and Aos (2011) quantified in their cost-benefit calculations for social interventions through the Washington State Institute for Public Policy.

Once the cost, benefits, and effectiveness of a particular treatment or intervention have been determined, a cost-benefit ratio (CBR) can be calculated to give

Table 26.2 Example of Costs and Benefits*

Potential Benefits of Intervention	Potential Costs of Intervention
Increased wages	Service delivery costs
Increased tax revenue	Staff training
Avoided prison/jail costs	Quality assurance
Avoided law enforcement costs	Administrative overhead
Avoided court costs	Transportation
Avoided medical costs	Assessment costs
Avoided investigations	Court costs
Avoided child placements	Case management costs

*As quantified by Lee and Aos (2011) in cost-benefit analysis of social interventions.

an idea of how much is returned in benefits versus costs (e.g., Spoth, Guyll, & Day, 2002). The formula for this calculation is as follows:

$$CBR = \frac{Present\ Value_b}{Present\ Value_c}$$

Here *Present Value*$_b$ represents the total calculated present value of the benefits, and *Present Value*$_c$ equals the total calculated present value of the costs associated with a treatment or program. (Note: Although not represented in the example to follow, total costs and benefits should be "discounted" *[cost or benefit / 1 + discount rate]* to arrive at the "present value" for each before applying this formula. Although discounting will be addressed more fully in the discussion below, it may help to understand that the discount rate is used to adjust future projections backward toward the value of current dollars). If the application of this formula returns a value greater than 1.0, the program or treatment is considered viable because the benefits outweigh the costs. Conversely, a value of less than 1.0 indicates that the program or treatment produces more costs than benefits. Continuing the example from above and assuming that a day of sobriety is worth $1,250 in benefits (including increased wages[1] from reduced absenteeism,

1 Determining the benefits of an intervention requires the researcher to sum as many of the potential dollars saved or produced as a result of the treatment as can be found. Sometimes the components can be acquired from existing studies. For example, Goetzel et al. (2004) calculated the value of one day of work as $185.20, which could then be used to estimate the value of reduced absenteeism. Likewise, a researcher can also determine the average salary in a sample and divide this amount by 365 to determine the specific amount in that study. Of course, in order to make this meaningful the researcher must measure both income and absenteeism in the study.

avoided divorce expenses, avoided legal fees and jail time, improved health for both members of the couple, etc.), a program that costs $15,000 and results in 93 days of sobriety would produce a cost-benefit ratio of $7.75, indicating that each dollar spent on the program resulted in a savings of $7.75 per dollar spent overall.

$$CBR = \frac{\$1,250 \times 93 \; days}{\$15,000} = \frac{\$116,250}{\$15,000} = \$7.75$$

Calculation of the cost-benefit ratio alone for a particular treatment can be used to argue for its implementation. For example, Klarreich et al. (1987) studied the costs associated with participation in an employee assistance program (EAP) that delivered rational emotive therapy (RET) for 295 employees of a large North American oil company. Klarreich et al. defined benefits in terms of reduced absenteeism and supervisor time saved and found that the total benefit of the EAP was a total savings of $356,062 to the company, in contrast to the $130,000 required to deliver treatment. The figures were used to calculate a cost-benefit ratio of $2.74, indicating that $2.74 was saved for every dollar spent to provide EAP benefits. Klarreich et al. used these findings to show that providing RET through an EAP was beneficial to the company in terms of both increased productivity and a healthier bottom line.

While the CBR can sometimes be useful by itself, it is usually used to support the findings of a full cost-benefit analysis. The core summary measure of cost-benefit analysis is the net present value (NPV) of the intervention or treatment. Although there are a few different ways to arrange the variables in the equation (e.g., Lee & Aos, 2011), for the sake of demonstration we will use the following:

$$NPV = \sum_{y=0}^{N} \frac{(Q \times B - C)_y}{(1 + Dis)^y}$$

In this formula, NPV stands for the net present value of the program or treatment, Q is the quantity of a particular benefit that is produced, B is the monetary value of the benefits of the treatment, C is the cost of the treatment, and *Dis* refers to the discount rate. The discount rate is used to bring projections back to current dollars, since a dollar that hasn't been spent yet theoretically increases in value until it is spent. Although the discount rate may vary depending on the nature of the project, a value of 3% can be considered acceptable for most applications (Gold, Siegel, Russell, & Weinstein, 1996; Miller & Hendrie, 2008). The summation sign is used to show that the values can be projected and totaled (*N*) across a number of individual years (*y*).Continuing with the substance use example above, if we carry over the assumption that the benefit for a day of sobriety was $1,250 (including increased wages, avoided legal fees and jail time, etc.) the *NPV* of the $15,000/93-day program would be $98,300.

$$Treatment\ A = \sum_{y=1}^{N} \frac{\left(93\ days \times \$1,250 - \$15,000\right)_y}{\left(1+.03\right)^y} = \$98,300$$

Likewise, the NPV of the $12,000/75-day program would be $79,368. Accordingly, it could be demonstrated that even though the two programs are essentially identical in terms of cost-effectiveness, Treatment A has a more overall positive economic impact because it results in more days sober. From these examples, it can also be seen how projecting these savings into the future for as long as the benefit is expected to last (e.g., 2 years) would increase the saving associated with the treatment.

$$Treatment\ B = \sum_{y=1}^{N} \frac{\left(75\ days \times \$1,250 - \$12,000\right)_y}{\left(1+.03\right)^y} = \$79,368$$

In a "real world" example, Klietz et al. (2010) applied cost-benefit analysis to multisystemic family therapy (MST) with juvenile offenders. In this study, Klietz et al. compared the costs and benefits of MST with treatment as usual, which, in this case, was individual therapy. The analysis showed that based on reduced recidivism after treatment, MST resulted in a total savings of as much as $199,374 per juvenile offender treated, with a cost-benefit ratio of $23.59. Furthermore, when intangible benefits (e.g., jury award to victims for pain/suffering) were factored in, a cost offset of $14,289 was found for MST compared with individual treatment. This is especially important given that the cost of delivering MST ($10,882 per participant) is substantially higher than the cost for delivering individual treatment ($2,055 per participant).

The savings demonstrated in MST studies like this led Sprenkle (2012) to conclude: "This fairly expensive program has been widely adopted, I am certain, because it has proved to save money on even more expensive alternatives like incarceration" (p. 9). Applying these methods to other types of MFT treatments would more than likely yield similar results and lead to substantial growth in the profession as a whole.

Defining Costs and Benefits of Treatment

Validity and reliability, as commonly understood in research methods, are not typically considered directly in cost evaluations (though "sensitivity analysis" is sometimes used to address related issues; e.g., Fals-Stewart et al., 2005). Instead, these concepts are more often indirectly considered within the context of whether the study upon which effectiveness was based possessed adequate internal and external validity. Stated another way, if the study used to determine effectiveness was flawed, then, by definition, cost evaluations will be flawed as well. Nevertheless, construct validity, as understood in the broader sense, can be readily applied to cost evaluations. This is particularly true when taking into account how costs and benefits are determined and quantified.

Before evaluation of costs can be considered complete, both direct and indirect costs need to be determined. Direct costs refer to expenditures related to the provision of services, while indirect costs refer to "the value of resources lost" (Hunsley, 2003, p. 63), such as would be incurred from absenteeism and decreased productivity related to participation in treatment. Failure to address both direct and indirect costs was actually one of the weaknesses of the study mentioned earlier by Gould et al. (1995), because these authors identified only the direct costs of providing treatment for panic disorder. Similarly, there is a multiplicity of potential direct and indirect benefits that could be included in the cost-benefit analysis. Fals-Stewart et al. (2005) list increased income (e.g., from steady employment), decreased costs associated with criminal activity, and reduced mental health care utilization (e.g., fewer hospitalizations) as the most common broad categories of types of benefits. Determining benefits for each of these categories comes with its own unique challenges, which can significantly impact the validity of the results. This is especially true the farther out benefits are calculated from when the actual treatment was delivered.

Even after selecting which costs and benefits to calculate (which often is limited by what is available in already existing data; e.g., Crane & Payne, 2011), the method for monetizing the variables needs to be carefully considered. Even small variations between the "estimated" value of a particular cost or benefit and the "actual" cost or benefit in the real world can result in dramatic differences in the final calculated costs. Additionally, the variable(s) used for determining effectiveness should be carefully considered. In a study comparing two treatments for depression, is decreased symptom presentation or increased work functioning a more appropriate outcome to investigate? Or should the researcher do the analysis for both outcomes? Such decisions will have a direct effect on the conclusion validity of related cost analyses. If a researcher fails to include important outcomes in the analysis, or poorly quantifies them, the likelihood increases of incorrectly concluding that a treatment is not cost-effective, when in actuality it was cost-effective. Likewise, if the researcher overestimates the benefits, by either using some that are not relevant to the treatment or overestimating the actual value, the likelihood of incorrectly judging a particular treatment to be cost-effective increases as well. Suffice it to say, what the researcher decides to include and evaluate in terms of effectiveness, costs, and benefits can have a dramatic effect on the quality of the cost evaluation, as well as how useful the findings are for consumers.

Considering the Family in Costs and Benefits

The examples presented thus far highlight a unique aspect of cost evaluation in marriage and family research; namely, that the systemic perspective that guides researchers in this field assumes that a change in one part of the system will affect other parts of the system. This understanding leads to the conclusion that cost-benefit analysis in MFT should include the benefits of treatment and intervention for other members of the system. Because most cost evaluations are not conducted by MFT researchers, there is a near absence of studies that include costs and benefits associated with family members. Fals-Stewart et al. (2005) argued that including family members should constitute one of the unique contributions of MFT research to the cost-benefit literature, in part because of the "multiplier effect" of MFT interventions. The multiplier effect highlights that MFT interventions extend beyond just the individual who is the focus of treatment. This multiplier effect could be observed in greater productivity by a client's spouse, as well as fewer sick days and need for costly mental health services (Fals-Stewart et al., 2005).

Take, for example, a couple relationship characterized by marital discord and occasional domestic violence perpetrated by the husband, and where the parents detour their problems through an adolescent child, who then exhibits depression and suicidal behavior resulting in hospitalization. If the father were to receive treatment for domestic violence in a clinical trial, and the researcher conducted a cost-benefit analysis based on "benefits" limited to him (e.g., reduced criminality), it stands to reason that the actual benefits would be significantly underestimated if the treatment also eliminated the adolescent's hospitalizations. It is likely that if MFT researchers were to apply their systemic perspective to cost-benefit analysis, the savings resulting from treatment would be greater than the impressive results already found by those promoting other treatment modalities.

Where this type of research becomes difficult is when dollar amounts have not been previously calculated for potential benefits. When this is the case, MFT researchers should collaborate with someone specializing in health economics. Using the above example to illustrate, even in the absence of data on the cost of police involvement in domestic violence, it is possible to contact the local hospital and determine the per day cost of an inpatient stay. Reductions in such health care utilization for family members could then be included as an outcome measure and used in some of the cost-analysis calculations outlined above. Although access to cost data may be limited, researchers can use insurance reimbursement rates, contact major employers, use precalculated estimates (e.g., Aos et al., 2001 provide data on costs related to different crimes, which can be found at: http://www.wsipp.wa.gov/pub.asp?docid=04-07-3901), consult national statistics, and more in the effort to uncover the monetary value of benefits.

Application and Advocacy

Although conducting cost analyses is difficult by itself, another issue that commonly arises after cost evaluations are completed is what to actually do with the information from such research. As highlighted above with MST, cost-benefits analysis can be used effectively to argue for the inclusion of services within the marketplace. Crane and Christenson (2012) and Crane (2008) argue that there are primarily two avenues for practitioners and researchers to disseminate the results of cost evaluation studies. First, it can disseminated at the grassroots level, where satisfied consumers make the case to their employers (who purchase health care plans for their employees) and directly to their insurance companies that the services MFTs provide are valuable. This type of effort has the potential to raise awareness among stakeholders about what services are in demand and which can ultimately affect decisions about what services to cover. Also, in some cases where services, such as family therapy, or where providers, such as MFTs, are denied participation in health care plans, the actual participants of the plan are the only persons who are eligible to appeal for consideration of claims for services that have been denied. In other words, patients are those who have been harmed, not providers. Patients then are able to appeal for coverage of this service or provider type, while providers do not have any standing to appeal such a decision for a person or class of persons.

The second commonly described method is advocacy on the part of individual practitioners, groups of professionals, and their professional organizations. When a particular service is not covered, practitioners can contact the policymakers in governmental offices or private insurance companies to argue for changes in their policies. Kessler (2008) described a number of examples of practitioners (armed with research) who have encouraged policymakers to modify their policies with positive results. These types of efforts are best carried out when the practitioner has at his/her disposal the evidence that (a) his/her services are as effective (or more so) as what is already being provided and that (b) the services result in cost savings to the organization. There are few policymakers who would not be interested in learning how to decrease costs while also providing high-quality services.

In addition to arguing for coverage of services and professional groups, cost-effectiveness data are also very helpful in making a case for grant applications where establishing the importance of a research topic is important. In a very competitive grant application process, applicants who can include a procedure to gather and report cost-effectiveness information can have an advantage over other applicants. Of course a well-designed study is a necessary foundation for any good research proposal, but applicants equipped to gather, analyze, and report cost-effectiveness information can have a significant advantage over other well-designed proposals. In fact, not only is it beneficial to include, but some federal grant opportunities now require that plans for cost evaluations be included in the application.

It is also helpful to consider that cost-effectiveness estimates can be developed once clinically effective interventions have been demonstrated in tightly controlled treatment outcome or comparative treatment studies. It should be reasonable to report what a laboratory study costs to run and then estimate what a similar intervention developed would cost to be implemented in a real-world setting. Further, beyond establishing measures for demonstrating clinical effectiveness, investigators could gather information on other potentially beneficial data such as health care utilization, changes in health status, improvements in disease management behaviors at the individual and family levels, as well as data related to employability and levels of absenteeism from school or work. Even if investigators are not interested in discussing issues beyond clinical effectiveness, other investigators would likely be willing to provide collaboration on understanding the cost and potential benefits of given treatment interventions.

Summary and Conclusion

In this chapter we have outlined the basic methods for conducting cost evaluations and have demonstrated the application of some of the methods used in this type of research. As should be evident from the discussion of validity and reliability, conducting cost-effectiveness and cost-benefit analysis requires consideration of numerous factors and influences. Accordingly, researchers who are interested in incorporating these concepts into their research will need to continue to expand their knowledge regarding cost evaluation beyond what is presented here. Fortunately there are a number of excellent references and books that can aid in acquiring the necessary skills (e.g., Aos, Phipps, Barnoski, & Lieb, 2001; Boardman, Greenberg, Vining, & Weimer, 2010; Drummond, Sculpher, Torrance, O'Brien, & Stoddart, 2005; Hargreaves, Shumway, Hu, & Cuffell, 1996; Levin & McEwan, 2000; Yates, 1996).

The methods discussed here constitute an extension of research regarding clinical effectiveness and outcomes. These methods can be used to augment and support research findings by demonstrating that a particular treatment is not only clinically effective, but also cost-effective as well. With the increase in government-sponsored health care and programs, demonstrating cost-effectiveness will only become more important. Accordingly, here are two suggestions for increasing the presence of cost evaluation in MFT. First, all researchers should become familiar with cost evaluation methods. Second, whether interested in cost evaluation or not, researchers can support this effort by gathering and reporting cost data (or at least state that it is available upon request) when investigating clinical outcomes. If the data are available, then those who are interested in cost evaluation can fill this need.

References

Aos, S., Phipps, P., Barnoski, R., & Lieb, R. (2001). *The comparative costs of and benefits of programs to reduce crime.* Olympia: Washington State Policy Institute. Retrieved from http://www.wsipp.wa.gov/pub.asp?docid=04-07-3901

Boardman, A., Greenberg, D., Vining, A., & Weimer, D. (2010). *Cost-benefit analysis* (4th ed.) Upper Saddle River, NJ: Prentice Hall.

Briggs, A. H., O'Brien, B. J., & Blackhouse, G. (2002). Thinking outside the box: Recent advances in the analysis and presentation of uncertainty in cost-effectiveness studies. *Annual Review of Public Health, 23,* 377–401. doi: 10.1146/annurev.publhealth.23.100901.140534

Crane, D. R. (2008). The cost effectiveness of family therapy: A summary and progress report. *Journal of Family Therapy, 30,* 399–410. doi:10.1111/j.1467-6427.2008.00443.x

Crane, D. R., & Christenson, J. D. (2012). A summary report of the cost-effectiveness of the profession and practice of marriage and family therapy. *Contemporary Family Therapy: An International Journal, 34,* 204–216. doi: 10.1007/s10591-012-9187-5

Crane, D. R., & Payne, S. H. (2011). Individual versus family therapy in managed care: Comparing the cost of treatment by the mental health professions. *Journal of Marital and Family Therapy, 37,* 273–289. doi: 10.1111/j.1752-0606.2009.00170.x

Dennis, M., Godley, S. H., Diamond, G., Tims, F. M., Babor, T., Donaldson, J., Liddle, H., Titus, J. C., Kaminer, Y., Webb, C., Hamilton, N., Funk, R. (2004). The Cannabis Youth Treatment (CYT) study: Main findings from two randomized trials. *Journal of Substance Abuse Treatment, 27,* 197–213. doi: 10.1016/j.jsat.2003.09.005

Detsky, A. S., & Naglie, I. G. (1990). A clinician's guide to cost-effectiveness analysis. *Annals of Internal Medicine, 113,* 147–154.

Drummond, M. F., Sculpher, M. J., Torrance, G. W., O'Brien, B. J., & Stoddart, G. L. (2005). *Methods of economic evaluation of health care programmes* (3rd ed.). New York: Oxford University Press.

Fals-Stewart, W., Yates, B. T., & Klostermann, K. (2005). Assessing the costs, benefits, cost-benefit ratio, and cost-effectiveness of marital and family treatments: Why we should and how we can. *Journal of Family Psychology, 19,* 28–39. doi: 10.1037/0893-3200.19.1.28

Goetzel, R. Z., Long, S. R., Ozminkowski, R. J., Hawkins, K., Wang, S., & Lynch, W. (2004). Health, absence, disability, and presenteeism cost estimates of certain physical and mental health conditions affecting US employers. *Journal of Occupational and Environmental Medicine, 46,* 398–412. doi: 10.1097/01.jom.0000121151.40413.bd

Gold, M. R., Siegel, J. E., Russell, L. B., & Weinstein, M. C. (1996). *Cost-effectiveness in health and medicine.* New York: Oxford University Press.

Gould, R. A., Otto, M. W., & Pollack, M. H. (1995). A meta-analysis of treatment outcomes for panic disorder. *Clinical Psychology Review, 15,* 819–844. doi: 10.1016/0272-7358(95)00048-8

Hargreaves, W. A., Shumway, M., Hu, T., & Cuffell, B. (1996). *Cost-outcomes methods for mental health.* San Diego, CA: Academic Press.

Hunsley, J. (2003). Cost-effectiveness and medical cost-offset considerations in psychological service provision. *Canadian Psychology, 44,* 61–73. doi: 10.1037/h0085818

Kessler, R. (2008). Integration of care is about money too: The health and behavior codes as an element of a new financial paradigm. *Families, Systems, and Health, 26,* 207–216. doi: 10.1037/a0011918

Klarreich, S. H., DiGiuseppe, R., & DiMattia, D. J. (1987). Cost effectiveness of an employee assistance program with rational-emotive therapy. *Professional Psychology: Research & Practice, 18*, 140–144

Klietz, S. J., Borduin, C. M., & Schaeffer, C. M. (2010). Cost-benefit analysis of multisystemic therapy with serious and violent juvenile offenders. *Journal of Family Psychology, 24*, 657–666. doi:10.1037/a00208.38

Lazar, S. G. (Ed.). (2010). *Psychotherapy is worth it: A comprehensive review of its cost-effectiveness.* Washington DC: American Psychiatric Association.

Lee, S., & Aos, S. (2011). Using cost-benefit analysis to understand the value of social interventions. *Research on Social Work Practice, 21*, 682–688. doi: 10.1177/1049731511410551

Levin, H. M., & McEwan, P. J. (2000). *Cost-effectiveness analysis: Methods and applications.* Thousand Oaks, CA: Sage Publications.

Miller, T., & Hendrie, D. (2008). *Substance abuse prevention dollars and cents: A cost-benefit analysis.* DHHS Pub. No. (SMA) 07-4298. Rockville, MD: Center for Substance Abuse Prevention, Substance Abuse and Mental Health Services Administration.

Noyes, K., & Holloway, R. G. (2004). Evidence from cost-effectiveness research. *NeuroRx, 1*, 348–355.

Pinsof, W. M., & Wynne, L. C. (1995). The efficacy of marital and family therapy: An empirical overview, conclusions, and recommendations. *Journal of Marital and Family Therapy, 21*, 585–613. doi: 10.1111/j.1752-0606.1995.tb00169.x

Pirraglia, P. A., Rosen, A. B., Hermann, R. C., Olchanski, N. V., & Neumann, P. (2004). Cost-utility analysis studies of depression management: A systematic review. *American Journal of Psychiatry, 161*, 2155–2162. doi: 10.1176/appi.ajp.161.12.2155

Quade, E. S. (1971). *A history of cost-effectiveness.* Unpublished paper presented at the IFORS International Cost-effectiveness Conference, Washington, DC.

Spoth, R. L., Guyll, M., & Day, S. X. (2002). Universal family-focused interventions in alcohol-use disorder prevention: Cost-effectiveness and cost-benefit analyses of two interventions. *Journal of Studies on Alcohol, 63*, 219–228.

Sprenkle, D. H. (2012). Intervention research in couple and family therapy: A methodological and substantive review and an introduction to the special issue. *Journal of Marital and Family Therapy, 38*, 3–29. doi: 10.1111/j.1752-0606.2011.00271.x

Yates, B. T. (1994). Toward the incorporation of costs, cost-effectiveness analysis, and cost-benefit analysis into clinical research. *Journal of Consulting and Clinical Psychology, 62*, 729–736. doi: 10.1037/0022-006X.62.4.729

Yates, B. T. (1996). *Analyzing costs, procedures, processes, and outcomes in human services.* New York: Sage Publications.

AUTHOR INDEX

Aboud, F. E. 110
Ackerman, R. A. 370, 381, 392, 399
Acock, A. 316, 327
Adams, M. 258, 262
Addis, M. E. 183, 193, 195
Adelman, H. S. 62, 74
Agarwal, I. 295–6
Agnew, C. R. 230, 243–4
Aguinis, H. 347, 357, 362
Aholou, T. M. C. 257, 262
Aiken, L. S. 355, 357, 359, 362–3
Ainsworth, M. D. S. 234, 236–7, 243, 384, 399
Alderfer, M. A. 98, 107, 235, 243
Alexander, G. E. 110, 143, 157
Algina, J. 105, 108
Ali, P. A. 79, 81, 84–5, 92
Allen, C. A. 41
Allen, J. J. B. 146, 150, 154–5
Allen, J. P. 235, 246
Allen, K. A. 243, 254, 262
Allen, W. D. 29, 43, 162, 177
Allison, P. D. 198, 206, 323, 327, 337, 345, 409, 415
Almedia, D. M. 220, 223
Aloia, M. S. 181, 194
Alonso-Arbiol, I. 17, 26
Alpert, J. 193
Altman, D. G. 189, 191, 194
Alvesson, M. 17–18, 21–3, 25–6
Amaro, H. 174, 177
Ames, M. H. 101–2, 109, 245
Anastasopoulou, P. 117, 122
Andersen, E. 80, 87, 91

Anderson, J. R. 79, 91
Anderson, M. P. 267, 281
Anderson, S 29, 42–3, 110
Anderson, S. R. 201, 206, 220, 224
Andreasen, N. C. 144, 154
Andrews, D. 103, 107
Andridge, R. R. 338, 341, 345
Anker, M. G. 211, 223
Antony, M. M. 151, 156
Aos, S. 423, 426–8, 431, 433, 435
Archbold, P. G. 270, 281
Aristotle 289, 295
Aronson, E. 22, 27, 154
Ashbourne, L. M. 262
Aspland, H. 230, 235, 244
Asscher, J. J. 349, 363
Atkins, D. C. 3, 11, 192
Atkinson, P. 249, 262
Austin, J. T 40–2, 113, 206
Azem, T. 125, 138

Babbie, E. 28–9, 32, 34–5, 37, 41, 316, 327
Babcock, J. 139
Babor, T. 434
Badiee, M. 271, 281
Baigis, J. 84, 91
Bailey, C. E. 149, 156
Bakeman, R. 230, 234–5, 244, 384, 388–91, 393–7, 399
Baker, J. K. 241, 243–4
Baldwin, S. A. 27
Bale, R. N. 181, 191
Barge-Schaapveld, D. Q. 212, 223

Bargiel, K. 236, 245
Barlow, D. H. 198, 206
Barnoski, R. 433
Baron, R. M. 222–3, 347, 351, 362–3
Barrera, M. 163, 176
Barrett, K. C. 316, 328
Barrett, L. F. 214, 224
Barrios, E. S. 125, 139
Barron, K. E. 347, 363, 365
Bartle-Haring, S. 18, 26, 379–82, 391–2
Barton, J. 28–9, 31, 41, 53, 58
Barton-Henry, M. L. 53, 58
Bateman, A. 116, 121
Bateson, G. 29–1, 37, 41
Battjes, R. J. 179, 194
Baucom, D. H. 97, 108, 187, 191–2, 235, 245
Bauer, M. 194
Baumann, A. A. 70, 75, 165, 169, 176
Beauchaine, T. 128, 138
Beck, A. T. 187, 191
Beck, J. S. 212, 224
Becker, A. 286, 296
Becvar, L. A. 33, 41, 118, 121
Beer, J. S. 144, 148, 153, 155–6
Beggs, M. A. 267, 281
Begun, A. L. 85, 91, 132, 142, 398
Beitin, B. 253–4, 262
Beldavs, Z. G. 165, 176
Bellido, C. 164, 175
Belwood, M. F. 198–9, 206
Ben-Ari, A. 211, 224
Benasutti, K. M. 194
Benson, K. 253, 264
Bentler, P. M. 376, 381
Berger, L. K. 85–6, 91
Berman, J. S. 53, 57
Bermudez, J. M. 272, 279
Bernal, G. 163–4, 166–8, 172–3, 175–7
Berns, S. B. 192, 324, 327
Berntson, G. 129, 138, 154, 156–7
Berry, E. 113, 115–16, 121
Berry, J. W. 18, 26
Berry, W. D. 321, 327
Bianchi, S. M. 79, 91
Bickman, L. 96, 107
Bierman, K. L. 190, 192

Biesta, G. 269, 278
Biggs, M. M. 194
Biggs, V. 295–6
Biocca, F. 118, 121
Bischoff, R. J. 292, 296
Blackburn, K. M. 142, 150, 154, 156
Blackhouse, G. 424, 434
Blaine, J. D. 179, 194
Blehar, M. C. 234, 243, 384, 399
Bloom, M. 198, 206
Blow, A. J. 183, 191, 247, 267, 278
Blumenfeld, W. J. 262
Boardman, A. 433–4
Bobko, P. 357, 364
Boik, R. J. 347, 362
Boles, S. M. 306, 311
Bolger, N. 208–9, 218–19, 224, 350–1, 364–5, 368, 382
Bollen, K. A. 352, 362
Bonilla, J. 164, 175
Bonvicini, K. A. 80, 86, 91
Boomsma, D. I. 137, 139
Borduin, C. M. 180, 192–3, 421, 435
Bornstein, M. 127, 138
Borrego, J., Jr. 163, 176
Bosch, J. 264
Bot, S. D. 110
Boutron, I. 189, 191
Bowen, M. 151, 154, 231, 381, 386
Bower, P. 79, 91
Boyd-Franklin, N. 100, 109
Bradbury, H. 251, 264, 283, 285, 295–6
Bradbury, T. N 349, 363, 375, 379, 381, 399–400
Bradley, B. 230, 239, 244, 398–9, 403, 416
Braithwaite, S. R. 355, 362
Brandon, A. R. 62, 75
Bratini, L. 162, 177
Bray, J. H. 320, 327
Brazil, K. 269, 281
Brenneman, G. 295–6
Brewer, M. B. 10–11
Brewster, R. 241, 244
Brick, J. M. 336, 338, 345
Briggs, A. H. 424, 434
Brimhall, A. S. 253, 262

Brindley, R. 116, 121
Brodal, A. 127, 138
Broderick, C. B. 112, 121
Brondino, M. J. 186, 192–4
Brooner, R. K. 190–1
Brown, C. H. 109, 297, 399
Brown, L. M. 274, 280
Brown, M. 100, 109
Brown, P. C. 131, 138
Brown, S. R. 320, 327
Brown, T. A. 104, 106, 108
Browner, W. S. 32, 42
Brownlee, K. 70, 75
Brunner, J. 121, 193, 253, 262
Bryant, C. M. 242, 245
Bryce, G. 97, 109
Bryman, A. 271, 279
Bucceri, J. M. 110
Buchanan, D. R. 294–5
Buchner, A. 404, 416
Bucholz, R. D. 154
Buitelaar, J. 129, 141
Bullock, B. M. 185, 192
Bunge, S. A. 143, 156
Burbules, N. C. 28, 32, 43
Burgess, N. 84, 91
Burgoon, J. K. 118, 121
Burk, W. J. 369, 382
Burleson, B. R. 185, 192
Burlew, K. 90–1
Burt, S. A. 393, 399
Busby, D. M. 48, 108
Butler, A. C. 212, 224–5
Butler, J. L 267, 269, 279
Butler, M. H. 393, 400
Bybee, D. 177, 280
Byrne, B. 101, 106, 108
Byrne, D. 115–16, 121

Cabero, A. 244
Cacioppo, J. 129, 138
Cain, H. I. 66, 72, 75
Calage, C. 144, 154
Callahan, C. 84–5, 92
Callan, V. J. 53, 57
Calogero, R. M. 225
Campbell, D. T. 32, 35–7, 41, 174, 177, 350, 364

Campos, M. 17, 26
Canli, T. 143, 154
Cano, A. 94, 108
Capodilupo, C. M. 110
Caracelli, V. J. 270–1, 279
Card, N. A. 369, 381
Carlson, M. R. 75
Carlston, D. E. 230, 243–4
Carpenter, J. 231, 244
Carroll, J. 286, 296
Carroll, K. M. 179, 181–2, 191–2, 194
Carstensen, L. L. 131, 139
Castaneda, C. 262
Castro, F. G. 163, 176
Catran, E. 129, 140
Cavell, T. A. 48, 58
Chambers, A. L. 57, 97, 109, 183, 193
Chambers, D. A. 162, 177
Chambless, D. L. 387, 400
Chamow, L. 99, 110
Chan, F. 41
Chao, R. K. 110
Chapman, J. E. 194, 416
Charlés, L. L. 253, 262
Charmaz, K. 248, 251–2, 262
Chavez, R. 91
Cheek, J. 259–60, 262
Chen, M. Y. 121, 161
Chen, Q. 351, 365
Chen, S. 333, 345
Chenail, R. J. 243–4, 264
Cheong, J. 362–3
Chibnall, J. T. 154
Chien, D. 103, 109
Childs, N. M. 201, 206
Chisholm, D. 161, 176
Christensen, A. 97, 108–9, 183, 192–3
Christensen, C. M. 19, 27
Christensen, H. 84, 91
Christensen, T. M. 21, 26
Christenson, J. D. 421, 432, 434
Christian, L. M. 80, 92, 257
Churchill, S. L. 266, 281
Clark, H. T 252, 263, 332, 346
Clarke, A. E. 252, 263
Coan, J. A. 150, 154, 235, 244

Cohen, J. 80, 82, 91, 315, 324, 327, 355, 358–9, 363, 371, 388, 390, 407–8, 416
Cohen, L. H. 221, 224–5
Cohen, P. 255, 258, 363
Cohen-Kettenis, P. 129, 141
Coker, A. D. 29, 35, 42
Cole, S. P. 122, 207
Coleman, J. U. 62, 75
Collins, L. M. 190, 192, 332, 409, 416
Collins, P. Y. 161, 176
Conger, R. D. 46, 55–6, 58, 236, 245, 377, 381, 392, 399
Connell, A. M. 125, 138
Conner, T. S. 11, 213, 219, 224
Conrad, A. 224
Consolvo, S. 116, 121
Contreras-Grau, J. 110
Conway, C. R. 144, 154
Cook, P. F. 181, 194
Cook, T. D. 32, 35–6, 41, 177, 350, 364
Cook, W. L. 3, 11, 41, 52, 56–7, 107–9, 268, 310–11, 362–3, 366, 381–2, 392, 400, 414, 416
Cooper, H. M. 324, 327
Cooper, M. L. 47, 56
Corbin, J. 292, 296
Córdova, D. 165, 177, 280
Cordova, J. 188, 193
Cornwall, A. 283, 296
Corrigan, P. W. 181, 192
Cortés, D. E. 174, 177
Cortez, P. 100, 108
Costa, P. T. 46, 57
Cottler, L. B. 84–5, 92
Cousins, J. B. 291, 296
Cowles, M. 407, 416
Cozolino, L. 142, 154
Crabtree, A. 118, 122
Craggs, J. G. 224
Craighead, L. W. 122
Craighero, L. 151, 156
Crane, D. R. 16, 27, 197, 199, 206, 432, 434
Creswell, J. D. 10–11, 248, 252–3, 255, 263, 266–8, 270–5, 277–9, 292, 296

Crocker, L. M. 105, 108
Crosby, R. D. 225
Cross, W. E. 110
Crotty, M. 249–50, 263, 268, 279
Crow, D. M. 113, 122
Crowell, J. A. 235, 246, 387, 399
Cuffell, B. 433–4
Cui, M. 377, 381
Cui, Y. 155
Culhane, S. E. 359, 363
Cummings, E. M. 32, 42, 129, 139
Cunningham, P. B. 180, 193
Curran, P. J. 374, 381
Curtin, J. J. 146–7, 154
Curtis, N. M. 180, 192
Cutuli, J. J. 107, 243

Daar, A. S. 176
Dabbs, J. 113, 122
Dagne, G. 109, 397, 399
Dahl, C. M. 267, 280
Dahlberg, B. 278–9
Dahlhamer, J. M. 331, 346
Dakof, G. A. 193
Dalais, C. 140
Dalgleish, T. L. 238, 246
Dalton, M. 157
Daly, K. J. 262
Dankoski, M. 2, 11
Dannals, R. F. 157
Dapretto, M. 151, 156
Darby, C. A. 82, 92
Darkes, J. 80–1, 86, 91
Dates, B. 177, 280
Davey, A. 29–31, 40, 42
Davey, M. P. 29–31, 33–7, 39, 42
Davidson, R. J. 143–5, 152–5, 187, 192
Davila, J. 212, 225
Davis, A. 208, 224
Davis, C. 407, 416
Davis, M. 90, 92
Davis, M. C. 212, 225
Davis, S. D. 239, 246
Day, R. D. 54, 56
Day, S. X. 435
de Boer, M. R. 110
De Geus, E. J. C. 137, 139

de Leeuw, E. 104–5, 108
de Vet, C. W. 110
Dearry. A. 282, 285, 296
DeGarmo, D. S. 165, 174, 176, 184, 186, 192
Dehle, C. 131, 134, 136, 140
DeJong, C. R. 203, 207
Dekker, J. 110
Dekovic, M. 349, 363
Del Boca, F. K. 80–1, 86, 91
Delamont, S. 249, 262
Delaney, B. 91
DelCampo, R. L. 101–2, 109
DeMets, D. L. 179, 192
Demos, J. H. 145, 155
Dennis, M. 424, 434
Denton, W. H. 184–6
Denver, J. W. 136, 139
Denzin, N. K. 249, 252, 262–4, 279
Derjak, M. 122
Desmond, J. E. 154
Deters, F. G. 114, 122
Detsky, A. S. 424, 434
DeVellis, R. 104–5, 108
Diamond, G. 434
Diener, E. 230, 244
DiGiuseppe, R. 421, 435
Dillman, D. A. 80, 87–90, 92, 103–4, 108
DiMattia, D. J. 421, 435
Dirk, J. 224
Dobson, K. S. 185, 193, 195
Dodd, R. H. 224
Dodson, L. 122
Dodson-Lavelle, B. 122
Doherty, A. 121
Doherty, W. J. 79, 91, 310–11
Dolbin-MacNab 2–3, 11, 40, 42, 62, 76, 98, 111, 247, 259, 262–6
Dollahite, D. C. 28, 32, 42
Domenech Rodríguez, M. M. 161, 163–9, 172–7, 280
Donaldson, J. 434
Donnellan, M. B. 46, 56, 370, 375, 377, 381–2, 392–3, 399
Donoghue, J. 43, 110
Dosser, D. A. 315, 324, 328

Draper, T. W. 48, 50, 56
Drummond, M. F. 433–4
Drury, M. 24, 26
Duffy, M. 244
Dugard, P. 198, 203–4, 206
Dugosh, K. L. 190, 194
Duman, S. 103, 109
Dumas, T. 108
Duncan, B. L. 211, 223
Duncan, S. C. 374, 381
Duncan, T. E. 374, 381
Dunne, J. D. 143, 155
DuPree, W. J. 267, 281
Duran, B. 70, 76, 283, 297
Durbin, E. 57
Dyer, J. 19–21, 23–5, 27, 54–6
Dzierzeqski, J. M. 224

Earl, L. M. 291, 296
Ebner-Priemer, U. W. 223, 225
Eddy, J. M. 173, 176, 387, 399
Edwards, D. L. 180, 193, 248, 253, 263
Edwards, J. R. 362–3
Edwards, T. 99, 110
Efron, B. 412–13, 416
Eid, M. 230, 244
Eide, E. 224
Eide, H. 224
Eisikovits, Z. 97, 108
Ekas, N. V. 241, 244
El-Sheikh, M. 97, 109, 129, 137, 139
Elashoff, R. M. 191
Eldridge, K. 188, 193
Elliott, R. 263
Ellis, M. V. 315, 324, 327
Emanuel, E. J. 63, 75
Emery, G. 187, 191
Emmerson, N. A. 225
Enders, C. K. 333–5, 345, 409–10, 416
Engblom-Deglmann, M. L. 253, 262
Engel, S. G. 225
Engelmann, J. M. 143, 155
Engelsing, T. M. 191
Erath, S. A. 129, 137–9
Erbacci, A. 122
Erdfelder, E. 404, 416

Escobar-Chew, A. R. 177, 280
Escudero, V. 231, 244
Esquilin, M. 110

Fabri, M. 122
Fahrenberg, J. 222, 224
Fairchild, A. J. 351, 364
Fairclough, N. 248, 253, 263
Falicov, C. J. 253, 263
Fallah, S. 84, 92
Fals-Stewart, W. 421–3, 429–31, 434
Fang, S. R. 70, 75
Farrer, L. 84, 91
Fauchier, A. 103, 109
Faul, F. 404, 416
Fava, M. 190, 192–4
Ferguson, S. G. 212, 225
Fernandez, I. 17, 26
Ferrer, E. 55, 58
Festinger, D. S. 190, 194
Fidell, L. S. 107, 110, 341, 346
Field, A. 316, 327, 397, 399
Fiese, B. H. 107, 243, 254, 263
Figueredo, A. J. 331, 345
File, P. 203, 206, 298
Fincham, F. D. 55–6, 355, 362, 381
Fine, M. 258, 263
Finset, A. 224
Fisch, R. 30–1, 43
Fischer, I. 121, 198, 206
Fishbane, M. 142, 155
Fiske, D. W. 37, 41, 382
Fitzgerald, H. E. 177, 280
Fixen, D. L. 304, 311
Flannery-Schroeder, E. 187, 193
Fleiss, J. L. 388, 390, 399
Flicker, S. 293, 296
Flisher, A. J. 176
Flores, G. 161–2, 176
Flyvbjerg, B. 268, 279
Forbes, L. J. L. 221, 224
Ford, M. 24, 27
Forgatch, M. S. 165, 174–7, 184–6, 192, 280
Forster, A. S. 224
Fowles, D. C. 128, 139
Fox, S. 337, 346
Francis, M. E. 84, 91, 108, 110, 262

Frankfort-Nachmias, G. 321, 323, 327
Franzen, C. 43
Frazier, P. A. 247, 256, 357, 359, 363
Frazier, S. L. 194
Freedland, K. E. 187, 192
Freedman, B. 186–7, 192
Fretz, B. R. 172, 176
Frey, L. M. 157
Fricker, R. 95, 108
Friedlander, M. L. 30, 42, 94, 109, 239, 244
Friedman, E. S. 194
Friedman, G. 57
Friedman, L. M. 179–80, 187, 192
Fritz, C. O. 324, 327
Fritz, M. S. 351, 363–4
Froehlich, J. 116–17, 121
Frye, R. L. 79, 92
Fuller, W. 338, 345
Funder, D. C. 230, 244
Funk, J. L. 99, 108, 321, 327, 434
Furberg, C. D. 179, 192
Furr, R. M. 230, 234, 244
Fyffe, C. 399

Gaboury, I. 194
Gabrieli, J. D. E. 143, 154, 156
Gale, J. E. 24, 27, 247, 251–60, 262–5, 272
Galea, S. 79, 89, 92
Gallo, J. J. 278–9
Gallo, L. C. 131, 140
Gambrel, L. E. 267, 269, 279
Gangwani, S. 154
Ganong, L. H. 48–9, 57
Gao, Y. 299, 312, 399
Garcia, M. 43, 110
Gardner, B. C. 47, 56, 108
Gardner, F. 230, 235–6, 244
Garland, A. F. 194
Garrett, A. L. 266, 281
Gates, S. 87, 89, 92
Gaynes, B. N. 190, 192
Geisinger, K. 100, 108
Gelernter, J. 86, 92
Gelso, C. J. 172, 176
George, C. 43, 234, 244, 382, 387, 399
Geske, J. 29, 42, 292, 296

Ghosh, C. M. 400
Gillham, B. 95, 109
Gilreath, T. D. 342, 345
Girden, E. R. 320, 327
Gjertsen, H. 93
Glaser, B. G. 248, 251–2, 264
Glaser, R. 131, 139
Glasgow, R. E. 301, 306, 311
Glenn, N. D. 55, 57
Glesne, C. 248, 250, 264
Gnisci, A. 234, 244
Goble, L. 131, 140
Godley, S. H. 434
Goessling, K. 70, 75
Goetz, J. 24, 27
Goetzel, R. Z. 427, 434
Gold, D. B. 129, 141
Gold, J. I. 107, 243
Gold, M. R. 428, 434
Goldbeck, L. 107, 243
Golden, R. N. 188, 192, 258
Goldman, E. 70, 75
Goldsmith, J. 57
Goldstein, M. J. 53, 56, 195
Gollan, J. K. 193
Goodman, J. S. 333, 345
Gordis, E. B. 103, 109, 400
Gordon, S. L. 25, 27
Gortner, E. 193
Gosch 187, 193
Gotlib, I. H. 150, 155
Gottman, J. M. 30, 42, 45, 57, 128, 131–4, 137, 139–40, 230–1, 234–6, 240, 244, 405, 417
Gould, R. A. 424, 430, 434
Goyder, J. 88, 93
Gracey, F. 116, 121
Grady, C. 63, 75, 85, 92
Grady, D. 32, 42
Graffy, J. 91
Graham, J. W. 331, 333–6, 338–46, 409–10, 416–17
Graham, W. F. 271, 279
Grawitch, M. J. 52, 57, 368, 381
Graziano, W. G. 230, 243–4
Green, B. L. 284, 296
Green, D. O. 266, 281
Green, S. 99, 111

Greenberg, D. 433–4
Greenberg, L. S. 30, 42, 94, 109, 245, 263, 398–400
Greene, J. C. 268–72, 279
Greenhalgh, C. 118, 122
Gregersen, H. 19, 27
Gregory, J. 195
Griffiths, K. M. 84, 91
Griner, D. 164, 176
Gross, J. J. 143, 154, 156, 299
Grossman, D. 295–6
Grossman, P. 113, 123
Guba, E. 255, 264
Gubrium, J. E. 259, 264
Guimbretière, F. 123
Gul, R. B. 79, 81, 84–5, 92
Gunthert, K. C. 209, 212, 224–5
Guta, A. 293, 296
Gutmann, M. L. 268, 279
Guyll, M. 82, 85, 92, 213, 224, 427, 435

Haase, R. F. 315, 324, 327
Haber, P. S 181, 195
Habib, T. 149, 155
Hackman, H. W. 262
Hahlweg, K. 187, 191
Hall, J. N. 268–9, 279
Halverson, C. F. 49, 58, 239, 246
Hamaker, E. L. 4, 11
Hampshire, A. 121
Handel, G. 267, 279
Hane, A. 125, 139
Hanley, J. H. 186, 192
Hanson, C. L. 193
Hanson, W. E. 267–9, 271, 273–5, 277, 279
Harger, J. 129, 139
Hargreaves, W. A. 433–4
Harkness, J. L. 66, 75
Harmon, L. R. 33, 42, 142, 144, 146, 148, 150, 153, 155
Harmon-Jones, E. 142, 144, 146, 148, 150, 153, 155
Harms, C. 104, 118, 121
Harper, J. M. 54, 56, 207, 236, 240–2, 244–6, 296, 383, 398
Harré, R. 253, 265

Harrison, B. 116, 121
Haslett, T. 28–9, 31, 41
Hatfield, B. E. 251, 265
Hatherly, R 156
Hauser, S. T. 235, 246
Hawkins, K. 434
Hawks, J. 150, 156
Hayes, A. F. 348, 350–5, 362–4
Haynes, S. N. 97, 110, 230, 245
Heatherington, L. 30, 42, 94, 109, 244
Heffer, R. W. 48, 58
Heffner, K. L. 131, 133–4, 136, 139
Heinrich, L. 84, 92
Heller, J. 65, 75
Hendrickson Christensen, D. 267, 280
Hendrie, D. 428, 435
Henggeler, S. W. 180, 186, 188, 192–4
Henker, B. 213, 225
Hepworth, J. 310–11
Herman, K. C. 33, 43
Herman, S. A. 62, 75
Herman, V. 284, 296
Hermann, R. C. 425, 435
Hernandez, L. 143, 157
Herr, N. R. 211, 225
Herrera, R. S. 101–2, 109
Hersen, M. 198, 206, 400
Hertlein, K. 292, 296, 307, 312
Hervis, O. E. 182, 194
Hesse-Biber, S. 112, 121–3
Hey, S. 117, 122
Heyman, R. E. 97, 110, 230, 245, 387–8, 397–9
Hill, C. E. 109, 194, 230, 242, 245, 364, 382
Hilton, J. 157
Hiroko, S. 117, 123
Hirschberger, G. 131, 140
Hitchcock, J. H. 274, 280
Hodges, S. 115–16, 121
Hodgson, N. 42
Hoffman, J. M. 351, 364
Hoffman, L. 209, 225
Hoffman, M. 84, 91
Hogue, A. 184, 193
Hohner, P. 89, 93
Holder, A. 110

Hollan, J. D. 118, 121
Holland, A. S. 124, 132–4, 136–137, 139
Hollander, M. 410–12, 416
Holleran Steiker, L. K. 163, 176
Holleran, S. E. 113–14, 122
Holley, S. R. 131, 141
Holloway, R. G. 425, 435
Holman, T. B. 47, 56
Holmbeck, G. N. 107, 243, 347, 357, 363
Holmes, B. 91
Holstein, J. A. 259, 264
Holtrop, K. 162, 165, 177, 280
Hoopes, M. H. 236, 241, 245
Horsford, S. 177, 280
Horton, N. J. 342, 345
Horvath, S. 244
Howard, L. 80, 93
Howe, G. 109
Howe, G. W. 397, 399
Howe, K. R. 268, 280
Hox, J. 104, 108
Hoyle, R. H. 356, 363, 416
Hoyt, W. T. 242, 245
Hu, L. 376, 381
Hu, T. 433–4
Huang, H. 29, 35, 42
Huddleston-Casas, C. A. 266, 281
Hudley, C. 110
Hudson, J. L. 187, 193
Huey, S. J. 186, 193
Hughes-Scalise, A. 125, 138
Huitema, B. 320, 327
Hulley, S. B. 32, 34, 42
Humbad, M. N. 393, 399
Hunninghake, D. B. 82, 92
Hunsley, J. 423, 430, 434
Hunter, S. V. 253, 264
Hutton, J. L. 87, 92

Iacoboni, M. 151, 156
IJsselsteijn, W. 118, 121
Inrig, S. J. 62, 75
Insel, T. R. 176
Isaacs, K. L. 75
Ishikawa, S. S. 225

Islam, N. Y. 243, 245
Israel, B. A. 286, 293, 296
Iversen, G. R. 320, 327

Jackson, D. C. 144–54
Jackson, D. D. 30–1, 42
Jacob, T. 236, 245
Jacobson, N. S. 107, 109, 125, 131, 133–4, 139, 183, 187–8, 193, 195, 315, 324–7, 405, 416
James, E. J. 59, 75
Järvelin, K. 121
Jasper, H. H. 145, 155
Jensen, M. 51, 57
Jewkes, R. 283, 296
Jiménez-Chafey, M. I. 176
Joestl, S. S. 176
Johanson, L. M. 17, 27
Johnson, D. R. 340, 345
Johnson, L. N. 24, 27, 201, 206, 220, 224, 414–15, 417
Johnson, M. D. 55, 57
Johnson, R. B. 42, 280
Johnson, S. K. 414–15, 417
Johnson, S. M. 97, 109, 182–3, 185, 192–3, 230, 238–9, 244, 246, 398–9
Johnston, J. A. 225
Jones, G. 121
Jonides, J. 143, 157
Jorstad-Stein, E. C. 87, 92
Joyce, J. 108
Judd, C. M. 11, 359, 362–4, 416

Kagen, N. I. 260, 264
Kakaradov, B. 123
Kalton, G. 336, 338, 345
Kam, C. M. 332, 345, 409, 416
Kane, R. 96, 109
Kang, E. 154
Kaplan, N. 234, 244, 387, 399
Kapur, N. 115, 121
Karam, E. 57
Karney, B. R. 349, 363, 375, 379, 381, 398–9
Karnik, R. B. 251, 265
Kaser-Boyd, N. 62, 74

Kashy, D. A. 3, 11, 50, 52, 57, 107, 109, 310–11, 351, 364, 366, 368, 370, 374, 381–2, 392–3, 399–400, 414, 416
Kasle, S. 114, 122
Katsumata, M. 117, 123
Katz, L. 128, 139
Kazdin, A. E. 110, 161–2, 176, 184, 186, 194, 196–206, 315, 328
Keeney, B. P. 31, 42
Keiley, M. K. 2, 11, 40, 42, 62, 76, 97–8, 109, 111, 132, 257, 259, 263, 265
Keith, D. V. 25, 27
Keller, P. 97, 109, 129, 139
Kelley, K. 324, 328, 355, 364
Kelly, J. R. 230, 243–4, 324
Kemp, J. 97, 109
Kendall, P. C. 187, 193, 412
Kennedy, J. 397, 400
Kenny, D. A. 3–4, 11, 52–3, 57, 107, 109, 222–3, 310–11, 347, 351, 356, 362–6, 368–71, 373, 381–2, 392–3, 400, 414–16
Keppel, G. 407, 417
Kerig, P. K. 235, 245, 400
Kerr, M. 369, 382
Kessler, R. C. 211, 220, 223, 421, 432, 434
Khanna, A. 70, 75
Khoo, S. T. 362–3
Kidorf, M. S. 191
Kiecolt-Glaser, J. K. 131, 139
Kiesler, D. J. 245
Kim, J. K. 338, 345
Kimball, T. G. 234, 246, 387, 400
Kimberly, C. 150, 155, 157
King, D. K. 301, 311
King, V. L. 191
Kinmonth, A. L. 91
Kinnunen, U. 213, 225
Kirchner, T. R. 212, 225
Kissil, K. 33, 42
Kitchener, K. S. 63, 75
Kito, M. 48, 57
Klarreich, S. H. 421, 428, 435
Klein, K. J. 303, 311

Klein, M. H. 238, 245
Klemmer, S. 123
Klietz, S. J. 421, 429, 435
Kline, R. B. 105–6, 109, 354, 357, 360–2, 364
Klostermann 125, 138, 421, 434
Klostermann, K. 421, 434
Klostermann, S. 125, 138
Klump, K. L. 393, 399
Knerr, M. 379, 382
Knoble, N. B. 253, 264
Knobloch-Fedders, L. M. 57
Knol, D. L. 110
Knutson, N. 174, 176
Knyazev, G. G. 151, 155, 157
Koch, G. G. 98, 109, 388, 400
Kochanska, G. 128, 139
Koerner, K. 183, 193, 195
Kolodner, K. 191
Koperwas, K. 241, 245
Koren, C. 97, 108
Kort, J. 117, 122
Kosutic, I. 43, 110
Kranzler, H. R. 86, 92
Kristjánsdóttir, Ó. B. 224
Kubota, C. 41
Kuhn, T. 28, 31, 42–3
Kuldau, J. M. 191
Kumanyika, S. 90, 93
Kumpulainen, S. 121
Kupfer, D. J. 193
Kuschel, A. 187, 191
Kuwabara, H. 157
Kwiatkowski, T. 16, 18–19, 27

La Taillade, J. J. 139
Labov, W. 248, 253, 264
Lachin, J. M. 181, 193
Ladany, N. 315, 324, 327
Lal, A. 379, 381
Lam, C. Y. 155
Lamb, S. E. 87, 92
Lambert, L. S. 362–3
Lambert, M. J. 32, 42, 230, 242, 245
Laming, R. 224
Lämsä, T. 213, 225
Lance, C. E. 55, 58, 363

Landay, J. A. 116, 121
Landis, J. R. 98, 109, 388, 400
Lane, R. 128, 141
Lang, A. G. 404, 416
LaPann, K. 193
Largent, E. A. 85, 92
Larios, S. 91
Larsen-Rife, D. 46, 56
Larson, C. L. 144, 154
Laslett, B. 258, 264
Lather, P. 251, 264
Latta, T. 57
Laurenceau, J. P. 209, 214, 218–19, 224–5
Laursen, B. 369, 381–2
Lavee, Y. 28, 32, 42, 211, 224
Lavori, P. W. 190, 193
Law, D. D. 16, 27
Law, M. 256, 264
Lazar, S. G. 422, 424, 435
Lebow, J. L. 57, 97, 109, 183, 193
Lee, B. 123
Lee, E. 41
Lee, G. K. 41
Lee, P. A. 190, 194
Lee, S. 62, 75, 423, 426–8, 435
Leech, N. L. 316, 328
LeFort, S. M. 270, 280
Leon-Guerrero, A. 316, 323, 327
Leong, F. T. L. 100, 109
Letourneau, E. J. 180, 193
Letts, L. 264
Levenson, R. W. 131–4, 137, 139–41, 234, 244, 405, 417
Levin, H. M. 433, 435
Lewin, K. 283, 296
Lewis-Beck, M. S. 319, 328
Lianekhammy, J. 150, 155, 157
Liao, C. 123
Liao, J. G. 180, 193
Liddle, H. A. 182, 193, 434
Lieb, R. 433
Lincoln, Y. S. 237, 249, 255, 259–60, 262–4, 279
Lindahl, K. M 235, 241, 244–5, 384, 400
Linden, M. K. 149, 155–6

Lindquist, M. 143, 157
Lindsay, J. 269, 281
Linfield, K. J. 55–6
Linville, D. 253, 264
Lipsey, M. W. 304, 311
Lipsitz, S. R. 342, 345
Little, R. J. A. 333–4, 337–8, 345, 409–10, 417
Little, T. D. 369, 381
Liu, T. 2, 11, 40, 42
Livi, S. 3, 11
Lock, A. 252, 264
Lockwood, C. M. 351, 364
Lohfeld, L. H. 269, 281
Long, S. R. 434
Lorber, M. F. 125, 140
Lorenz, F. O. 236, 245, 377, 381
Loving, T. J. 131, 139
Lozano, D. L. 146–7, 154
Lubar, J. F. 149, 155–6
Lucy, L. 245
Lund, C. 176
Lundervold, D. A. 198–9, 206
Luther, J. F. 194
Lutz, A. 143, 155
Lykken, D. T. 324, 328
Lynch, J. G. 351, 365
Lynch, L. 33, 42
Lynch, W. 434
Lyness, K. P. 67, 75
Lyons, K. S. 379, 382

MacCallum, R. C. 40–2
Maccoby, E. E. 53, 57
MacKinnon, D. P. 350–1, 355, 362–5
Madison, A. M. 29, 42
Main, M. 234, 244, 387, 399
Makinen, J. A. 238, 246
Malarkey, W. B 131, 139
Malhotra, N. K. 333, 345, 409, 417
Malinen, K. 213, 225
Mancini, J. A. 303–4, 311
Manders, W. A. 349, 363
Mangen, D. J. 270, 280
Mangrum, L. F. 48, 58
Mannetti, L. 3, 11
Manouilenko, I. 156

Manusov, V. 235, 245
March, D. 155, 176
March, K. 277, 280
Marcos, A. C. 48, 50, 56
Marek, L. I. 303–4, 311
Margolin, G. 103–4, 109, 188, 193, 384–5, 387, 389, 400
Margraf, J. 224
Markowski, E. M. 66, 75
Marlowe, D. B. 190, 194
Marsiske, M. 224
Martens, M. P. 244
Martin, J. A. 53, 57
Martin, N. C. 2, 10–11, 42
Martinez, C. R. 173, 176
Martoni, M. 122
Marvasti, A. 248, 252, 265
Mason, S. 90, 92
Mason, W. 337, 346
Massey, D. S. 97, 109
Mastropieri, M. A. 202, 207
Mathieu-Coughlan, P. 238, 245, 348, 350, 364
Matthews, E. E. 181, 194
Matthys, W. 129, 141
Mattson, R. E. 55, 57
Matveev, M. 129, 140
Maxwell, S. E. 320, 324, 327–8
Mazziotta, J. C. 151, 156
McAllister, C. L. 284, 296
McCabe, R. E. 151, 156
McCaffrey, D. 337, 346
McCarthy, M. 131, 141
McClelland, G. H. 347, 359, 363, 365
McCollum, E. E. 62, 75
McCrae, C. S. 221, 224
McCrae, R. R. 46, 57, 235, 245
McDaniel, S. H. 58, 310–11
McDonald, S. 207
McDowell, T. 70, 75
McEwan, P. J. 433, 435
McGlinchey, J. B. 324, 327
McGonagle, K. A. 220, 223
McGrath, K. 393, 395, 397, 400
McKay, H. G. 207, 306, 311
McKnight, K. M. 330–2, 345
McKnight, P. E. 330–2, 345

McLeod, B. D. 234, 243, 245
McNamara, J. P. H. 224
McNulty, J. K. 356, 364
McSpurren, K. 89, 93
McWey, L. M. 59, 75, 391–2
Meagher 293, 296
Medina, A. M. 400
Mednick, S. A. 140
Mehl, M. R. 11, 51, 57, 113–14, 121–2, 213, 219, 224
Meiers, M. W. 287, 292, 297
Meiran, N. 129, 140
Melamed, L. E. 320, 327
Melby, J. N. 236, 239–42, 245
Melendez,T. 43, 70, 75, 110
Mellingen, K. 140
Melton, G. B. 186, 192
Menchaca, D. 131, 134, 136, 140
Mendes, W. B. 146, 156
Mennenga, K. D. 220, 224
Messinger, D. S. 241, 244
Meuret, A. E. 223–4
Meyer, A. H. 224
Meyer, K. 18, 26
Meyer, P. S. 331, 346
Miall, C. E. 277, 280
Michel, B. D. 197, 207
Miklowitz, D. J. 182, 185, 191, 194–5
Milenkovic, N. 224
Milkie, M. A. 79, 91
Miller, F. G. 85, 92, 294–5
Miller, J. 91
Miller, R. B. 81, 92
Miller, T. 428, 435
Minnis, H. 97, 109
Minnix, J. A. 155
Mintun, M. A. 154
Miskovic, V. 151, 156
Mitchell, E. 117, 122
Mitchell, J. E. 225
Mitchell, M. 100, 109
Moher, D. 189, 191, 194
Mohr, D. C. 187, 192
Mokrova 251, 265
Monaghan, D. 117, 122
Monastra, V. J. 149, 156
Monette, D. R. 203, 207

Moore, J. J. 239, 246
Morgan, C. 80, 93
Morgan, D. L. 269, 273, 280
Morgan, G. A. 316, 328
Morland, L. 400
Morley, K. C. 181, 195
Morris, P. E. 264, 324, 327
Morrison, A. 194
Morrison, N.C. 278
Morry, M. M. 48, 57
Morton, S. C. 312
Moscovitch, D. A. 151, 155–6
Motil, K. J. 75
Moustakas, C. 248, 254, 264
Mt-Isa, S. 92
Mulder, I. 117–18, 122–3
Mulvey, L. 284, 296
Munro, C. A. 157
Munsch, S. 212, 224
Munz, D. C. 52, 57, 368, 381
Murphy, E. 273, 280
Murphy, S. A. 190, 192
Murray, J. D. 30, 42
Murray, K. 128, 139
Murray, L. W. 315, 324, 328
Murthy, D. 119–20, 122
Muthen, B. 106, 108
Myers, T. A. 348, 363
Myrtek, M. 222, 224

Nachev, C. 129, 140
Nadal, K. 110
Nadaud, A. 278
Nagireddy, C. 254, 260, 264
Naglie, I. G. 424, 434
Nakash, R. A. 87, 92
Napierala, M. A. 7, 11
Nastasi, B. K. 274, 280
Natale, V. 117, 122
Negi, L. T. 122
Nelson, C. C. 301, 311
Nelson, K. L. 131, 140
Nes, A. A. 214, 224
Neufeld, K. J. 191
Neumann, P. 425, 435
Neupert, S. 209, 225
Newfield, N. 253, 263

Newman, T. B. 32, 42
Newton, T. L. 125, 130, 134, 137, 140
Ngu, L. Q. 131, 140
Nichols, M. P. 23, 27, 43
Nicoll, J. 273, 280
Nicolson, N. A. 212, 223
Niehuis, S. 47, 56
Nock, M. K. 197, 205, 207
Noller, P. 53, 57, 139
Nonnecke, B. 103, 107
Norpoth, H. 320, 327
Northey, W. F. 149, 156
Noyes, K. 425, 435
Nunnally, J. C. 95, 98, 109
Nuro, K. F. 181–2, 184–5, 191–2

O'Brien, B. J. 424, 434
O'Brien, K. 84, 92
O'Brien, M. 267, 280
O'Cathain, A. 273, 280
O'Connor, N. E. 117, 122
O'Fallon, L. R. 282, 285, 296
O'Hearn, H. G. 400
O'Leary, D. S. 144, 154
O'Leary, K. 94, 108
O'Leary, S. G. 125, 140
Oberman, L. M. 151, 156
Odell, M. 254, 260, 264
Odh, R. 156
Oka, M. 220, 224, 398
Okazaki, S. 101, 109, 195
Olchanski, N. V. 425, 435
Olchowski, A. E. 335, 342, 345
Oliver, P. H. 400
Olson, D. H. 48, 50, 57, 108
Olson, L. 161, 176
Olson, M. M. 267, 280, 292, 296
Onken, L. S. 179, 194
Onwuegbuzie, A. J. 34, 42, 269, 272–3, 280
Orme, J. G. 198, 206
Ortega, A. 90, 93
Ortiz, E. 312
Otte, R. 117, 123
Otto, M. W. 85, 91, 194, 424, 434
Otto-Salaj, L. L. 85, 91
Owen, A. M. 121

Ozawa-de Silva, B. 122
Ozminkowski, R. J. 434

Pace, T. W. W. 122
Paez 17, 26
Pagani, M. 144, 156
Paldino, D. 55, 57
Pampel, F. C. 319, 328
Pan, H. 399
Pan, W. 324, 328
Parker, E.A. 286, 296
Parker, T. S. 142, 150, 154–7
Parra-Cardona, J. R. 70, 75, 162, 165–6, 172, 177, 280
Parrish, B. P. 212, 224–5
Parzen, M. 342, 345
Pasch, L. A. 398, 400
Pascual-Leone, A. 398, 400
Patel, V. 176
Patterson, C. 100, 109
Patterson, G. R. 165, 174–6, 184–5, 192
Patterson, J. 99, 107, 110, 243
Paul, C. 282, 337–9, 341, 346
Pawlik, K. 223–4
Payne, S. H. 425–6, 430, 434
Peddemors, A. 117, 123
Pedhazur, E. J. 34, 42
Pennebaker, J. W. 113–14, 122, 137, 140
Peracchio, L. 32, 35, 41
Perdices, M. 207
Perepletchikova, F. 184, 186, 194
Perlesz, A. L. 269, 281
Perrez, M. 223–4
Perumbilly, S. 43
Peters, M. L. 262
Peters, S. 108
Peterson, C. K. 146, 155
Peterson, C. M. 267, 281
Peterson, F. R. 201, 206
Petska, K. S. 267, 279
Petty, R. E. 351, 364
Pfeifer, J. H. 151, 156
Phillips, D. 28, 32, 43
Phipps, P. 433
Photos, V. 197, 207, 253

Pickrel, S. G. 186, 192–3
Pierce, C. A. 347, 362
Piercy, F. P. 2, 11, 32, 42–3, 59, 64, 75, 230, 244–5, 253–4, 262, 264, 267, 281, 292, 296, 307, 312, 399
Pierro, A. 3, 11
Piette, J. D. 306, 311
Pineda, J. A. 151, 156
Pinsof, W. M. 56–7, 245, 420–1, 435
Pirraglia, P. A. 425, 435
Pizzagalli, D. A. 144–5, 152–3, 156
Plano Clark, V. L. 266–75, 277–9, 281
Pleis, J., R. 331, 346
Plint, A. C. 189, 194
Pokrywa, M. L. 86, 92
Pollack, M. H. 424, 434
Pollastri, A. R. 86, 92
Pollock, N. 264
Popp, D. 369, 382
Porges, S. W. 124, 126–9, 136, 139–40
Posada, G. 387, 400
Potter, J. 248, 253, 261, 263–4
Preacher, K. J. 324, 328, 348, 350–5, 362–5
Preece, J. 103, 107
Price, J. H. 113, 122
Price, J. L. 154
Priem, J. S. 48, 57
Prince, S. E. 188, 193
Prins, P. J. M. 349, 363
Pritchett, R. 97, 109
Probstfield, J. L. 79, 82, 92
Prokopova, R. 129, 140
Pruzinsky, T. 53, 58
Puffer, S. 79, 92
Putman, P. 151, 156

Quade, E. S. 420, 435
Quera 234, 244, 384, 388–91, 393–7, 399
Quintana, S. M. 96, 100, 110

Radojevic, V. 149, 155
Rafaeli, E. 208, 224
Raghunathan, T. E. 337, 339, 346
Raine, A. 129, 138, 140
Rains, L. A. 174, 176
Ramachandran, V. S. 151, 156

Ramirez, A. J. 224
Rand, M. 95, 108
Ranganath, C. 150, 155
Rao, J. N. K. 338, 346
Rapoport, R. 258, 264
Ravaud, P. 189, 191
Ray, J. M. 231, 235, 245
Ray, R. D. 231, 235, 245
Rayner, R. 403, 417
Rea, M. 195
Reason, P. 251, 264, 283, 285, 295–6
Reddy, S. D. 113, 115, 122
Redmond, C. 82, 92, 213, 224
Reed, S. F. 136, 139, 213, 225
Reich, J. W. 212, 225
Reich, T. 48, 57
Reis, H. T. 4, 11, 416
Remen, A. L. 387, 400
Renneberg, B. 387, 400
Repinski, D. 245
Rettie, R. 118, 122
Reuter, M. 245
Reynolds, C. 140
Reynolds, K. D. 306, 311
Rhodes, S. 312
Richler, J. J. 324, 327
Riggs, B. 234, 246, 387, 400
Ritz, T. 224
Rivett, M. 231, 244
Rizvi, S. L. 197, 205, 207
Rizzolatti, G. 151, 156
Robbins, M. L. 114, 122
Roberts, L. J. 324, 327
Roberts, M. J. 317, 320–1, 328
Roberts, T. A. 137, 140
Robinson, B. F 397, 399
Robinson, J. D. 155
Robinson, P. W. 198, 207
Robinson, W. D. 286, 292, 296
Robles, T. F. 114, 122
Robuck, P. R. 75
Rodick, J. D. 193
Rodney, C. C. 220, 223
Rodriguez, J. 90, 92
Rodriguez, M. D. 70, 75, 90, 92
Roelofs, K. 151, 157
Rog, D. 96, 107
Rogge, R. D. 99, 108, 321, 327

Rogoff, B. 29, 33–4, 43
Rogosa, D. 138, 140
Rohrbaugh, M. J. 51, 57
Roisman, G. I. 124–5, 131–4, 136–7, 139–40
Ronan, K. R. 180, 192
Rönkä, A. 213, 225
Rose, W. 108
Rosen, A. B. 425, 435
Rosen, K. H. 62, 75
Rosenbaum, J. F. 194
Rosenblatt, P. C. 258–9, 264
Rosenfeld, J. P. 150, 155
Rosenfield, D. 224
Rosenthal, J. A. 397, 400
Roth, P. L. 332, 336, 346, 409, 417
Roth, W. T. 222, 224–5
Roulston, K 249, 265
Rounsaville, B. J. 179, 194
Rovine, M. J. 214, 224
Rowan, J. A. 145, 156
Rowe, C. 193
Rowe, J. 121
Rowe, M. A. 224
Rowland, M. D. 180, 186, 193–4
Rubin, D. B. 333–4, 338, 341–2, 345–6, 409–10, 417
Rucker, D. D. 351, 362, 364
Rush, A. J. 187, 190–4
Russell, C. J. 357, 364
Russell, C. S. 267, 280–1
Russell, L. B. 428, 434
Russo, R. 317, 320–1, 328
Ryan, L. 143, 157

Sachs, G. S. 191, 194
Sadler, J. Z. 62, 75
Sale, J. E. 269, 281
Salmaso, D. 156
Salzer, M. S. 181, 192
Sandberg, J. G. 17–18, 21–3, 25–6
Sandelowski, M. 270, 277–8, 281
Sanderson 37, 43, 97, 99–100, 110
Sanford, J. M. 125, 130, 134, 137, 140
Sanford, K. 55, 57
Sannibale, C. 181, 195
Sarbin, T. R. 253, 265
Savage, S. 207

Savla, J. 29, 42
Saxena, S. 176
Sayer, A. 379, 382
Sayers, S. L. 393, 395, 397, 400
Scaramella, L. 245
Schaafsma, M. 278
Schaeffer, C. M. 421, 435
Schafer, J. L. 331–2, 334–6, 338–40, 342, 344–6, 409–10, 416–17
Scharf, D. N. 212, 225
Schenker, N. 339, 346
Scherer, D. G. 186, 192
Schlup, B. 224
Schmelkin, L. P. 34, 42
Schmidt, L. A. 151, 156
Schoenwald, S. K. 180–1, 184, 186, 193–4
Schrader, S. S. 112, 121
Schroeder, L. D. 187, 193, 319, 328
Schultz, A. J. 291, 296
Schultz, A. S. 221, 225
Schultz, R. 207
Schulz, A. 286, 296
Schulz, K. F. 181, 191, 194
Schulz, M. S. 235, 246
Schutter, D. J. 151, 157
Schwartz, A. L. 165, 169, 176
Schwartz, S. J. 182, 187, 192, 194
Schwarz, J. C. 53, 58
Scruggs, T. E. 202, 207
Sculpher, M. J. 433–4
Seedall, R. B. 162, 177, 236, 240, 245, 387, 391, 393, 400
Seider, B. H. 131, 133–4, 140
Seilhamer, R. A. 236, 245
Selig, J. P. 362, 364, 369, 381–2
Sellars, S. 224
Shadish, W. R. 17, 27, 174, 177, 350, 364
Shahar, B. 211, 225
Shao, J. 338, 346
Sharpe, T. 241, 245
Shavelson, R. 106, 108
Shaw, B. F. 185, 187, 191, 195
Sheets, V. 351, 364
Sheidow, A. J. 194
Shekelle, P. G. 308, 312
Sheldon, M. S. 47, 56

Sheline, Y. I. 154
Sheppes, G. 129, 140
Shiffman, S. 212, 225
Shimizu, T. 117, 123
Shivakumar, G. 62, 75
Shoham, V. 51, 57
Shortt, J. 139
Shron, T. 236, 245
Shrout, P. E. 350, 365
Shumway, M. 433–4
Sidani, S. 331, 345
Siegel, J. E. 428, 434
Silverman, D. 34, 43, 248, 252, 265
Silverman, R. 16, 18–19, 27
Silverman, W. K. 149, 156
Silverthorn, B. C. 18, 26
Simon, G. 28, 43
Simpson, L. E. 192
Sindik, J. 100–1, 110
Singer, J. D. 218–19, 225
Singh, R. 253, 265
Sjöberg, L. 17–18, 23, 25, 27
Sjoquist, D. L. 319, 328
Skoyen, J. A. 51, 57
Slatcher, R. B. 114, 122
Slater, L. M. 257, 262
Sliwinski, M. J. 225
Sluzki, C. E. 253, 265
Smeaton, A. 121
Smith, A. L. 66, 75
Smith, G. T. 36–7, 43
Smith, L. 162, 177
Smith, T. B. 167, 173, 176–7
Smith, T. W 131, 137–8, 140
Smock, S. A. 59, 75
Smyth, G. 121
Smyth, J. D. 80, 92
Smyth, J. M. 221, 225
Snieder, H. 137, 139
Snyder, D. K. 48, 50, 52, 57–8, 97,
    99, 108, 110, 230, 233, 235–6, 241,
    245, 362–3, 399
Sobel, M. E. 352–3, 365
Solomon, D. H. 48, 57
Sorra, J. S. 303, 311
Southam-Gerow, M. A. 194
Sparks, J. A. 211, 223

Spinhoven, P. 151, 157
Spiro, A. 209, 225
Spoth, R. L. 82, 92, 213, 224, 427, 435
Sprenkle, D. H. 2, 11, 32, 42–3, 59,
    64, 67, 75, 162, 177, 183, 191, 230,
    244–5, 262, 267, 281, 296, 312,
    399, 420–1, 429, 435
Springer, P. R. 42, 192, 246, 292, 296,
    400
St. George, S. 244
Stanton, M. 29, 37, 43, 97, 110
Stanton, S. 97, 108
Stark, K. A. 131, 140
Starr, L. R. 212, 225
Steen, I. S. 224
Steketee, G. 387, 400
Stephan, P. E. 319, 328
Steuber, K. R. 48, 57
Stevens, J. P. 105, 110
Stewart, B. J. 270, 281, 292, 421–3,
    429–31, 434
Stewart, D. 264
Stine, R. 352, 362
Stith, S. M. 62, 75
Stoddart, G. L. 433–4
Stoller, K. B. 191
Stone-Elander, S. 156
Strand, K. 267, 272–7
Strauss, A. L. 248, 251–2, 264, 292,
    296
Striley, C. L. W. 84–6, 92
Strong, T. 251–2, 264–5
Strycker, L. A. 301, 311, 374, 381
Stumpp, J. 117, 122
Suarez-Morales, L. 91
Sue, D. W. 103, 110
Sue, S. 97, 100–1, 109–10
Suess, P. 127, 138
Sullivan, C. 177, 280
Sullivan, K. T. 398, 400
Sullivan, T. J. 203, 207
Sun, S. 324, 328
Suveg, C. 187, 193
Swanson, C. C. 30, 42
Swanson, G. M. 82, 92
Swanson, K. R. 30, 42
Swindle, R. 225

Switzer, D. M. 336, 346
Switzer, F. S. 336, 346
Symons, F. 238–9, 246, 393, 396, 400
Szapocznik, J. 182, 194

Tabachnick, B. G. 107, 110, 341, 346
Takagi, E. 40, 42
Tamaren, L. 278
Tambling, R. B. 220, 224, 414–17
Tams, L. 177, 280
Tan, B. H. 253, 265
Tashakkori, A. 267–9, 272, 274,
 278–81
Tate, R. L. 197, 206–7
Tavris, C. 22, 27
Taylor, B. J. 335, 345
Taylor, G. 96, 110
Taylor, L. 62, 74
Taylor, S. R. 348, 350, 364
Teddlie, C. 267–9, 272–4, 278–81
Teesson, M. 181, 195
Templeton, G. B. 201, 206
Tennenbaum, D. 236, 245
Tennent, P. 118–20, 122
ter Hofte, G. 117, 122–3
Terada, M. 181, 194
Terry, M. 284, 296
Terwee, C. B. 99, 110
Thase, M. E. 190, 194
Thayer, J. 128, 141
Thomson, C. L. 181, 195, 207, 327
Thorngren, J. M. 21, 26
Thornicroft, G. 176
Thyer, B. A. 59, 75
Tibshirani, R. J 412–13, 416
Tims, F. M. 434
Tix, A. P. 347, 363
Todman, J. 198, 203, 206
Togher, L. 207
Tolunsky 145, 156
Tolvanen, A. 213, 225
Tomany-Korman, S. C. 161, 176
Tomlinson, M. 176
Tomm, K. 244
Tomoyuki, K. 117, 123
Tompson, M. C. 195
Tonetti, L. 122

Torgerson, D. J. 79–80, 85, 92–3
Torino, G. C. 110
Tormala, Z. L. 351, 364
Torraco, R. J. 29, 33, 43
Torrance, G. W. 433–4
Tourangeau, R. 97, 109
Toviessi, P. 18, 26
Tracy, M. 79, 89, 92
Tran, T. V. 97, 99, 110
Travers, R. 293, 296
Treat, T. A. 184, 188
Treboux, D. 399
Tremaine, W. J. 67, 75
Trivedi, M. H. 190, 192–4
Trochim, W. M. K. 5–7, 10–11, 316,
 326, 328
Troyano, N. 96, 110
Truax, P. A. 107, 109, 193, 315, 324–7,
 405, 416
Trull, T. J. 223, 225
Tse, T. 188, 195
Tubbs, C. 29, 42
Tucker, C. M. 33, 43, 224
Tucker, L. 224
Tudge, J. R. H. 251, 265
Turner, L. A. 34, 42
Turner, R. M. 193
Turner, W. L. 29, 43, 162, 177
Tyson, R. 30, 42

Uchino, B. 129, 138
Uebelacker, L. 94, 110
Unger, S. 84, 92
Urey, J. R. 193

Vallis, T. M. 185, 195
van Baren, J. 118, 121
van de Vihver, F. J. R. 17, 26
van der Windt, D. 110
van Dulmen, S. 224
van Engeland, H. 129, 141
van Goozen, S. 129, 141
van Lanen, F. 118, 121
Van Langenhove, L. 253, 265
Van Maanen, J. 252, 265
van Peer, J. M. 151, 157
Van Stone, W. W. 191

Vandenberg, R. J. 55, 58
Venables, P. H. 129, 140
Venner, K. 91
Versace, F. 155
Vietze, D. L. 110
Villarruel, F. A. 165, 177
Vining, A. 433–4
Visser, A. 118, 123
Visser, Y. L. 287, 292, 297
Vivian, D. 387, 399
Vogt, T. M. 306, 311
Von Bertalanffy, L. 29, 31, 37, 43, 367, 382
von Hippel, P. 343, 346
Vu, C. T. 97, 108

Wager, T. D. 143, 157
Wagerman, S. A. 230, 244
Waldinger, R. J. 235, 241, 243, 246
Wall, S. 234, 243, 384, 399
Wallace, P. 91
Wallerstein, N. 70, 76, 283, 294–5, 297
Wallis, F. 174, 177, 412
Walsh, C. R. 293, 297
Walsh, S. J. 86, 92
Walsh, S. R. 67, 75
Walters, L. H. 239, 246
Waltz, J. 139, 183–4, 195
Wamboldt, F. S. 254, 263
Wampler, K. S. 49, 58, 234, 236, 238–40, 244–6, 383, 387, 398, 400
Wand, G. S. 157
Wang, L. L. 324, 328
Wang, S. 434
Ward, A. J. 82, 92
Ward, E. 91
Ward, M. R. 267, 281
Ward, T. J. 32, 346
Warden, D. 192
Warriner, K. 88, 93
Waters, E. 59, 234, 243, 310, 384, 387, 399–400
Watkins, R. 287, 292–3, 297
Watson, J. B. 403, 417
Watson, J. M. 80, 85, 93
Watson, P. 121
Watson, S. M. 193
Watson, W. 286, 296

Watzlawick, P. 30–1, 43
Weakland, J. H. 30–1, 43
Weerts, E. M. 144, 157
Wegner, D. M. 129, 141
Weimer, D. 433–4
Weinstein, M. C. 428, 434
Weisman, A. G. 185–6, 195
Weiss, A. 235, 245
Weiss, R. L. 287, 399
Weisz, J. R. 234, 243, 245
Wells, K. C. 149, 156
Welsh, R. 29–30, 37, 43, 97, 110
Wendler, D. 63, 75
Wenze, S. J. 209, 224
Werner-Wilson, R. J. 152–7
Wertheimer, A. 85, 92
Wessen, S. 258, 263
West, S. G. 351, 355, 357, 359, 362–4
Westmorland, M. 264
Wetherall, M. 264
Wethington, E. 220, 223
Whalen, C. K. 212–13, 225
Wheeler, J. 192
Whisman, M. A. 94, 110, 347, 359, 365
Whitaker, C. A. 25, 27
Whitaker, T. 111
Whitson, S. 129, 139
Widaman, K. F. 55, 58
Wieling, E. 29, 43, 162, 164–5, 172, 174, 176–7
Wiener, N. 31, 43
Wiley, R. H. 42, 92, 108, 245, 264, 324, 327–8, 345–6, 416–17
Wilhelm, F. H. 113, 123, 222, 224–5
Willett, J. B. 110, 219, 225
Williams, J. 350–351, 364–365
Williams, L. 99–100, 110, 121
Williams, M. A. 92, 129, 140
Williams, R. J. 188, 195
Williamson, E. 92, 225
Wilson, P. 97, 109, 142, 144, 146, 148, 150, 152–7
Winkielman, P. 142, 155
Wis, L. 258, 263
Wisniewski, S. R. 192–4
Withers, E. 92
Wittenborn, A. K. 62, 76, 98, 111, 188, 192, 259, 265

Wittink, M. N. 278–9
Wolfe, D. A. 410–12, 416
Wonderlich, S. A. 225
Wong, L. 258, 263
Wood, N. D. 115, 121, 142, 150, 154, 156–7
Woodall, A. 80, 85, 93
Woolley, S. R. 239, 246
Worrall, J. 28, 31, 43
Worthington, R. 104, 111
Wright, D. 81, 92
Wright, K. 278
Wulff, D. 244
Wurzelmann, J. I. 75
Wylie, L. 84, 92
Wynne, L. C. 435

Yancey, A. 90, 93
Yang, Y. 99, 111
Yap, P. M. E. H. 253, 265
Yates, B. T. 420–1, 433–5

Yeh, R. 118–20, 123
Yoder, P. 238–9, 246, 393, 396, 400
Yorgason, J. B. 208–10, 224–5
Young, C. G. 70, 75
Young, R. 340–5
Yuan, J. W. 131, 133–4, 141

Zarcone, V. P., Jr. 191
Zarin, D. A. 188, 195
Zautra, A. J. 212, 225
Zayas, L. H. 163, 177
Zhang, Z. 353, 364–5
Zhao, X. 351, 365
Zhao, Z. 154
Zhou, E. 224
Zimmerman, J. F. 65, 76
Zinbarg, R. E. 57
Zuccarini, D. 238, 246
Zuniga, X. 262
Zyphur, M. J. 353, 364–5

SUBJECT INDEX

ABAB design 199, 203
Actor–Partner Interdependence Model
108, 363, 371–4, 377, 381, 392–3,
403, 414, 416–17
adaptive treatments 190
alpha level 406, 408
analyze change 2, 133
association and causation 326
attrition bias 81, 92
auxiliary variables 343–4

baseline phase 199–200, 202, 206
between-family 209
between-person 209–10, 214, 216,
218–19
bootstrapping 350, 352–4, 412–13, 418
brand 86

casewide deletion, 336
categorical codes, 235–6
census, 81–2, 338
clinical significance, 109, 280, 315, 321,
324–8, 416
clinical trials 17, 67–8, 75, 79, 84,
90–2, 174, 178–81, 183–93, 195,
197, 205, 270, 275, 366, 415
ClinicalTrials.gov 188–9, 195
Cohen's kappa 388–90
community champions 291
community-based participatory research
69–70, 76, 90–1, 276–7, 282–97
CONSORT 189, 191, 194
conspicuous sampling 238
constructionism 250, 256, 264
continuous codes 235, 240

control groups 69, 81, 187–8, 191–2, 367
convergent parallel design 274
correlation 10, 39, 53, 139, 150–1,
153, 211, 214, 216, 219, 315–16,
318–19, 321, 332, 338, 343–4, 363,
367, 388–91, 399, 412
cost/benefit: cost allocation 422; cost-
benefit analysis 420, 422, 426–31,
433–5; cost-benefit ratio 426, 428–9,
434; cost-effectiveness 91, 420–6,
429, 432–5; cost-unit analysis 422,
425; direct costs 424, 430; estimated
426; incremental ratio, 422 424–5;
indirect costs 422, 430; net present
value 422, 428–9; quality-adjusted life
years 425; types of costs 422
cultural adaptation process model 164
cultural bias 100, 107, 242

daily assessments 208, 212, 221
daily processes 211–12, 221
data analysis 3, 7, 32, 40, 57, 64–5,
107, 109–10, 119, 189, 208,
213–14, 219, 225–6, 268, 273, 290,
300, 310–11, 345, 363–4, 366–7,
369, 371, 373–5, 377, 379–82, 391,
393, 400, 405–6, 411, 416
decisional balance matrix 82
deep structure adaptations 163
discourse analysis 248, 250, 252–3,
260–1, 263
distinguishability 369
dyadic data analysis 7, 39, 52, 57, 107,
109, 310–11, 366, 369, 371, 374,
380, 382, 391–2, 400, 416

dyadic growth curves 377–8
dyadic research design 98

ecological validity framework 164,
167–8, 174–5
effectiveness 17–18, 34–5, 62, 72–3,
91, 102, 104, 107, 133, 178–80,
182, 186, 191, 193, 196, 200–2,
205–6, 211–12, 230, 243, 251,
266, 275, 283–4, 288–9, 298–9,
301–3, 305, 332, 337–8, 366, 420–6,
429–30, 432–5
efficacy 56, 94, 107, 165, 178–80, 182,
186, 201, 251, 275, 277, 304, 306,
345, 401, 416, 435
embedded design 275
epistemology 28, 31, 34, 42, 248–51,
254–6, 259–60
ethics: AAMFT Code of Ethics 59–60,
66–7, 71–4; autonomy 59–63, 83,
259, 294; *The Belmont Report* 60,
63, 65–66, 71, 75–7; beneficence
60, 63–5, 259; informed consent
59, 62, 73, 119, 136, 258–9, 294;
institutional review board 64, 73, 92,
259–60, 293; justice 60, 65–73, 75,
172, 175, 177, 251, 259, 262, 423;
nonmalfeasance 63, 65; respect for
persons 60; Tuskegee Syphilis
experiments 60; voluntary 85,
129, 368
ethnic minorities 71, 90, 109, 133,
161–2
ethnography 116–20, 250, 252, 254,
263, 265
evidence-based treatments 161, 176
explanatory sequential design 274–75

factor analysis 39, 101, 105, 108, 387,
399–400; confirmatory 101, 108
feasibility 18–19, 102, 170, 182, 224,
276, 401, 415
fidelity 38, 71, 173–4, 176–7, 183–6,
192–5, 230–1, 280, 304–5, 329, 332,
379, 401
fidelity rating scale 184–5
first-order change 30–31
focal sampling 238

focus groups 34, 274, 276–7, 283, 287,
290, 292, 296, 303–4, 307, 312
follow-up reminders 89
funnel effect 81

generalizability 8, 33, 80–1, 95, 134,
236, 245
grounded theory 248, 250–2, 254,
262–4, 274, 296
growth curve modeling 374, 381–2

hierarchical linear modeling 40, 355,
373, 403

incentives 62–63, 73, 82–9, 92–3, 205,
211, 213, 224
The Innovator's DNA 19–22, 24–5, 27
interactional coding 135
interrater agreement 233, 241, 387–9
intervention phase 199, 202
interview constellation 256–8
intraclass correlation 214, 216, 388–91,
399
Iowa Family Interaction Rating Scales
(IFIRS) 239–42
item nonresponse 331

key informants 290

latent variable 53, 335, 361, 381
listwise deletion 336, 409–10
longitudinal research 34, 52, 54–5, 58,
92, 103, 109–10, 125, 131–3, 140,
165, 208, 219, 224–5, 244, 254, 300,
308, 331, 333–4, 345, 350, 361–4,
374, 378–9, 381–2, 392, 399–400
lotteries 88, 93

magnitude 164, 315, 321–4, 327–8,
355, 360
measurement and surveys: culturally
appropriate measures 99, 291; Internet
surveys 89–90, 108; Qualtrics 89,
220; questionnaire selection 98–9;
questionnaires 5, 15, 38–9, 87–90,
92, 95–6, 98–107, 109, 118, 120,
154, 245, 335; Survey Monkey 89;
survey research 38, 49, 59, 87–90,

105, 107–8, 117, 220–1, 266, 272–5, 283–4, 290, 292–3, 296, 299, 306–8, 331, 333–5, 340, 345–6, 387, 400
measurement error 308, 324, 326, 357, 405–6
measurement invariance 46, 53–4, 58, 108
mediator 32, 154, 223, 347, 349, 351–4, 362–4
medical family therapy 310–11
mental health disparities 161–2, 171, 282, 284, 287
missing data: conditional mean imputation 338–40, 409; full-information maximum likelihood 329; hot deck imputation 338, 340, 345–6; mean substitution 329, 337–8, 409–10; missing at random 331, 334, 339–40, 409; missing completely at random 334–5, 337, 339–40, 345; missing data 2, 7, 99, 209, 213, 329–33, 335–7, 339–46, 354, 402, 405, 408–10, 415–17; missing not at random 334; missing values analysis 333–4; multiple imputation 335, 341, 345–6, 409–10, 415–17; planned missingness 334–5; single imputation 337–40, 409–10; unconditional mean imputation 339–40; wave nonresponse 331
mixed methods design 276, 278, 280
moderator 32, 129, 139, 154, 222–3, 292, 347, 355–3, 365
mono-method bias 95–6, 401
motivational interviewing 83
multiphase design 275
multiple perspectives 37, 47–8, 56, 301, 380

narrative 125, 185, 197, 234, 241, 248–50, 252–4, 263, 265, 361
needs assessment 284, 287, 292, 295
networking 24, 26, 112
nonindependent 2–3, 52, 57, 96, 108, 363, 368, 380–1, 391, 403
nonparametric statistics 410–1

objectivism 250–1
One-With-Many design 392

pairwise deletion 336
paradigmatic stance 269, 271
participatory action research 250, 283
phenomenology 247–8, 250, 252, 254
physiology: autonomic nervous system 124–7, 129–31, 137–9, 147, 156; biological artifact 152; blood pressure 124, 130; electrical brain activity 143–4, 148; electrocardiogram 124, 130; electroencephalography 142–3, 145, 147, 149, 151, 153–7; functional magnetic resonance imaging 143–4, 154–6; heart rate 117, 124, 126–31, 133, 138–9, 147, 223, 423; laboratory design 146–7; mirror neuron system 151, 156; nonbiological artifact 152; parasympathetic nervous system 124, 126–7, 129–30, 132; participant setup 135; physiological research 2, 125, 127, 129–31, 133–5, 137–9, 141, 157; Positron emission tomography 143–4, 154, 156–7; sin conductance level 124, 126–9, 132–3, 136, 139; sympathetic nervous system 124–30, 132; vagal reactivity 127–8; vagal tone 127–8, 138–9
piecewise improvement 375
pooled regression 414, 417

random assignment 6, 62, 173, 192, 198
randomization 180–1, 186, 190, 193, 203, 206
randomized controlled trial 166, 170–1, 174, 277
Reach Effectiveness–Adoption Implementation Maintenance (RE-AIM) 299, 301–2, 305–6, 311
recruitment 35, 79–85, 87, 89–93, 134, 170, 181, 195, 208, 213, 293, 404
regression 3, 9, 39, 105, 315, 318–20, 322–3, 327–8, 338–41, 345–6, 350–2, 354–6, 358–60, 362–4, 366–7, 373, 380, 409–11, 413–15, 417–19
relational engagement 87, 91
relational measure 96
reliability 6, 8, 10, 37, 39, 46, 53, 95–9, 102, 105, 110–1, 135, 156, 185, 202, 205, 234–5, 241, 250–1,

255, 332, 335, 357, 363, 387–90, 399–400, 406, 414, 429, 433
research question 15–18, 22, 26–7, 29, 34, 44–5, 62, 79, 95–6, 99, 154, 231, 234–6, 239, 247, 249, 256–7, 262, 267, 269, 271, 309, 315, 358, 402–6, 408
response rate 88–9, 95, 329
retention 79–83, 85–7, 89–93, 163, 168, 208, 213, 277

sample size 7, 16, 67, 79–82, 105, 134, 153–4, 181, 190, 277, 321, 324, 328, 332, 335–7, 351–3, 357, 363, 371, 377, 388, 401–2, 404–6, 408, 410–1, 416
second-order change 29–31
selection bias 80, 85, 87, 308
sequential design 274–5
significance testing 324, 366, 416
single-case design 196, 198, 201, 205
small sample 81, 363, 402, 406, 410, 413, 415–16
social justice 70–2, 75, 172, 175, 177, 251, 262
Social Relations Model 392
STAR*D 190, 192, 194
statistical power 80–1, 87, 187, 332, 335–7, 340, 357, 362, 371, 403–4, 406, 411, 416
statistical significance 80, 153, 315, 321, 324, 326, 328, 355, 415–16
structural equation modeling 2, 11, 40–2, 101, 108–9, 315, 335, 345, 350, 363–5, 371, 381, 387, 392, 403, 416
subjectivism 250
surface level adaptations 163

technology, use of: accelerometers 117, 122; ButterflyNet 118, 120, 123; digital pens 118; electronically activated recording (EAR) 113; Ethno-Goggles 118–20, 122; MyExperience 116–18, 120–1; SenseCam 113, 115–16, 120–1; SocioXensor 117–18, 120, 122–3; WiShare 117–18

theory: and measurement choices 37; and methodology 34
tracking system 86
transformative design 275
treatment as usual 421, 423–4, 429
treatment manual 179, 181–5
trustworthiness 250, 255–6, 262
type I error 7, 205, 320, 337, 369, 402, 407
type II error 6–8, 10, 46, 80–1, 205, 338, 369, 404, 407–8

underserved populations 162–3, 172, 284
unidimensional measurement 46, 55
unit nonresponse 331
unit of analysis 34, 51, 80, 97, 197–8, 203, 284–5, 367, 371, 378, 380, 384, 392, 404–5
unit of interest 46, 48–53
unit of measurement 48–50, 52

validity: conclusion validity 5–7, 9, 29, 35, 46–7, 53, 80–1, 98, 100, 153, 174, 178, 181, 204–5, 304, 308, 332, 336, 369–70, 379–80, 402, 411, 413, 420, 430; construct validity 5–6, 29, 35–7, 43, 45, 57, 96–7, 99–100, 135, 137, 149, 152–153, 204, 234, 306, 332, 335, 370, 386–7, 430; cultural validity 96, 100, 102, 109–10; ecological validity 41, 164, 167–8, 172, 174–5, 209; external 5–8, 29, 35, 80–1, 95–6, 102, 104, 134–6, 152–3, 174, 178, 180, 190, 204, 236, 306, 308–9, 334, 379, 401, 415, 429; internal 6, 8, 29, 35, 46, 96, 152, 173, 179–81, 192, 196, 203–4, 309, 369, 379–80, 401
variability 5, 8, 10, 127–8, 182, 202–3, 205, 209, 211, 216, 237, 321–3, 336–8, 341, 362, 373, 406–7, 413
variance 1, 3–4, 45, 53, 101, 105, 203, 216, 218, 228, 317, 320, 322–3, 327–8, 332, 337–8, 342, 346, 360, 366, 372–3, 377–9, 389, 407, 409, 412
vulnerable populations 60, 70–1